fundamentals of CREATURE DESIGN

How to create successful concepts using functionality, anatomy, color, shape & scale

3dtotal Publishing

3dtotalPublishing

Correspondence: publishing@3dtotal.com
Website: store.3dtotal.com

Fundamentals of Creature Design © 2020, **3dtotal Publishing.** All rights reserved. No part of this book can be reproduced in any form or by any means, without the prior written consent of the publisher. All artwork, unless stated otherwise, is copyright of the featured artists. All artwork that is not copyright of the featured artists is marked accordingly.

Every effort has been made to ensure the credits and contact information listed are present and correct. In the case of any errors that have occurred, the publisher respectfully directs readers to **store.3dtotal.com/pages/information** for any updated information and corrections.

First published in the United Kingdom, 2020, by 3dtotal Publishing.

Reprinted in 2024 by 3dtotal Publishing.

Address: 3dtotal.com Ltd, 29 Foregate Street, Worcester, WR1 1DS, United Kingdom.

Soft cover ISBN: 978-1-912843-12-1
Printed and bound in China
by C&C Offset Printing Co., Ltd

Visit **store.3dtotal.com** for a complete list of available book titles.

Managing Director: Tom Greenway
Studio Manager: Simon Morse
Lead Designer: Fiona Tarbet
Lead Editor: Samantha Rigby
Editor: Marisa Lewis
Designer: Matthew Lewis
Editorial Assistant: Tilly Barnett

Cover images © Individual artists as listed throughout the book

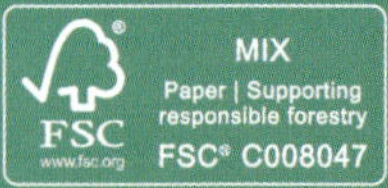

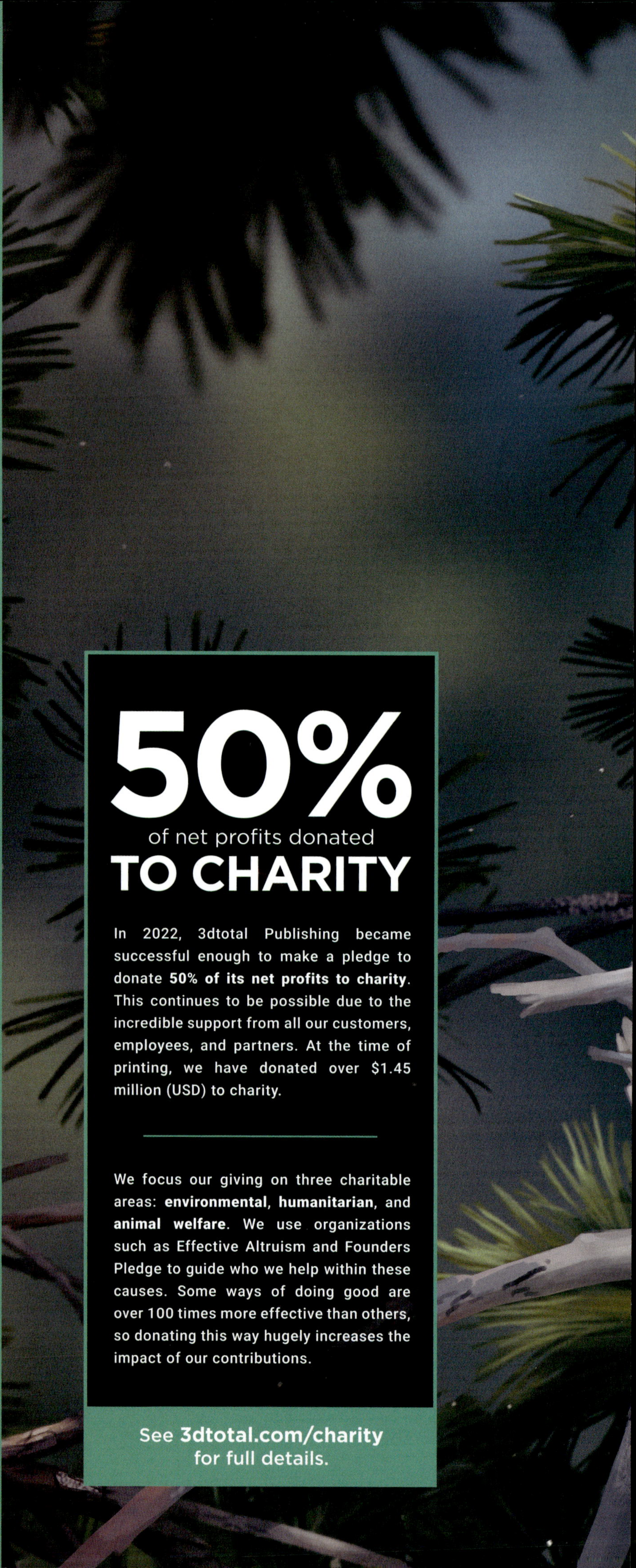

50%
of net profits donated
TO CHARITY

In 2022, 3dtotal Publishing became successful enough to make a pledge to donate **50% of its net profits to charity**. This continues to be possible due to the incredible support from all our customers, employees, and partners. At the time of printing, we have donated over $1.45 million (USD) to charity.

We focus our giving on three charitable areas: **environmental**, **humanitarian**, and **animal welfare**. We use organizations such as Effective Altruism and Founders Pledge to guide who we help within these causes. Some ways of doing good are over 100 times more effective than others, so donating this way hugely increases the impact of our contributions.

See **3dtotal.com/charity**
for full details.

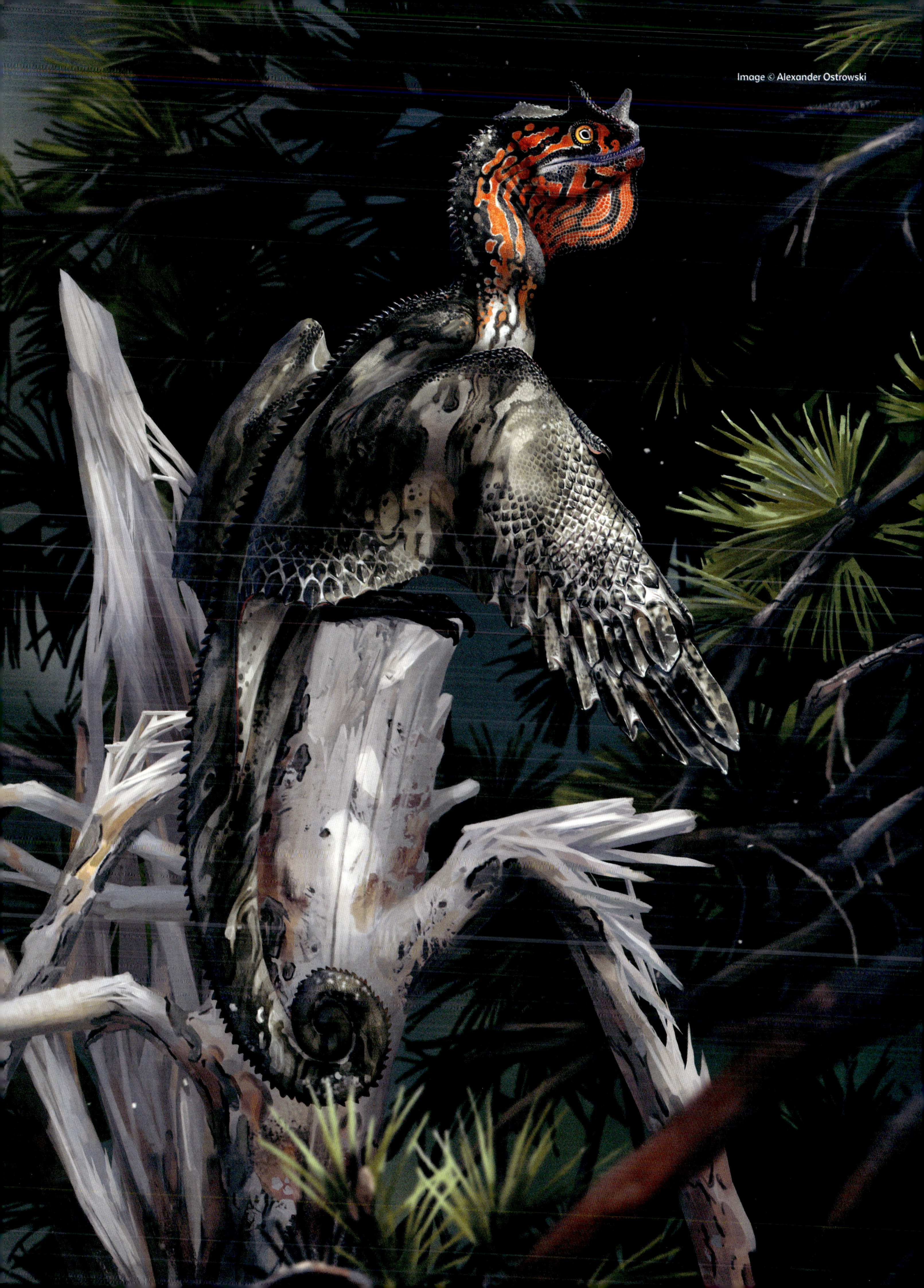
Image © Alexander Ostrowski

CONTENTS

Image by Dominique Vassie

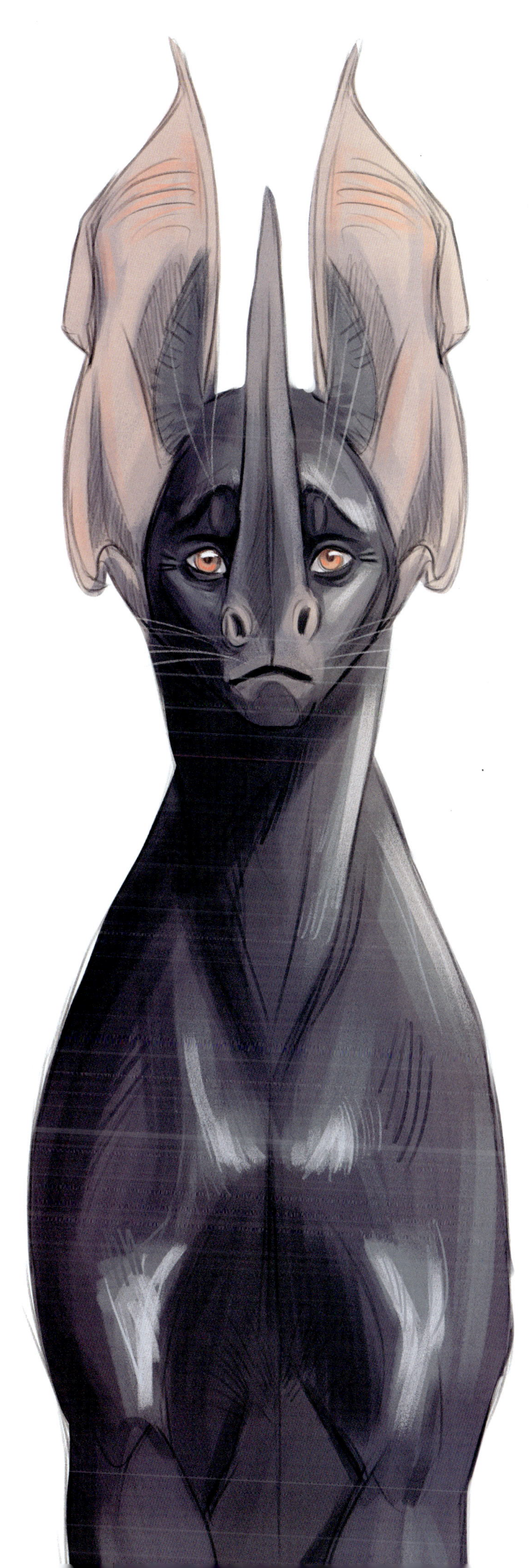

FOREWORD

Planet of the Apes, Chewbacca, "Baby Yoda," Gollum, the Ents, Na'vi, T-Rex, Rocket Racoon, Groot... the list goes on and on. Strange aliens from distant galaxies, fantastical beasts from another dimension, or your favorite hero's pet sidekick. There are an infinite number of amazing creatures starring in our favorite entertainment experiences; creatures that we have grown up with and that make our favorite stories more exciting and memorable. Sometimes they are used as set dressing, or as a way to bring ancient creatures to life. Sometimes they are a way for artists and storytellers to talk about difficult subjects such as racism, inequality, environmentalism, and other themes that might have been impossible to bring up otherwise in fictional stories of the time. Science fiction and creature design have been a way for creators to tell amazing stories that can touch people's hearts and change their points of view about things happening in the world, through subtle or not-so-subtle allegory and metaphor. That being said, they can also be used as simply a fun way to expand a fictional universe and make a mundane story more fantastical.

To me, creature design is a natural result of my hobbies and interest in studying nature, and trying to recombine and imagine what other forms of life might possibly exist in the universe. It seems like a simple task at first, but the more you get into it, the deeper the rabbit hole goes, and the amount of things to think about and create expands exponentially. Understanding on a deep level how biological life has grown and evolved on Earth is fundamental to becoming a good creature designer. The more you study and understand, the more you realize how related everything is; studying comparative anatomy and other in-depth analyses will open up many doors and enable all your imaginary designs to be infinitely more believable to an audience. This understanding will allow your characters and creatures to engage and entertain an audience. Without this understanding, your designs can have the opposite effect, taking the viewer out of the experience because "something doesn't look quite right." When you have a solid grasp of these

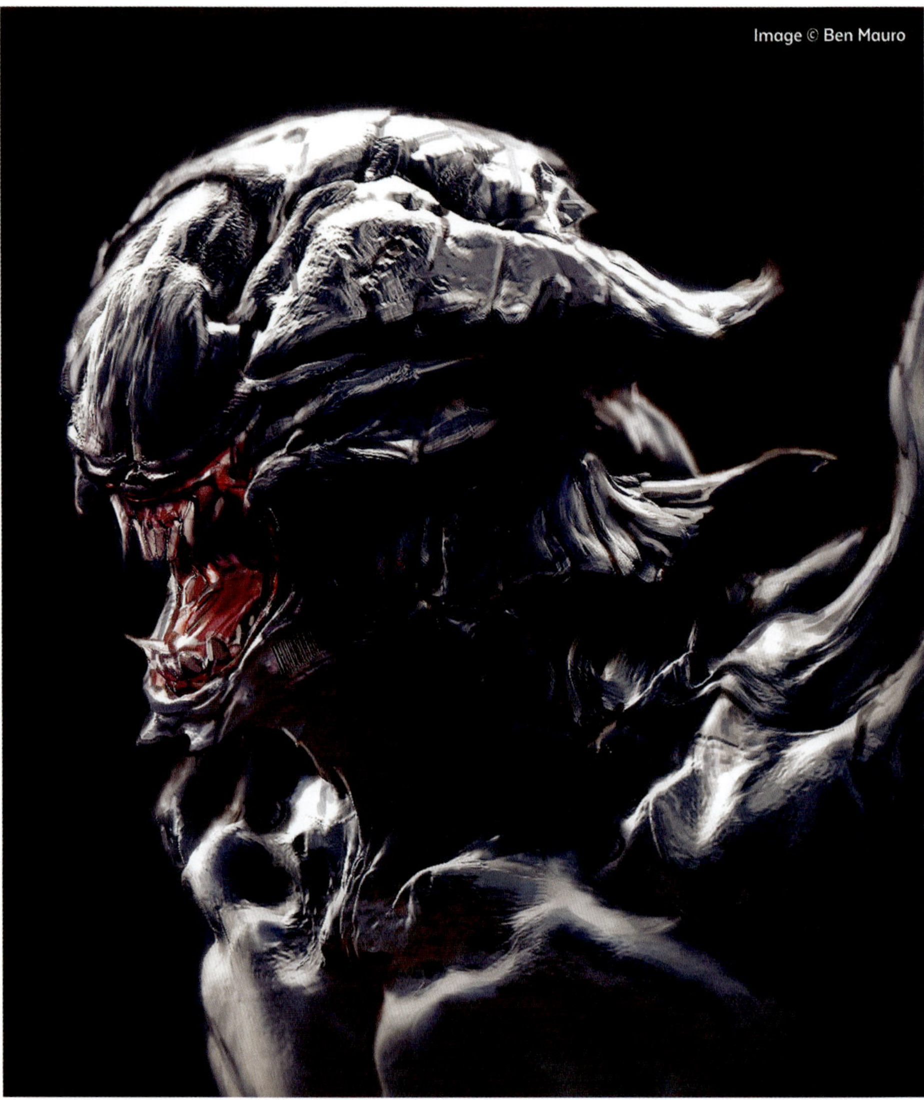

Image © Ben Mauro

principles, the sky is the limit for creation. Need to design an aquatic-inspired humanoid bounty hunter? No problem. A giant lizard-lion creature that chases the heroes through an alien market? Piece of cake! Having that understanding makes all of this fun, and it becomes more about imagining the coolest idea possible and bringing it to life.

These key foundation skills are a very important starting point on your way to becoming a good creature designer. This book will be a good introduction and reference guide to help you down the path of exploring and understanding these principles, as you grow and expand your skills as a creature designer in the entertainment industry. I hope you enjoy this book and have a great time creating amazing creatures.

Ben Mauro
Senior concept designer
benmaurodesign.com

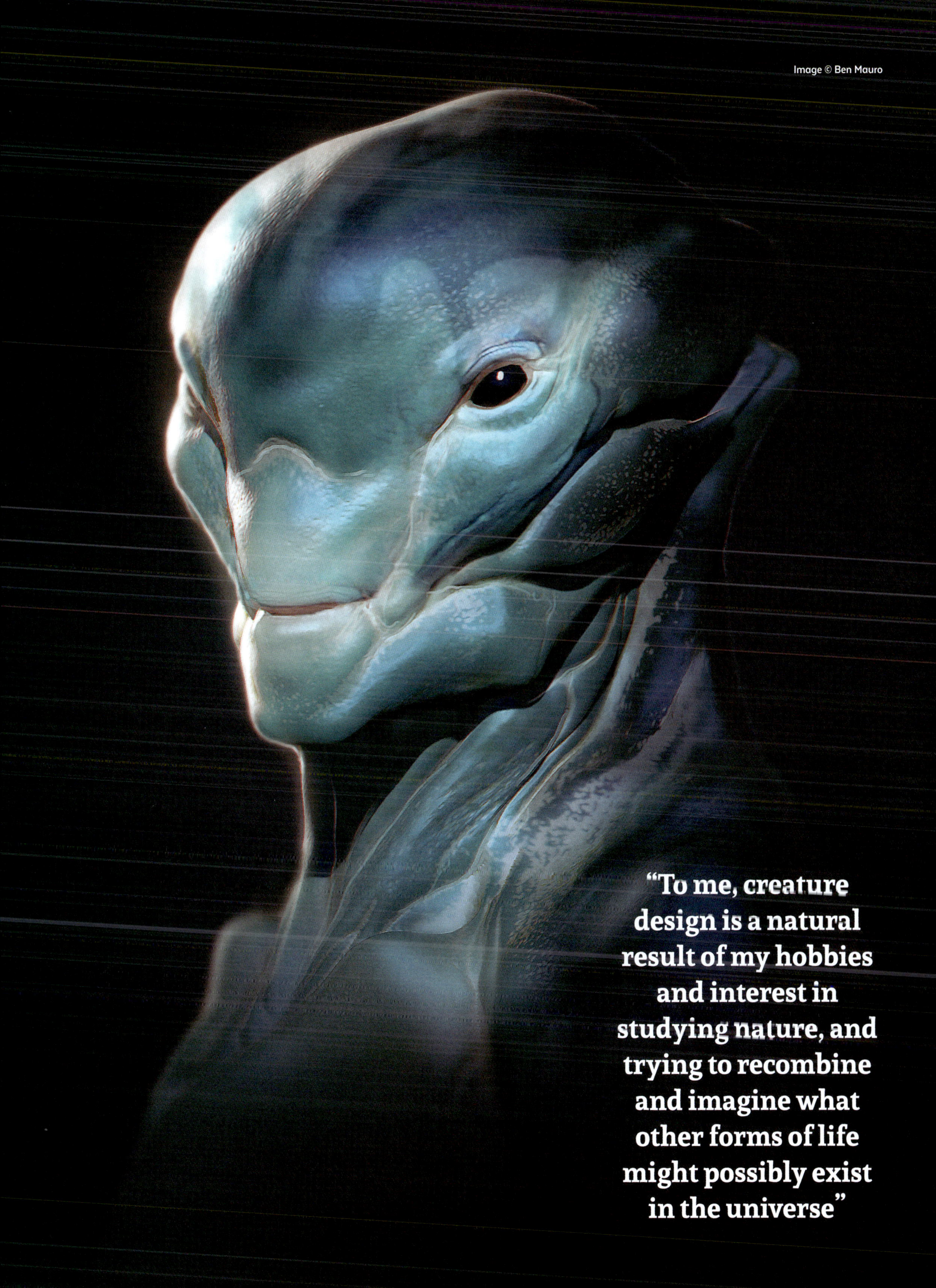

"To me, creature design is a natural result of my hobbies and interest in studying nature, and trying to recombine and imagine what other forms of life might possibly exist in the universe"

HOW TO USE THIS BOOK

For years we have watched, engaged with, and been enthralled by fascinating creature design. As the worlds of cinema, television, and video games become ever more inhabited by these unique creatures, the more designers and creatives will need to make them! This book is an accessible and engaging guide for those who want to delve into the world of creature design, and expand upon their knowledge and talents in order to create believable fictional beasts.

This book is divided into two main sections: reference chapters and creature design projects. To get started, we recommend following the reference chapters, which include **Research & imagination**, **Functionality & adaptation**, and **Anatomy**. These informative chapters will guide you through topics such as biodiversity, evolution, the anatomy of real-world creatures, and how all these can be applied to fictional creatures. Following these are the concept design theories and professional insights of **General design principles** and **Creature design in the industry**, which will help you to troubleshoot and elevate your creative approaches on your path to creature-design success.

You will then be ready to tackle the **Design processes** chapter, in which eight professional artists demonstrate the creation of eight imaginary creatures, each following their own individual brief. These projects, ranging from "Ungulate herbivore" to "Post-apocalyptic swamp fish" show a range of unique perspectives on how to approach creature design, and how to use the knowledge and principles outlined in the first half of the book to produce engaging, original creations.

The brief and its challenges are highlighted at the beginning of each project, and are then thoroughly investigated by each artist, in a clear process that you can follow along with if you wish. A wealth of annotations and tips provides extra insight into each creative decision, from sourcing real-world inspirations to choosing believable color palettes.

Next, the **Gallery** section condenses the steps carried out in the **Design processes**, showcasing research and development sketches alongside final portfolio designs. The **Exercises** section can be used as practice for your next projects, providing you with some bite-sized briefs to engage with and inspire your own designs. Finally, the **Glossary** will clarify technical terms to help you understand unfamiliar words or phrases.

We hope the tasks provided in this book will engage and inspire you as you explore the exciting realm of creature design. There will always be a fascination and demand for beasts and monsters, for as long as humans continue to be captivated by them, and the talented professionals in this book will help you make your creatures the best they can be.

Image © Ken Barthelmey

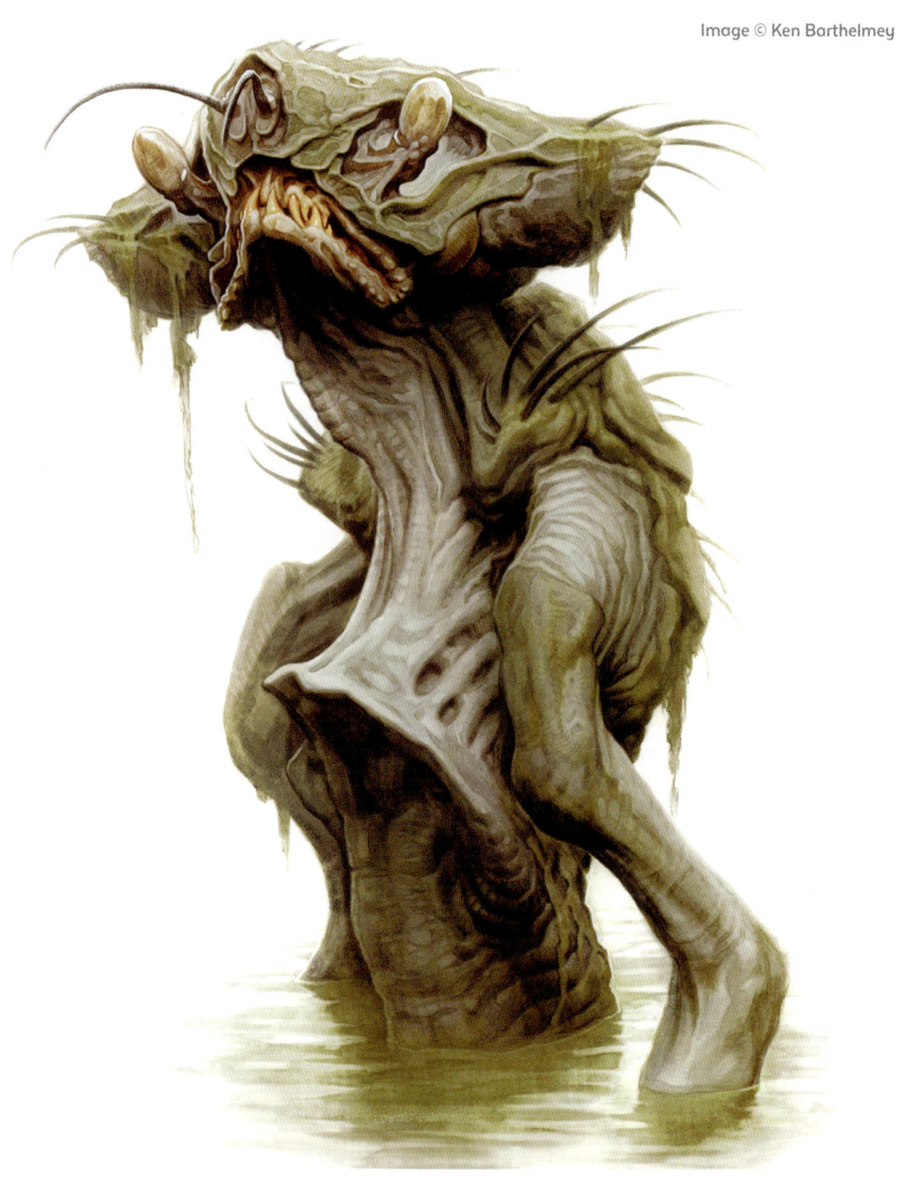

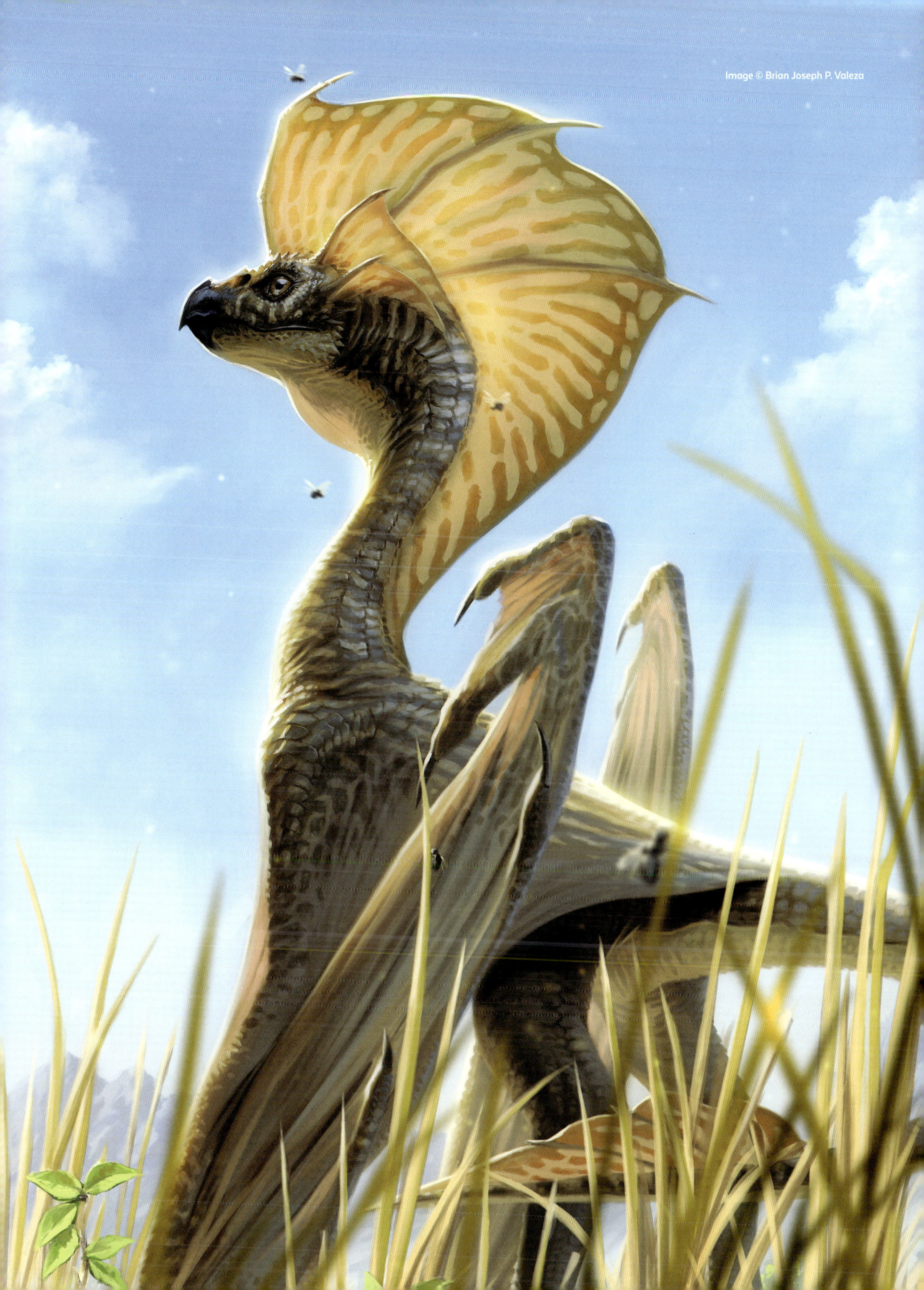
Image © Brian Joseph P. Valeza

Research & imagination

"When designing creatures, you will span genres from high fantasy to hard science fiction, and the degree to which reality informs your design must match the nature of that creature's world"

By Alex Ries

GATHERING RESEARCH

When designing creatures, you will span genres from high fantasy to hard science fiction, and the degree to which reality informs your design must match the nature of that creature's world. For example, a dragon, which may have been created through acts of magic, need not follow the rules of evolution as closely as an alien that evolved following natural laws on its home planet.

References for creature design are more accessible now than at any time in history. It is tempting to simply collect pictures of creatures by other artists that you love and use them as your entire source of inspiration. However, you must remember that truly new ideas are unlikely to come from *within* existing artistic tradition. Nature easily provides inspiration in infinite form and variety.

The internet is a titanic repository of resources for real-world wonders, but it should be supplemented with more in-depth sources. A useful resource is, perhaps surprisingly, older biology textbooks, which you can find first- or second-hand. Collect textbooks on invertebrate biology, paleontology, and general biology – the more variety, the better.

Avoid the natural temptation to only gather images of familiar creatures such as mammals, birds, and reptiles. While these groups are important, they are an almost comically tiny fragment of the possible inspirations available from life on Earth.

The importance of gathering references of unfamiliar groups (marine worms, microscopic crustaceans, plants, and fungi) is that without this broader exploration, you would perhaps never know these forms existed at all, and thus become trapped in the familiar tropes that dominate creature art.

REAL-WORLD CREATURES

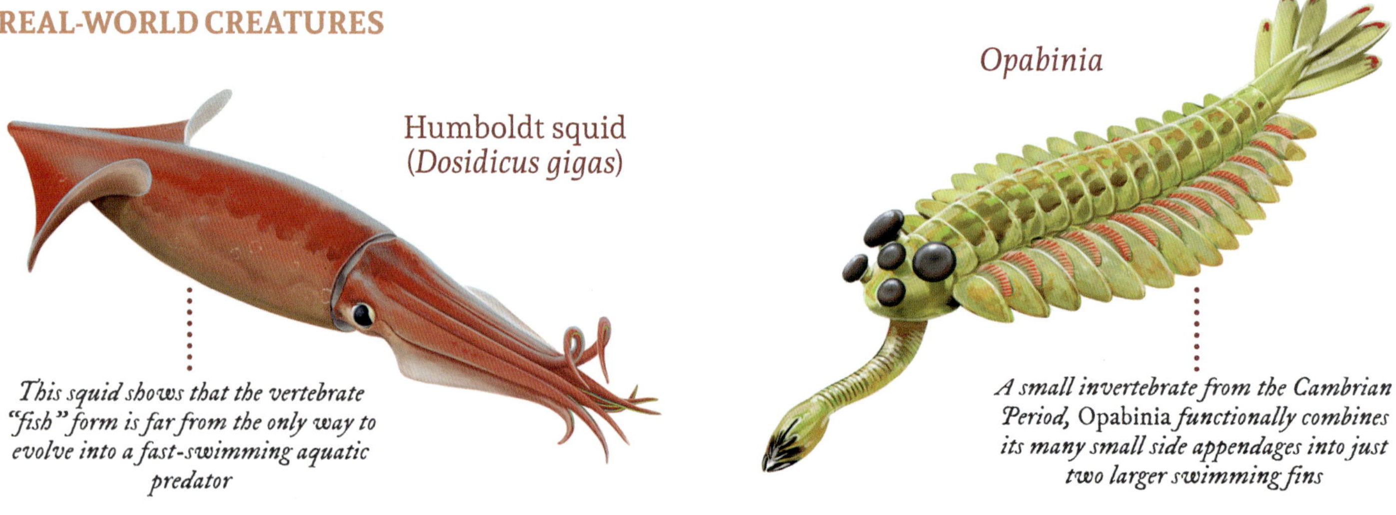

Humboldt squid
(*Dosidicus gigas*)

This squid shows that the vertebrate "fish" form is far from the only way to evolve into a fast-swimming aquatic predator

Opabinia

A small invertebrate from the Cambrian Period, Opabinia functionally combines its many small side appendages into just two larger swimming fins

IMAGINARY CREATURE

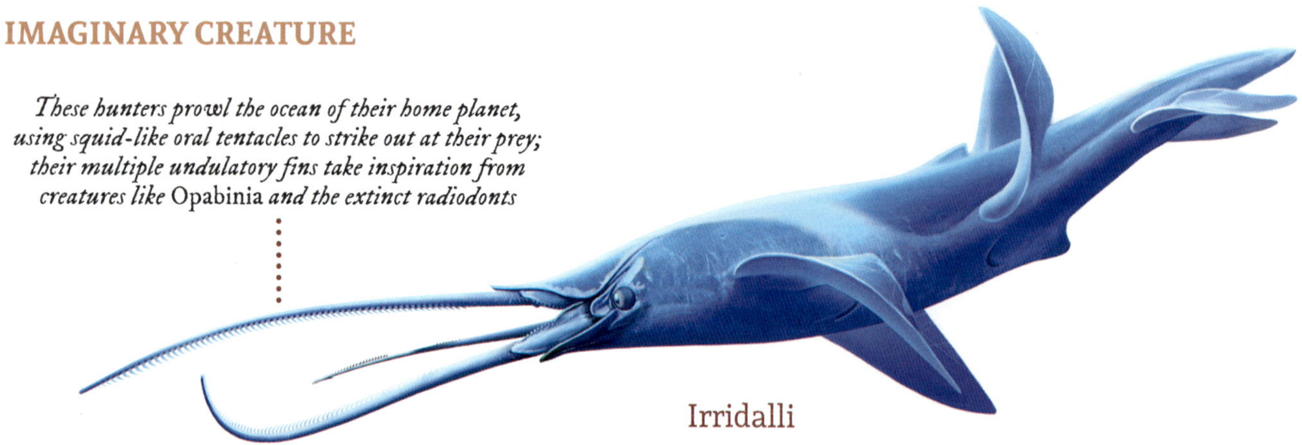

These hunters prowl the ocean of their home planet, using squid-like oral tentacles to strike out at their prey; their multiple undulatory fins take inspiration from creatures like Opabinia and the extinct radiodonts

Irridalli

REAL-WORLD CREATURES

Vampire bat (*Desmodontinae*)

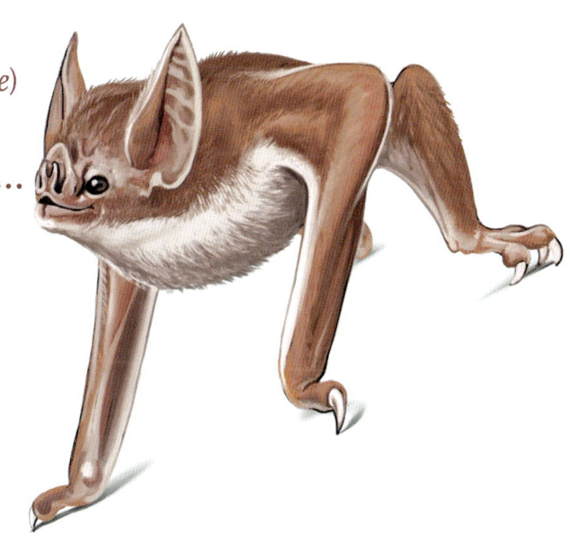

The vampire bat demonstrates complex wing-folding mechanisms that allow it to both fly and walk effectively on land

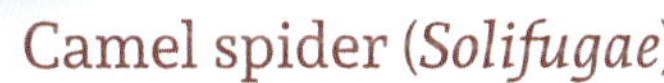

Camel spider (*Solifugae*)

Small but ferocious: the huge parallel jaws of the solifugid (a type of arachnid) show how different mouthparts can be among existing animals

IMAGINARY CREATURE

Bluestick flyers

Tiny colonial flying hunters; the sharp paired jaws link back to the solifugids while the elegantly folding wings combine elements of bats and the extinct pterosaurs

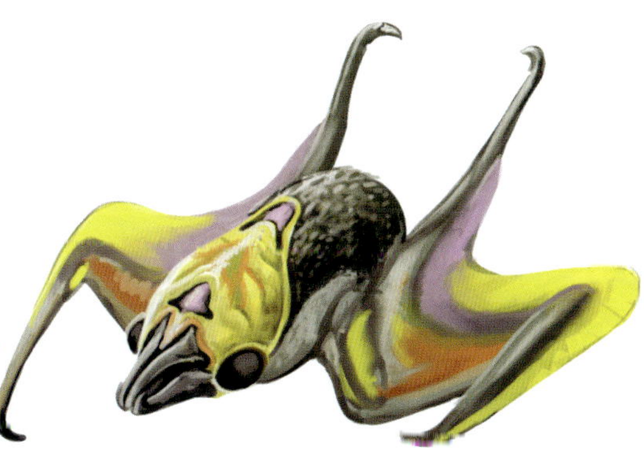

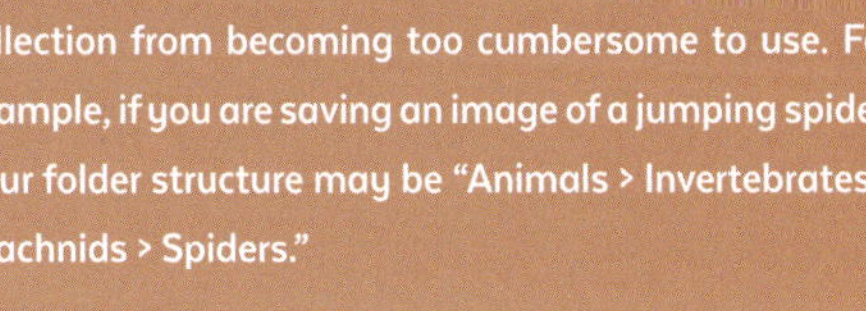

Organizing files

If you are gathering digital references, keep them well ordered. Subfolders of useful groups will keep your collection from becoming too cumbersome to use. For example, if you are saving an image of a jumping spider, your folder structure may be "Animals > Invertebrates > Arachnids > Spiders."

IMAGINATIVE DESIGN

Having gathered your research, you will have the raw materials for your designs; it is now up to you as an artist to synthesize this information into a novel, coherent creature. Again, the rules of the world for which you are designing must be considered. In a fantasy context, or with "synthetic" creatures in science fiction, the rules of evolution and phylogeny may not apply. For example, a griffin combines aspects of mammalian lions and dinosaurian birds – combinations that do not occur naturally. The creatures on these pages are examples of fictional designs inspired by real-world evolution.

In exploring possible design directions, there is in truth no single "correct" method. The only criterion is that your method ultimately delivers the design you need. Thumbnailing is the most common method at the earliest stage; these simple sketches can fill a page and be used to explore numerous broad ideas as quickly as possible for you or your client.

The advent of digital art has added another potent dimension to the process; as well as thumbnailing, you can develop designs on the fly. It is possible to move, warp, resize, and completely overhaul artwork as you create it. In this way, the drawing *itself* is dynamically designed, sometimes avoiding entirely the need for endless thumbnailing. Save your working files iteratively as you go, before any major changes, so that you have multiple numbered versions archived. You may find yourself dipping back into older files for elements to copy and paste into the newest.

As you begin the design process, it can be tempting to search just a little longer for that perfect reference image - one with slightly better lighting, a more useful camera angle, or a different dynamic pose. However, this is a trap that easily leads into procrastination. You may never find the "perfect" reference for your creature. In truth, you do not need it.

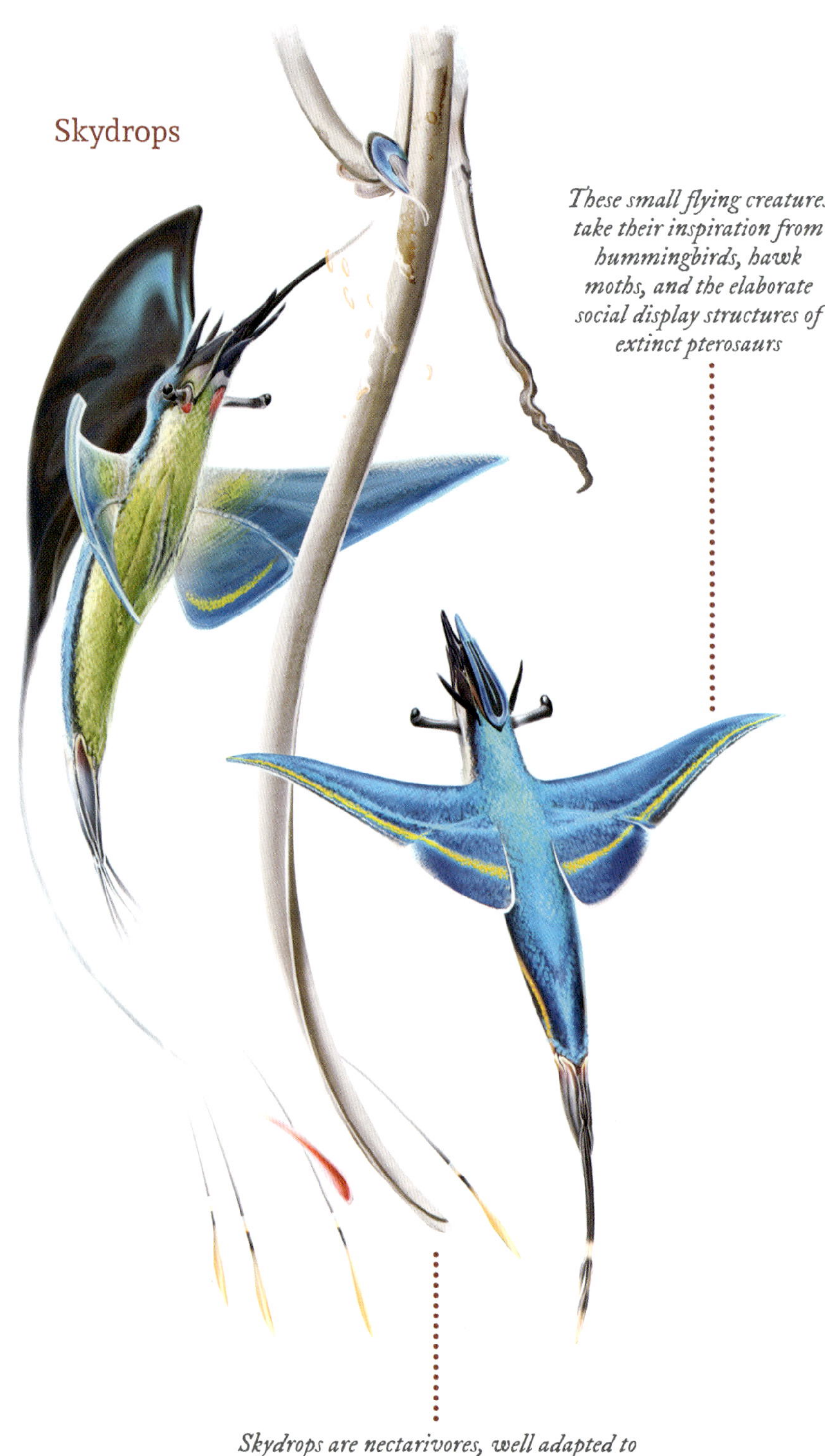

These small flying creatures take their inspiration from hummingbirds, hawk moths, and the elaborate social display structures of extinct pterosaurs

Skydrops are nectarivores, well adapted to thrive in a humid rainforest environment

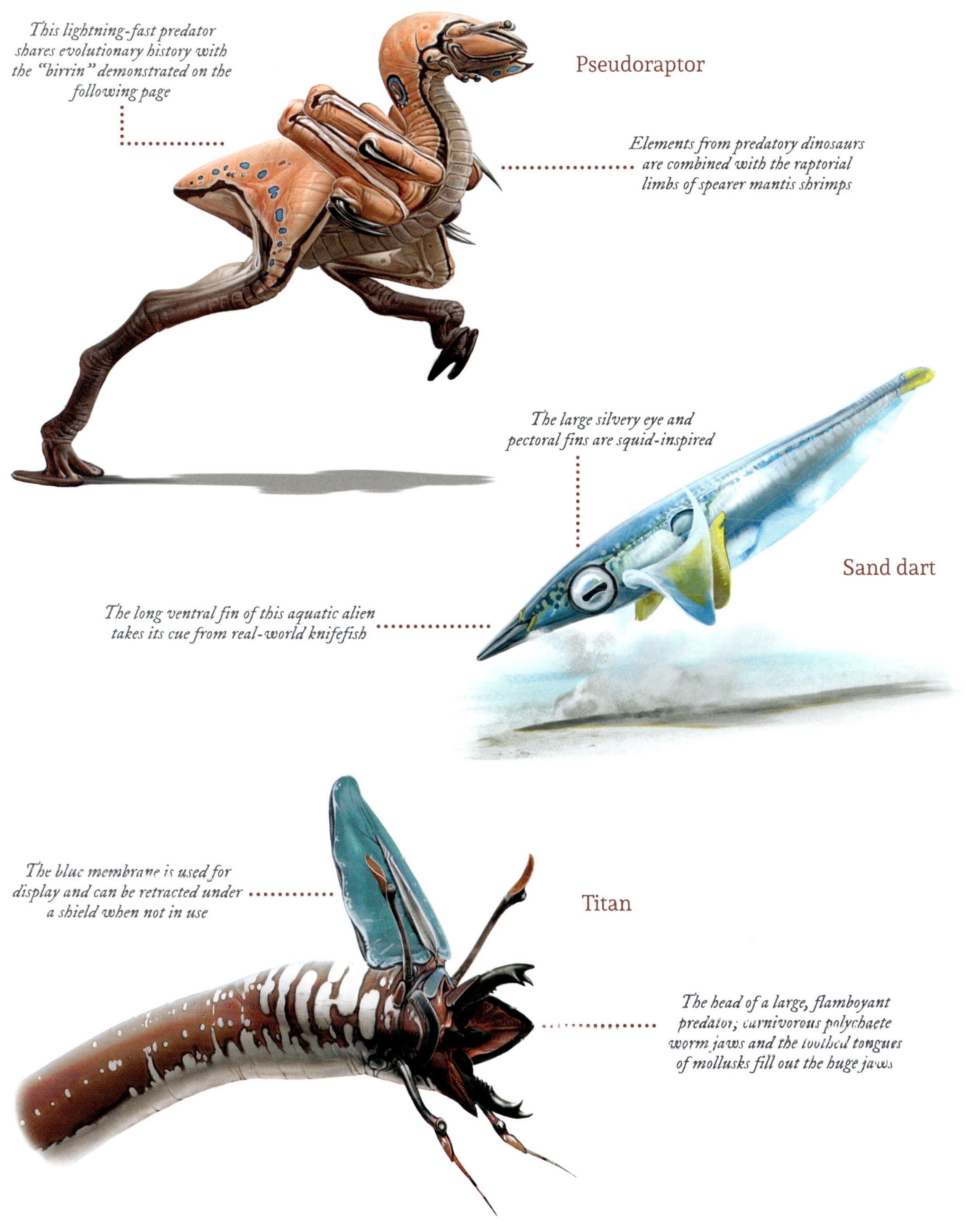

This lightning-fast predator shares evolutionary history with the "birrin" demonstrated on the following page

Pseudoraptor

Elements from predatory dinosaurs are combined with the raptorial limbs of spearer mantis shrimps

The large silvery eye and pectoral fins are squid-inspired

Sand dart

The long ventral fin of this aquatic alien takes its cue from real-world knifefish

The blue membrane is used for display and can be retracted under a shield when not in use

Titan

The head of a large, flamboyant predator; carnivorous polychaete worm jaws and the toothed tongues of mollusks fill out the huge jaws

Example creature design: Birrin

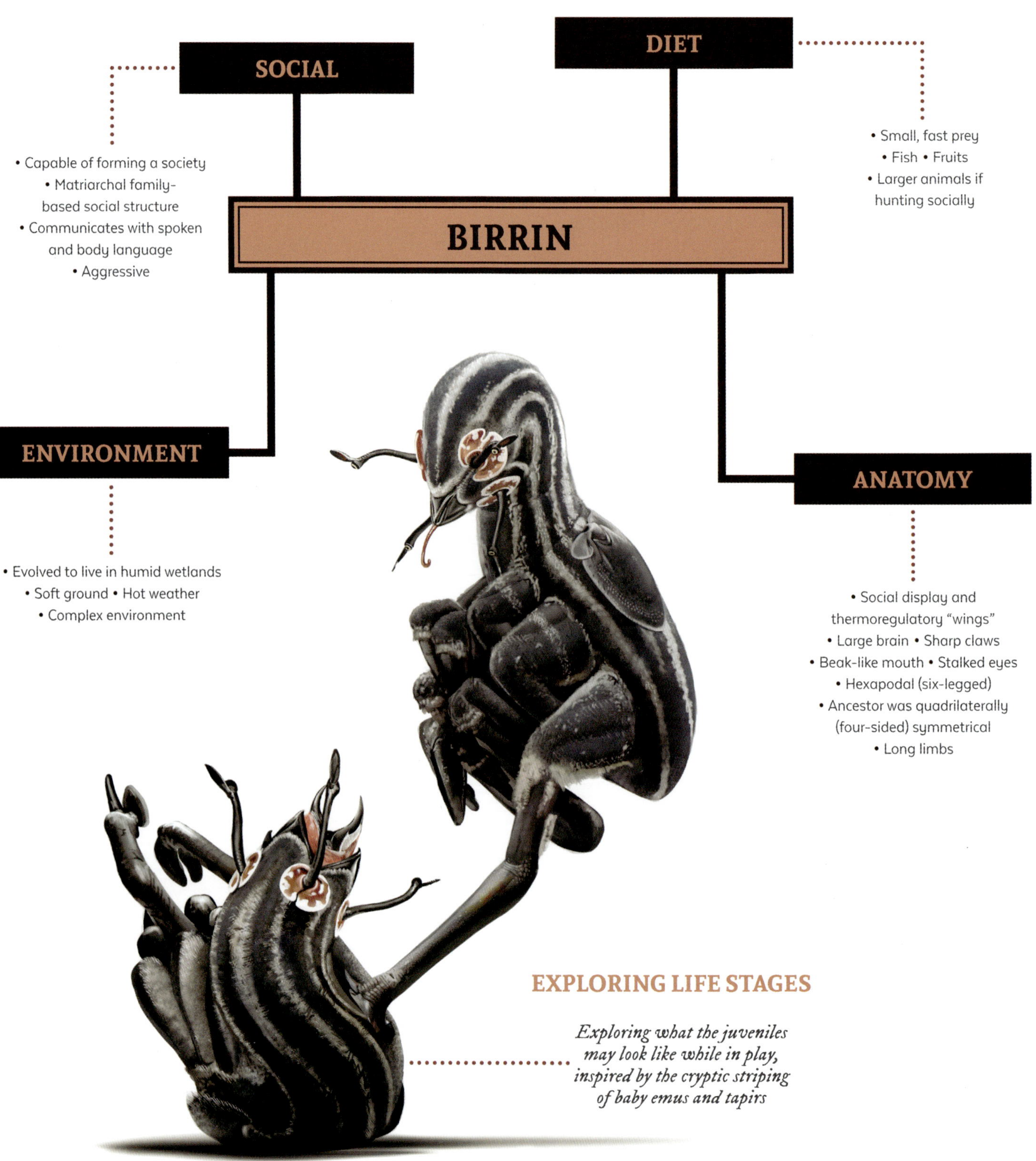

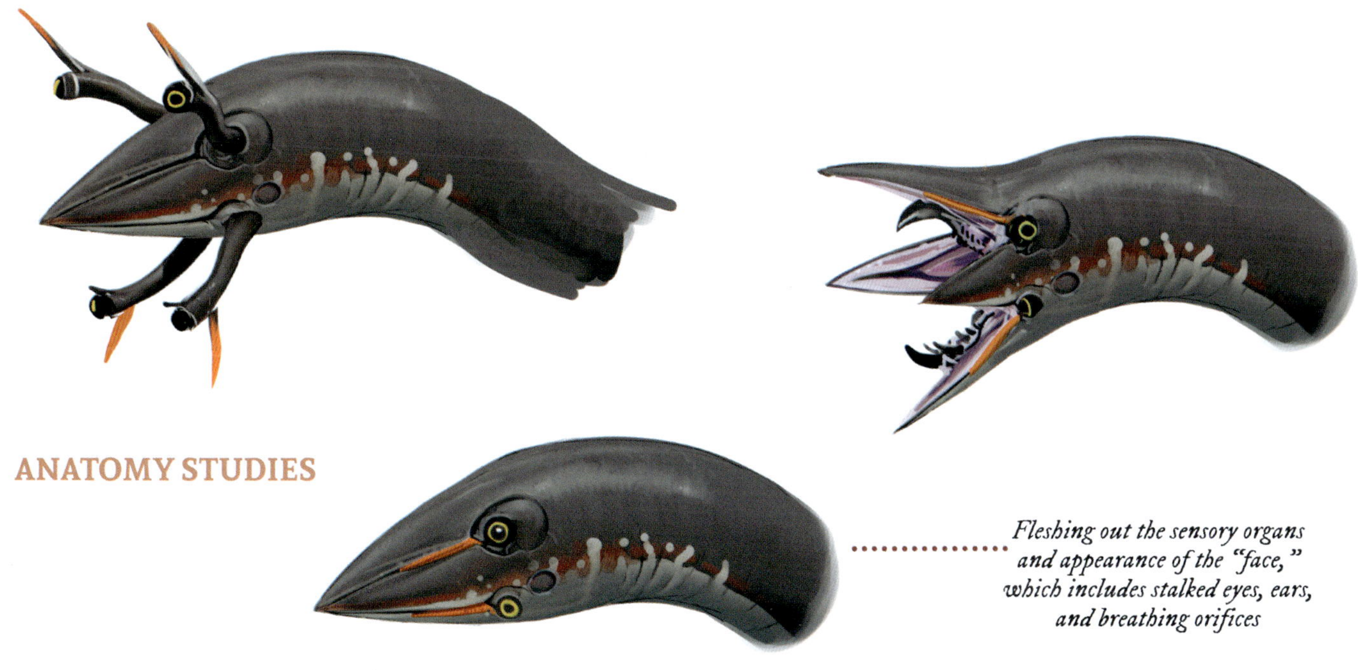

ANATOMY STUDIES

Fleshing out the sensory organs and appearance of the "face," which includes stalked eyes, ears, and breathing orifices

A dynamic image of the smaller male displaying for an (unimpressed) female to examine possible social behaviors

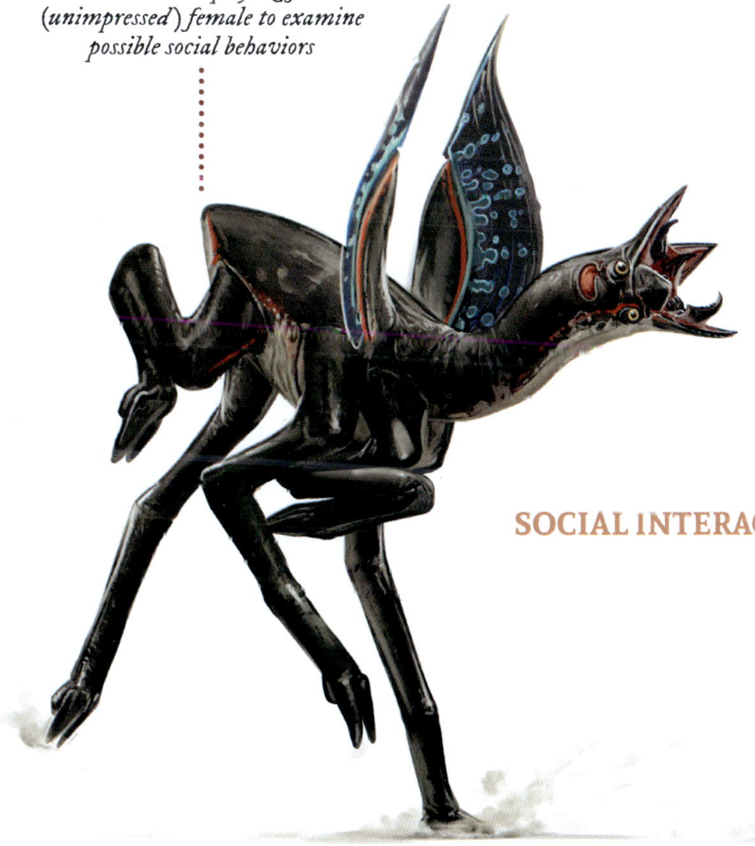

SOCIAL INTERACTIONS

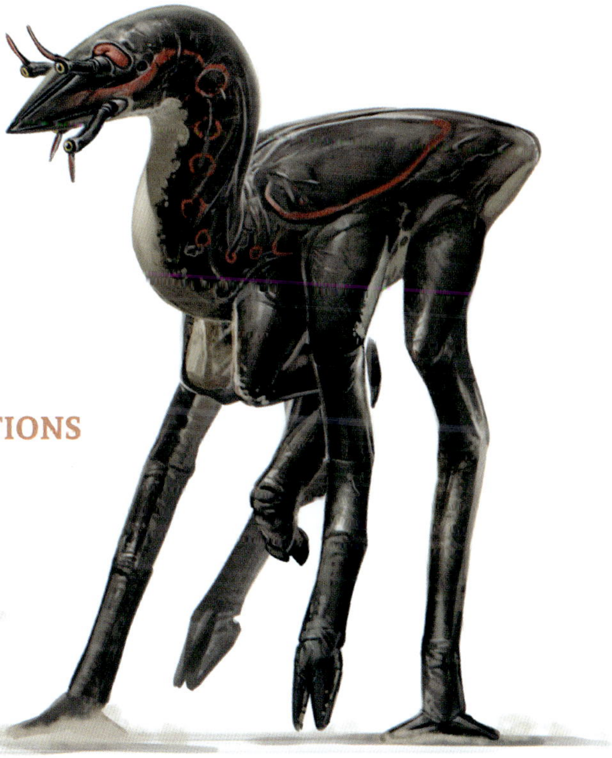

ANATOMY STUDIES

A close-up of birrin appendages; if your creature is to be part of an ongoing project, working out these details early can be important

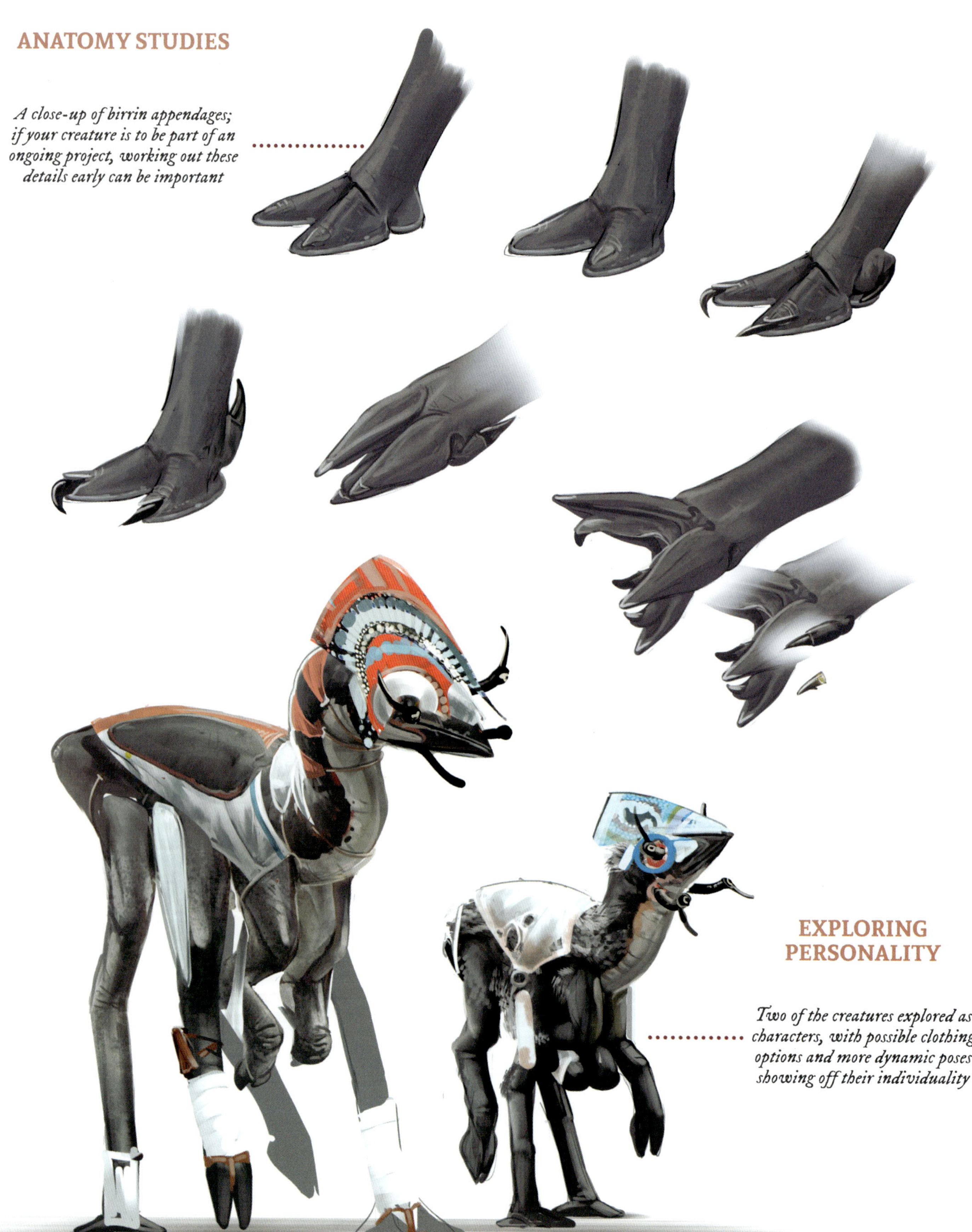

EXPLORING PERSONALITY

Two of the creatures explored as characters, with possible clothing options and more dynamic poses showing off their individuality

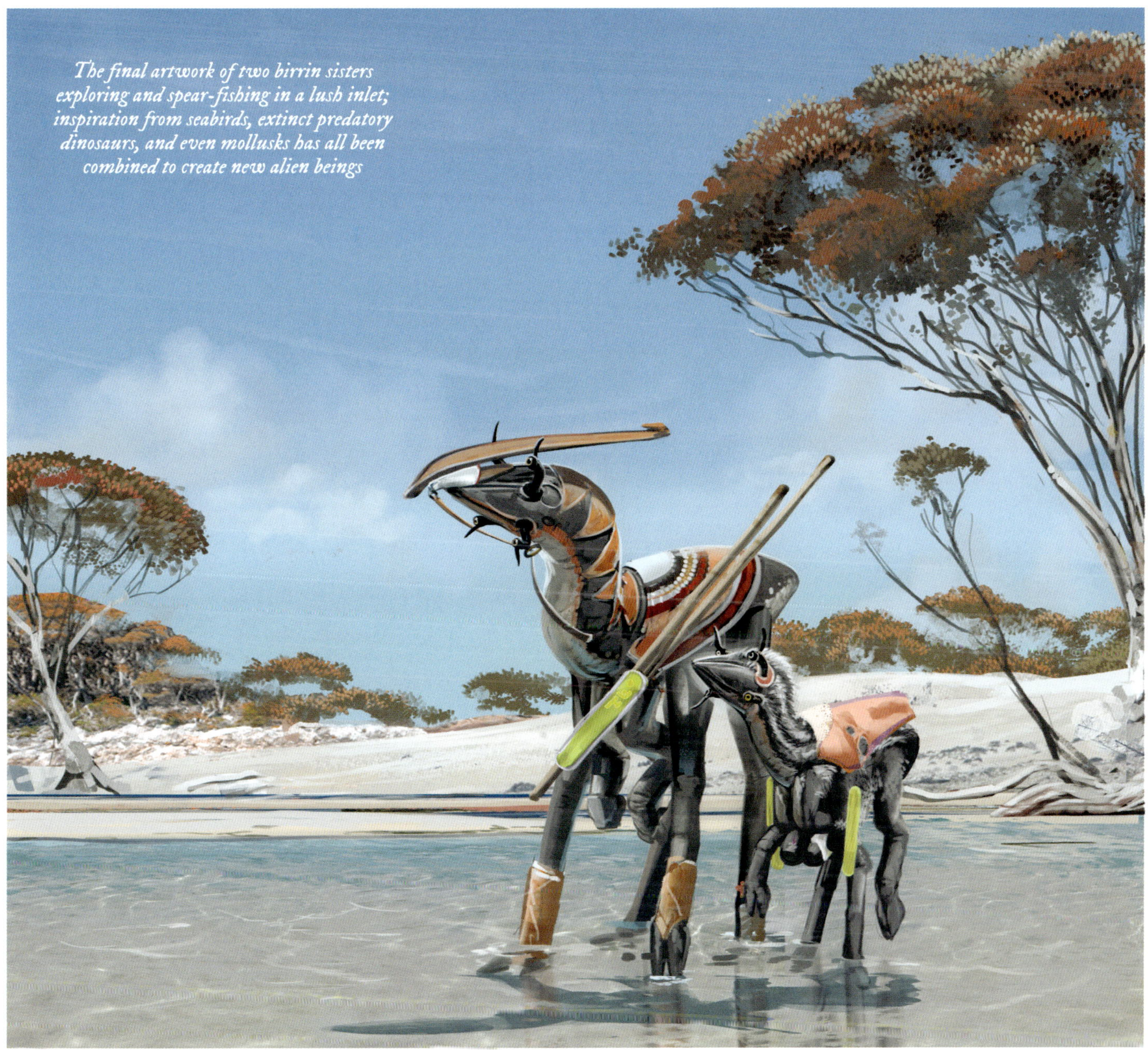

Study from reality

Draftsmanship is not the be-all and end-all of design. However, improving your drawing skills *will* help you communicate the ideas you are trying to convey more effectively, and so is worth pursuing. Few methods of training are more effective than life drawing. It will give you a feel for how organisms are put together, how they carry themselves, and even aspects of their behavior. While it is often advised to seek out and draw animals in the real world, you can also use photographic wildlife books and the internet to reference animals you would never otherwise be able to access. Remember, if you wish to publish observational drawings based on photos, to respect any use restrictions placed on them by the copyright holder.

Functionality & adaptation

"Functionality is one of the most grounding and important aspects of your creature design. It not only connects your creature to a place, but it helps describe why it is there, what role it plays, and how it survives. Ultimately it will connect your creature with the audience"

By Brynn Metheney

BIODIVERSITY: THE VARIETY OF LIFE

Form should always follow function. There is no doubt that you have heard this phrase before. It is a key principle to consider when designing creatures and characters alike. It allows us to ask the questions:

- What does functionality mean in the realm of creature design?

- How significant is functionality?

- What is it about functionality that can help us design more interesting creatures?

The function of a creature can be tied to many variables. Real-world animals do not evolve in a vacuum. They are affected by the changing climates, the environment they occupy, their own behavioral tendencies and reactions, and other animals and plants that inhabit or invade the same spaces. So many factors go into shaping animals on our own planet, it is no wonder that we, as designers, are keen to use these observations as principles when we design imaginary creatures.

When we begin designing a creature, the infinite possibilities can seem overwhelming. Asking ourselves questions about **how our creature moves and survives in the world it inhabits** can help us focus on a design solution. Realizing the functionality of your creature is key to relating to your audience.

Our job as designers is to reach an audience that has a connection to our characters and creatures. Using real animals as references helps our audience relate to the creatures we create, because of the **real-world associations** those animals bring. If you use key features and adaptations found in nature in your own designs, such as long fur in a cold climate, the audience will link the creature with something they have seen before. Perhaps a musk ox or a polar bear will come to mind, along with all the connotations those animals invoke.

Similarly, when we think of a lion, we think of the mane first. If you give your creature a mane, your audience may think of a lion and its associations; for example, social hierarchy and physical power. Being aware of the decisions you make in these design aspects is important, as they can **affect the audience's perception** of your design. In this chapter, we will be exploring the facets of function,

REAL-WORLD BISON

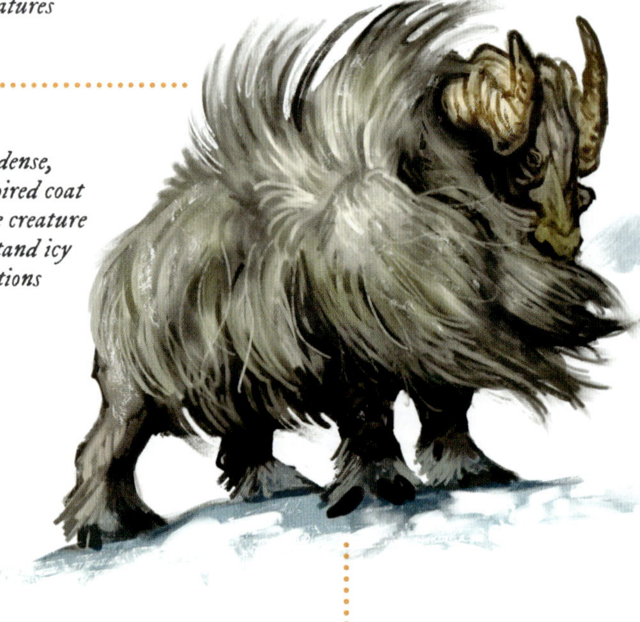

Bison are able to withstand some of the harshest weather the American Midwest has to offer, enduring scorching summer heat and below-freezing temperatures

IMAGINARY CREATURE ADAPTED TO A COLD CLIMATE

Long, dense, bison-inspired coat enables the creature to withstand icy conditions

Bison are characterized by their size and build — males can weigh over 2,000 lb. They have long vertebrae that are supported by strong muscles inside their hump; these features help the bison plough through snow to access vegetation in the winter

Wide, flat hooves allow easy traversal of snowy or slippery terrain

how creatures adapt to survive, and how we can use what we know about animals here on Earth to help us design imaginary creatures. We will be asking ourselves questions such as:

- **Where does it live?**

- **What does it eat?**

- **Is it female, male, or neither?**

In each section we will discuss some key examples of how animals adapt. The exploration will not be exhaustive, so as part of your creature design process you should continually research real-world animals to fuel your concepts.

Functionality is one of the most grounding and important aspects of your creature design. It not only connects your creature to a place, but it helps describe why it is there, what role it plays, and how

it survives. Ultimately it will connect your creature with the audience. Use these principles as a guide and enjoy exploring all of the amazing, innovative, and seemingly impossible solutions that nature has come up with for the problem of survival. The natural world is never boring and will always be more alien and more incredible than we can imagine.

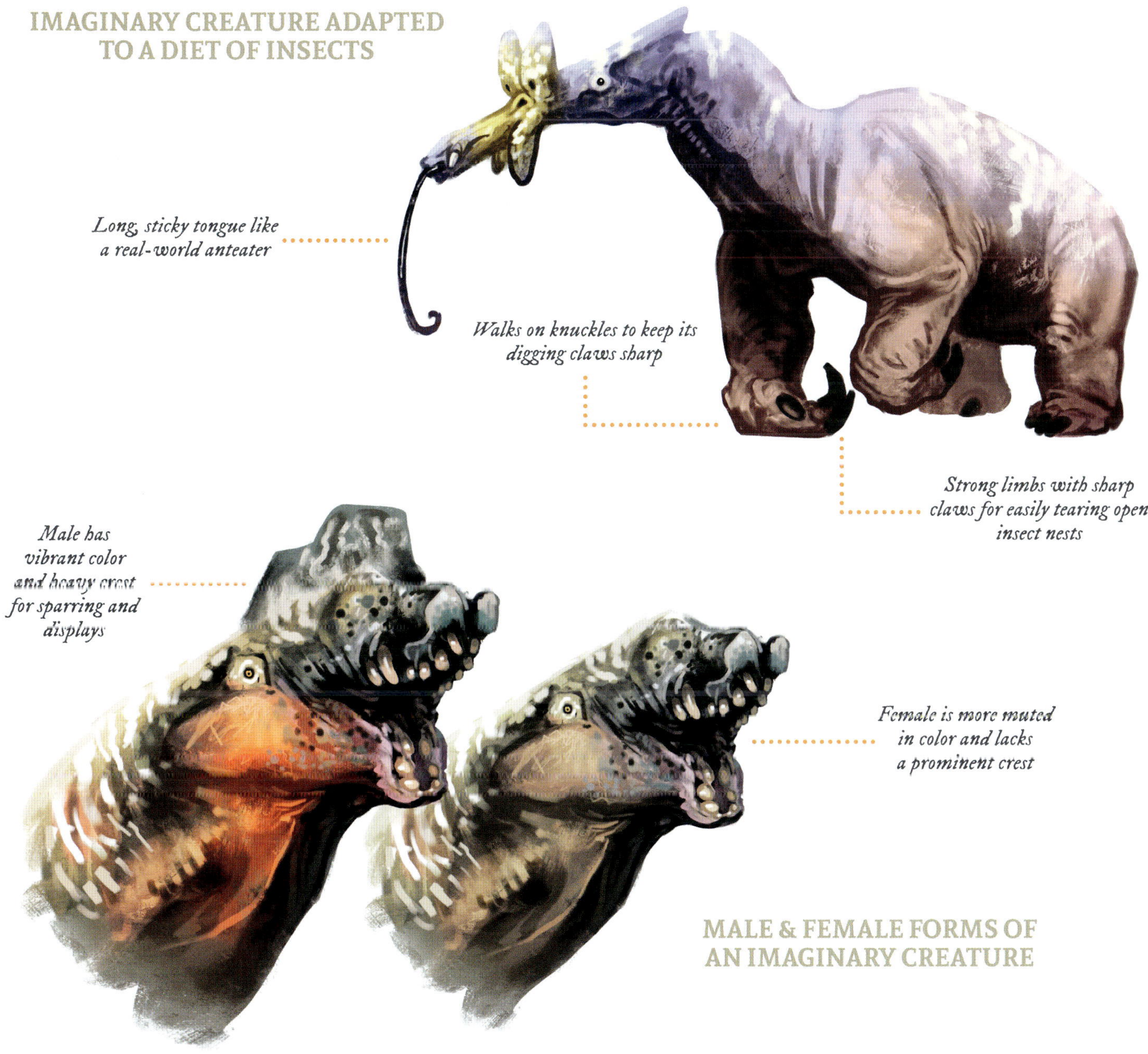

Climate

The very first question to ask yourself when you begin to design a creature is: "**Where does it come from?**" This question begins the process of setting up a successful design and finding solutions to the creature's survival. Asking yourself about where the creature comes from is a great way to give yourself, and your audience, a place to feel grounded.

Let us stay within the cold climate we discussed as an example on **page 22**. Here on Earth, we expect animals to look a certain way when they inhabit a cold climate. Animals might have a lot of body fat or be covered in fur or feathers. Surviving in a cold environment means prioritizing body heat and energy, so these animals use as little energy as possible to gather or hunt food, and their bodies adapt to retain heat.

Different animals retain heat in different ways. Seagulls use their feathers to trap body heat close to their bodies, while walruses use thick blubber to keep their internal organs and muscles warm. Other animals adapt in real time to survive. Reindeer simply move to warmer places when the weather becomes too harsh, migrating to a different area to take advantage of food and warmth elsewhere. Certain fish slow their metabolisms to endure the most extreme times of the season.

REAL-WORLD ADAPTATION TO A COLD, WET CLIMATE

Walrus (*Odobenus rosmarus*)

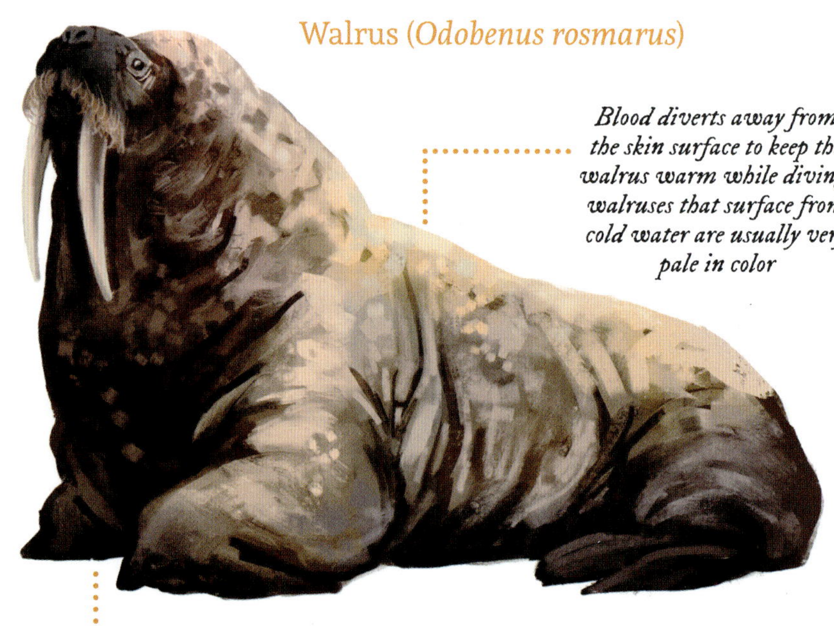

Blood diverts away from the skin surface to keep the walrus warm while diving; walruses that surface from cold water are usually very pale in color

Thick blubber keeps the walrus's organs warm while it dives deep for food

IMAGINARY CREATURE ADAPTED TO A COLD CLIMATE

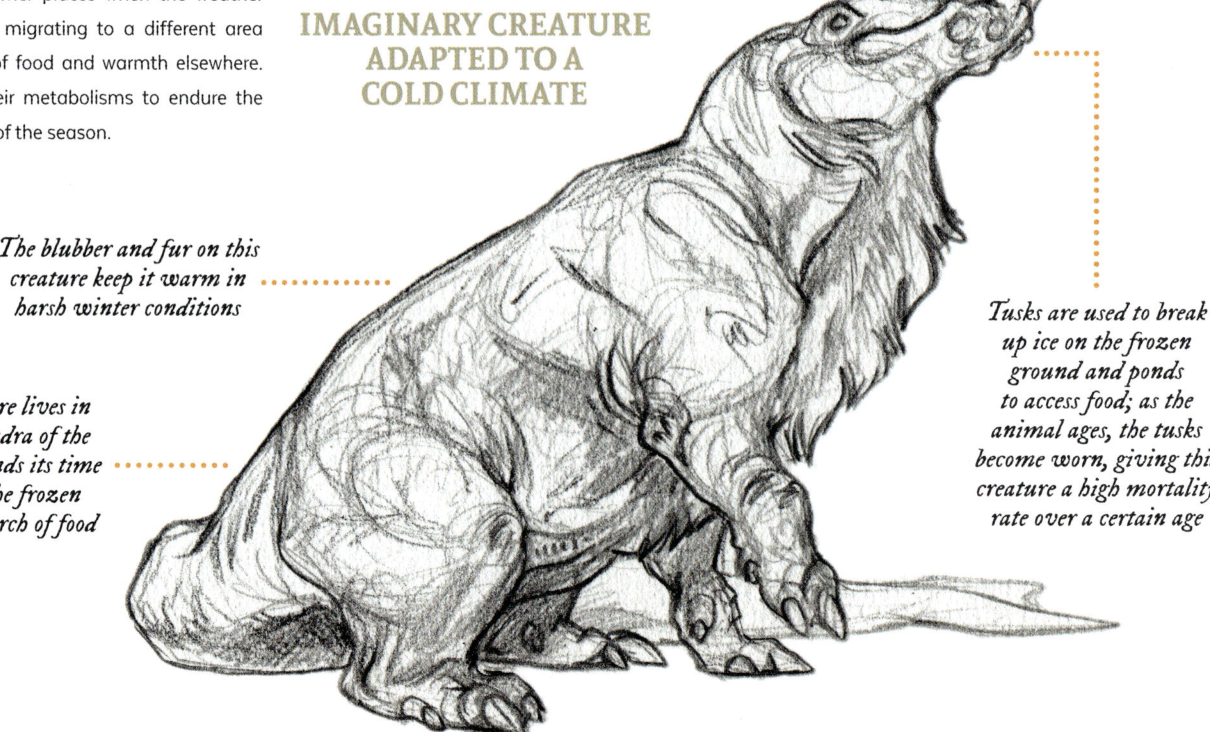

The blubber and fur on this creature keep it warm in harsh winter conditions

This creature lives in the cold tundra of the north; it spends its time roaming the frozen plains in search of food

Tusks are used to break up ice on the frozen ground and ponds to access food; as the animal ages, the tusks become worn, giving this creature a high mortality rate over a certain age

Bottom image © Brynn Metheney

This just covers one kind of temperature in one kind of place. The possibilities for adaptation related to temperature are endless. If we compare hot and cold climates, we see drastic changes in physiology, even within the same species. Take, for example, a snow leopard and an African leopard. The snow leopard has long, thick fur for surviving in the cold. Its body is compact to keep all of the warmth close to the core of its body. Its face and ears are short to keep them from becoming frostbitten. It possesses a long tail for balance as it jumps and explores the rough terrain of the Himalayas, and its paws are wide to give it a lot of surface area so as not to sink into the snow.

In contrast, the African leopard is supple and built to be larger. It can take down much bigger prey and pull them up into trees, so it is equipped with powerful forelegs and shoulders. Its body is longer and larger, with shorter fur to help keep it cool in the heat of the African savanna.

Comparing even just these two animals shows the profound effects that the temperature of an environment can have in the real world – and gives you some idea of how you might apply the same logic to your creature designs.

REAL-WORLD ADAPTATION TO A HOT, DRY CLIMATE

African elephant (*Loxodonta*)

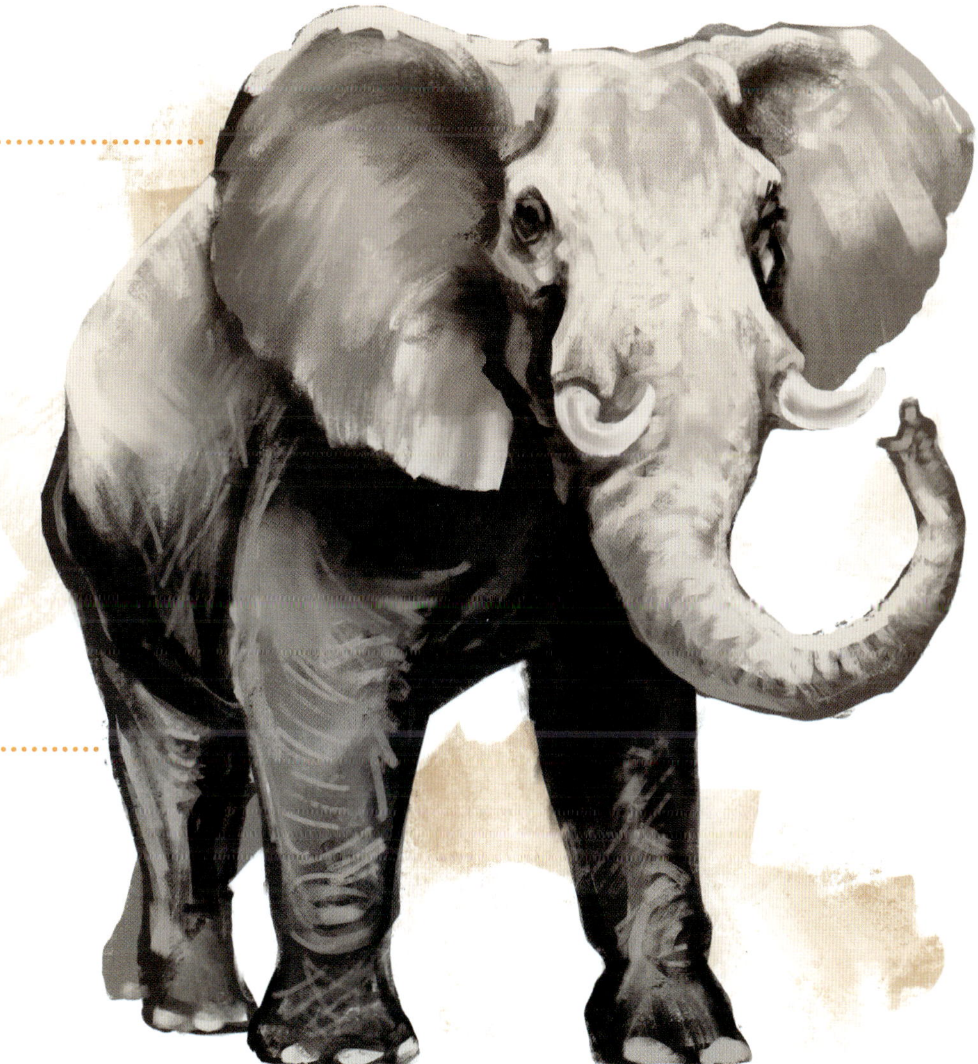

Large ears help the elephant regulate its body temperature by dissipating heat

Elephants are herbivores, but are able to forage for a large variety of plants, and can even survive on tree bark in the dry seasons

REAL-WORLD ADAPTATION TO A HOT, DRY CLIMATE

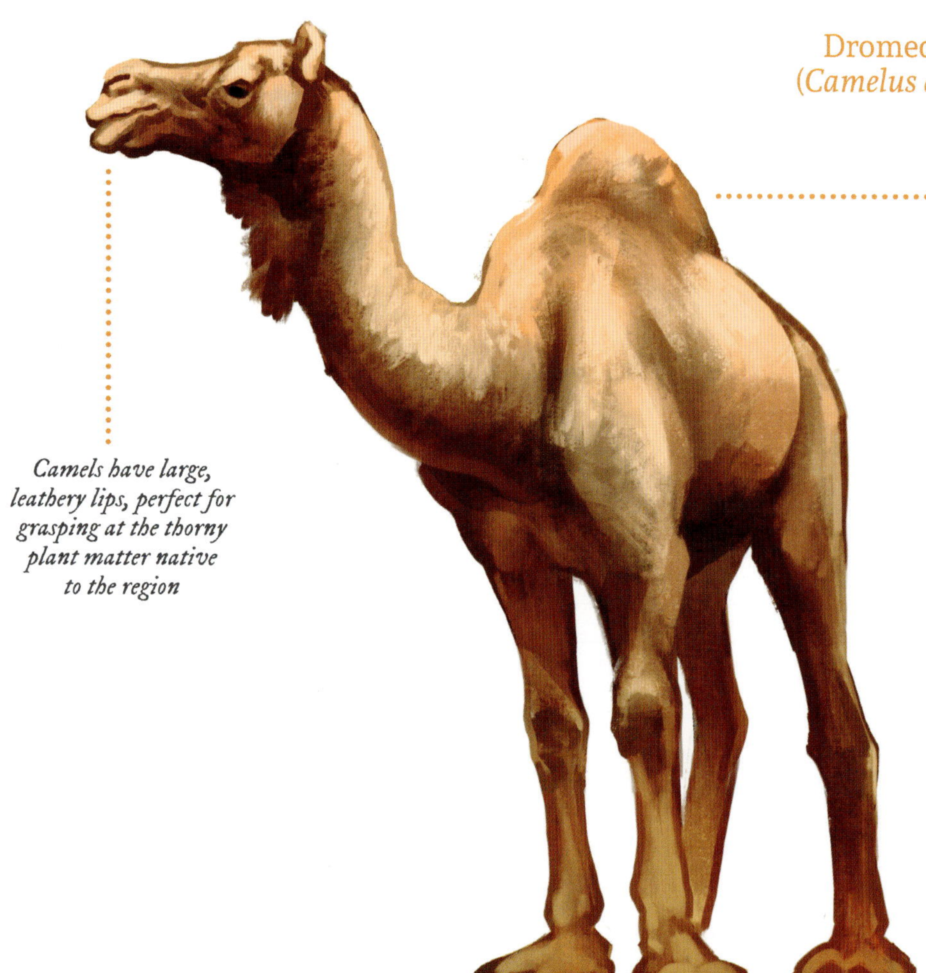

Dromedary camel
(*Camelus dromedarius*)

The camel stores fat in its hump that helps it to survive months of drought and hardship; camels also have unique digestive tracts, able to absorb almost all of the liquid inside the plants they consume

Camels have large, leathery lips, perfect for grasping at the thorny plant matter native to the region

Dromedary camels are iconic desert inhabitants for a reason – they are perfectly adapted to their habitat, with large, flat feet that help them stay on the tops of sand dunes by increasing their surface area

Adaptation ideas

Cold climate

- More body fat
- Slower metabolism
- More hair/fur/feathers
- Potential migration
- Compact body
- Flattened facial features

Hot climate

- Larger surface area to dissipate heat
- Less hair/fur/feathers
- Ability to retain and absorb water
- Large feet or paws for walking on sand
- Nocturnal behavior

IMAGINARY CREATURES ADAPTED TO A HOT, DRY CLIMATE

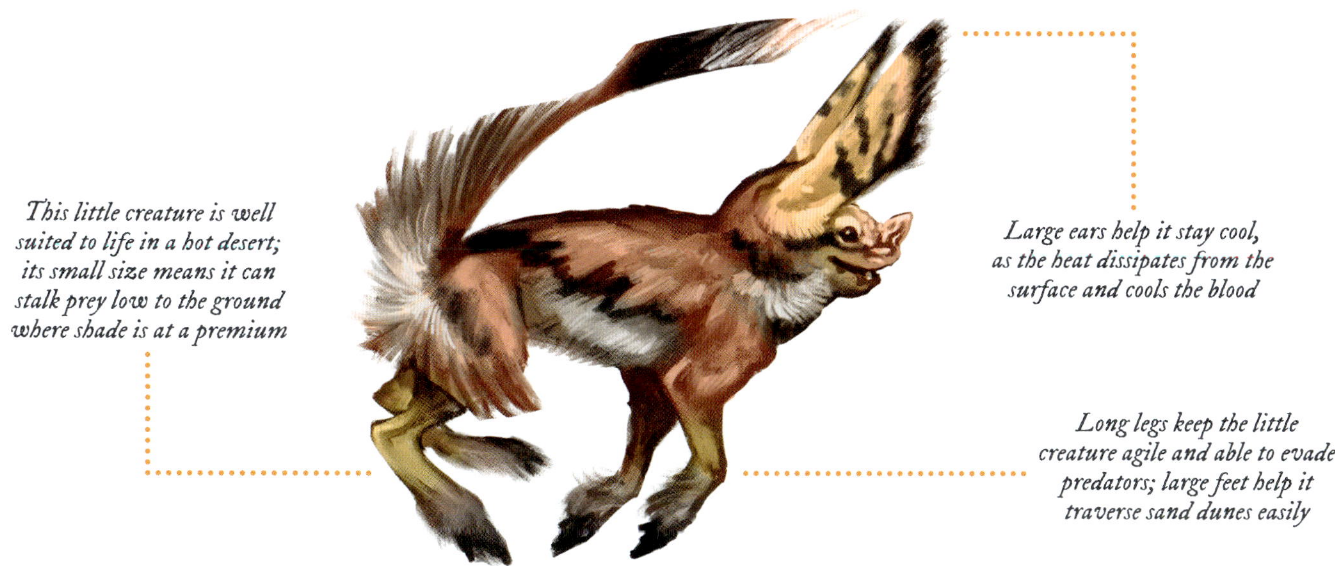

This little creature is well suited to life in a hot desert; its small size means it can stalk prey low to the ground where shade is at a premium

Large ears help it stay cool, as the heat dissipates from the surface and cools the blood

Long legs keep the little creature agile and able to evade predators; large feet help it traverse sand dunes easily

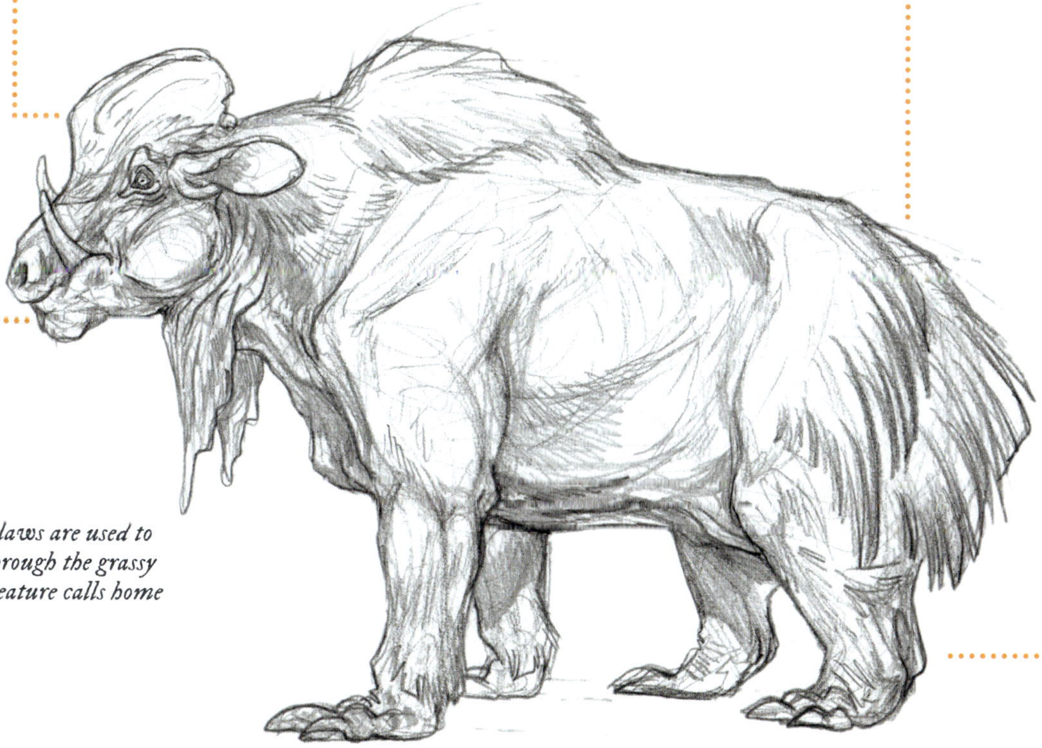

This creature's large crest is used for intimidation and is filled with large blood vessels to help cool the animal

The fur of this animal is mostly short, as the majority of its year is hot and dry

Tusks and claws are used to rummage through the grassy plains this creature calls home

The feet are well equipped with large claws for scavenging for plant matter under the dry ground and logs

Habitat

All animals on Earth encounter different types of terrain, sometimes multiple kinds, in their day-to-day lives. There are a huge variety of habitats on our planet: rainforests, rivers, deserts, tundra, coasts, open ocean, grassy plains - the list goes on. Each of these environments has a direct effect on how an animal is shaped and what adaptations are needed for its survival.

It is not a stretch to understand that a creature that lives **on land** will differ from one that lives **in the ocean**, and from those that spend time **in the air**. Habitats on Earth fall into these basic categories, and most animals exist in them or between them.

Sometimes traits will cross species lines and environments, because the solution is simple and makes the most sense. For example, multiple animals, ranging from fish and reptiles to birds and mammals, use flippers and fins to move around in water. This type of common adaptation among different groups of animals is called **convergent evolution**. If you pay close attention, you will begin to see similarities in adaptations among different species of animals. For example, the snow leopard mentioned earlier in this chapter has large, wide feet to help it stay on top of snow drifts. You will find the same adaptation present in snowshoe hares and even in reindeer to help with the same problem.

Even animals that do not deal with snow will have the same solution if the surface they are walking on is similar in composition. For example, a camel also has large feet to help it walk on sand without sinking, and Jacana birds have large feet to enable them to walk lightly on the tops of floating lily pads.

Next time you watch a nature documentary, ask yourself *why* the animals look the way they do. A lot of it has to do with the way they move around their world, and how the habitat has shaped their body and evolution.

Air

Animals that spend time in the air feature wings or enlarged skin membranes to aid in flight or gliding. They need adaptations for retaining blood pressure and oxygen levels at high altitudes, and bodies that are shaped to glide through the air effectively. When it comes to migration, the ways in which birds navigate is fascinating, and there is much debate on whether this ability comes from olfactory, auditory, visual, or even magnetic capability. Turn to **page 86** for a more anatomical overview of how birds are adapted to flight.

REAL-WORLD ADAPTATION TO AN AERIAL SETTING

Pigeon (*Columbidae*)

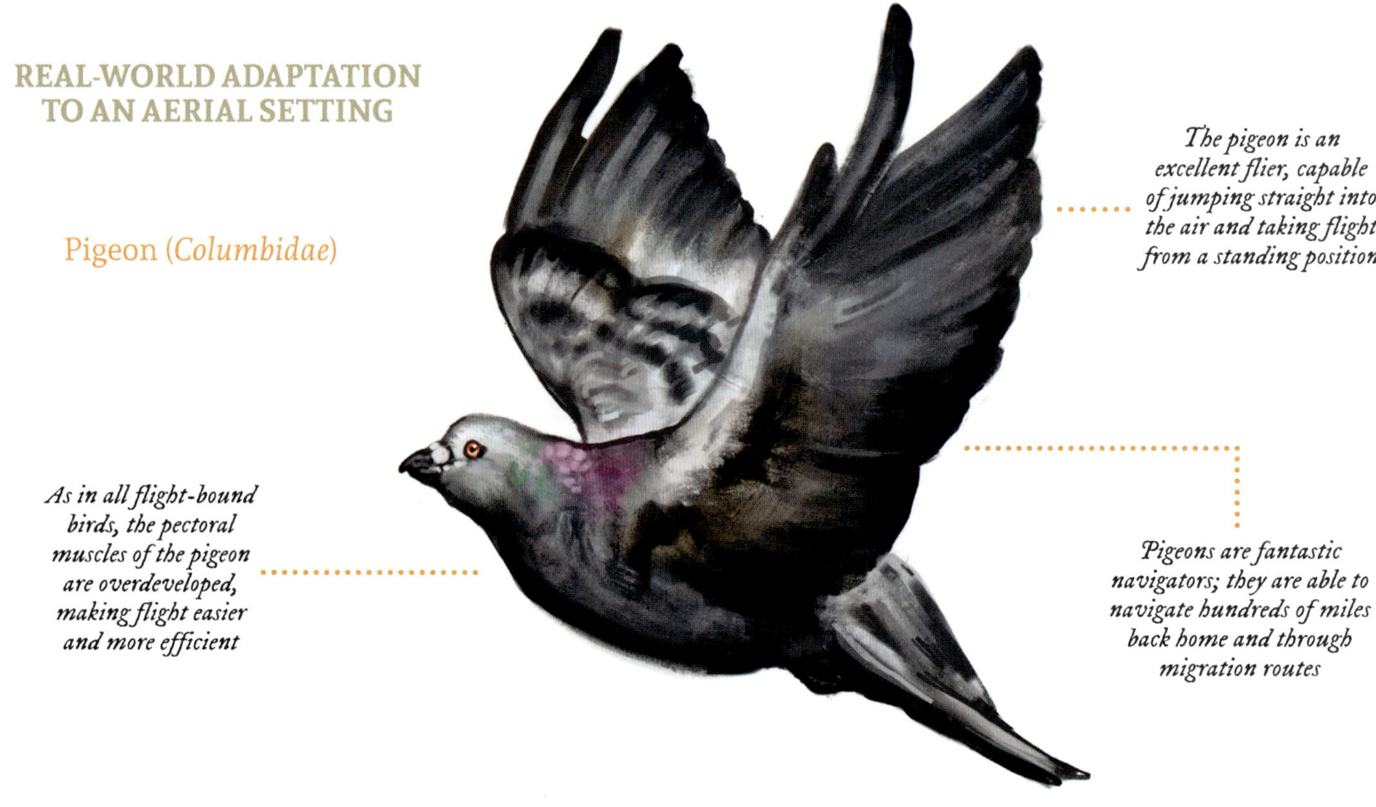

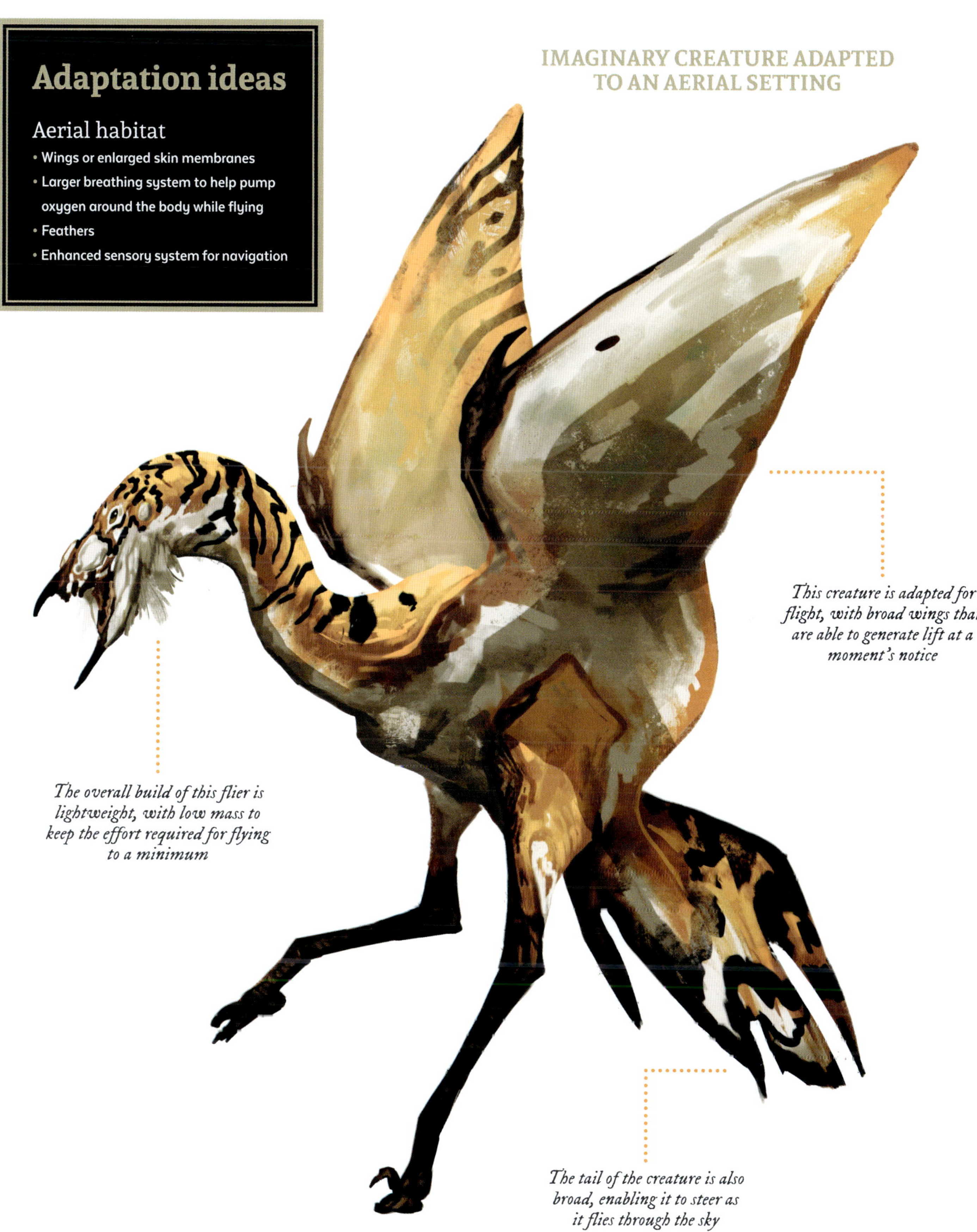

IMAGINARY CREATURE ADAPTED TO AN AERIAL SETTING

Above image © Brynn Metheney

Water

Animals adapted to the ocean will most likely exhibit bodies that are shaped like torpedoes for ease of movement through water, and fins or flippers for added steering and mobility. They will need adaptations to allow them to breathe underwater, or they will need to obtain air by returning to the surface. Refer to **pages 82** and **90** for a closer look at how cetaceans and fish are adapted to thrive in an aquatic environment.

REAL-WORLD ADAPTATION TO AN AQUATIC SETTING

Bluefin tuna (*Thunnus thynnus*)

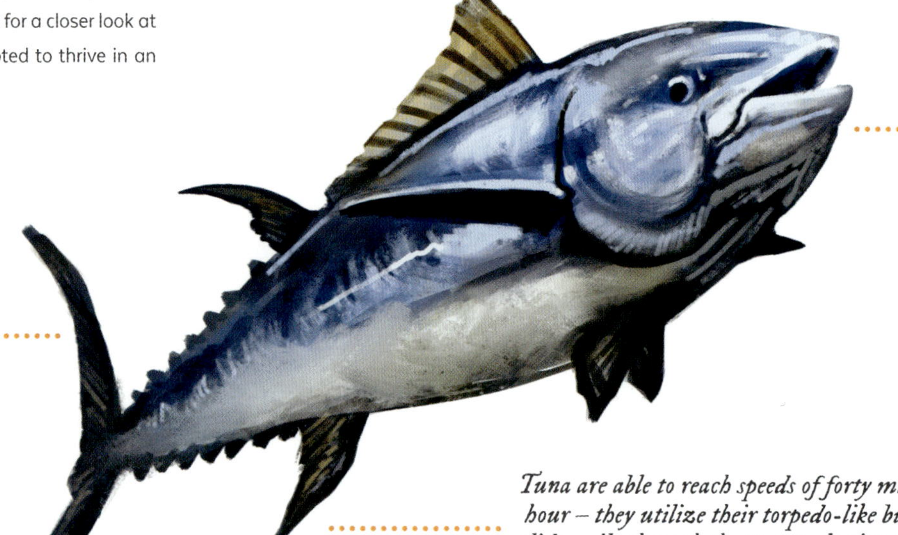

The bluefin tuna is a large open-ocean predator that swims in schools, hunting small fish

Tuna are adapted with high hemoglobin counts in their bloodstream, making it easier to supply their muscles with oxygen needed for fast and efficient movement

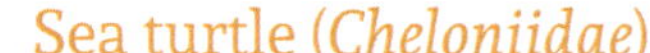

Tuna are able to reach speeds of forty miles per hour – they utilize their torpedo-like build to glide easily through the water, altering the fins along their body to reduce drag

Sea turtle (*Cheloniidae*)

The sea turtle still has to breathe air from the surface; its nostrils are positioned high on its head for easy access

The overall shape of the turtle is very streamlined – we see this shape repeated often in aquatic animals, as it reduces water resistance and increases speed

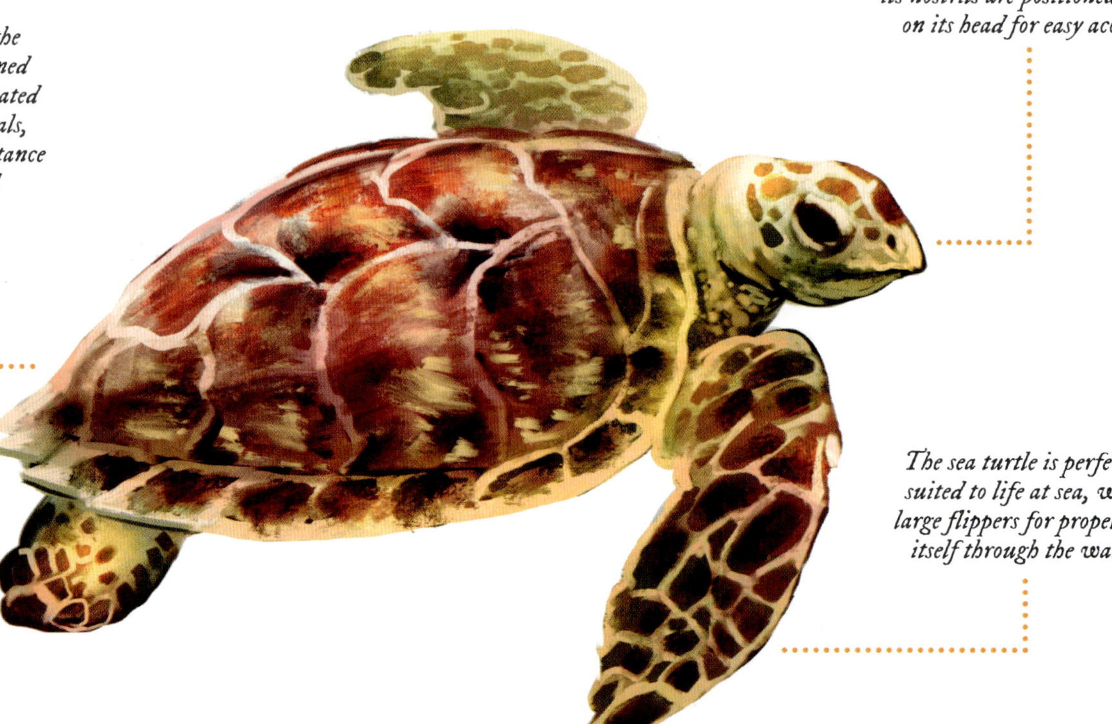

The sea turtle is perfectly suited to life at sea, with large flippers for propelling itself through the water

IMAGINARY CREATURE ADAPTED TO AN AQUATIC SETTING

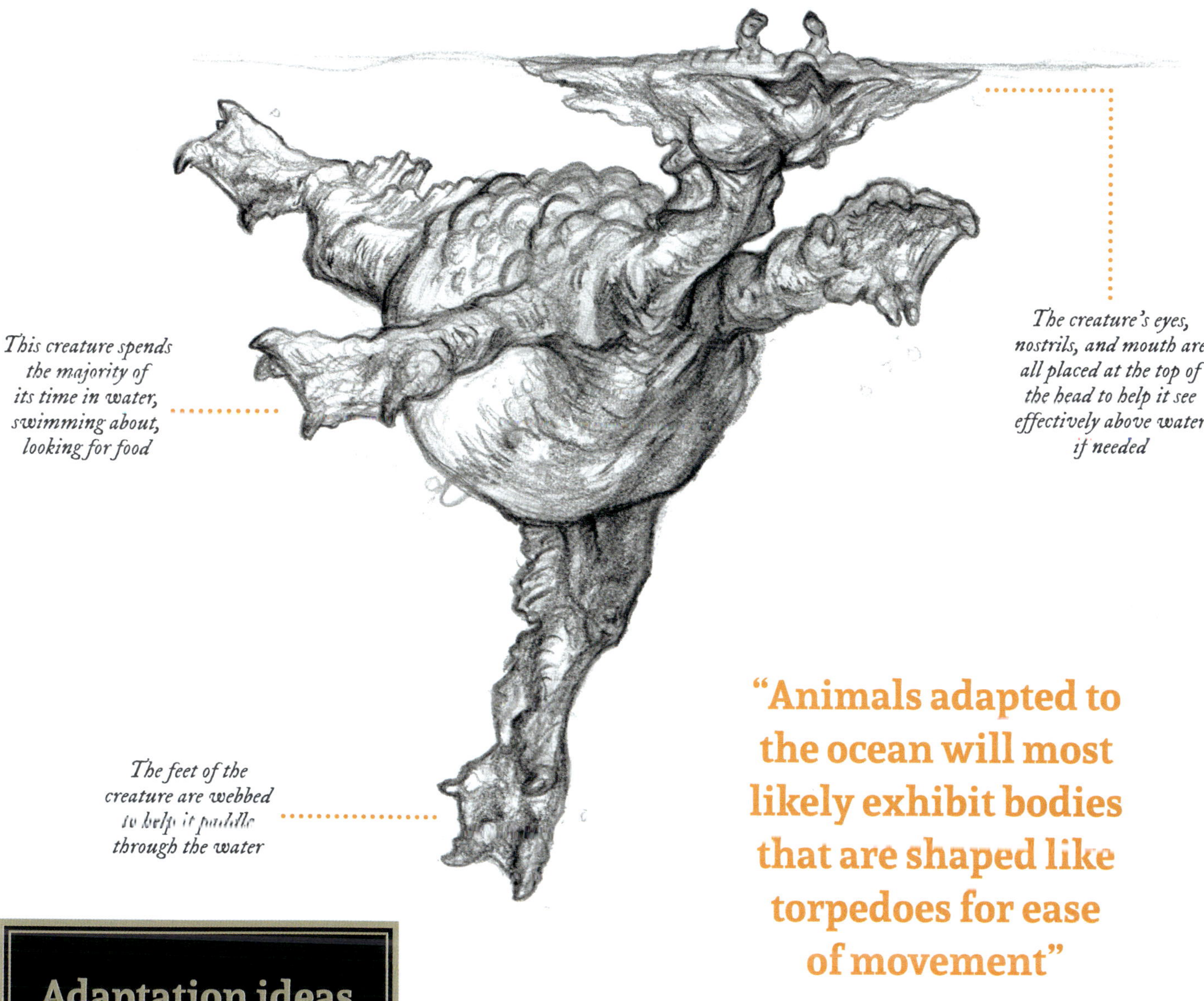

"Animals adapted to the ocean will most likely exhibit bodies that are shaped like torpedoes for ease of movement"

Adaptation ideas

Water

- Streamlined body
- Fins and flippers for underwater mobility and steering
- Gills or blowholes
- Scales or waterproof fur/feathers

Land & terrain

Animals that live on land will exhibit a range of adaptations depending on what kind of terrain they are traversing, but they will usually have legs or be able to manipulate their bodies to move. Land animals have a wide variety of body shapes and sizes, as they are not inhibited by the limitations that adaptations for the air and sea require. Terrain has endless influence on an animal's physiology.

The way a creature moves around the space it inhabits will determine a lot about its design overall. When you ask yourself "**Where does it come from?**", consider the kind of terrain your creature will encounter in its daily life. For example, animals that live on mountain ranges will require the ability to grip onto rocks and breathe limited oxygen. Animals that live in trees will have dexterous paws, perhaps a tail, and a flexible and/or strong body.

Keeping these adaptations in mind, we can begin to expand on those possibilities and bring variance in habitat into our observations. For example, tree climbers will vary depending on the kinds of trees they inhabit. Animals that live in tropical rainforests, such as the orangutan, look very different from those that inhabit pine forests, such as the pine marten.

ADAPTATION TO A WOODLAND SETTING

European badger (*Meles meles*)

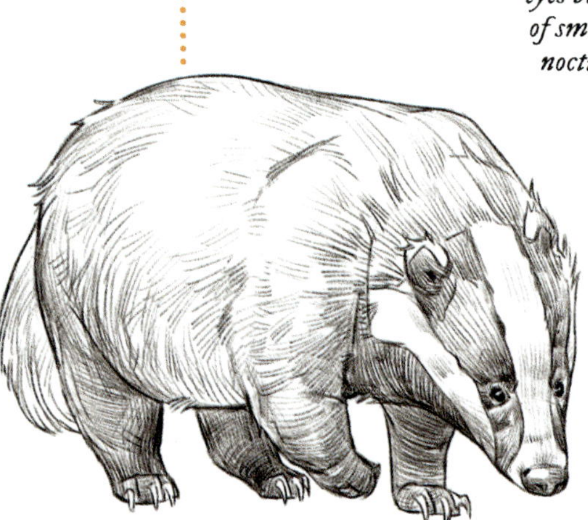

The European badger's body is stocky and low to the ground – an ideal physique for a digging and foraging omnivore

The badger has small, weak eyes but a powerful sense of smell that supports its nocturnal wanderings

Muscular limbs with wide paws and non-retractable claws are used for burrowing and maintaining dens

ADAPTATION TO AN ARCTIC SETTING

Polar bear (*Ursus maritimus*)

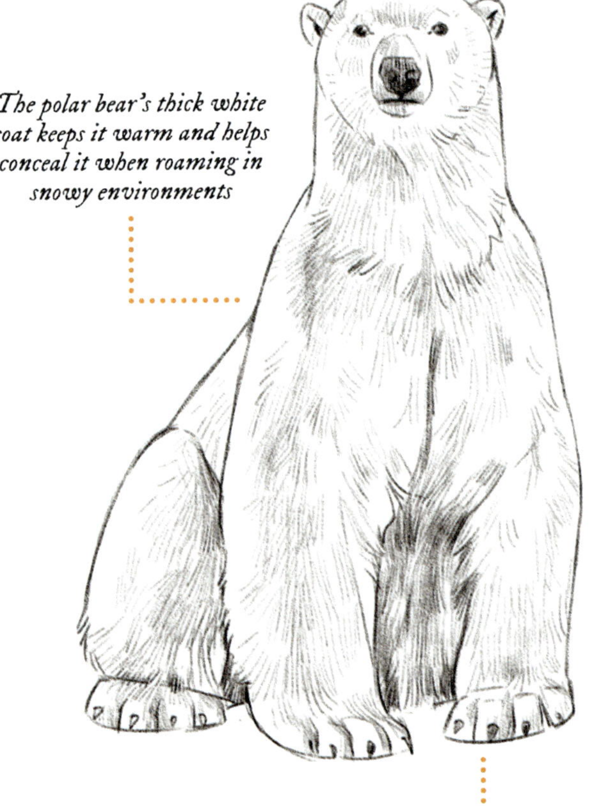

The polar bear's thick white coat keeps it warm and helps conceal it when roaming in snowy environments

Massive paws help spread the bear's weight when walking on snow and ice, as well as making it a formidable swimmer

Worldbuilding

Designing multiple creatures for the same place requires attention to things like relationships between species, food sources, habitat, and terrain. Animals here on Earth have carved out spaces for themselves in ecosystems that adjust to and absorb their presence. For example, if you design a predator, you should think about what kinds of animals it is hunting and what those animals look like, what kind of world it inhabits, what seasons affect it, and how it adapts to change over time. Worldbuilding can be vast, but some of the principles covered in this chapter will help you find a starting place.

Above images by Alexandra Fastovets (hanukafast)

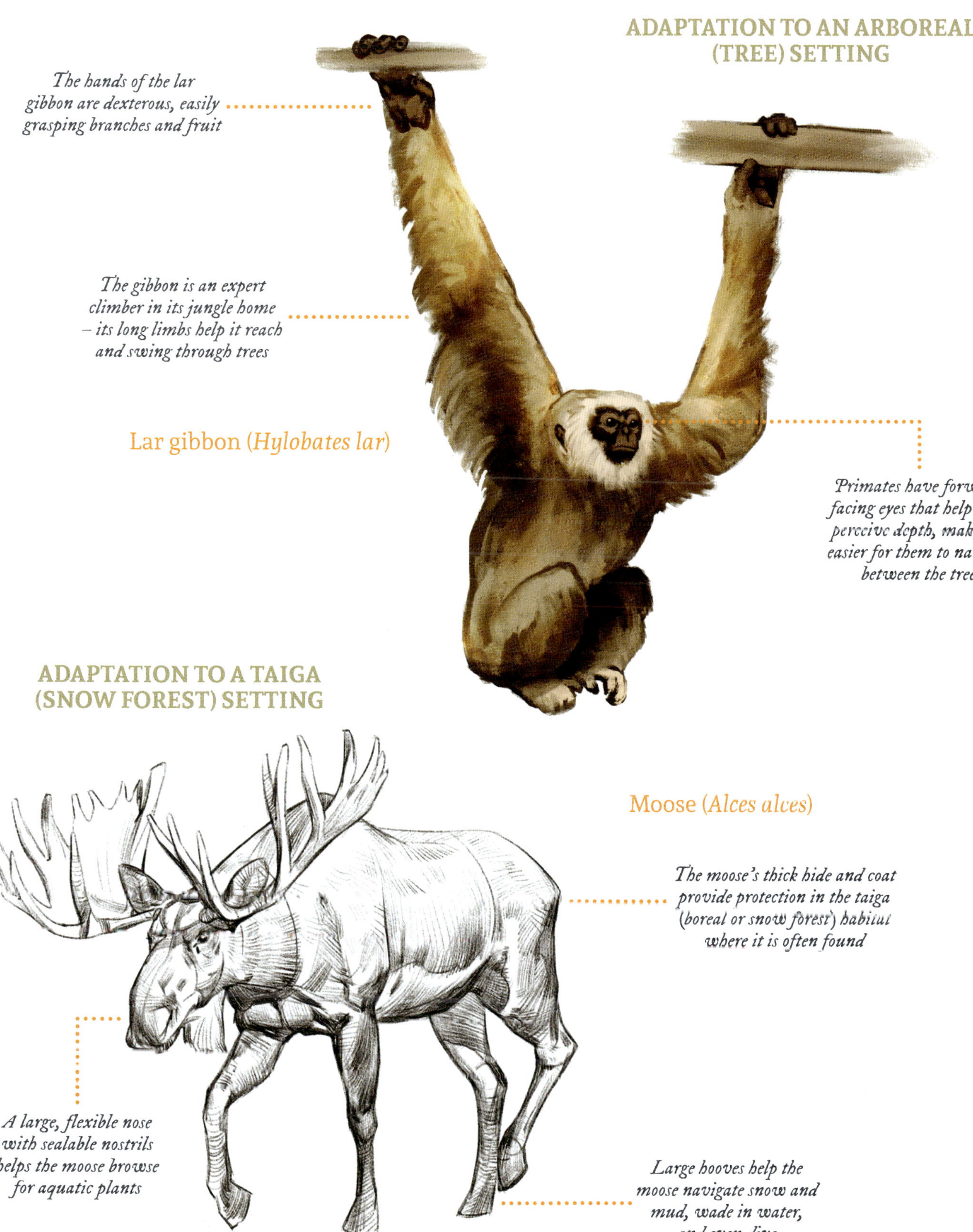
ADAPTATION TO AN ARBOREAL
(TREE) SETTING

The hands of the lar
gibbon are dexterous, easily
grasping branches and fruit

The gibbon is an expert
climber in its jungle home
– its long limbs help it reach
and swing through trees

Lar gibbon (Hylobates lar)

Primates have forward-
facing eyes that help them
perceive depth, making it
easier for them to navigate
between the trees

ADAPTATION TO A TAIGA
(SNOW FOREST) SETTING

Moose (Alces alces)

The moose's thick hide and coat
provide protection in the taiga
(boreal or snow forest) habitat
where it is often found

A large, flexible nose
with sealable nostrils
helps the moose browse
for aquatic plants

Large hooves help the
moose navigate snow and
mud, wade in water,
and even dive

IMAGINARY CREATURE ADAPTED TO AN ARBOREAL SETTING

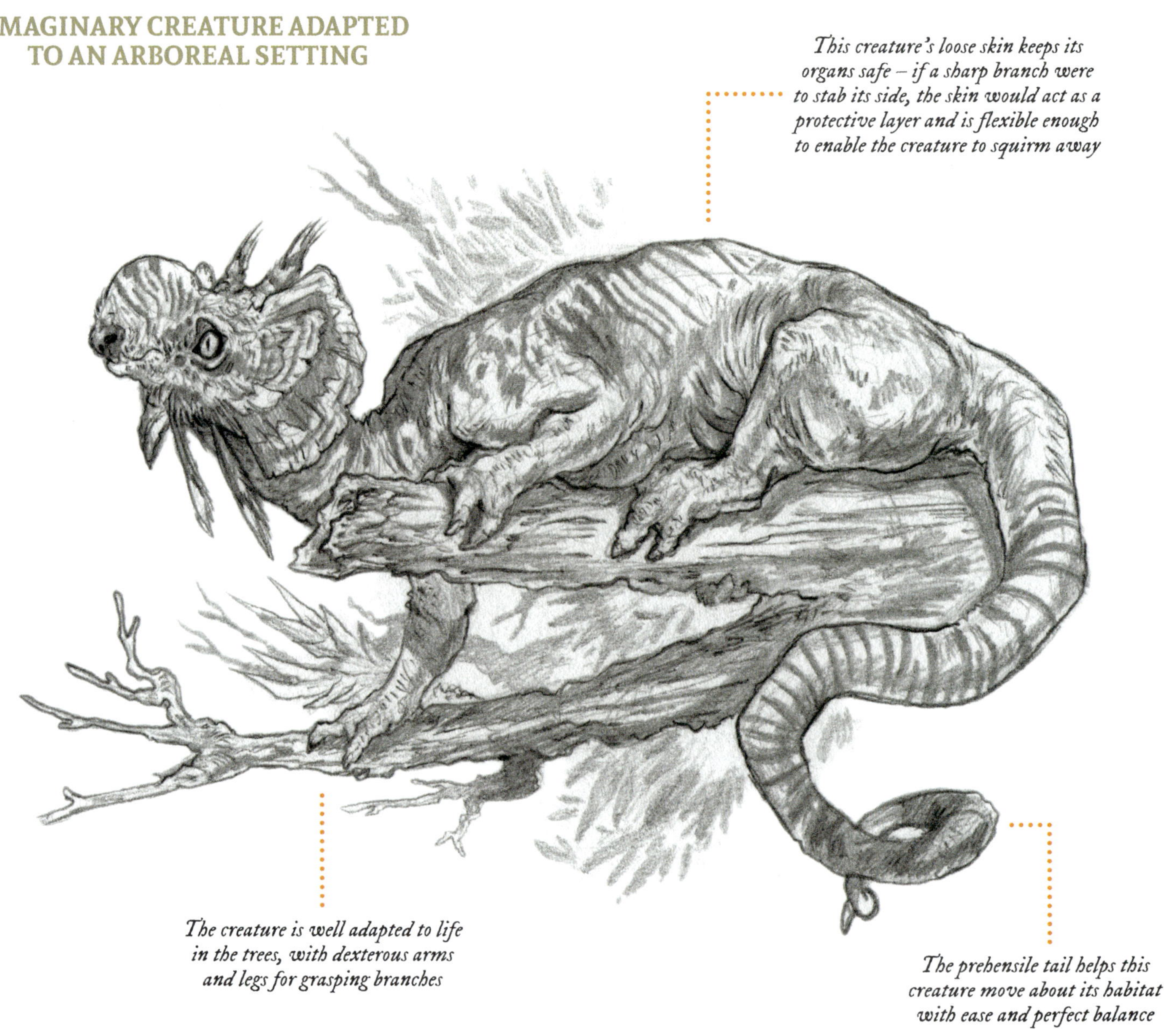

Adaptation ideas

Sand
- Wide feet to distribute weight
- Alternative means of hydration
- Ability to regulate temperature
- Ability to burrow for food or shelter

Mountain
- Agile feet and limbs
- Long tail for balance
- Thick weatherproof coat
- Seasonal coats with different colors

Forest
- Prehensile tail
- Mottled or striped camouflage
- Dexterous arms and legs
- Keen low-light vision

IMAGINARY CREATURE ADAPTED TO A COASTAL SETTING

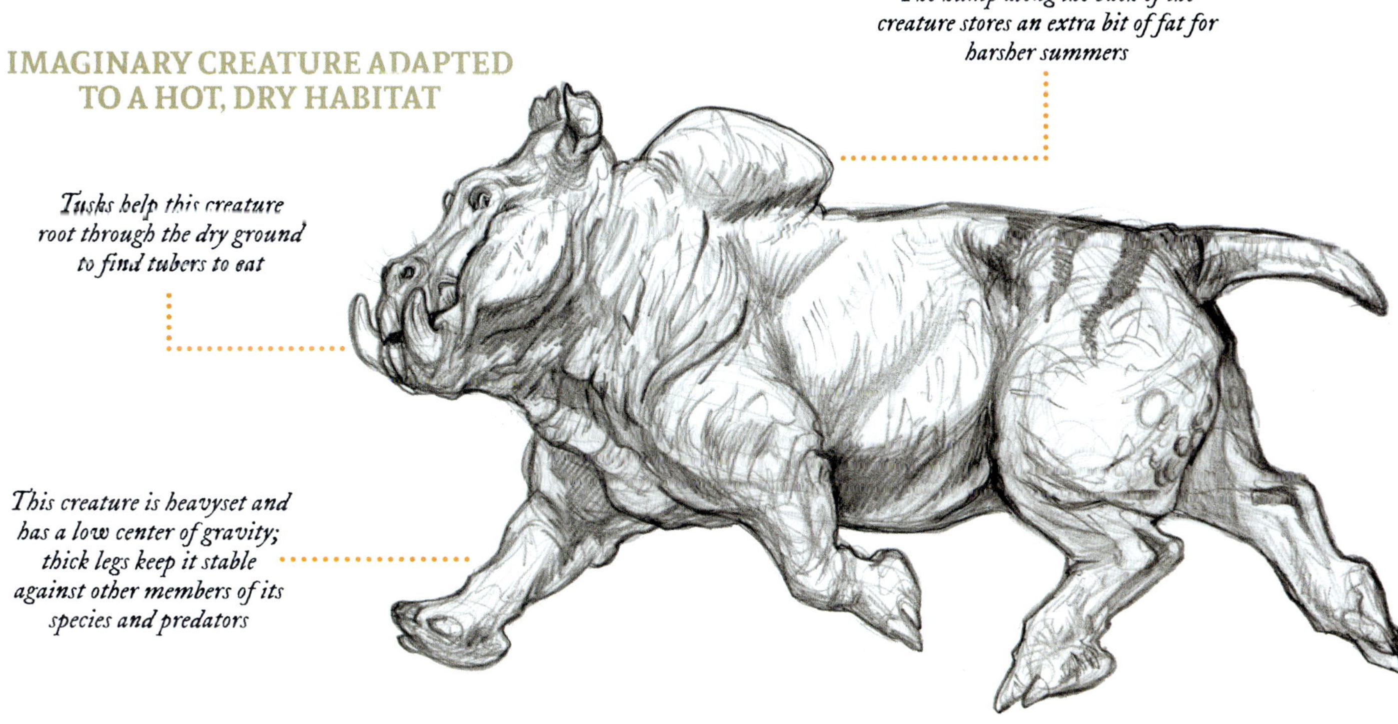

With eyes high on top of its head, this creature is able to see all around it

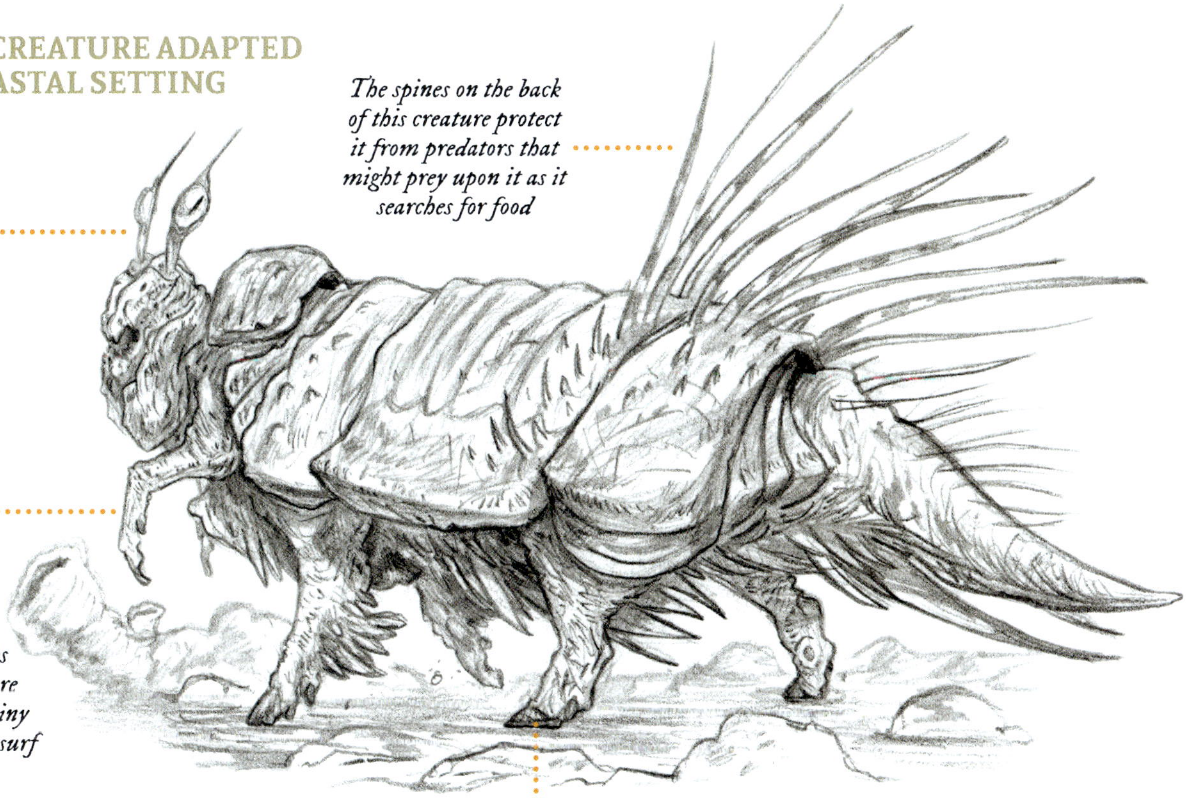

The spines on the back of this creature protect it from predators that might prey upon it as it searches for food

The smaller limbs toward the front are used for gathering tiny organisms along the surf

Living along the coast can be a harsh existence – this little creature is well equipped with feet that are able to traverse all sorts of terrain

IMAGINARY CREATURE ADAPTED TO A HOT, DRY HABITAT

The hump along the back of the creature stores an extra bit of fat for harsher summers

Tusks help this creature root through the dry ground to find tubers to eat

This creature is heavyset and has a low center of gravity; thick legs keep it stable against other members of its species and predators

35

Diet

Another of the foremost questions to ask yourself when you begin a creature design is: **"What does this creature eat?"** All life needs to consume something for energy, and animals often have specific diets that keep them functioning and thriving. What an animal eats has a huge effect on its physiology and overall behavior. There are lots of ways to eat in the natural world, as well as lots of *things* to eat: meat, fish, insects, fruit, vegetation, and nectar.

Activity level has a lot to do with how and what an animal eats. Some animals have metabolisms that allow them to eat less often. Crocodiles are carnivores with such a slow metabolism that they can go for a year without eating food. In contrast, hummingbirds have the highest metabolism of any animal on Earth. Their food source is pure sugar and they have to eat constantly.

Different diets require different tools for eating, drinking, and hunting. The diets of real-world animals have a direct effect on their physiology and the toolkits with which they work.

Teeth are one small example of how diet can determine how an animal can look. Animals that eat meat tend to have sharp teeth for holding on to, killing, and consuming prey. In contrast, animals that eat plants have teeth that are either flat or specialized for eating the kind of vegetation they consume. Flamingos have specially-shaped beaks with combs inside for filter-feeding. Anteaters have elongated jaws that house a long, sticky tongue for slurping up insects.

As you design your creatures, think about the kinds of food they eat. It is one of the most important questions you can ask yourself about your design, as it will determine a lot about the creature's size, shape, adaptations, and features.

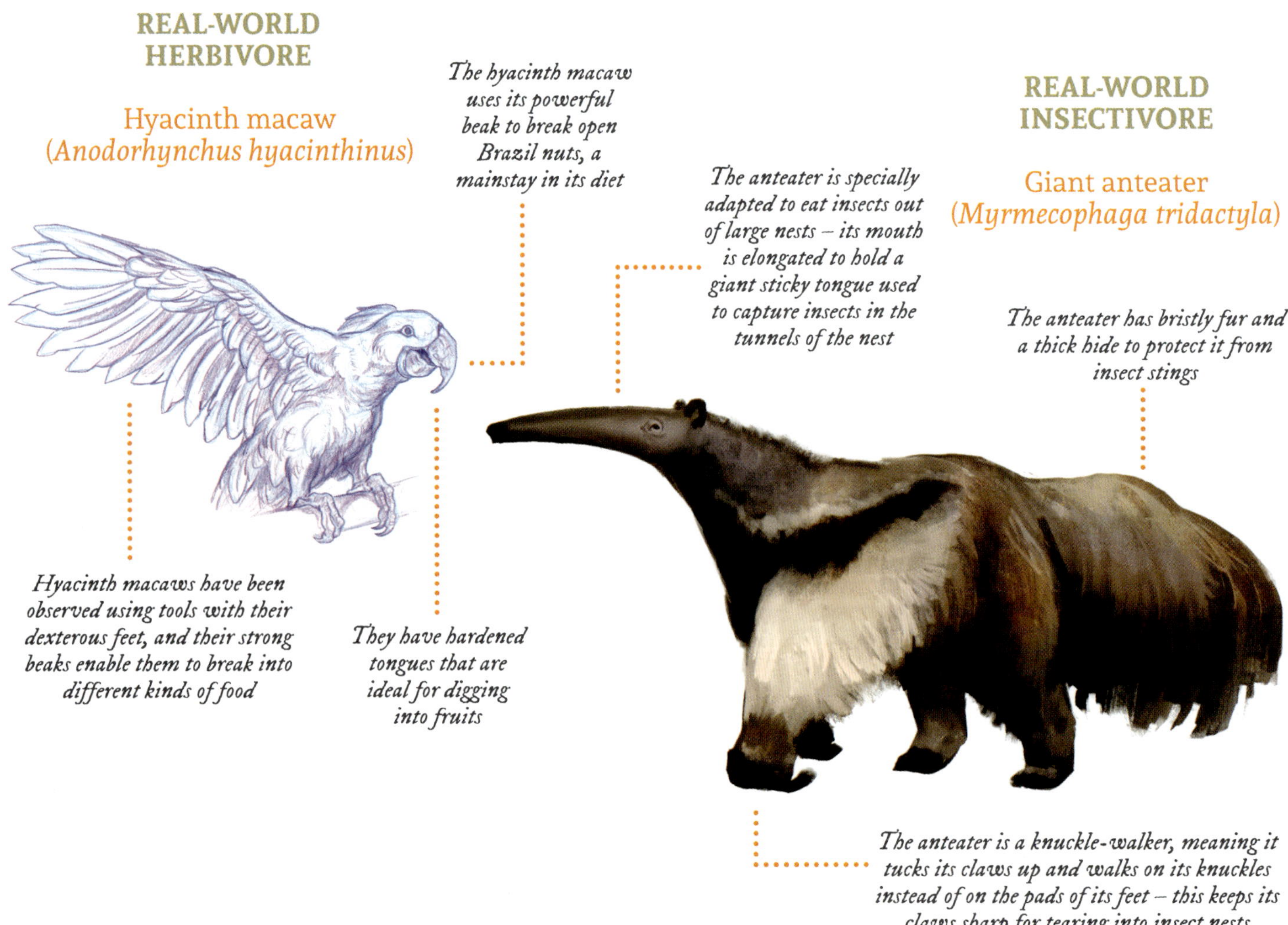

REAL-WORLD HERBIVORE

Hyacinth macaw (*Anodorhynchus hyacinthinus*)

The hyacinth macaw uses its powerful beak to break open Brazil nuts, a mainstay in its diet

The anteater is specially adapted to eat insects out of large nests — its mouth is elongated to hold a giant sticky tongue used to capture insects in the tunnels of the nest

REAL-WORLD INSECTIVORE

Giant anteater (*Myrmecophaga tridactyla*)

The anteater has bristly fur and a thick hide to protect it from insect stings

Hyacinth macaws have been observed using tools with their dexterous feet, and their strong beaks enable them to break into different kinds of food

They have hardened tongues that are ideal for digging into fruits

The anteater is a knuckle-walker, meaning it tucks its claws up and walks on its knuckles instead of on the pads of its feet — this keeps its claws sharp for tearing into insect nests

REAL-WORLD CARNIVORE

Spotted hyena (*Crocuta crocuta*)

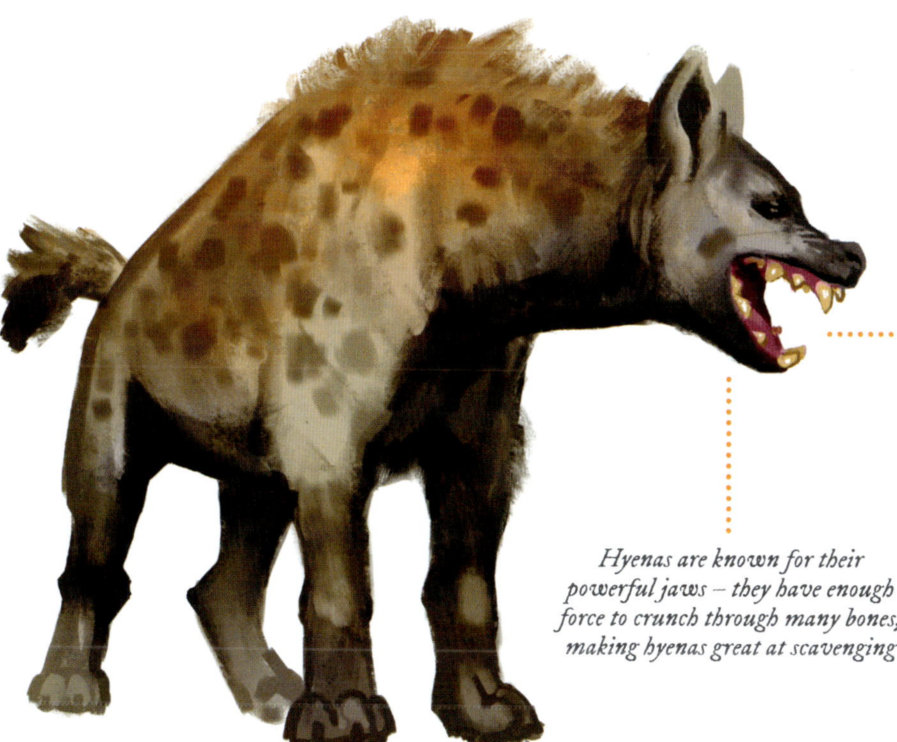

The hyena is a carnivore, with sharp and specialized teeth for killing and consuming prey

Hyenas are known for their powerful jaws – they have enough force to crunch through many bones, making hyenas great at scavenging

IMAGINARY CARNIVORES

These carnivores would tear their food apart like birds of prey (such as eagles and vultures) and swallow pieces whole due to a lack of carnassial teeth (back teeth used for shearing meat)

These predators are also equipped with heat pits along their faces to locate their prey's body heat – this makes up for their poor eyesight

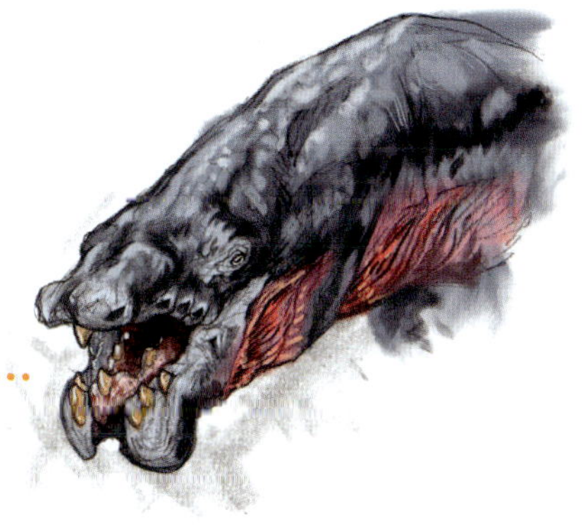

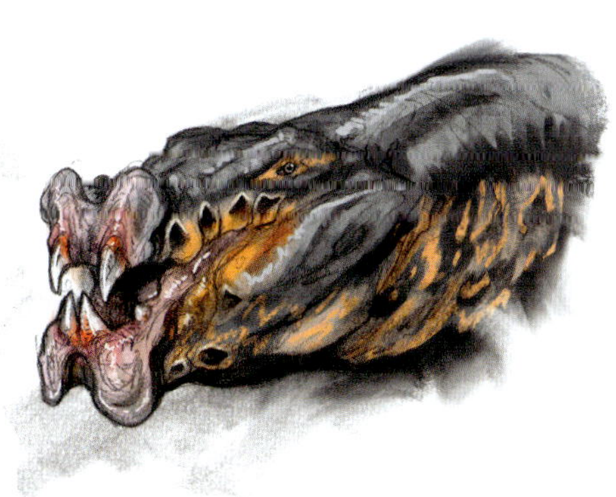

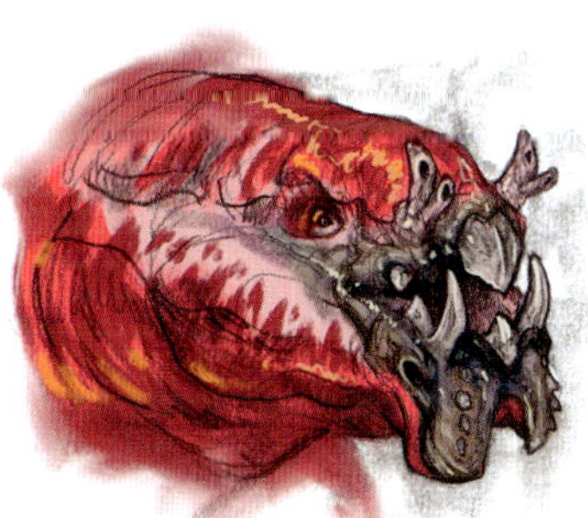

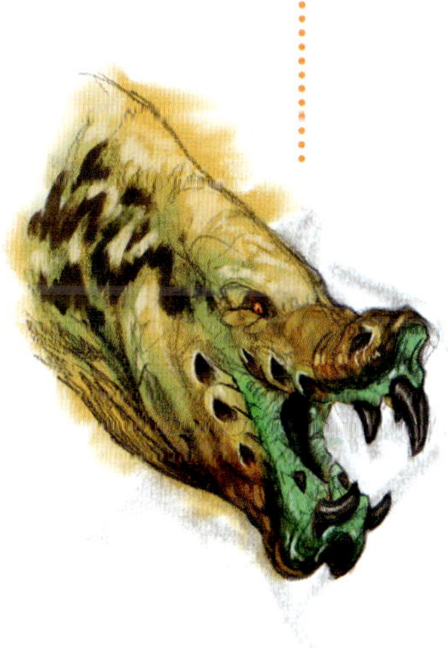

37

IMAGINARY HERBIVORE

This large herbivore uses its specialized tongue to reach into flora and eat the nectar inside

The modified secondary limbs at the front of the animal help to select only the best stems and flowers

This creature is large and does not have any natural predators; it can stand tall and enjoy its meal without having to worry about being hunted – being tall pays off!

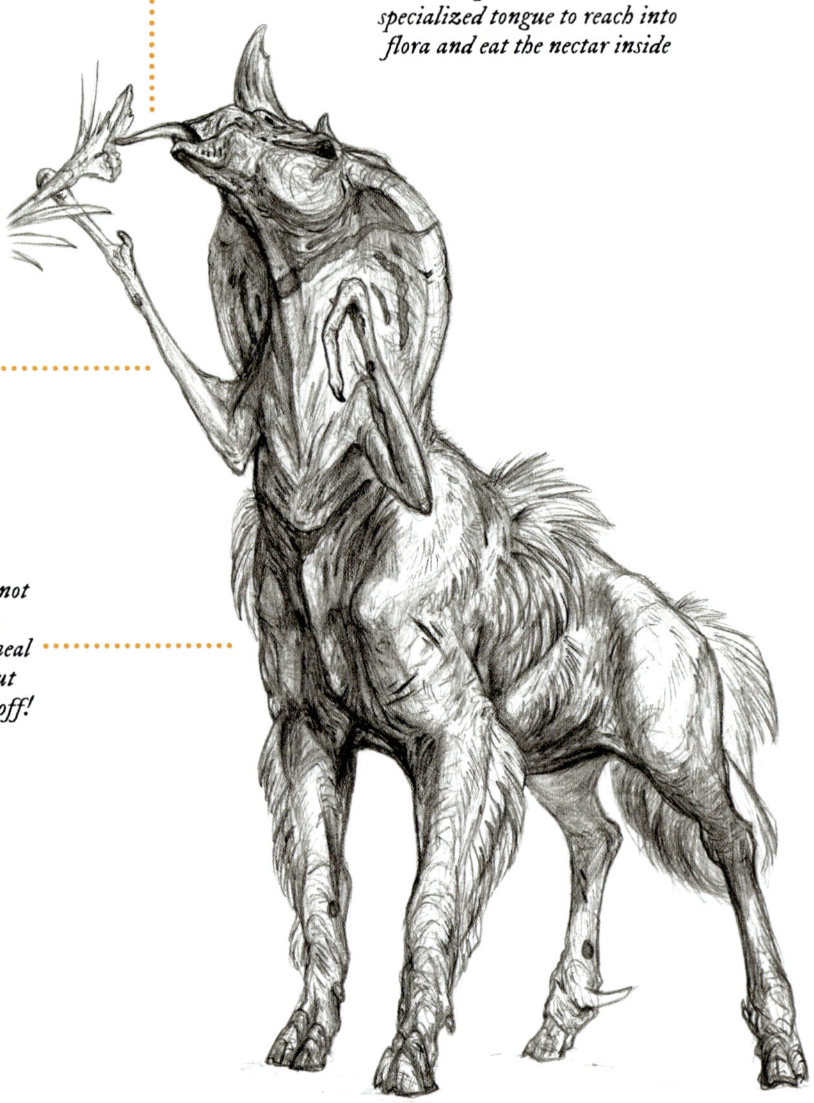

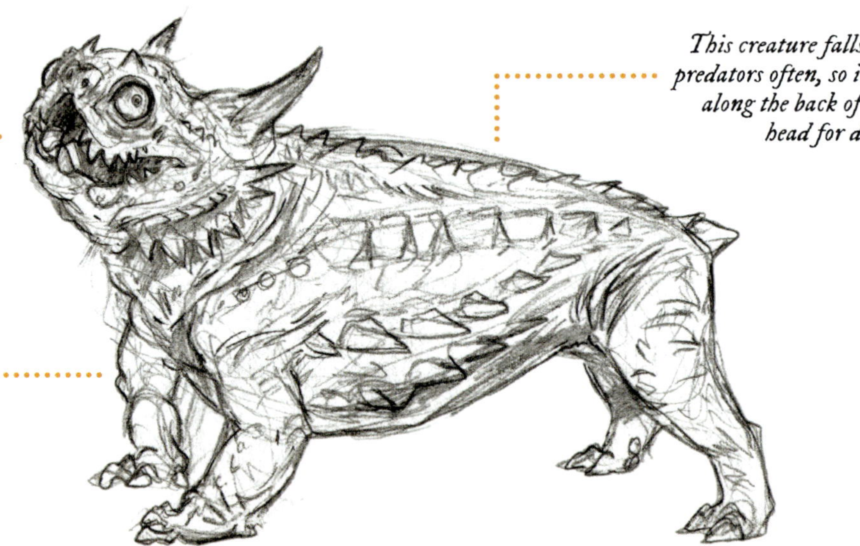

IMAGINARY INSECTIVORE

This small creature is an insectivore that uses its barb-like teeth to grasp its prey

This creature falls prey to larger predators often, so it uses the spines along the back of its body and head for defense

This creature's stocky build and low stature mean that it can fit into small spaces low to the ground – it routinely scampers through fallen logs in search of food

Predator or prey?

Related to diet, we should also consider adaptations caused by an animal's position in the food chain. Apex predators are often larger in size, have sharp claws and teeth, and possess a lot of power to allow them to successfully attack prey. For example, crocodiles have especially strong muscles around their jaw to help them bite down with up to 5,000 lb of force. You can think of some creatures as having weapons, such as horns, stingers, and venom. Some predators use camouflage to sneak up on their prey; sharks are usually dark on top with pale undersides, so from above they blend with the darkness of the water, and from below they blend with the lightness from the sky ("**countershading**").

Camouflage can also be used by prey animals to help them avoid detection from creatures trying to eat them. Other animals use **aposematism** to ward off predators by suggesting they are harmful – think of toxic tropical frogs and many arthropods. Over time, predators associate the bright and contrasting colors with a bad taste. Mimicking the appearance of aposematic animals is another tactic - an example is the hoverfly appearing like a wasp or bee.

The position of a creature's eyes can also be a good indicator of whether it is predator or prey. Many predators such as tigers, wolves, owls, and humans have forward-facing eyes that allow them to judge depth and attack well. Conversely, prey animals such as rabbits, gazelles, and small birds have eyes on the sides of their heads that allow them a better peripheral view through which to spot predators.

REAL-WORLD PREDATOR

Tiger (*Panthera tigris*)

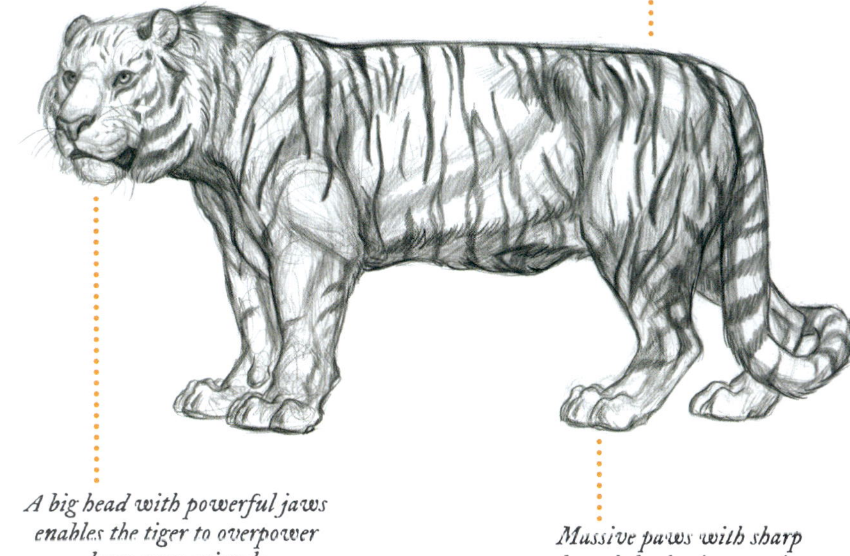

The tiger's vertically striped coat helps conceal it when prowling the undergrowth

A big head with powerful jaws enables the tiger to overpower large prey animals

Massive paws with sharp claws help the tiger to seize or incapacitate its prey

REAL-WORLD PREY

Arctic hare (*Lepus arcticus*)

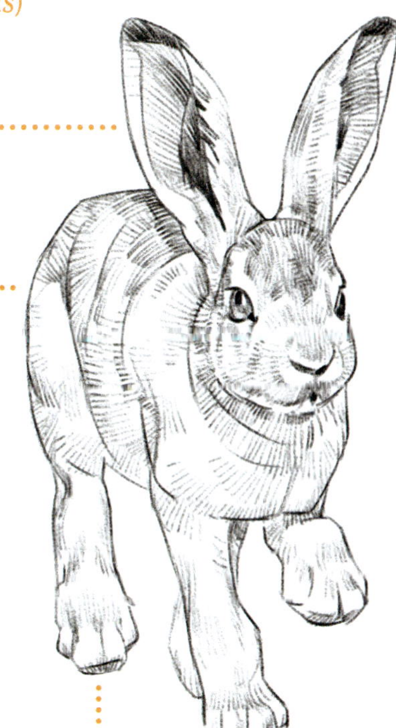

Large ears and high-set, side-facing eyes offer keen hearing and wide peripheral vision

A white coat offers camouflage in the snow from predators such as foxes and falcons

Powerful hind legs give the hare great speed and agility for making its escape

Adaptation ideas

Carnivorous predator

- Large, sharp teeth and claws
- Strong musculature
- Camouflage for hunting
- Venomous
- Ways to access smaller creatures such as insects

Herbivorous prey

- Flat teeth for breaking down vegetation
- Ability to crack into nuts
- Ways to deter, hide from, or defend against predators
- Camouflage for protection

Social behavior

The way an animal socializes with members of its own species, or others outside of its species, can have an effect on the way it looks, its size, and how it survives in the wild. Adding a social aspect to your creature is an interesting way to add to its design. It can mean that your creature is smaller, larger, more intelligent, or more dangerous.

Animals that are solitary will likely be shaped or act differently than animals that live in groups. For example, animals such as the grizzly bear are solitary, mainly because they are large and temperamental with their territory. They need to be large to pull down the huge elk, which makes up part of their diet, on their own. They are also grazers, and will spend most of their days eating to feed their big bodies. Because they are so large, they hibernate for half of the year, when conditions are too harsh for them to be outside looking for food.

Wolves hunt the same prey in the area, but in contrast are much smaller and work as a team. The wolf is a social carnivore, using pack members and female and male leaders to bring down large prey such as the elk. This strength in numbers means they can be much smaller in size than the solitary bear. It also means they can stay active throughout the year, as they do not need to fuel such a gigantic body.

Some animals use groups as a way to stay safe. Schools of sardines group together in huge numbers for protection - if you have thousands of others around you, you are less likely to be singled out by a predator.

Communication

Social animals need to have a method through which to communicate. The most obvious is sound. Many animals use vocalization for a variety of different reasons: to warn that a predator is nearby; as a sign of aggression; to signal to the other sex during a mating ritual; or to indicate that food has been found. Other animals rub body parts or strike them against each other to communicate. For example, crickets rub parts of their forewings to produce sound, while gorillas beat their chests. Fish can create noise by using sonic muscles to cause vibrations in their swim bladders.

Other ways of communicating include by sense of smell, through visual signaling including body language and color-changing, and even by generating an electric field and varying the wavelength and frequency of it. This is a fascinating area to research, and exaggerating key features of your design for communication purposes can add depth and interest.

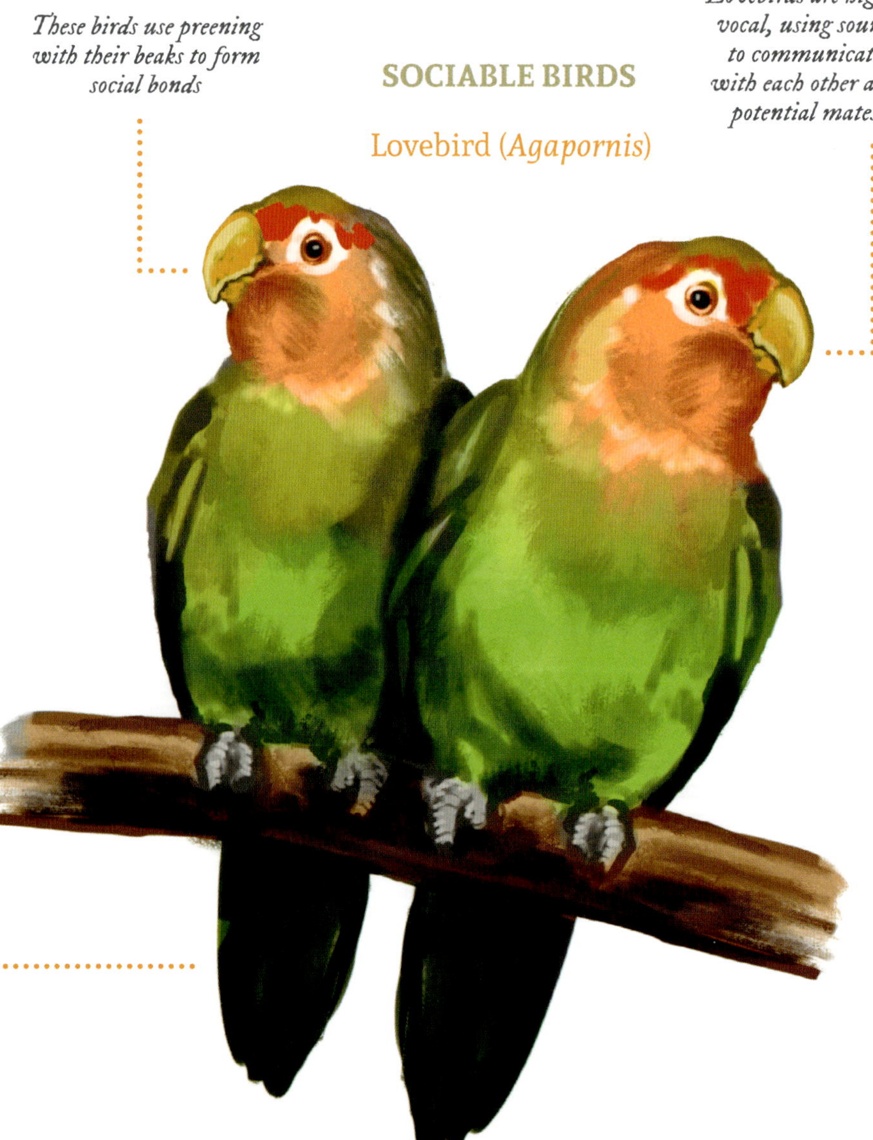

These birds use preening with their beaks to form social bonds

SOCIABLE BIRDS

Lovebird (*Agapornis*)

Lovebirds are highly vocal, using sound to communicate with each other and potential mates

Lovebirds are highly social – so social, in fact, they are monogamous for life

LARGE SOCIAL GROUPS

Ring-tailed lemur
(*Lemur catta*)

These primates have extremely expressive faces and eyes for communicating with each other

Ring-tailed lemurs live in social groups of up to thirty members

Scent glands on the wrists help lemurs mark territory and communicate with other members of their troop

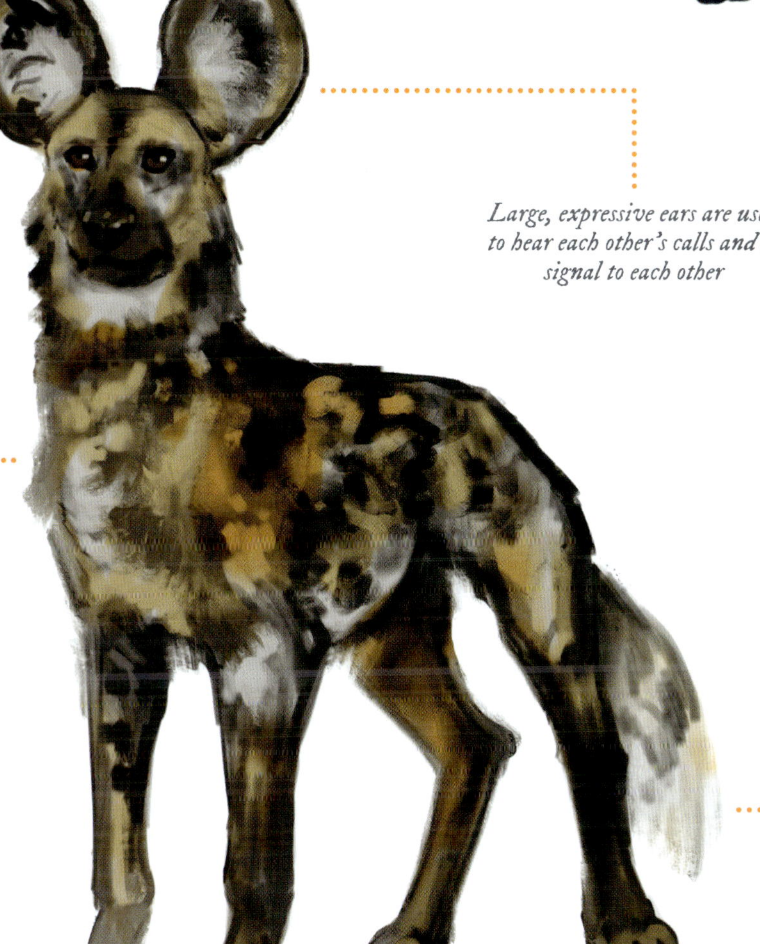

PACK HUNTERS

African wild dog
(*Lycaon pictus*)

Large, expressive ears are used to hear each other's calls and to signal to each other

African hunting dogs are extremely intelligent canids that hunt together in highly organized packs

The hunting dogs' white tails help them spot one another as they pursue prey together

IMAGINARY CREATURES
ADAPTED TO LIFE IN GROUPS

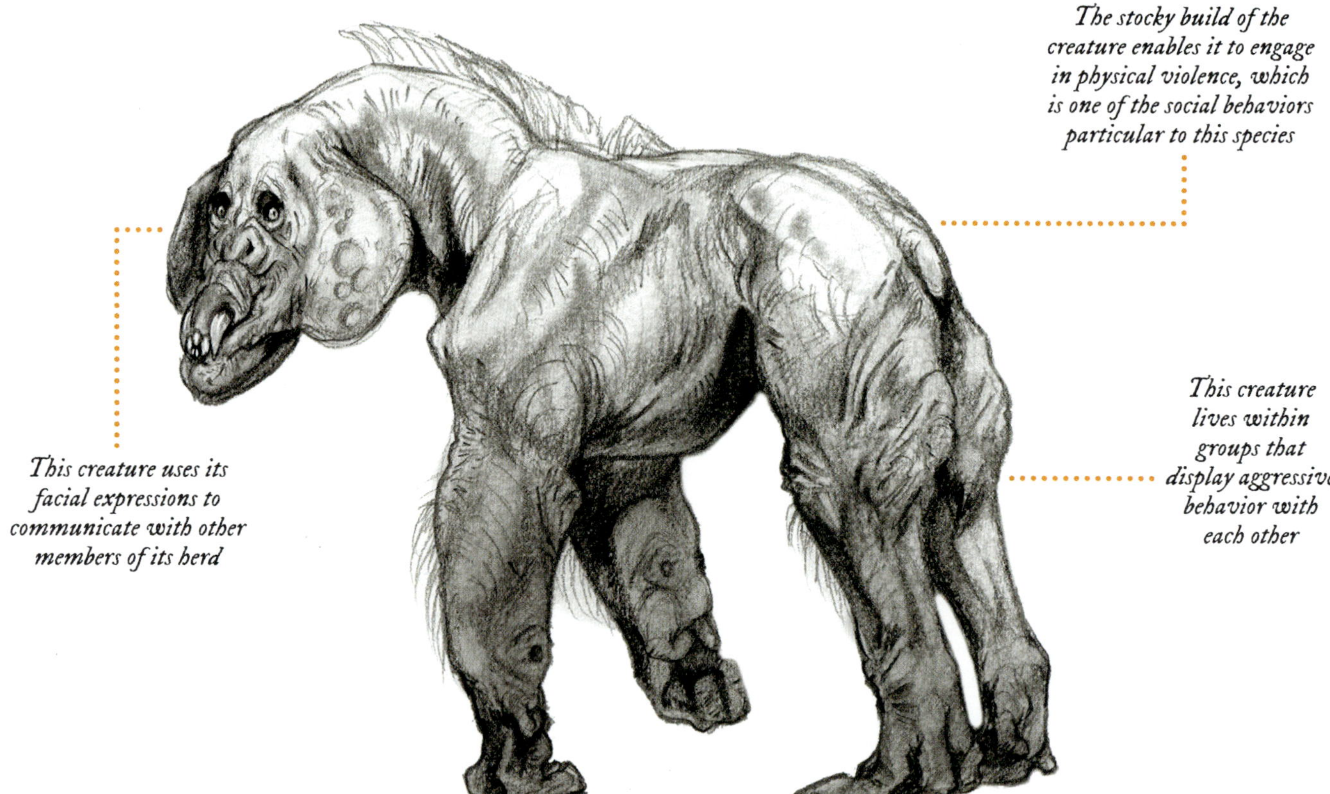

The stocky build of the creature enables it to engage in physical violence, which is one of the social behaviors particular to this species

This creature uses its facial expressions to communicate with other members of its herd

This creature lives within groups that display aggressive behavior with each other

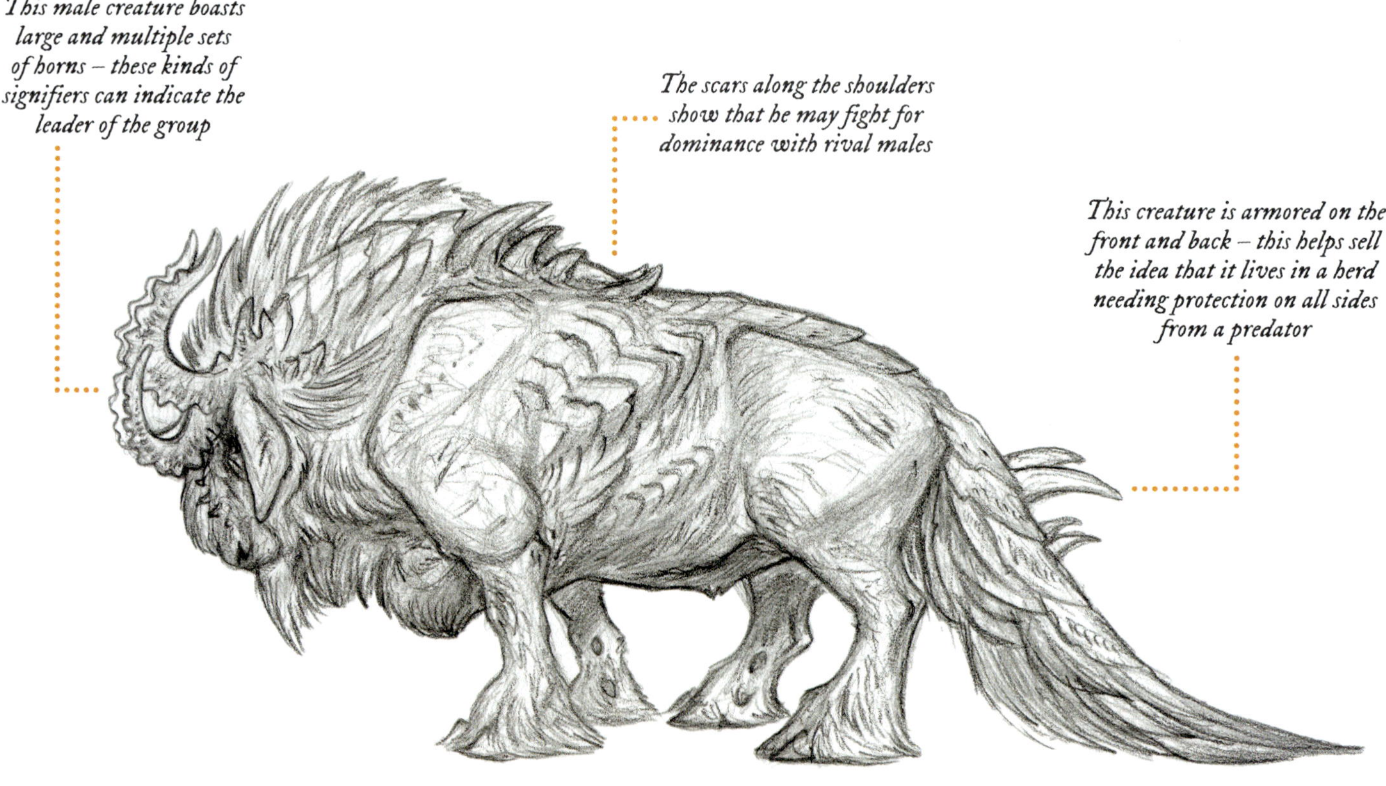

This male creature boasts large and multiple sets of horns – these kinds of signifiers can indicate the leader of the group

The scars along the shoulders show that he may fight for dominance with rival males

This creature is armored on the front and back – this helps sell the idea that it lives in a herd needing protection on all sides from a predator

Top image © Brynn Metheney

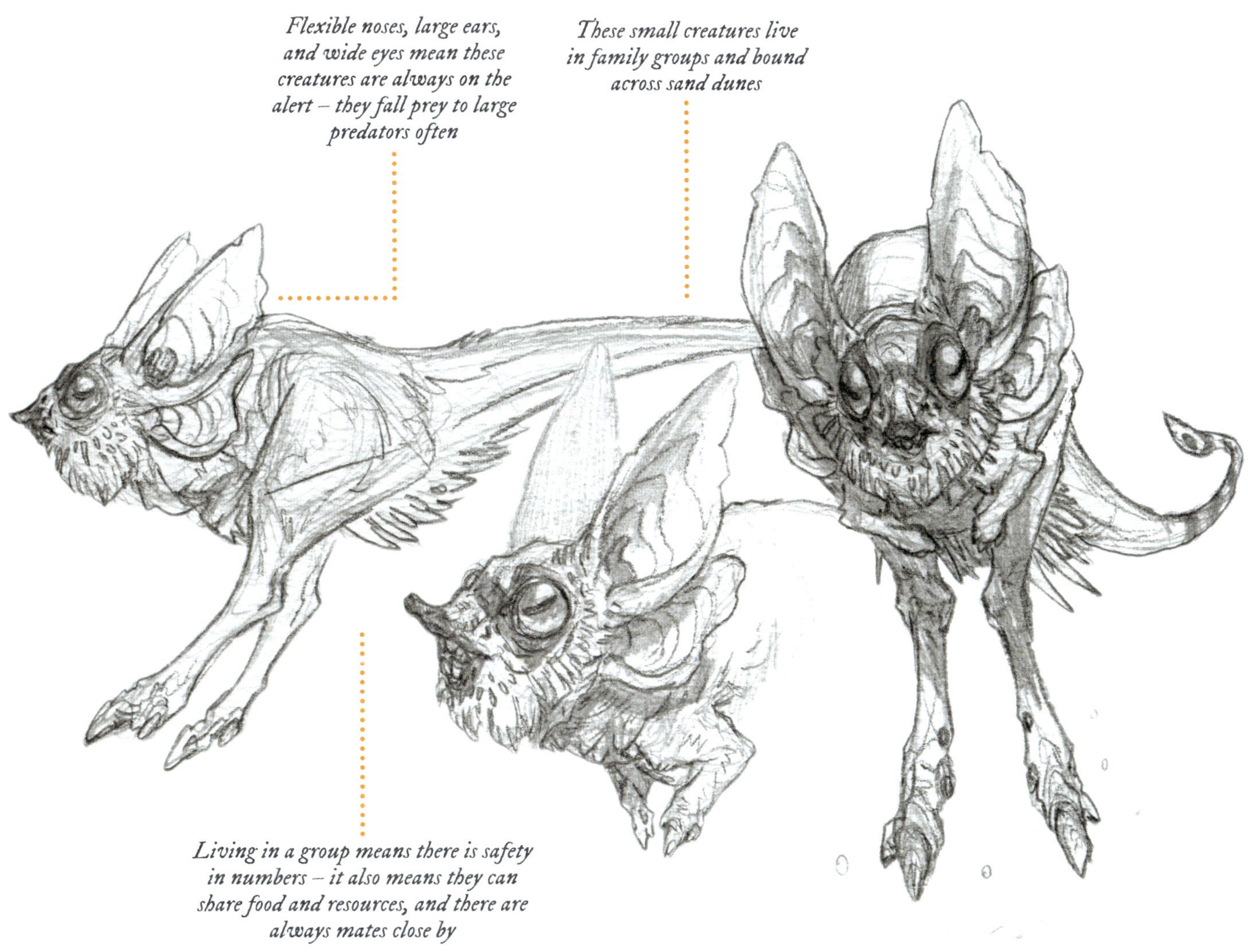

Adaptation ideas

Visual communication

- Bright warning markings
- Signaling with ears, tail, or feathers
- Posturing and ritual displays
- Color-changing ability

Auditory communication

- Vocalizations such as whistling or howling
- Generating sound with other body parts, such as wings or a rattle
- Ultrasound (high frequency) or infrasound (low frequency) noise

Olfactory communication

- Producing scent to attract a mate
- Stink glands that deter predators
- Territorial scent-marking
- Sensing pheromones using the mouth or other body parts

Reproductive attributes & behaviors

Animals are built to survive, and part of surviving is reproducing. All life reproduces itself, either through mating with a member of the opposite or same sex, by reproducing alone, or by duplicating itself. Passing on genetic material to a new generation is as old as life itself. Some animals showcase differences between different sexes (**sexual dimorphism**) and others show none at all.

Birds of paradise are an excellent example of sexual dimorphism. The males exhibit bright plumage and complex feather structures, while the females tend to be on the conservative side in color and shape. In contrast, animals like the clownfish exhibit no outward physical differences between the sexes, and are even able to switch between male and female reproductive organs. Gender roles we tend to associate with males and females break down in the natural world as well, with females and males switching roles to survive.

Animals also care for their young differently among species. Some care for their young for years and others leave them to survive on their own. The way we understand gender and sex in our own world is very different (and even limited) compared to the natural world, where roles are not binary. Considering this when designing your creature will add another level of believability and originality.

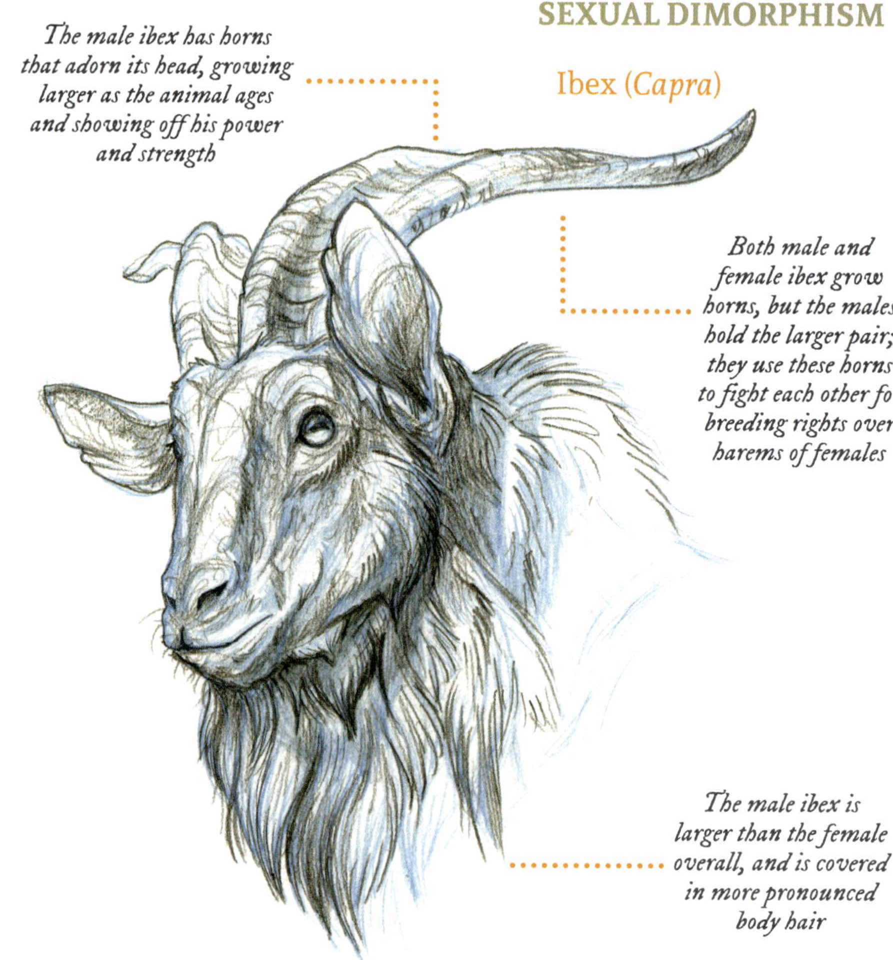

The male ibex has horns that adorn its head, growing larger as the animal ages and showing off his power and strength

Both male and female ibex grow horns, but the males hold the larger pair; they use these horns to fight each other for breeding rights over harems of females

The male ibex is larger than the female overall, and is covered in more pronounced body hair

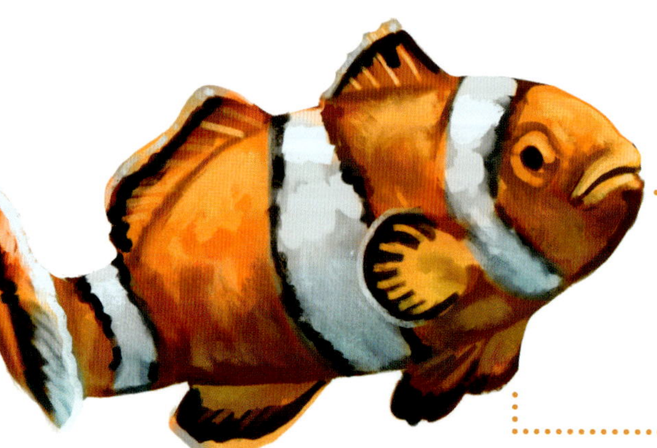

Clownfish are governed by a dominant female, and if she disappears, the dominant male in line will switch his sex to female and assume her position

The clownfish is able to transition between male and female when needed

While clownfish are hermaphroditic, they have no outward sexual dimorphism – males and females appear identical

REPRODUCTIVE ATTRIBUTES OF IMAGINARY CREATURES

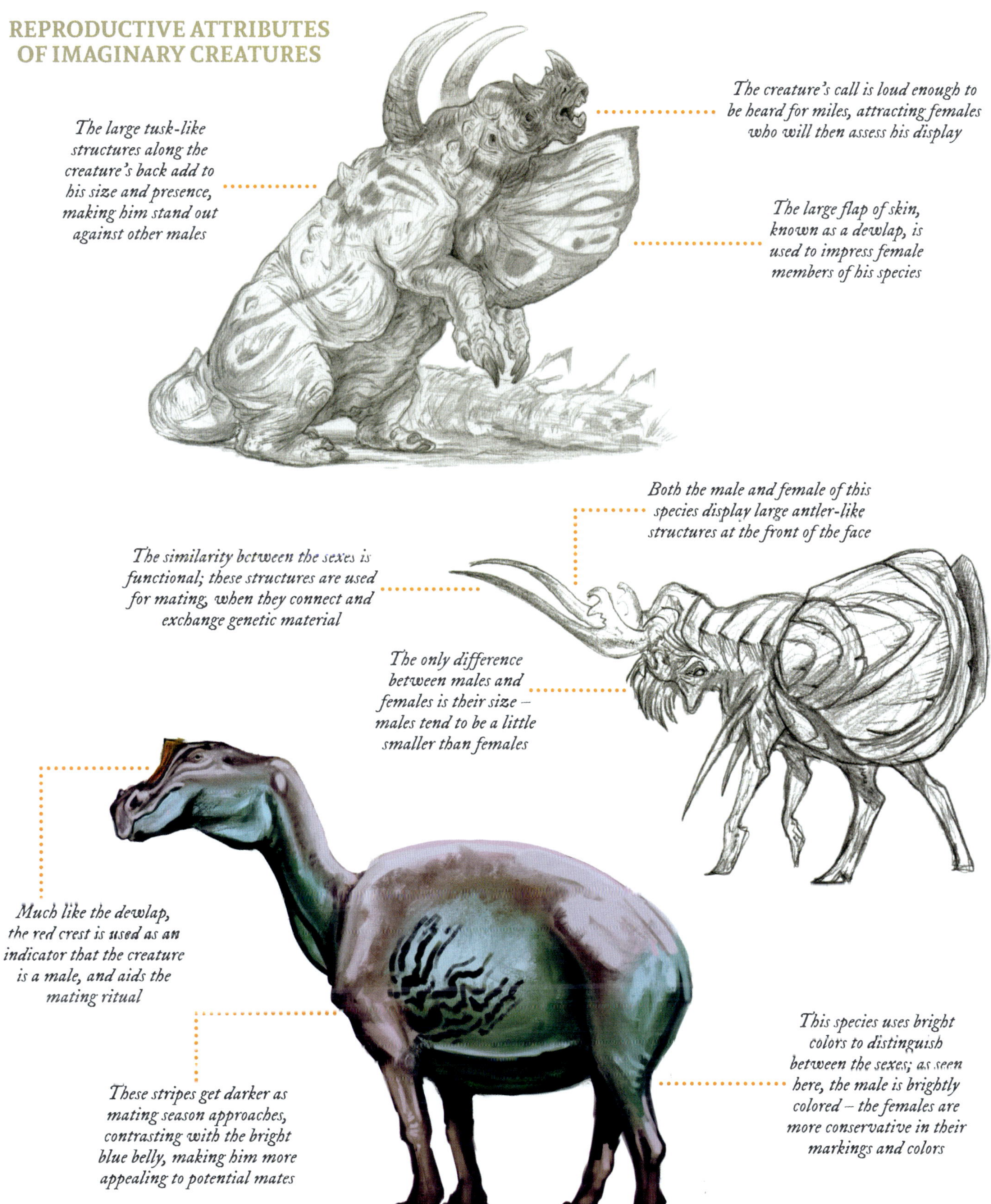

Life cycles

All life on Earth has a life cycle. We age, as do the animals and plants around us. It is important to think about your creature's age and how it can affect the *character* you are designing. We may be designing species, but we are also designing *individual* creatures of that species.

Age can be a great way to show a certain kind of character. For example, as the male ibex ages, his horns grow larger and larger, becoming more impressive and imposing. This is a way to show that your creature is older, wiser, or more weathered than the rest. Alternatively, you can use **shape language**, like rounded and softer shapes, to show that a creature may be young and inexperienced. We associate these soft shapes with human babies, and many animals are smaller, more rounded, and softer in shape when they are young, too (see more on shape language on **page 116**).

Thinking about how your creature ages and weathers through life is also a great way to add believability. Adding elements of wear and tear can convey the idea that your creature exists in a place and is affected by it. Chipped teeth, broken horns, matted fur, and missing scales are good indicators that a creature has had a life of action. Nothing on our planet makes it out unscathed, so this should apply to fictional creations as well.

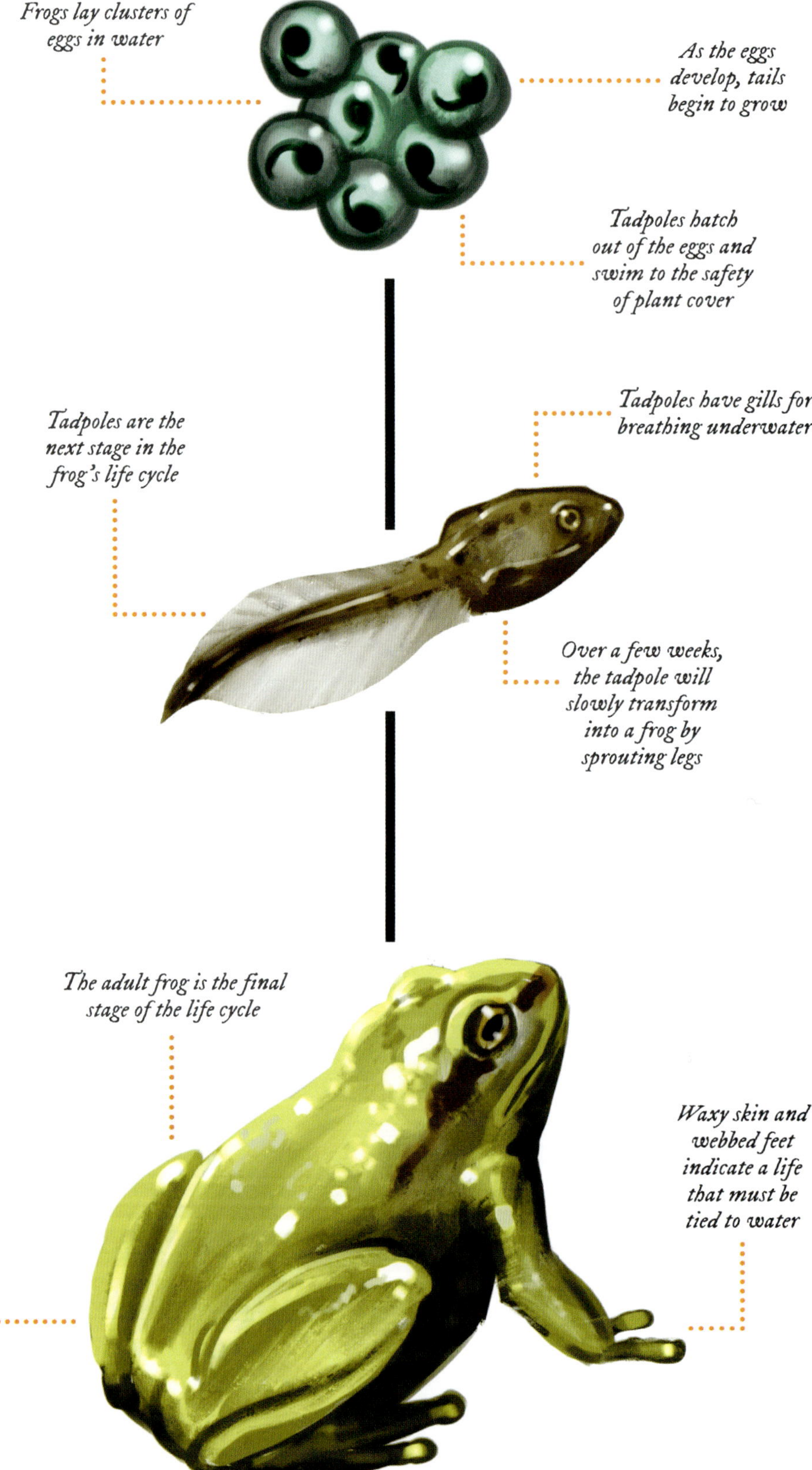

LIFE CYCLE OF AN IMAGINARY CREATURE

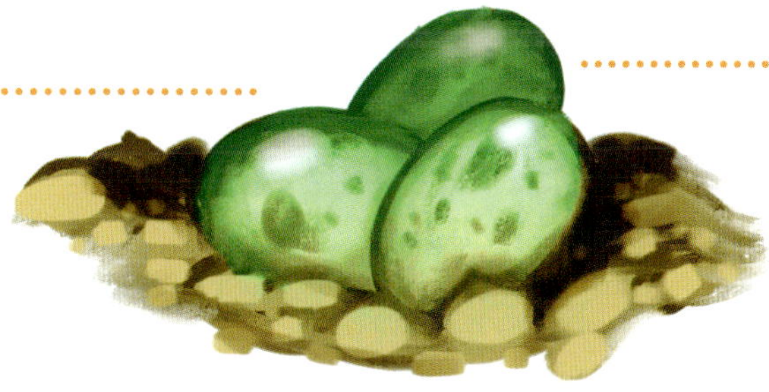

This creature lays its eggs in rocky nests – the eggs have a hard shell to protect them from danger

The mother will guard her nest from predators and egg thieves

Once the eggs hatch, the mother leaves her young to fend for themselves

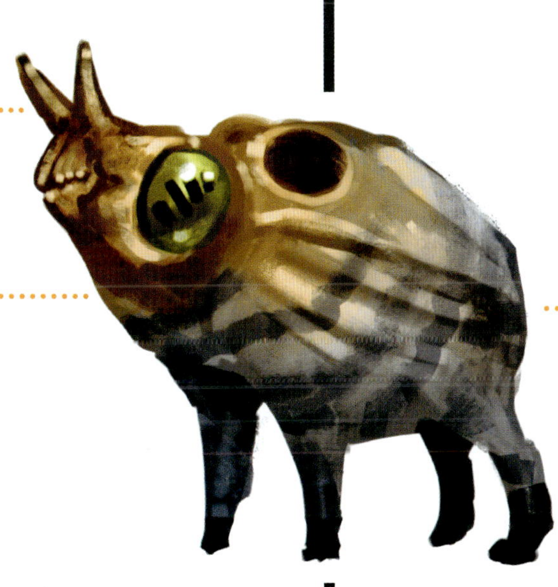

The creature hatches ready to stand and find food using the sensory organs on top of its head

This creature looks young because of its large eyes and rounded shape

The markings along the creature's body help it to stay camouflaged in the underbrush

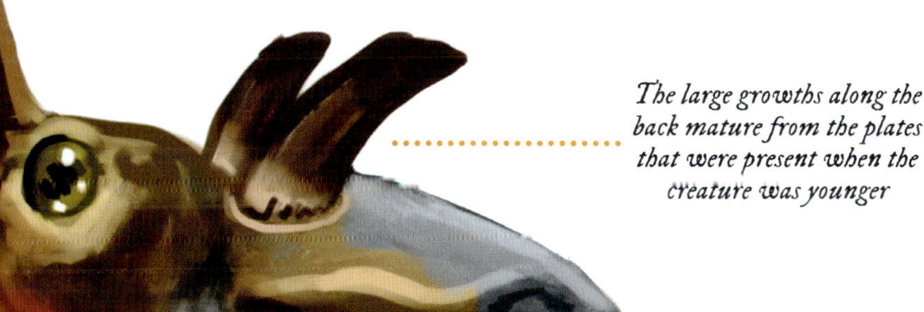

The large growths along the back mature from the plates that were present when the creature was younger

The creature uses its size to intimidate predators instead of hiding

When the creature reaches adulthood, the markings fade away as they are not needed

Domestication

Domestication can be an interesting exercise in creature design. It allows for very exaggerated features that would otherwise be a liability in the natural world. You do not need to look further than dogs to understand the impact that human influence can have on the look and function of an animal. It is estimated that around 20,000 to 32,000 years ago, humans began domesticating dogs from wolves. Humans saw the potential in having a companion that could help with hunting and protection early on. The roles of dogs expanded into herding, retrieving, flushing, sport, and even just sitting on our laps.

The shape, size, temperament, intelligence, and features of each dog breed are determined by the perceived value of those traits by the humans who breed them. For example, herding dogs like the border collie are built to be lightweight and excellent runners. They have a low center of gravity to help them turn at a moment's notice. They are extremely intelligent and have a lot of energy, making them excellent problem-solvers and planners.

Breeds such as the greyhound are built for speed and coursing game. They have a high prey drive and will chase anything that moves. They can reach speeds of forty-five miles per hour and have excellent eyesight compared to other breeds.

Dogs such as the Chihuahua were bred for companionship in early Mexico. They are small, easy to care for, and loyal to a fault. They are often alert, making them great alarm systems, while also being excellent couch potatoes. Not only are dogs' physical appearances affected by our preferences, but their actual personalities are too.

Dogs are one example of where humans have had a huge hand in the shape and function of an animal's physiology. There are many other animal species that have been touched by our tastes and preferences. Horses, sheep, cattle, pigs, birds, cats, and fish have all been shaped by humans. Applying some of these selected traits to your creature can be a fun way to incorporate outlandish features that would not make sense in the wild.

COMPANION ANIMALS

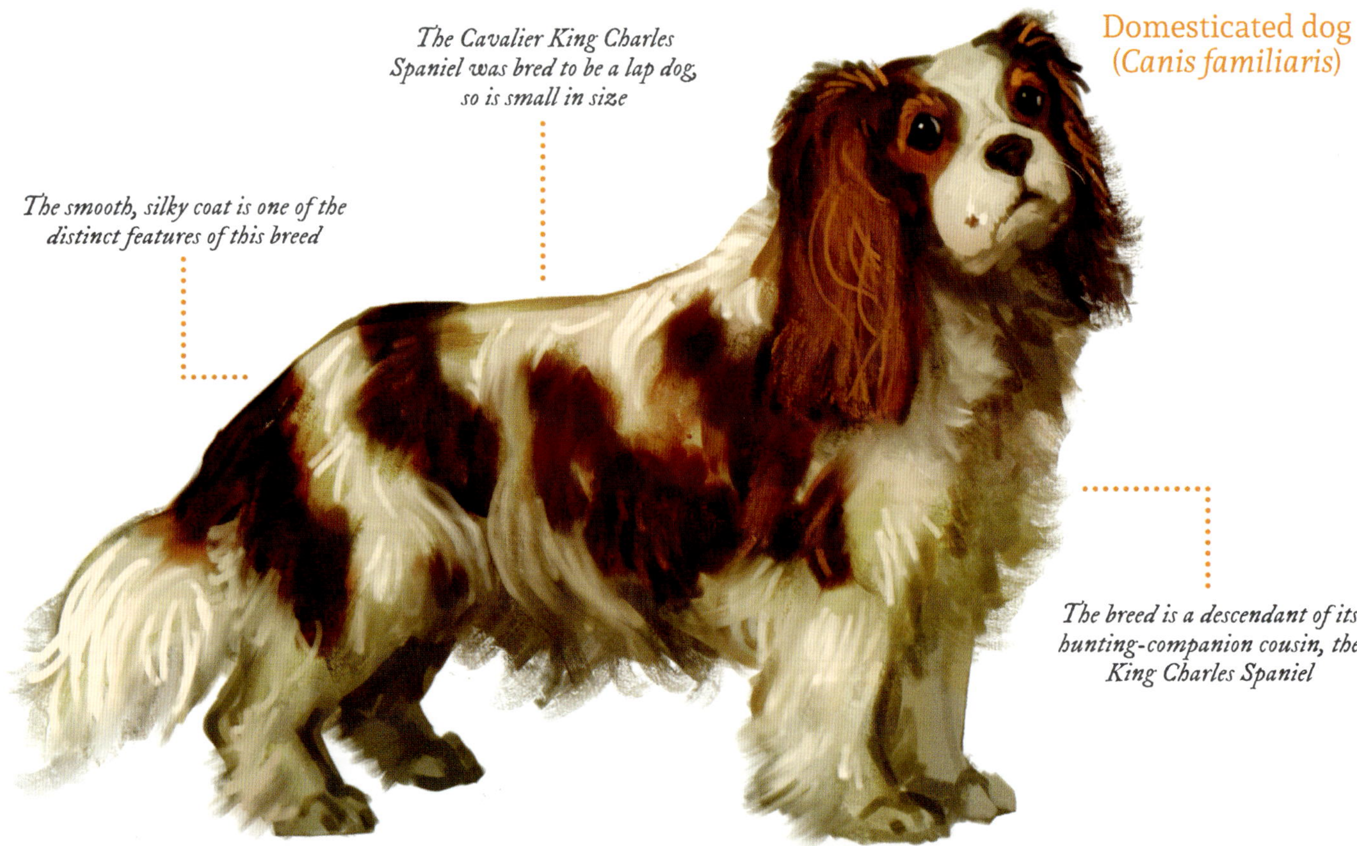

The Cavalier King Charles Spaniel was bred to be a lap dog, so is small in size

The smooth, silky coat is one of the distinct features of this breed

The breed is a descendant of its hunting-companion cousin, the King Charles Spaniel

LIVESTOCK & AGRICULTURE

Domesticated horse
(*Equus ferus caballus*)

Humans began riding and domesticating horses about 6,000 years ago

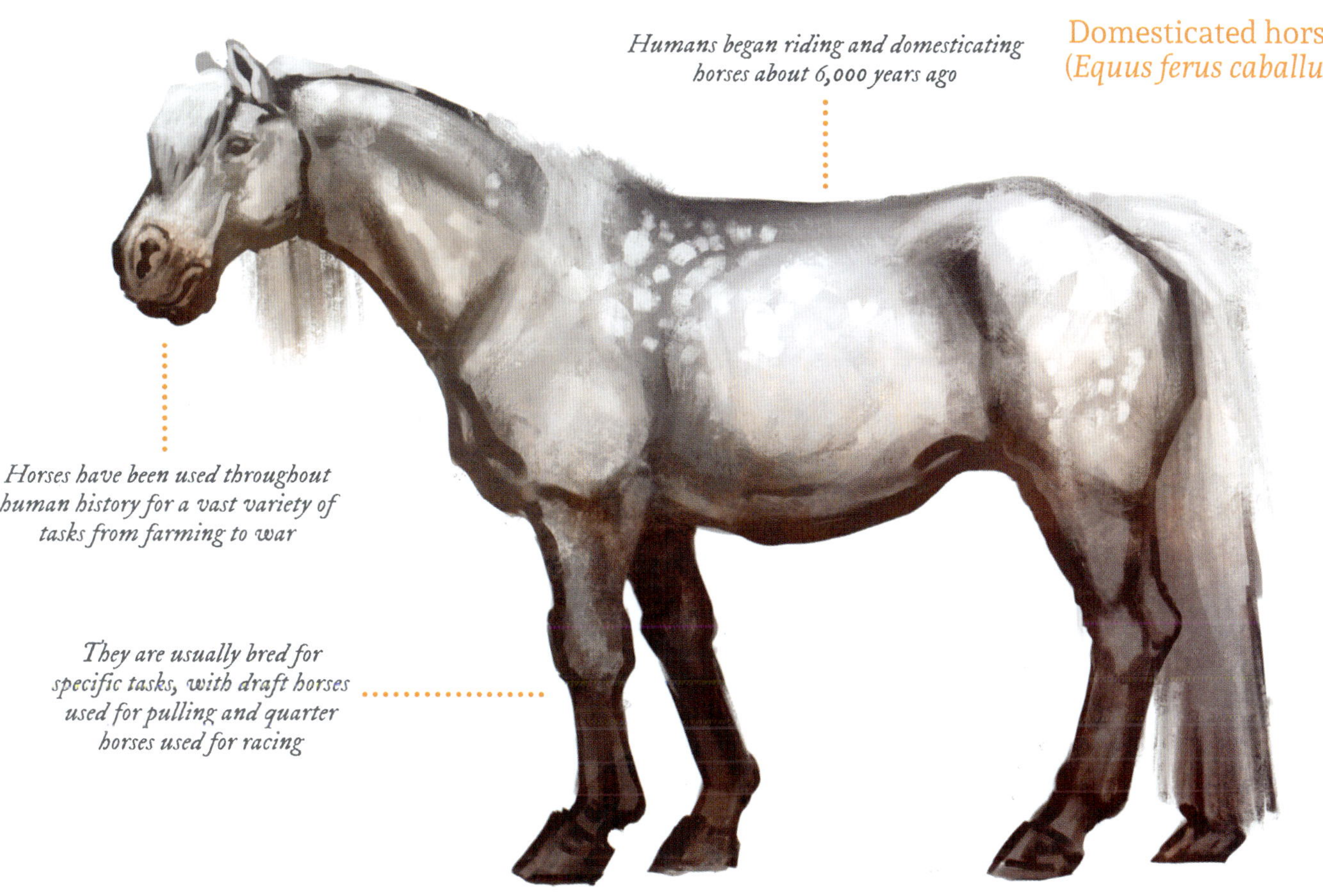

Horses have been used throughout human history for a vast variety of tasks from farming to war

They are usually bred for specific tasks, with draft horses used for pulling and quarter horses used for racing

BREEDING FOR AESTHETIC VALUE

Goldfish
(*Carassius auratus*)

Fish from all different species have been bred for many different things – they are not domesticated like dogs or horses, but they can be bred in captivity and their appearance altered

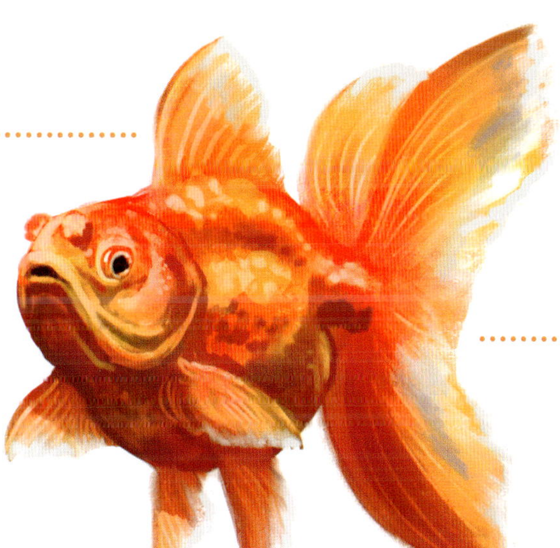

Goldfish were bred for their beauty and purely for display; unfortunately, the fancy varieties are riddled with health problems due to in-breeding

The goldfish finds its origin in the carp fish

IMAGINARY CREATURES BRED FOR AESTHETIC VALUE

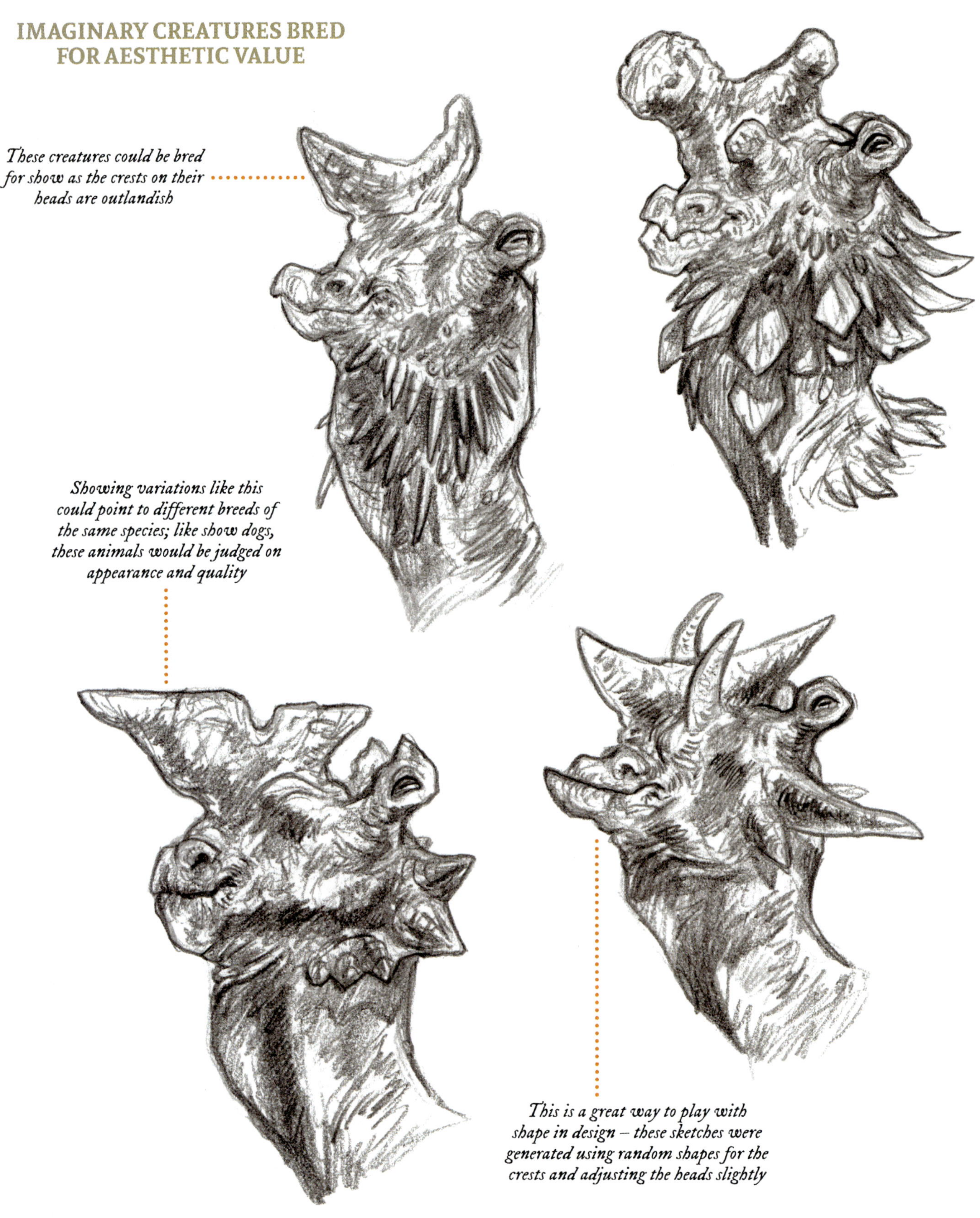

These creatures could be bred for show as the crests on their heads are outlandish

Showing variations like this could point to different breeds of the same species; like show dogs, these animals would be judged on appearance and quality

This is a great way to play with shape in design – these sketches were generated using random shapes for the crests and adjusting the heads slightly

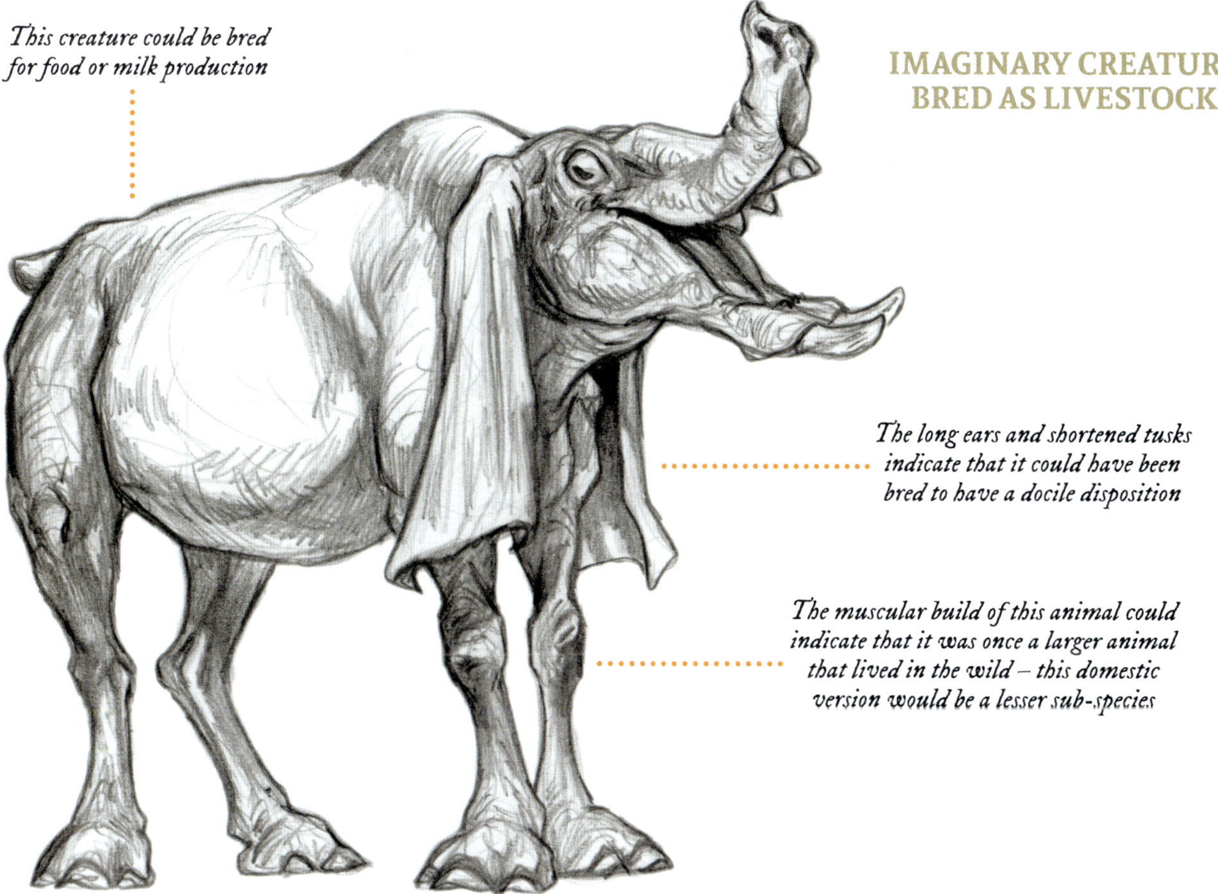

This creature could be bred for food or milk production

IMAGINARY CREATURE BRED AS LIVESTOCK

The long ears and shortened tusks indicate that it could have been bred to have a docile disposition

The muscular build of this animal could indicate that it was once a larger animal that lived in the wild – this domestic version would be a lesser sub-species

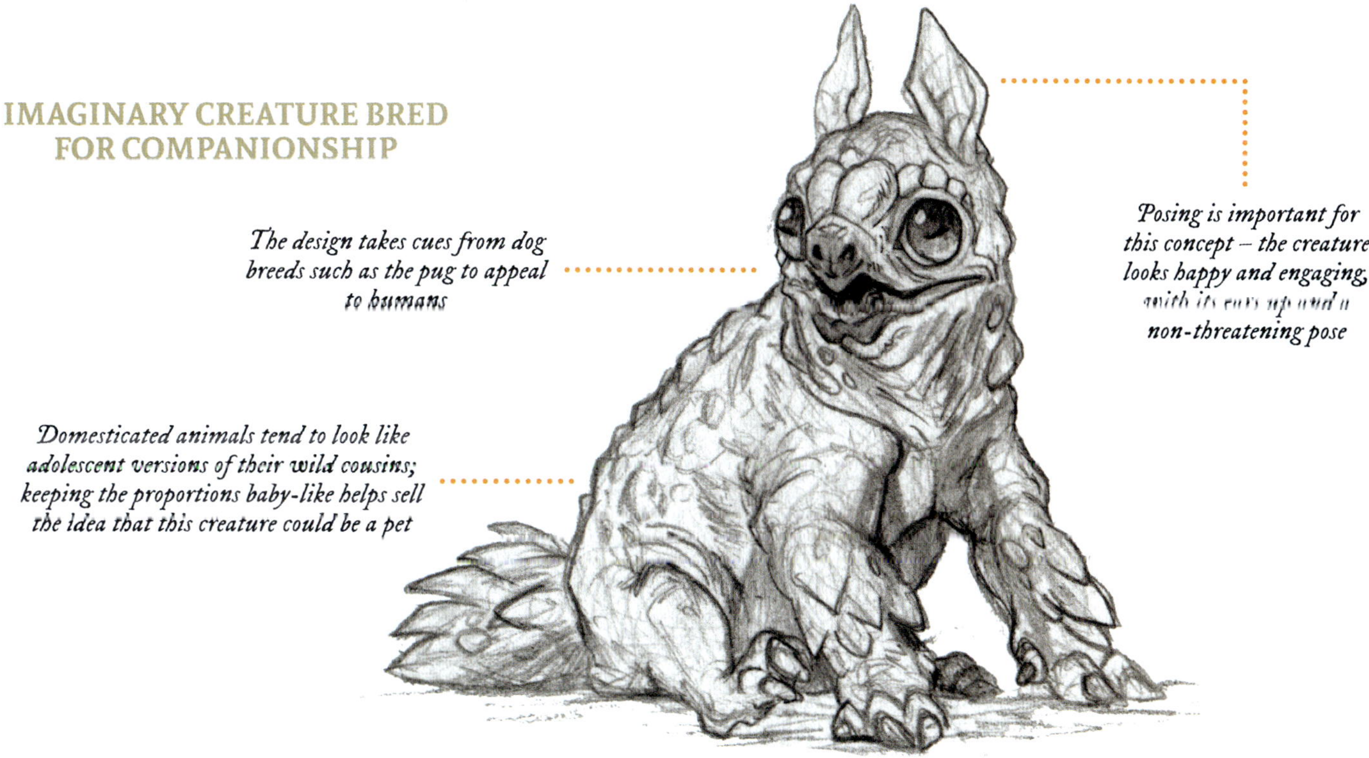

IMAGINARY CREATURE BRED FOR COMPANIONSHIP

The design takes cues from dog breeds such as the pug to appeal to humans

Posing is important for this concept – the creature looks happy and engaging, with its ears up and a non-threatening pose

Domesticated animals tend to look like adolescent versions of their wild cousins; keeping the proportions baby-like helps sell the idea that this creature could be a pet

EVOLUTIONARY BIOLOGY

Life on Earth is always adapting. When animals adapt and make heritable changes to their behavior and appearance over generations, we refer to this as evolution. All of the aspects discussed in this chapter add to the evolutionary history of the creature that you are designing. Having an idea of where your creature lives, what it eats, its social life, if it has a sex, and how old it is, can add to the believability of your design. Take that a step further and think about clues you can add to its evolutionary history, and suddenly you have something really special.

Vestigial traits

Real-world animals hold clues to their past all over their bodies. Even humans have vestigial traits that point back to life as early primates. Vestigial traits are attributes that are left over from previous generations. For example, in humans, our tailbone remains from our evolutionary past spent in trees, and our appendix is a "left over" organ from our ancestors' diet.

Whale skeletons show a long history of life on land before taking to the sea, with the presence of pelvic bones and hand structures inside their flippers. Horses have toes fused inside their legs from when they were small multi-toed animals. Ostriches have wings left over from an ancestor that once flew through the skies. Take a look at animals a little closer and read about their histories. You will begin to see traits left over from previous generations everywhere. What traits can you add to your creature that hint at an interesting evolutionary past?

Evolutionary history

After you have determined some basic factors of your design, you can begin to delve into its evolutionary past by asking questions such as:

- How long ago did this creature start climbing through trees?

- When did this creature take to the sea?

These kinds of questions can help you determine what sort of traits to make present in your design. For example, if you have a creature that is semi-aquatic in nature, it may still have traits that are more suited to moving around on land. Sea lions look as though they are suited to both land and sea in their physiology. They have flippers and their bodies are adapted to be almost completely waterbound. Sometimes this means moving around on land can be cumbersome.

Another example of evolutionary history could be found by comparing your creature to another member of its species. Marine iguanas spend the majority of their time in the ocean. Little has changed on their bodies since they began taking to the sea; their anatomy worked well for the kind of swimming and eating they take part in. That said, certain traits have changed. Their skin is darker and changes color depending on the algae they eat. Their teeth have changed from being suited to catching prey, to being perfect for eating algae off of rocks. They have more robust tails for swimming and stockier builds for enduring cold water. These are significant changes that inform us of their life as seafaring lizards, even if at first glance they appear similar to their land-dwelling cousins.

When designing an evolutionary tree for your creature, think about gradual change over time. What aspects of the creature need to change to better suit its new environment? Does your creature need longer legs for dealing with the terrain? Perhaps it needs eyes located higher on its head to see over the water it wades through. Maybe it also needs webbed feet to handle a watery environment. Small, gradual changes are key to making a believable evolutionary history.

Questions to ask

As you will have seen throughout this chapter, there are many questions you can ask yourself to help you create well-considered designs. Here are a few useful ones to remember:

- What did this creature's predecessors look like, where did they live, and how did they behave?

- What could this creature evolve into, and why?

- Is it related to land mammals, cetaceans, birds, fish, insects, or something else entirely?

- Has domestication or selective breeding affected the development of this creature?

- Has a changing habitat, climate, or diet affected the development of this creature?

- What is its relationship to other creatures that share its habitat?

- How does this creature compare to other members of its own species? How similar or different are they, and why?

- Does this creature have any vestigial remains from its evolutionary past?

REAL-WORLD EVOLUTION

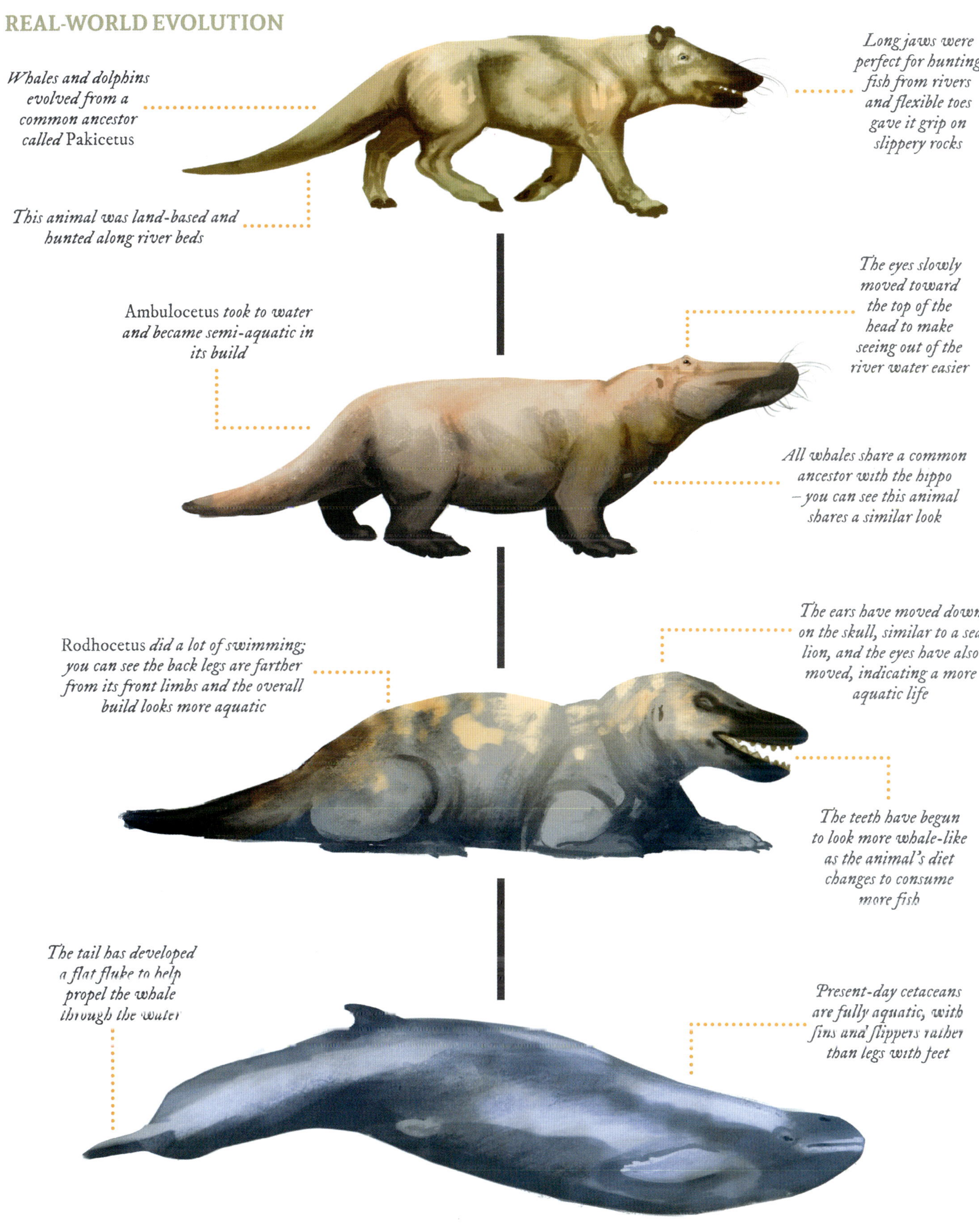

REAL-WORLD TO IMAGINARY EVOLUTION

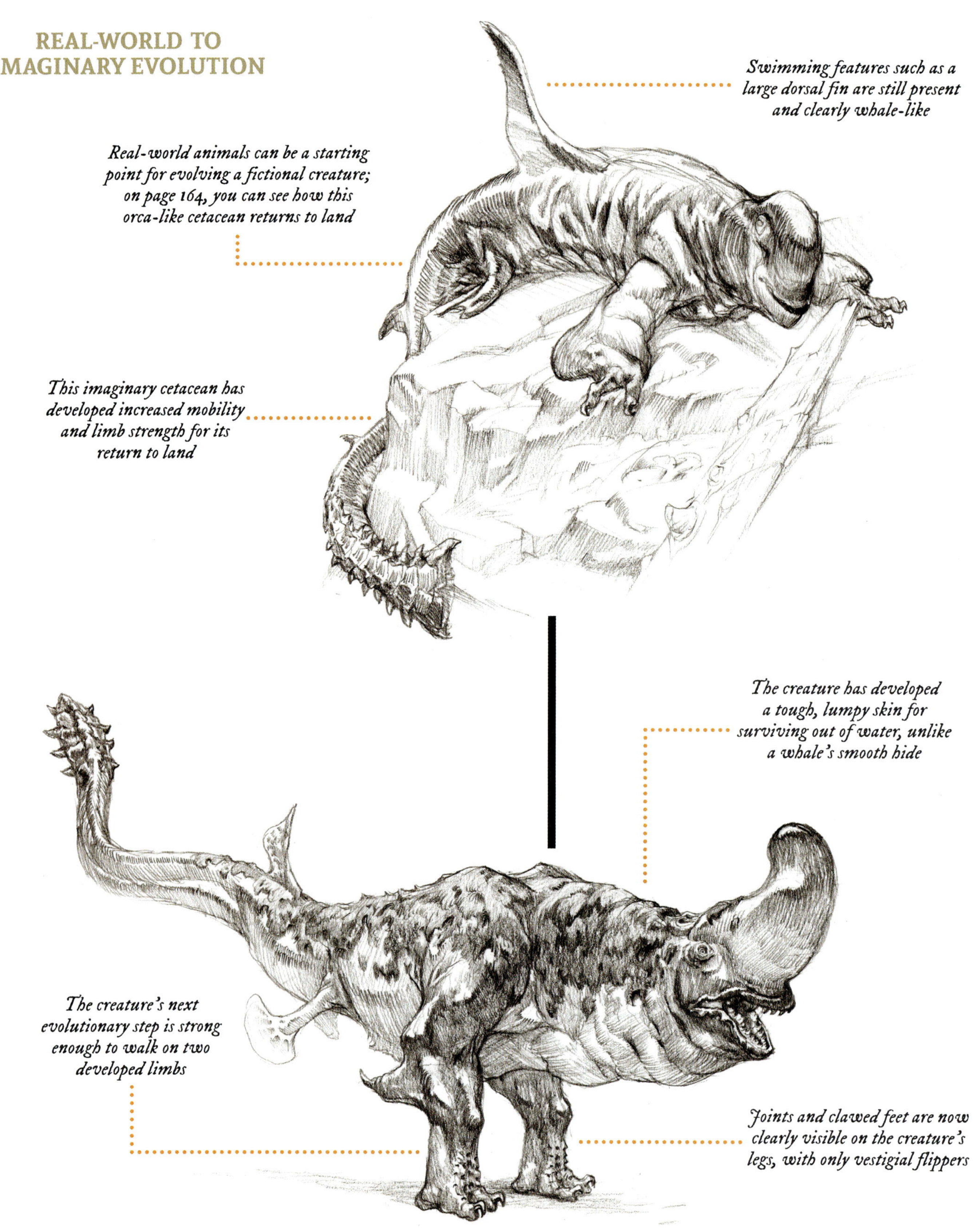

Above images by Jordan K. Walker

IMAGINARY EVOLUTION

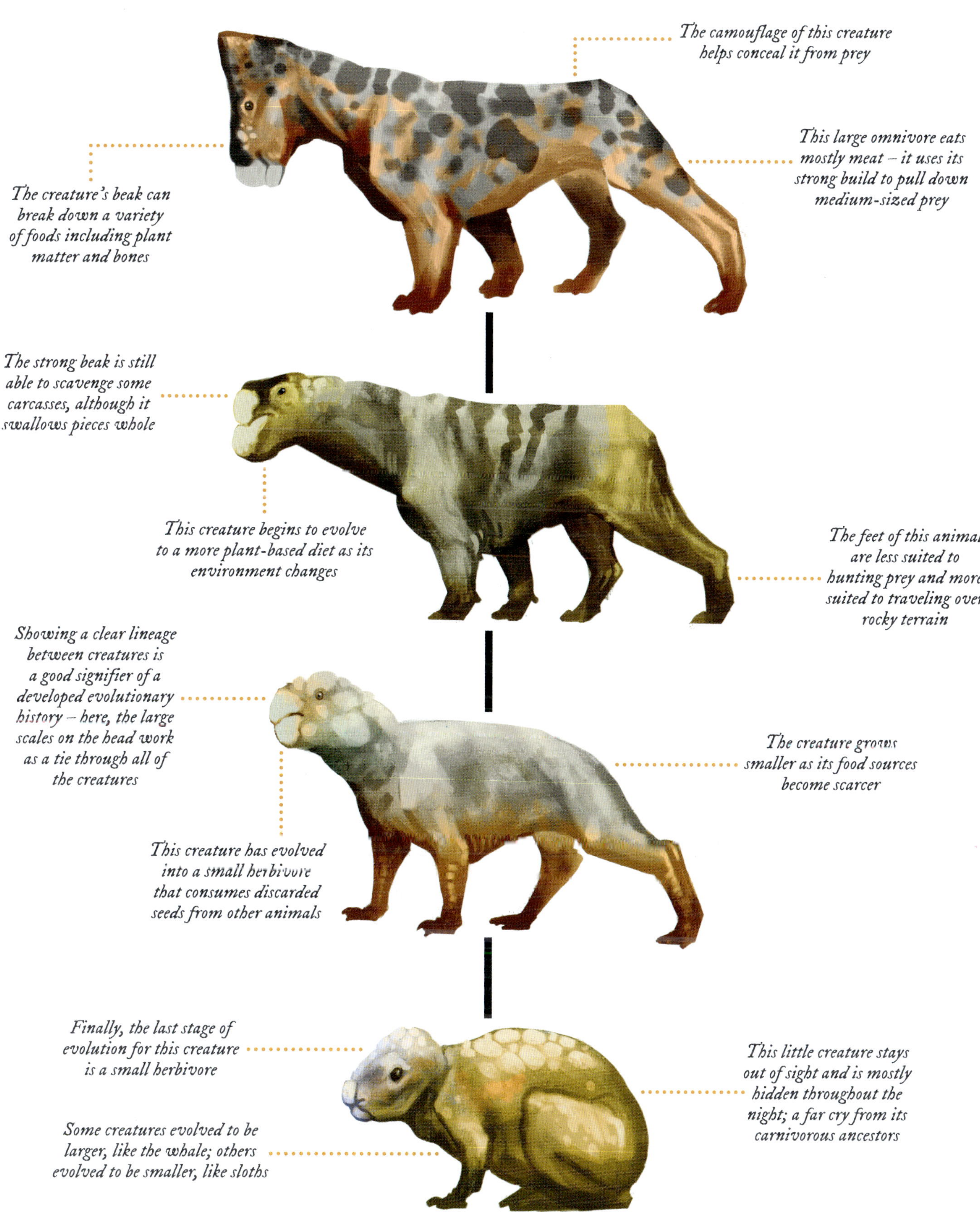

Anatomy

"Extensively studying the anatomy of real species gives artists a vast mental library of how real animals are organized and function"

By Dominique Vassie

WHY IS ANATOMY IMPORTANT?

Creature design takes a wide range of different forms. Some projects need creatures that are crudely anatomically assembled for an intentional cute or comedic effect, but if the aim is to produce creatures that look like they have their own functioning anatomy and evolutionary history, then understanding animal anatomy well is essential. This process starts with drawing and studying as many different real-world animal species as possible, gathering a mental database of those forms that are adapted so well for their life on Earth.

It is also important to consider an animal as a **complete, moving entity**. Simply sticking on limbs and body parts without consideration for how the creature grows and moves will create a design that is not believable. Take a look at the examples shown below. Little thought has been given to how the limbs might function and attach to the body, or how features such as gills actually appear and work in reality. In creature design, you need to consider practical elements such as the balance of the animal, how it feeds, where its muscles are, and how the limbs are powered and supported. The examples on the opposite page take these considerations into account to create cohesive, believable designs. Take time to draw inspiration from the amazing life forms all around you, and understand how their anatomy makes them suited to their lifestyle.

INCOHESIVE ANATOMY

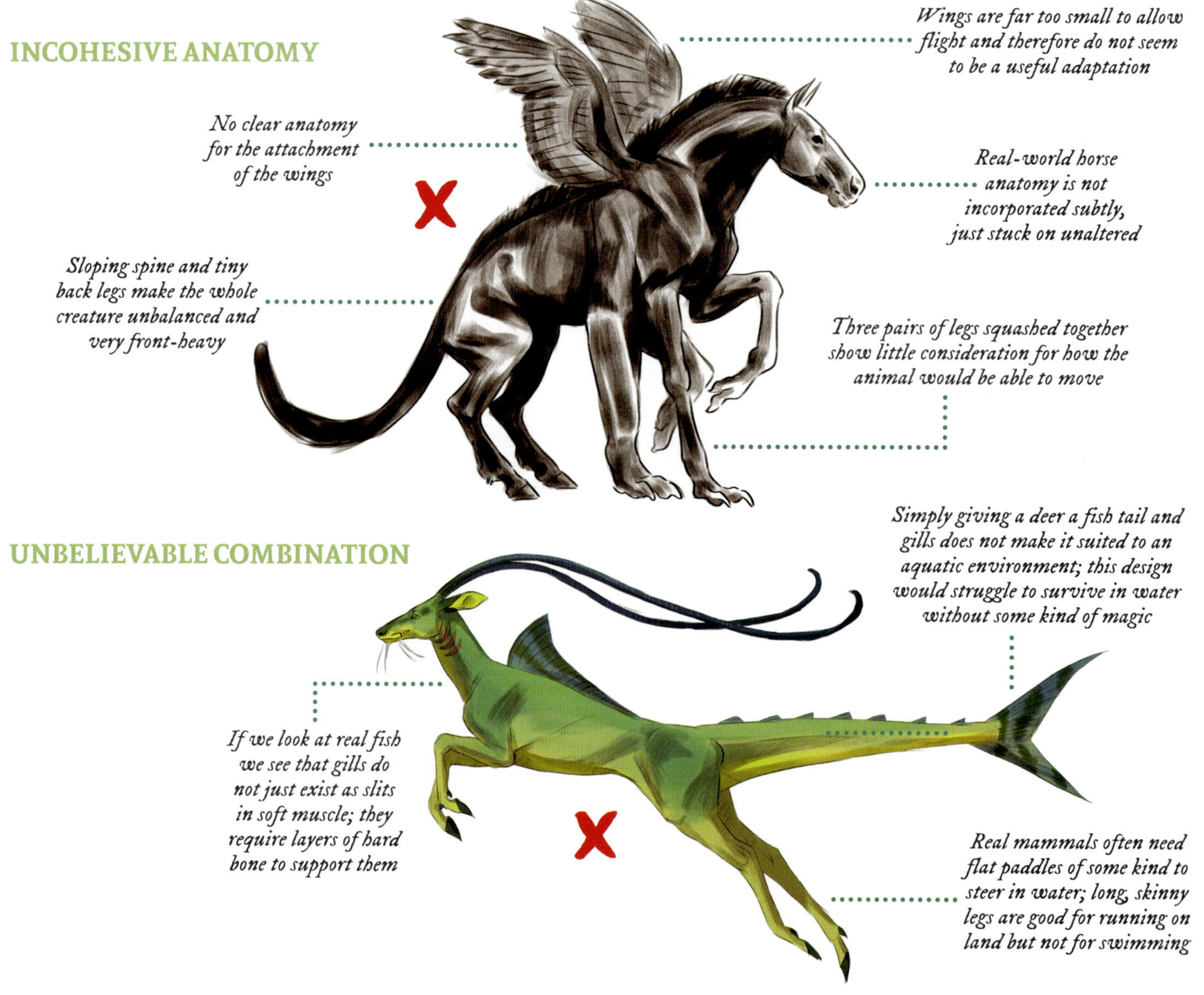

UNBELIEVABLE COMBINATION

BELIEVABLE COMBINATION

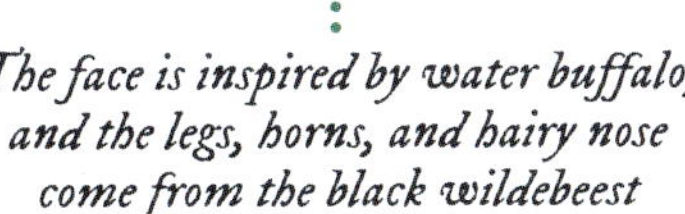

Its shaggy neck fur, forelegs, and tail take from bison and yak

This creature could be ridden by humans, hence the focus on animals with more rigid spines for comfortable travel

This design blends five different hoofed animals fluidly together to create something that is new and not quite like any of them

The overall shape, especially the hindquarters, is very horse-like

The face is inspired by water buffalo, and the legs, horns, and hairy nose come from the black wildebeest

COHESIVE ANATOMY

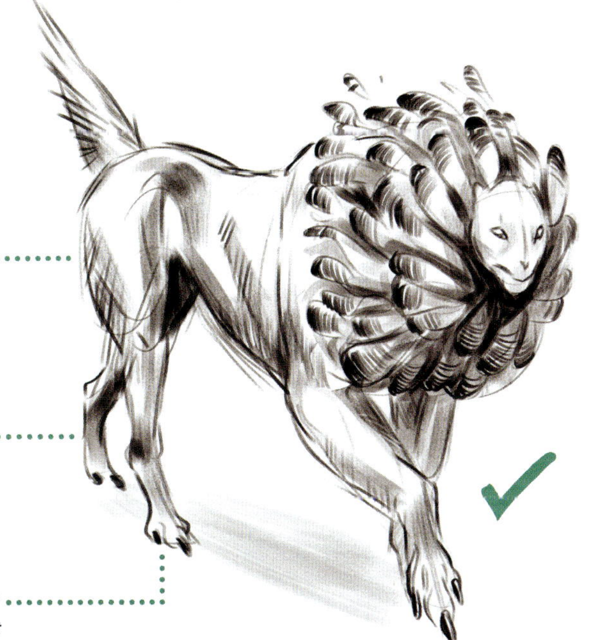

This creature is well structured and balanced, with anatomy that is not distinctly any real-world animal – it is also not obviously different animals stitched together

It appears to have a cohesive anatomy of bone and muscle supporting it from within

The limbs are in the appropriate place for believable movement

Essential anatomy

In this chapter we will first look at the techniques of blending and exaggeration, which form a large part of incorporating real-world anatomy into imaginary creature design, and how you can use these effectively in your designs. We will then study the anatomy of a range of different animals to give you an overview of their underlying structure. The animals have been chosen to give a basic and broad coverage of key groups for creature design. You can refer back to these pages at any time to help bring accuracy and believability to your creations.

Evolution

It is useful to have a basic understanding of the evolutionary relationships between species, as this enables you to determine the anatomy of new animals more easily. If you know that whales and dolphins are mammals, and that their closest relative is the hippopotamus, then understanding their anatomy and adaptations becomes easier than if you think they are fish. Once you are conscious of which animals are related, you can also identify which anatomical features make them a distinct group, and take those interesting features into your designs. Find out more about evolution on **page 52**

BLENDING ANATOMIES

Throughout history there have been folk tales and legends of many fantastical creatures, but these are often in the form of chimeras, where pieces of real species are stitched together in a rather inorganic way. An example of this is the centaur, where the creature is simply the upper body of a human attached to the body of a horse with little modification. However, modern creature design tends to steer away from this, instead **blending the anatomy** of different species more smoothly. This results in something new and functional that looks like it has its own evolutionary history.

Successful blending of animals requires **avoiding the cut-and-paste approach** and instead looking more closely at the anatomy of the animals for interesting aspects. From there, the artist can work out how to merge those aspects into a design in a way that looks more natural. An understanding of how bones and muscles connect and support areas of the body is key to this.

It helps to choose a solid basic body plan for your creature that you can then modify, exaggerate, and blend with the anatomy of other living things. Then consider questions such as, "How does the animal move? How many legs does it walk on? Does it swim?" Answering such questions early gives you a framework from which you can work out the ecology and lifestyle of your creature. With that framework, you can blend in anatomical features that help the animal to adapt successfully.

You can also use the skin coverings, colors, and knowledge of how animal bodies connect to make your creature fluid and seamlessly assembled, ready for life in its world.

The examples here show designs for a wild boar crossed with a European badger. The first is basically a badger's head with a boar's body, which has an unimaginative, slightly laughable effect. The second uses different elements from each animal and considers the impact of each body part on the animal's functionality.

Blending tips

- Familiarize yourself with real-world anatomy to understand how bones and muscles connect

- Consider the effect that each area of anatomy will have on the functionality of the creature - make sure it can move and eat effectively

- Avoid the cut-and-paste approach

- Use pattern, coloration, and skin coverings such as scales, feathers, and fur to unify areas

See more design tips on **page 104**.

INCOHESIVE ANATOMY

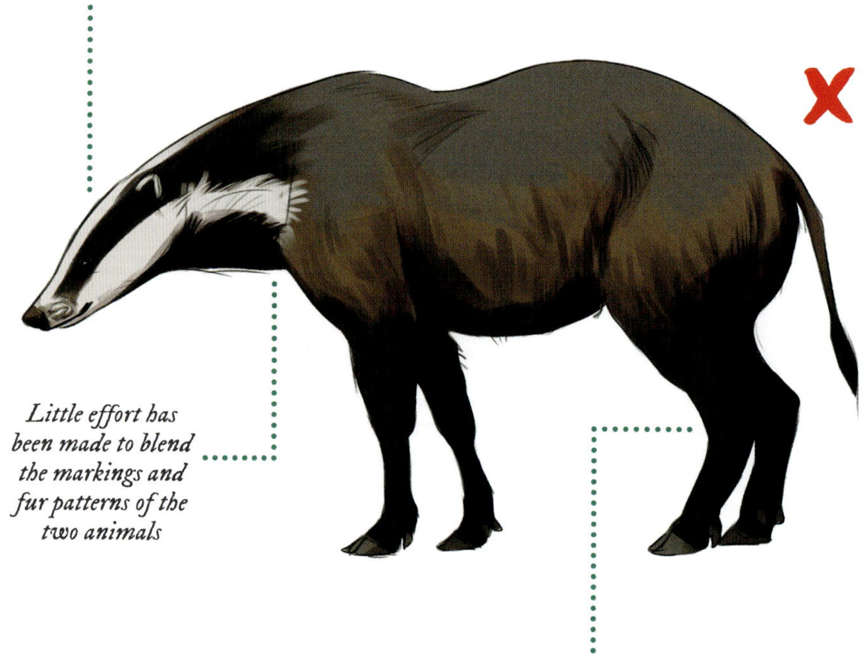

The badger head has not been modified in any way, making this a comedic chimera rather than a well-blended creature design

Little effort has been made to blend the markings and fur patterns of the two animals

Like a centaur, the badger's head and back have simply been stuck to the legs of a wild boar

COHESIVE ANATOMY

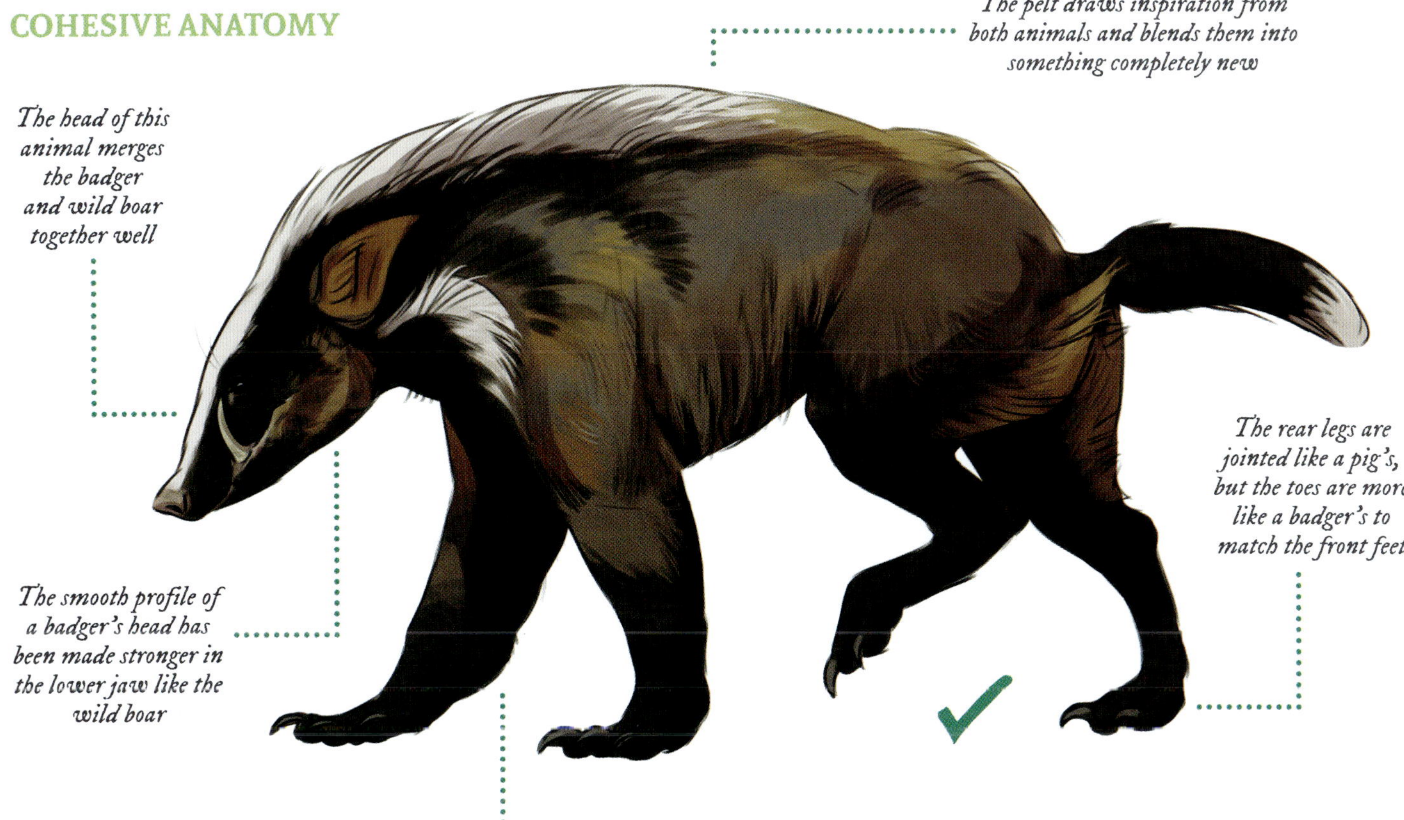

Consider what's underneath

This is a rough sketch of a fictional creature's musculature to help solidify a design and ensure it is functional as an animal. It can be helpful to rough out the internal anatomy for a design, especially one with a thick layer of hair or feathers that obscures the form.

Each of the anatomy sections in this chapter includes an image of the animal reduced to its basic shapes, along with skeletal and muscular overviews to help create a foundation for your creature designs.

Combining multiple references

Remember that you do not have to limit yourself to two beasts – combining the snout of one, the claws of another, and the body of another can bring originality to your design – as long as they are blended accurately and believably from an evolutionary and functional point of view. You can also use non-animal elements such as plants and man-made materials.

REAL-WORLD CREATURES

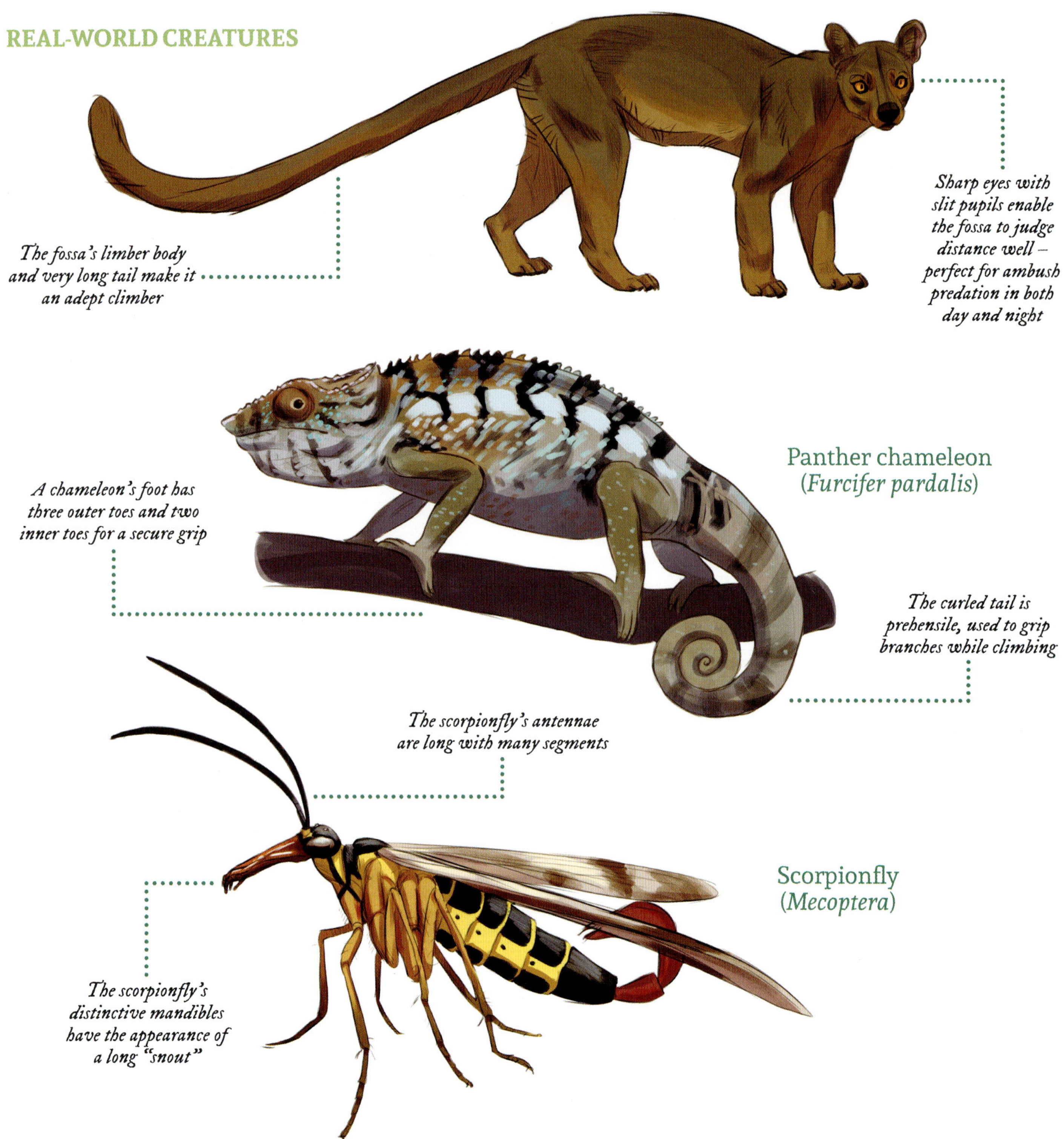

Fossa
(*Cryptoprocta ferox*)

Sharp eyes with slit pupils enable the fossa to judge distance well – perfect for ambush predation in both day and night

The fossa's limber body and very long tail make it an adept climber

A chameleon's foot has three outer toes and two inner toes for a secure grip

Panther chameleon
(*Furcifer pardalis*)

The curled tail is prehensile, used to grip branches while climbing

The scorpionfly's antennae are long with many segments

Scorpionfly
(*Mecoptera*)

The scorpionfly's distinctive mandibles have the appearance of a long "snout"

IMAGINARY CREATURE

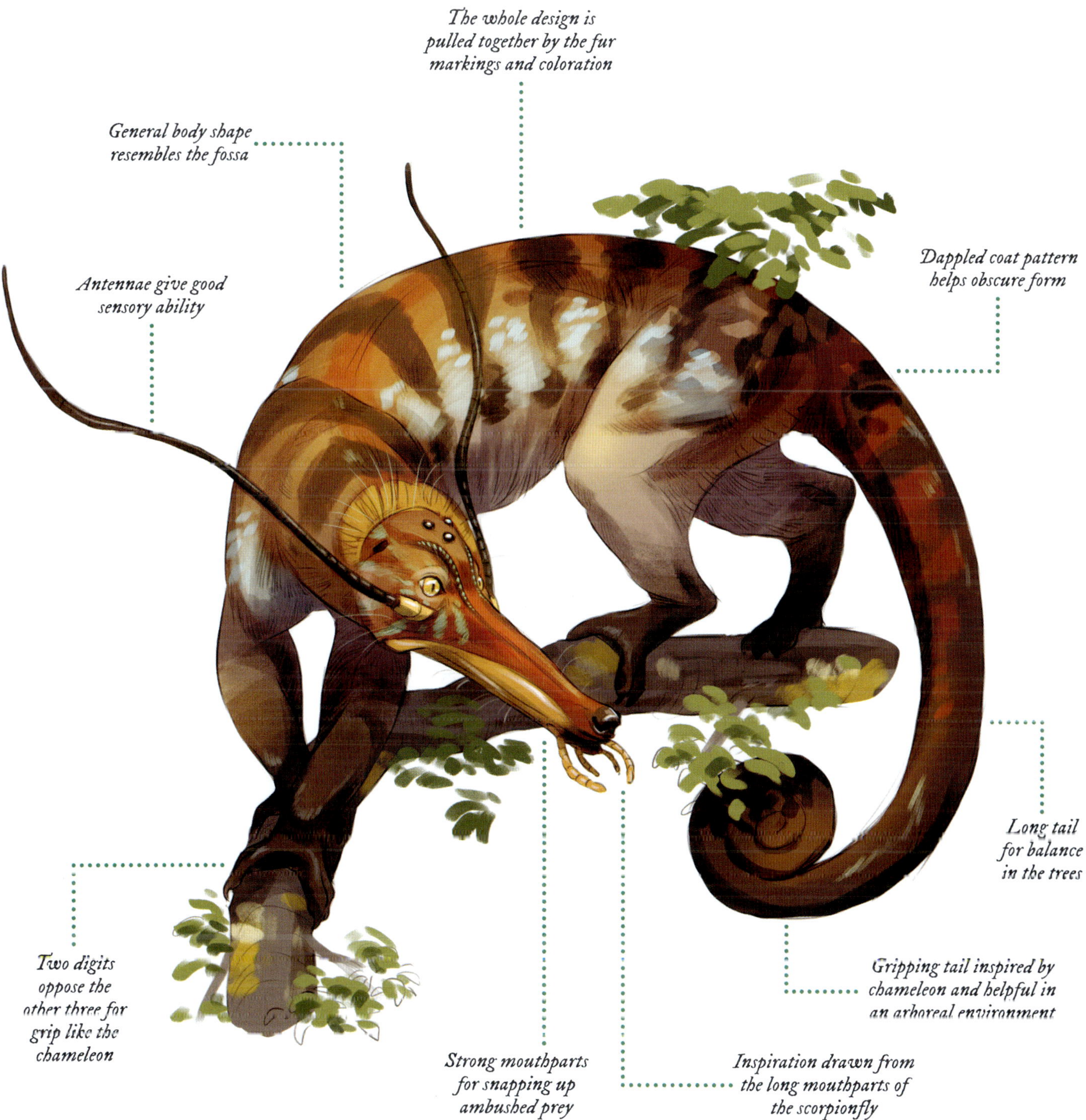

EXAGGERATING ANATOMIES

Real animals have had millions of years to evolve into a huge variety of forms, and all have interesting features that can be **exaggerated into caricatures** or used in a creature design. As artists, we can push the boundaries of evolution a little and manipulate reality into something weirder and more wonderful to fit our design requirements or desires. However, the more you learn about nature, the more you realize that it has already developed its fair share of ridiculous animal anatomies and adaptations to inspire us.

Exaggeration of real-world anatomies is a very useful technique for creating designs based on real animals, or for giving fantastical creatures believable features. For example, many even-toed ungulates, such as sheep and goats, have large elaborate horns. As creature designers, not only can we borrow those pieces of anatomy, we can play with them by either making them huge or extending their coils far beyond the creature's body in imaginative ways.

However, any exaggeration that we do must also be balanced. Exaggeration for the sake of it does not necessarily work; if you exaggerate one area of a design, you may need to alter another to compensate for it and ensure that the creature can still function. For instance, if your animal now has horns the length of its body, it will also need muscle in its neck to accommodate and support that weight.

The exaggeration on the near right has failed to make the creature look like something new. In some contexts, this is the kind of slightly comedic exaggeration needed, but it does not result in an interesting, functional creature design. If we are considering the anatomy of the creatures we design, we must note **how an animal feeds, moves, and functions**. There has been little effort to make it look like anything other than a rhino with long legs. Other areas need to be exaggerated in a more creative way to make this a good creature design that looks like it has its own anatomy and ecology.

BALANCED EXAGGERATION

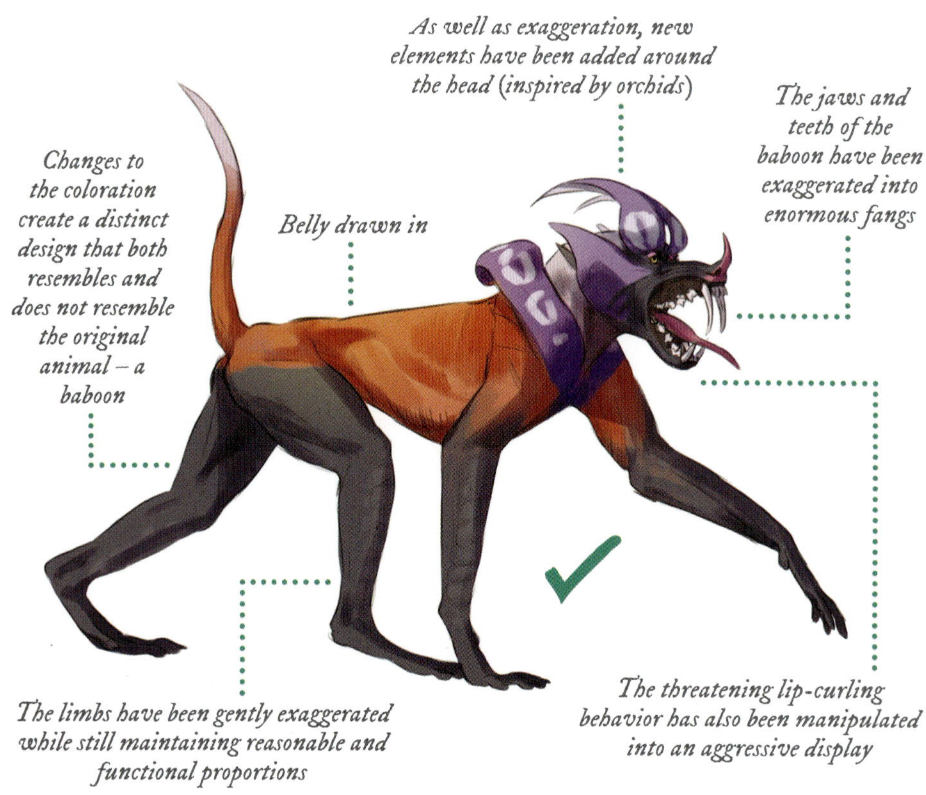

UNBALANCED EXAGGERATION

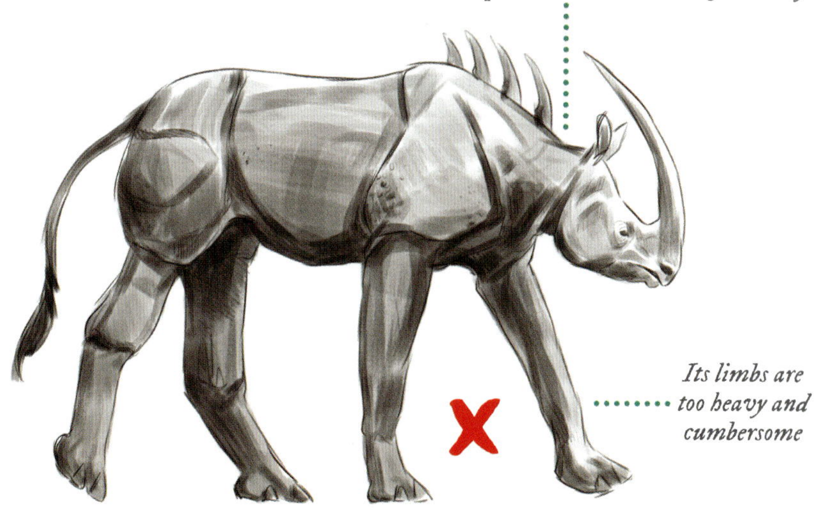

REAL-WORLD CREATURE

Topi (*Damaliscus lunatus jimela*)

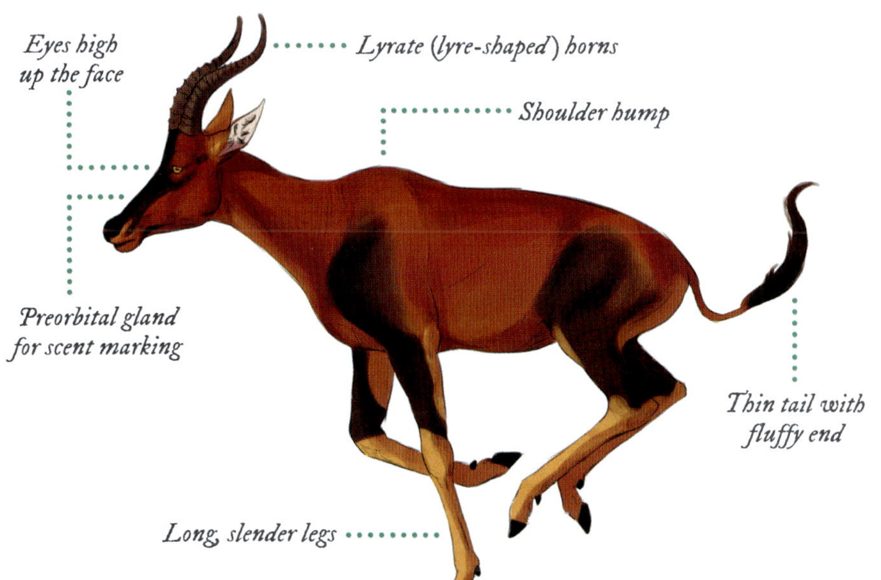

Exaggeration tips

- Do not use exaggeration alone – introduce new elements and colors to bring originality to your design

- Remember you can exaggerate an animal's behavior, posture, and patterning in addition to its anatomy

- Consider the effect any exaggeration will have on the creature's functionality

- Use skin coverings and patterns to unify areas of the design

IMAGINARY CREATURE

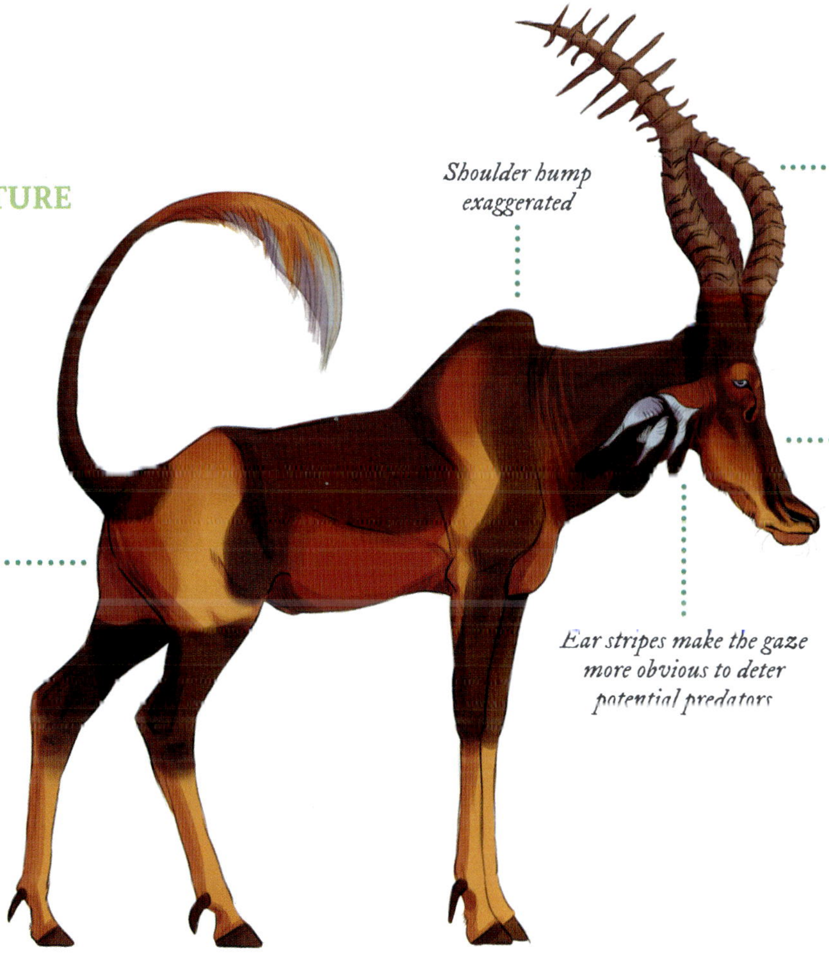

HUMAN ANATOMY

We, *Homo sapiens*, find ourselves among our fellow "great apes" in the tree of life. Chimpanzees, gorillas, bonobos, and orangutans are the animal species with the most similar anatomy to our own, and together we form an evolutionary family, the **Hominids**. However, human anatomy can be related to all vertebrates in some way, as we all evolved from a common ancestor. This is especially true for terrestrial vertebrates such as dogs, horses, birds, and frogs, but also for certain animals that later returned to the water, such as dolphins.

For creature designers, it is important to have a solid understanding of human anatomy in terms of its place among that of other animals. Once you understand the **connection with other animals**, you will be able to comprehend anatomy for all species - not just those pictured in this book. This knowledge will help you create cohesive designs when combining the anatomies of different creatures, as you will have an in-depth understanding of how animal bodies fit together and function mechanically.

Another reason it is important to understand human anatomy is that it features prominently in several classic fantasy creatures, such as centaurs and mermaids. It is also a useful tool for making creatures with believable characters and personality – creatures that are relatable to people and able to perform human gestures, activities, and expressions.

This section will provide a few examples of how the human body relates to other vertebrates. You can use this knowledge to help you apply the concept to other mammals, birds, reptiles, amphibians, and, more distantly, fish.

HUMAN MUSCULATURE

Adult female

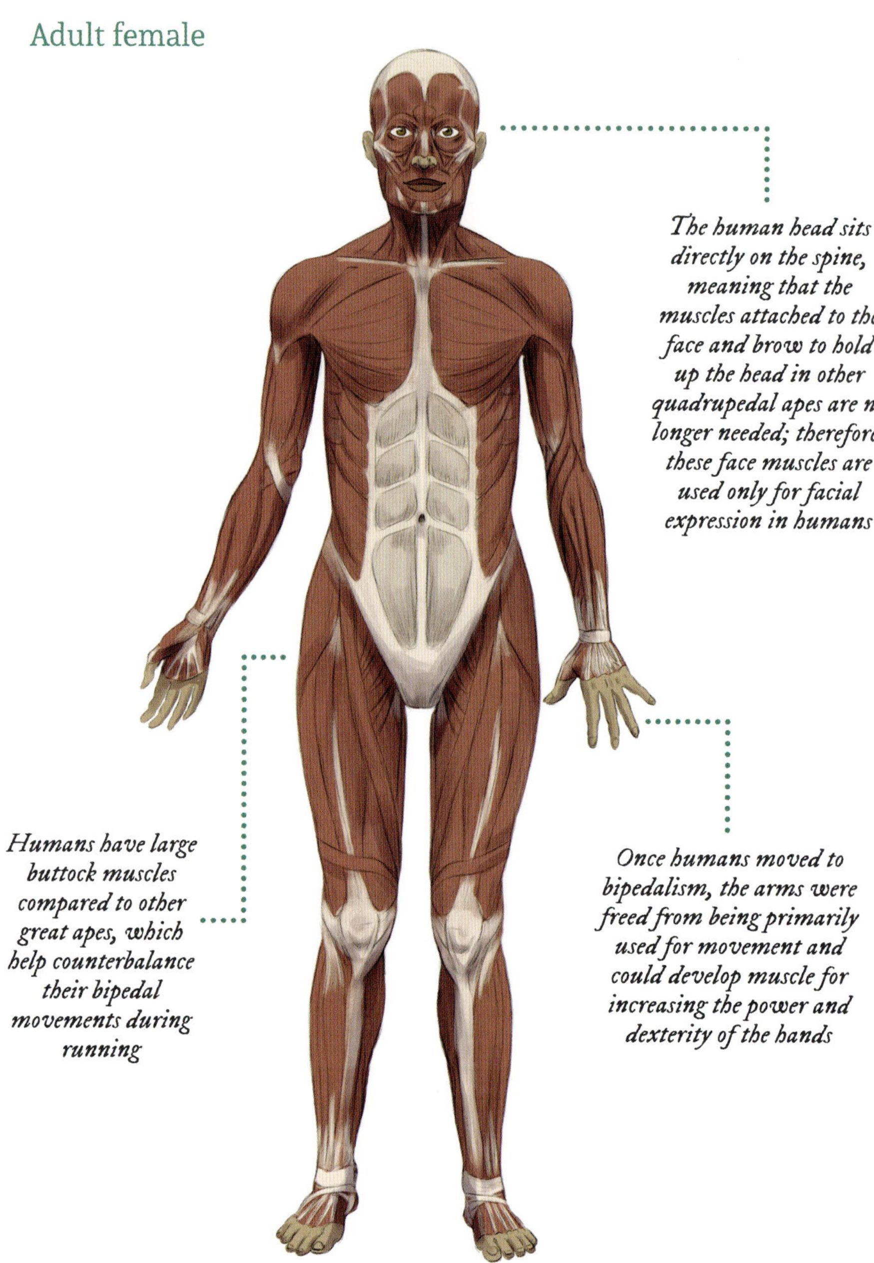

HUMAN SKELETON

An inward curve in the lower spine (lumbar) allows humans to walk with a straight back and not lean forward like other great apes do during short bipedal bursts; the upright posture uses far less muscle input by bringing the center of mass more directly above the feet

The shoulder blades float across the back of the broad, shallow ribcage rather than supporting it like in quadruped animals

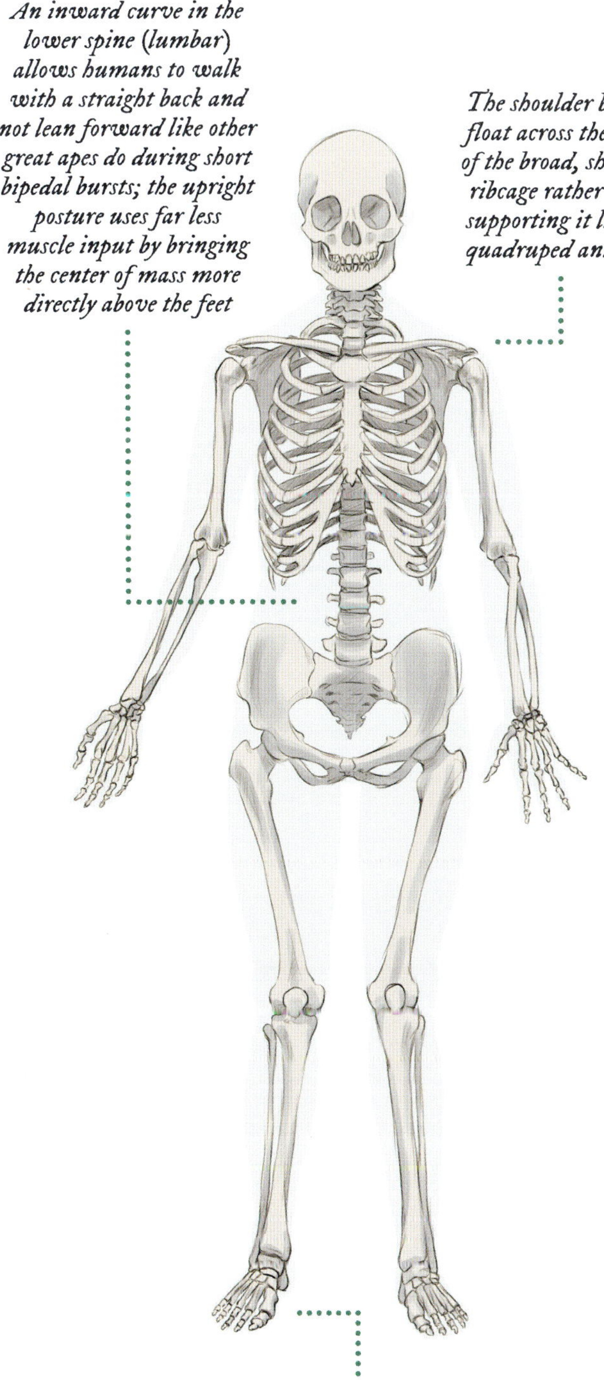

Humans have a prominent heel and a foot arch, which means the feet are adapted to bear the body's entire weight for prolonged periods

HUMAN BASIC SHAPES

Humans have a large brain in relation to body size, when compared to other primates

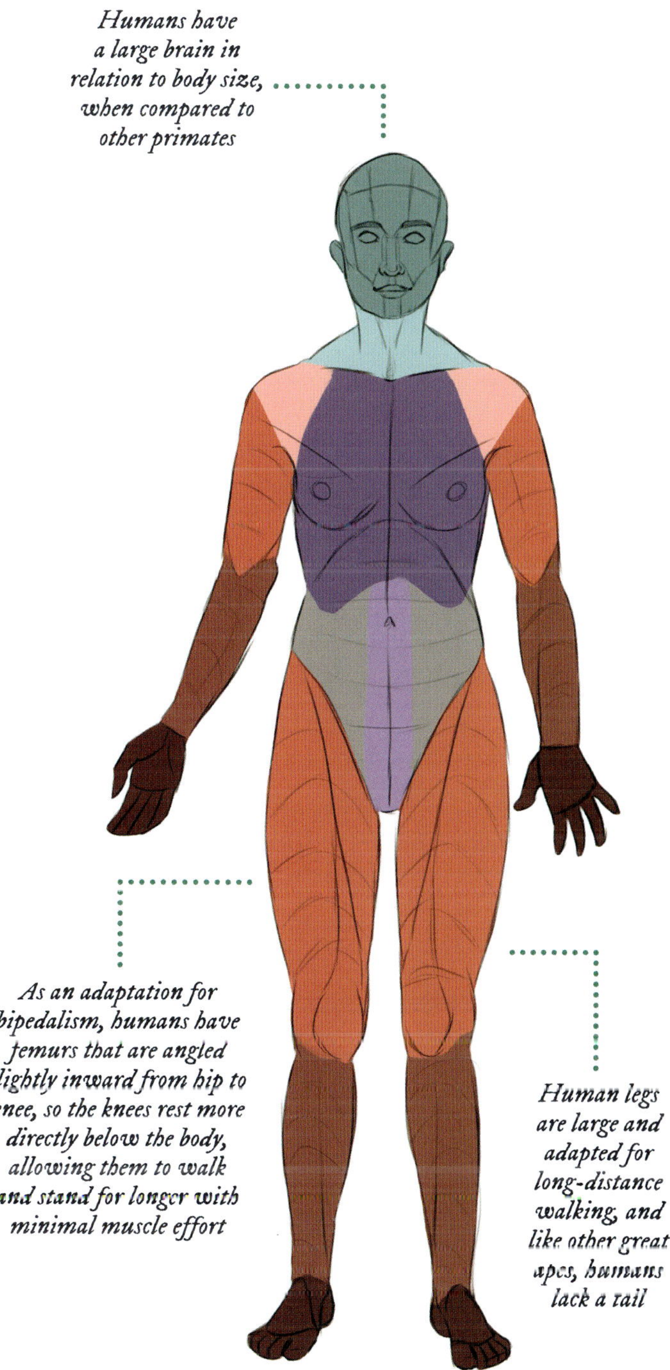

As an adaptation for bipedalism, humans have femurs that are angled slightly inward from hip to knee, so the knees rest more directly below the body, allowing them to walk and stand for longer with minimal muscle effort

Human legs are large and adapted for long-distance walking, and like other great apes, humans lack a tail

QUADRUPED / HUMAN COMPARISON

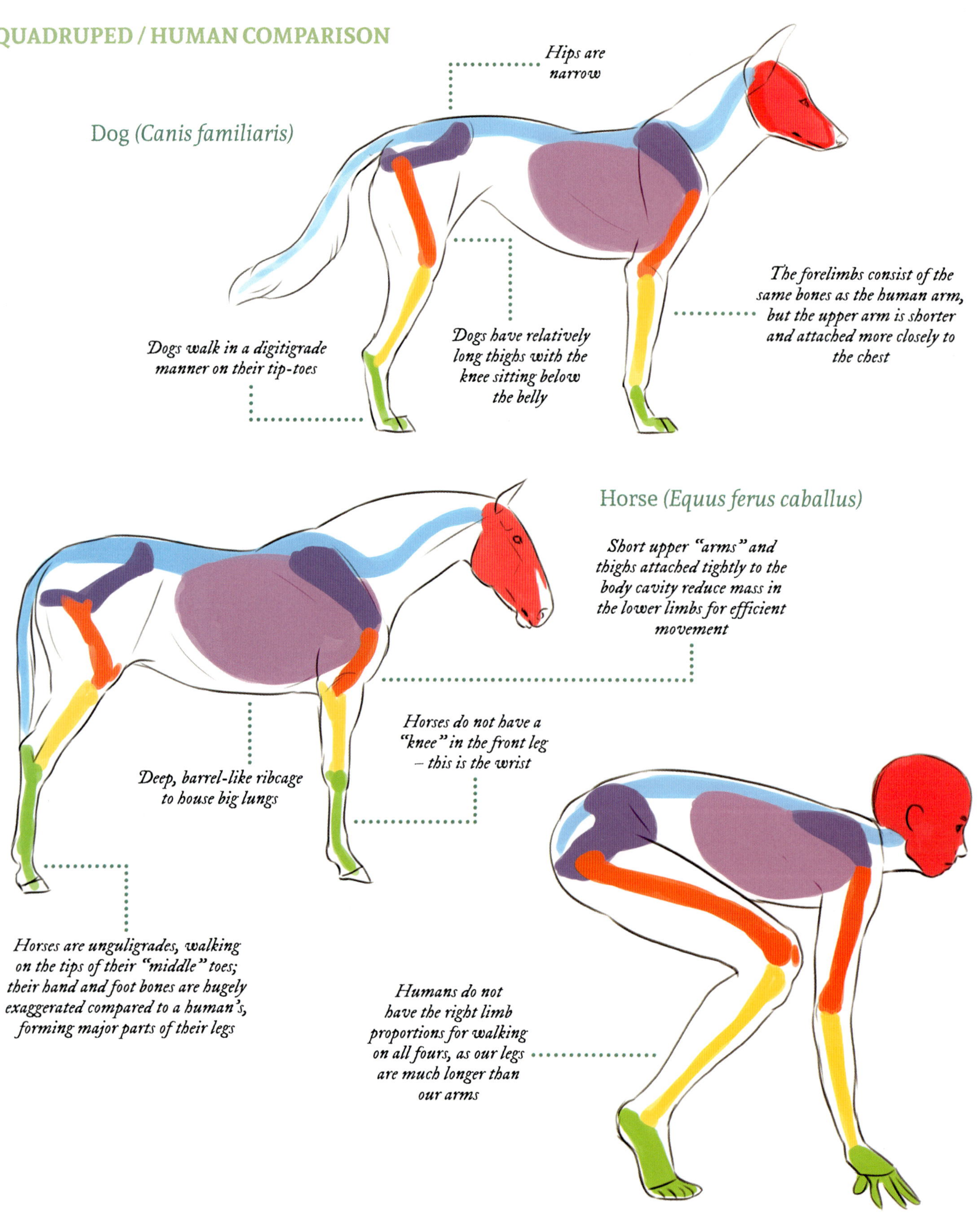

AVIAN / HUMAN COMPARISON

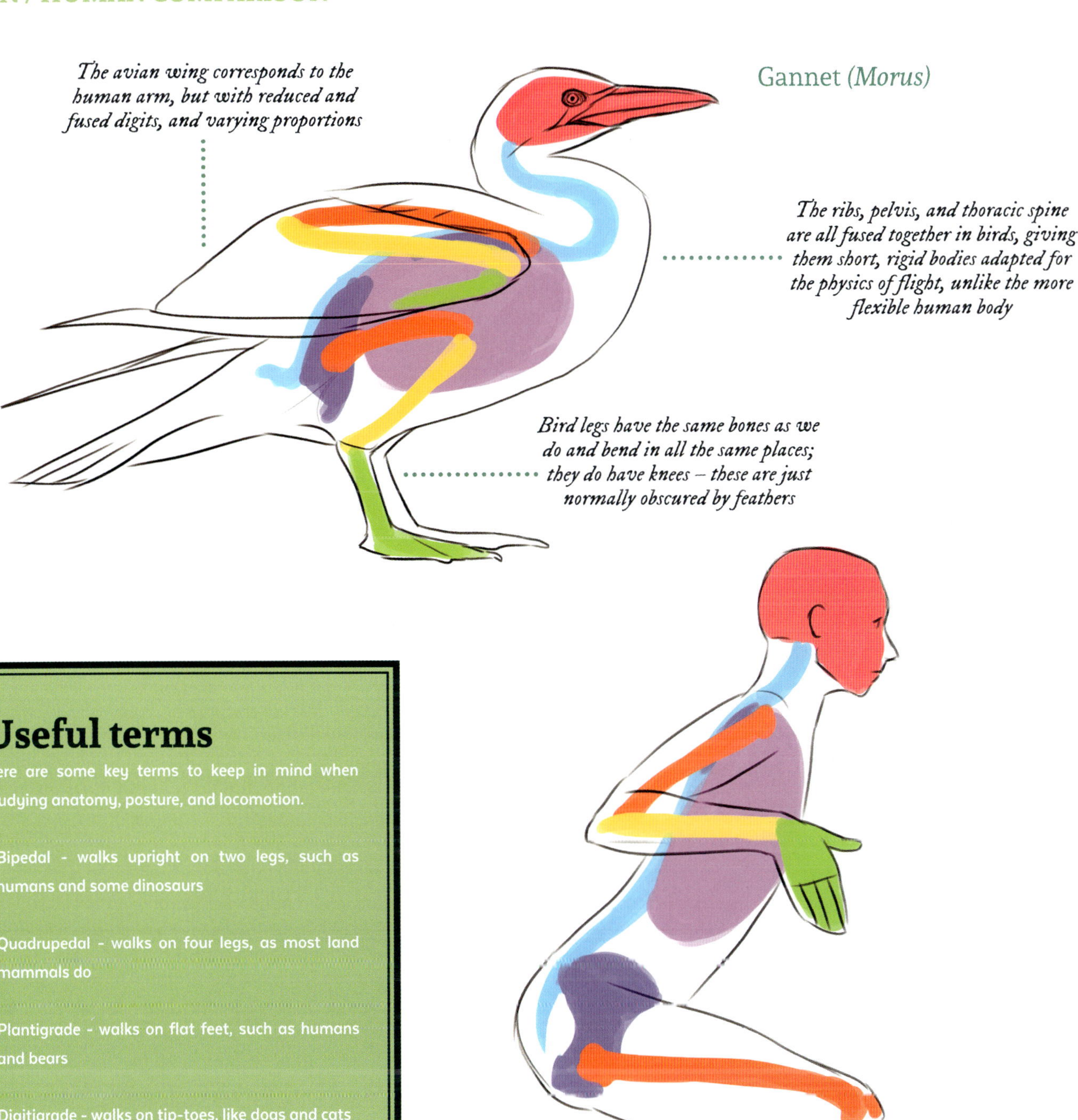

Useful terms

Here are some key terms to keep in mind when studying anatomy, posture, and locomotion.

- Bipedal - walks upright on two legs, such as humans and some dinosaurs

- Quadrupedal - walks on four legs, as most land mammals do

- Plantigrade - walks on flat feet, such as humans and bears

- Digitigrade - walks on tip-toes, like dogs and cats

- Unguligrade - walks on hooves, such as horses, rhinos, and deer

These are just a few examples from common terrestrial mammals. Many animals fall between these groups, or move in different ways altogether!

Anthropomorphism

As humans, we have a stronger reaction to human forms and faces than to any other animal. Our draw to human faces is so powerful that we routinely find them in all sorts of inanimate objects, to the extent that car manufacturers take the "expression" a car conveys with its front end into account during the design process. The farther removed a creature is from a human, the harder it is to form an emotional connection with it. In terms of animals, we relate most to other mammals, which is why designs that are based around horses or dogs may be more successful than ones based on sea sponges.

Humans are highly reliant on eyesight, and we express so much through our eyes that they can immediately bring personality into a creature design. A real-life example of this is seen in insects. Most insects have eyes and faces that seem expressionless to a human viewer, as we cannot draw any emotional cues from their compound eyes or rigid exoskeleton. However, insects with a pseudopupil (a false pupil caused by a trick of the light), such as praying mantises, immediately connect more with people, as they appear to be watching you with moving eyes like a mammal. Their false pupils give a sense of personality and sentience that other insects lack.

Creatures can also be made bipedal, given human-like activities to do, or provided with complex cultures and civilizations of their own - all of which help make them more relatable. If even a tiny thing like a moving pupil can make an otherwise very non-human creature more relatable, then there is a broad spectrum of anthropomorphism to play with in your designs.

Eyes & brows

Humans as a species have highly developed eyesight and communicate with their eyes, as do many other primates. Incorporation of human-like eyes into a creature of any kind, however alien, can immediately help the audience to connect. A defined brow in a creature design can also make the face more human and expressive. Therefore, cartoon animal characters are often given eyebrows, even when their real-life equivalents do not have them.

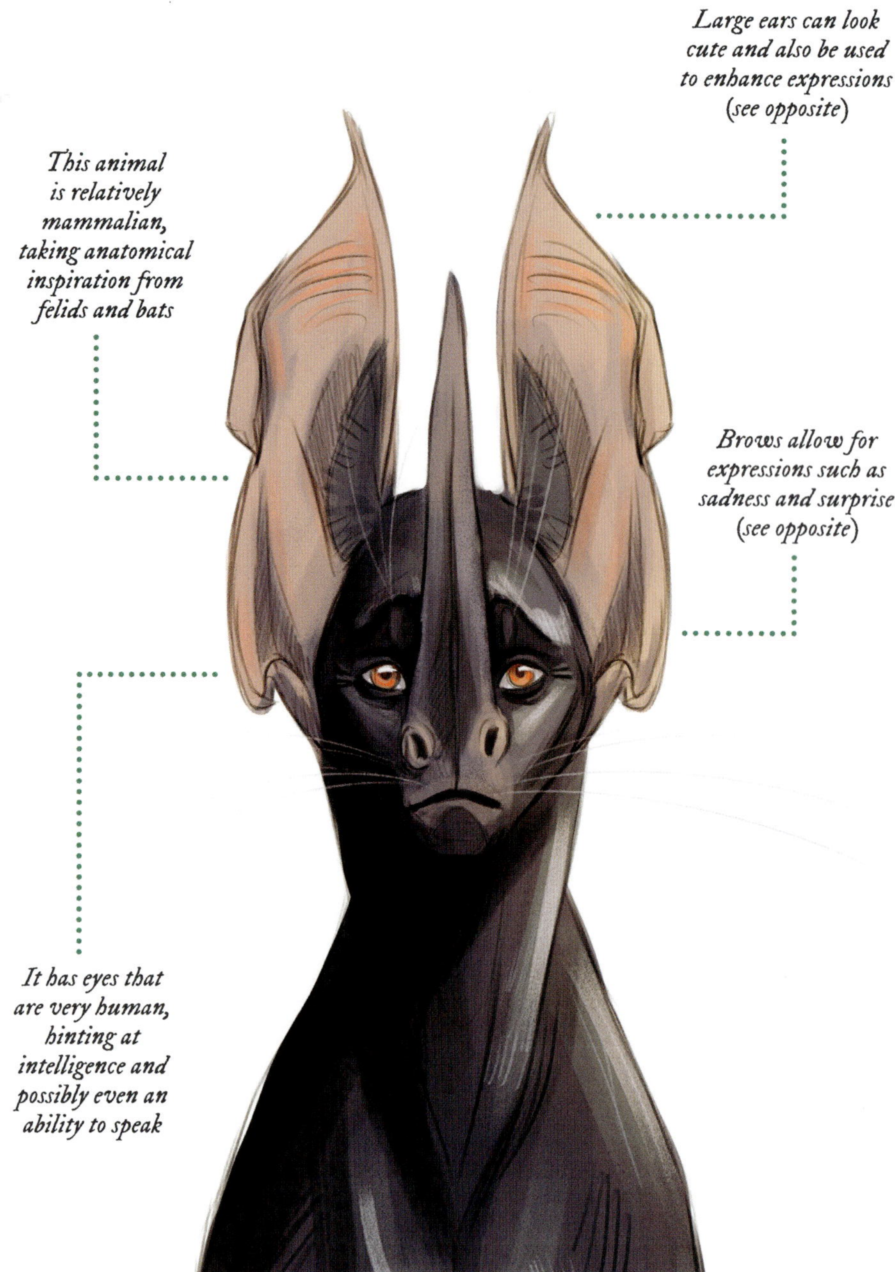

Facial expressions

Creatures can be made more appealing to a human audience and given personality through facial expressions. These can transform a creature from seeming like it is just part of the background to being a character that is part of a story. Many real-world animals do not have the facial musculature and flexibility to make complex expressions. Creatures based on animals such as insects need to have some mammalian facial anatomy if they are to convey personality in this way. The images shown here include elements adapted from human facial expressions.

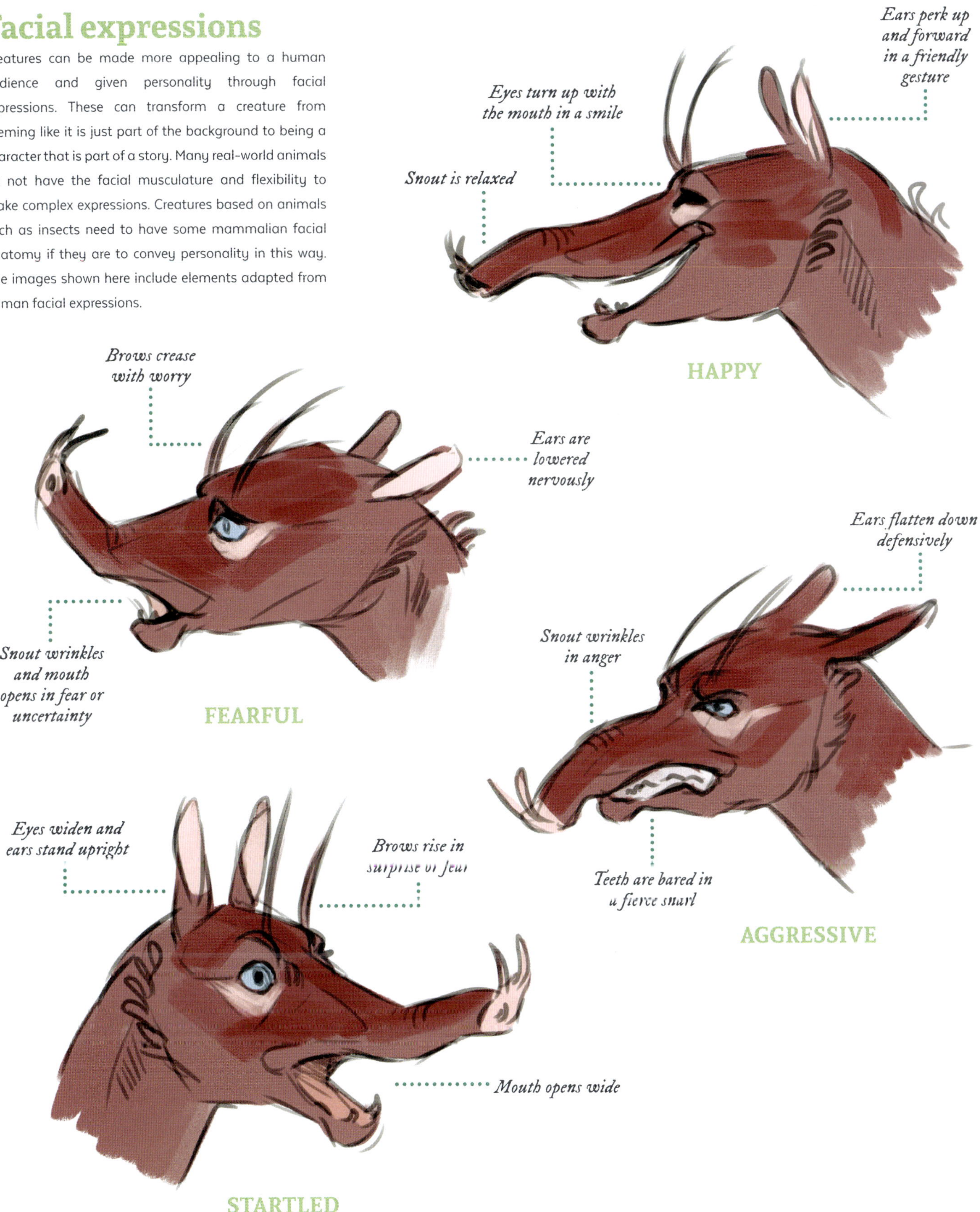

Bipedalism

Some alien-like creature designs can be made more relatable if they take an approximate bipedal human form. This basic human shape can then be altered and mixed with different species to become something fantastical. The bipedal form acts as a good base upon which to add anatomy and inspiration from real creatures that are harder to emotionally engage with, such as invertebrates. This way it is easier to make a character that can perform human-like actions and interact with other humanoid characters.

This creature's face and fins draw inspiration from the cuttlefish, a kind of marine mollusk

Tail for balance

Bipedal stance, turning to look at viewer with some intelligence

Facial hair

Clothing and decoration

Evidence of harvesting

Jewelry

Bipedal stance

Clothing & activities

Another way that artists can make fantasy creatures more relatable is by giving them clothing and human activities to do - be that buying groceries or flying spaceships. Often, but not always, this involves introducing some humanoid anatomy, such as bipedal walking or human-like arms or hands, to help them manipulate objects.

Gestures & form

The little fairy creatures below are based on real-world animals called salps - a type of "sea squirt" that stick together to form long, drifting chains. Although salps are among our closest invertebrate relatives, they are not able to connect with a human audience well. They have no eyes, hands, or ability to use body language. This is sufficient if you want a creature that simply exists in an environment, but it is extremely difficult to show character and cuteness without some vertebrate or human characteristics. characteristics. The imaginary adaptations shown here include simple humanoid forms added to the salp-like structure, making them more relatable.

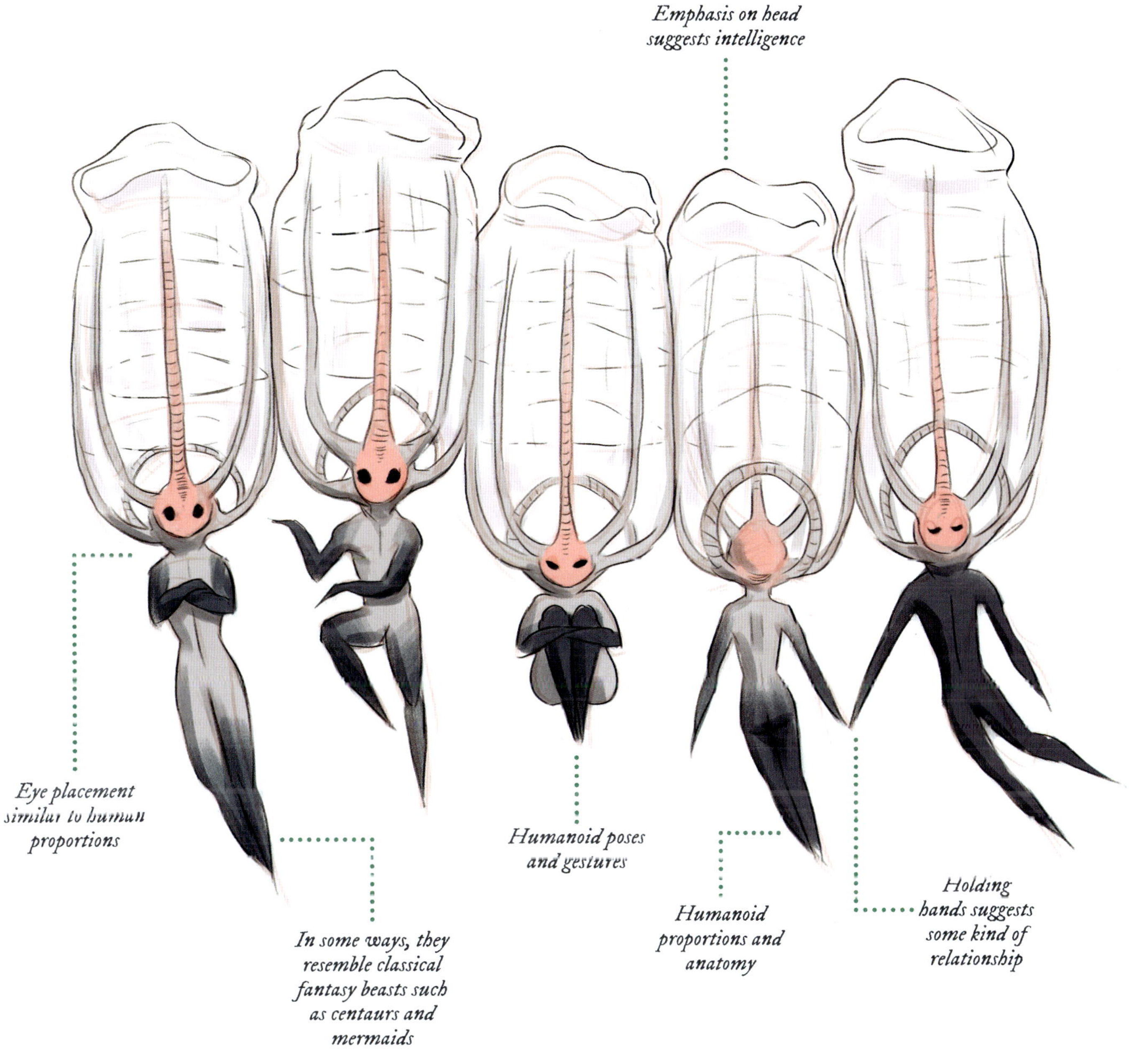

PRIMATE ANATOMY

Primates are a group of mammals mostly found in tropical forest climates. They can be divided into:

- **Prosimians** (lemurs, lorises, and tarsiers)

- **New World monkeys** of the Americas (such as spider, squirrel, howler, tamarin, and capuchin monkeys)

- **Old World monkeys** of Asia and Africa (such as baboons, langurs, macaques, and mangabeys)

- **Apes** (gibbons, orangutans, chimps, gorillas, and humans)

All primates are **plantigrade**, meaning that they walk on the flats of their feet with their heels on the ground. Most are **excellent climbers** because their hands and feet are well adapted to grip, and most spend time sitting upright so their **dexterous hands** are free to manipulate objects. Most primates have **long tails** and many are intelligent and adaptable. Nearly all primates are **highly social** and live in groups. Trichromatic color vision has also evolved in several primates, meaning they often use colorful signals, as birds do. Therefore, many primates have coats or skin that feature **bold and colorful patterns**.

Primate skulls feature a large brain case, **forward-facing eye sockets**, and generally a flattened facial profile (except for certain groups like lemurs and baboons). Primates are largely reliant on eyesight at the expense of an acute sense of smell. Good binocular vision means they can judge distance accurately, which is important for a tree-dwelling animal. Although most primates have long tails for balance, only a very small number of New World monkeys have evolved **prehensile tails** - ones that can be used to hold onto objects. The capuchin has a prehensile tail that is used in conjunction with the legs for balance when foraging, but is not used to hold the entire animal's weight. Such extreme prehensile tails are found only in the spider, howler, and woolly monkeys.

Primates have upper arms that are free from the main body rather than tucked against it like a horse or dog. This, combined with the ability to twist their forearms, gives them a greater range of movement that is especially useful for climbing. The relative length of the fore and hind limbs differs according to their lifestyle; for example, those that move by **brachiation** (swinging), such as gibbons, have arms that are far longer than their legs. Species that tend to cling to trees in an upright posture, such as the indri or sifaka lemurs, are more likely to have larger legs for big leaps between trees and hopping along the ground.

MUSCULATURE

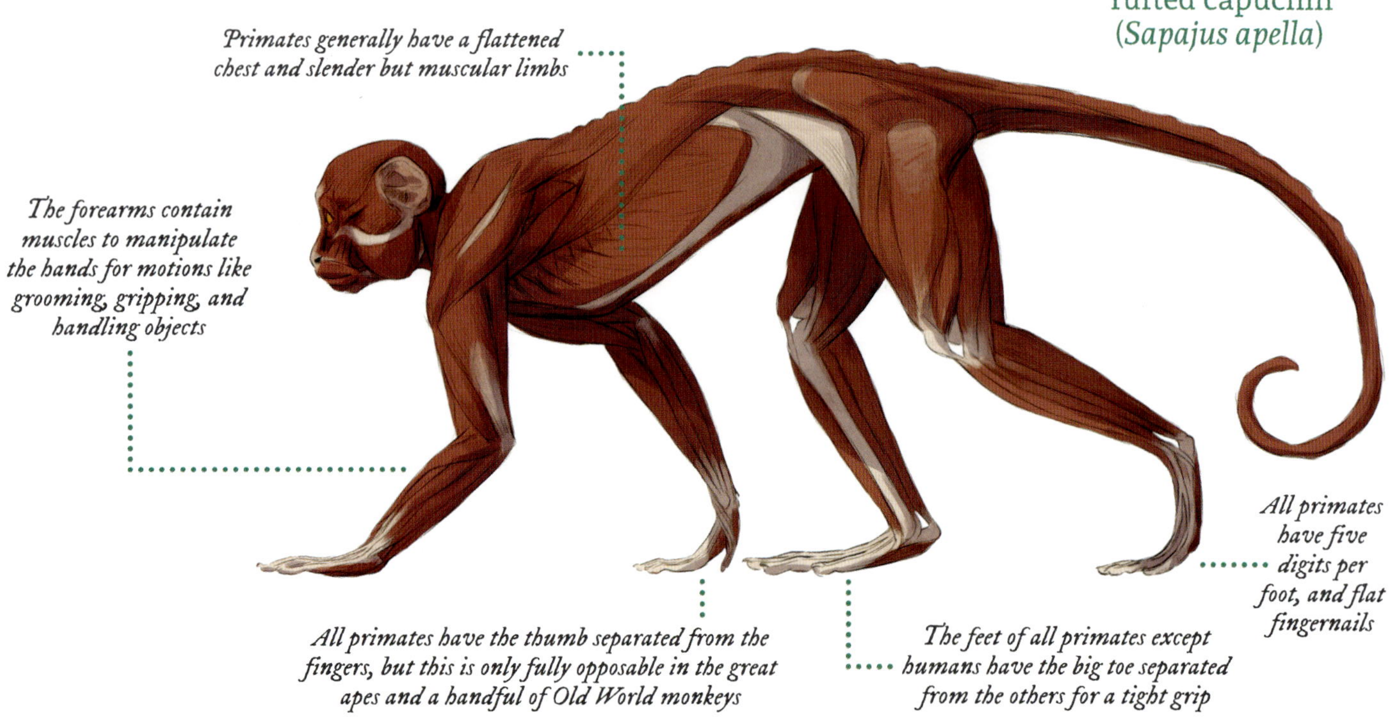

SKELETON

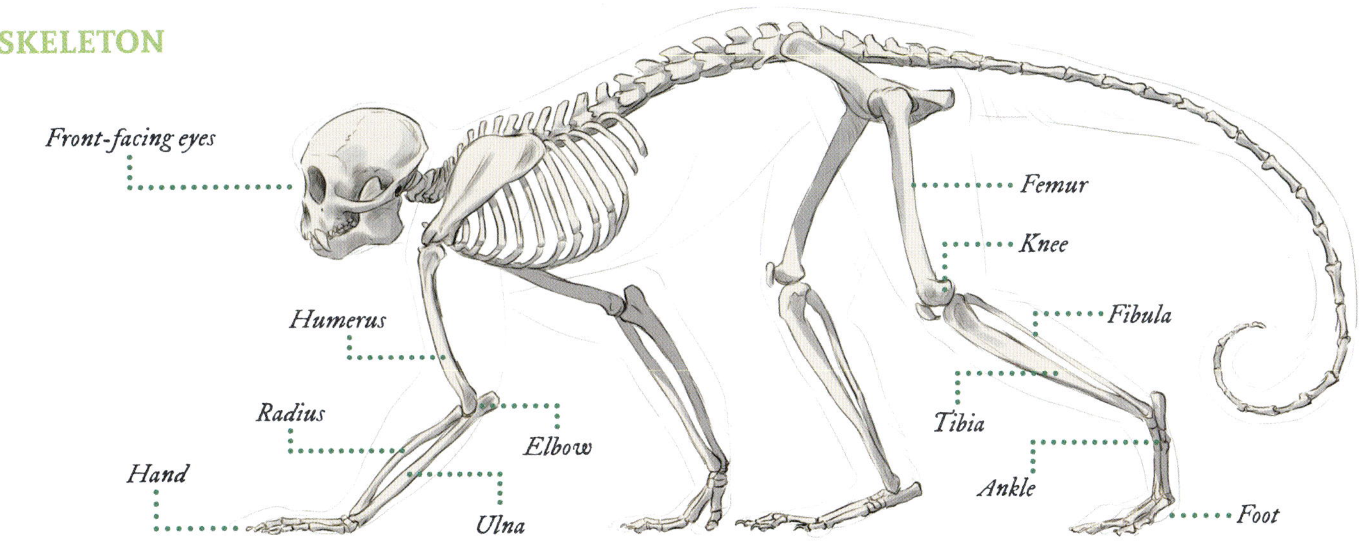

BASIC SHAPES

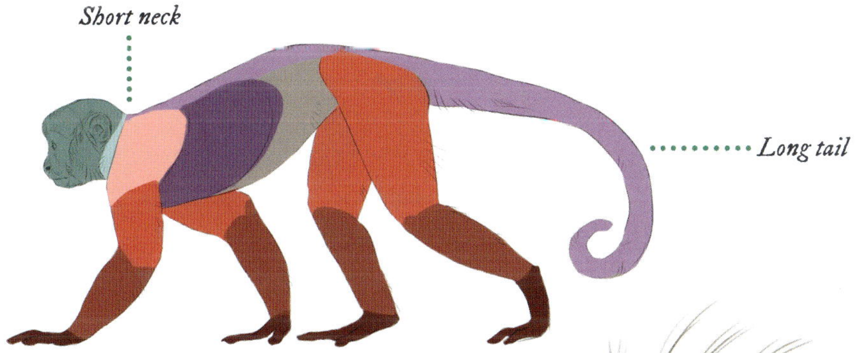

IMAGINARY PRIMATE

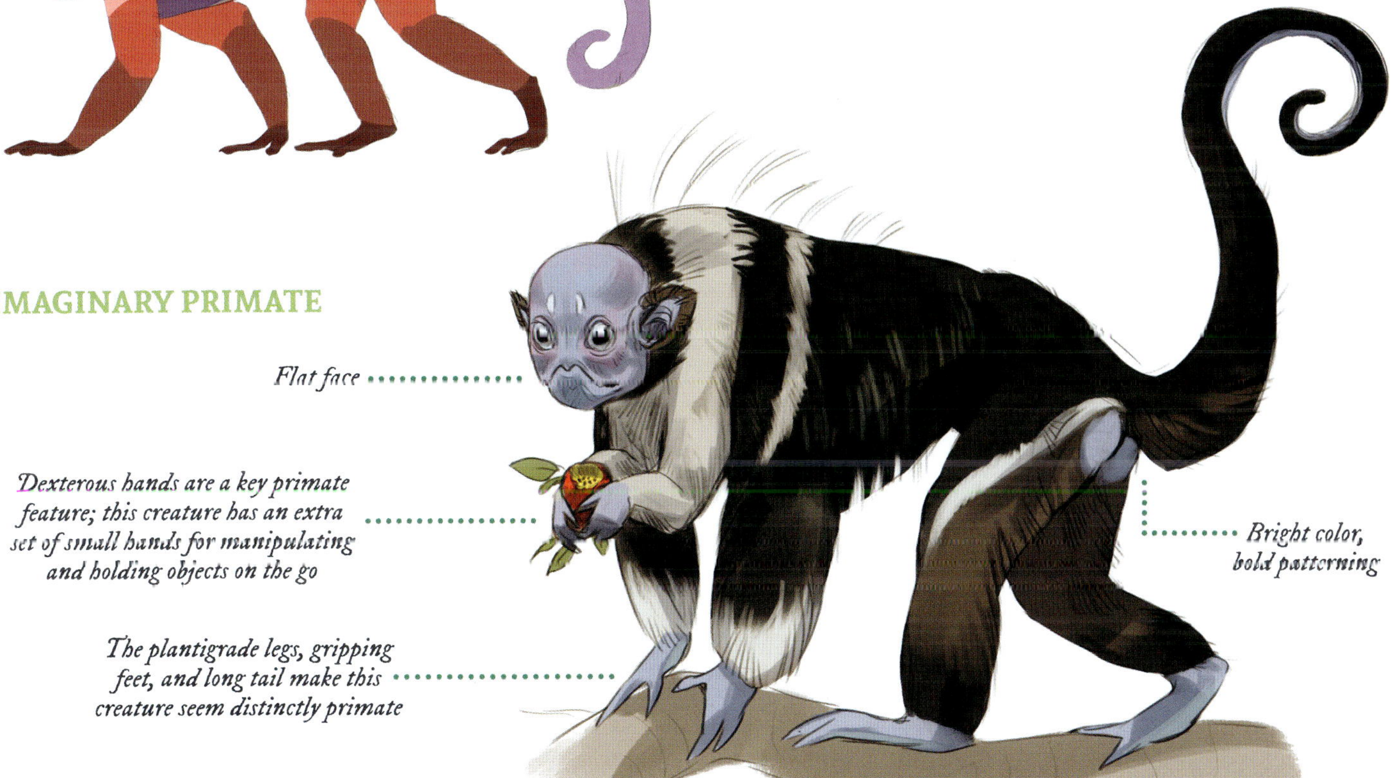

FELINE ANATOMY

Felines are a highly specialized family of carnivorous mammals, consisting of about forty species ranging from large (such as tigers, lions, leopards, pumas, and jaguars) to small (such as lynx, Scottish wildcats, bay cats, ocelots, and domestic cats). Nearly all feline species are **solitary**.

They have **flexible spines**, **muscular limbs**, and relatively **large eyes** with good binocular and night vision. All cats have **claws** that passively retract into sheaths and are actively protracted, except for the cheetah, whose claws are always protracted. Cat paws have hard pads like those of dogs; however, these pads are surrounded by hair. Combined with their retractable claws, this enables them to stalk prey silently. They have very **diverse patterns**, colors, and lengths of fur, and are adapted to a range of habitats and niches across the world.

Many cat species have a skull with a pronounced **sagittal crest** (a bony central ridge) along the top. This is typical of many carnivores that have a **strong bite force**, as it allows attachment of the large muscles used to close the jaw. They generally have quite **short**, **domed heads** with many **long whiskers** used for sensing on the muzzle, cheeks, and brow.

Felines are mostly adapted to be ambush predators. They have relatively short, muscular limbs (with a few exceptions) and are not built for long-distance running, relying instead on stealth and strength. The forearm bones of cats can be twisted so their paws face each other. This enables them to climb trees and grip prey with a lot of strength, in a way that dogs cannot. The **shoulder blades** always slide above the line of the spine when weight is put on a limb, giving their shoulders a fluid appearance.

MUSCULATURE

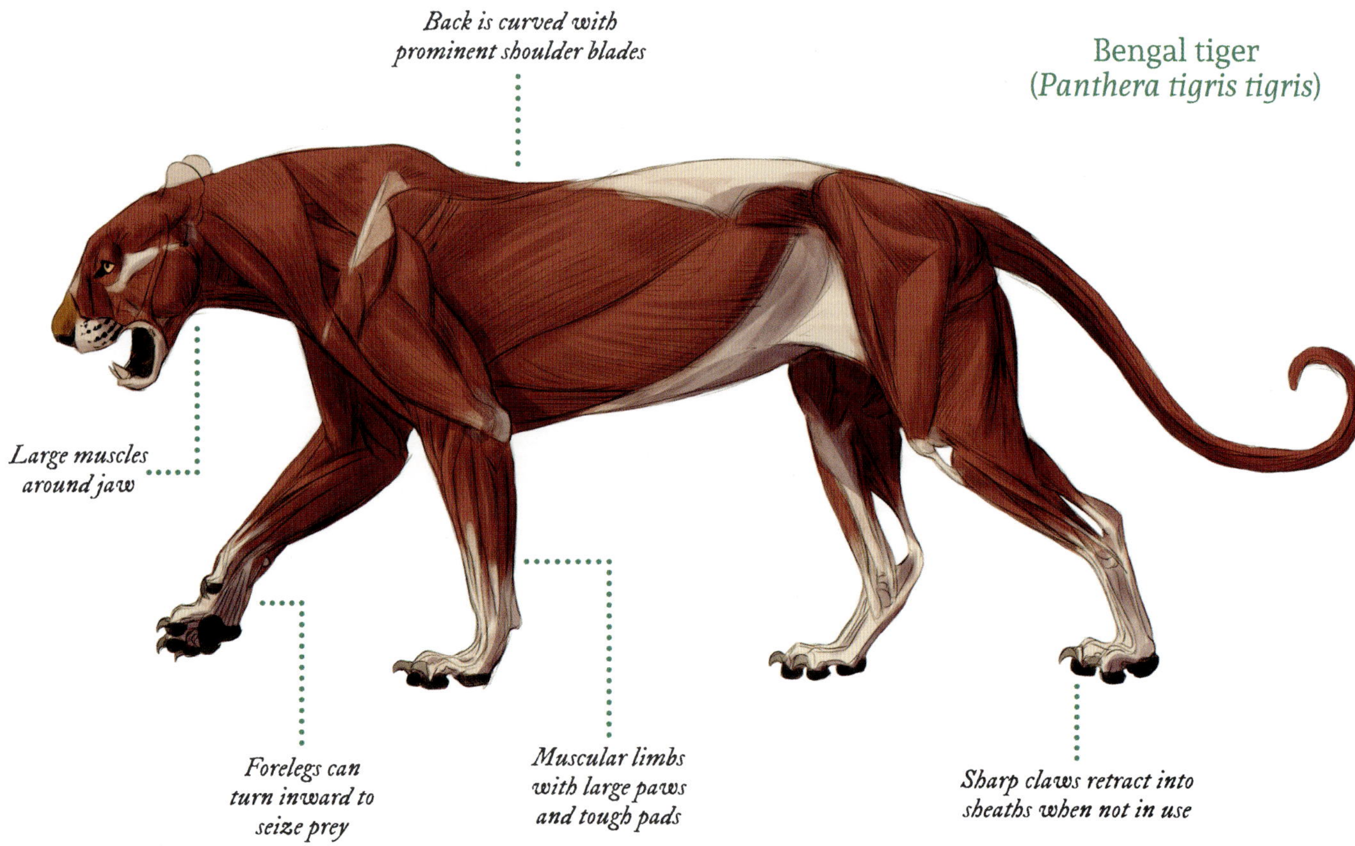

SKELETON

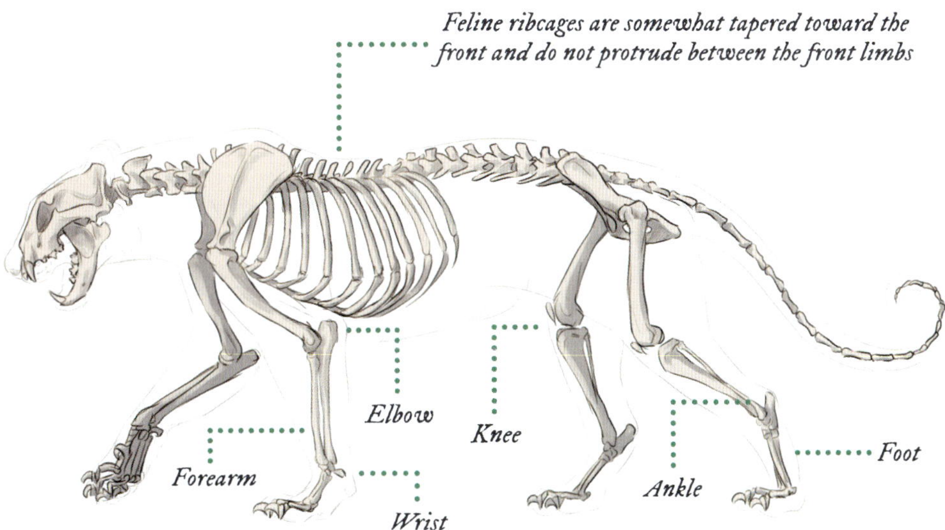

BASIC SHAPES

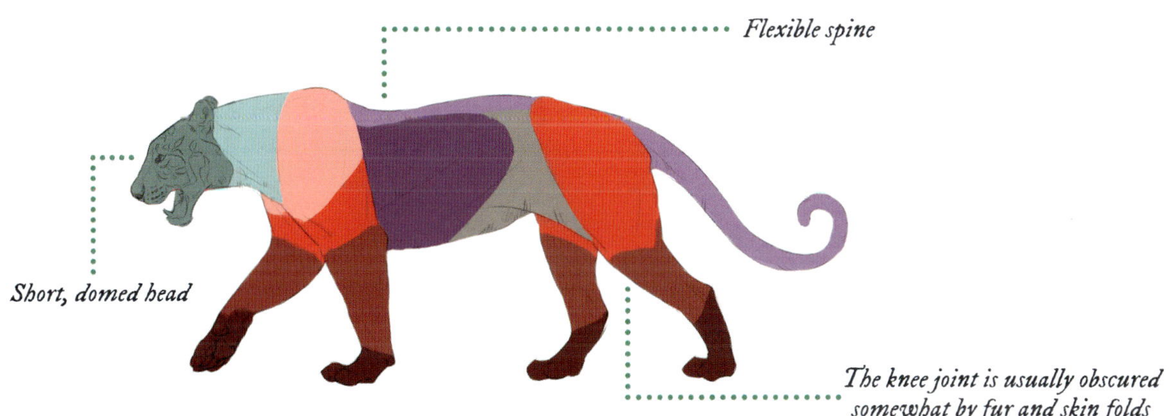

IMAGINARY FELINE

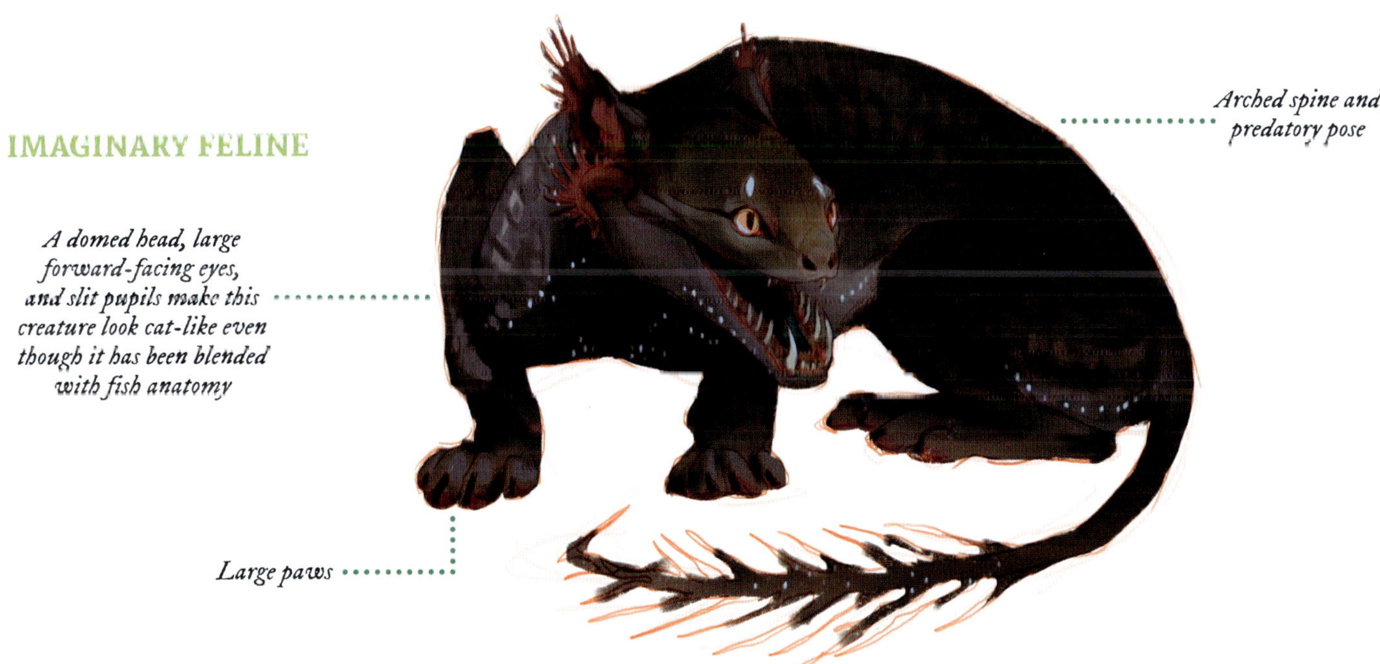

77

CANINE ANATOMY

Canids are a family of around thirty-five living species of predatory mammal, containing a range of species such as the gray wolf, jackal, fox, African wild dog, bush dog, and raccoon dog. Generally, they are adapted to be excellent long-distance travelers with **high endurance**, and are highly opportunistic.

Domestic dogs have lived alongside humans for over 15,000 years and have been **selectively bred** into a range of unnatural shapes, many of which are not useful adaptations in nature but can provide some visual inspiration for creature design.

Dogs walk on their toes (**digitigrade**) and extra bends in their legs add spring to their step for efficient long-distance travel. In the diagram below, note how the muscle stops partway down each limb and attaches to tendons, which pull the toes from above. This keeps the feet light and easier to move, like running in bare feet rather than heavy boots.

Dogs are unable to twist the bones of the forearm like cats can, as some of their wrist bones are fused. This improves their ability to run long distances efficiently, but limits their capacity to grip non-flat surfaces and climb.

Wild canids all have **long, tapered skulls**. These long snouts are essential to house the large **olfactory organs**, which dogs need to hunt down prey by smell. Dogs also possess defined **canine teeth** (fangs) for stabbing, and have developed **carnassial teeth** (back teeth) for shearing meat.

MUSCULATURE

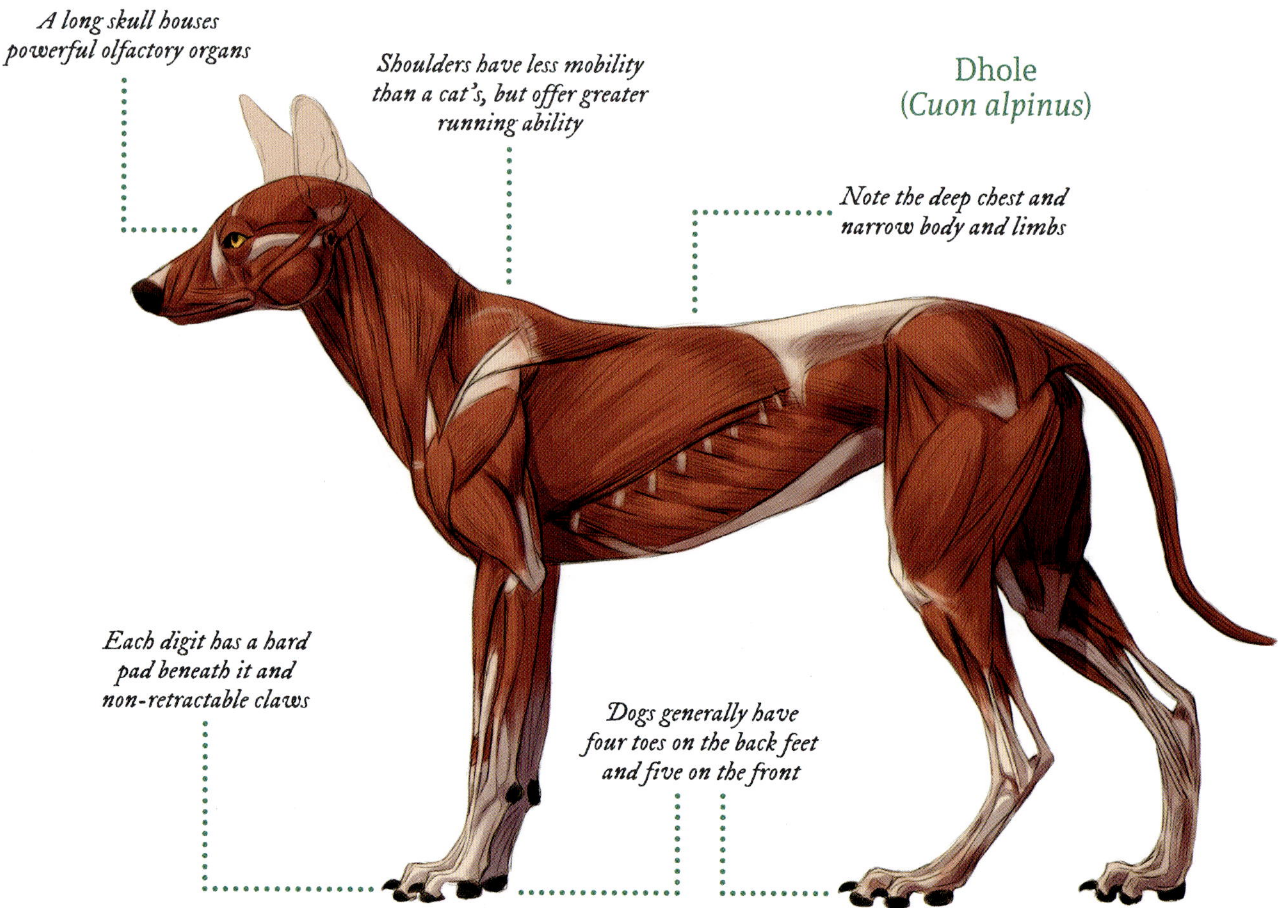

SKELETON

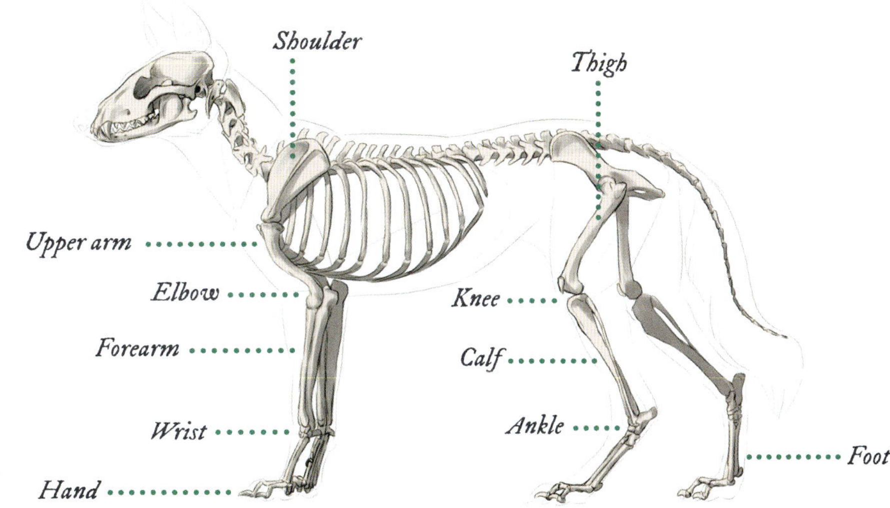

BASIC SHAPES

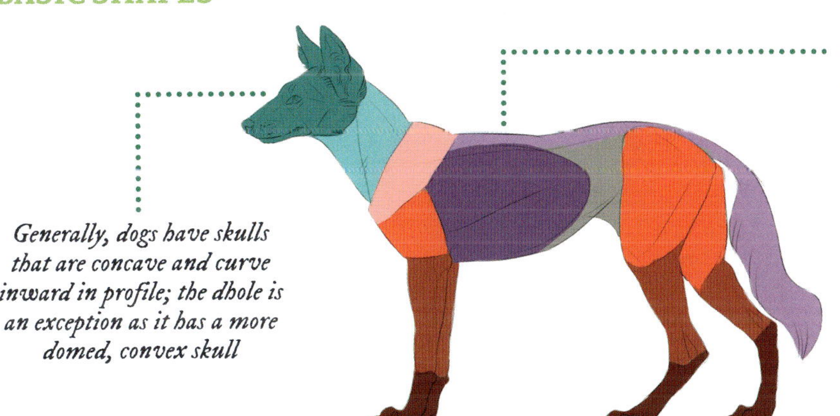

IMAGINARY CANINE

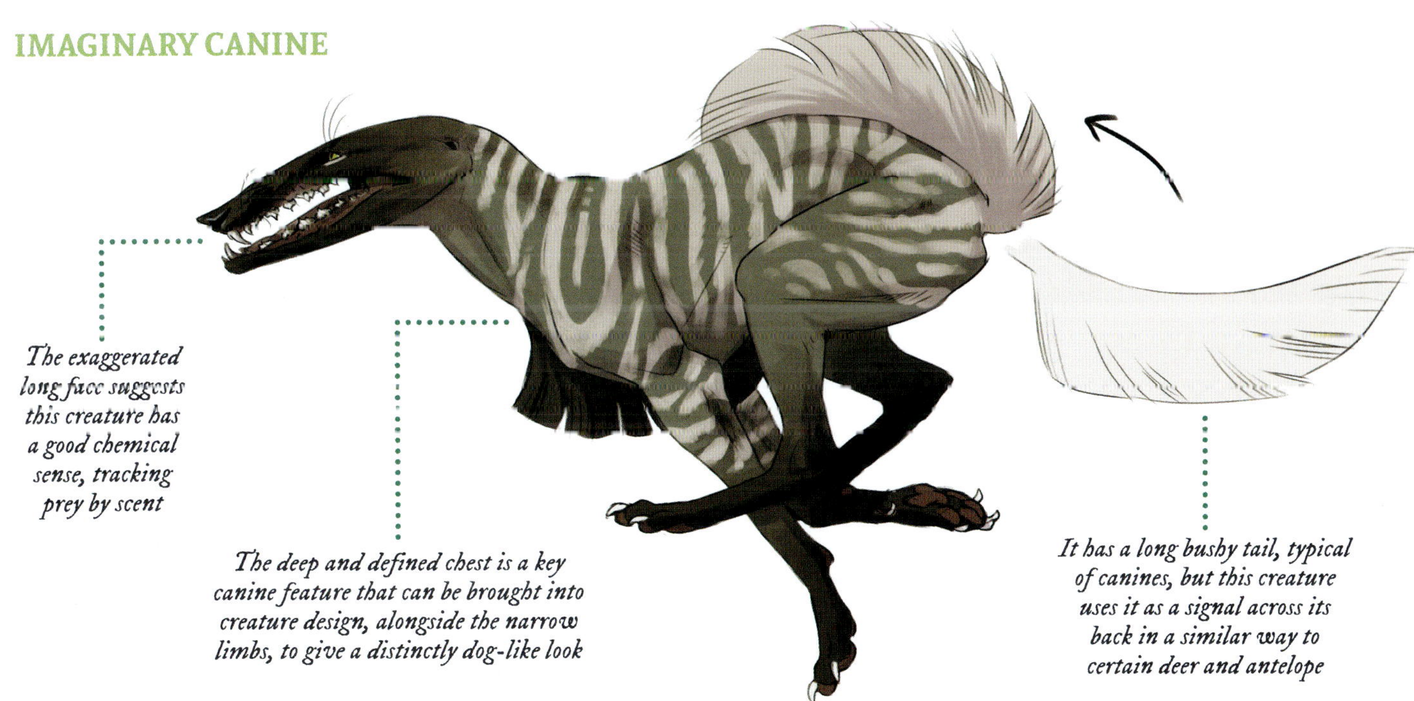

EQUINE ANATOMY

Horses are large, herbivorous mammals that walk upon a single toe on each foot. They are members of the order *Perissodactyla* (**odd-toed ungulates**), which also includes tapirs and rhinos. Although today's wild equids (such as zebras and wild donkeys) are relatively uncommon due to habitat loss, the domestic horse has lived alongside us for around 6,000 years, and first appeared in cave paintings in Europe around 17,000 years ago.

In terms of creature design, the horse is arguably one of the most important animals to study for its anatomy, as so many imaginary worlds require rideable animals.

Horses do not have any muscle in their legs below the wrist and ankle. Most of the muscle used to move the limbs is tightly packed in the main body area. This concentration of weight higher up means the feet are light, making movement of the long limbs much more efficient. They also have **wide nostrils** for taking in plenty of oxygen when running.

Through their evolution, horses have **lost all but one digit** on their "feet." They stand solely upon their third toe, with just remnants of two other toes on either side of the third metacarpal (known as splint bones). It is the equivalent of humans walking *en pointe* like ballerinas, but on their middle toes and fingers. Each

foot is protected by a single tough **hoof**. Horses are useful for riding as their backs remain relatively rigid throughout most gaits, allowing for comfortable seating. An animal such as a cat would be difficult to ride with a saddle in the same place as a horse, because its spine and shoulders move much more.

MUSCULATURE

Przewalski's horse (*Equus przewalskii*)

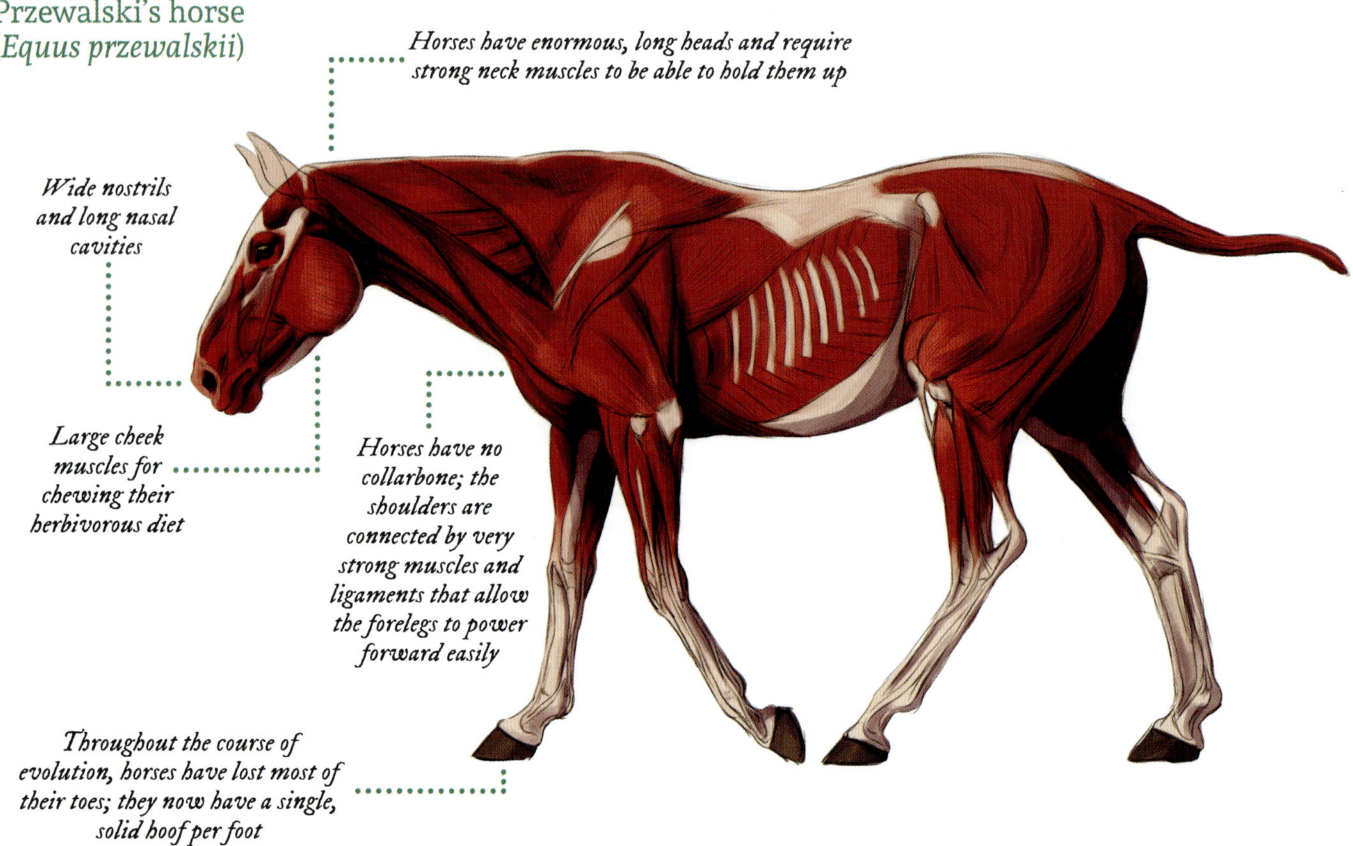

SKELETON

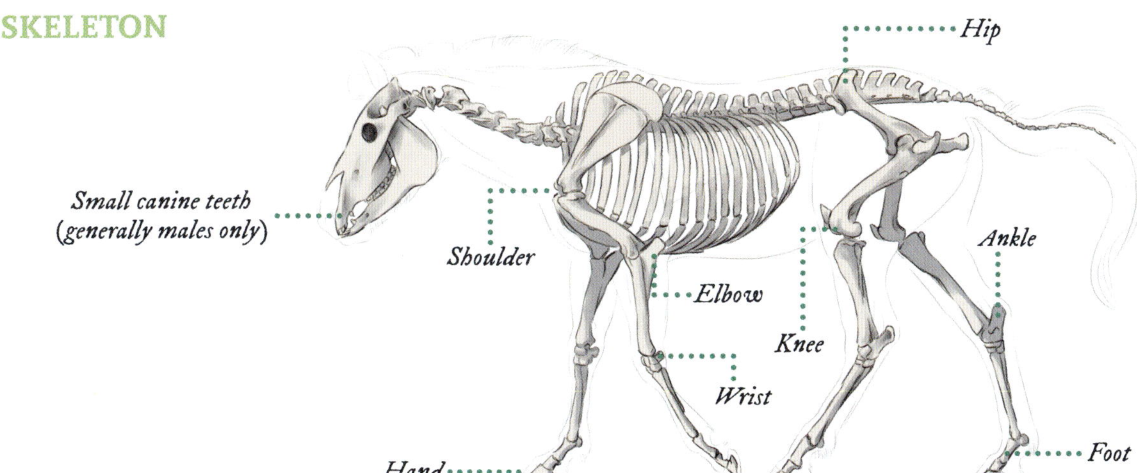

BASIC SHAPES

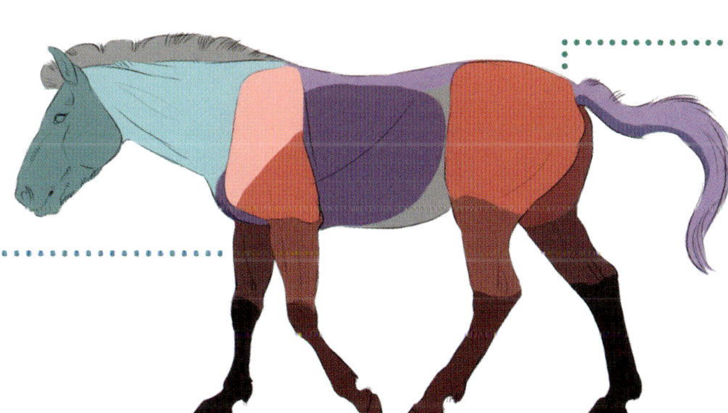

IMAGINARY EQUINE

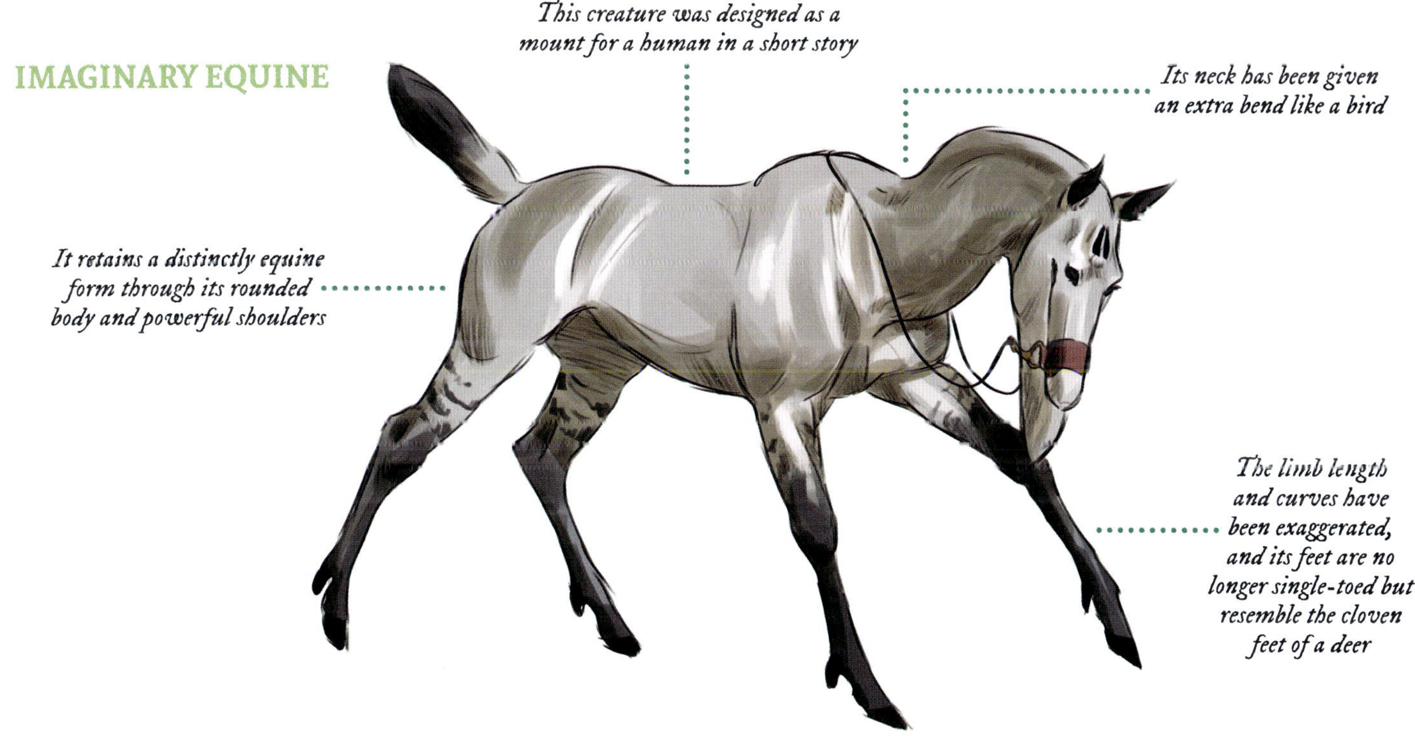

CETACEAN ANATOMY

Cetaceans are a group of mammals that includes whales, dolphins, and porpoises. The group is split into "baleen whales" (such as humpback and blue whales), which filter-feed tiny prey with hairy plates in their mouths called baleen; and "toothed whales" (such as dolphins, porpoises, orca, and sperm whales), which have sharp teeth for actively catching prey. Cetaceans evolved from a terrestrial ancestor that returned to the water, and so retain mammal-like skeletons, muscles, and the need to breathe air – but with major modifications for a completely aquatic lifestyle. Their anatomy is much more like a dog, horse, or cat than that of a fish.

The body of a cetacean is **streamlined** and **hairless** to reduce drag in water. The only protrusions are the essentials: a **dorsal fin** for stability, two strong **pectoral fins** for steering, and two horizontal **tail flukes** for propulsion. Most of a cetacean's muscle is in its hugely powerful tail, which is essential for its movement in water. They have lost their hind limbs but retain forelimbs containing muscle and bone, which are adapted into flippers. The muscle is surrounded by a thick layer of insulating **blubber**.

All toothed whales hunt and navigate using **echolocation**. They have a fatty organ in the head called the **melon**, which helps focus the sound beams that bounce off objects and return through the lower jaw to the middle ear. Toothed whales have only one **blowhole**, while baleen whales have two. All cetaceans lack a sense of smell.

The neck vertebrae are tightly packed or fused for swimming stability, meaning most cetaceans cannot move their necks freely. Most cetaceans have multiplication of the finger bones, which extend farther than other mammals'. In the skeleton diagram opposite, note the similarity of the forelimb to other mammals, as well as the remnant of the pelvis. The dorsal fin and tail fluke do not contain bones - they are made from strong cartilage and vary in shape and size between species.

MUSCULATURE

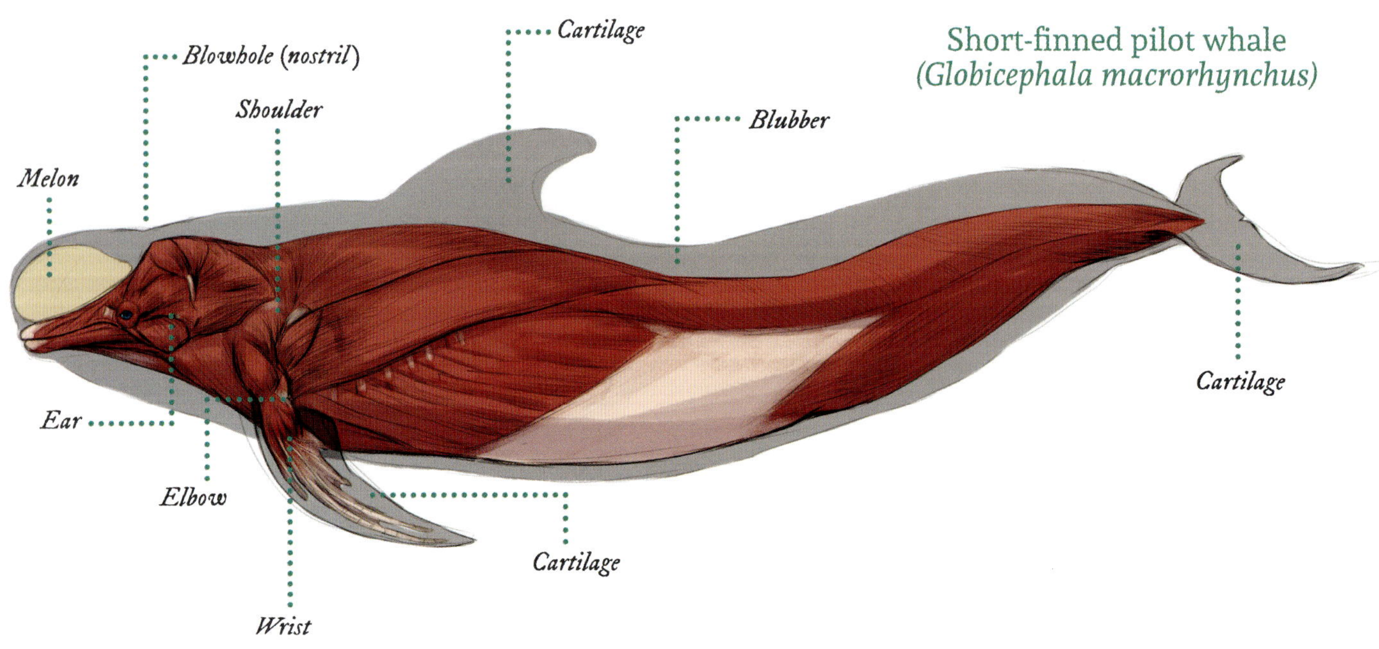

SKELETON

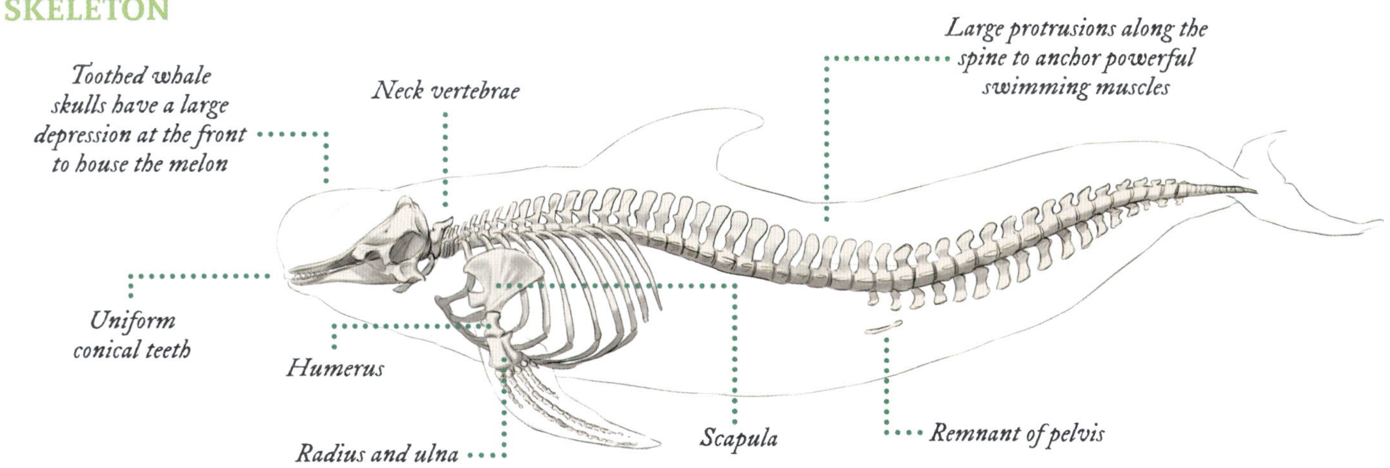

BASIC SHAPES

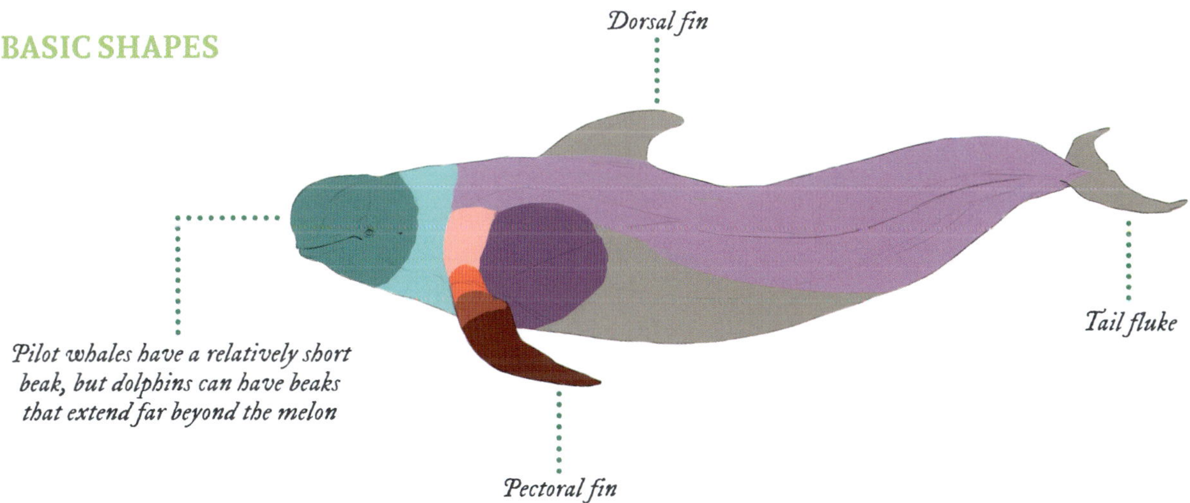

IMAGINARY CETACEAN

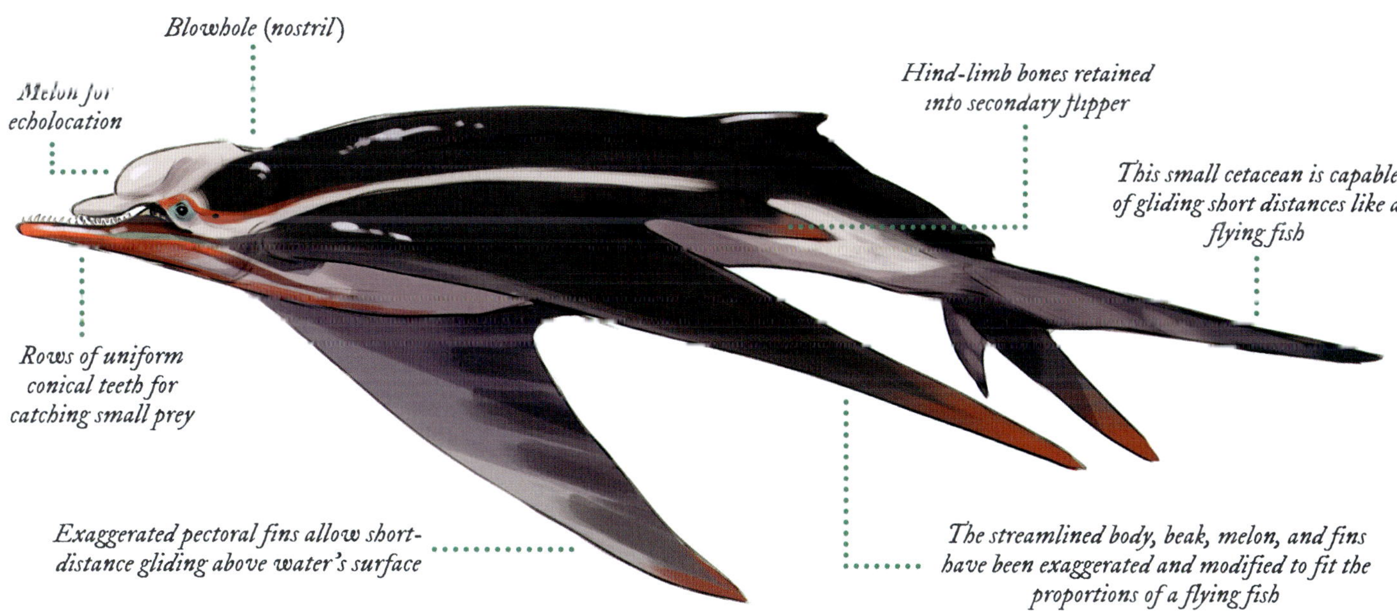

LIZARD ANATOMY

Lizards are a highly diverse group of over 5,500 species of reptile that do not fit neatly into one lineage. Like other reptiles, they are **cold-blooded** and are covered in a dry layer of hard, overlapping **scales**. Reptile scales are all connected by the skin and cannot be removed individually, so reptiles replace their scales by shedding the entirety of their old outer skin. A typical lizard has four legs with five toes on each and a long tail, but some have no legs at all. Most lizards walk on all four legs, but some species lift their front legs off the ground for fast running, with some even able to run across water in this way.

Lizards have **limbs positioned to the sides of the body** rather than beneath them like mammals. This means they have a distinct side-to-side motion as they walk, because the weight of the body is thrown from left to right. They have a long **muscular tail** that acts as a counter-balance.

Lizards generally do not have a range of specialized teeth or fangs, and instead have rows of uniform teeth used for gripping prey. They have pronounced spines branching off the tops of the tail vertebrae and chevron bones beneath. These help anchor the tail muscles and protect the nerve cord and major blood vessels. Like snakes, many lizards have **forked tongues** that allow them to taste chemicals in the air and determine the direction they are coming from.

MUSCULATURE

Nile monitor lizard
(*Varanus niloticus*)

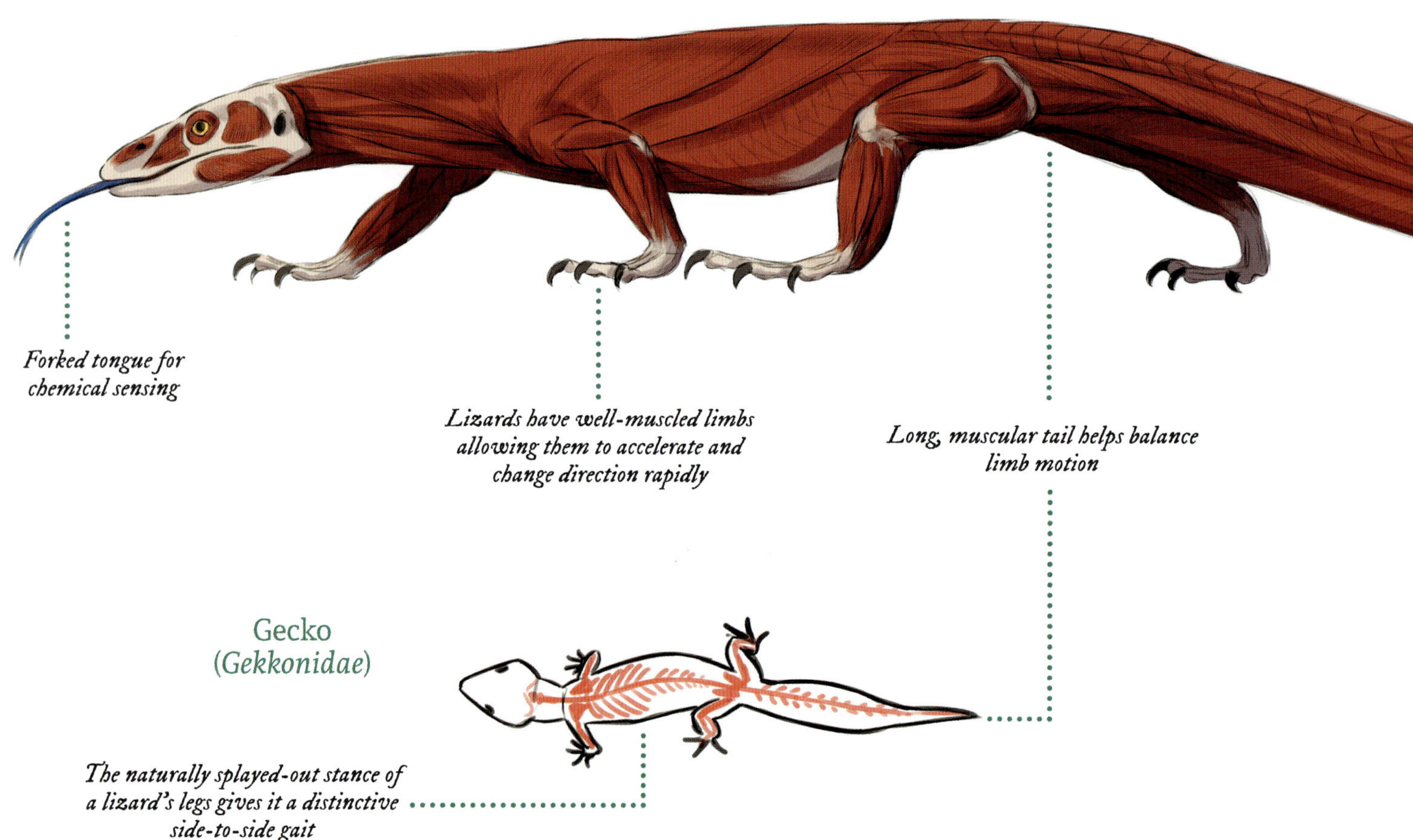

SKELETON

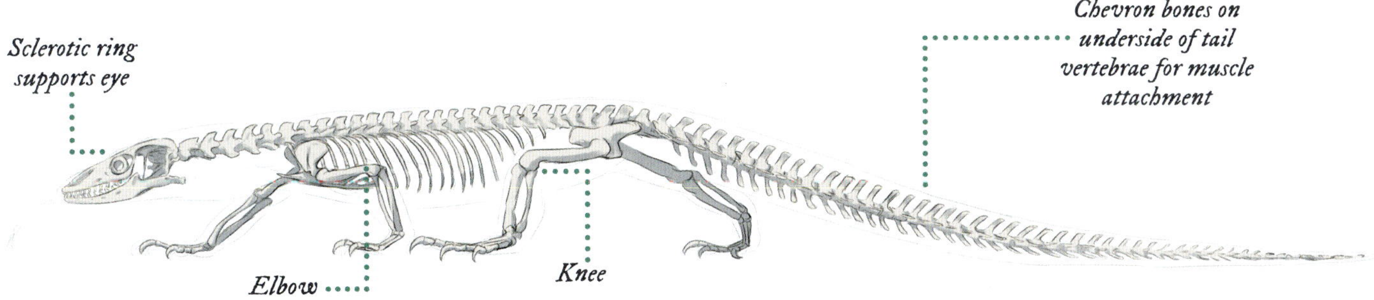

Sclerotic ring supports eye

Chevron bones on underside of tail vertebrae for muscle attachment

Elbow

Knee

BASIC SHAPES

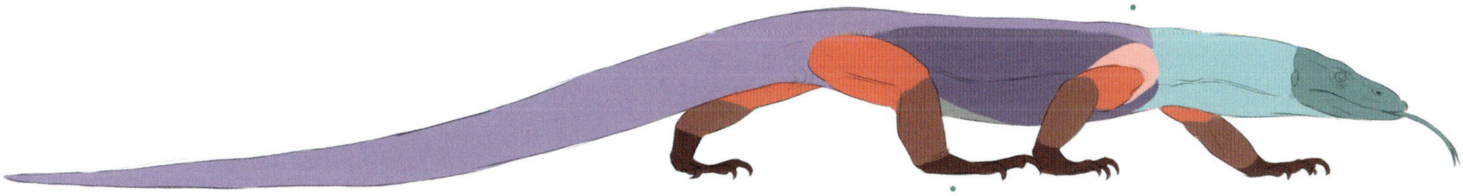

Like primates, the upper arm of a lizard is detached from the main body wall, allowing the foreleg to move more freely

Lizards walk on the flats of their hands and feet

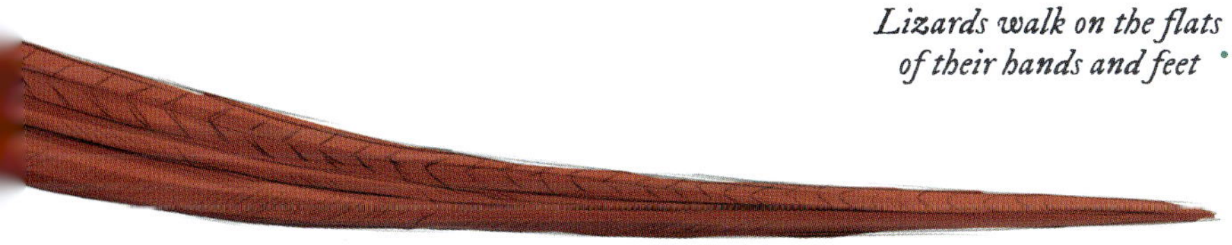

IMAGINARY LIZARD

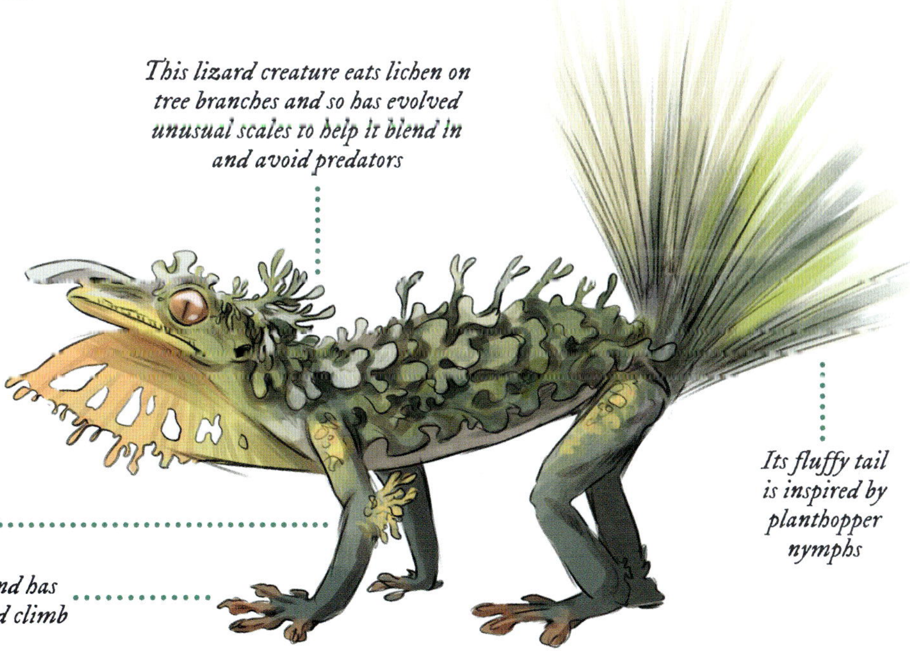

This lizard creature eats lichen on tree branches and so has evolved unusual scales to help it blend in and avoid predators

It has legs to the side of its body and external ear openings

Its fluffy tail is inspired by planthopper nymphs

This creature is very gecko-like and has toes adapted to stick to surfaces and climb

AVIAN ANATOMY

Birds are a group of about 10,000 species of warm-blooded vertebrates that are highly adapted for flight. They evolved from a lineage of theropod dinosaur and their closest living relatives are crocodiles. Their anatomy is different to that of mammals in many ways. In order to fly, birds have:

- **compact bodies**

- **lightweight yet strong bones**

- **feathers**

- **wings**

- **highly efficient respiratory and circulatory systems**

The strict demands of flight have resulted in relatively little variation in basic body structure across the group. All birds have **reduced jaws** that are covered in lightweight horny **beak sheaths** (rather than teeth).

The skeleton of a bird's main body cavity is almost entirely fused together, cutting out the need for additional bones or the muscles and ligaments to connect them. Bird bones are also mostly hollow, but are strengthened by internal struts. This reduces body weight and provides a rigid, compact frame ideal for withstanding the physical pressures of flight.

Unlike bats, whose flight surface is made from skin stretched between the limbs, the flight surface of birds comprises layers of specially adapted **feathers** that form an aerofoil. To compensate for the rigid, **unbendable torso**, birds have a much longer and more **flexible neck** with more vertebrae than mammals, so they can see around, preen, and reach things more easily.

MUSCULATURE

Grey heron (*Ardea cinerea*)

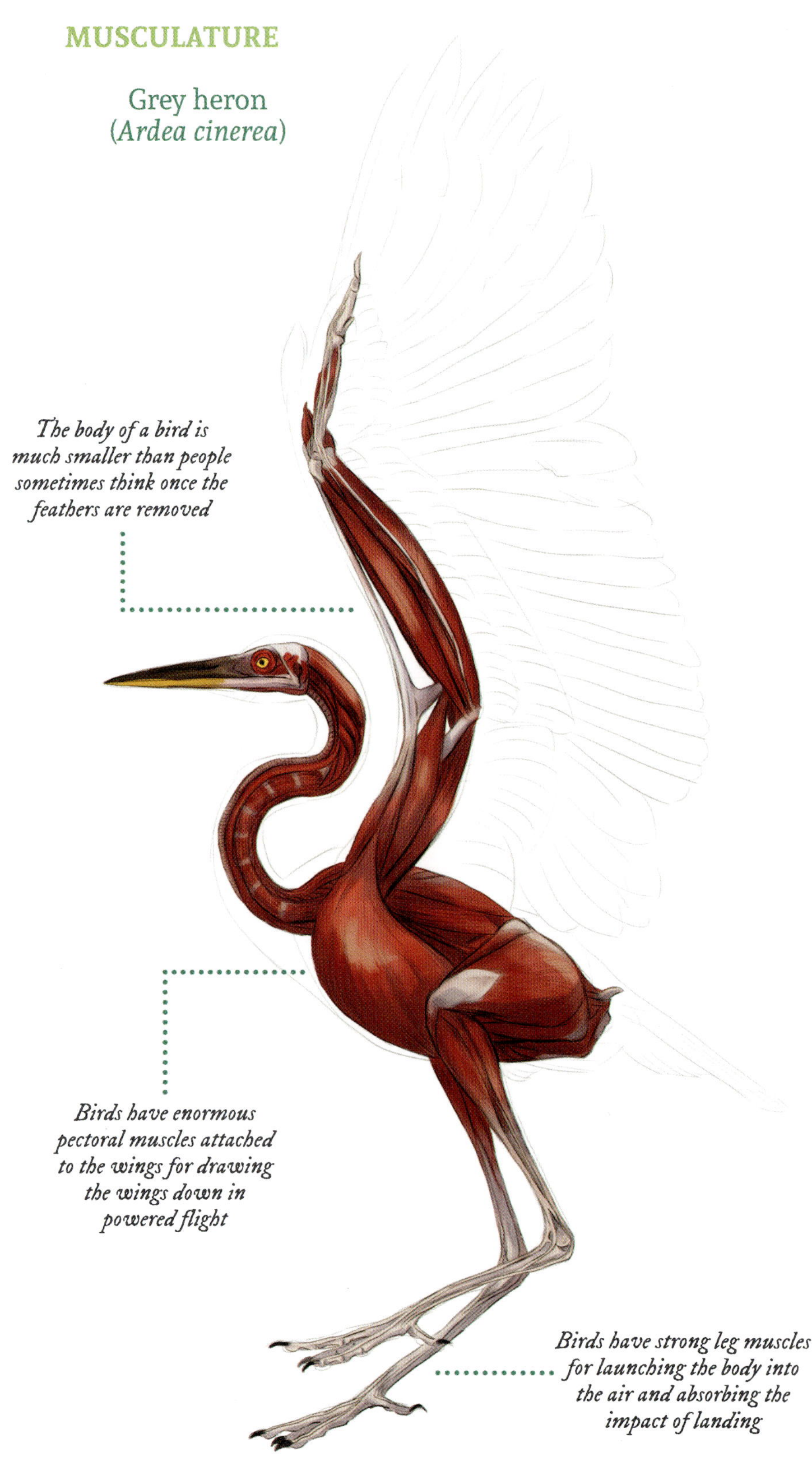

SKELETON

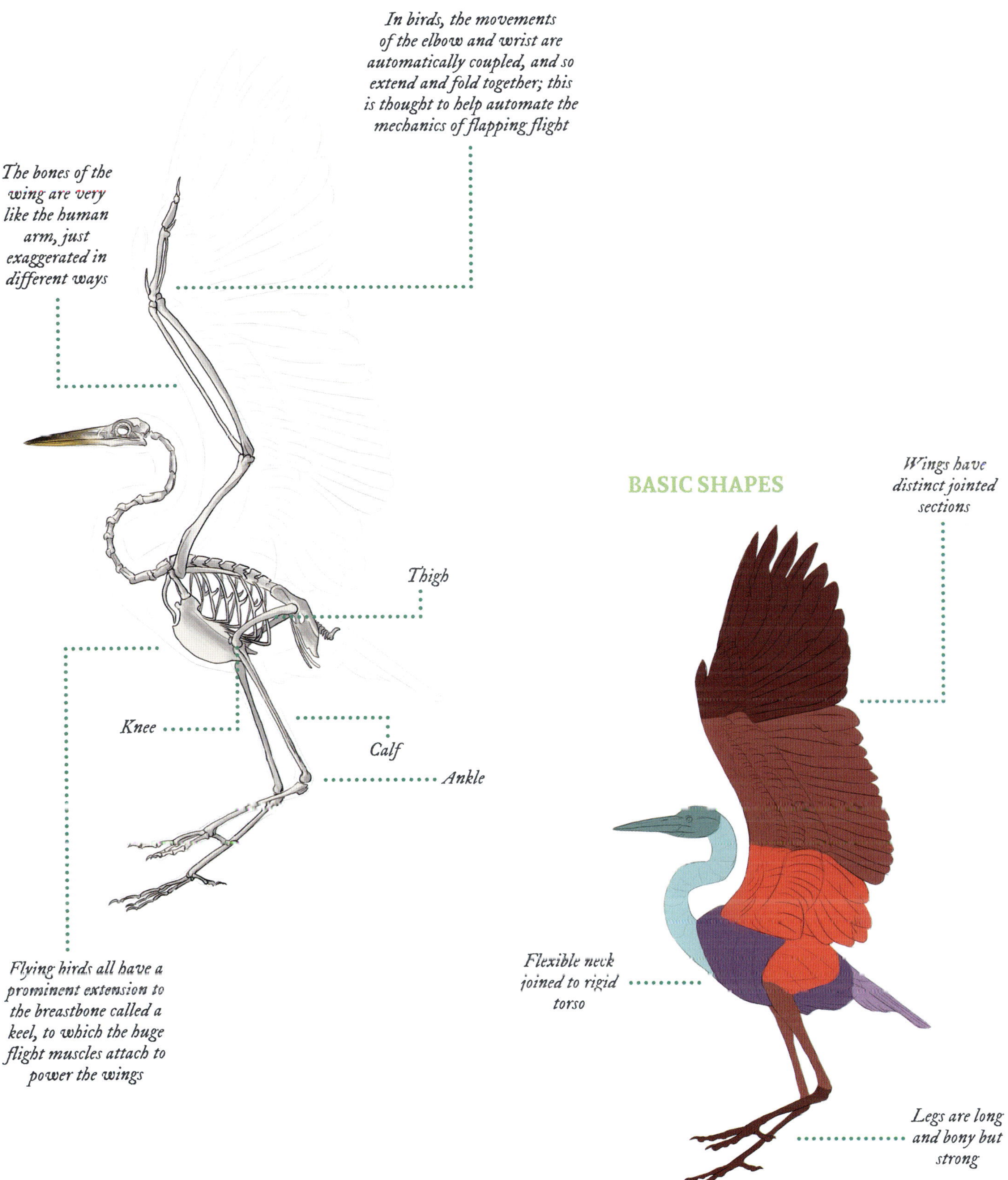

BASIC SHAPES

Wings

The flight feathers on the outer edge of a bird's wing are rigid and help provide lift and thrust for flight. All the basic feather groups are the same for all birds, but they take different shapes based on the lifestyle of the species. For examples, birds that fly long distances over the ocean have different wings to those that only fly short distances between trees in a forest. The wing of a bird folds with the outermost section (**primary** flight feathers – dark blue in the images below) tucked beneath the section closest to the body (**secondary** flight feathers – shown in red below). In terms of human anatomy, folding a wing is a bit like tucking your hand up against your armpit. Smaller feathers called **coverts** cover the bases of the flight feathers. Below you can see the different feather sections of a heron's wing and a barn owl's wing, and how those sections fold and overlap when the wing is closed.

DORSAL VIEW OF A WING

Grey heron (*Ardea cinerea*)

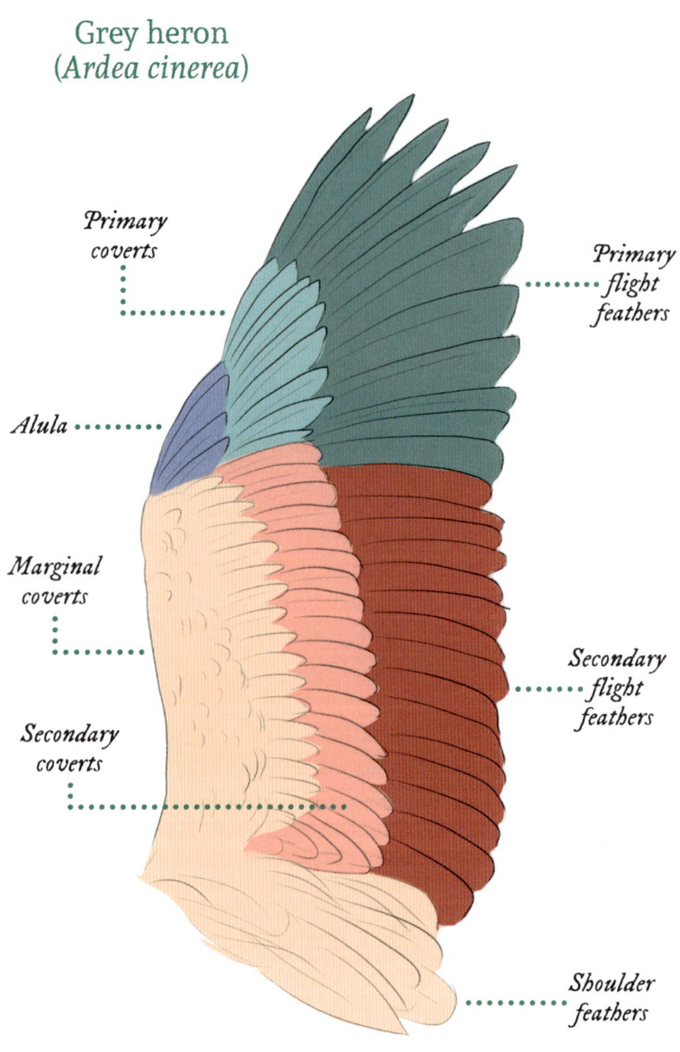

FOLDING WING

Barn owl (*Tyto alba*)

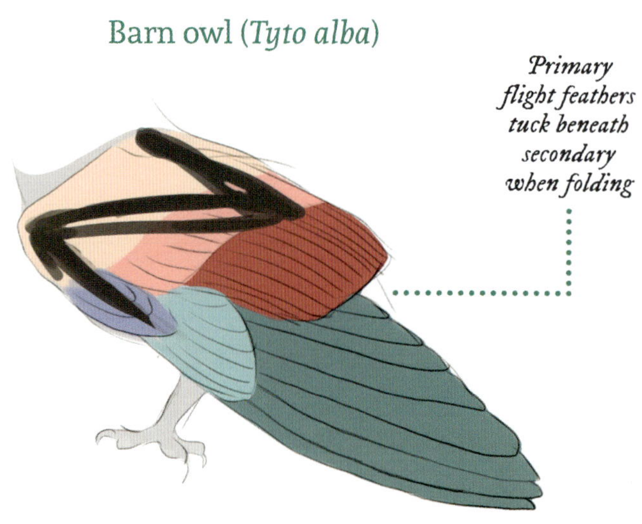

FULLY FOLDED WING

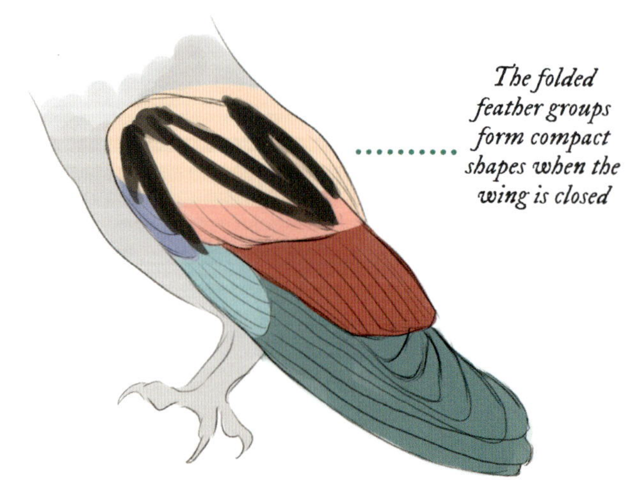

Beaks

Beaks are all adapted for different purposes, so consider beak shape carefully when using avian anatomy in creature design. Here are some examples from which you can draw inspiration.

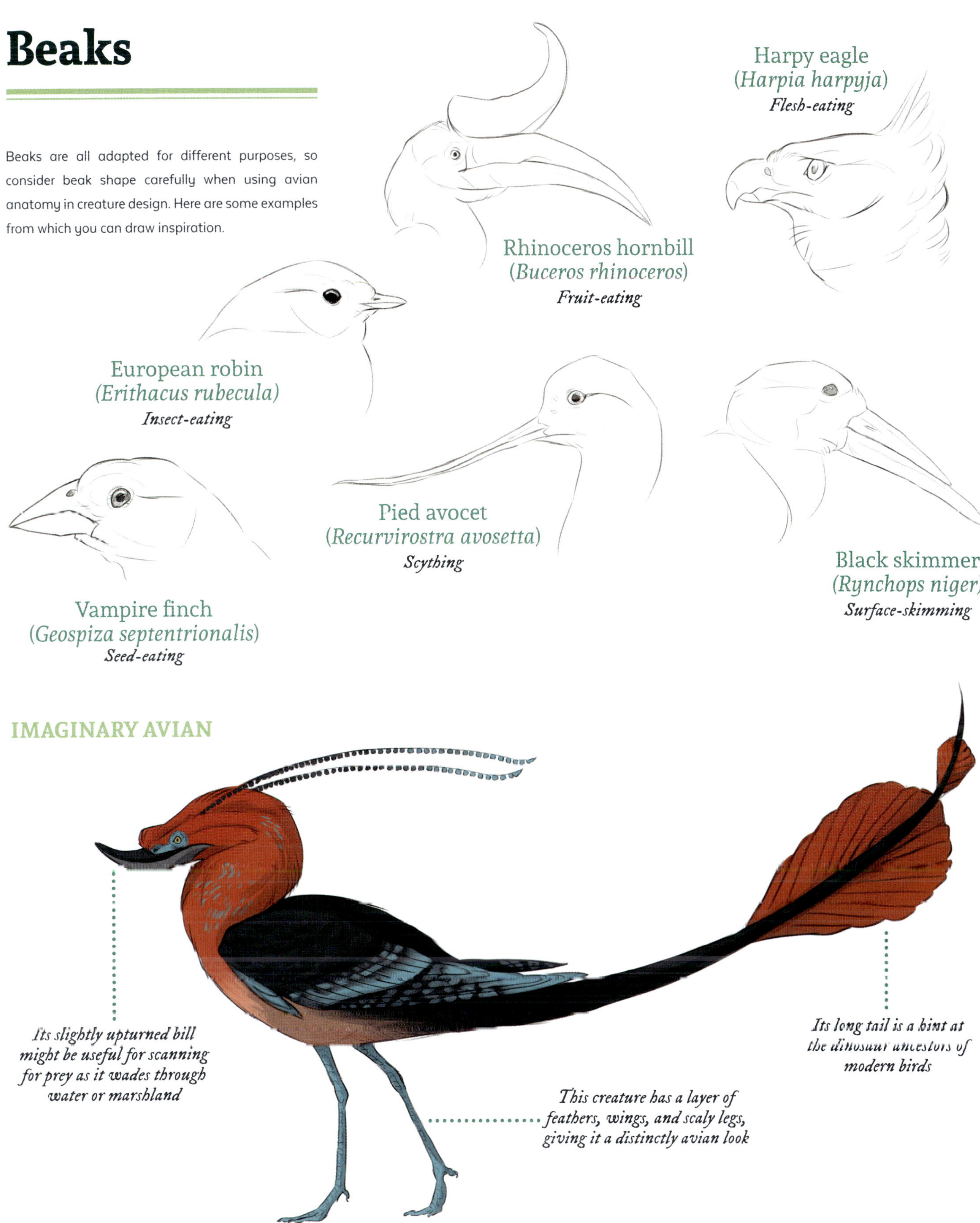

Harpy eagle
(*Harpia harpyja*)
Flesh-eating

Rhinoceros hornbill
(*Buceros rhinoceros*)
Fruit-eating

European robin
(*Erithacus rubecula*)
Insect-eating

Pied avocet
(*Recurvirostra avosetta*)
Scything

Black skimmer
(*Rynchops niger*)
Surface-skimming

Vampire finch
(*Geospiza septentrionalis*)
Seed-eating

IMAGINARY AVIAN

Its slightly upturned bill might be useful for scanning for prey as it wades through water or marshland

This creature has a layer of feathers, wings, and scaly legs, giving it a distinctly avian look

Its long tail is a hint at the dinosaur ancestors of modern birds

FISH ANATOMY

Scientifically, there is no formal group that is "fish." The animals we think of as fish are actually about 33,000 species spread over several different evolutionary lineages. These lineages are only distantly related to each other, rather than being a distinct group all descended from a common ancestor, as with birds, for example. Fish can be divided into three types:

- **Jawless fish** (hagfish, lampreys)

- **Cartilaginous fish** (sharks, rays, chimeras)

- **Bony fish** (most "fish" species, such as goldfish, tuna, salmon, and seahorses)

A typical fish has **scaled skin**, **fins**, breathes with **gills**, and is **cold-blooded**. They have a large mass of muscle relative to their body size. Their main body consists of sheets of overlapping muscles known as myotomes. These muscles are adapted for the fast side-to-side movements of swimming by contracting smoothly in sequence down the body, creating a powerful wave from head to tail. Remnants of this kind of muscle are present in the tails of some reptiles and amphibians.

The main purpose of the **dorsal fin** is to stabilize the fish. The **pectoral** and **pelvic fins** assist with movement and steering. The **anal fin** also helps with stabilization. Some fish also have an **adipose fin**, the purpose of which we are still unsure about.

Fish skulls are far more complex than mammalian ones and are made up of many more intricate pieces. The skulls are mainly structured around the need to support the gills. The spine of most bony fish passes through the middle of the body, with spikes above and below to support the swimming muscles. The pectoral and pelvic fins are supported by simple girdles often attached to the skull. The dorsal and anal fins, however, are supported by spines.

Fish possess a network of receptors on their bodies called the **lateral line system**. These tiny receptors (neuromasts) are sensitive to water movement and pressure changes. They lie in pits below the skin and help fish orient themselves and swim. Most fish have a network of such receptors on the head and in a canal along each side of the body. The grooves in the muscle along a fish's body are normally quite pronounced on the outside of the fish, as they do not have thick blubber like marine mammals.

MUSCULATURE

Sockeye salmon (*Oncorhynchus nerka*)

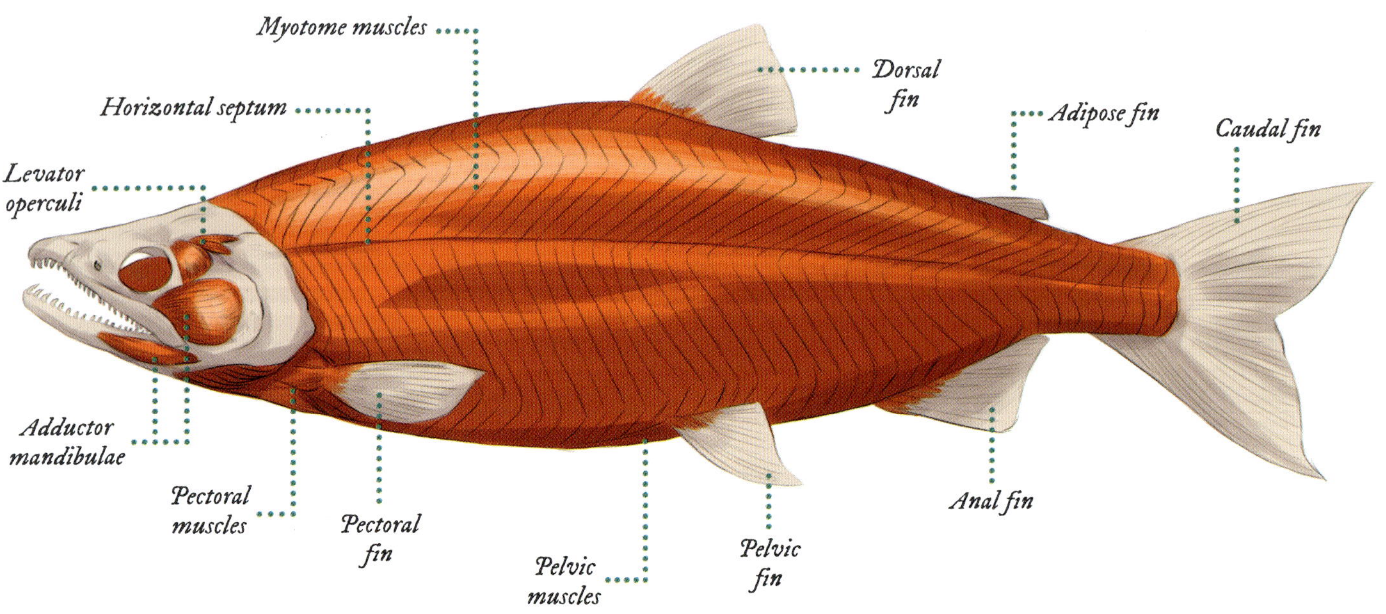

SKELETON

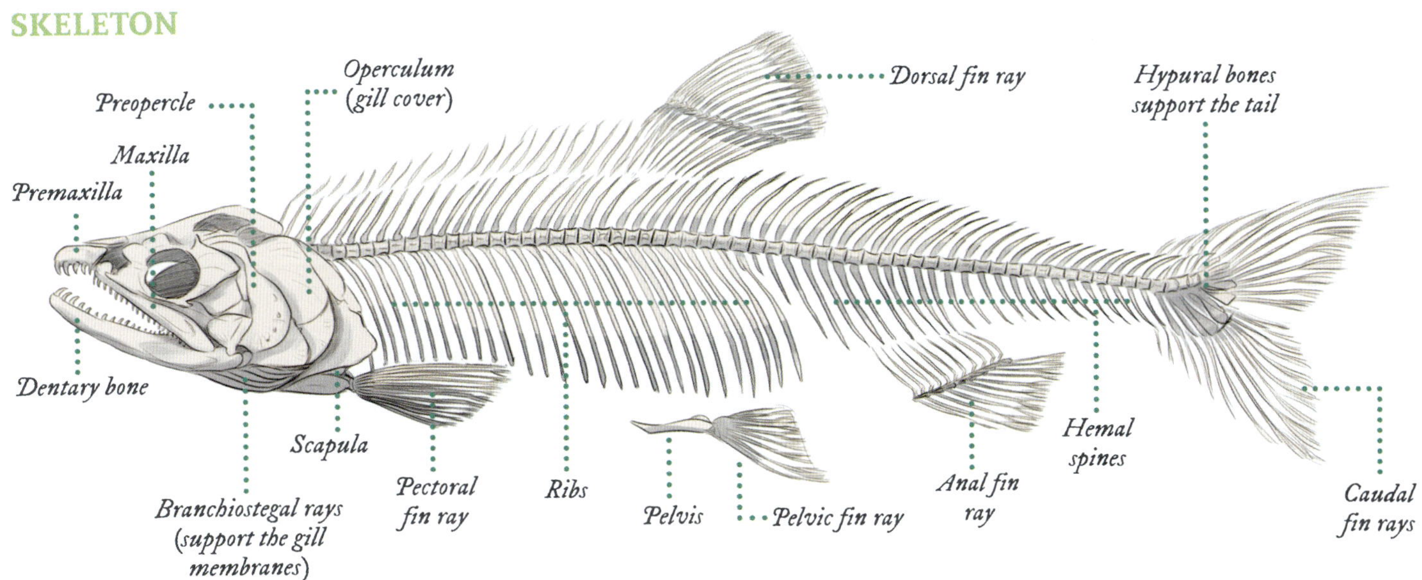

BASIC SHAPES

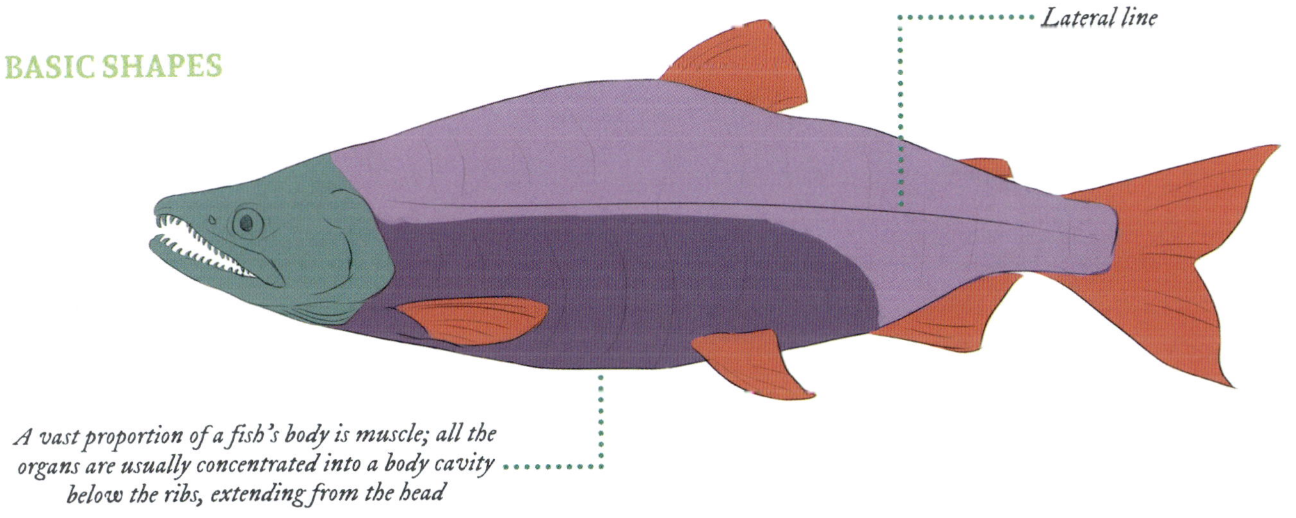

*A vast proportion of a fish's body is muscle; all the
organs are usually concentrated into a body cavity
below the ribs, extending from the head*

Cartilaginous skeletons

Sharks, rays, and chimeras make up a class of fish with skeletons made of cartilage, rather than bone like the salmon's above. These skeletons lack ribcages but are very flexible, allowing sharks to make quick, sharp turns.

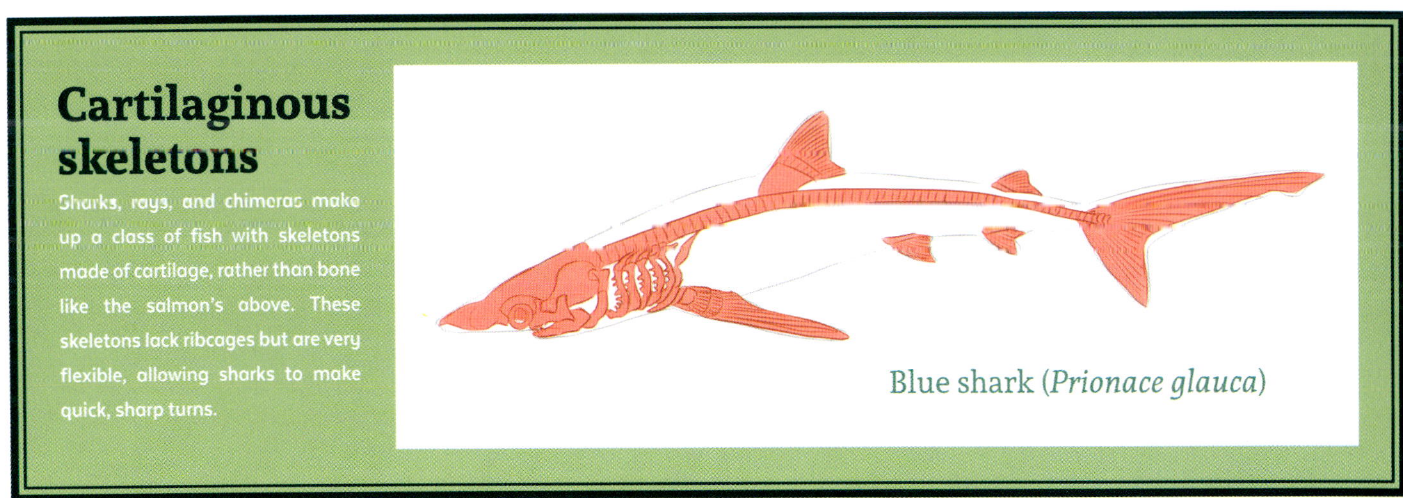

Swimming

With any design, it is important to think about how the creature moves. Fish have been around for millions of years and have a range of swimming techniques to meet their ecological requirements. Most fish swim by passing a wave down a portion of the body (such as the **body-caudal fin propulsion** examples below), but others use only certain fins (see the **median paired fin propulsion** fish below). For most fish, the wave starts part-way down the body, but some, such as eels, pass it along the full length of their bodies and can even swim backward. Fast, long-distance-swimming fish such as tuna keep most of the body rigid and beat only the tail fin itself for propulsion.

BODY-CAUDAL FIN PROPULSION

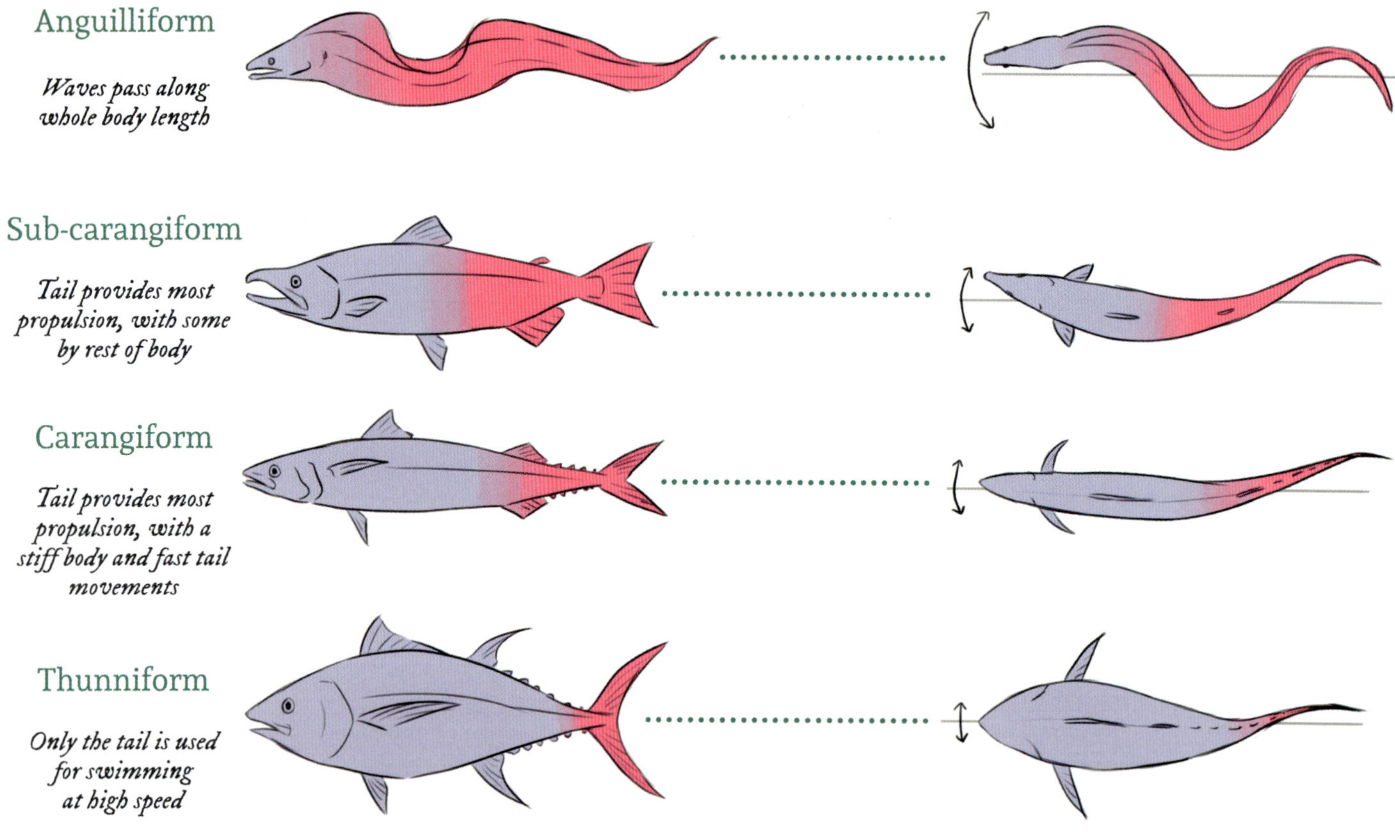

Anguilliform

Waves pass along whole body length

Sub-carangiform

Tail provides most propulsion, with some by rest of body

Carangiform

Tail provides most propulsion, with a stiff body and fast tail movements

Thunniform

Only the tail is used for swimming at high speed

MEDIAN PAIRED FIN PROPULSION

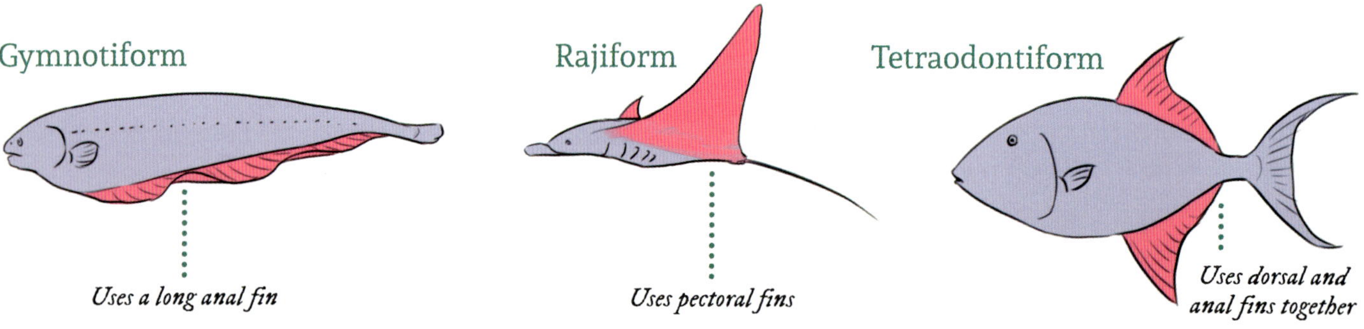

Gymnotiform

Uses a long anal fin

Rajiform

Uses pectoral fins

Tetraodontiform

Uses dorsal and anal fins together

Fish heads

Bony fish have complex skulls that can have a huge range of adaptations to inspire countless creature designs. Here are just a few examples of the unusual and fascinating heads and jaws that can be found in real-world fish.

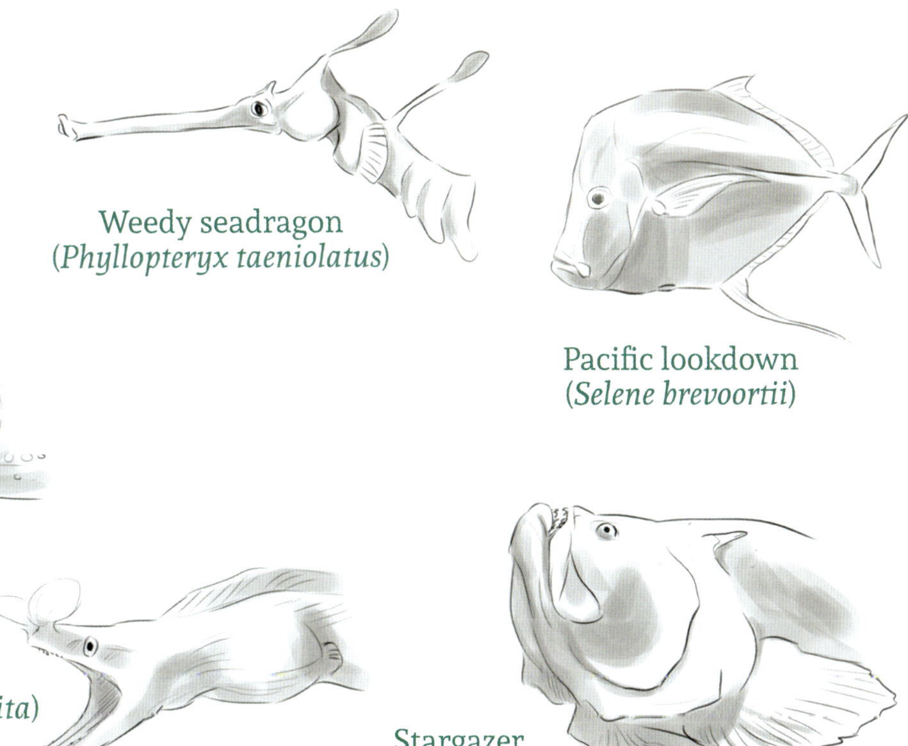

Weedy seadragon
(*Phyllopteryx taeniolatus*)

Pacific lookdown
(*Selene brevoortii*)

Viperfish
(*Chauliodus*)

Ribbon eel
(*Rhinomuraena quaesita*)

Stargazer
(*Uranoscopidae*)

IMAGINARY FISH

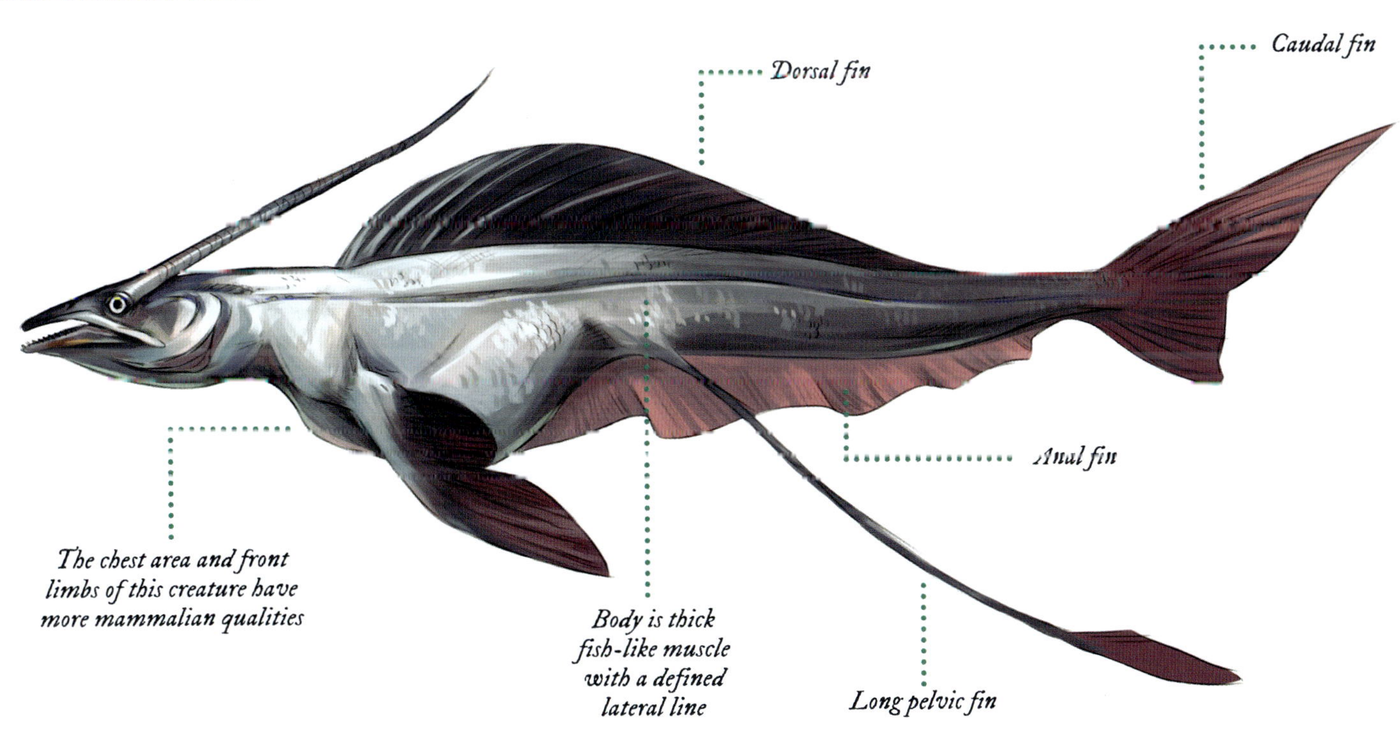

ARTHROPOD ANATOMY

All the animals studied so far in this chapter have been vertebrates – animals with backbones. However, these are just a tiny fraction of animal life, with some studies suggesting that up to ninety-seven percent of animal species on Earth are invertebrates, making them a treasure trove of creature design inspiration. Arthropods are a group of over one million known species of invertebrates, which are characterized by their hard exoskeletons, jointed limbs, and segmented bodies. As their exoskeletons are hard, all these animals grow by molting their skins. There are four main groups of arthropods: **chelicerates**, **crustaceans**, **myriapods**, and **insects**. Each has distinct anatomical features.

Chelicerates

Chelicerates are a subdivision of arthropods that includes groups such as spiders, scorpions, whip scorpions, ticks, harvestmen, horseshoe crabs, and sun spiders. Chelicerates are named after the appendages nearest to their mouths: the **chelicerae**. In true spiders, these are fangs, but in other groups such as scorpions these are more like miniature pincers near the mouth. The next appendages out from the mouth, unique to chelicerates, are the **pedipalps**. In spiders, these look a bit like extra legs, but are in fact used for reproduction. In scorpions, however, these are developed into huge pincers. It is the same body part, just exaggerated into many forms across different species.

Most chelicerates have bodies divided into two segments: the **cephalothorax** and the **abdomen**. They also generally have **four pairs of legs** and no wings or antennae. Note that spiders have an extra segment in their legs, the patella, compared to insects. Spiders also have specialized organs on their abdomens called **spinnerets**, used for making silk.

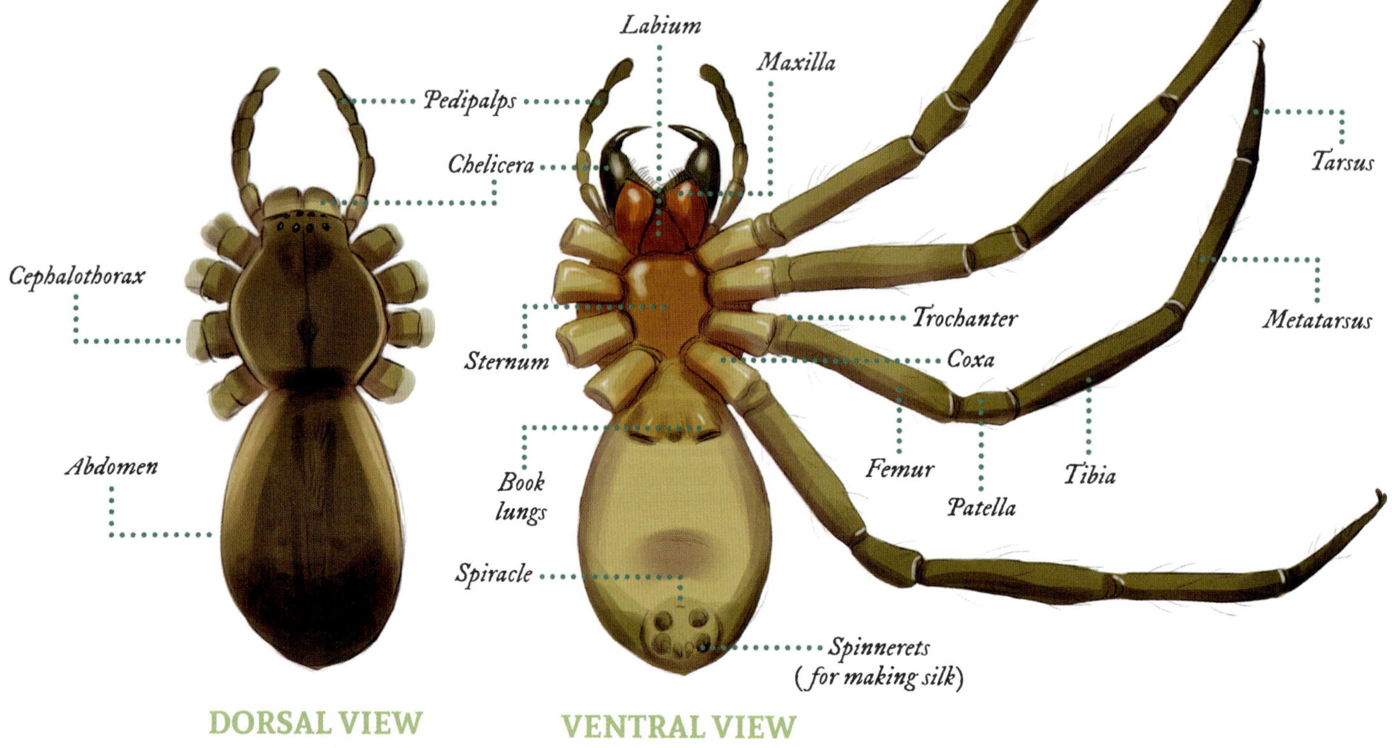

DORSAL VIEW

VENTRAL VIEW

Spiders

Spider species have their eight eyes arranged in different ways as adaptations to their various lifestyles. In jumping spiders, the eyes form an "eye-crown" around the top of the head to give almost 360-degree vision. The front two eyes are highly developed for actively hunting prey. In wolf spiders, the eyes are arranged in three rows. The central row has two very large eyes and these spiders, like jumping spiders, see relatively well for arachnids.

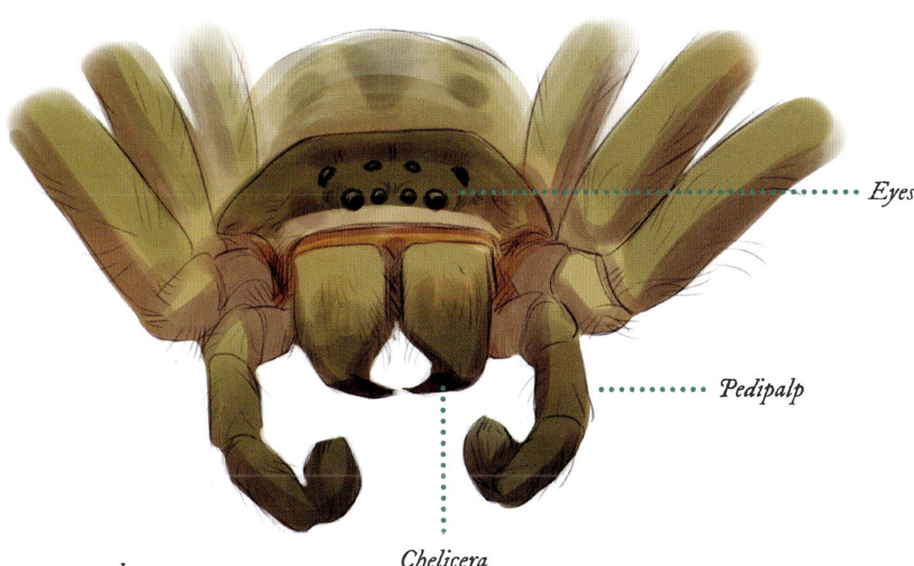

Huntsman spider
(*Sparassidae*)

Wolf spider
(*Lycosidae*)

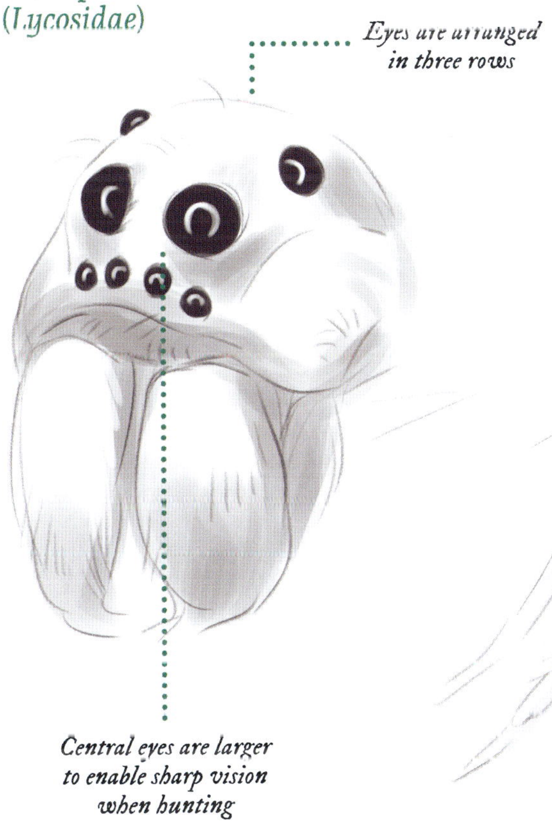

*Eyes are arranged
in three rows*

*Central eyes are larger
to enable sharp vision
when hunting*

Jumping spider
(*Salticidae*)

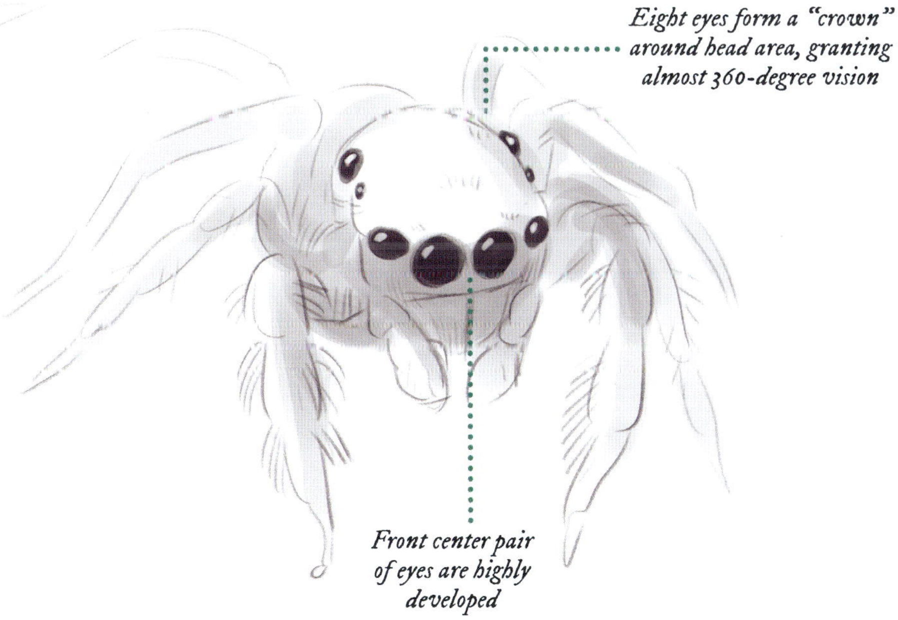

*Eight eyes form a "crown"
around head area, granting
almost 360-degree vision*

*Front center pair
of eyes are highly
developed*

Scorpions

Scorpions are another example of a chelicerate. Scorpion abdomens are split into seven **"body" segments** and five **"tail" segments**, ending in a sharp, **venomous sting**. Scorpions also possess unique comb-like structures on their undersides, called **pectines**, which sweep the ground with sensory hairs and act as a chemical sensing system. The pedipalps are adapted into **pincers** for defense and catching prey. Scorpions also have **three clusters of eyes**: a central one and two lateral clusters.

SCORPION ANATOMY

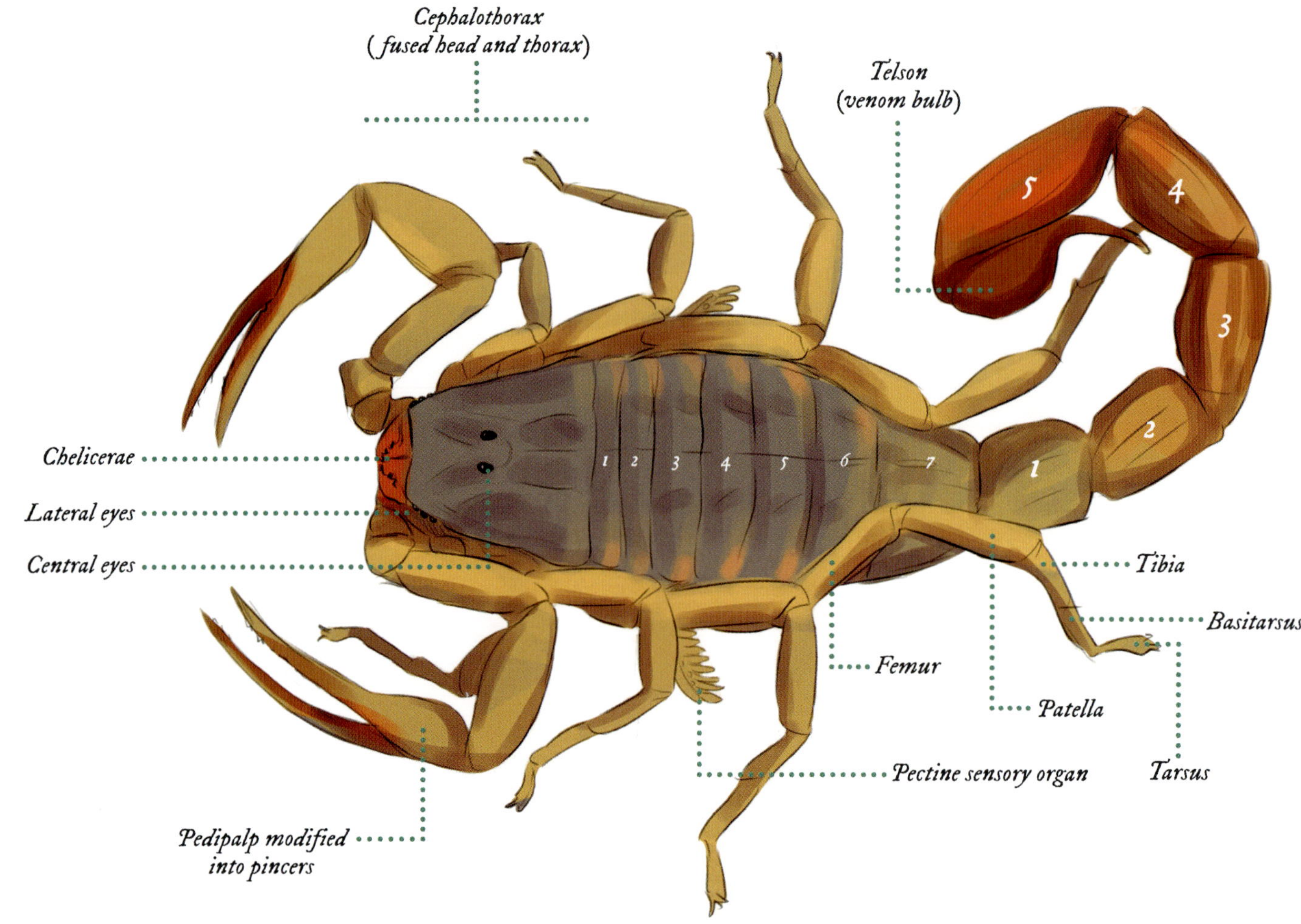

Crustaceans

Crustaceans are a diverse group of arthropods, most of which are aquatic, although some have adapted to life on land. They include animals such as **crabs**, **lobsters**, **crayfish**, **shrimp**, **woodlice**, and **barnacles**. Crustaceans have many appendages along the body used for many purposes: sensory antennae, feeding mouthparts, defensive claws, walking legs, and swimming fins.

Most crustaceans have limbs that branch at a certain point to perform two different functions (they are biramous). For example, **gills** branch off the upper legs under the outer exoskeleton, and movement of the legs helps stimulate flow of water over these gills to aid breathing.

Crabs, lobsters, and close relatives generally have several layers of modified **feeding appendages**. The outermost mouthparts of a crab consist of the maxillipeds, and these all fold in neatly on top of each other and help channel pieces of food into the jaws farther within.

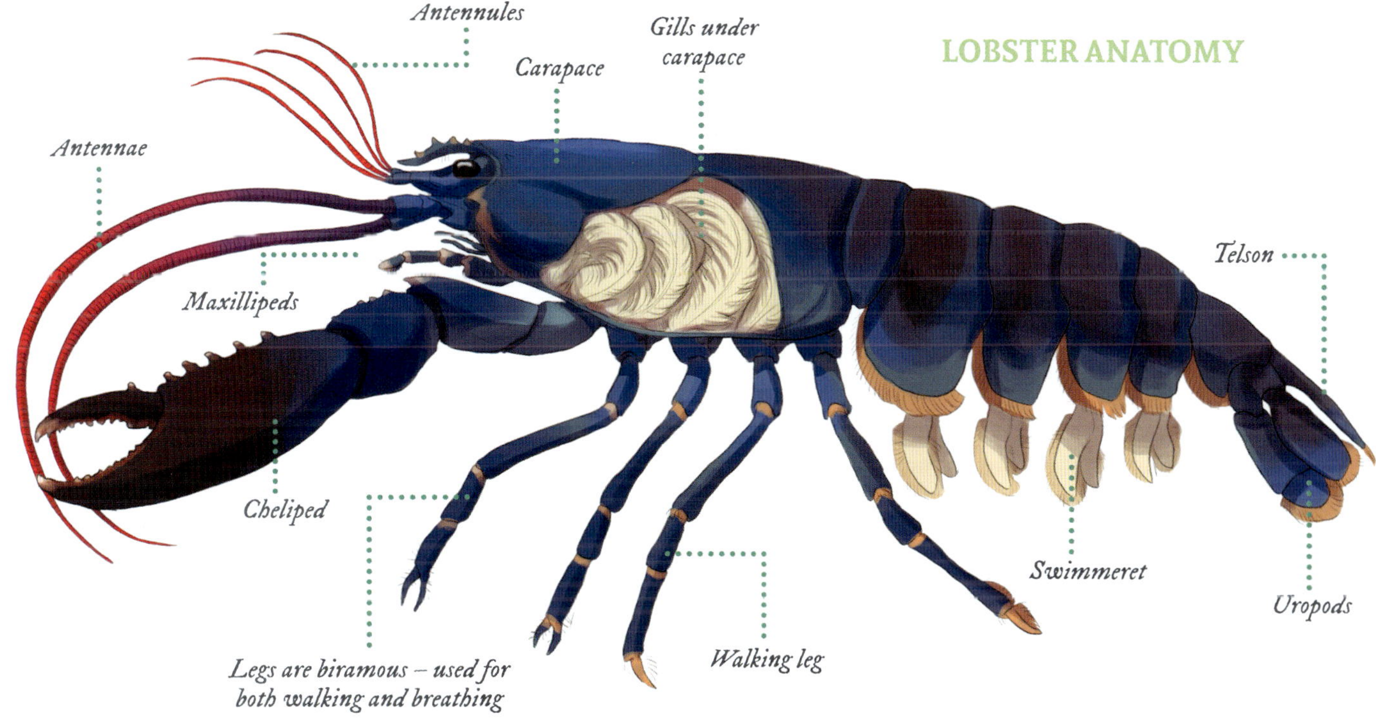

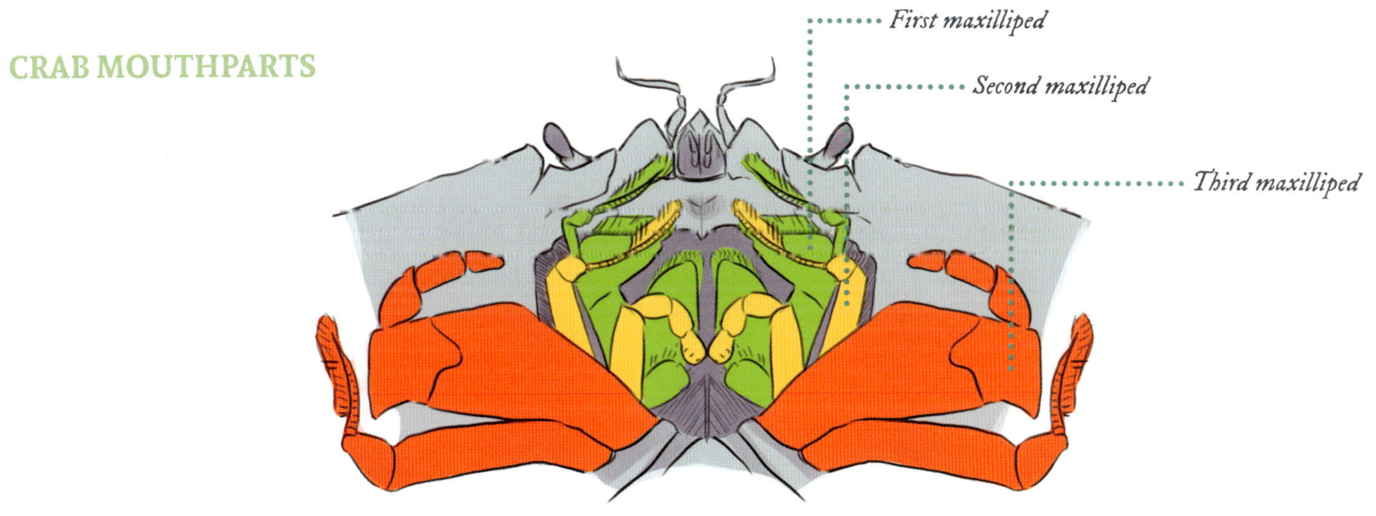

Myriapods

There are over 16,000 known species of myriapod. These are mostly terrestrial arthropods characterized by their abundance of legs.

Millipedes

Millipedes usually have **long, cylindrical bodies** with **many segments**, but some are shorter, such as pill millipedes. All millipedes are slow and have no sharp weapons with which to defend themselves, so they coil up into a tight spiral or ball when under threat, and rely on their armor and release of foul fluids for self-defense.

Millipedes also have poor eyesight, possessing just clusters of simple eyes called **ocelli**. Their **jaws** consist of the epistome, the mandibles, and the gnathochilarium for chewing their diet of decaying plant matter.

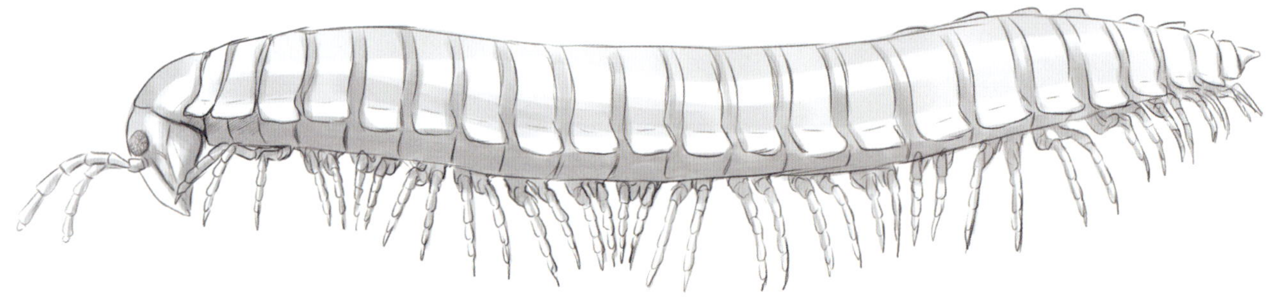

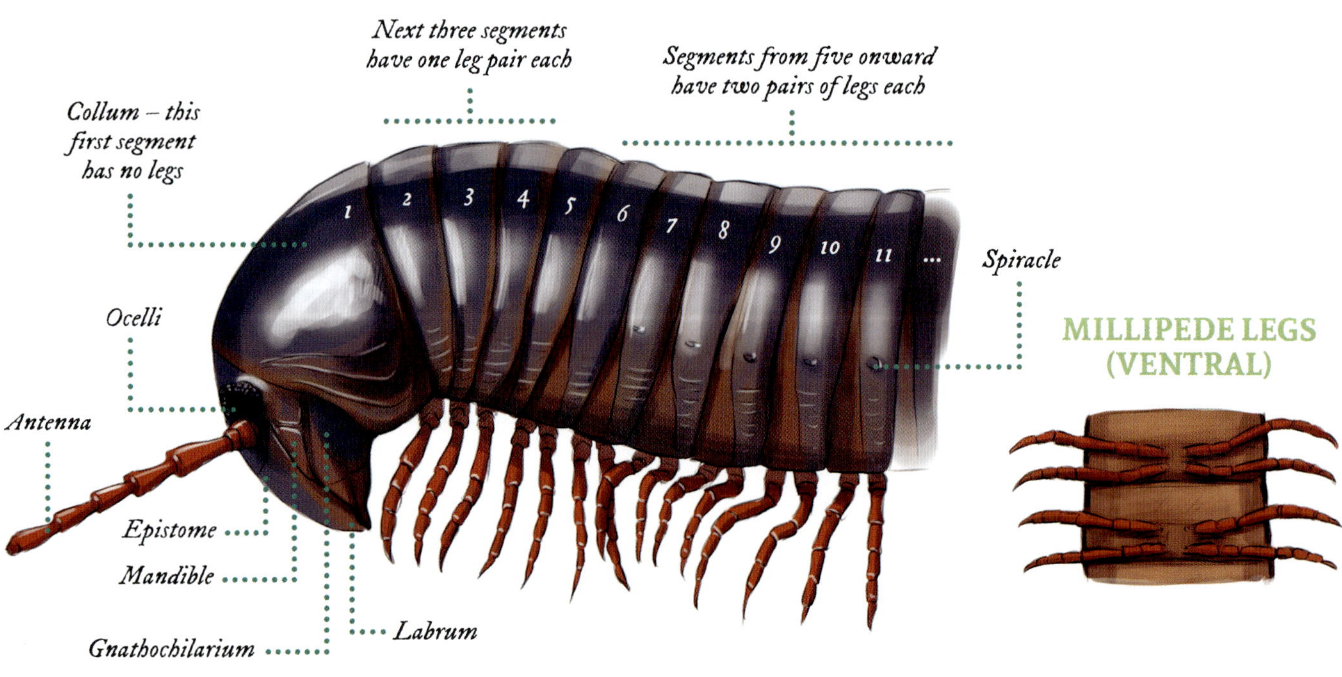

Centipedes

Centipedes are a group of fast, predatory myriapods with **flattened heads and bodies** and one pair of legs per body segment. Many lack eyes entirely but others have simple **ocelli**. All rely instead on their **antennae** to navigate, and have large spiracles, through which they breathe, along the length of the body.

Centipedes have modified legs called the **forcipules** under and behind their main mouthparts; these are used to inject venom.

CENTIPEDE ANATOMY

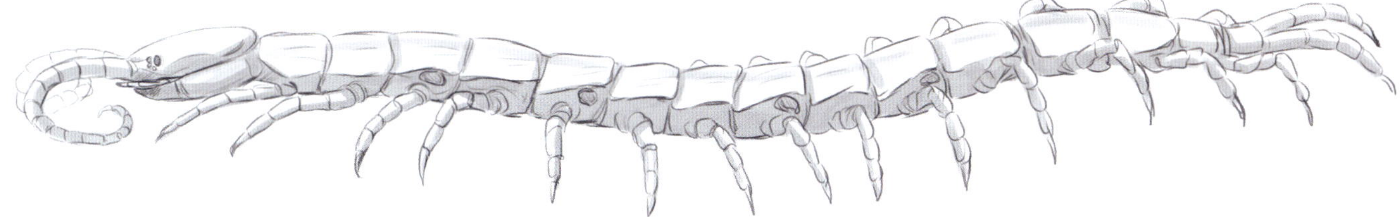

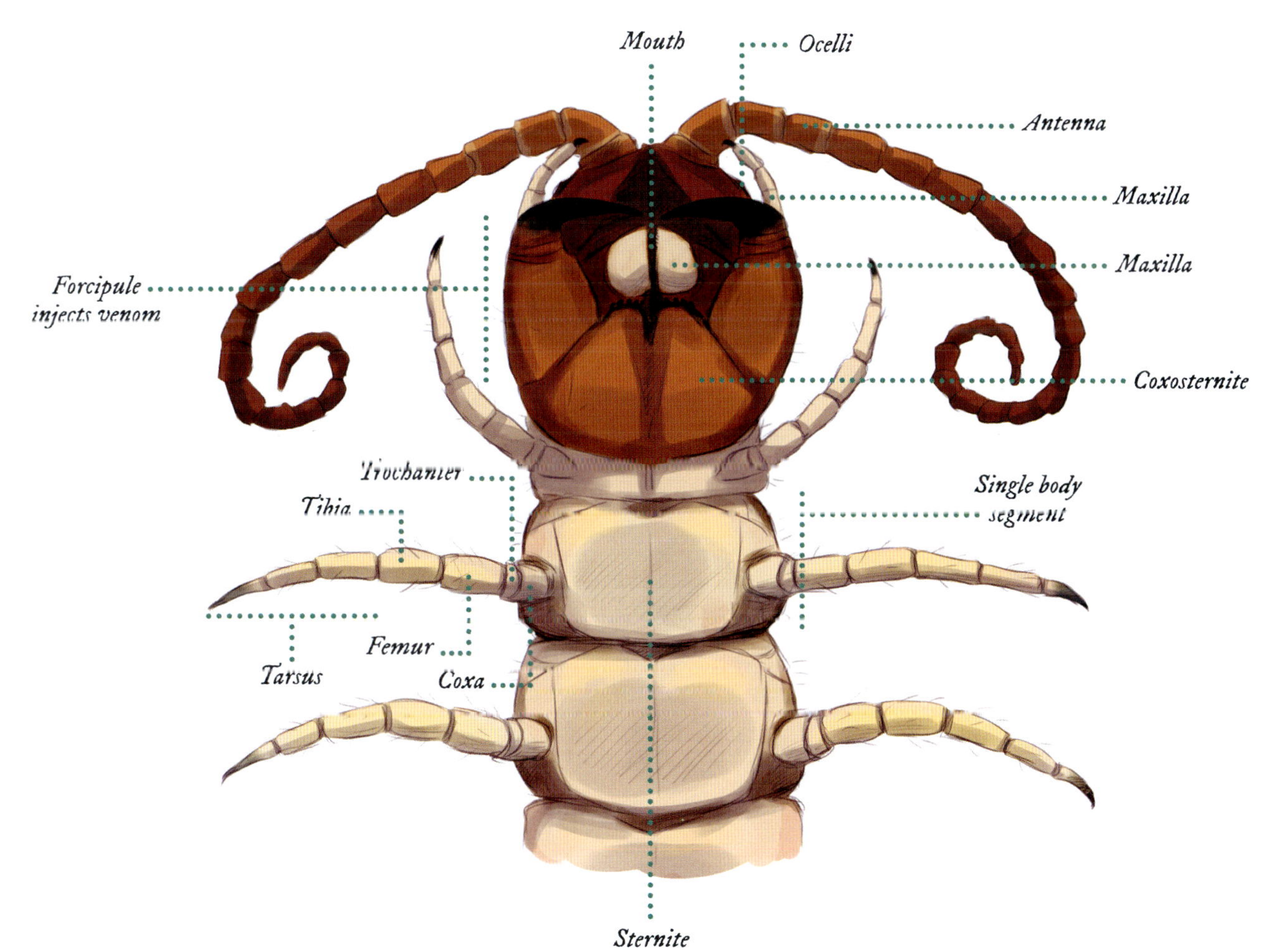

Insects

There are more than one million described insect species, but the total number is estimated at over six million. These animals are often overlooked due to their size, yet they show incredible diversity of form and adaptation. Take some time to understand these animals and you will find endless inspiration for creature design.

The basic hexapod insect form has **three pairs of walking legs** and **two pairs of wings**. In beetles, the forewings have evolved into hard elytra that protect the wings beneath. In true flies, the hind wings are adapted into organs called halteres, which help them perform incredible aerial acrobatics. Most insects can fold their wings to a certain extent except for dragonflies and mayflies. Insects have legs jointed differently to our own, and having six legs allows for good stability and fast movement. Some have legs adapted for leaping, others for swimming, and some for moving across the surface of water.

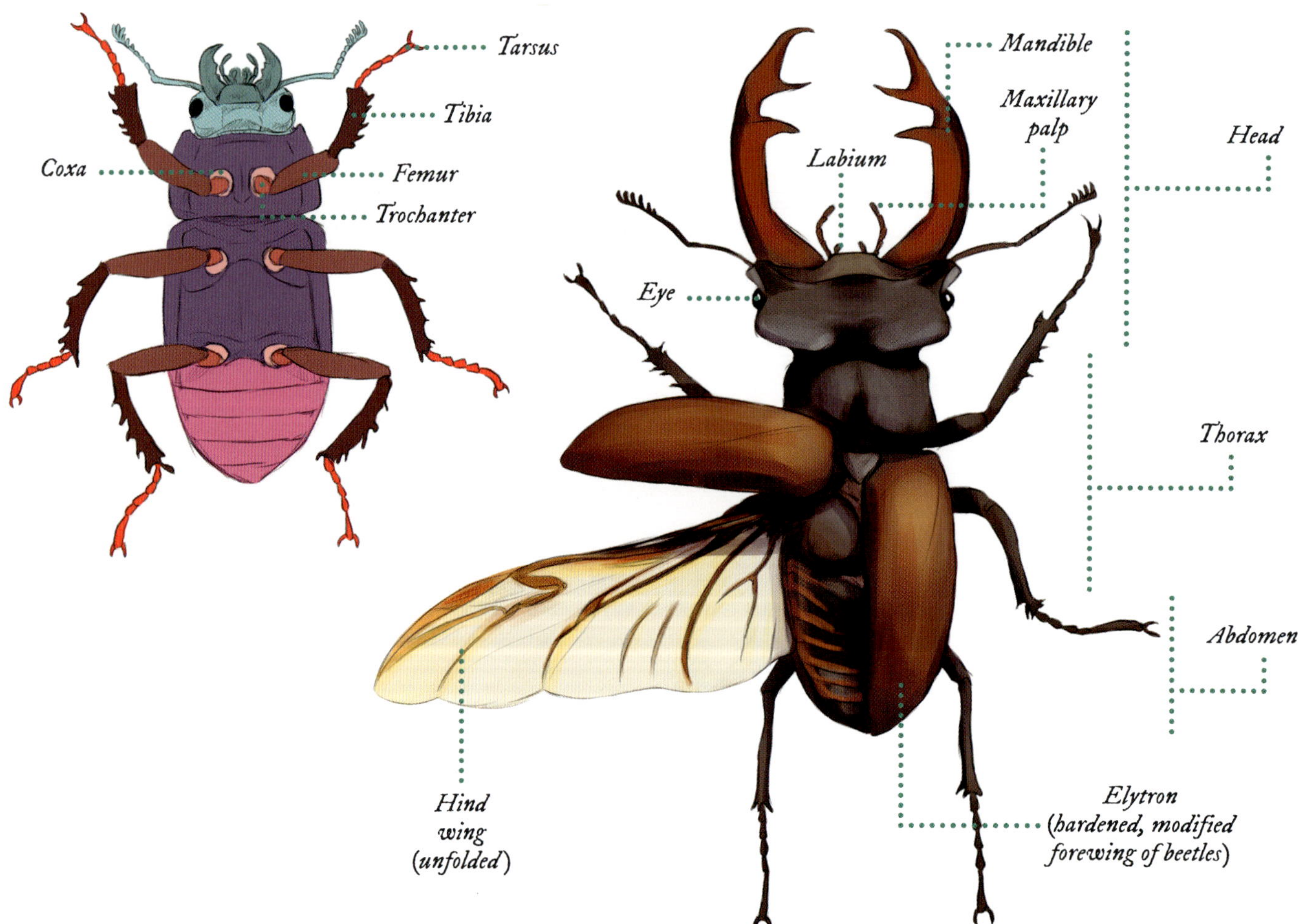

Insect mouths

Chewing insects

Insect mouths are more complex than mammalian jaws. The first two diagrams on the right show the main sections of all insect jaws as found on a typical chewing insect (a praying mantis). The labrum forms the top of the mouth. The mandibles are tough and used for crushing and slicing from either side. The maxillae help handle and process food. The labium forms the floor of the mouth, and both the maxillary and labial palps help with tasting and touching potential food. Many insects have two main compound eyes, plus three small simple ocelli eyes in the middle of the head.

Lapping insects

Bees have the same basic mouthparts but they are adapted for lapping at nectar rather than chewing plant matter or prey. The maxillae form a tube-like structure around the labium.

Siphoning insects

Butterflies and moths have highly adapted mouthparts for siphoning fluids without piercing. The maxillae have evolved into a long, coiled tube called a proboscis. Some insects have mouthparts designed to both pierce and suck internal fluids, such as the true bugs (like aphids, cicadas, and stinkbugs) and female mosquitoes.

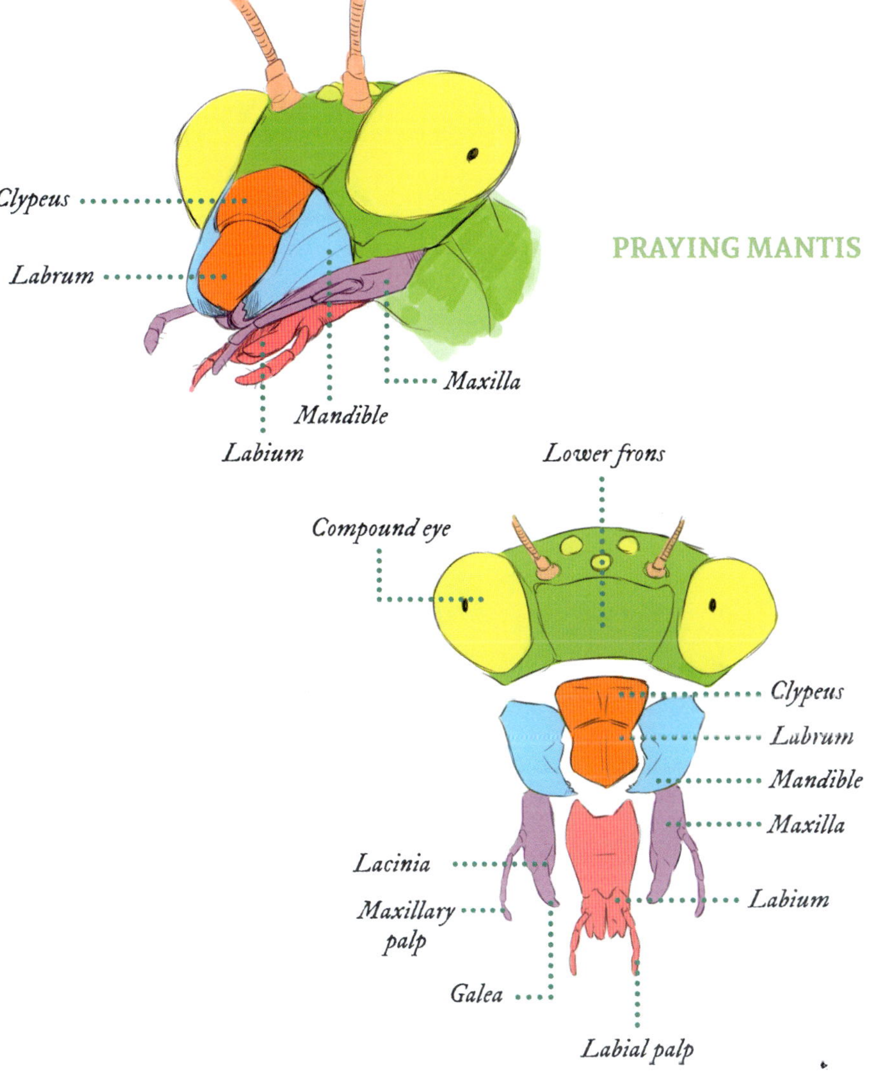

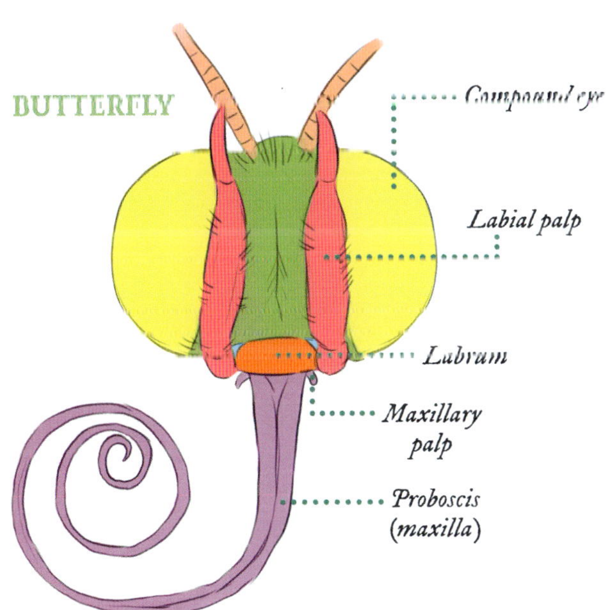

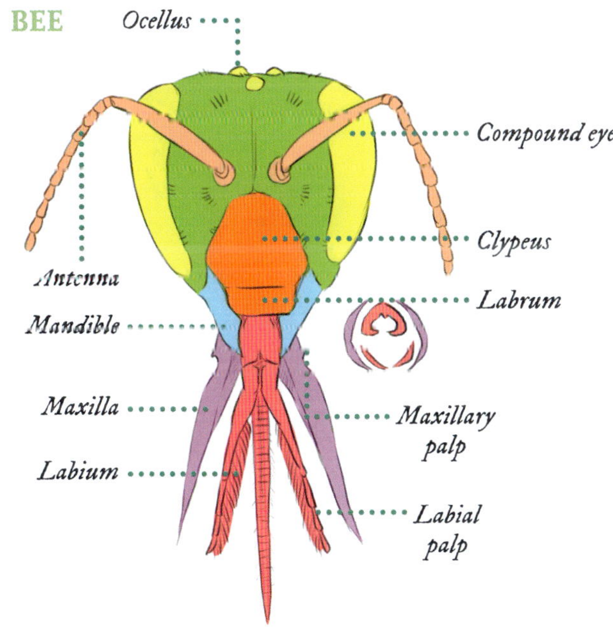

Insect larvae

Insects can be categorized based on their life cycle, and thinking about a creature's life cycle can add unique details to your designs. Some insects undergo **incomplete metamorphosis**: they hatch from eggs as tiny nymphs that molt several times to reach maturity, which is the case with mantises, grasshoppers, and cicadas.

However, most insect species undergo **complete metamorphosis**. This involves the insects hatching from eggs as larvae. Larvae are essentially adapted to be eating machines. They normally look very different to the adults and molt several times to accommodate growth. These then enter a non-feeding pupal stage during which metamorphosis occurs using the energy stored as larvae. The adult insects then emerge from these pupae. Having a larval stage is a useful strategy because larvae are often adapted to a completely different environment and food source to the adult, thus reducing competition within species.

Polypod insect larvae

Polypod insect larvae have three pairs of true legs like the adult insect, but also have several pairs of soft "prolegs" along the abdomen. Examples of insects with such larvae are butterflies, moths, caddisflies, and sawflies.

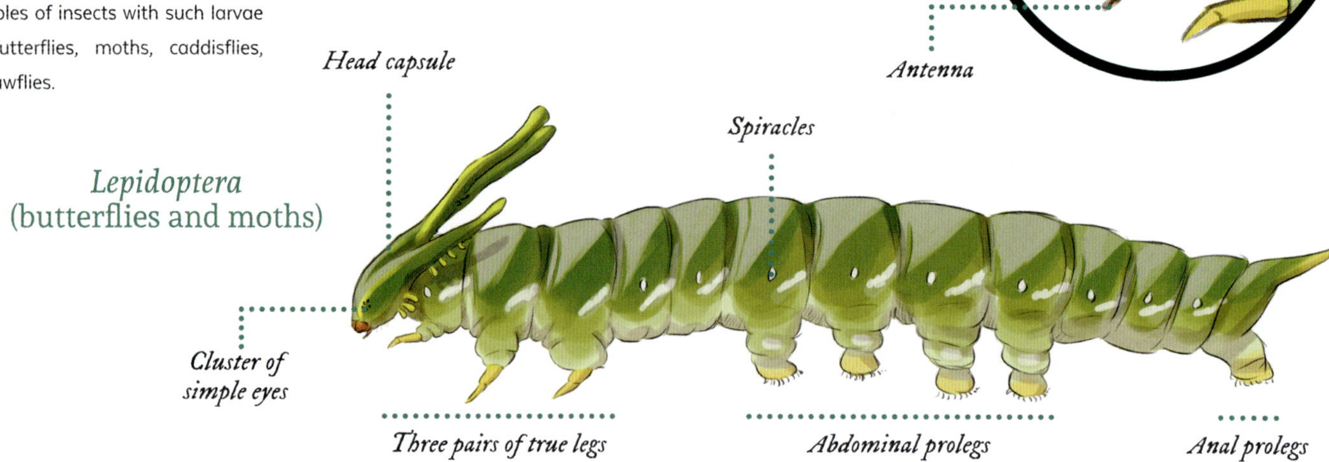

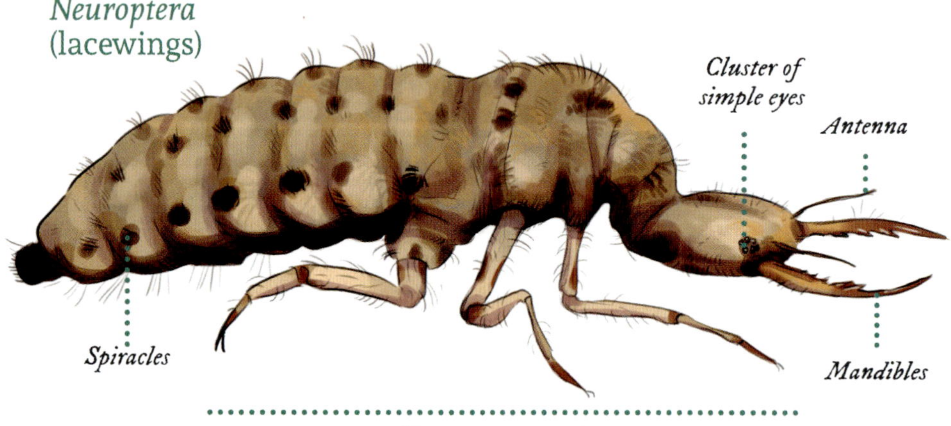

Oligopod insect larvae

Oligopod insect larvae possess just three pairs of true legs and hard, developed mouthparts. Some, like this antlion, are ambush predators with long mandibles and are covered in hairs to help lodge them in their substrate. Examples of insects with oligopod larvae are the lacewing flies and scarab and ground beetles.

Apod insect larvae

Some insect larvae are apod, meaning they have no legs at all. These larvae are well adapted for burrowing through their food source, be that plant or animal, living or dead. Fly maggots like this one have tough little teeth at one end and a spiracle for breathing at the other. They have no true eyes but studies suggest that some can detect light through most of their skin.

Diptera (true flies)

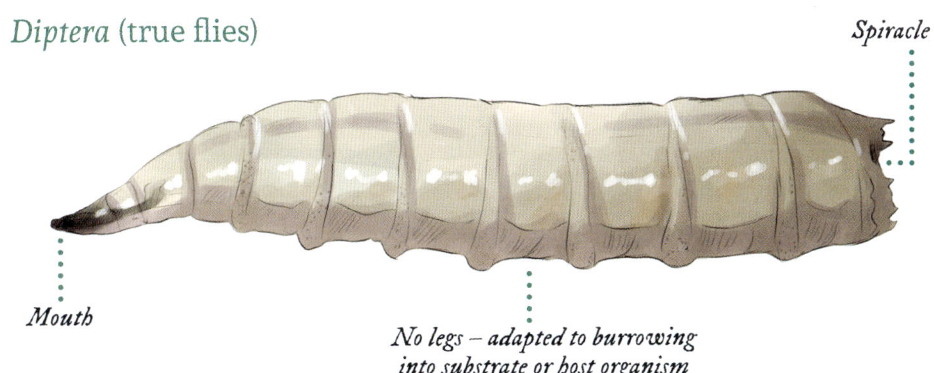

IMAGINARY INSECTS

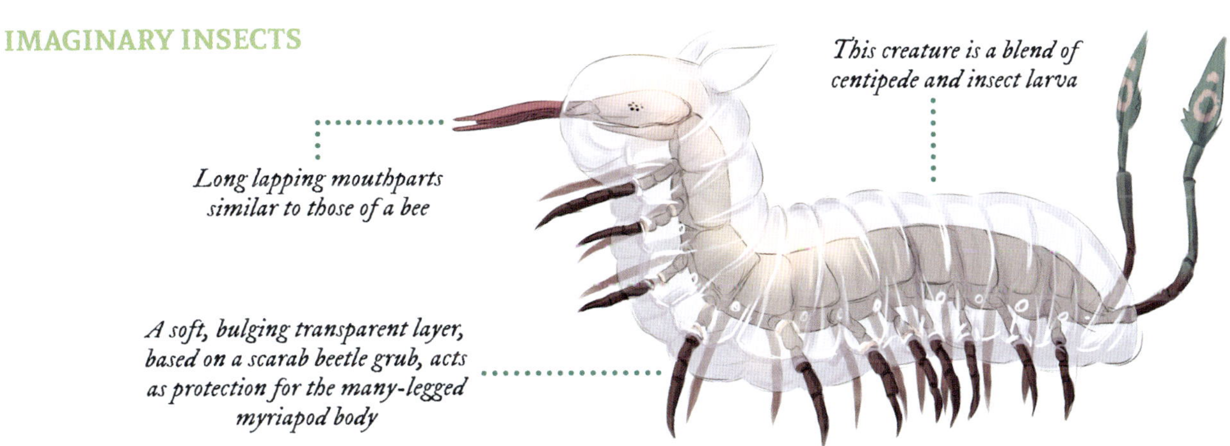

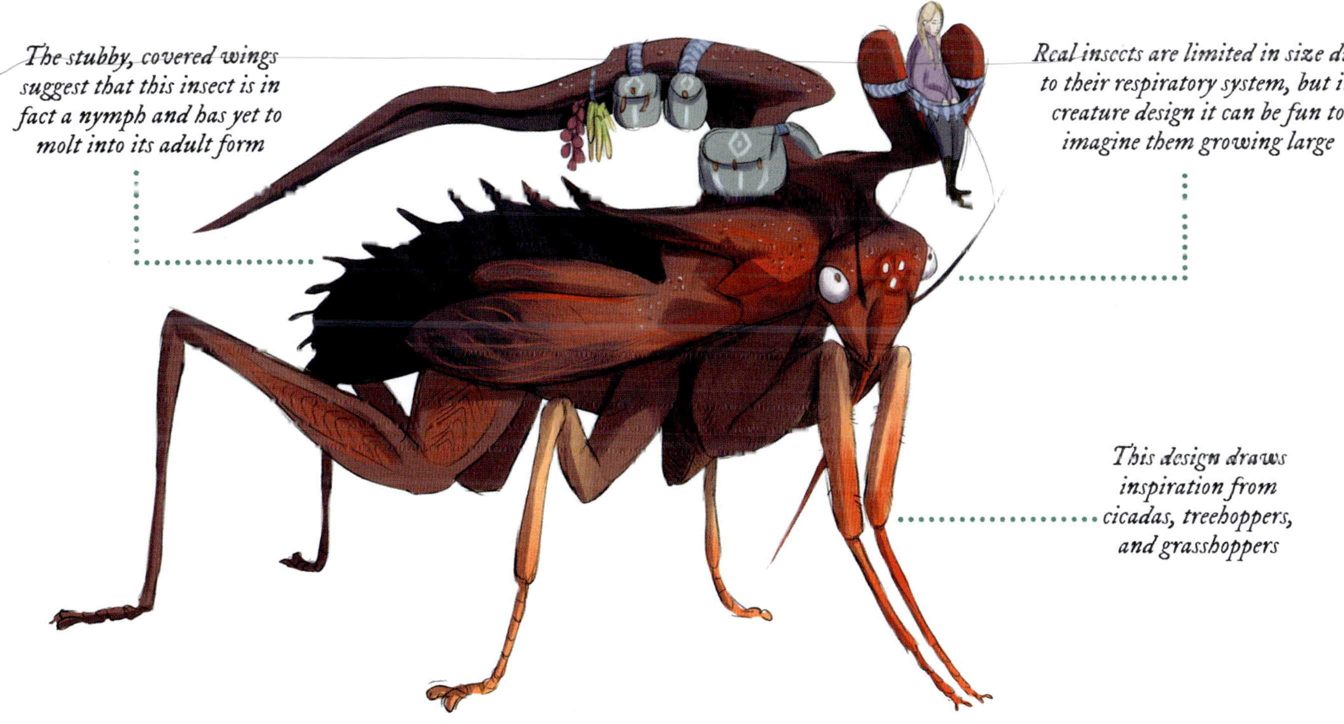

General design principles

"Mastering these principles is crucial for an artist to develop an image that communicates successfully to the viewer"

By Kyle Brown

AN ARTIST'S BLUEPRINT

Creature design, like any other type of concept design, is built on the foundation of essential technical principles. It is crucial for an artist to master these principles in order to develop artwork that communicates successfully with the viewer. They will serve as the blueprint and foundation of your work. Though some may seem simple, each has a level of detail that must be understood. An artist must implement the principles correctly to ensure their creature achieves its purpose within a project. This chapter will discuss a checklist of best practices when communicating your ideas to clients. This will ensure your design does not go against the visual needs of a project. The creatures on these pages show the various design principles in action.

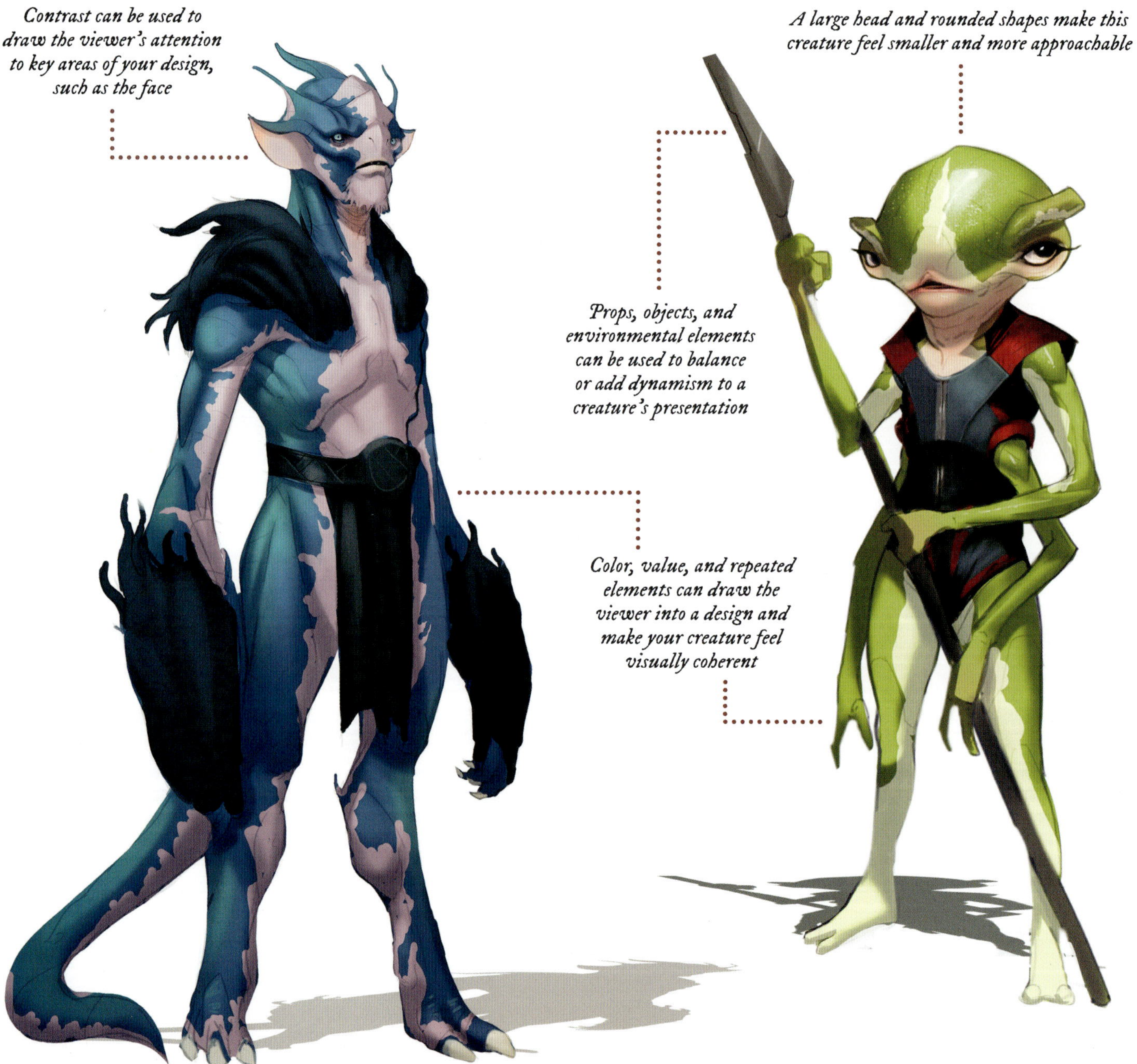

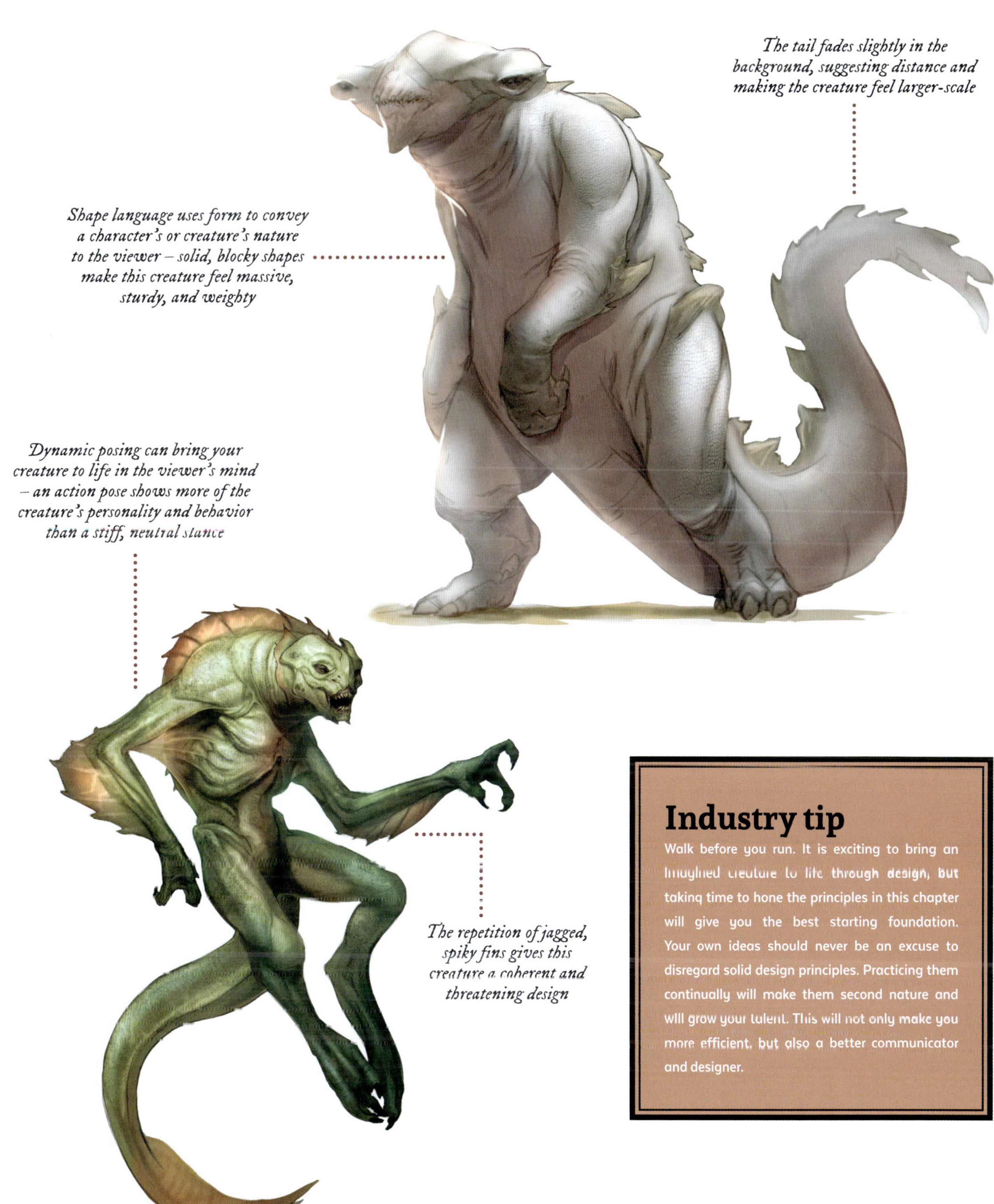

Industry tip

Walk before you run. It is exciting to bring an imagined creature to life through design, but taking time to hone the principles in this chapter will give you the best starting foundation. Your own ideas should never be an excuse to disregard solid design principles. Practicing them continually will make them second nature and will grow your talent. This will not only make you more efficient, but also a better communicator and designer.

BALANCE

Balance is the idea of stability or support in an object. An artist can use balance by applying it in the literal sense, giving their creatures "real-world" weight, position, and stability within the two-dimensional image. Balance of detail or value can also be used to draw the viewer's eye to specific elements of the creature that are important for them to see. It is just one of the balls in the design juggling act that you must think about as you work.

Balance, along with perspective (discussed on **page 114**), is the building block on which to establish your creatures, or any designs for that matter. It provides the foundation for more objective decisions early in the process, supporting the creative and subjective choices you make as you work. When using balance to distribute the physical attributes of a creature, you can create an image that is more appealing, focused, stable, and clear. When you are satisfied with a piece on a technical level, you can then present your creature for subjective review. This means asking: "How does the character read? What is its story? What is its function? Is it successful?"

Balance does not mean boring or plain, but rather the opposite. A large, traditional form can be juxtaposed against a smaller, extreme design element to bring balance to a piece. Pops of contrasting value can intensify areas of focus among areas of lesser importance. When you add elements of value and detail together, you can amplify and reinforce the balance to solidify a design.

This section will guide you through different ways to utilize value, color, detail, and pose to bring balance to a creature design.

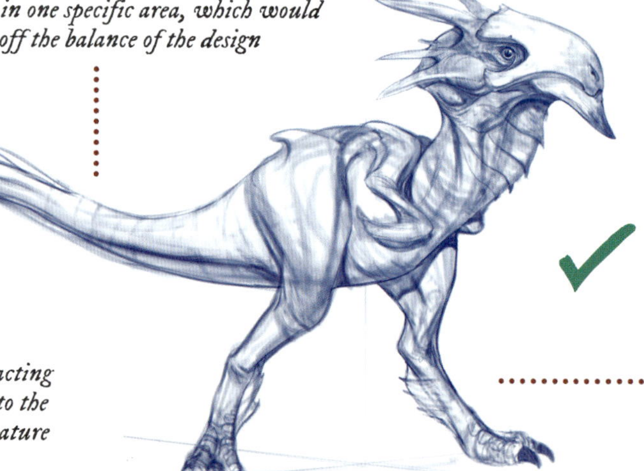

DETAIL LEVELS ✔

The mane is communicated to the viewer mainly through its volume indicating that it is fur – rather than every hair being rendered, which could be distracting

The head of the creature has been rendered to a higher level of detail to draw the viewer's eye – although viewers will naturally gravitate to the face of a character or creature, this technique helps reinforce that

FLOW & WEIGHT

The creature is comprised of a series of "S" and "C" curves that provide a natural flow to the design and pose, preventing the viewer from getting stuck in one specific area, which would throw off the balance of the design

The legs are large and feel as though they make up half of the creature's size; only primary forms (the structure of the leg as a whole) have been rendered, as well as some secondary details (tendons and plating)

The tail is upright, acting as a counterweight to the large skull of the creature

The legs are split evenly and planted firmly on the ground, helping distribute the weight of the torso and head that rest in the middle, giving balance to the pose

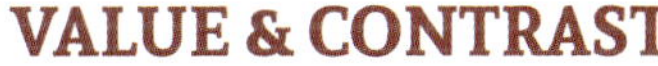

VALUE & CONTRAST

COLOR & SATURATION

Value ranges are smaller, meaning a lesser variety of values on the lower portion of the creature to avoid conflicting with the areas the viewer should focus on

The head is the most contrasting in terms of value range to ensure viewers connect with this the most — the value range will drive the eye to it

Like value, utilize chroma, or the saturation of color, to direct the viewer's eye to the face of the creature

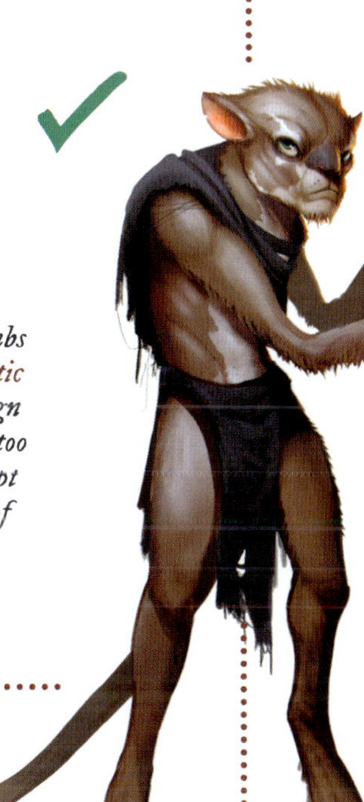

The pops of value from the areas of negative space between the shapes offer balance to the piece, without fighting the values of the creature itself

Larger areas like the limbs and tail are less chromatic — as they are larger design elements, making them too chromatic would disrupt the balance of the rest of the creature

Muted colors knock back shadowed areas and elements of lesser importance; specific accents of color harmonize the creature, reinforcing the balance

LACKING BALANCE

The value range is completely equal throughout the entire body; the eye has nowhere to focus and everything competes for the viewer's attention at once

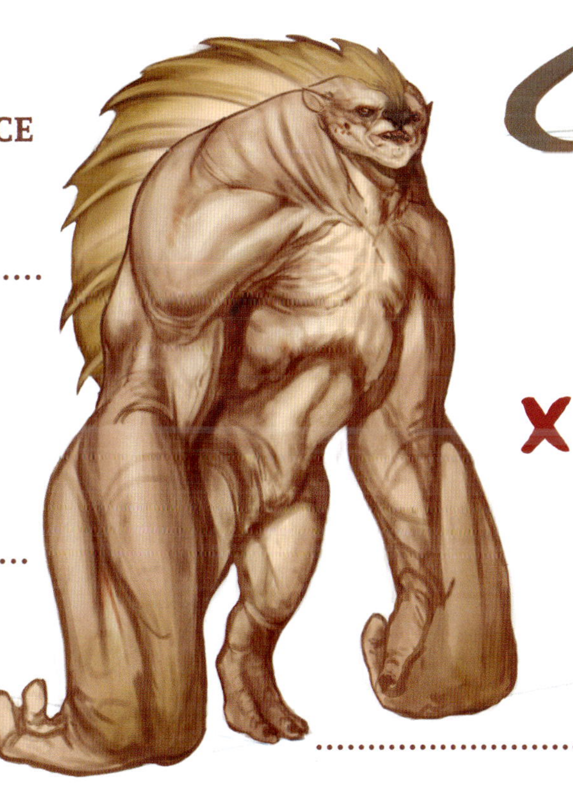

The massive forearms are isolated from the anatomy of the rest of the body, making the creature feel cartoonish and ill-defined — nothing else on it is as dominant, making it look proportionally unbalanced

The feet are positioned and posed behind the central mass of the body, which gives the impression that the creature is going to fall forward, literally throwing off the balance of the design

REPETITION

Repetition serves as a symbolic roadmap to direct the viewer's eye throughout a design. By repeating elements, we create a rhythm that harmonizes the creature. Elements that repeat at strategic points on a design can unify the piece. Even if we make extreme design choices, duplicating them at specific points and varying their sizes will link a piece together and make a cohesive and purposeful creature.

Repeating elements could take the form of progressively larger spikes that run down the dorsal plates of a building-sized lizard. They could be grotesque bulbous growths on a mutated carnivore, which at first feel isolated and unique, but are unified by their shape and material. Repetition helps prevent a concept from falling into what is referred to as the "chimera" pitfall of design, where isolated design elements appear to be stuck together without any discernible unifying quality.

Often we think of repetition on tertiary design elements, such as scales, feathers, or spikes. However, we can also use secondary forms like muscle groups to create new and interesting anatomical structures, adding believable function to our imagined beasts.

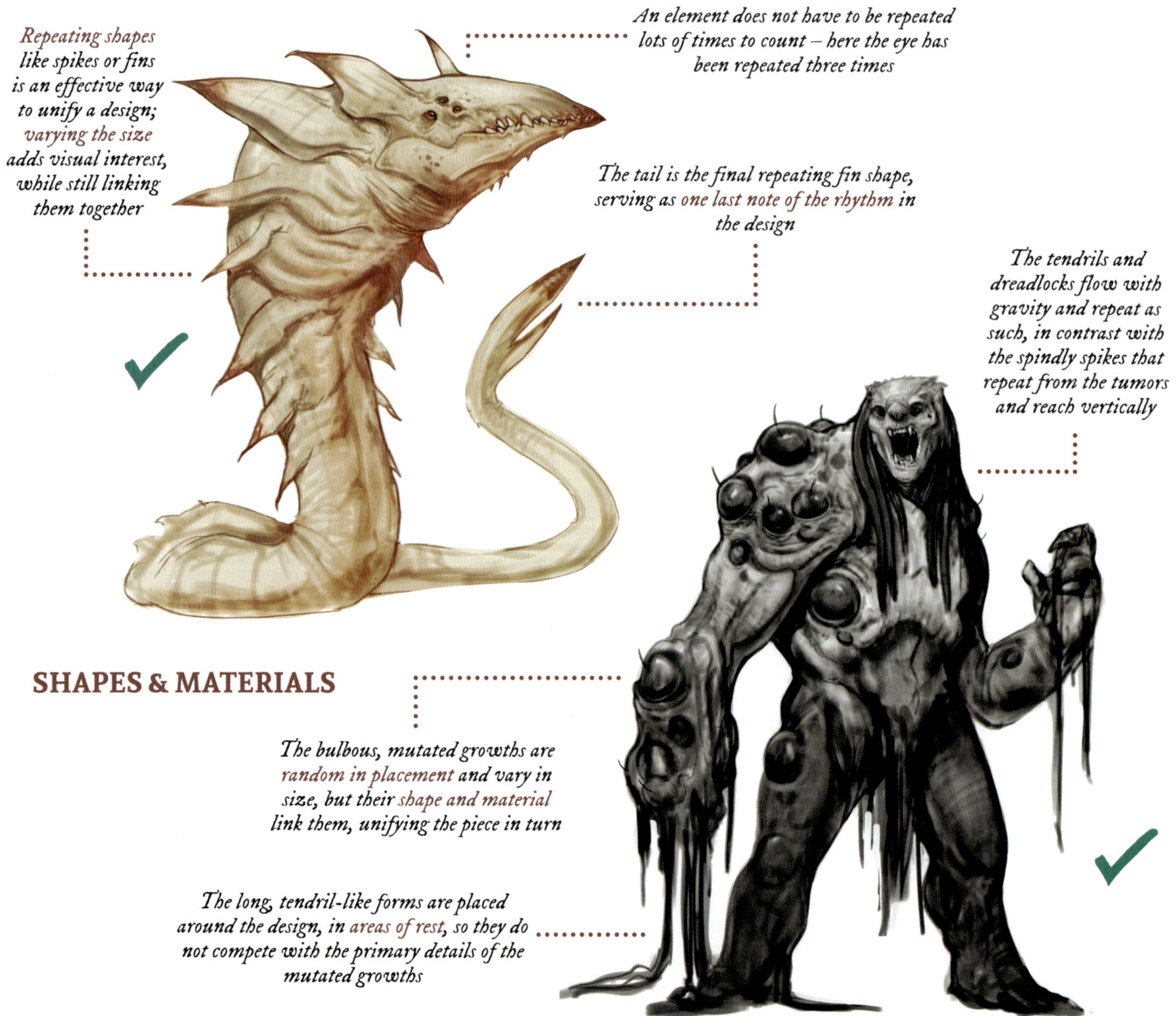

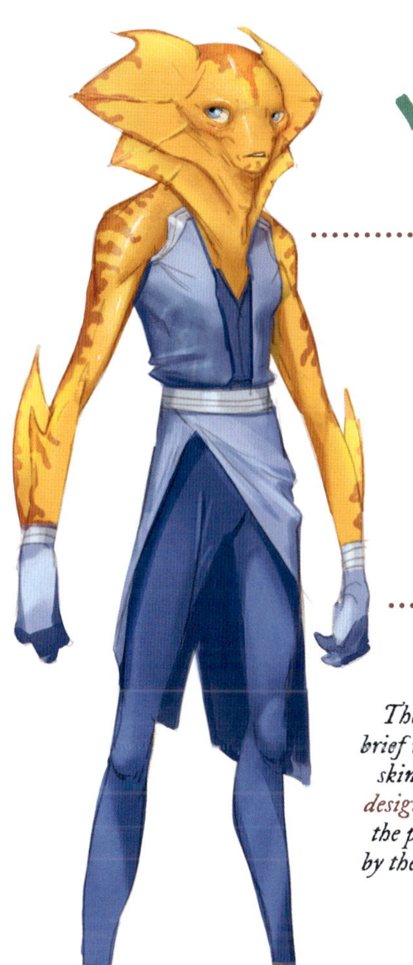

PATTERNS & COLORS

Repeating patterns of dark orange unify the skin surface of this alien

Blue is the dominant color of the design, but it is broken up into different values that repeat throughout the design to break up the uniformity

The gap in the trousers offers a brief repetition of the golden yellow skin to harmonize the top of the design with the bottom – likewise, the piercing blue eyes surrounded by the golden alien complexion link to the blue costume

The long feather-like tails are not only isolated in terms of their material, but the colors are isolated and are not found anywhere else in the design

The rear legs have a hoof-like structure, whereas the front limbs have cat-like pads and claws – this design difference isolates both elements, preventing the piece from feeling cohesive

Industry tip

You do not have to depict every wrinkle or hair, but the intended audience needs to be able to understand the form and function of the creature fully. A design that is unclear to the intended audience will usually be disregarded. Communication of shape is crucial to the success of any design, so be sure to present your design in a way that clearly demonstrates its form.

NO REPETITION

The green feathers represent both a shape language and color choice that are isolated to this one specific area and found nowhere else – this makes them stand out in an odd way, rather than as an interesting design choice

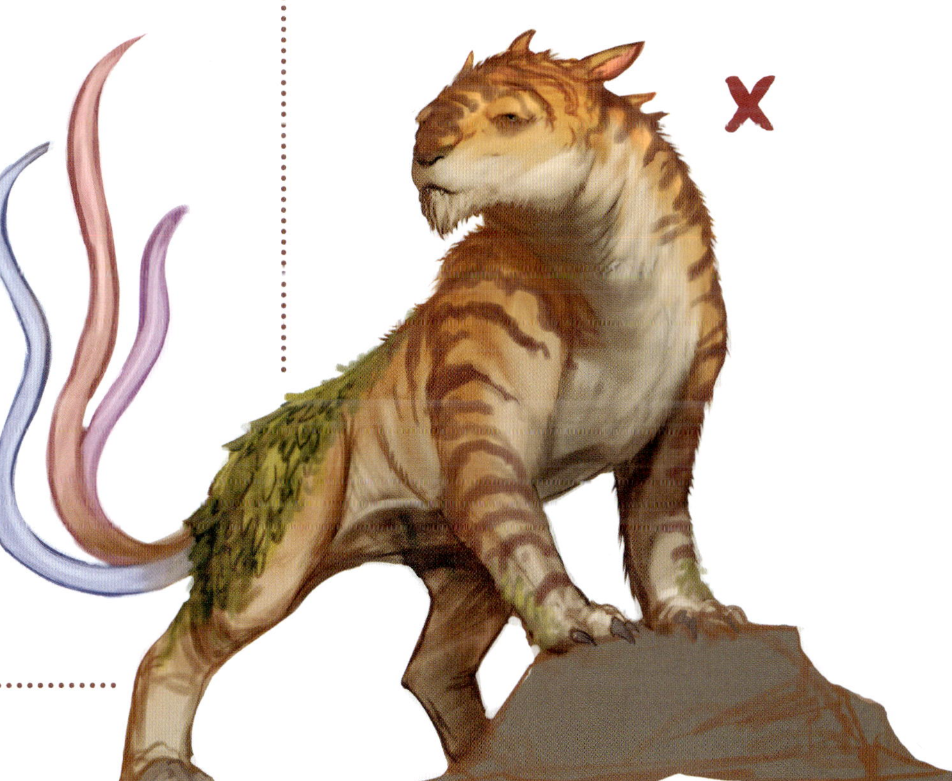

CONTRAST

Contrast is the proverbial "spice" in the design recipe that adds visual interest and guides the viewer's attention around an image. Contrast can present itself in numerous ways:

- **Contrasting the values** of an image focuses the audience's attention

- **Contrasting color** creates vibrancy or even reveals traits of the creature's characteristics

- **Contrast in detail** serves as visual relief, allowing the viewer to focus on specific elements the designer has chosen, then offering moments of rest on elements non-essential to the overall design

- **Different shapes** can be contrasted against one another for visual appeal, but can also be used to add complexity to their character

For example, well-described details around a character's eyes, against a simpler construction of the head, allow the viewer to connect and read emotion with clarity and ease. A creature with hard, razor-sharp plates on its back can be made interesting by contrasting those plates with a soft, fleshy underbelly.

These different elements of value, color, detail, and shape can be used together to make the visual contrast even stronger. An area of focus can utilize more refined detail and a deeper chromatic color juxtaposed against a broader, simpler shape, muted in color, to add complexity. Aggressive, sharp angles can be contrasted against soft curves, rendered with different values, to draw the viewer's eye.

Alternating and modifying these combinations can produce countless results. Utilizing them will not only make a piece more visually appealing, but can strengthen the substance of your concept too. Contrast is a key element for remaining in control of your piece and guiding the viewer through it, which is crucial when verbal or written influence is not available.

VALUE & COLOR

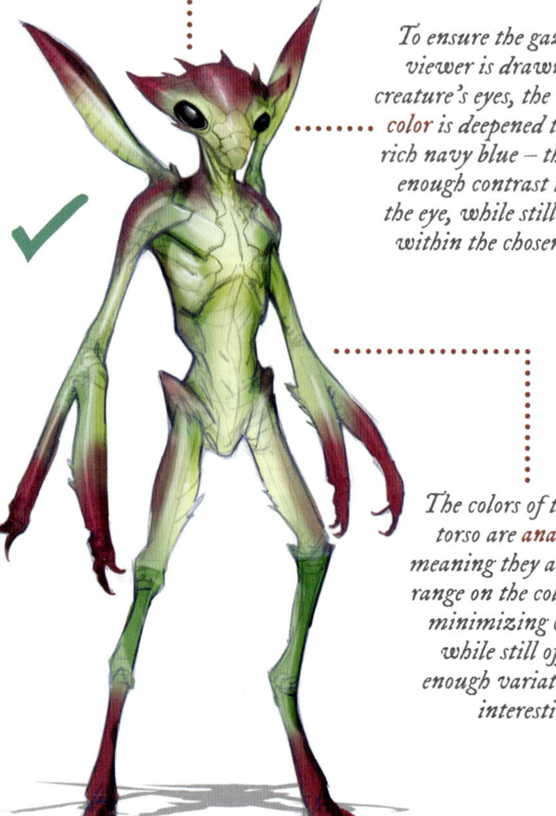

The largest value range, from light to dark, is rendered within the face of the character, guiding the viewer's eye to it

The claws are kept within a limited value range, so as not to compete or conflict with higher-contrast areas that require the viewer's focus (such as the face)

The value range minimizes near the feet and tail of the creature – areas that do not necessarily require the viewer's attention

Complementary color schemes add visually appealing contrast; adding them to your creature will harmonize and unify the design

To ensure the gaze of the viewer is drawn to the creature's eyes, the value and color is deepened to a dark, rich navy blue – this creates enough contrast to guide the eye, while still working within the chosen palette

The colors of the inner torso are analogous, meaning they are close in range on the color wheel, minimizing contrast while still offering enough variation to be interesting

DETAIL & DEFINITION

Areas like the arms and legs are rendered with enough definition and detail to resolve the functionality of the anatomy, while serving as a transition into areas of lesser detail and focus

The level of detail is increased around the head of the creature to guide the viewer's attention to it

Areas of less importance are not rendered as fully – this is purely an aesthetic choice and not a definitive rule; it is just something to experiment with to avoid conflict with detailed areas

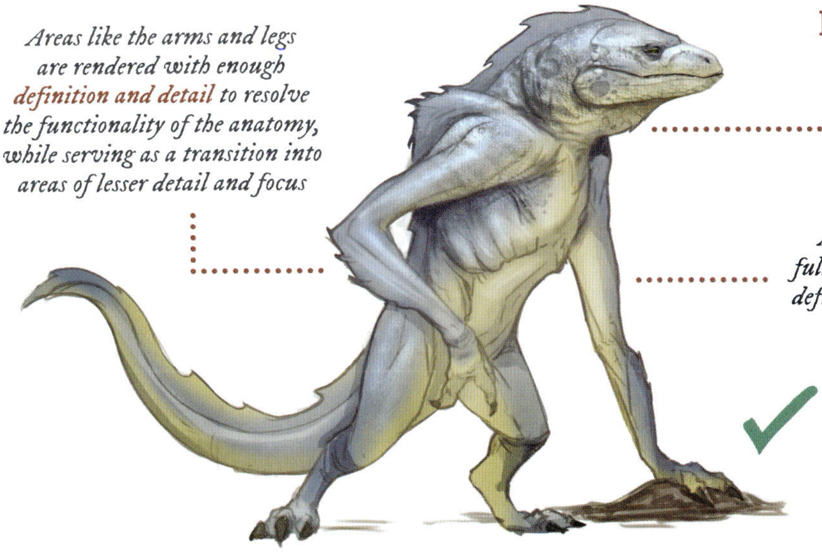

SHAPE & FORM

The creature's face is rounder in shape, contrasting with the angular plating around the skull and chin, and the sharp angles of the ears

The sharp plates contrast with the soft, round underbelly of the design; not only is this visually engaging, but the distinct difference in form also adds vulnerability, which makes the design more interesting

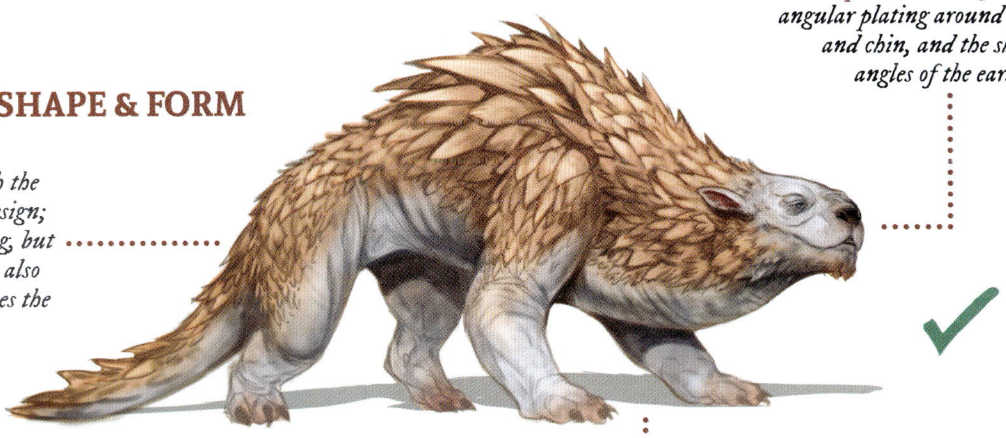

The feet, though part of the fleshy underbelly, are contrasted against the sharpness of the claws

NO COHERENT CONTRAST

The colors are analogous for the most part, with a couple of pops of color – overall, the color scheme is muted and boring

There are details all over the design (in the face, shoulders, and tail) in equal measure, competing for the viewer's attention, with no bridging areas in between those elements to create flow

There is no clear contrast in shape or scale – everything is fairly equal, resulting in no clear indication of hierarchy in importance

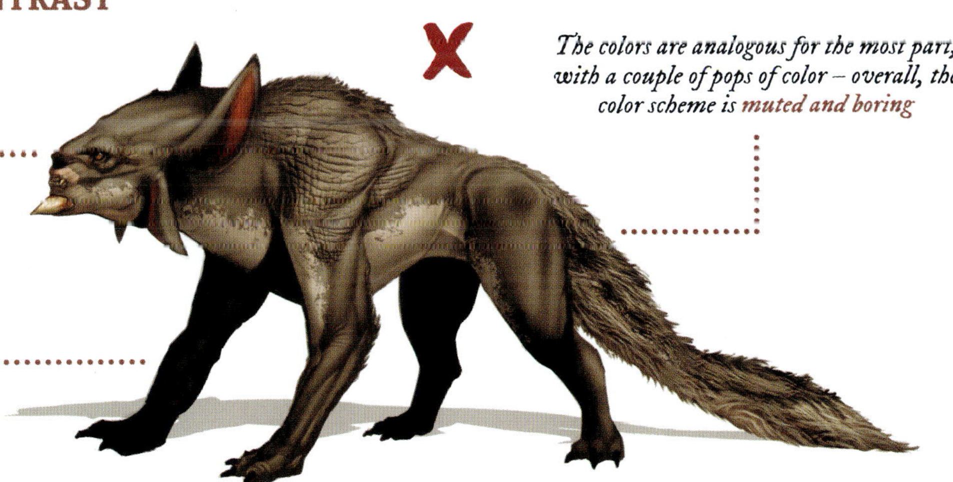

SCALE & PERSPECTIVE

Perspective, one of the most crucial design principles, is often ignored in creature design. On hearing the word perspective, people often think of educational exercises, locating a left and a right vanishing point to frame windows and doors on a city street, or mapping ellipses in space to block out the intricate wheel of a car. However, the moment students or beginner artists switch to organic forms such as characters or creatures, this essential design process is often overlooked.

Beginners are often intimidated by the organic forms of tissue, muscle, and bone wrapping, intersecting, and enveloping each other, unsure of how to visualize these in three-dimensional space. It is one thing to draw a box in perspective, but another thing entirely to map out an intricate creature, especially one that does not exist yet. However, complex forms can be reduced to simpler "primitive shapes," and you can use what you know about blocking these shapes in perspective to start creating more complex forms.

Perspective is essential to demonstrate the scale of a creature. Low vantage points can make a creature feel massive. Conversely, a higher vantage point can make a creature look smaller. Perspective is important when describing scale, but we can also use the size of forms and details, and their relationship to one another, to convey size. Increasing a creature's eyes to occupy the majority of their skull shape tends to make the creature feel smaller. Making tertiary details such as wrinkles extremely small, or removing them altogether, can make a creature feel massive. Pay close attention to these elements to convey the proper scale of a creature, especially when you do not have the benefit of an environment or accompanying character to use as a scale indicator.

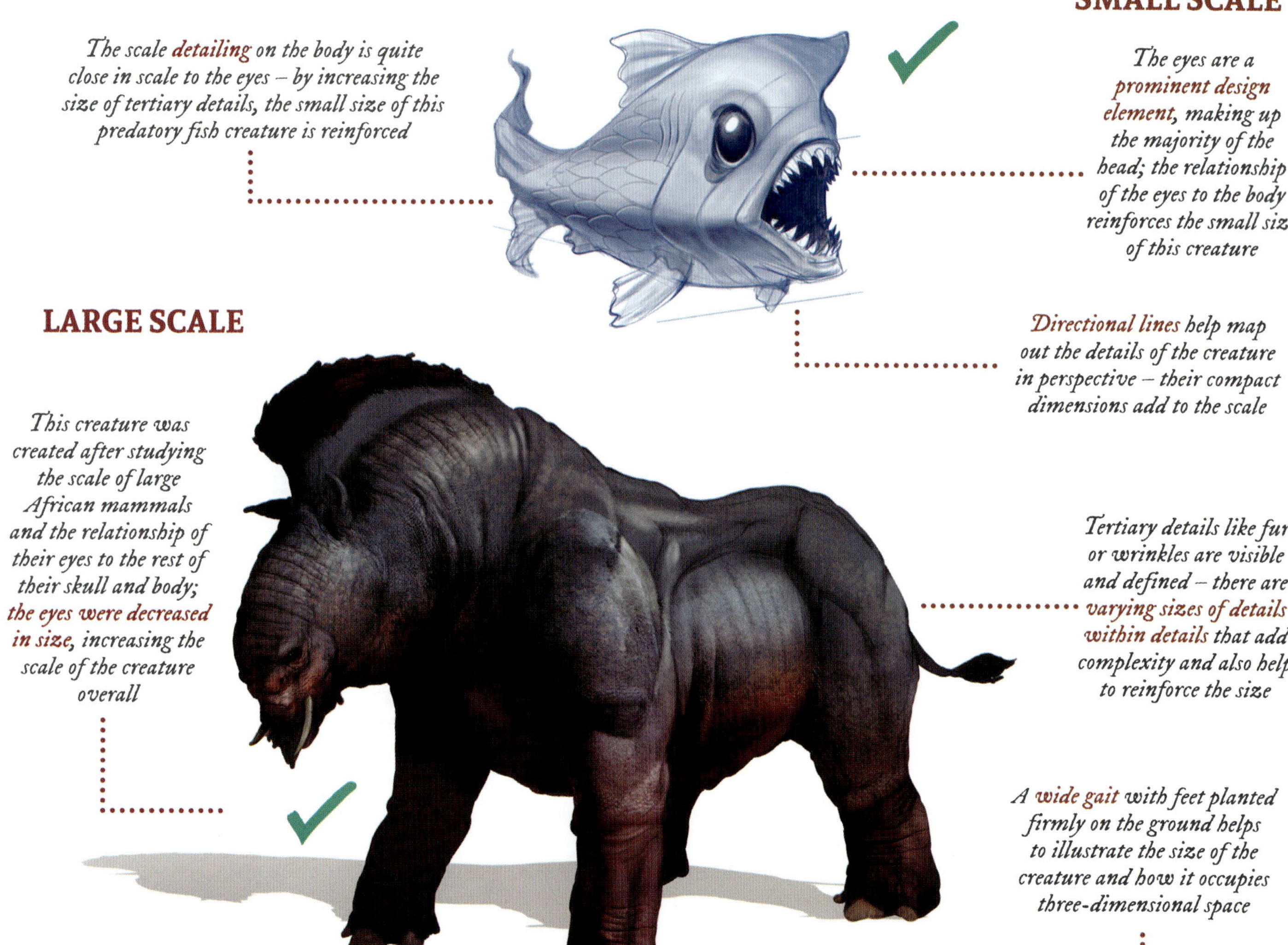

SMALL SCALE

The scale detailing on the body is quite close in scale to the eyes — by increasing the size of tertiary details, the small size of this predatory fish creature is reinforced

The eyes are a prominent design element, making up the majority of the head; the relationship of the eyes to the body reinforces the small size of this creature

Directional lines help map out the details of the creature in perspective — their compact dimensions add to the scale

LARGE SCALE

This creature was created after studying the scale of large African mammals and the relationship of their eyes to the rest of their skull and body; the eyes were decreased in size, increasing the scale of the creature overall

Tertiary details like fur or wrinkles are visible and defined — there are varying sizes of details within details that add complexity and also help to reinforce the size

A wide gait with feet planted firmly on the ground helps to illustrate the size of the creature and how it occupies three-dimensional space

Bottom image © Kyle Brown

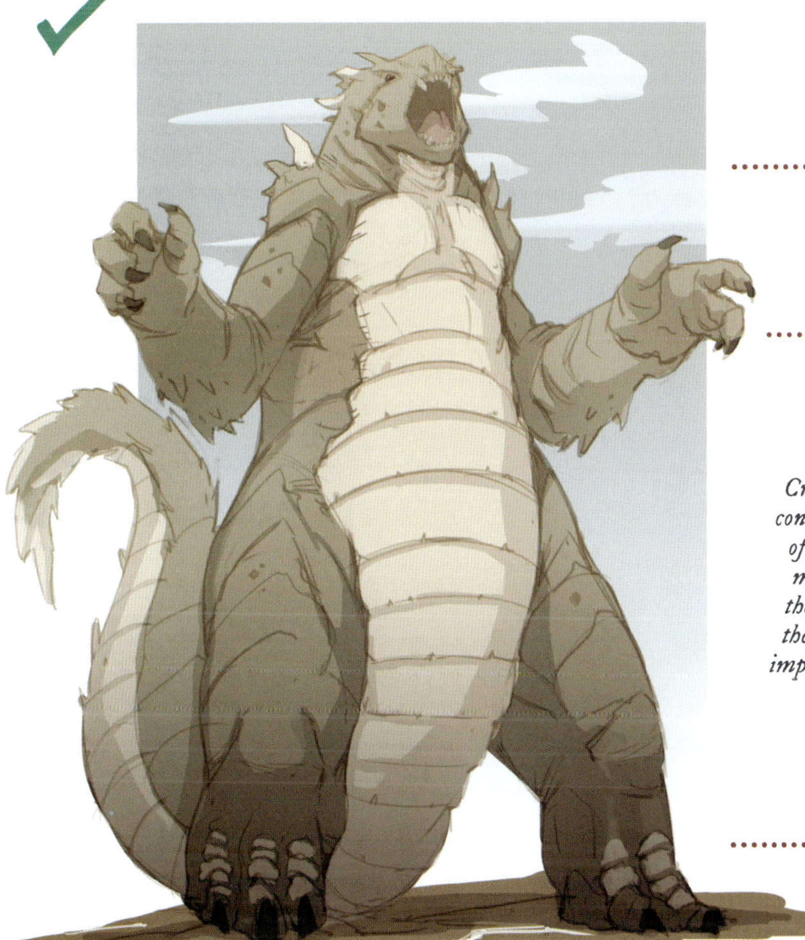

DRAMATIC PERSPECTIVE

Atmospheric perspective is added toward the top of the creature, near its head, to illustrate that the viewer, from their low vantage point, is witnessing a creature so massive that the atmosphere affects how it is viewed

Three-point perspective is used to exaggerate the direction of the creature and to reinforce the idea that it is the size of a building

Crisp shadows help convey the sheer scale of this *kaiju-sized* monster, creating the impression that the only light source impacting it is the sun

Visual interest

Varying the scale of details also adds visual interest, making a design more engaging and intriguing to the viewer. Do not forget to balance areas of visual interest with areas of visual rest, or the results may appear too busy and distracting.

INCOHERENT SCALE & PERSPECTIVE

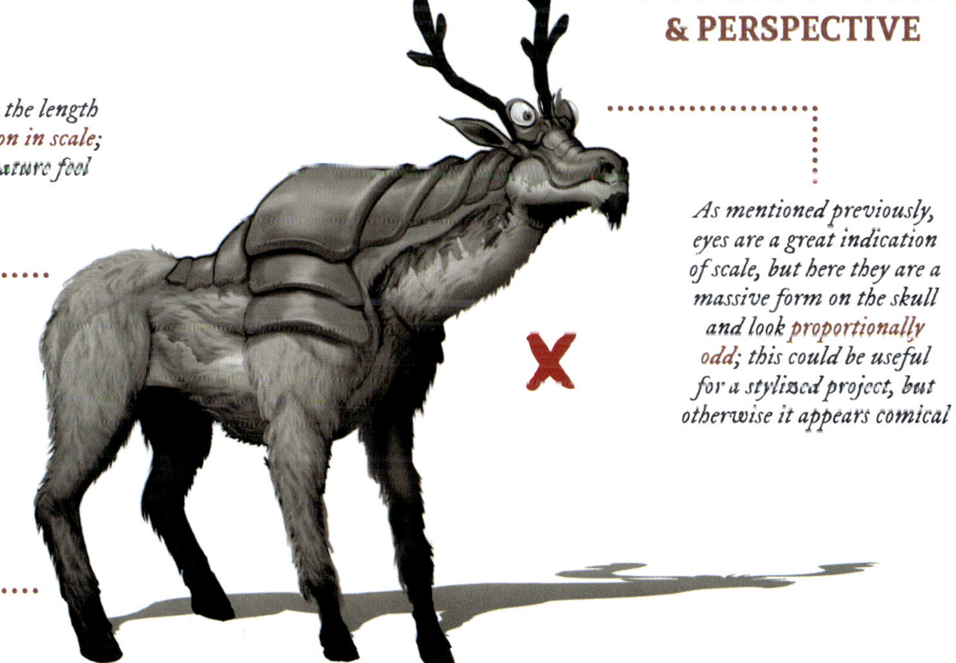

The strands of fur and the plates that run the length of the spine are both large and *lack variation in scale;* the length of these elements makes the creature feel smaller than the intended scale

As mentioned previously, eyes are a great indication of scale, but here they are a massive form on the skull and look *proportionally odd;* this could be useful for a stylised project, but otherwise it appears comical

The background legs appear longer than the foreground legs because they extend past what is visually intended as the *ground plane;* this is a common perspective mistake, and immediately breaks the illusion that this design inhabits a three-dimensional world

SHAPE LANGUAGE

Shape language is not just a tool for stylized work, but can be a hugely beneficial starting point for any creature design, whether for an animation project or a grisly photo-realistic monster. As humans we have been educated on how to read these basic shapes. They subconsciously inform us of the nature of a character or creature. Building a creature out of sharp angles and strong action lines can create a design that is intimidating, aggressive, and deadly. Shifting the angles down, to make a top-heavy, upside-down triangle, will demonstrate courage and strength. Curved edges evoke confidence and kindness; a character you can rely on, empathize with, and trust. A square or blocky build promotes stability, strength, and reassurance.

But what does shape language mean when creating an alien beast of burden or a carnivorous insectoid?

Shape does not just help reinforce personality, but can also evoke emotion in the viewer, whether that emotion is trust, kindness, fear, or caution. A creature's "on-screen" actions demonstrate its function and role in the story, but its shape helps the audience clearly understand its purpose within a frame or moment in time - thanks to a set of specifically designed shapes.

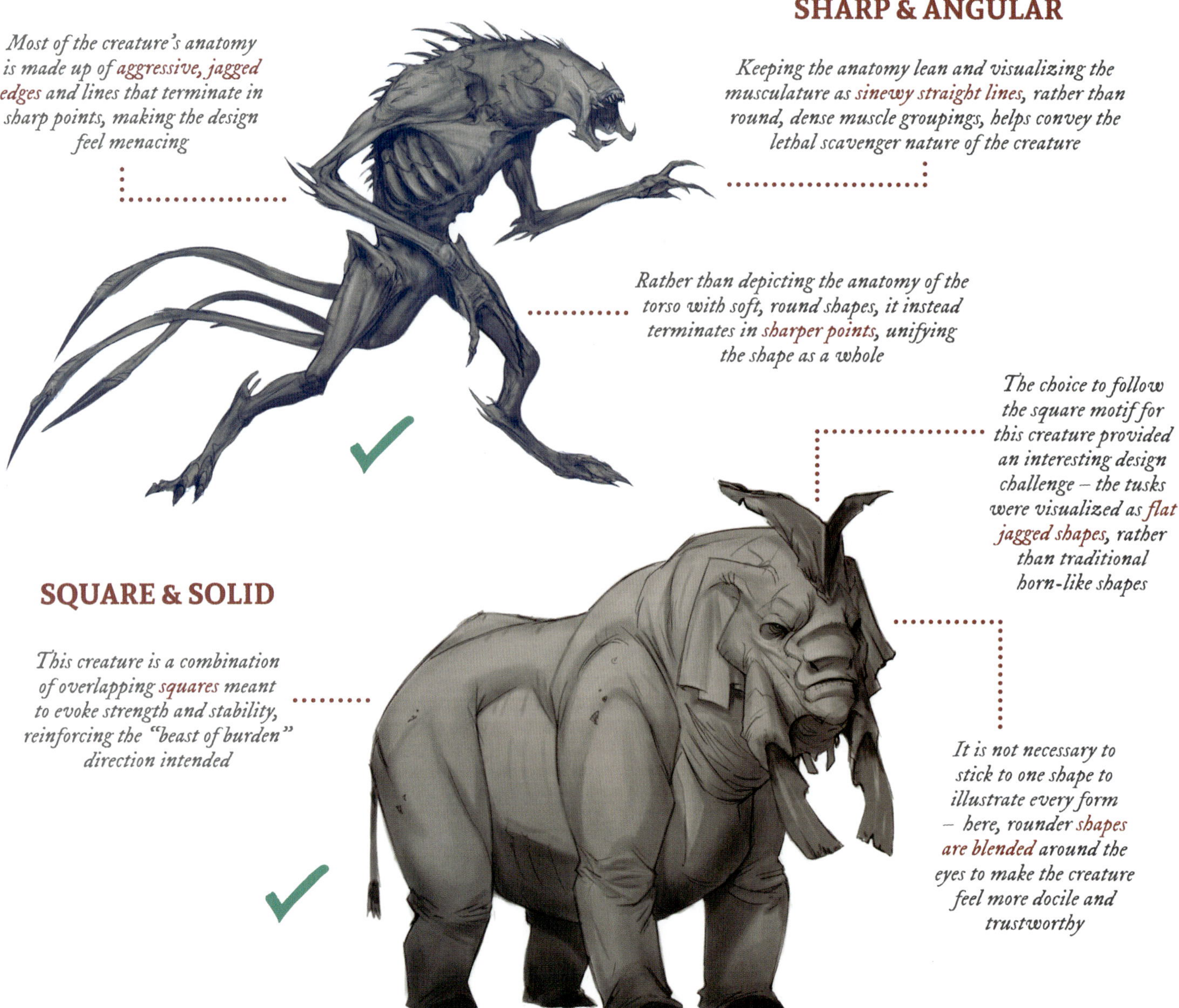

SHARP & ANGULAR

Most of the creature's anatomy is made up of aggressive, jagged edges and lines that terminate in sharp points, making the design feel menacing

Keeping the anatomy lean and visualizing the musculature as sinewy straight lines, rather than round, dense muscle groupings, helps convey the lethal scavenger nature of the creature

Rather than depicting the anatomy of the torso with soft, round shapes, it instead terminates in sharper points, unifying the shape as a whole

The choice to follow the square motif for this creature provided an interesting design challenge — the tusks were visualized as flat jagged shapes, rather than traditional horn-like shapes

SQUARE & SOLID

This creature is a combination of overlapping squares meant to evoke strength and stability, reinforcing the "beast of burden" direction intended

It is not necessary to stick to one shape to illustrate every form — here, rounder shapes are blended around the eyes to make the creature feel more docile and trustworthy

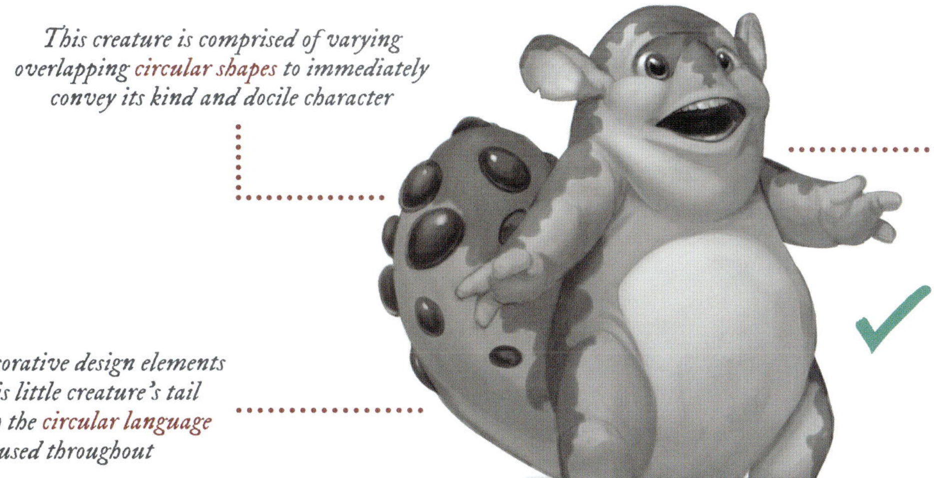

This creature is comprised of varying overlapping *circular shapes* to immediately convey its kind and docile character

Care was taken to ensure elements like the mouth and teeth also followed the *oval shape language*

SOFT & ROUND

The decorative design elements of this little creature's tail follow the *circular language* used throughout

INCOHESIVE SHAPES

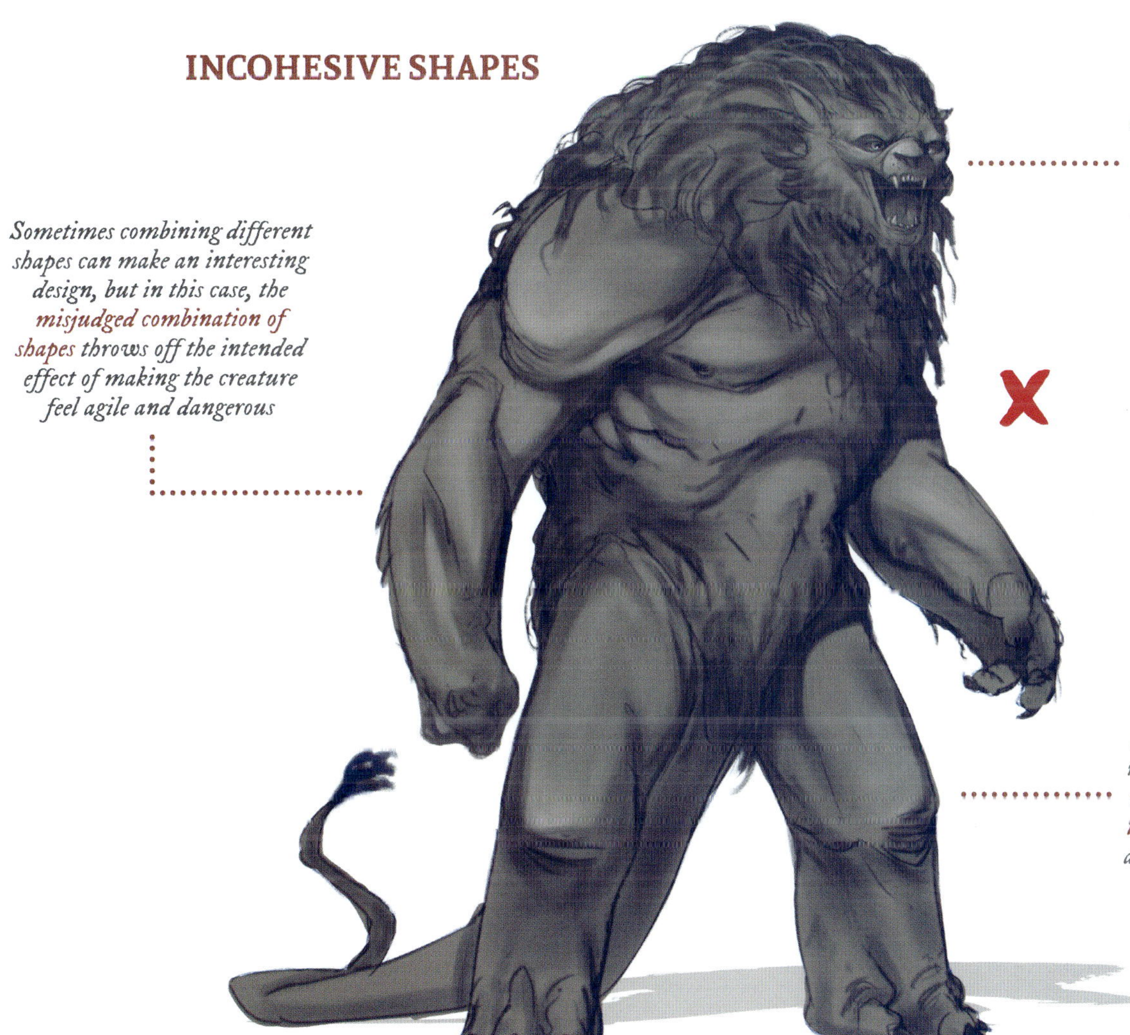

Sometimes combining different shapes can make an interesting design, but in this case, the *misjudged combination of shapes* throws off the intended effect of making the creature feel agile and dangerous

The T-zone of the face is based on a sharp, triangular shape to demonstrate the creature's ferocity, but the surrounding mane *does not accentuate* this choice

The legs are blocky in construction, which makes them sturdy and strong, but not fast and limber; on top of that, the arms *do not mirror the same form language*, and are long and rounded instead, confusing the design's logic

DYNAMISM

Creature design is all about communication. What is the best way to showcase the design, its characteristics, and its locomotion, without presenting it in a way that obstructs the form or confuses the silhouette? So much of a creature's energy can be conveyed with adjustments to the posture, position, and pose of the design. This process should not be confused with key-frame illustration, which is the process of putting characters in a specific scene from the project.

It is more important to present a creature in a clear and concise manner, rather than force it into an extreme pose. A slight turn of the head, the lowering or raising of the limbs, and the shift of the hips into a *contrapposto* position can add life to a design. Some details, such as wisps of hair or dripping saliva, can provide a sense of force or direction.

It is important that when placing limbs or features such as tails, spikes, or feathers, you avoid visual tangencies and parallel placement. This means that shapes should not all run in the same direction or abut each other in a visually confusing way. Instead, they should overlap and intersect clearly to give the impression of natural movement. If elements of your design do not vary in direction, shape, and scale, they can feel stiff and unnatural.

If the creature is meant to be intelligent, life and energy can be infused into the design by posturing the hands. Elements such as tails and spikes can also be used to emote and energize the creature. The more you can do to add energy into a piece, the more the viewer can connect with the creature and visualize it as a living, breathing entity.

DYNAMIC ACTION

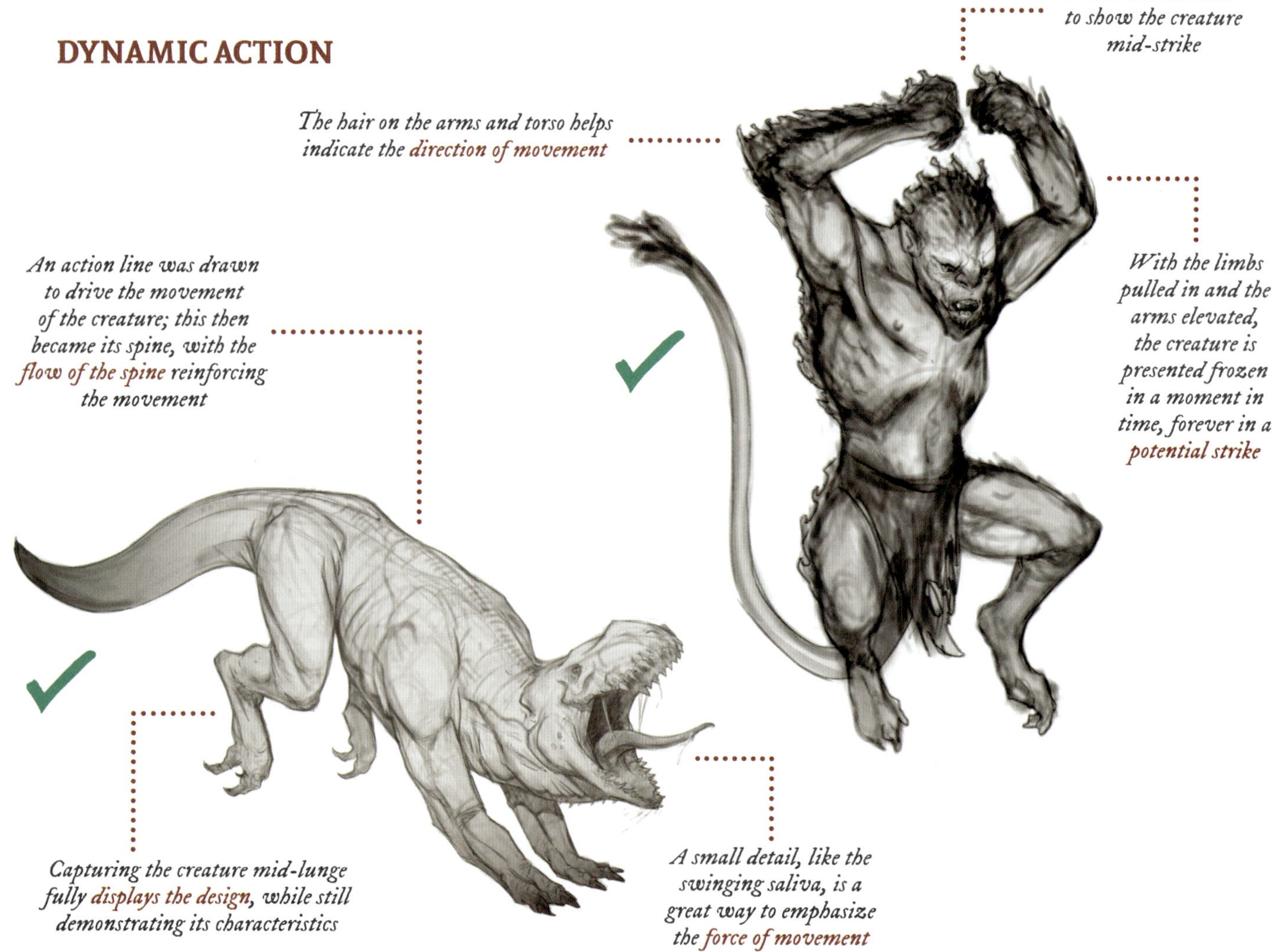

Arms are elevated to show the creature mid-strike

The hair on the arms and torso helps indicate the direction of movement

An action line was drawn to drive the movement of the creature; this then became its spine, with the flow of the spine reinforcing the movement

With the limbs pulled in and the arms elevated, the creature is presented frozen in a moment in time, forever in a potential strike

Capturing the creature mid-lunge fully displays the design, while still demonstrating its characteristics

A small detail, like the swinging saliva, is a great way to emphasize the force of movement

SUBTLE FLOW

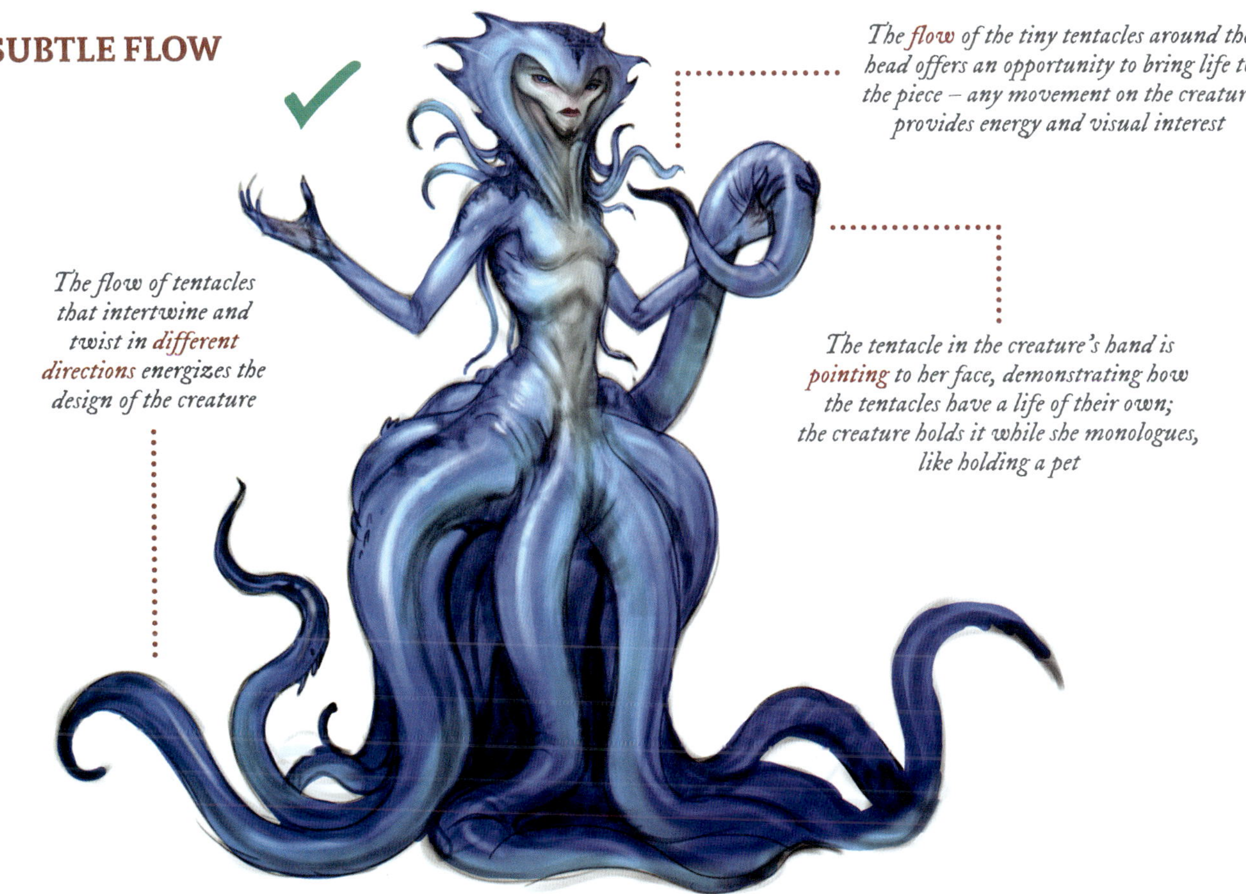

The flow of the tiny tentacles around the head offers an opportunity to bring life to the piece – any movement on the creature provides energy and visual interest

The flow of tentacles that intertwine and twist in different directions energizes the design of the creature

The tentacle in the creature's hand is pointing to her face, demonstrating how the tentacles have a life of their own; the creature holds it while she monologues, like holding a pet

RIGID & UNNATURAL

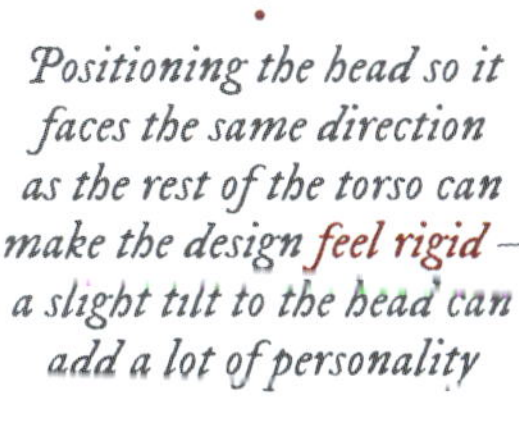

Here the arms are mirrored and stuck to the sides of the body, making the design feel stiff

Positioning the head so it faces the same direction as the rest of the torso can make the design feel rigid – a slight tilt to the head can add a lot of personality

The legs and feet are parallel to one another – this makes the creature look more like a statue than a living being that would naturally shift its weight and position

Industry tip

You can use the principles shown in this chapter to create a checklist of needs that the client may have for your design. Disregarding their needs shows a lack of understanding, and a breakdown in communication, and will mean you cannot provide a visual answer to what they require for their project.

Creature design in the industry

"Depending on who you are working with and what content you are working on, certain expectations about your designs will need to be met in order for you to fulfill the client's brief"

By Andrew Baker

DESIGNING FOR EXECUTION & BUDGET

In this chapter we will look at some of the factors to consider when creating designs for the entertainment industry. Creating creature designs can be exciting and feel limitless at times, but creating for certain professional briefs and projects presents many challenges that must be considered in order for the designs to be successful.

When working within the industry it is important to consider the final execution of the creature, as well as the budget, as these will greatly affect the end result. Most creature designs when produced will fall into two categories: **physical or practical effects**, or **digital effects**.

With physical or practical effects, where the creature is made with real materials, the limitations generally revolve around the design fitting **a performer's body**, or the ability to perform **puppetry or animatronics** on set. This means a creature must be built around a human silhouette or a physical rig that needs to be incorporated into the design. The creator must consider what the performer can and cannot do, as this affects how the creature will move and interact with others.

Whether using a suit, puppetry, animatronics, or a combination of these, building and maintaining these physical designs must be accounted for in the project's cost. Pushing the boundaries of physical effects can result in remarkable achievements with the use of human actors, and to this date, one of the most iconic creatures was a man in a suit: H.R. Giger's Alien.

Digital effects offer **fewer limitations in movement and design**, but provide their own set of considerations. Weight and physical presence need to be created in the image or model to make the design feel believable – they are not innately present like they are in practical effects. Studying the movement and characteristics of real creatures or humans will help you add weight and presence to your creatures, making them move and act more realistically. While a digital design may require no physical construction, it will still require teams of artists to make it, with access to sufficient resources, including **software and hardware**. Motion capture technology combines the physical and digital worlds by using a suited actor as the basis for a computer-generated design.

Either of these techniques will create challenges for you as the designer, but the most important thing to consider is how to make your creature believable. Your design should belong in the world it was created for. Any genre or style will require all of its participants to follow the same rules, as they exist in the same environment. If these rules appear broken, they must be broken for a good reason. If your design is going to stand alongside real-life actors, it is important for the texture, weight, and movement of that creature to be as believable as the characters with whom it will share the screen.

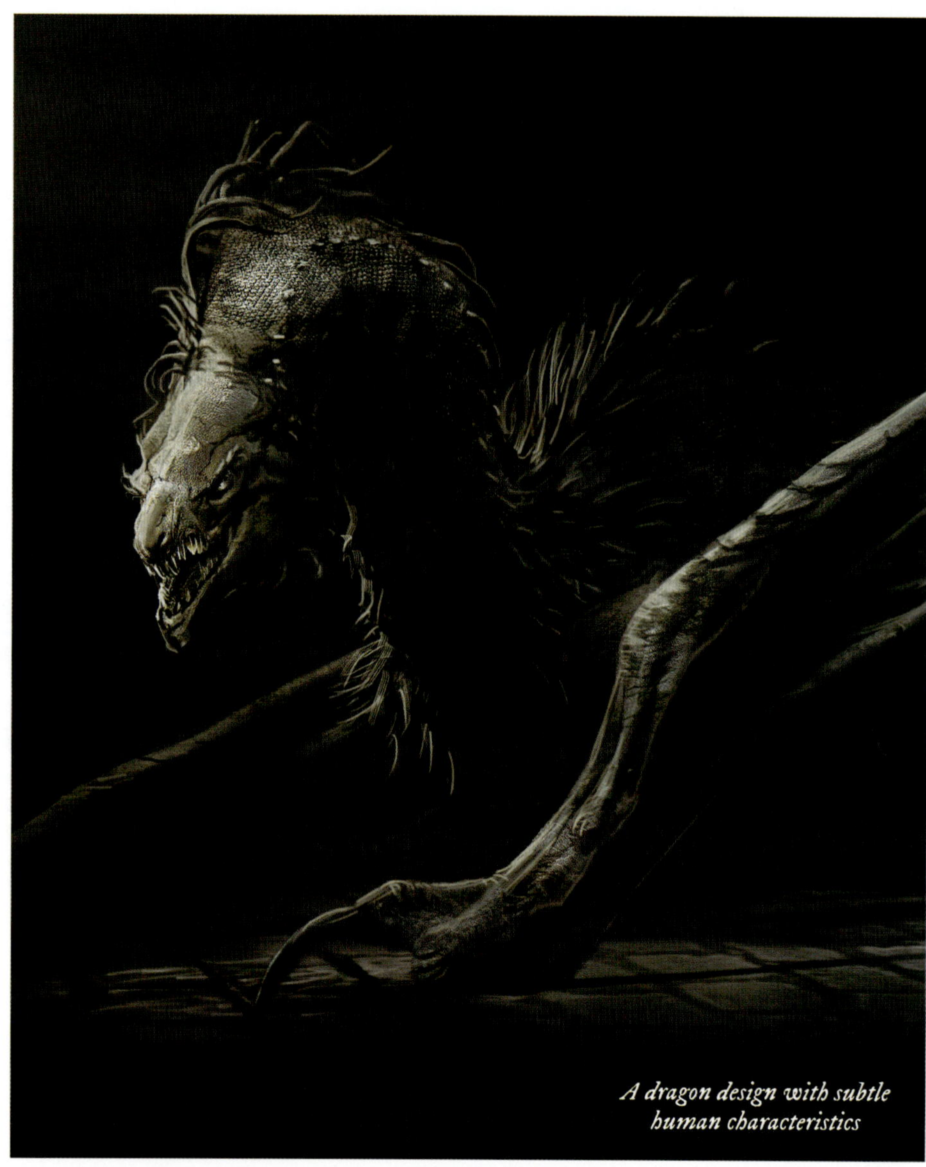

A dragon design with subtle human characteristics

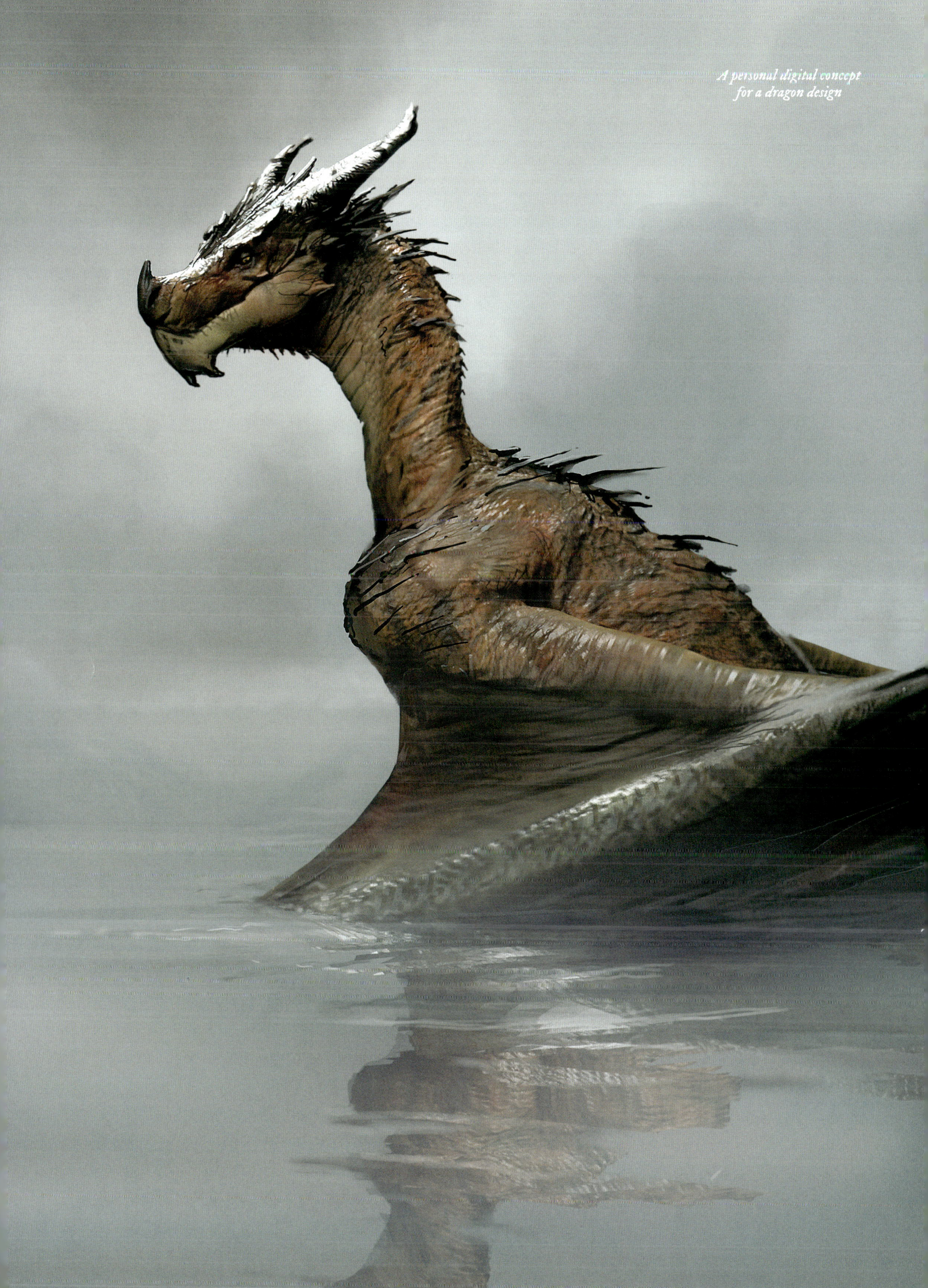

A personal digital concept
for a dragon design

CREATURES THAT ARE CHARACTERS

Designing for the industry often requires the artist to incorporate intelligence and personality into a creature. The brief will often outline characteristics and traits that need to be translated into the final concept. Basing your design on real-world interpretations of these traits can make your creature feel genuine. As an example exercise, find an actor or personality you find appealing and try to capture their performance style or look within your creature design.

One industry example of this is the dragon Smaug from *The Hobbit* films – without knowing who was cast for the role, you can define the key characteristics of the creature. From the original book, we know that Smaug is intelligent and able to speak, and this information can start to inform our design choices. For example, having slightly softer lips instead of a beak-like mouth would allow him to perform certain phonemes, helping to convince the viewer of his ability to speak and his intelligence. The ability of the eyes to look straight on, much like an eagle, would also allow the dragon to feel like a character without relying too much on typical humanoid cues, which would take away from his menacing presence.

Popular culture is full of creature designs that are also unique characters, ranging from beasts like Smaug to designs that are more clearly humanoid, like Yoda.

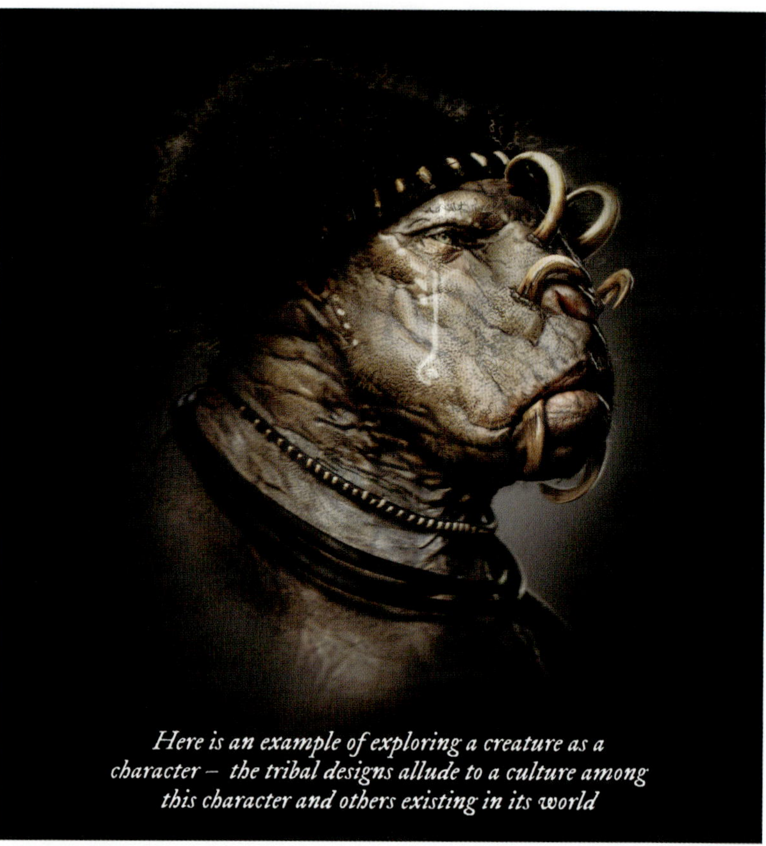

Here is an example of exploring a creature as a character – the tribal designs allude to a culture among this character and others existing in its world

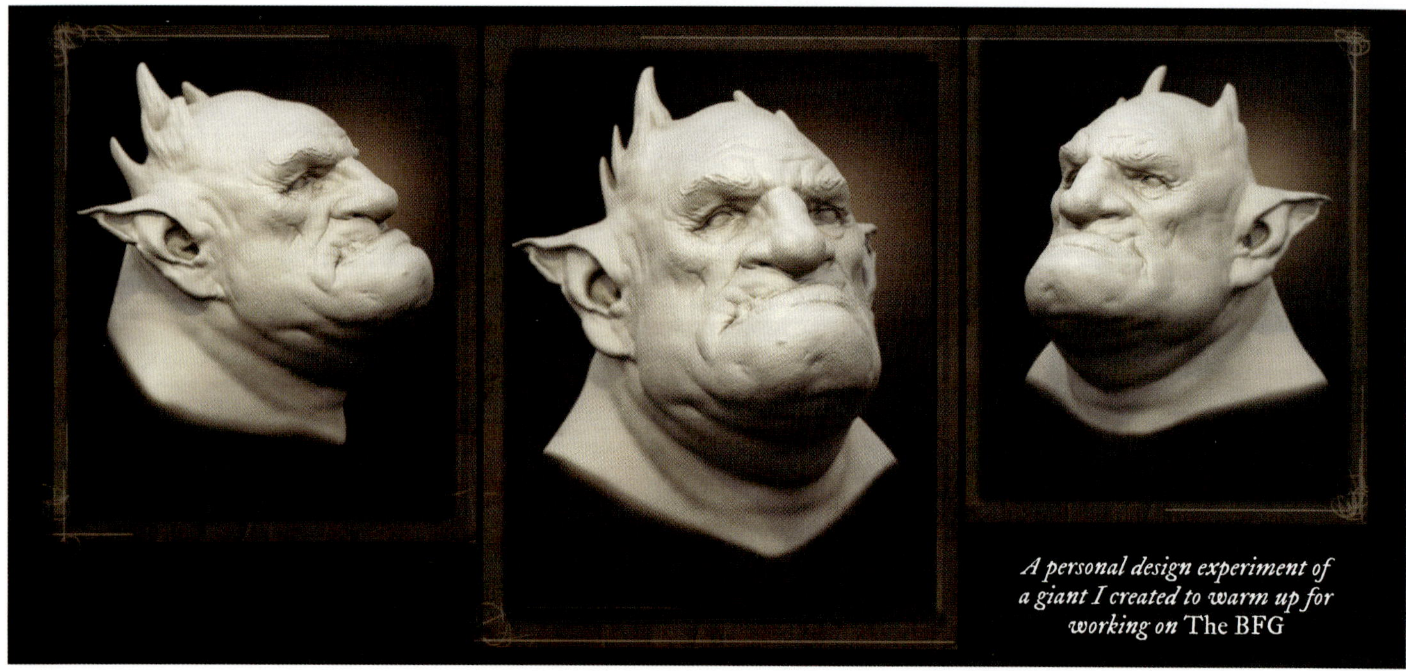

A personal design experiment of a giant I created to warm up for working on The BFG

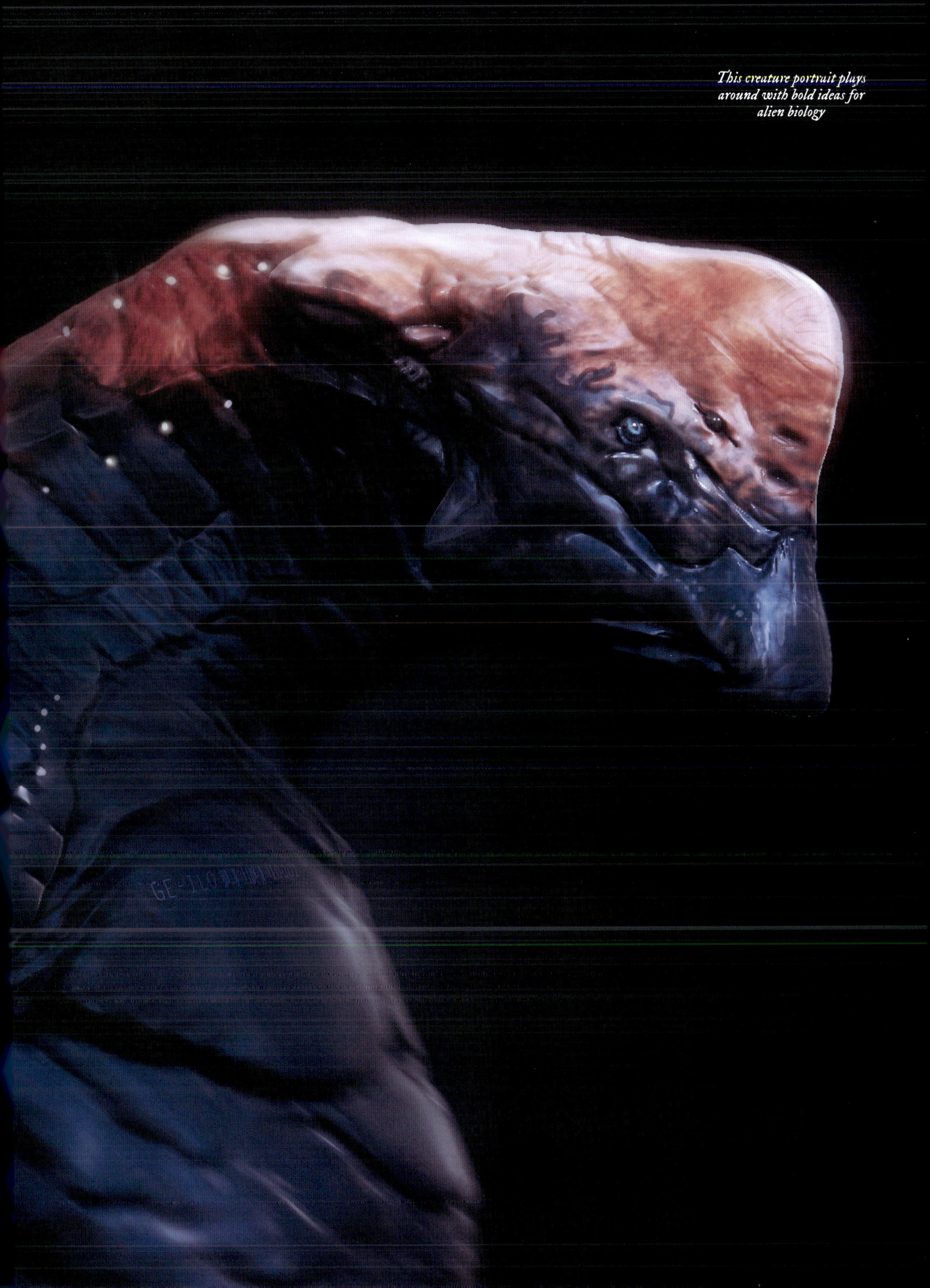

This creature portrait plays around with bold ideas for alien biology

DESIGNING FOR GENRE

Although genres can be very different from each other, your approach to creating a creature to live within any world can be relatively similar. Your creatures should follow the rules of their ecosystem. When building an alien planet, grounding certain concepts in reality, while playing around with aesthetics, can help the system and its inhabitants feel more realistic.

Though genres such as fantasy can feel like a far reach, fantastical creatures can still be based in reality. Supernatural or horror briefs allow for more exploration into elements beyond the rules of our world, such as lack of gravity or the use of "magic." Playing with the rules of design and reality can enrich the characters and transform them into something beyond our world. Even in these cases, basing your

designs on relatable shapes or textures will help your creatures feel believable, even if you subvert them and put them in different contexts. You can experiment with materials, features, and textures across many different genres.

Putting something where you least expect it can create a unique or surprising design. For example,

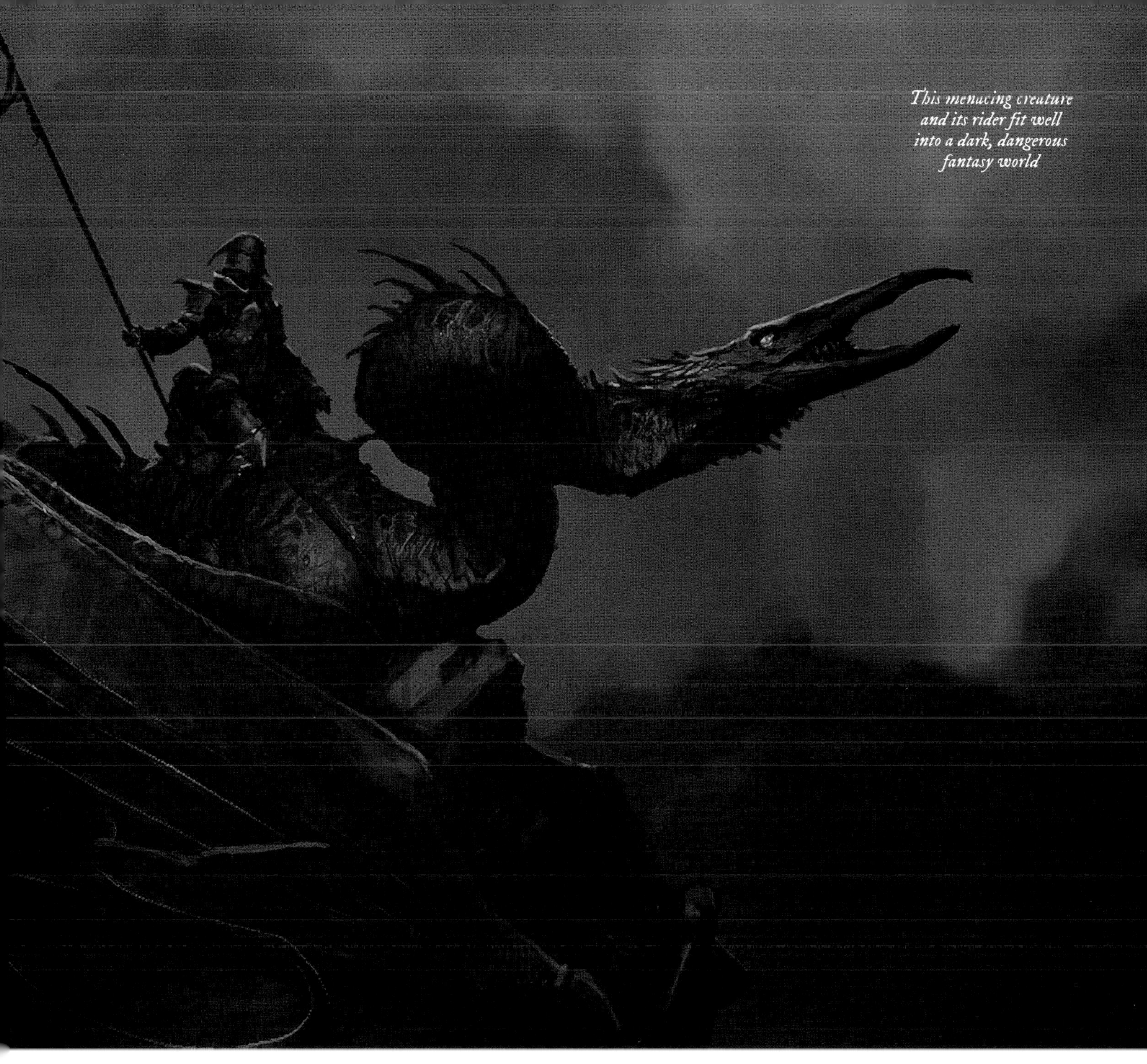

you could put a furry creature or a scaly character with horns in a sci-fi scenario, subverting how they are stereotypically tied to fantasy or horror genres. The same can be applied when creating horror creatures – it may seem counterproductive to give a horror creature a friendly characteristic, such as a smile, but if used effectively it has the potential to make the creature appear even more terrifying.

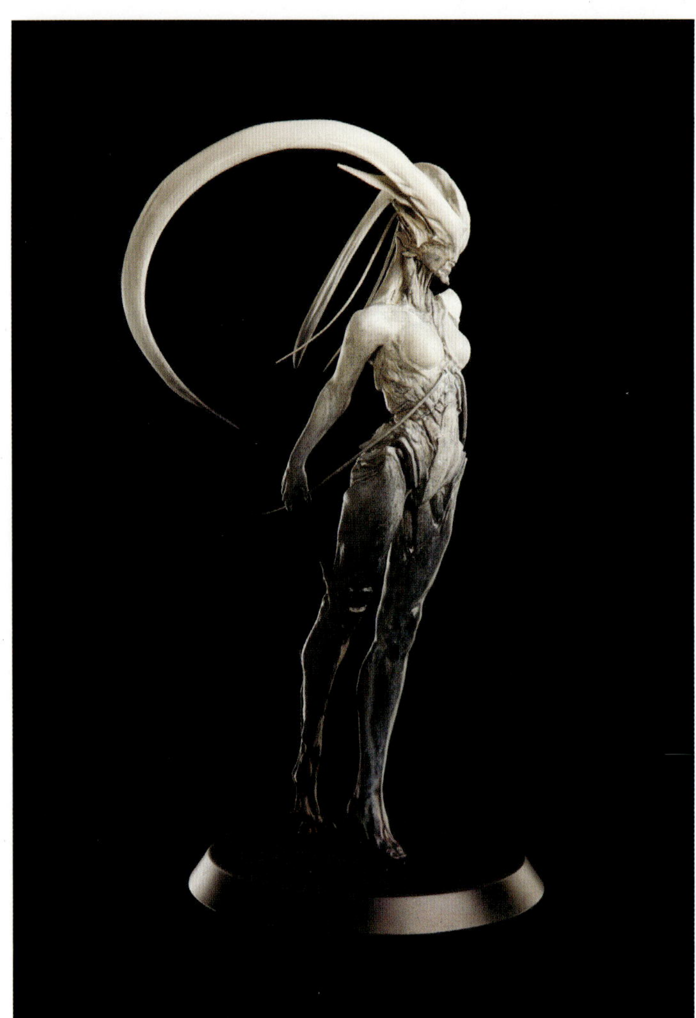
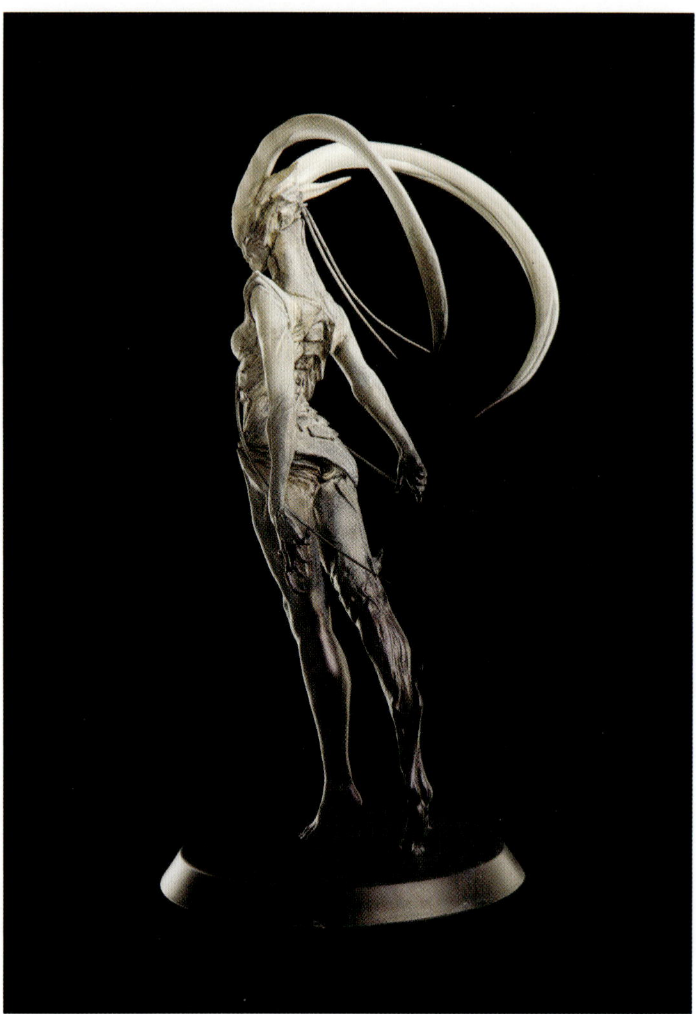

DESIGNING FOR CLIENTS

Designing for a specific client will present you with different challenges and approaches to your design process and outcome. Depending on who you are working with and what content you are working on, certain expectations about your designs will need to be met in order for you to fulfill the client's brief. Approaches will vary from industry to industry, and from one company to another.

Generally, the film industry tends to have a higher expectation of the image appearing as a final design when you present it. In this field it is common to use 3D software, even at the conceptual stage, in order to achieve this. This is not the best way to approach design for every industry, but it increases productivity, allowing more designs to be developed and considered for the final product.

When designing for the video game industry, you may encounter a slightly different approach. The design process may be extended, allowing more time for the rough idea, which is then slowly generated into the final design. It can often feel like you have spent more time on ideation (exploring the idea behind the piece), rather than rushing to the finish line. For example, a 3D modeler will need to know what a character or creature will look like from the back, so a design must be explored and developed thoroughly from different viewpoints before it is passed on to that stage.

Often, for client presentation, creating a series of designs that show your creature in a pose or *in situ* will help sell your design. Think of it as showing your client what your creature does when it is not "on camera," as this can add to the narrative of your design. Picturing how your creatures live, what they do, and who they are will make them feel more natural in their environment. Once you have developed this skill in your professional design process, it can be transferred to your personal projects and help your own creatures become more believable.

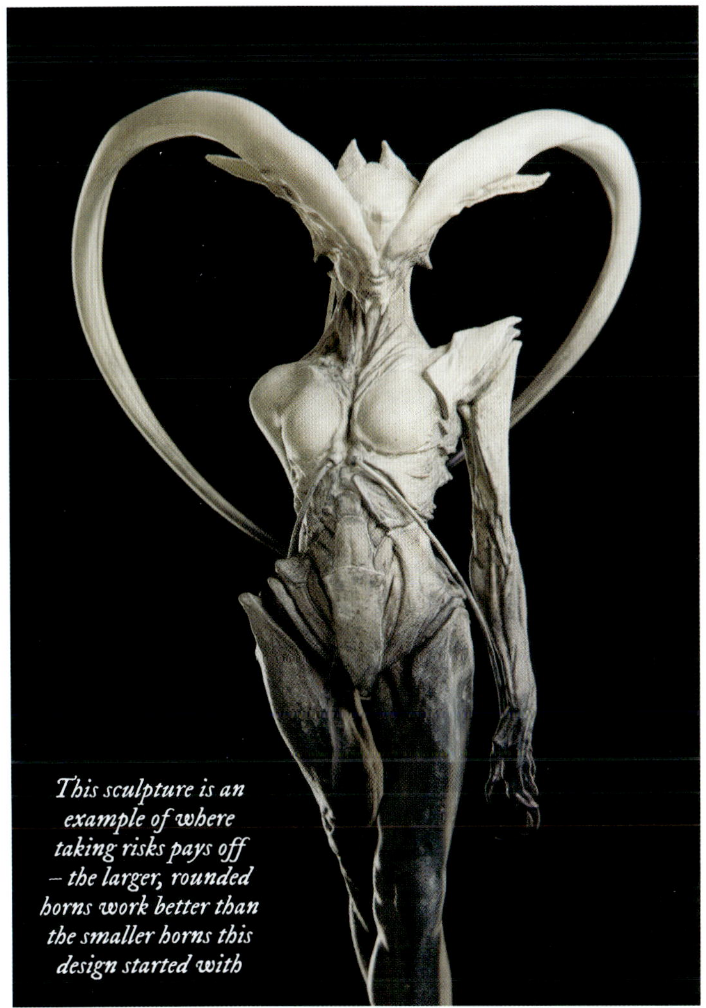

This sculpture is an example of where taking risks pays off – the larger, rounded horns work better than the smaller horns this design started with

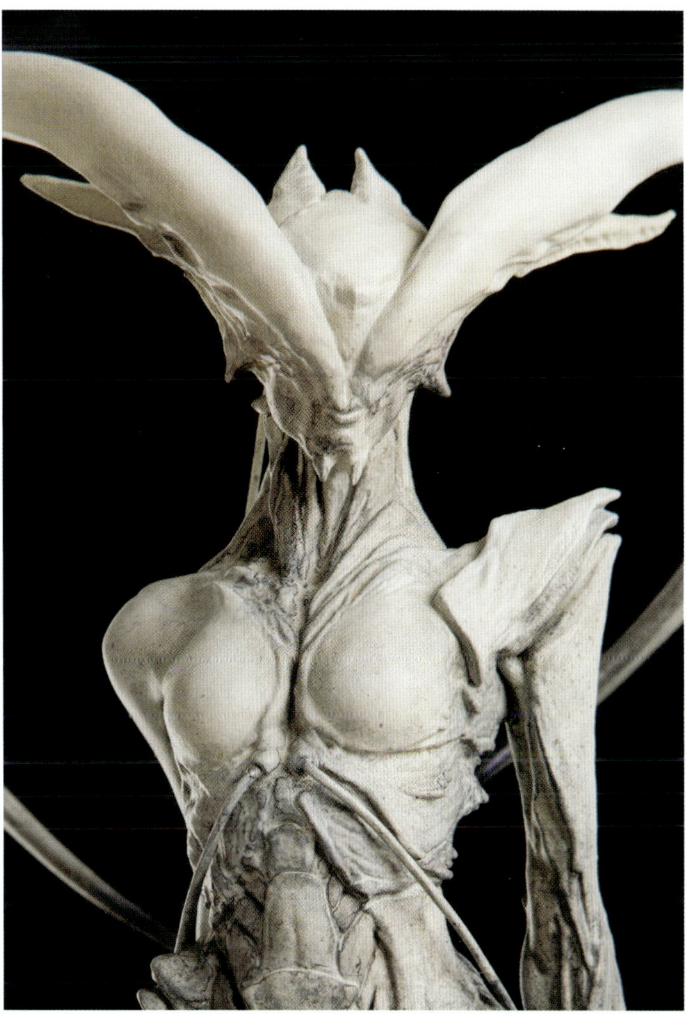

TACKLING BRIEFS

What is the best way to approach a brief, and how can this take your designs further? When given a brief, it is important to loosen up and take some risks. Often, good design comes out of doing things you would not normally do.

Practice giving yourself a brief; it will often seem limiting before it becomes liberating. When working on the personal project shown above, *Demon Girl*, I had settled on quite a "safe" horn design that I was dissatisfied with for months. Out of frustration, I grabbed the SnakeHook brush in ZBrush, my 3D modeling software, and pulled the horn out to create an iconic "looped" shape. Sometimes taking chances

may seem illogical, but it can help you create something unique, and hopefully it will not always come out of frustration. Taking ideas and exploring them a little more can help you figure out what will make sense in the final design. Playing with size, color, and shape, even if not specified by the brief can help you delve into more interesting designs.

Basing designs in anatomical research is important if your creature will move, but sketching out multiple ideas that take some anatomical risks can result in iconic design features. Give yourself the time to study real-world creatures, but keep these studies and sketches separate from your fictional design

tasks. The former will act as a catalog that you can use as a starting point for your designs before you try something new. Gather reference images and store them for future reference on sites like Pinterest.

Taking risks can be exciting, but going too far off-brief can sometimes hurt your work and result in a dissatisfied client. To avoid this, make sure you are always listening, asking questions, and not losing sight of the original purpose of the design. From my personal experience, a client always appreciates you showing interest and ensuring you fully understand the brief.

Design processes

Arboreal reptile

Alexander Ostrowski

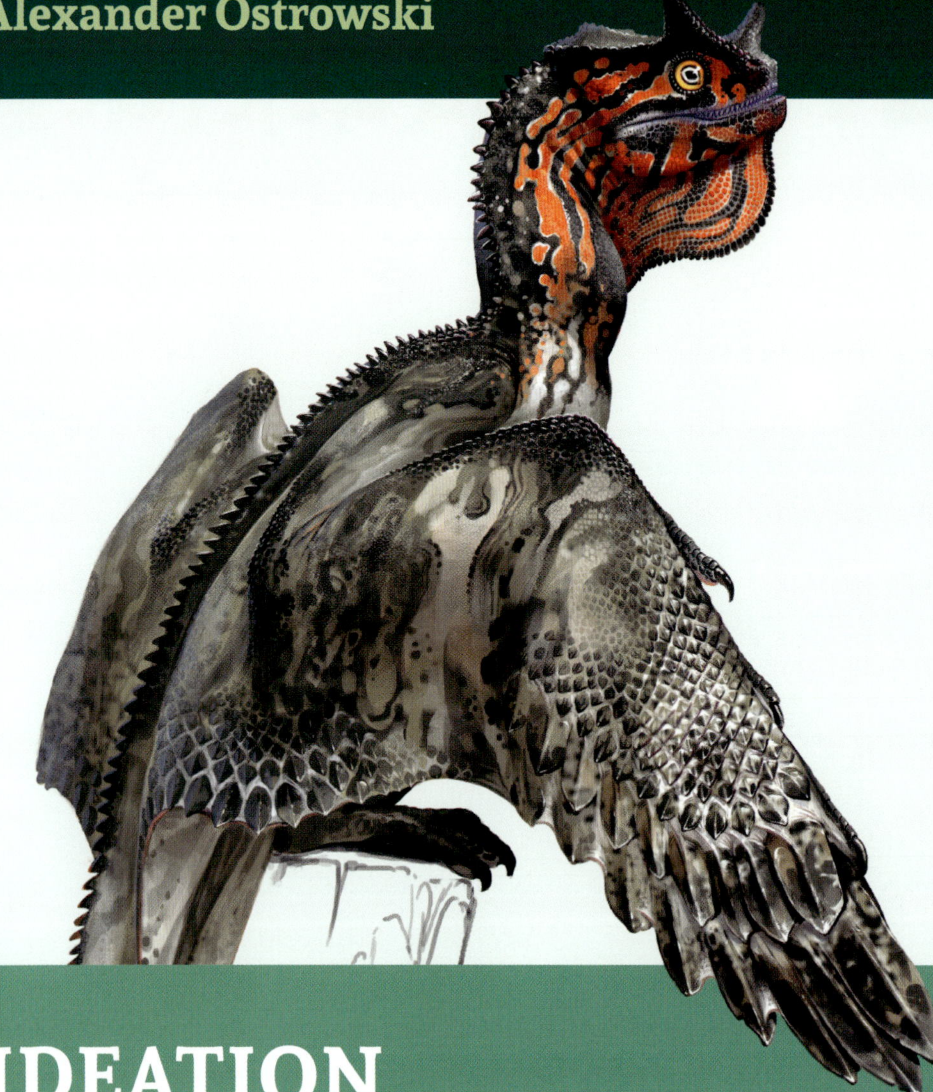

Key facts

- A reptile that spends its entire life in the treetops

- Can fly or glide and conceal itself in an arboreal setting

- Catches prey using a lure, and can camouflage to both hunt and hide from larger predators

- Territorial; known to prey on nests and eggs of its own kind when claiming a new tree

IDEATION

For this particular creature design, we will be creating an arboreal reptile with bird-like attributes. We should avoid obvious ideas such as a chimera-like mashup of a bird and a lizard. Instead, we could design an overall reptilian creature that has evolved convergent to birds. This means conveying how, over the course of evolution, this creature has developed similar features to birds, due to occupying and adapting to a comparable ecological niche.

A bird's most striking feature is the capacity for powered flight. Incorporating flight, as well as bird-like behavior, intelligence, and movement, will lend some avian qualities to the overall reptilian creature described in the brief. As a flying reptile, this creature would be well equipped for an arboreal lifestyle, but spending its entire life in the treetops will come with several challenges to keep in mind. If the creature needs to be able to climb, for example, features like a prehensile tail or strong claws would be possible adaptations for arboreal movement.

Another adaptation is its ability to camouflage. We can draw inspiration from real-world examples, such as the color-changing abilities of a chameleon or an octopus. Its camouflage could also be used for hunting, attracting prey with a lure or bait while still being perfectly concealed, no matter where in the dense treetops it lurks. This color-changing would allow for some fascinating displays such as territorial behavior and mating rituals.

Besides all the biological adaptations, it is also important to know when and where the creature lives. Taking inspiration from mythology as well as reality, this design will be reminiscent of wyverns - legendary bipedal dragons. This particular wyvern might spend its entire life in the treetops of a pine forest in a fantasy setting.

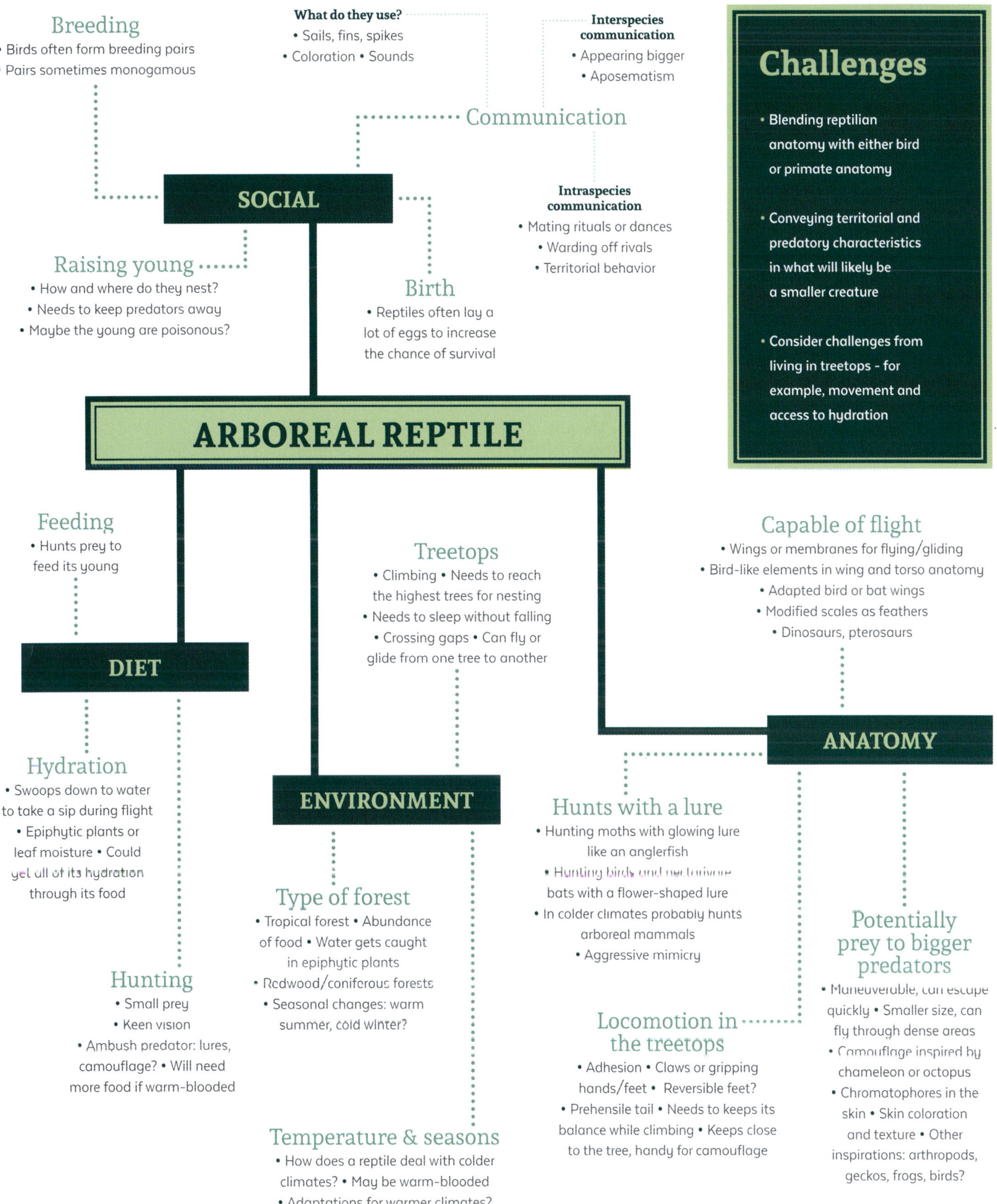

Breeding
• Birds often form breeding pairs
• Pairs sometimes monogamous

What do they use?
• Sails, fins, spikes
• Coloration • Sounds

Interspecies communication
• Appearing bigger
• Aposematism

Communication

Challenges
• Blending reptilian anatomy with either bird or primate anatomy
• Conveying territorial and predatory characteristics in what will likely be a smaller creature
• Consider challenges from living in treetops - for example, movement and access to hydration

SOCIAL

Intraspecies communication
• Mating rituals or dances
• Warding off rivals
• Territorial behavior

Raising young
• How and where do they nest?
• Needs to keep predators away
• Maybe the young are poisonous?

Birth
• Reptiles often lay a lot of eggs to increase the chance of survival

ARBOREAL REPTILE

Feeding
• Hunts prey to feed its young

Treetops
• Climbing • Needs to reach the highest trees for nesting
• Needs to sleep without falling
• Crossing gaps • Can fly or glide from one tree to another

Capable of flight
• Wings or membranes for flying/gliding
• Bird-like elements in wing and torso anatomy
• Adapted bird or bat wings
• Modified scales as feathers
• Dinosaurs, pterosaurs

DIET

ANATOMY

Hydration
• Swoops down to water to take a sip during flight
• Epiphytic plants or leaf moisture • Could get all of its hydration through its food

ENVIRONMENT

Hunts with a lure
• Hunting moths with glowing lure like an anglerfish
• Hunting birds and nocturnal bats with a flower-shaped lure
• In colder climates probably hunts arboreal mammals
• Aggressive mimicry

Type of forest
• Tropical forest • Abundance of food • Water gets caught in epiphytic plants
• Redwood/coniferous forests
• Seasonal changes: warm summer, cold winter?

Potentially prey to bigger predators
• Maneuverable, can escape quickly • Smaller size, can fly through dense areas
• Camouflage inspired by chameleon or octopus
• Chromatophores in the skin • Skin coloration and texture • Other inspirations: arthropods, geckos, frogs, birds?

Hunting
• Small prey
• Keen vision
• Ambush predator: lures, camouflage? • Will need more food if warm-blooded

Locomotion in the treetops
• Adhesion • Claws or gripping hands/feet • Reversible feet?
• Prehensile tail • Needs to keeps its balance while climbing • Keeps close to the tree, handy for camouflage

Temperature & seasons
• How does a reptile deal with colder climates? • May be warm-blooded
• Adaptations for warmer climates?

Anatomy research

Reptiles

Studying basic reptilian anatomy is a key starting point, as this creature will be an adapted reptile. Lizards have very distinctive feet that are well adapted for climbing - fitting for the arboreal lifestyle of the creature. They also have a lot of aesthetic features, such as spikes, sails, horns, and crests, that will be perfect for designing an interesting wyvern.

Reptiles have evolved into many different shapes and sizes, so in terms of evolution, it is plausible that they would evolve into a creature similar to our fictional wyvern. Within the reptile family there are, among others, lizards, snakes, birds, marine reptiles, pterosaurs – a small "winged lizard" dinosaur - and non-flying dinosaurs, all featuring different shapes and characteristics.

Birds

To make the bird-like characteristics of the wyvern more believable, it is useful to look at the ways birds behave and move. Their general posture and movements – such as folding away their wings – are a unique set of characteristics that are recognized as "bird-like." Plumes of feathers can be used for courtship or territorial behavior, similar to how some lizards use their features for display.

Birds are very intelligent and display some of the strangest hunting strategies in the animal kingdom. A good example of this is how herons hang from low branches above the water to catch fish; some even use bait to entice their prey.

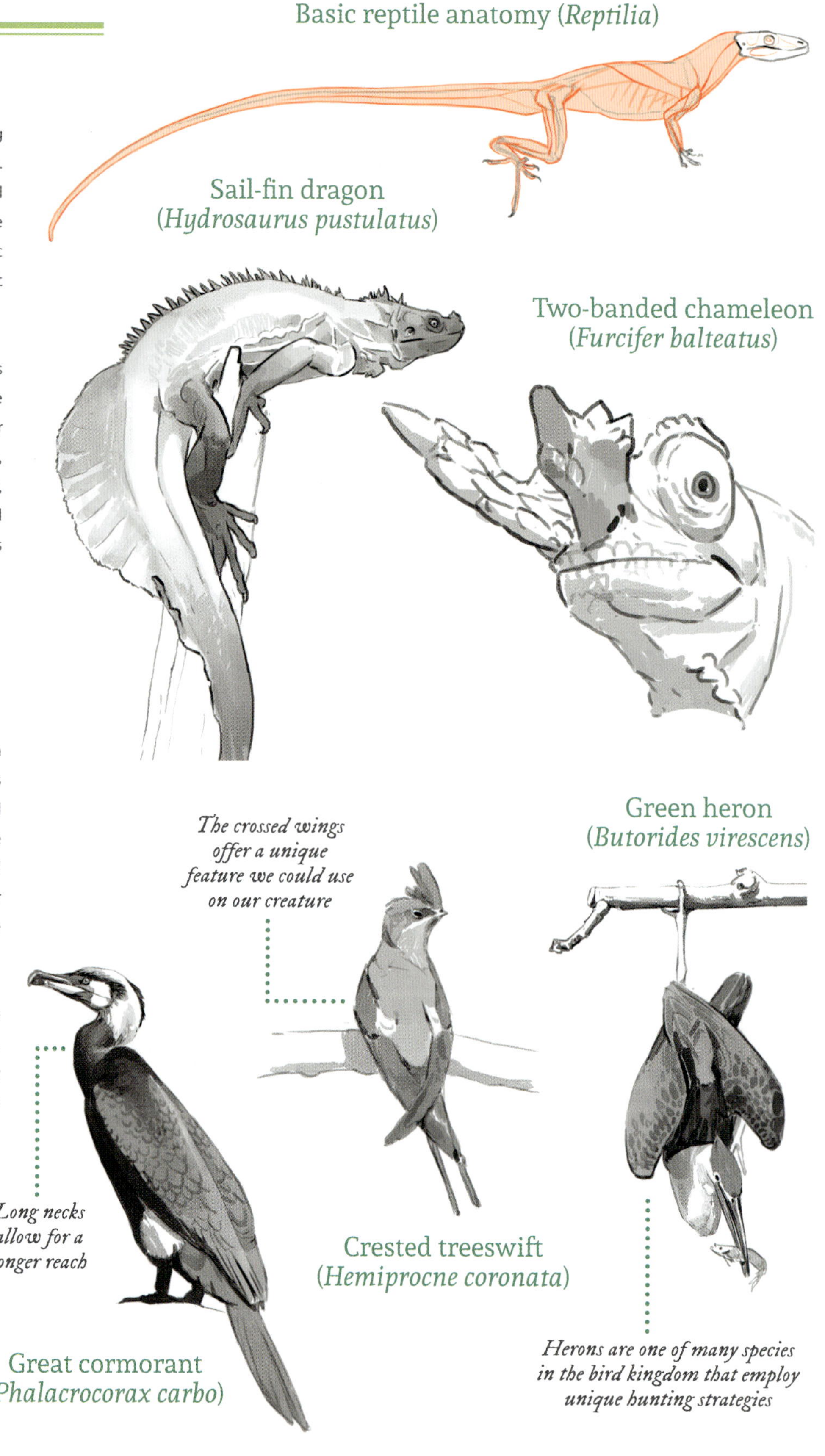

Wings

The three examples of flying animals shown here all feature different wing types: birds, bats, and the extinct flying reptiles, the pterosaurs.

In basic terms, a bird's wing can be seen as a jointed arm with a hand whose spread fingers are covered in feathers. You can read more about wing anatomy on **page 86**.

Bats, in contrast, have what is known as a "hand-wing." As the name suggests, this features a hand-like bone structure with very long fingers, all connected with a membrane. These generally allow for more maneuverability because they are more flexible than bird wings.

The wings of pterosaurs were formed by a membrane as well, but it extends from the body to the tip of the extremely elongated fourth finger.

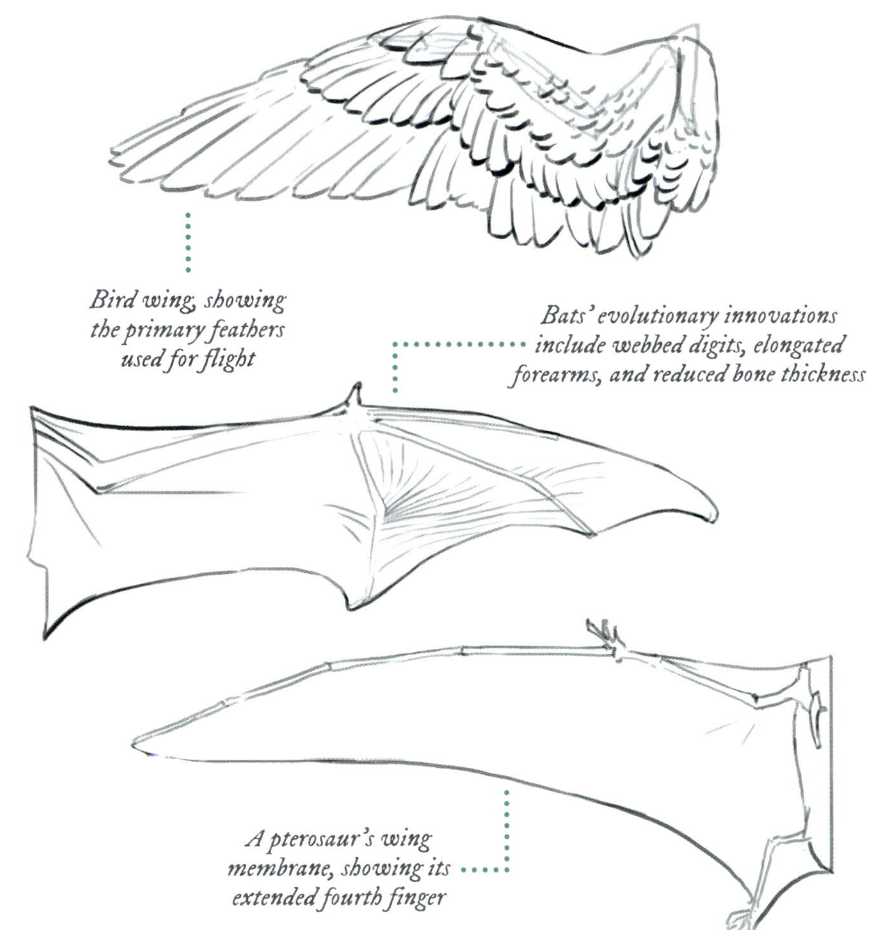

Bird wing, showing the primary feathers used for flight

Bats' evolutionary innovations include webbed digits, elongated forearms, and reduced bone thickness

A pterosaur's wing membrane, showing its extended fourth finger

Evolution

Pictured right, the Chinese dinosaur *Yi qi* ("strange wing") is an interesting example that could inspire some of the wyvern's features. This small creature evolved leathery hand-wings, similar to those of a bat, and those associated with mythological creatures such as dragons.

These wings were likely not adapted for powered flight, but this species resembles a midway point between the myth of the dragon and a dinosaur. *Yi qi* as a non avian dinosaur is more closely related to birds than other reptiles, and was probably also covered in feathers. This is another unique design feature that combines reptilian and avian traits that could be incorporated into the final creature design.

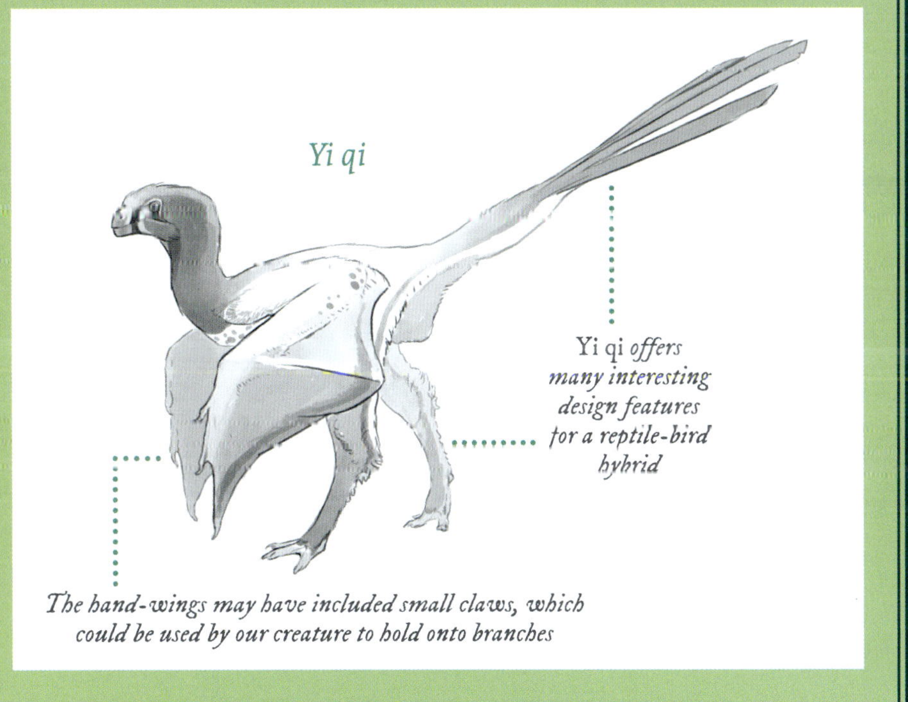

Yi qi offers many interesting design features for a reptile-bird hybrid

The hand-wings may have included small claws, which could be used by our creature to hold onto branches

Functionality research

Vision

When considering design elements that will make the creature appear intelligent, eyes offer many interesting ideas. This particular design requires bird-like attributes, and an important evolutionary feature of birds is their eyesight. There are two distinct differences in how birds' eyes are oriented on their heads, depending on whether they hunt or are hunted. The common buzzard, for example, has eyes that are angled toward the front. This allows for increased depth perception when seeking out prey. On a dove, however, the eyes are positioned on either side of the head. This creates a wider field of vision, allowing it to spot predators earlier on.

Regardless of how their eyes are oriented, all birds possess nictitating membranes. These are third, transparent eyelids that protect the eyes during flight or while fishing and diving.

Camouflage

According to the design brief, this particular creature requires the ability to conceal itself in an arboreal setting. There are several animals that are able to change the color of their skin, but chameleons are probably the best known for this ability.

Chameleons use color changes not only to camouflage, but also to communicate. Some species can adjust their colors according to the eyes of specific predators in order to hide, but most commonly they use color-changing to signal their physical condition and intentions to other members of their species.

While camouflaging is essential for the wyvern's survival, it is also important to show its ability to communicate. A highly territorial creature like this one needs to be able to perform acts of aggression or mating displays. Anole lizards, for example, use brightly colored dewlaps – extendable skin flaps on their neck or throat – to scare off rivals or attract mates. Combined with camouflaging abilities similar to a chameleon's, this will make the wyvern feel more reptilian and help achieve the criteria outlined in the design brief.

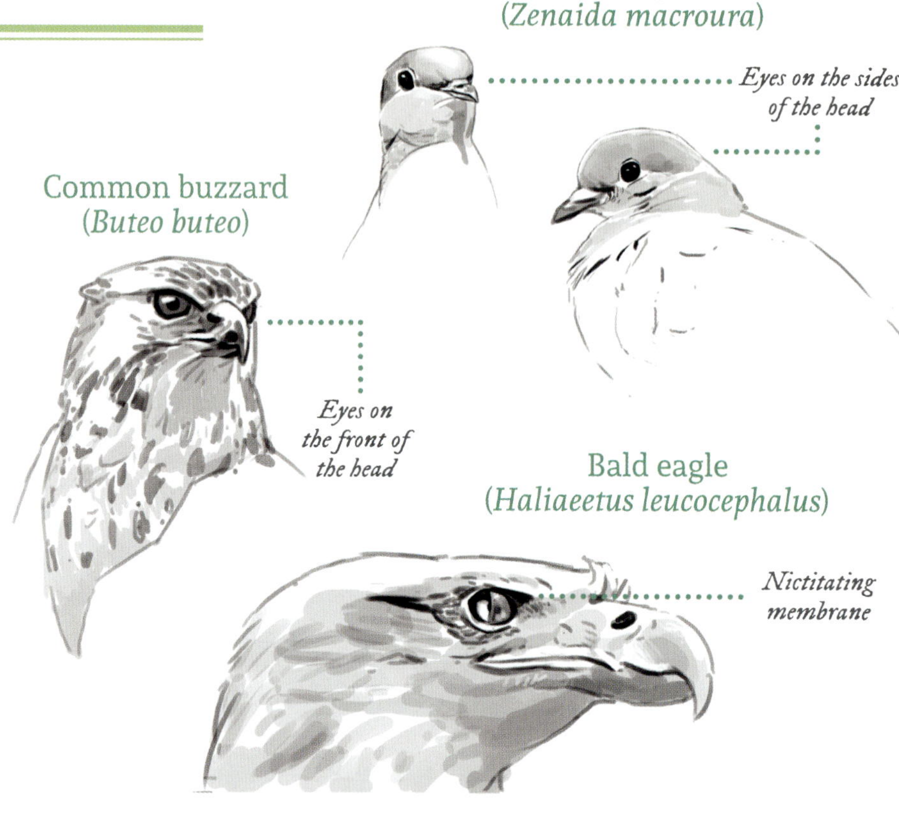

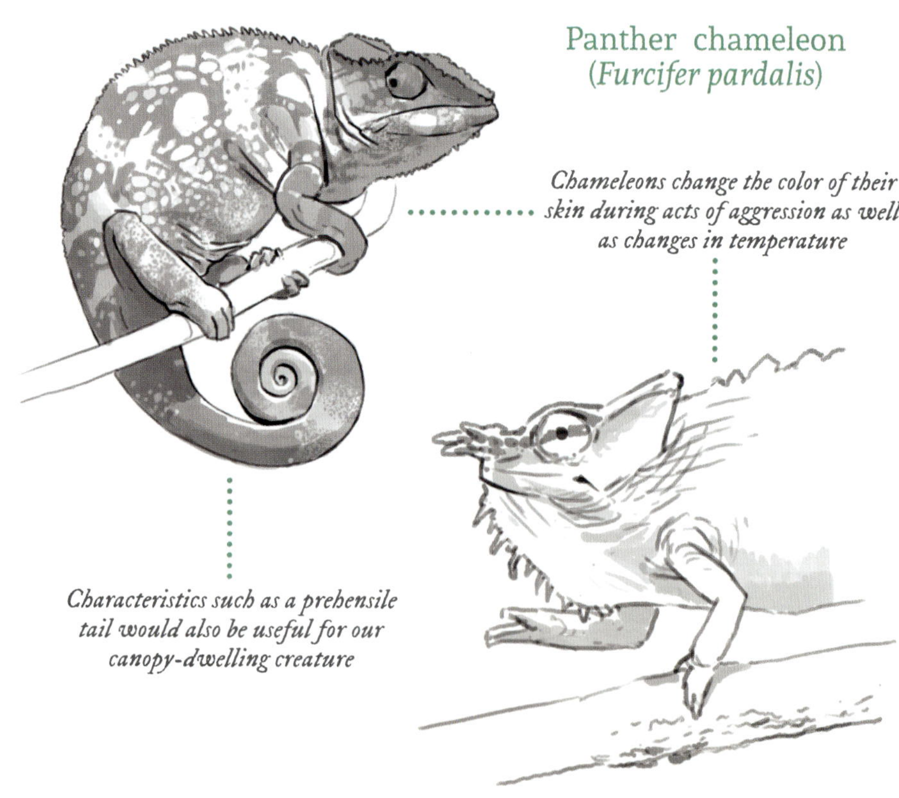

Hunting

As an ambush hunter, good camouflage is not enough for this creature to thrive. The wyvern requires a technique for attracting possible prey. Some snakes, like the spider-tailed horned viper from Iran, have unique tail tips that resemble small animals. The viper uses this special tail to lure insectivorous birds close enough to strike. A similar tactic could be employed by the wyvern to catch prey in the treetops of its forest home. This could be in the form of an insect-shaped tail or tongue, or a lure as seen in other predatory species such as the anglerfish.

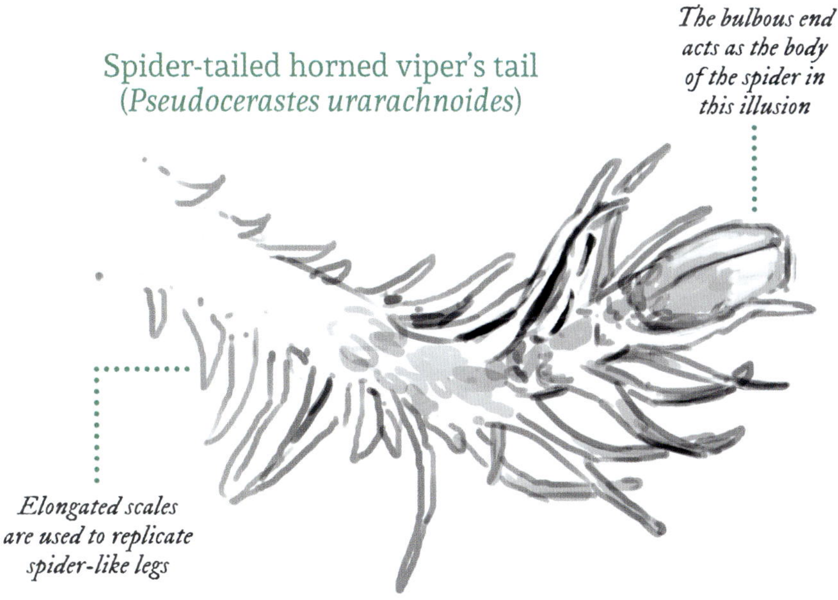

Spider-tailed horned viper's tail
(*Pseudocerastes urarachnoides*)

The bulbous end acts as the body of the spider in this illusion

Elongated scales are used to replicate spider-like legs

Coloration

When considering the environment and climate inhabited by your creature, it may be useful to search for animals that have created unique adaptations to similar settings. The tawny frogmouth (see right), a bird native to Australia and Tasmania, has developed a unique camouflage technique that allows it to become almost indistinguishable from its environment. Its plumage is patterned to mimic tree bark, and when frozen in place, these birds appear to be part of a broken tree branch.

The design of the wyvern could incorporate this kind of cryptic camouflaging. Changing its skin color to mimic the color and texture of the pine forest it inhabits would allow it to hide from prey and predators, and also open up some interesting behaviors regarding courtship and aggressive displays. As it lives in the forest, the creature's coloration would be various shades of brown and gray, with patterning that emulates the bark of trees, much like the tawny frogmouth.

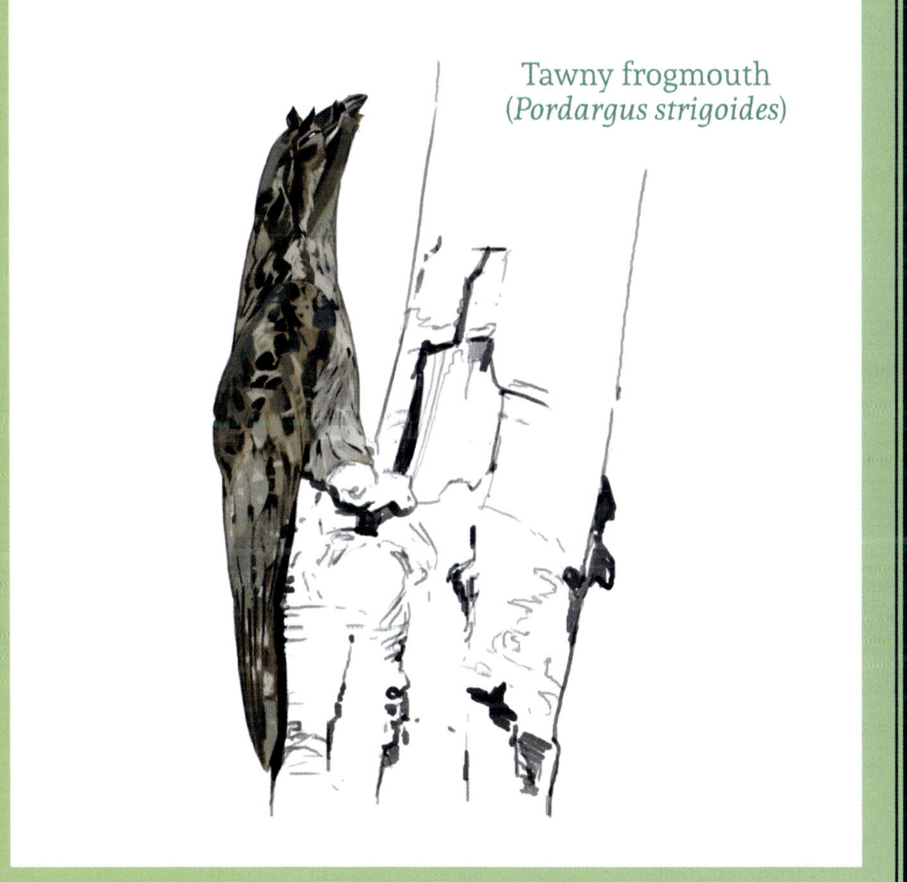

Tawny frogmouth
(*Pordargus strigoides*)

Thumbnails

The goal is to design a wyvern that is not just a winged reptile, but a creature that also behaves and moves similarly to a bird. Since this creature spends its entire life in the treetops, the way it navigates and maneuvers around its arboreal environment is an important point to consider.

Potential solutions could be found by experimenting with bird-like poses and shapes, elegant necks like those of cormorants or herons, and even elongated scales that act like primary feathers in a bird's wing. The wings are especially important because they are the creature's primary way of navigating its environment. Claws or adhesion pads on the wings could be added to help the wyvern when it climbs. It is also important to keep in mind that its eyes need to be adapted for flight, and that it should have increased depth perception to help with hunting.

Unlike most reptilians, this creature will need to be warm-blooded due to its active lifestyle in the treetops. To sustain itself, it will also need a lot of food, and therefore needs to be an efficient hunter. The most striking adaptation for this creature is the ability to camouflage, which could be conveyed further to the viewer with the inclusion of some chameleon-like features. This opens up an avenue of interesting shapes for the head, crest, or horns, and even some curly prehensile tails.

Based on our research, there are a few different hunting techniques to explore. One solution is an appendage that is used as a lure, such as a spider-shaped tail-tip, tongue, or glowing lure to attract nocturnal insects. Another option is through bird-like behavior, such as using bugs or nuts as bait to lure birds, martens, or squirrels to within striking distance.

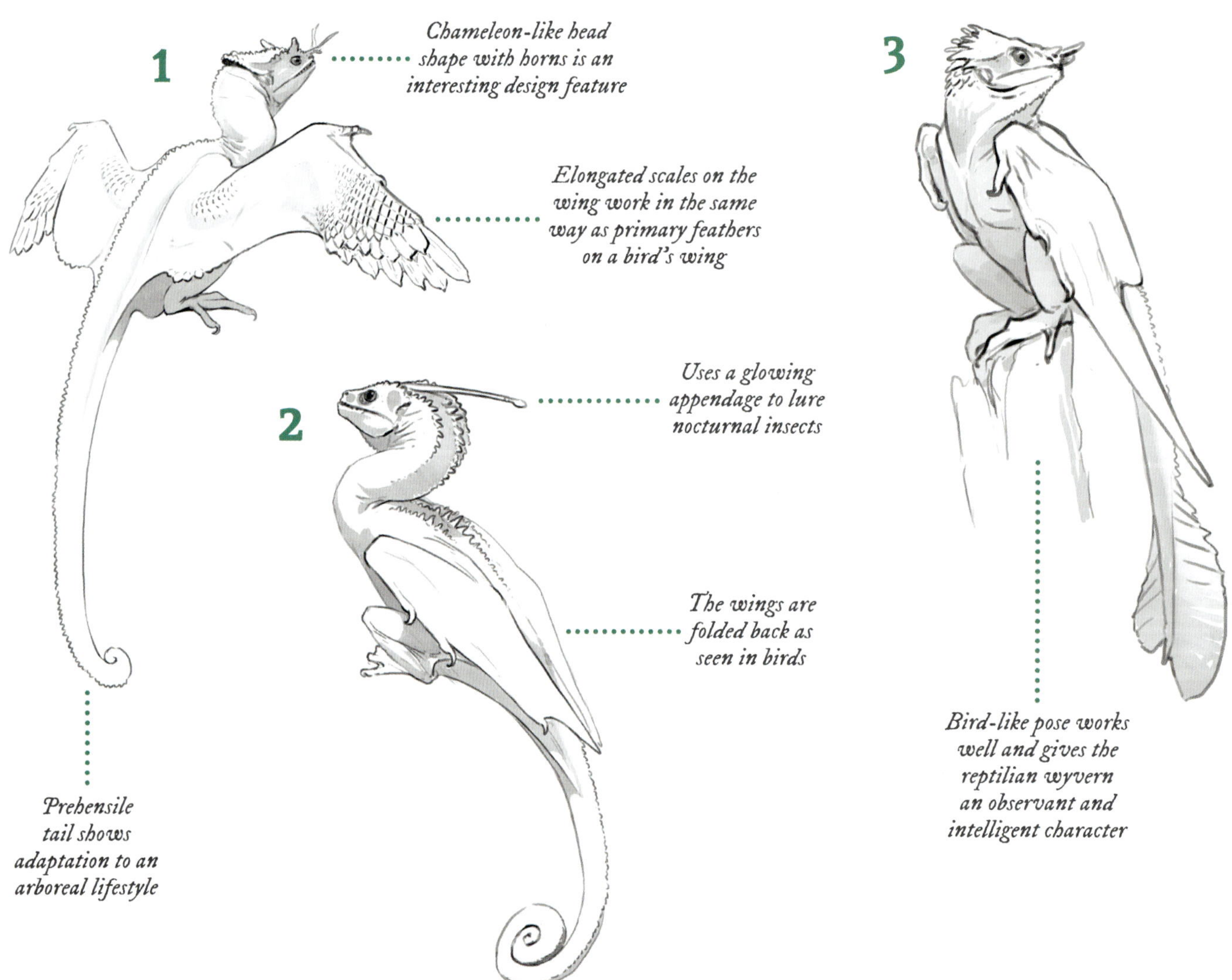

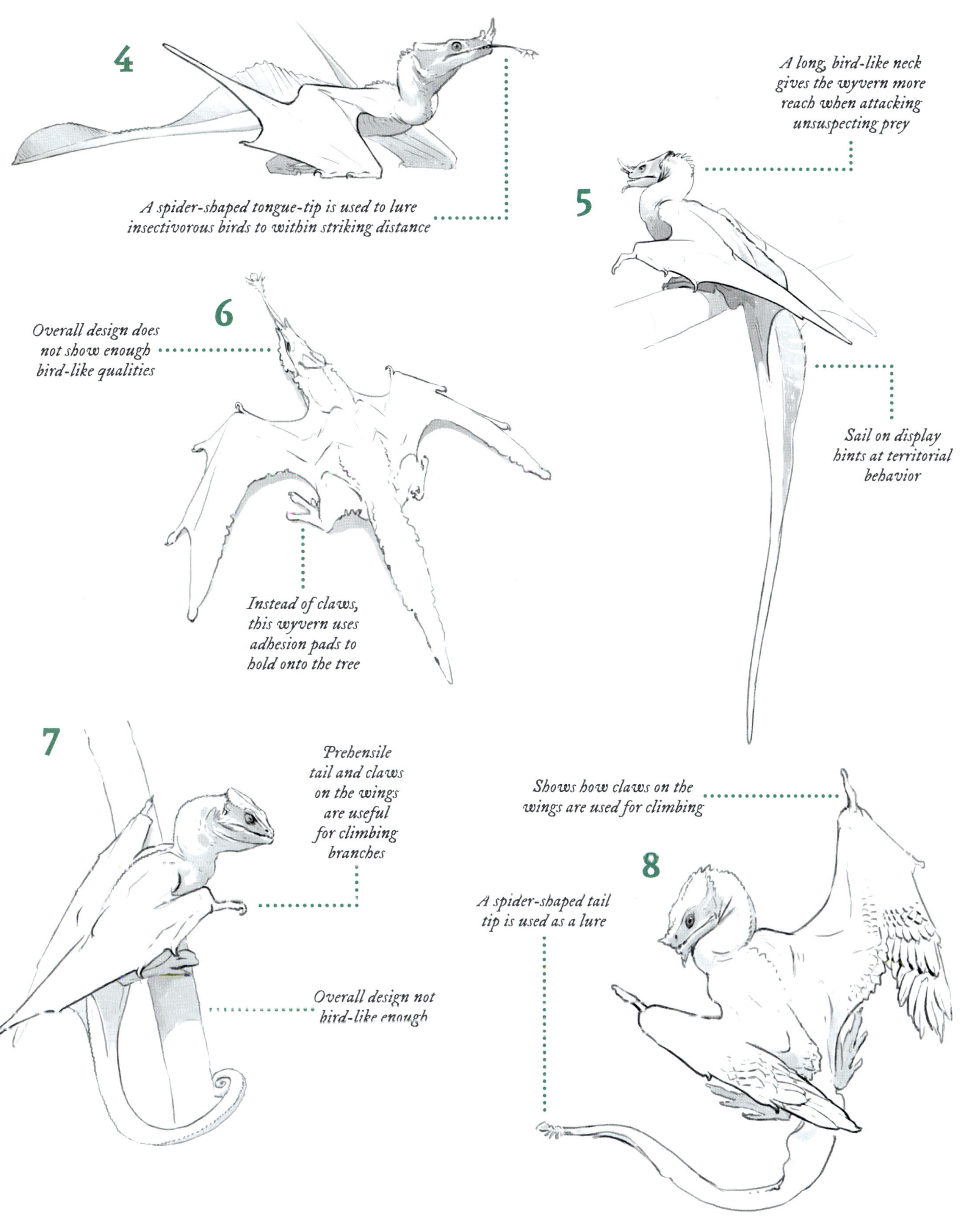

4

A spider-shaped tongue-tip is used to lure insectivorous birds to within striking distance

5

A long, bird-like neck gives the wyvern more reach when attacking unsuspecting prey

Sail on display hints at territorial behavior

6

Overall design does not show enough bird-like qualities

Instead of claws, this wyvern uses adhesion pads to hold onto the tree

7

Prehensile tail and claws on the wings are useful for climbing branches

Overall design not bird-like enough

8

Shows how claws on the wings are used for climbing

A spider-shaped tail tip is used as a lure

DEVELOPMENT

Thumbnail 1 is selected as the design to move forward with as it features many of the aspects that were highlighted in the brief. This design appears coherent as a blend between reptilian and bird-like anatomical features, without being a chimera. It clearly shows adaptations that the wyvern would develop in an arboreal ecosystem.

Certain features echo a chameleon shape, which hints at its reptilian nature and camouflaging abilities. Meanwhile, the way it perches on the branch, its long neck, and elongated scales show its avian attributes, which are also functional adaptations to the challenges it faces in its environment. In order to showcase its need to hunt prey, the design features sharp claws and teeth that allude to the wyvern's carnivorous diet.

The incorporation of display structures such as horns, dewlaps, and its ability to change skin color, show how the wyvern has developed ways to communicate. These features allow it to interact with members of its own species and perform territorial displays. The color-changing ability will become more apparent in the color stages of the design.

As a flying creature, most of the problems of arboreal movement are solved. The wyvern can fly from one tree to the next to escape predators, or swoop down to a pond or river and take a sip mid-flight. Its clawed wings and feet are well adapted for climbing, as well as the prehensile tail, which it uses to grab branches.

Front view

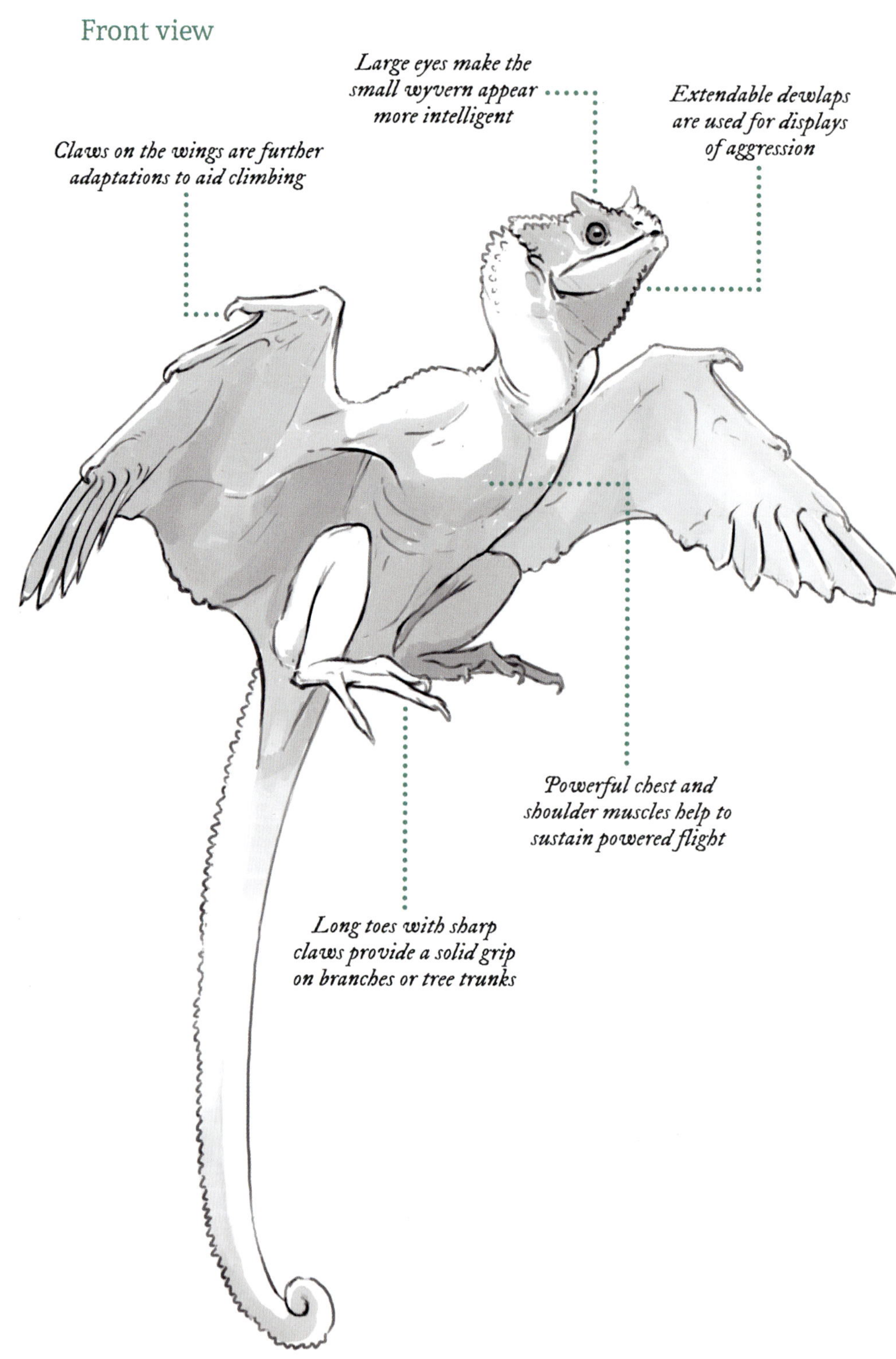

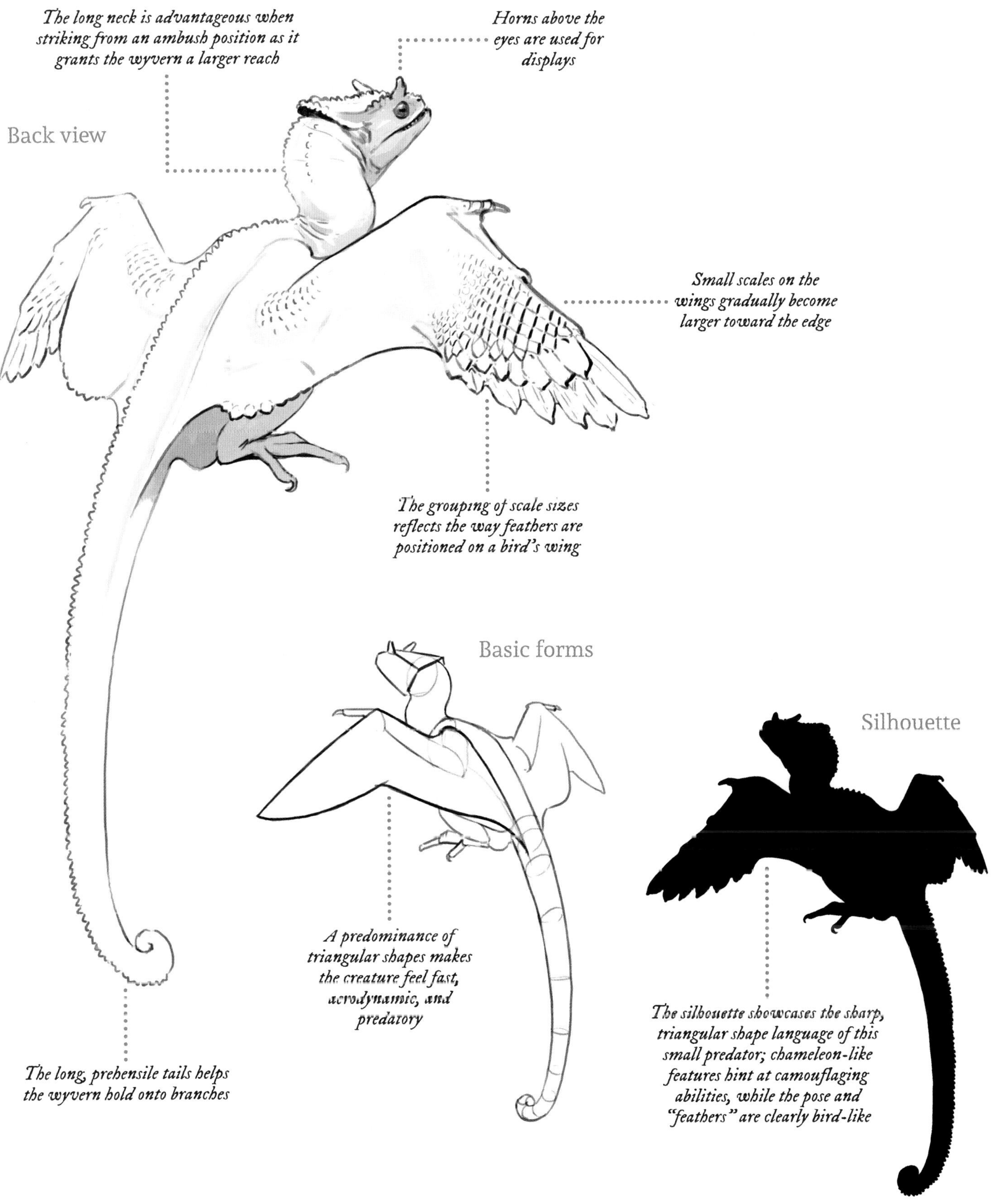

The long neck is advantageous when striking from an ambush position as it grants the wyvern a larger reach

Horns above the eyes are used for displays

Small scales on the wings gradually become larger toward the edge

The grouping of scale sizes reflects the way feathers are positioned on a bird's wing

The long, prehensile tails helps the wyvern hold onto branches

A predominance of triangular shapes makes the creature feel fast, aerodynamic, and predatory

The silhouette showcases the sharp, triangular shape language of this small predator; chameleon-like features hint at camouflaging abilities, while the pose and "feathers" are clearly bird-like

Poses

The criterion for these poses is to check the wyvern's ability to move within its arboreal ecosystem. One way the wyvern stays stable when navigating the canopies is by using its prehensile tail. Pose A shows how the creature uses its tail to hold tightly onto the branch when it wants to camouflage itself. Being able to wrap its length around the tree provides it with increased control and enables the wyvern to stay motionless for extended periods of time.

Pose B shows how the claws on the wings can help the wyvern to hold onto and climb trees. This can be used when the creature applies its ingenious hunting strategy: using bait and its ability to camouflage itself to lure potential prey up into the branches. Having reinforcements such as these will give it stability when high up in the treetops.

Pose C showcases the creature during flight. The neck is straightened, the tail is stretched out, and the legs are tucked in, highlighting the aerodynamic adaptability of the design. This also helps reinforce the creature's flight ability, as it appears naturally suited to the size and shape of the wings.

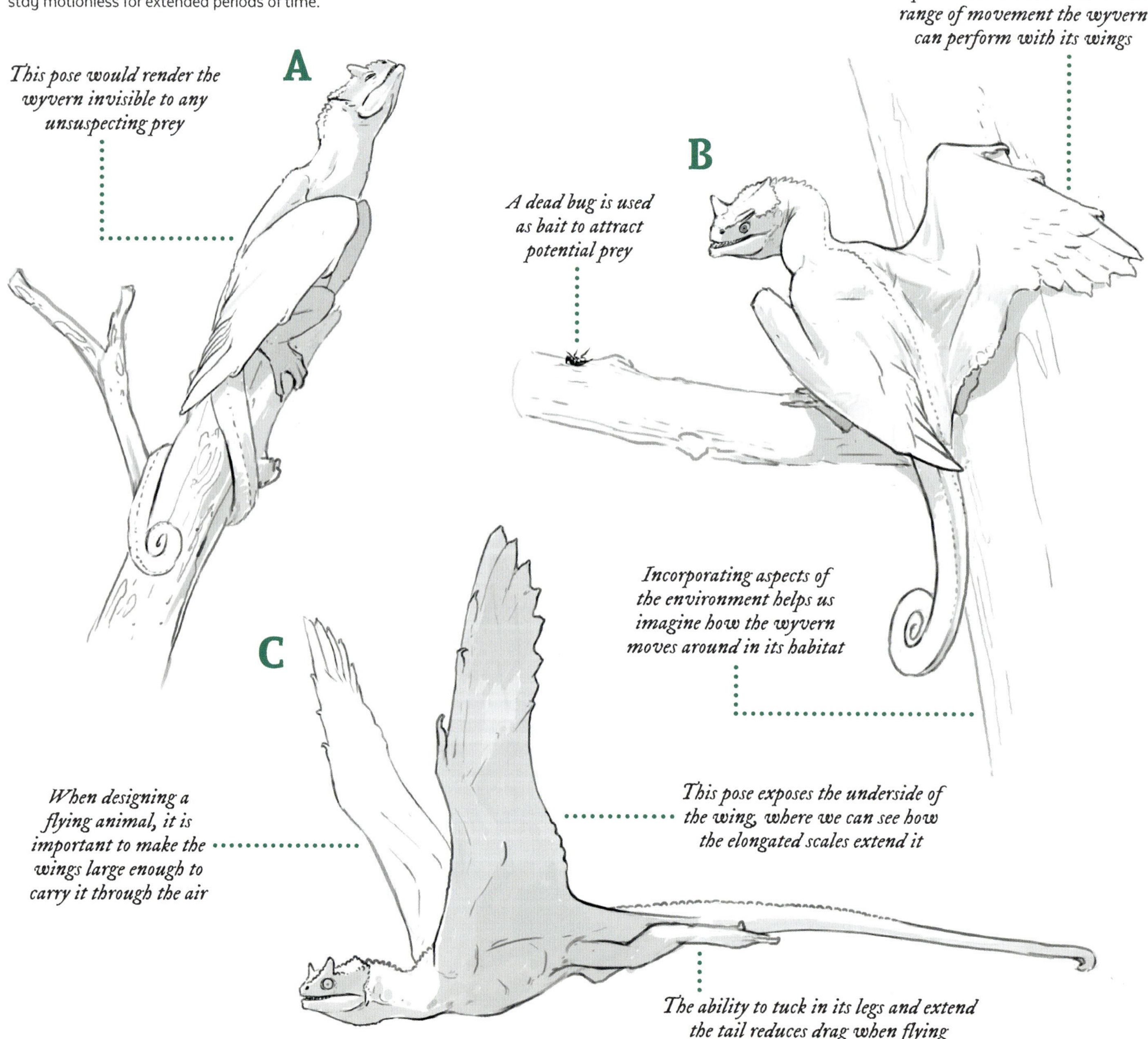

This pose would render the wyvern invisible to any unsuspecting prey

A

A pose such as this one shows the range of movement the wyvern can perform with its wings

B

A dead bug is used as bait to attract potential prey

Incorporating aspects of the environment helps us imagine how the wyvern moves around in its habitat

C

When designing a flying animal, it is important to make the wings large enough to carry it through the air

This pose exposes the underside of the wing, where we can see how the elongated scales extend it

The ability to tuck in its legs and extend the tail reduces drag when flying

Color & pattern

The wyvern's ability to change its skin color has multiple uses that must be considered when finalizing the design. Color-changing can be used for camouflaging and threatening displays - important behavioral patterns that need to be portrayed in the final color palette.

The goal of color sketches is to find the most logical coloration for this creature and its environment. In the images below, the wyvern has its wings partially spread out and its dewlap extended to make it appear larger and more threatening; by exploring variations in color, this behavior can be reinforced and made to feel more dramatic.

To effectively blend into its environment, the body should mimic the tree the creature sits on. A combination of browns and grays would allow the body to blend in and emulate the texture of the bark through delicate patterning.

The bright color patches are reminiscent of chameleons' warning signals when they feel threatened. Including this coloring in the design shows how the creature uses threatening displays to ward off rivals and settle territorial disputes; the bright warning colors contrasted with dark patterns on the head facilitate this.

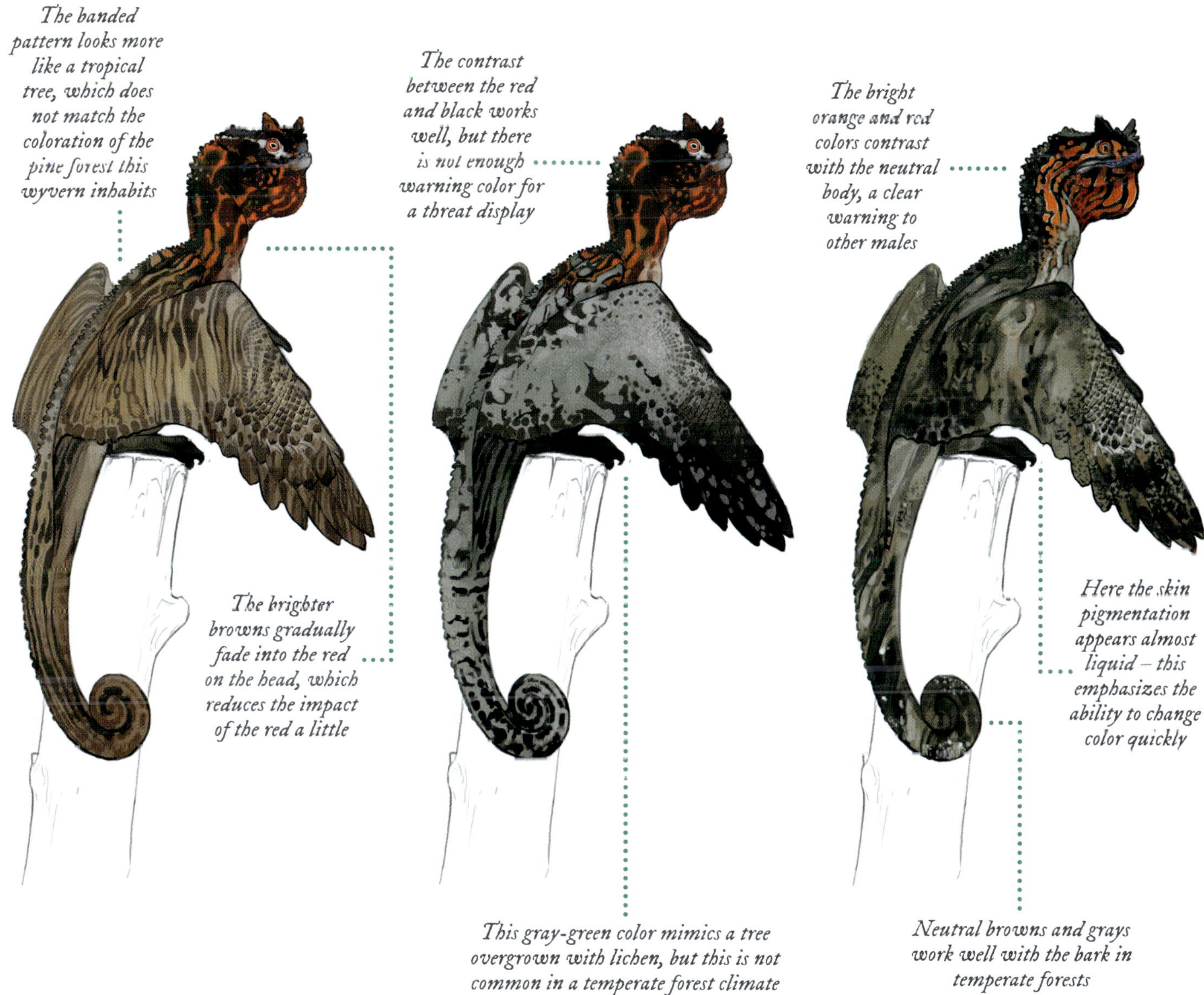

The banded pattern looks more like a tropical tree, which does not match the coloration of the pine forest this wyvern inhabits

The contrast between the red and black works well, but there is not enough warning color for a threat display

The bright orange and red colors contrast with the neutral body, a clear warning to other males

The brighter browns gradually fade into the red on the head, which reduces the impact of the red a little

Here the skin pigmentation appears almost liquid – this emphasizes the ability to change color quickly

This gray-green color mimics a tree overgrown with lichen, but this is not common in a temperate forest climate

Neutral browns and grays work well with the bark in temperate forests

FINAL DESIGN

The final design of the common forest wyvern is a strange little dragon that is highly adapted to its arboreal home. As a warm-blooded reptile, its perching posture and elongated scales are reminiscent of distinctly avian traits, while its shape and size remain reptilian. It appears intelligent due to its alert, bird-like shape and its large yellow eyes, which allow it to easily observe its surroundings. Though the research process explored different hunting techniques, such as a snake-like lure appendage, the final design uses an avian approach of collecting bait to lure its prey instead.

To emphasize the camouflaging abilities of the forest wyvern, the skin patterning has a liquid look, with round, flowing shapes that shift underneath the scaly skin. This fluidity contrasts with the sharper triangular structure of the body.

The research provided many interesting real-world animal features that were brought into the final design. The shape of chameleons, for example, is reflected in the prehensile tail that demonstrates the wyvern's arboreal lifestyle. The wing anatomy, inspired by a combination of living creatures and the dinosaur *Yi qi*, features elongated scales to help with flight. The claws on the wings are suited to climbing, providing the wyvern with added maneuverability when moving through the canopy, while also conjuring up mythical allusions to dragons. These features combined result in a unique and memorable dragon design that successfully meets the criteria of the original brief.

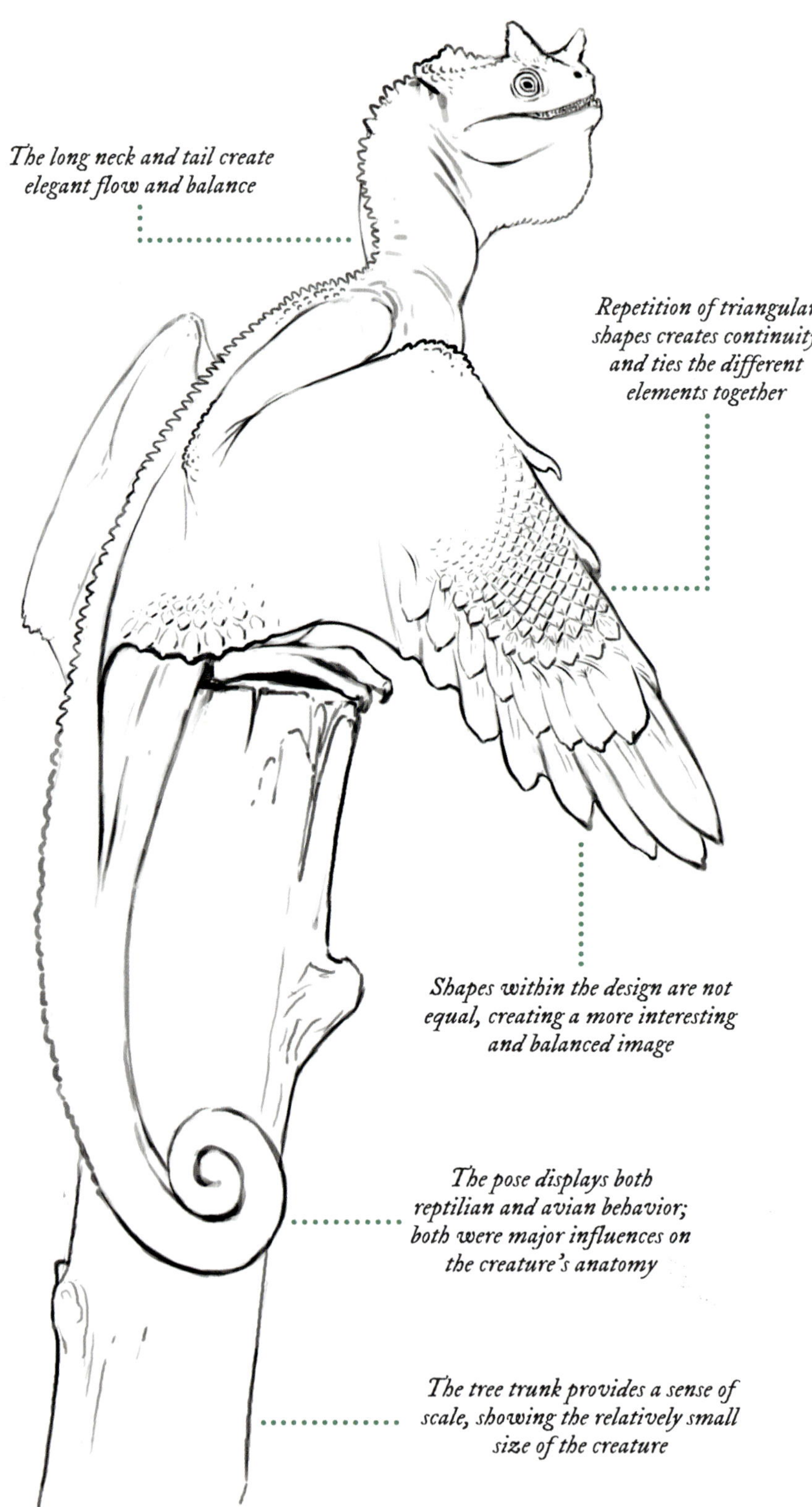

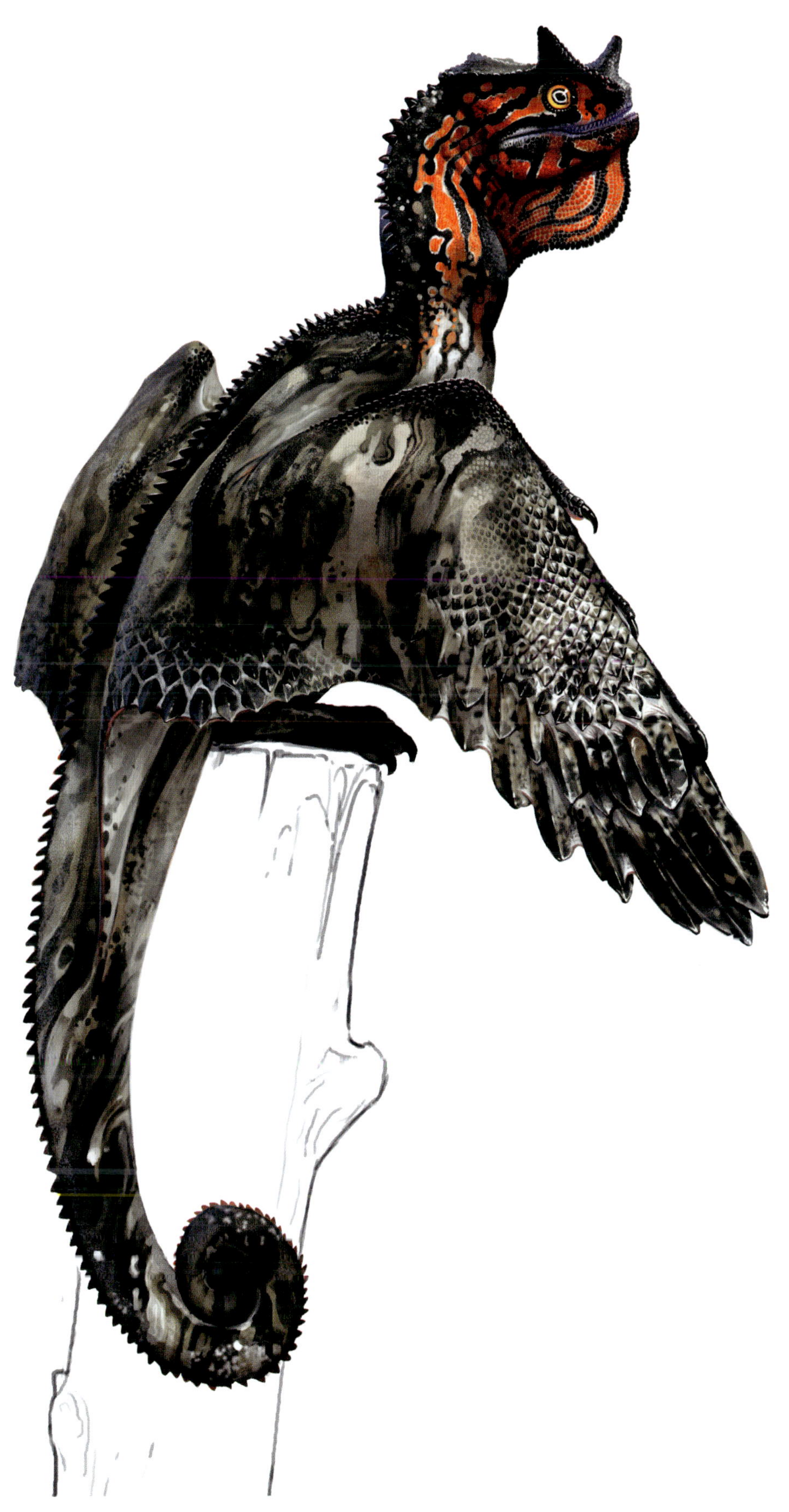

Final image © Alexander Ostrowski

LIFE CYCLE EXPLORATION

Hatchling

The hatchlings of the common forest wyvern are completely helpless. They are known as "nidicolous animals" – animals that remain in their birthplace for a relatively long time due to their dependence on their parents for food and protection.

The hatchlings cannot fly, hunt, or open their eyes. Their wings are small, but they have a large appetite. Since the wyvern is warm-blooded, they require more food to sustain their active lifestyle.

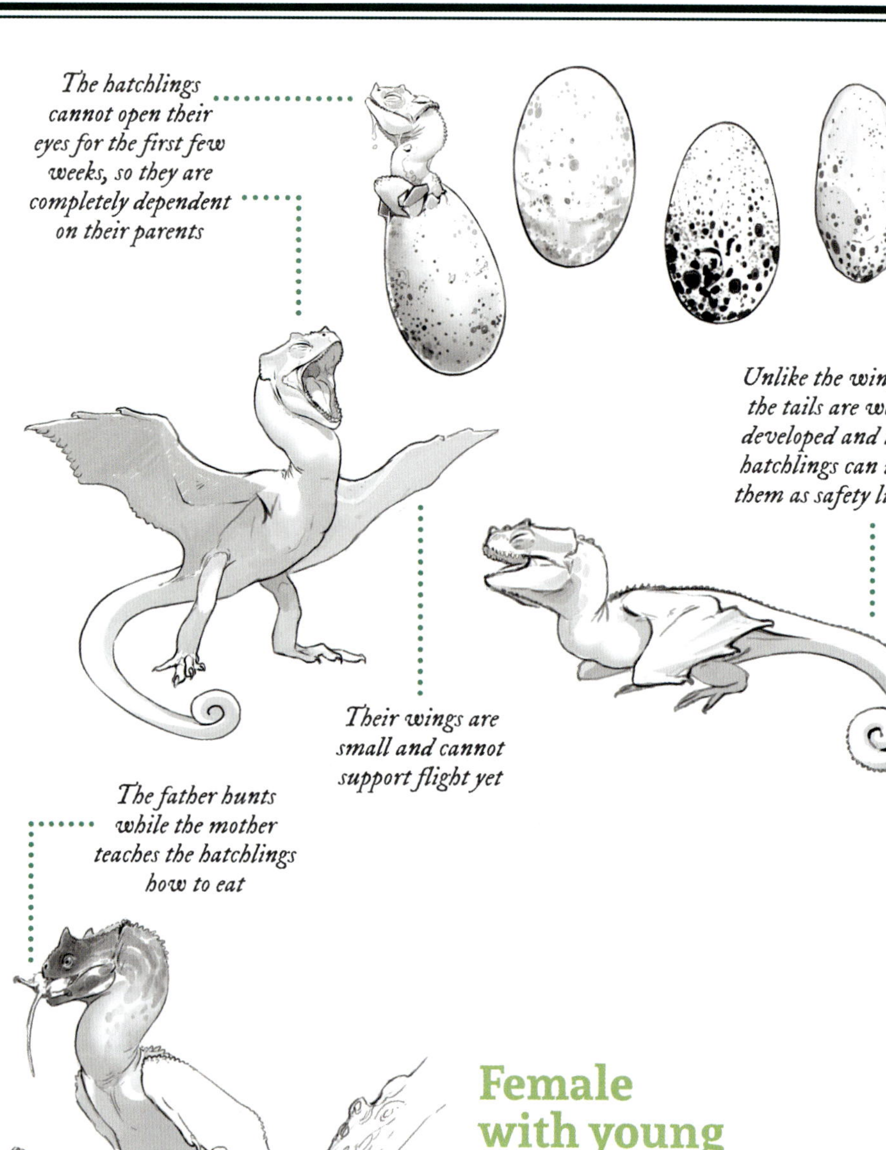

The hatchlings cannot open their eyes for the first few weeks, so they are completely dependent on their parents

Unlike the wings, the tails are well developed and the hatchlings can use them as safety lines

Their wings are small and cannot support flight yet

The father hunts while the mother teaches the hatchlings how to eat

The youngsters use their prehensile tails to hold onto the nest

The nest the parents built can only do so much to keep the hatchlings safe; the mother keeps watch for predators

Female with young

The sexes of the forest wyvern share similarities, but the females are lighter in build and have smaller horns that are angled backward slightly. Common forest wyverns form breeding pairs and remain together until their hatchlings are independent.

As part of the mating ritual, two wyverns make a nest together in the crown of an old pine tree, using pine needles, moss, feathers, and sticks. The female lays three to five eggs and incubates them until they hatch. After they hatch, the male hunts for food while the female stays in the nest, where she teaches her young how to eat and protects them from predators – especially other forest wyverns.

Old age

Old individuals are easily identified: the larger the horns, the older the wyvern. Some of the scales also continue growing and so the skin gets more textured with age. The scales start to lose their vibrant color and in some cases no pigment remains. Older wyverns are riddled with scars from numerous territorial battles. This affects their ability to camouflage, so older individuals sometimes change their hunting strategy. As older wyverns are also bigger and bulkier, they can overpower larger prey such as rabbits or young turkeys. Using berries as bait, they observe the forest floor from a branch until the prey approaches, then swoop down and carry their prey into the treetops to eat.

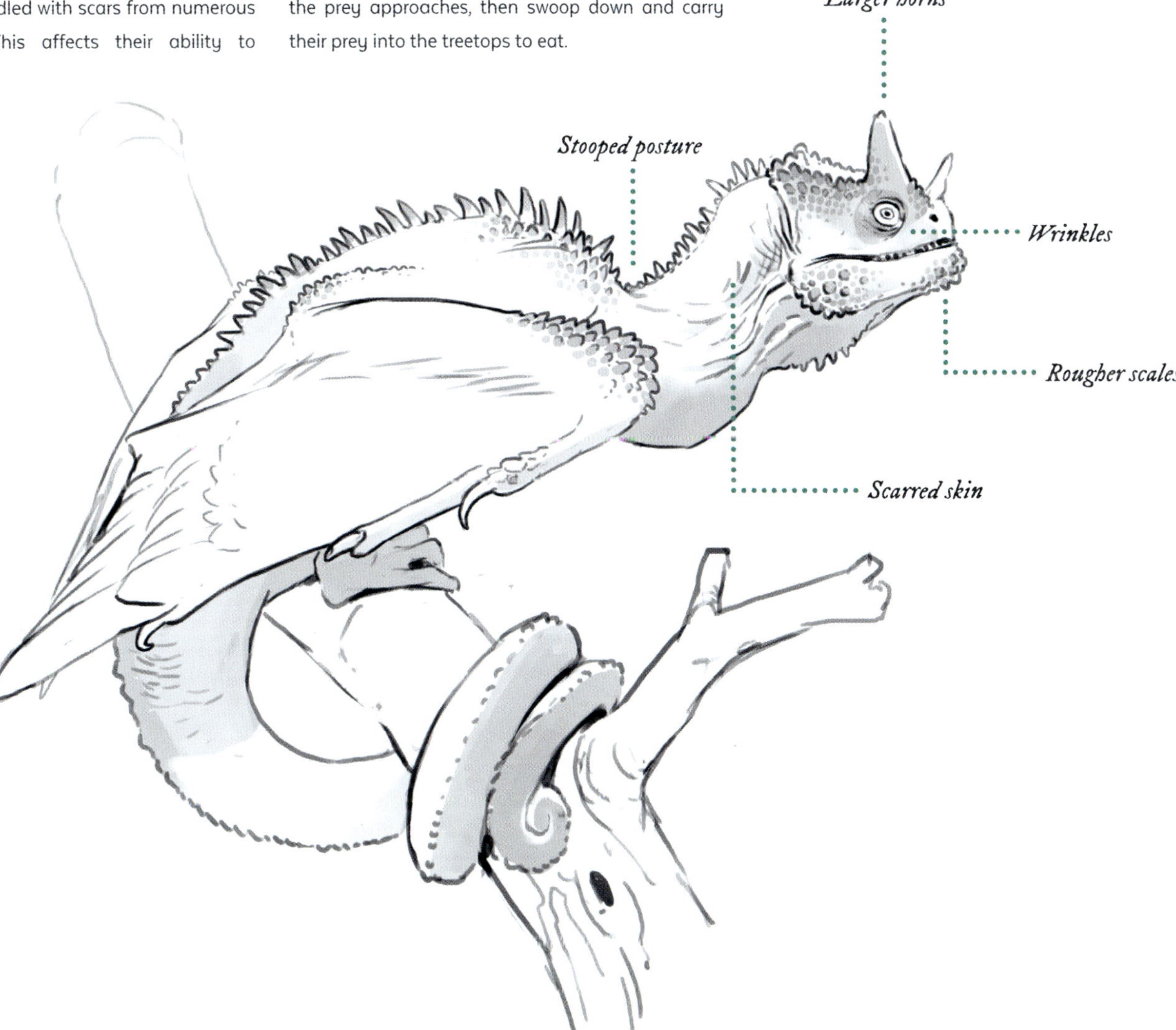

Industry tip

Knowing the basic principles of biology, ecology, and evolution is crucial for designing believable creatures. Every animal's anatomy has a reason. A bat's sense of hearing and large ears, for example, are solutions to the specific problem of hunting at night and flying through a dark forest. Ask yourself, "Why did my creature evolve this way? What does it eat? How does it get its food? Where does it live? What environmental challenges does it face, and how has it adapted to deal with them?" Doing your research based on questions like these, and looking at how real animals solved similar problems, will ground your creature design in reality and make it that much more believable.

Ungulate herbivore

Kate Pfeilschiefter

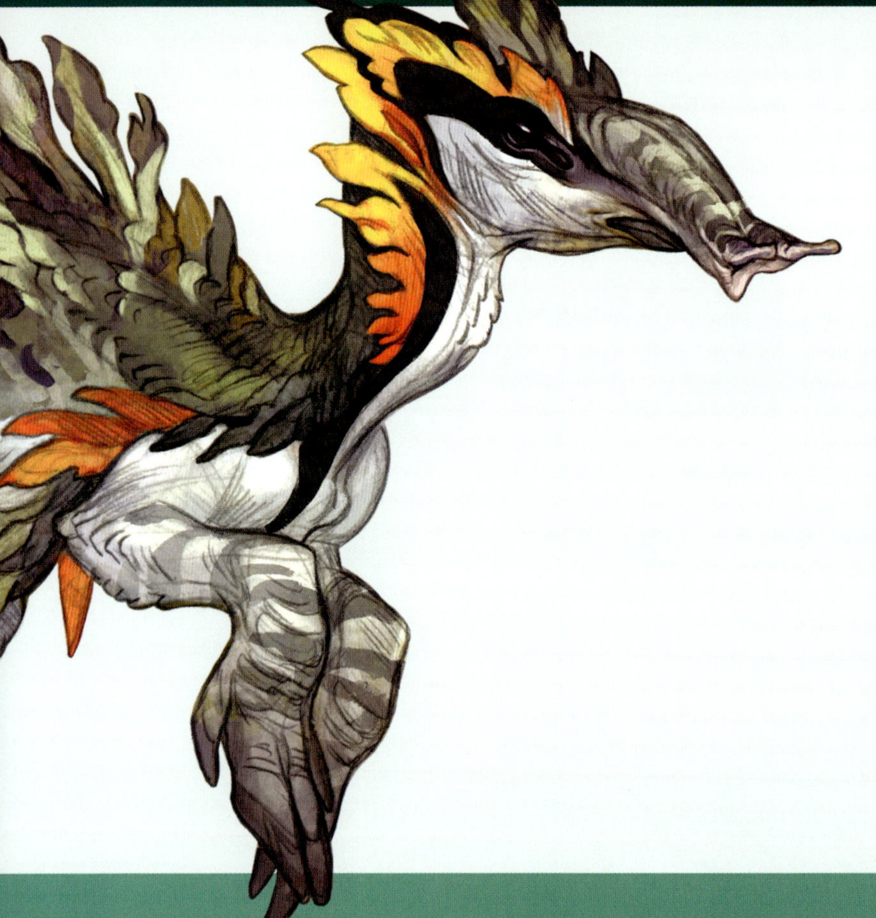

Key facts

- Foraging herbivore with a flexible snout and claw-like hooves for digging

- Generally lives in wooded or grassland areas that offer a wealth of plants and fruit

- Its high tolerance for poisonous plants can make its meat unappetizing to predators

- Largely solitary, each with a wide-ranging territory that is usually respected by others

- Poor vision but strong sense of smell that enables it to forage in any weather or at any time of day

- Plant-like features provide camouflage when feeding

IDEATION

The word "ungulate" may bring to mind images of majestic horses and leaping herds of gazelle, but the ungulate clade - the group comprising all hoofed mammals - features species functioning in many different niches, and with varying shapes and sizes. As far as descriptive usage goes, the term ungulate refers to being "unguligrade," which simply means the animal walks on its nails or hooves (or *ungulae* in Latin). Hooves are useful for traction and are generally found on animals that need to run but do not need to capture prey. Thus, hooves are mainly seen on herbivores that have many predators. It is common in evolutionary history to find animals that

evolve adaptations for one purpose and later modify them for other uses - this is called "exaptation." In this creature's case, hooves that evolved for mobility purposes are repurposed for digging.

Having front hooves devoted to use as foraging tools explains why the creature relies on camouflage and toxicity as defense mechanisms, instead of escape like most ungulates. Perhaps the front hooves are too cumbersome to run with. This also helps imply a size range, likely a small to mid-sized herbivore that is prey to many species. Smaller creatures can conceal themselves more successfully when feeding.

To determine the design's proportions, the research will start by focusing on small ungulates, then turn to exploring hoof shape through classic digging animals such as badgers and moles. Smell is this creature's primary mode of perceiving the world, so tapirs, star-nosed moles, saiga, and pigs are all possible reference points for facial anatomy. The plant structures will be a fun theme to incorporate as an interesting "integument" (skin structure) across the body. Aside from proportions, the snout and the plant-mimicking camouflage will likely be the key visual points of this design.

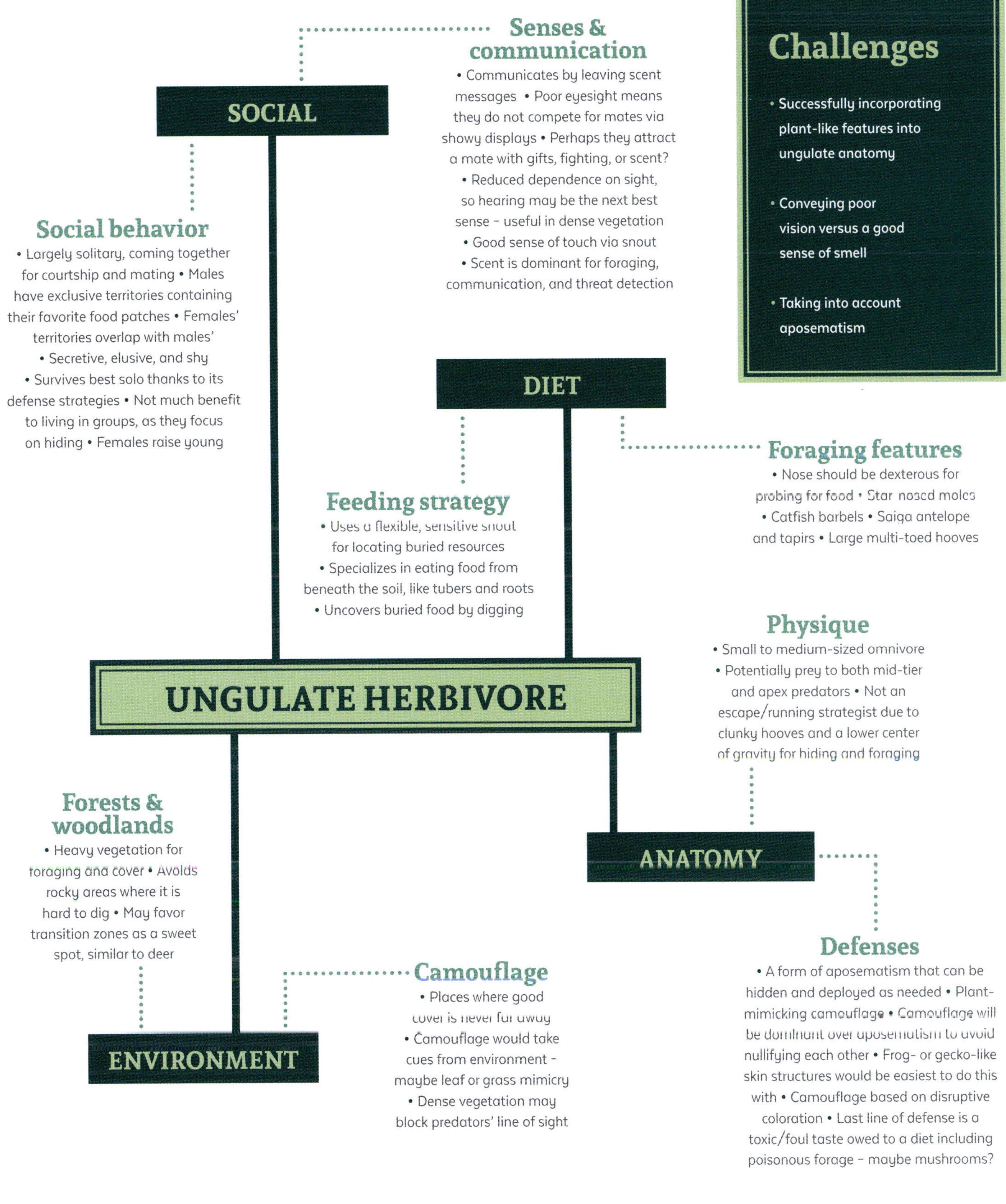

Senses & communication
• Communicates by leaving scent messages • Poor eyesight means they do not compete for mates via showy displays • Perhaps they attract a mate with gifts, fighting, or scent? • Reduced dependence on sight, so hearing may be the next best sense – useful in dense vegetation • Good sense of touch via snout • Scent is dominant for foraging, communication, and threat detection

SOCIAL

Social behavior
• Largely solitary, coming together for courtship and mating • Males have exclusive territories containing their favorite food patches • Females' territories overlap with males' • Secretive, elusive, and shy • Survives best solo thanks to its defense strategies • Not much benefit to living in groups, as they focus on hiding • Females raise young

Challenges
• Successfully incorporating plant-like features into ungulate anatomy
• Conveying poor vision versus a good sense of smell
• Taking into account aposematism

DIET

Feeding strategy
• Uses a flexible, sensitive snout for locating buried resources • Specializes in eating food from beneath the soil, like tubers and roots • Uncovers buried food by digging

Foraging features
• Nose should be dexterous for probing for food • Star-nosed moles • Catfish barbels • Saiga antelope and tapirs • Large multi-toed hooves

Physique
• Small to medium-sized omnivore • Potentially prey to both mid-tier and apex predators • Not an escape/running strategist due to clunky hooves and a lower center of gravity for hiding and foraging

UNGULATE HERBIVORE

Forests & woodlands
• Heavy vegetation for foraging and cover • Avoids rocky areas where it is hard to dig • May favor transition zones as a sweet spot, similar to deer

ANATOMY

Defenses
• A form of aposematism that can be hidden and deployed as needed • Plant-mimicking camouflage • Camouflage will be dominant over aposematism to avoid nullifying each other • Frog- or gecko-like skin structures would be easiest to do this with • Camouflage based on disruptive coloration • Last line of defense is a toxic/foul taste owed to a diet including poisonous forage – maybe mushrooms?

Camouflage
• Places where good cover is never far away • Camouflage would take cues from environment – maybe leaf or grass mimicry • Dense vegetation may block predators' line of sight

ENVIRONMENT

Anatomy research

Small ungulates

The general proportions and anatomy of existing smaller-sized ungulates will be strong reference points for our design. This basic research will indicate what commonalities are present across the species of ungulates, and where on the scale this design will fall. Shown here are the pudú, dik-dik, and a collared peccary. The dik-dik is a species of small antelope with an elongated, flexible snout thought to be used for cooling the air in intense heat; the pudú is the world's smallest deer; and the peccary is a slightly larger omnivorous ungulate with a habit of sniffing out and digging for roots and tubers.

The baby-like features of the pudú and dik-dik also help indicate their diminutive size without needing background elements for a point of reference. This is because proportions do not scale uniformly across large and small animals, due to differences of mass and other biological considerations.

Dik-dik
(*Madoqua*)

A key indicator of herbivory is a convex stomach. This is because plant matter takes far more processing power and time to digest than meat; in contrast, sleek concave abdomens are associated with fast, carnivorous predators

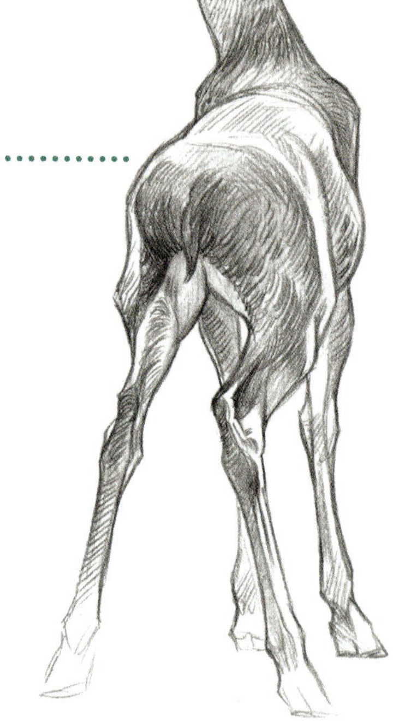

Pudú
(*Pudu*)

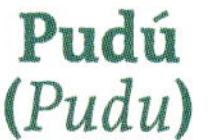

Features such as a high forehead, bent legs, large eyes, and large skull in proportion to the rest of the body make the pudú and dik-dik appear small in size

Collared peccary
(*Pecari tajacu*)

Rounded convex backs, most visible on the peccary, are another trait shared across each of these small mammalian herbivores; it may also be related to mass, as the inverse seems to happen on large mammals

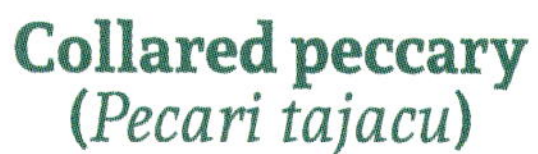

Part-time bipeds

Giant anteaters and pangolins could offer good inspiration for ideas about posture, digging, and how to implement interesting integument structures. The giant anteater is an unusual animal with a unique body shape. Features such as the specialized snout and forelimbs for digging and breaking into termite mounds suit the brief. The powerful shoulders and arms may be useful for communicating this creature's reliance on its forelimbs for digging. The bushy tail acts as a counterbalance when it is rearing up to defend itself, and the wiry hair is reminiscent of grass or bushy vegetation. Our design could incorporate a similar tail and use the planned plant-mimicking integument in place of hair.

The pangolin does many of the same things as the anteater, but on a smaller scale. This lighter creature is a facultative (optional) biped that regularly picks up its bulky front claws and walks upright. Its scale armor also trails around it and breaks up its shape in a similar way to the giant anteater's fur.

A bipedal stance may be a good solution for a creature design featuring forelimbs specialized for digging

Giant anteater (*Myrmecophaga tridactyla*)

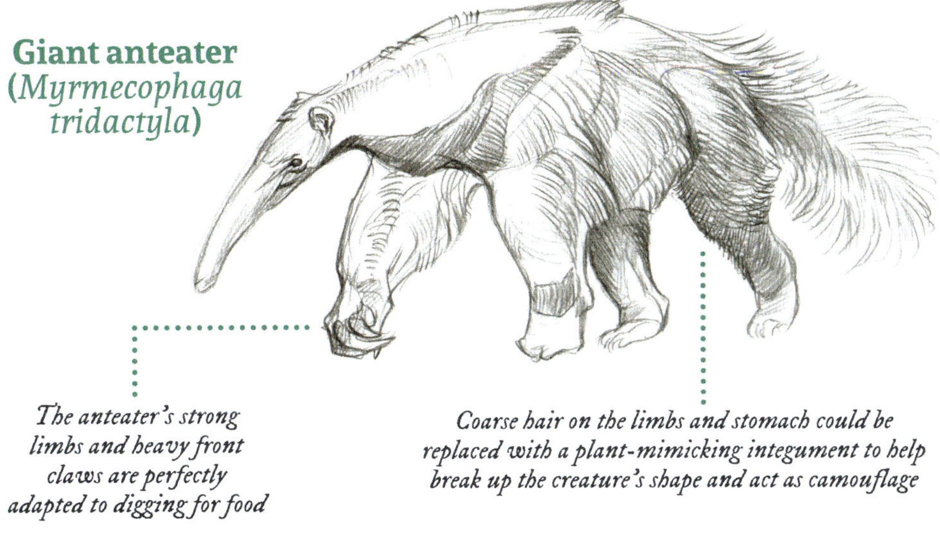

The anteater's strong limbs and heavy front claws are perfectly adapted to digging for food

Coarse hair on the limbs and stomach could be replaced with a plant-mimicking integument to help break up the creature's shape and act as camouflage

Pangolin (*Manidae*)

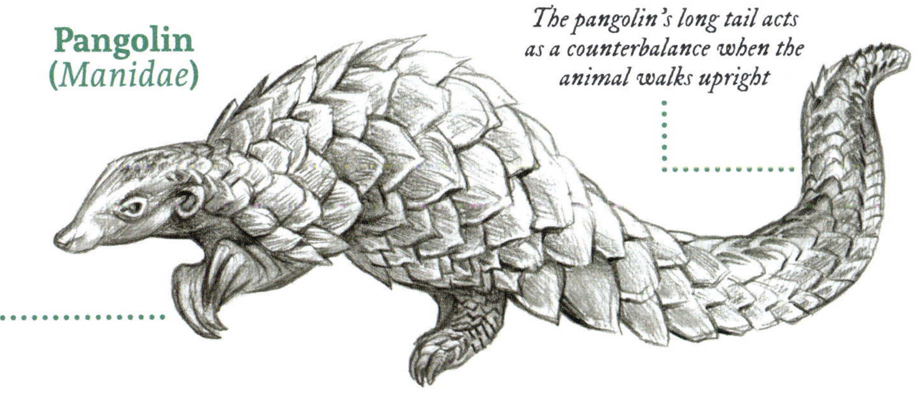

The pangolin's long tail acts as a counterbalance when the animal walks upright

Evolution

Psittacosaurus, an early relative of *Triceratops*, was an herbivorous non-avian dinosaur that was found with impressions of hollow bristles along the upper surface of its tail. Extinct animals such as this offer alternative examples of how to construct a creature, rather than using only known surviving species. Following discoveries in paleontology is a great way to find new sources of inspiration and expand your mental library of forms.

Psittacosaurus represents a dinosaur genus - a taxonomic group between family and species - that is thought to have originated from a quadrupedal form, with some theories suggesting its young were not exclusively bipedal until their hind limbs grew long enough. Our creature's front limbs will be clunky and adapted for digging, so perhaps it could stand up on its hind legs like *Psittacosaurus* for quicker getaways. The bristles also present another reference point for the creature's pseudo-plant structures, and the beak is an effective adaptation for cropping tough plant matter.

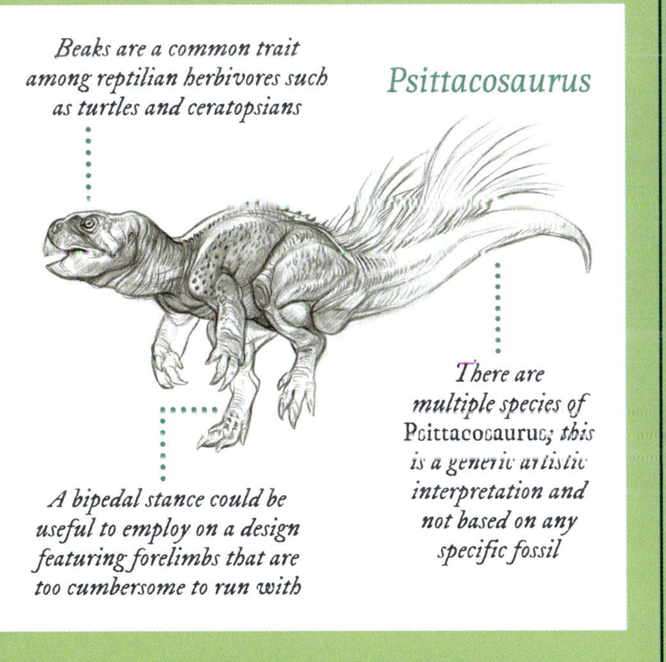

Beaks are a common trait among reptilian herbivores such as turtles and ceratopsians

Psittacosaurus

There are multiple species of Psittacosaurus; this is a generic artistic interpretation and not based on any specific fossil

A bipedal stance could be useful to employ on a design featuring forelimbs that are too cumbersome to run with

Functionality research

Snout

Scent is the creature's dominant sense and therefore its main method of navigating the world. The nose is flexible, and needs to be tactile and sensitive to help with foraging. Perhaps one of the most extreme examples of touch-sensitive noses belongs to the star-nosed mole. The mole uses a uniquely tentacled nose packed with touch receptors to find insects in complete darkness. It is so effective that it essentially acts as vision, allowing the animal to identify whether the object it has touched is edible within eight milliseconds. Using similar structures may help convey our creature's tactile aspect.

The saiga antelope's nose is a multipurpose structure used to cool down on hot days, like the dik-dik's, as well as filtering out dust and warming intakes of cold air. In fact, the skull features an extremely high nasal bone to make room for the huge appendage. These features could be transferable to our creature; the snout could be located high up on the skull in order to emphasize its importance. The nose when relaxed will overhang the mouth, as it does on the saiga or elephant, and can be lifted up for expression or to reach higher food sources.

Hooves

Hooves are specialized for running and traction. Normally legs become smaller and lighter toward the distal end - the farthest end from the body - to reduce the amount of force needed to overcome inertia. Most animals living on firm terrain have hooves that are as small as possible for their body mass. The creature for this brief, however, does not rely on running for its defense and instead uses its front hooves for foraging. It will need long, overgrown, spade-shaped hooves, similar to the claws found on moles and badgers, in order to effectively dig for its food. The creature's hind hooves should be proportioned so they do not take design prominence away from the front limbs, and to keep the creature as a whole more mobile.

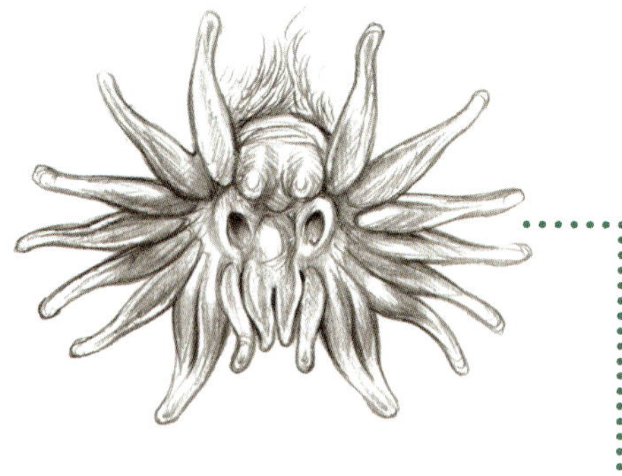

The relatively small star-shaped nose of this mole is covered in over 25,000 minuscule touch receptors known as Elmer's organs, and is roughly six times more sensitive than the human hand

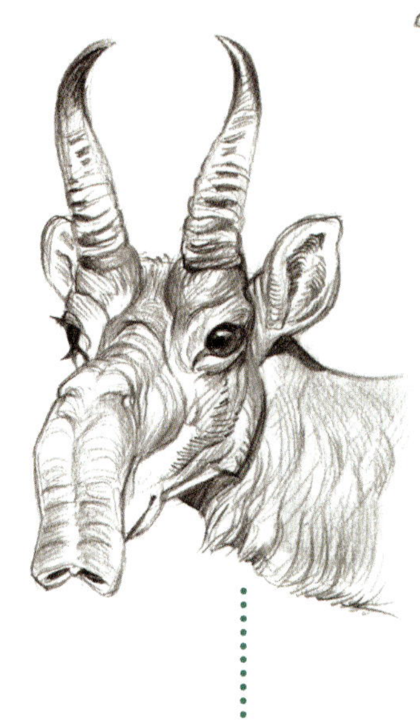

Wrinkle details are visible when the saiga's nose tenses up or is used for vocalization

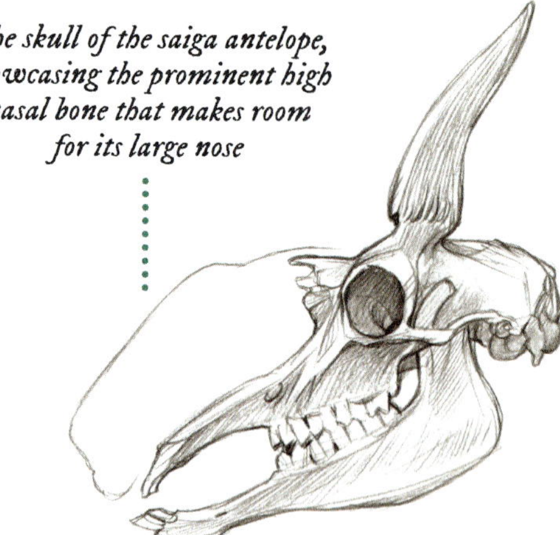

The skull of the saiga antelope, showcasing the prominent high nasal bone that makes room for its large nose

The overgrown front hoof of a goat

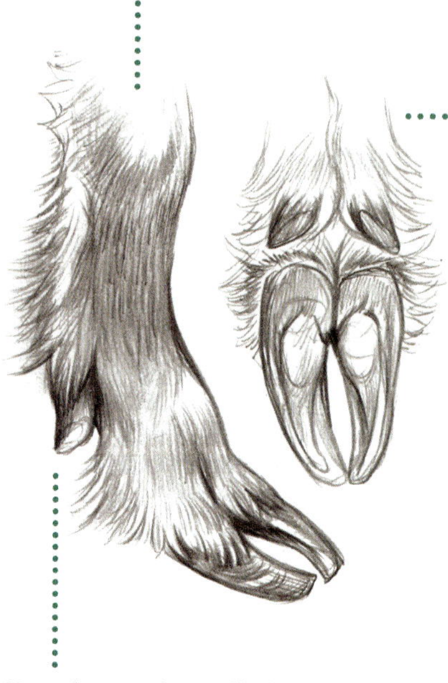

This bottom view shows the typical position of the dewclaws relative to weight-bearing digits

Dewclaws — the small digits held off the ground — are usually vestigial but will be larger on our creature to aid digging

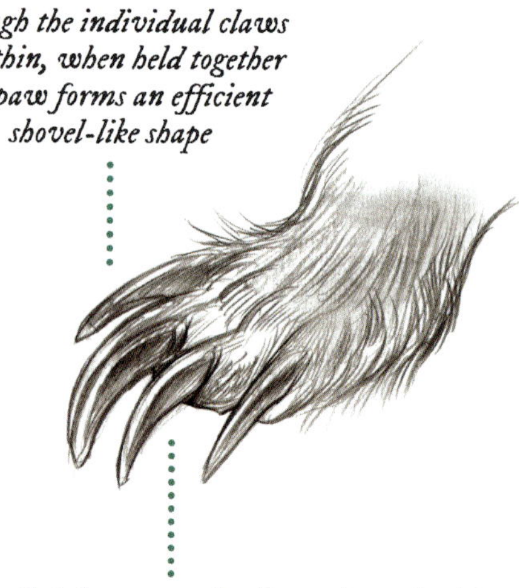

Though the individual claws look thin, when held together the paw forms an efficient shovel-like shape

Subtle concave details on the underside of the claw help scoop away dirt

Integument camouflage

There are several examples of real-world creatures with plant-mimicking integuments that can be used as reference for this design. The leafy sea dragon could be the primary influence for the main structures and how they attach to the body, while various camouflaged geckos can provide inspiration for smaller integument details used to break up the body outline. Many reptiles and amphibians use skin structures to create spines, lobes, frills, and spikes. Our creature will do the same. Its epidermis - the outer skin layer - will consist of a bumpy, gecko-like surface in order to smoothly blend and incorporate these plant-like structures throughout the body.

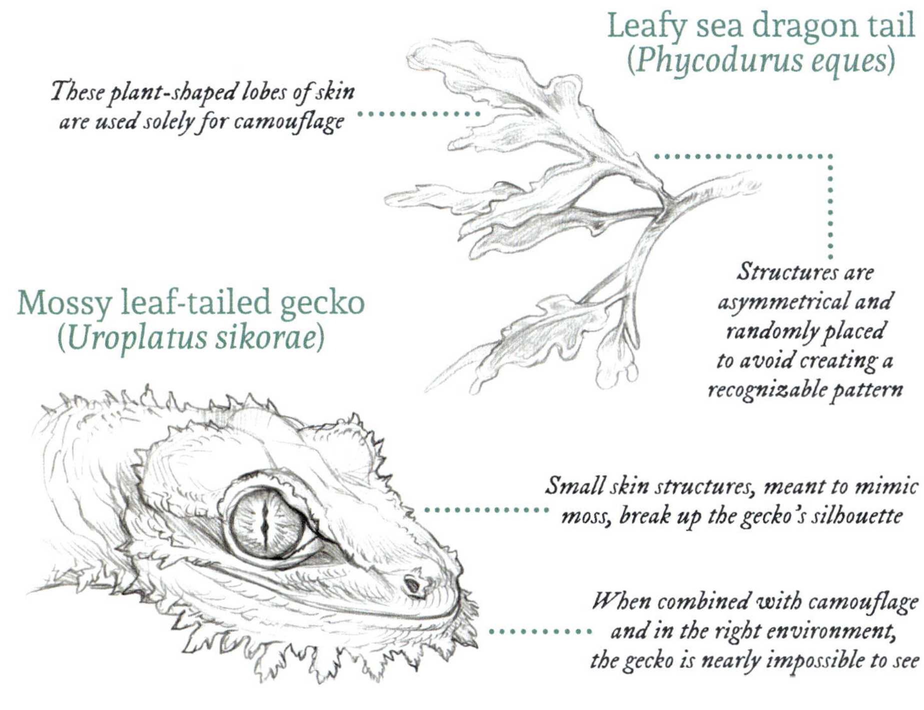

Leafy sea dragon tail (*Phycodurus eques*)

These plant-shaped lobes of skin are used solely for camouflage

Structures are asymmetrical and randomly placed to avoid creating a recognizable pattern

Mossy leaf-tailed gecko (*Uroplatus sikorae*)

Small skin structures, meant to mimic moss, break up the gecko's silhouette

When combined with camouflage and in the right environment, the gecko is nearly impossible to see

Coloration

This creature design needs to carefully combine two extremes in the realm of animal coloration; aposematism and camouflage. Aposematism relies on creating contrasting values and popping colors to draw attention and intimidate, while camouflage intends to do the opposite by blending an animal into the background. From the research, the creature design would benefit from taking inspiration from the herpetological area of the animal kingdom: reptiles and amphibians. This means referencing animals such as geckos and salamanders for color-scheme ideas, in order to meet the challenges of the brief.

The fire salamander (below right) represents the aposematic tactic by using bright saturated markings atop a dark background to create contrast that warns of its high toxicity. The mossy leaf-tailed gecko (above right) breaks up its form using disruptive camouflage, casting mottled splotches of brown and black in irregular ways across its limbs and face in order to confuse the contours of its body.

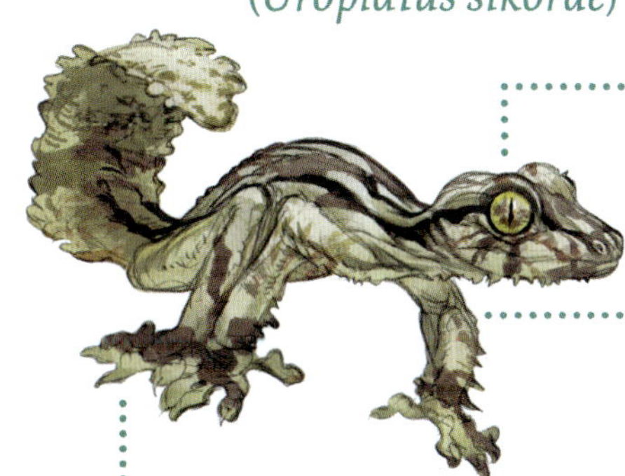

Mossy leaf-tailed gecko (*Uroplatus sikorae*)

Dark eye stripes are used by many animals to hide their faces; this gecko even has striped irises

The gecko expands and contracts different pigment cells to adjust to different backgrounds

Green colors are useful for tropical areas where the vegetation does not vary seasonally

Fire salamander (*Salamandra salamandra*)

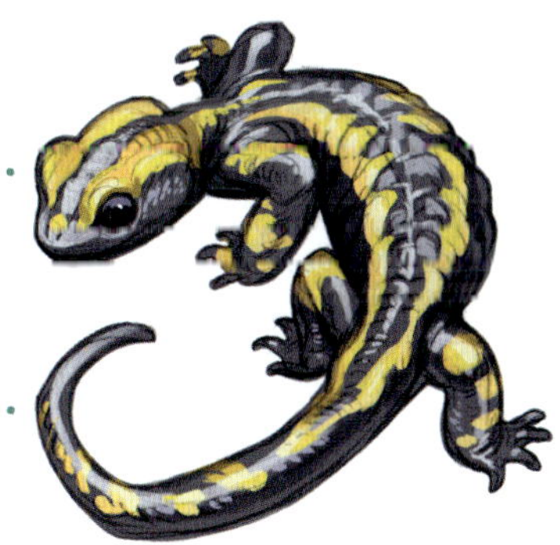

Bright yellow tends to coincide with poison glands; yellow and red are common colors for indicating toxicity

A dark underside emphasizes the yellow and makes the animal stand out from the background (the opposite of countershading)

Thumbnails

Taking what we have learned through research in the anatomy and functionality sections, the general goal for thumbnails will be to explore and narrow down the finer details of the plant structures and the creature's size and proportions.

The creature should feel small in order for its reliance on camouflage as its primary defense to feel plausible. If it appears too big or too durable, it may call into question the evolutionary adaptation of camouflage- and toxicity-based survival strategies; in nature, these are usually defense mechanisms for when escape or confrontation are not realistic survival techniques.

The plant structures will be most prominent along the spine, but their shapes should be repeated elsewhere throughout the body in varying sizes, so they do not feel unexpected whenever they do take greater prominence in the design. The largest leafy fronds should be supported throughout the body by smaller tertiary details such as scales and skin lobes. Having other structures such as these to compare and contrast against will make the larger primary shapes in the design feel more important.

For the same reason, varying the proportions of the front and back limbs, and keeping the hind limbs slimmer, will emphasize the importance of the digging limbs for the creature's survival. The snout should also take up a large amount of room on the face to convey its importance as the primary sensory feature. The creature would likely have a shy and nervous disposition - a personality trait that can be portrayed within the design. As a creature that takes great effort to not draw attention to itself, it meets up with others only when necessary and communicates by leaving discreet olfactory cues around its environment.

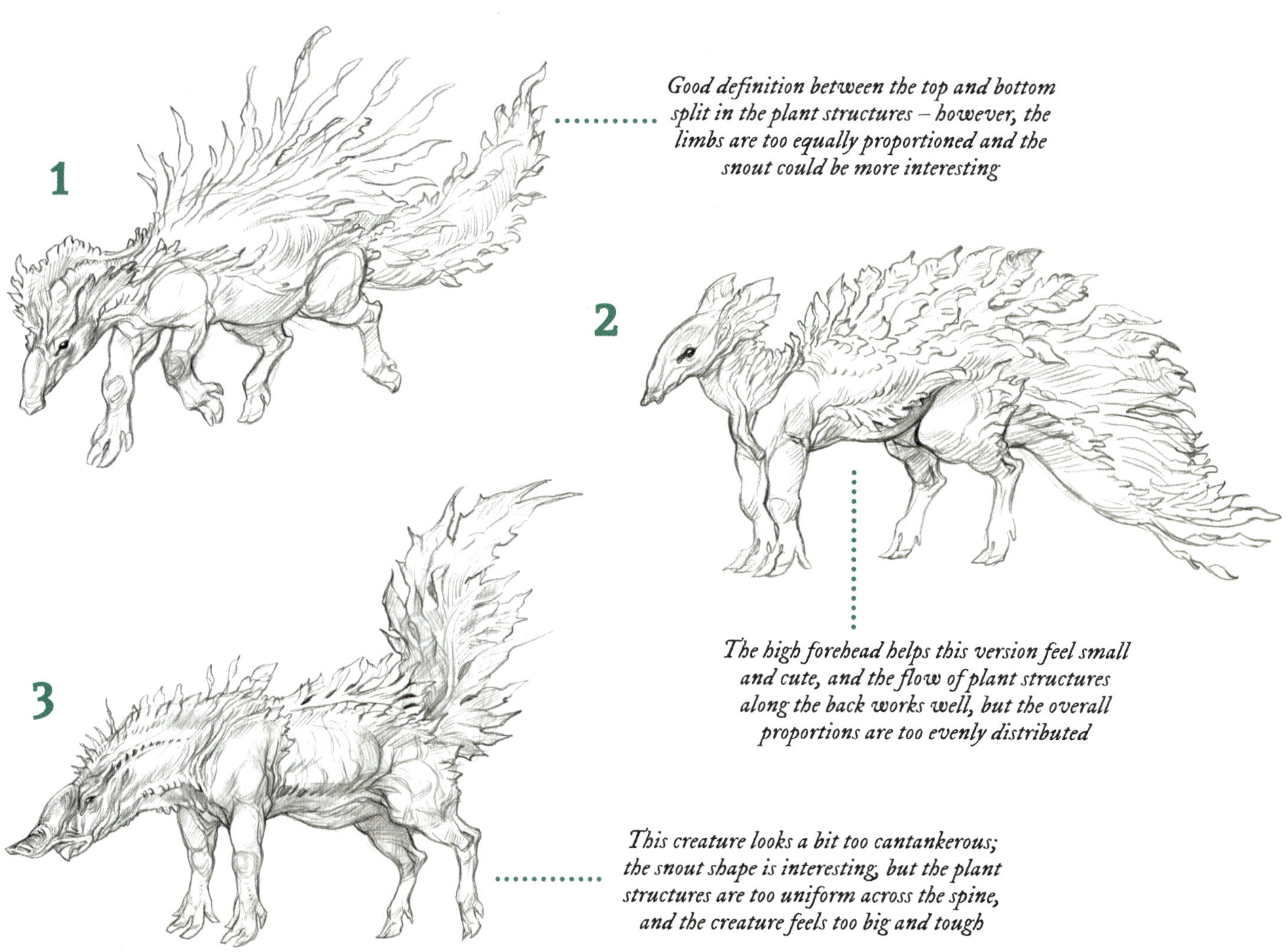

Good definition between the top and bottom split in the plant structures — however, the limbs are too equally proportioned and the snout could be more interesting

The high forehead helps this version feel small and cute, and the flow of plant structures along the back works well, but the overall proportions are too evenly distributed

This creature looks a bit too cantankerous; the snout shape is interesting, but the plant structures are too uniform across the spine, and the creature feels too big and tough

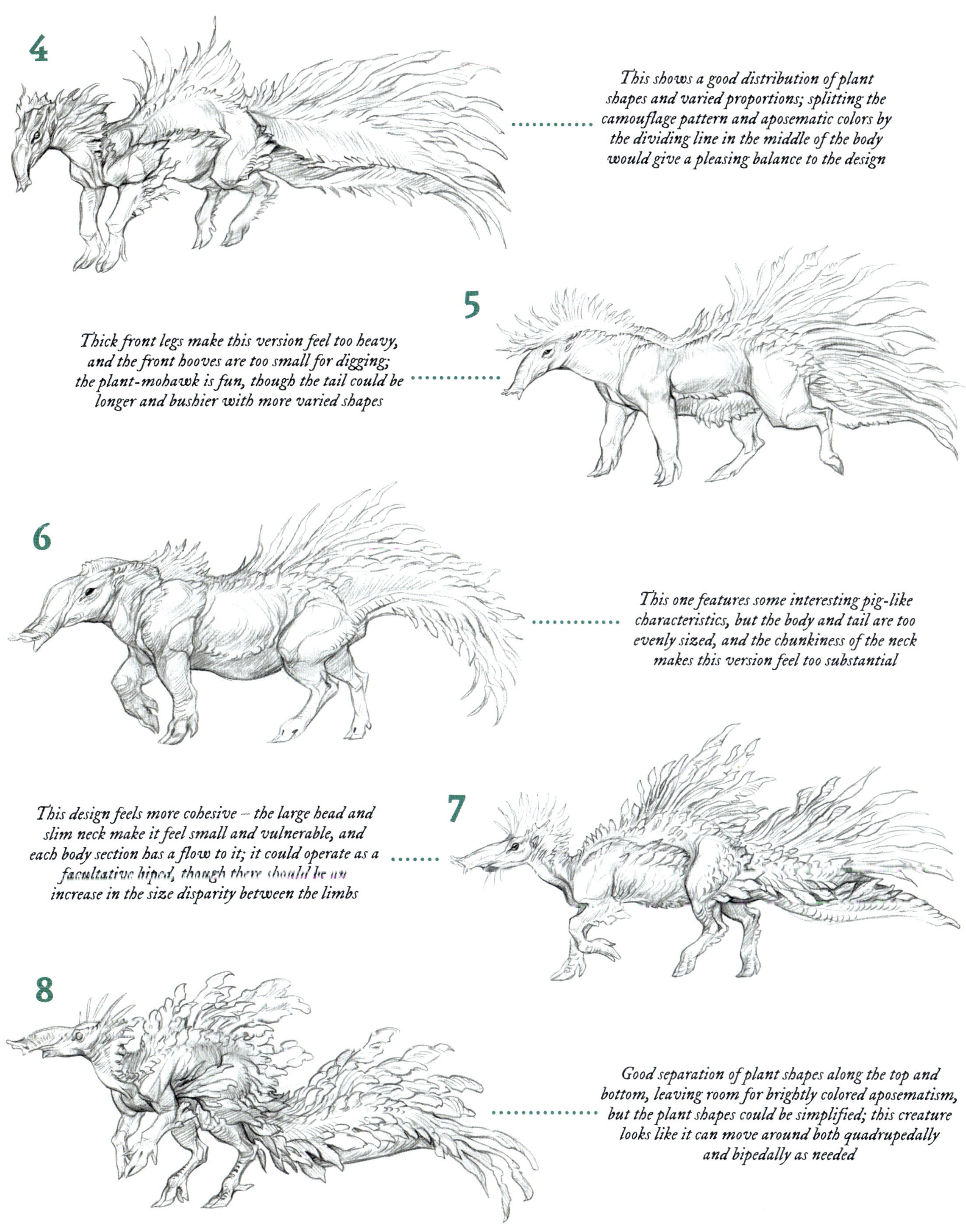

4

This shows a good distribution of plant shapes and varied proportions; splitting the camouflage pattern and aposematic colors by the dividing line in the middle of the body would give a pleasing balance to the design

5

Thick front legs make this version feel too heavy, and the front hooves are too small for digging; the plant-mohawk is fun, though the tail could be longer and bushier with more varied shapes

6

This one features some interesting pig-like characteristics, but the body and tail are too evenly sized, and the chunkiness of the neck makes this version feel too substantial

7

This design feels more cohesive – the large head and slim neck make it feel small and vulnerable, and each body section has a flow to it; it could operate as a facultative biped, though there should be an increase in the size disparity between the limbs

8

Good separation of plant shapes along the top and bottom, leaving room for brightly colored aposematism, but the plant shapes could be simplified; this creature looks like it can move around both quadrupedally and bipedally as needed

DEVELOPMENT

The chosen design direction is a combination of elements from a number of the thumbnail designs. Committing the creature to a bipedal stance allows for its front limbs to specialize more exclusively in foraging. This also allows for more interesting poses and movement, as the creature can switch walking methods depending on the activity. The chosen thumbnails each have a clear break-up of body segments, with shape language specific to the neck, torso, and tail united by a through-line of the plant structures flowing between them.

An early design focus was that the creature would have reptilian skin in order to smoothly blend the plant-structures and the rest of the creature's exterior. The silhouette is frayed and obscured by lobes of skin, but the placement and distribution of the plant-like structures is informed by the underlying anatomy.

A large portion of the head is devoted to the snout as it is the creature's primary sense organ. Having it rooted fairly high on the head and protruding far off the face contributes to the silhouette. The size of the eyes is balanced out by the creature's proportions: smaller eyes would be more suggestive of poor sight, but also might incorrectly suggest a larger body size. Instead, making the eyes just slightly smaller than average for a typical mammal of this size, while also adding features such as a slight squint and some rhino-like wrinkles (as rhinos are a real-world example of a poor-sighted herbivore), helps to suggest nearsightedness without conveying the creature as too large.

Aposematism is tricky to incorporate, given that the prompt suggested a reliance on camouflage as well. The same plant-like structures intended for disguise can serve as dual-purpose warning signs: the top coloration would consist of disruptive camouflage, and the underside would contain warning colors that could be hidden or flared as needed. These features would allow easy transition between the two defensive faculties.

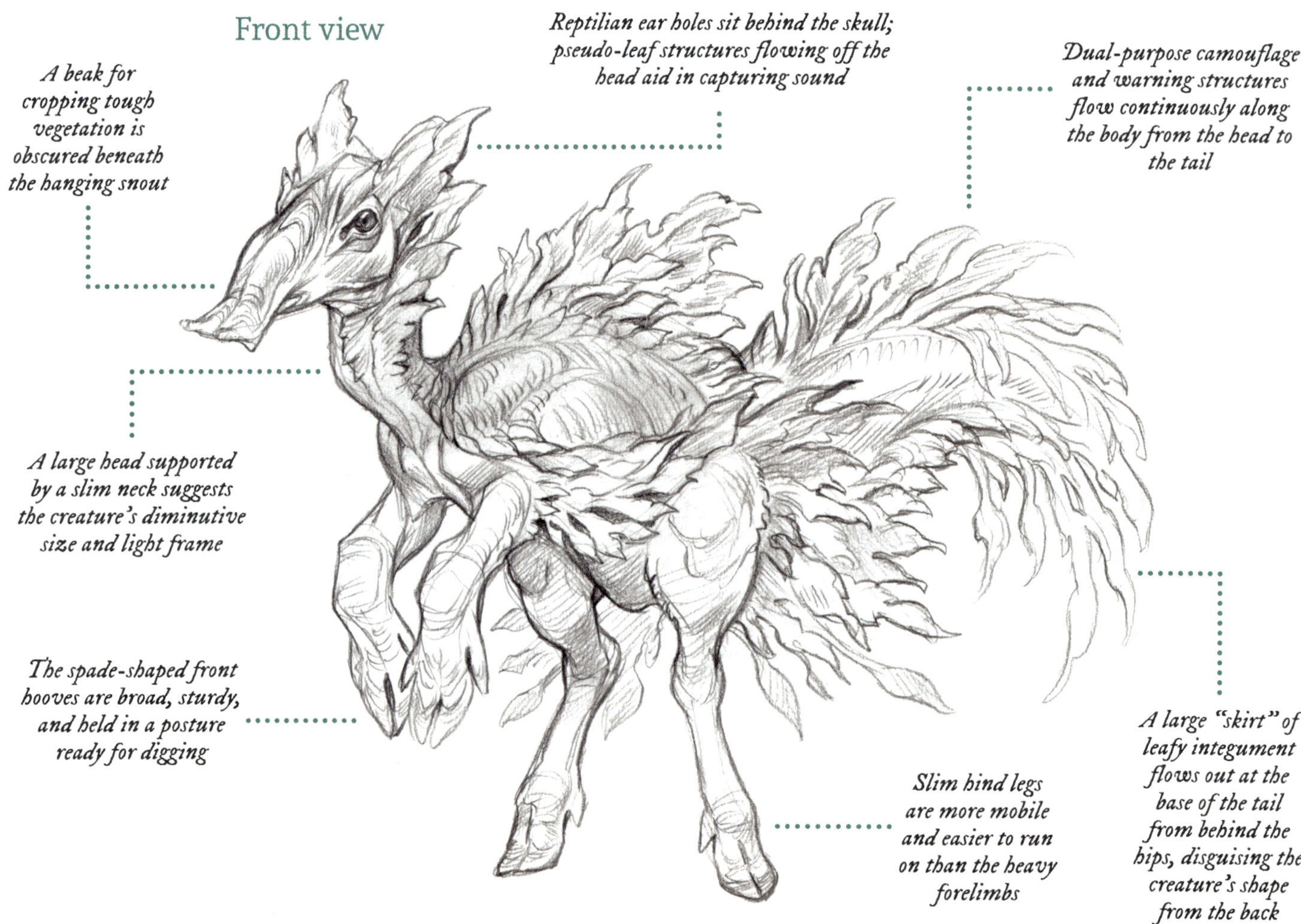

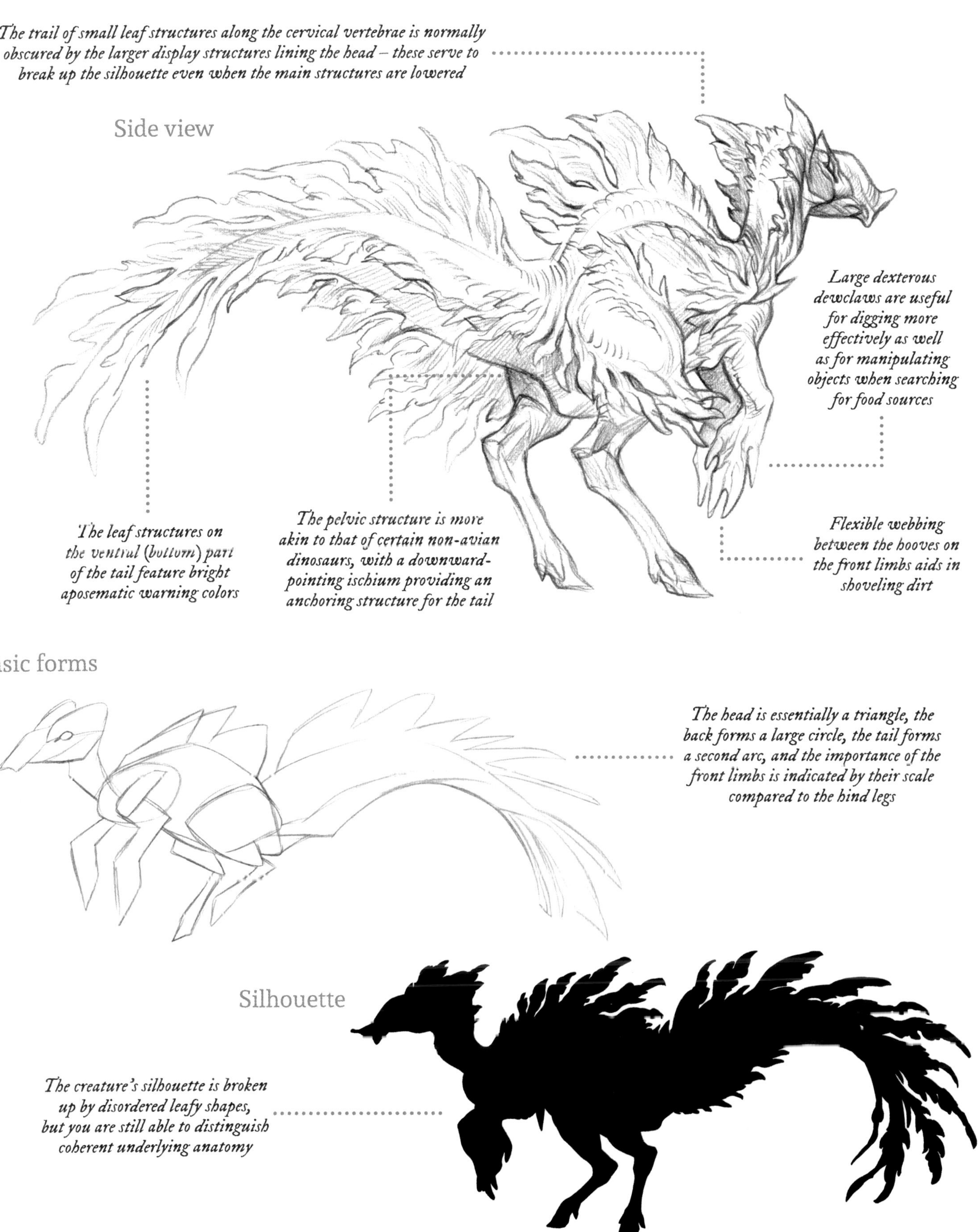

The trail of small leaf structures along the cervical vertebrae is normally
obscured by the larger display structures lining the head – these serve to
break up the silhouette even when the main structures are lowered

Side view

Large dexterous
dewclaws are useful
for digging more
effectively as well
as for manipulating
objects when searching
for food sources

The leaf structures on
the ventral (bottom) part
of the tail feature bright
aposematic warning colors

The pelvic structure is more
akin to that of certain non-avian
dinosaurs, with a downward-
pointing ischium providing an
anchoring structure for the tail

Flexible webbing
between the hooves on
the front limbs aids in
shoveling dirt

Basic forms

The head is essentially a triangle, the
back forms a large circle, the tail forms
a second arc, and the importance of the
front limbs is indicated by their scale
compared to the hind legs

Silhouette

The creature's silhouette is broken
up by disordered leafy shapes,
but you are still able to distinguish
coherent underlying anatomy

Poses

Here are three poses depicting common behaviors. For the majority of its time, especially when resting, the creature would keep its warning coloration hidden, relying primarily on its camouflage and leafy integument to keep itself safe. When being cautious or lying down, the leafy "cape" and "skirt" would droop to hide the outline of its body, and its head fronds would be pressed flat against the skull to hide the bright coloration underneath.

When foraging the creature would do most of the digging work with its large front hooves, using its back legs to brace itself for stability as it pulls away mounds of earth. Its nose is busy probing the loosened earth for food rather than sniffing for predators, making it vulnerable during this time. The "leaves" along its spine would be raised and moved in accordance with the wind, mimicking the movement of any surrounding vegetation and helping it blend in, even while walking.

If the vegetation mimicry fails and it is approached by a predator, the creature lifts up the leafy integument lining its underside to flare the bright warning colors underneath. It raises and thrashes its tail, curling it up to show the similar colors along its underside, and spreads its legs into a wide stance to make itself appear larger and more threatening. It could possibly flap the leaf "cape" along the neck as well, creating a disorienting blinking display. If all else fails, it will either fight or flee depending on the size and speed of the threat.

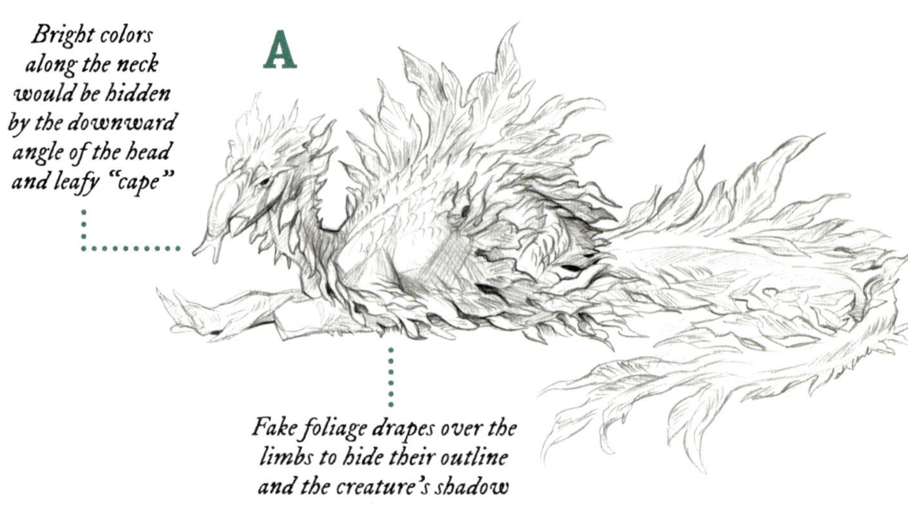

Fake foliage drapes over the limbs to hide their outline and the creature's shadow

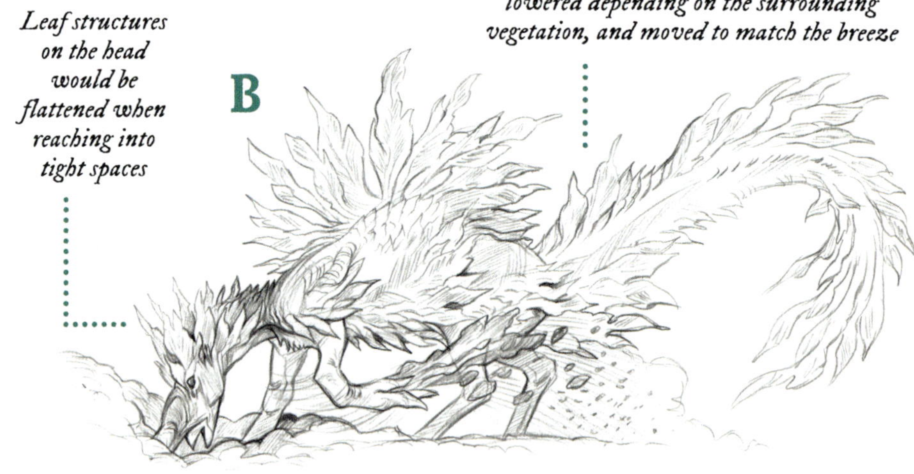

Beak is exposed for eating as the snout probes the earth ahead for food

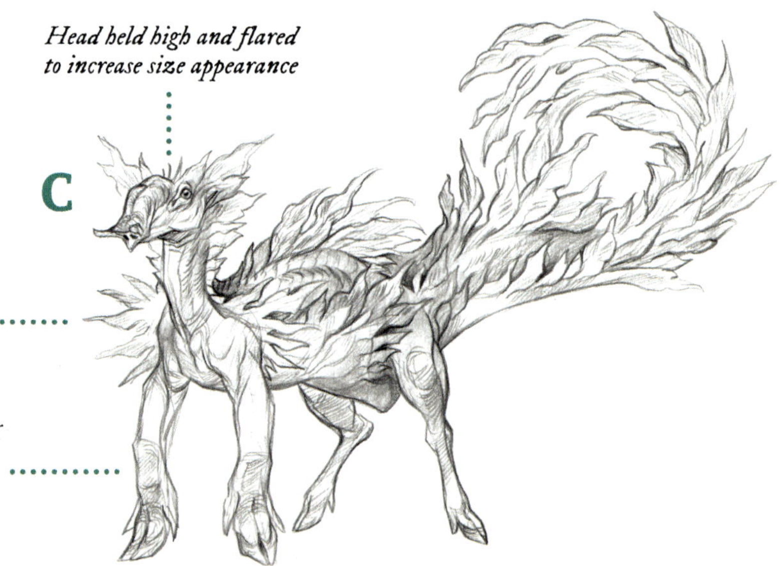

Color & pattern

Each color option explored here is approached with the intention of balancing the dominant survival strategy of camouflage with the secondary survival strategy of aposematism. The dorsal surface of the creature utilizes disruptive camouflage, breaking up anatomical forms with stripes and blobs of different values atop a muted color scheme, while the underside features colors sharply contrasted or brightly hued.

Different color schemes may be useful in different environments. Considering the leafy camouflage structures cannot change with the seasons as easily as fur or pigment cells, setting this creature in a subtropical zone closer to the Equator makes sense. Green coloration may be useful for such an environment, but the main color also needs to function as a contrasting backdrop to the typically red and yellow aposematic colors when they are exposed in a threat display.

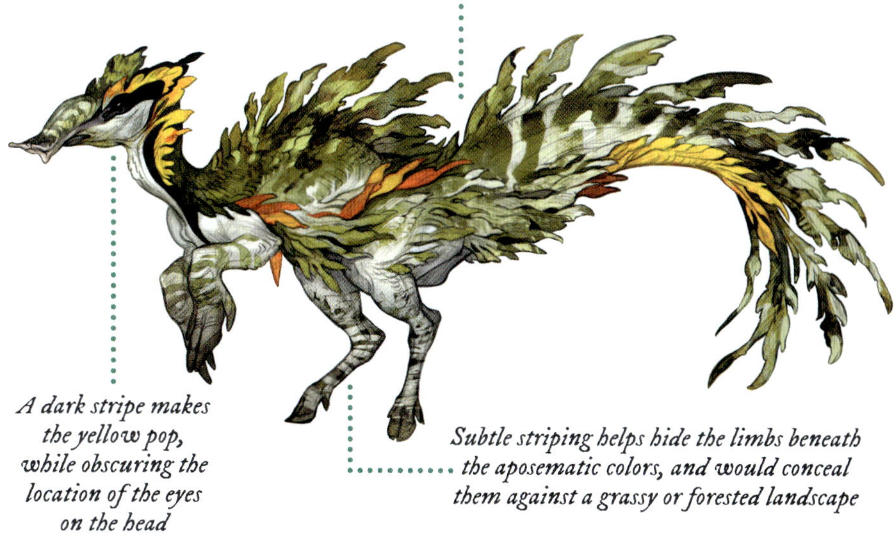

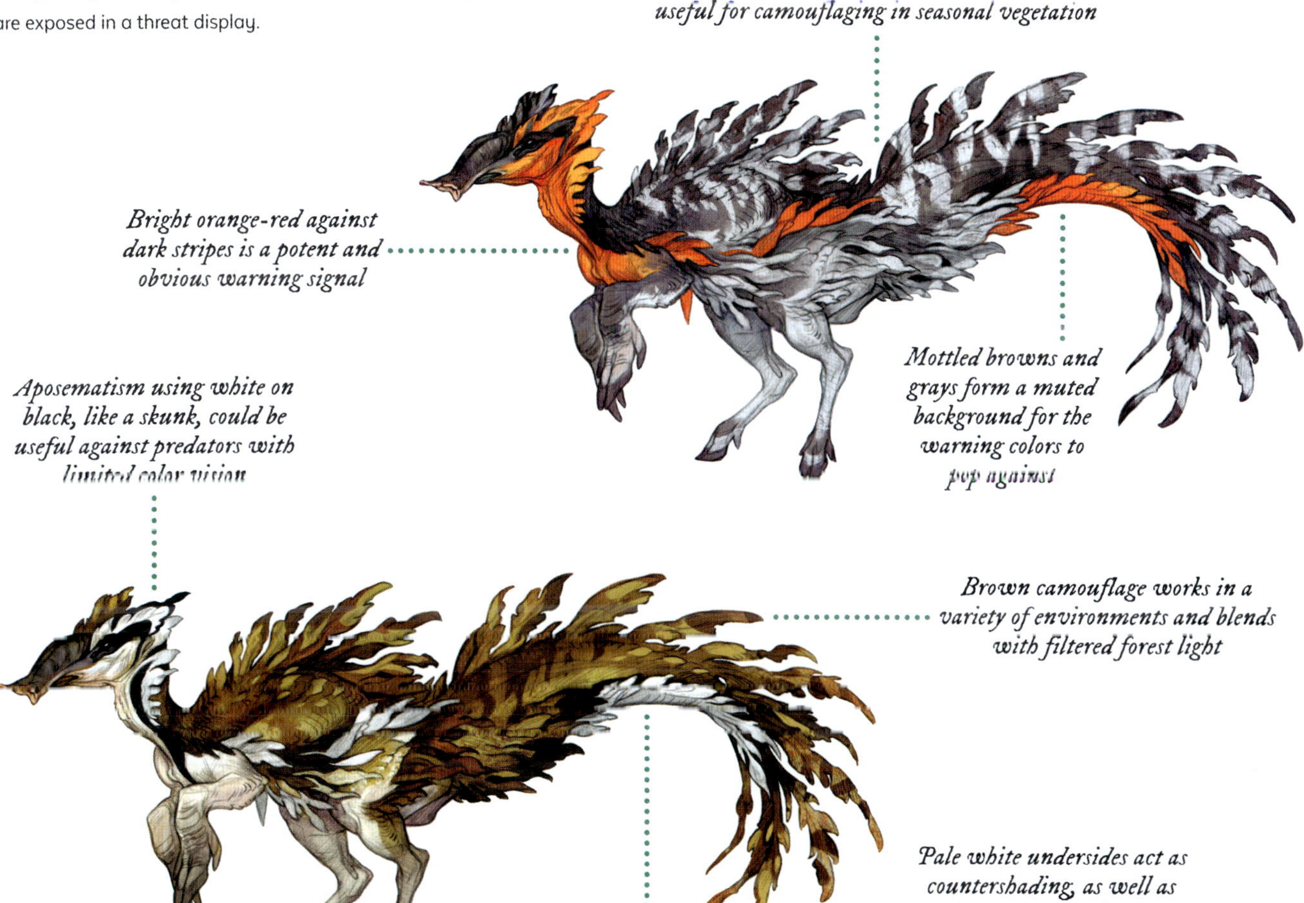

FINAL DESIGN

This design is a good example of how following a brief can result in a really exciting, original design. The deeper the exploration into different facets of the design brief and what they entailed, the more varied the references and influences for this creature became. The final design was far removed from the initial impression and interpretation of the brief and ungulate herbivores. Instead, what came as a result is this funny little creature named the "bramblesnoot."

Anatomical features from both bipedal reptiles, such as dinosaurs, and facultative mammalians have been used to create a cohesive creature design. Research into mammals with similar proportions and lifestyles, such as the pangolin and giant anteater, pushed the creature into a bipedal design and influenced the proportions used for the tail and leaf structures.

The ungainly snout, large head, thin neck, and the way the creature carefully cradles its forelimbs to its chest, convey an unassuming character; perhaps these creatures are eager to avoid confrontation, and a little comical. The flared warning colors on the head and slight triangular angles indicate this creature is still capable and ready to hold its ground if a threat does appear. In a fictional setting, these animals might be encountered as a piece of foliage or vegetation that a character accidentally steps on, only to have it let out a surprised squeak or chirp as it hops out from underneath them, scuttling hastily into the underbrush.

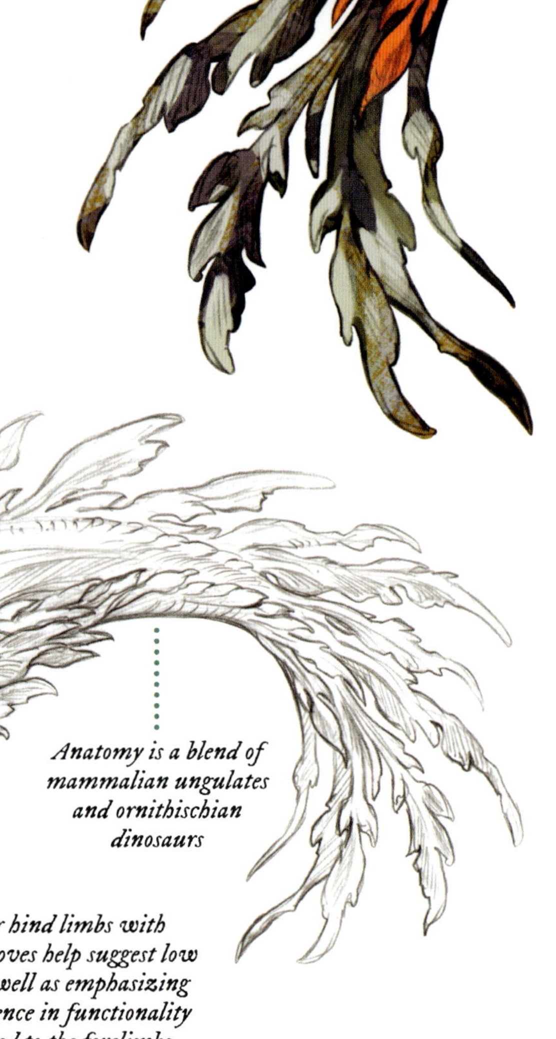

Large, flexible snout provides a powerful sense of touch and smell for finding food, sensing danger, and olfactory communication

Leafy integument lobes are distributed throughout the body at varying sizes and densities to break up the creature's silhouette

Sturdy shovel-like forelimbs are attuned to their work as foraging tools

Anatomy is a blend of mammalian ungulates and ornithischian dinosaurs

Slender hind limbs with smaller hooves help suggest low mass, as well as emphasizing the difference in functionality compared to the forelimbs

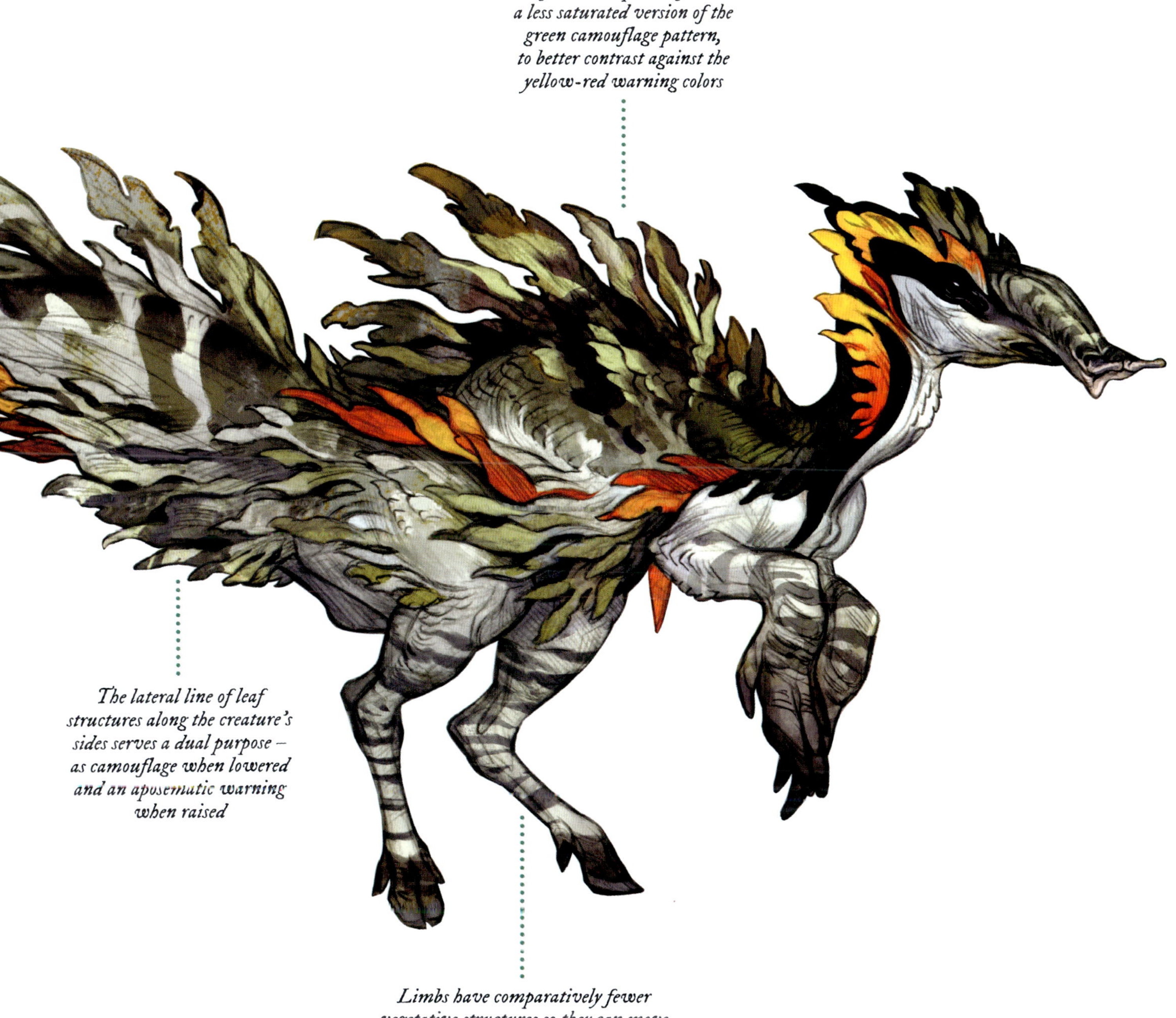

Final image © Kate Pfeilschiefter

ADAPTATIONS

Desert

The desert version (below) lives in hot scrubland with sparse vegetation, and has a larger body for defense to make up for the limited cover. The integument structures have evolved to resemble local plants; in this case, spiky, fleshy agave leaves. The leaves provide shade, help the creature disappear among cacti, and also serve as an additional spiky defense. The snout is bigger to aid in filtering out dust, and the front hooves are more substantial - perfect for breaking up compacted dried soil and stones.

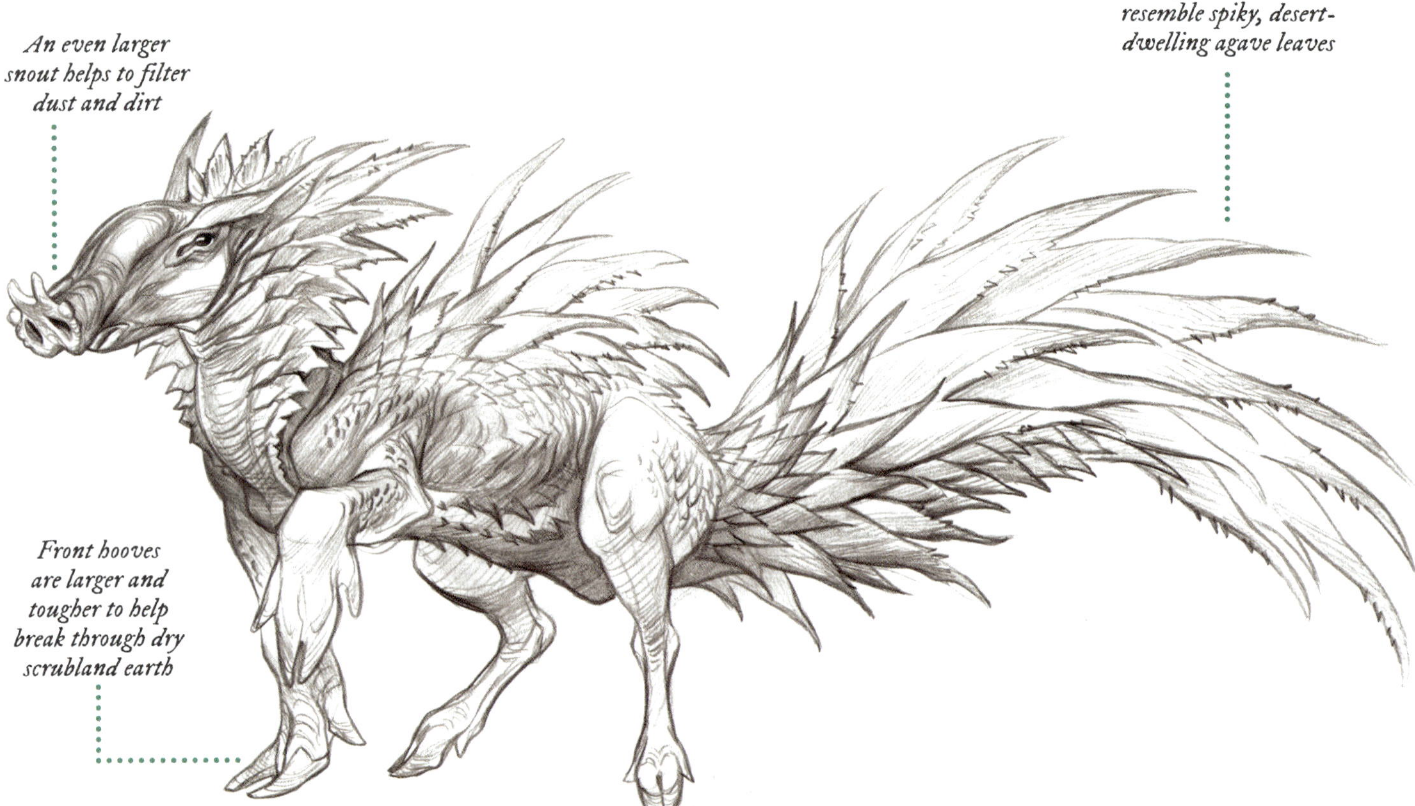

Industry tip

Follow the seemingly tangential subjects related to whatever field you are interested in and see where they lead. For creature design this will likely start with anatomy, but will branch off into biology, ecology, paleontology, biomechanics, natural selection, and speculative evolution. The more you learn about the factors shaping and influencing real animals, the more design options will open up to you, and the faster your decision-making will become. Your imagination is limited by the things you know, so learning and exposing yourself to new information is bound to bring more creativity to your designs. Nature is always stranger than fiction.

On a more targeted note, when approaching a brief with seemingly contradictory requests, such as in this example of balancing camouflage with aposematism, try to isolate one factor as the "hero" trait to focus on. If every trait is evenly represented, without something else to contrast against, then no single element will feel important.

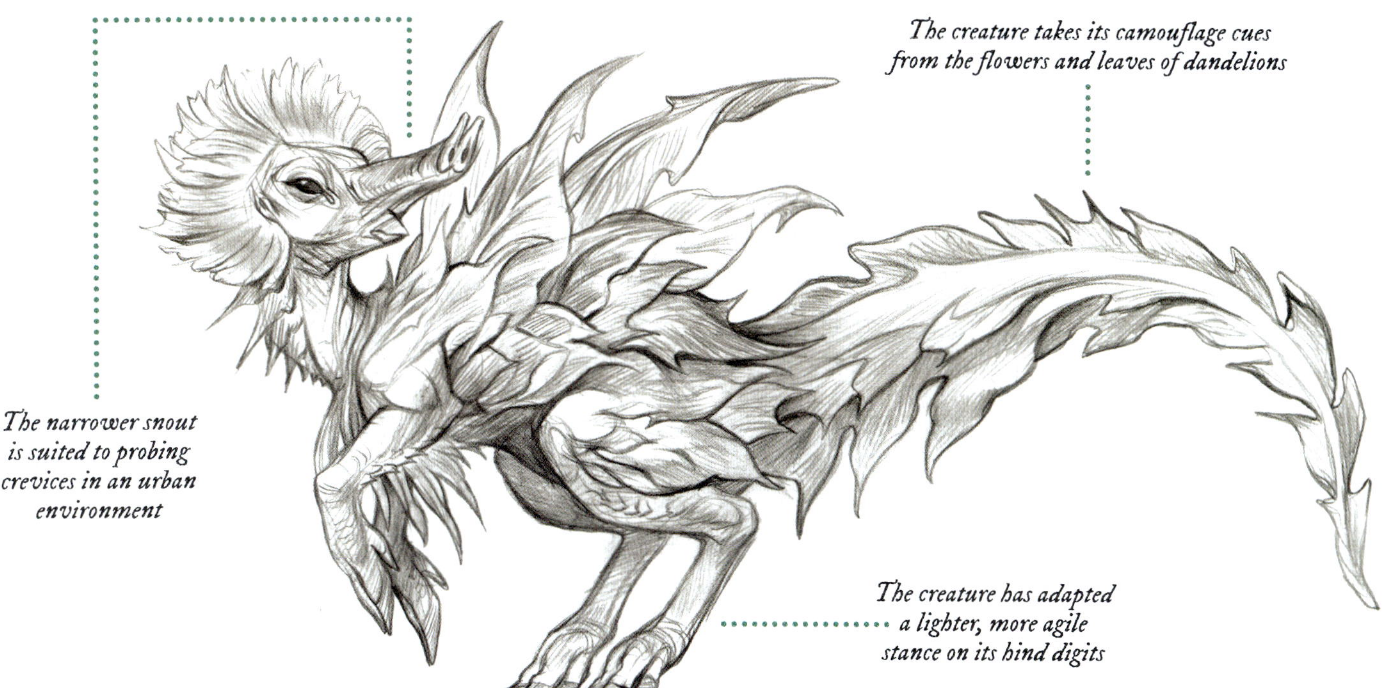

Urban

The urban version (above) has undergone selective pressure to become nocturnal and shrink in size, in order to avoid drawing attention to itself. Its warning colors would remain bright yellow, concentrated around the head to resemble a dandelion flower, while the remaining vegetation structures shift to resembling dandelion leaves. The snout is more slender for probing tiny cracks in human structures, and it has switched to bearing its weight on all four digits of the hind limbs - giving it better dexterity when climbing over irregular surfaces.

Male

The male (right) has a larger snout for producing a vocal honk in order to attract a mate or scare off a competitor. The flared leaf structures around the head are larger for display purposes and are used for warning off predators and intimidating rivals.

The primary difference between the male and female, however, is the male's possession of a bulbous scent gland at the end of its tail. This is dragged along the ground to announce his presence to rivals, as well as advertise to females. Females typically pay little attention to the males' squabbles, and choose the mate with the best aroma, though males can skew the odds in their favor if they successfully scare off the competition.

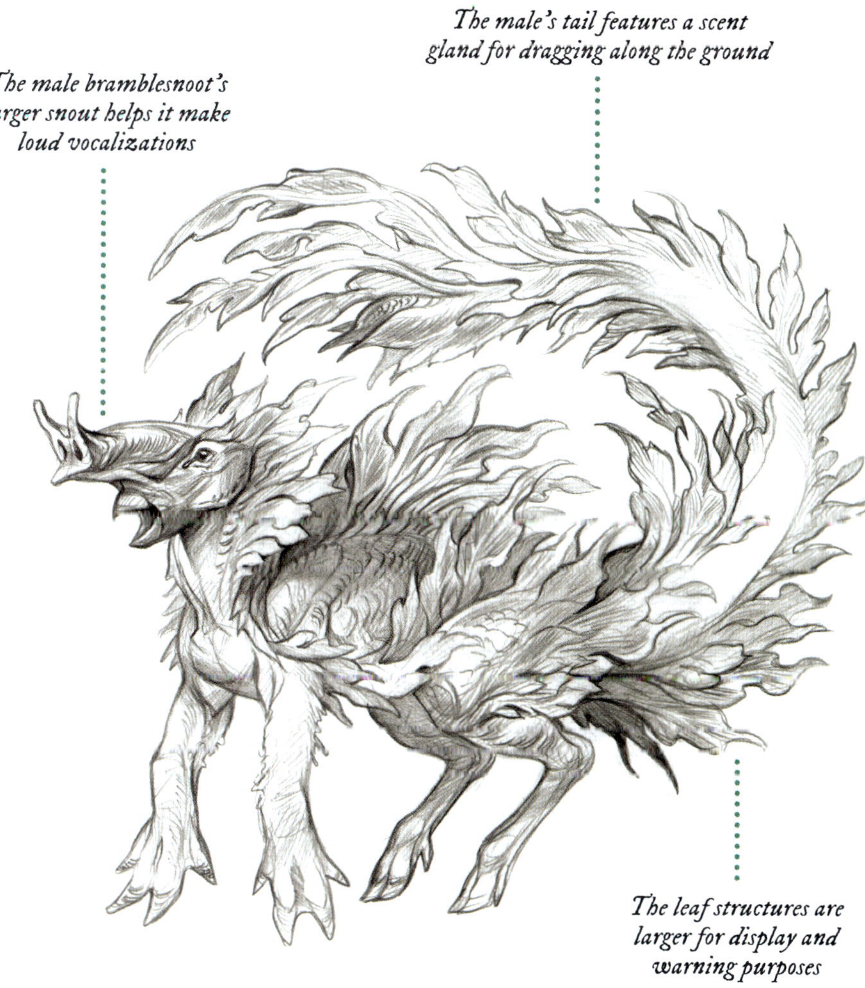

Cetacean hunter

Jordan K. Walker

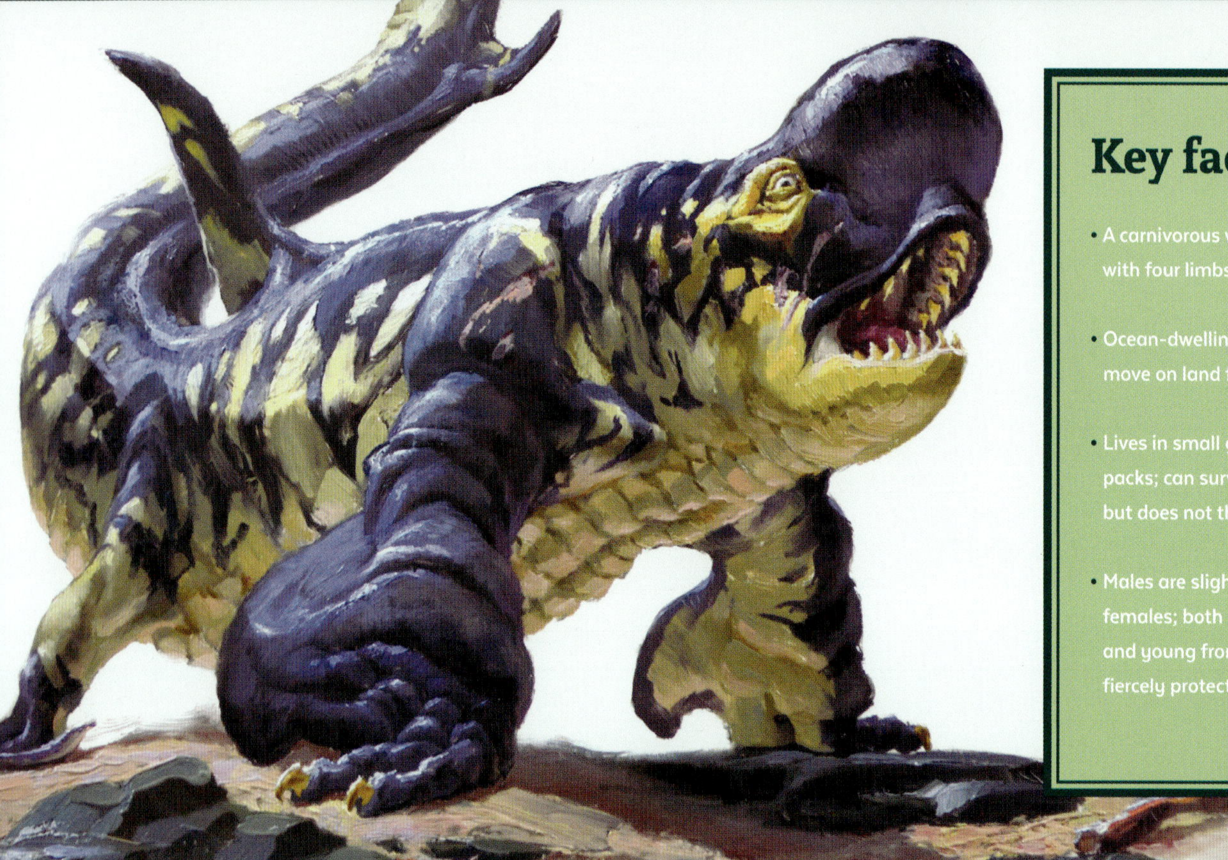

IDEATION

Modern cetaceans are fascinating animals with a rich evolutionary history. This group of animals includes whales, porpoises, and dolphins – many of which are highly intelligent and maintain close family bonds throughout their lives. Their ancestors walked on land, and given the right environmental conditions, it is possible a new species in the group might evolve to do the same in the future.

With this scenario in mind, the goal here is to design an amphibious cetacean that is highly social and comfortable moving on land. It will use these attributes to hunt prey and protect its young.

Such a species might evolve in a shallow sea full of archipelagos, such as the Salish Sea off the coast of Washington and British Columbia. Large animals like elk inhabit some of these islands, and would serve as enticing prey for an amphibious super-carnivore. The design will be influenced by the anatomy of orcas, a modern cetacean species found in this region. Orcas have been known to slide onto beaches to catch prey, and this behavior could be the basis of their eventual transition into amphibious hunters.

Other vertebrates that have a mainly aquatic life, but spend time on land, include some species of fish, turtles, and crocodilians. Aspects of these animals' anatomy will influence the design of my "cetacean hunter," especially in terms of limb development.

Many modern cetacean species live and hunt in family groups called pods. Cetacean hunters will ambush their land-dwelling prey in packs, driving their victims into the ocean to be devoured. They will rear their calves in the shelter of reefs and kelp forests, and take turns watching over these crèches. Competition between rival pods for territory and resources will be fierce, so the creatures must be equipped with the means to defend themselves.

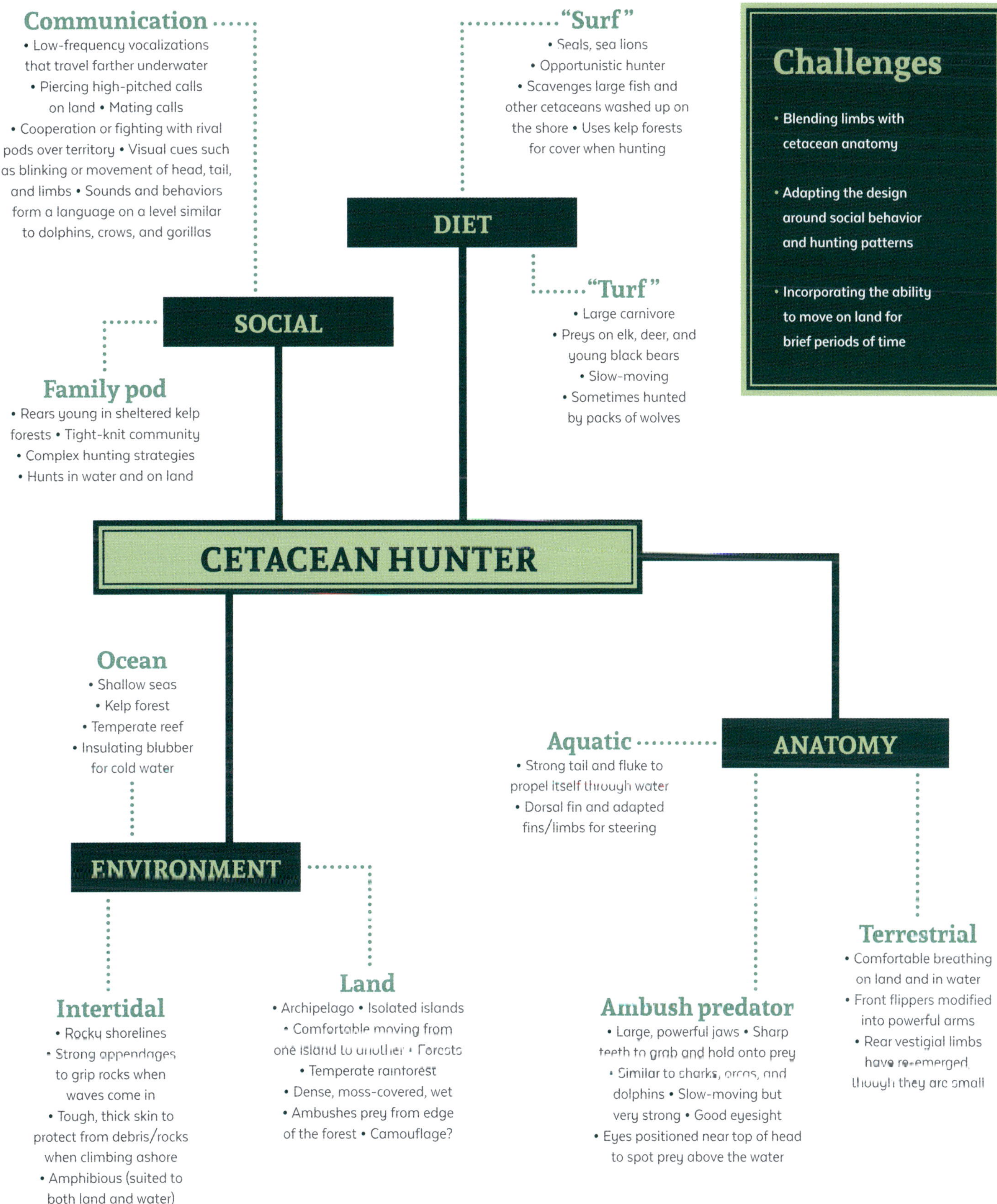
Communication
• Low-frequency vocalizations that travel farther underwater
• Piercing high-pitched calls on land • Mating calls
• Cooperation or fighting with rival pods over territory • Visual cues such as blinking or movement of head, tail, and limbs • Sounds and behaviors form a language on a level similar to dolphins, crows, and gorillas

"Surf"
• Seals, sea lions
• Opportunistic hunter
• Scavenges large fish and other cetaceans washed up on the shore • Uses kelp forests for cover when hunting

DIET

Challenges
• Blending limbs with cetacean anatomy
• Adapting the design around social behavior and hunting patterns
• Incorporating the ability to move on land for brief periods of time

SOCIAL

"Turf"
• Large carnivore
• Preys on elk, deer, and young black bears
• Slow-moving
• Sometimes hunted by packs of wolves

Family pod
• Rears young in sheltered kelp forests • Tight-knit community
• Complex hunting strategies
• Hunts in water and on land

CETACEAN HUNTER

Ocean
• Shallow seas
• Kelp forest
• Temperate reef
• Insulating blubber for cold water

Aquatic
• Strong tail and fluke to propel itself through water
• Dorsal fin and adapted fins/limbs for steering

ANATOMY

ENVIRONMENT

Terrestrial
• Comfortable breathing on land and in water
• Front flippers modified into powerful arms
• Rear vestigial limbs have re-emerged though they are small

Intertidal
• Rocky shorelines
• Strong appendages to grip rocks when waves come in
• Tough, thick skin to protect from debris/rocks when climbing ashore
• Amphibious (suited to both land and water)

Land
• Archipelago • Isolated islands
• Comfortable moving from one island to another • Forests
• Temperate rainforest
• Dense, moss-covered, wet
• Ambushes prey from edge of the forest • Camouflage?

Ambush predator
• Large, powerful jaws • Sharp teeth to grab and hold onto prey
• Similar to sharks, orcas, and dolphins • Slow-moving but very strong • Good eyesight
• Eyes positioned near top of head to spot prey above the water

Anatomy research

Orca

The cetacean hunters will be direct descendants of orcas, so it is important to have an understanding of orca anatomy. Orcas, also known as "killer whales," are predatory cetaceans with many subspecies found throughout the world's oceans. Their bodies are streamlined and hydrodynamic, allowing them to swim over great distances with speed and ease. They propel themselves by moving their large tail flukes up and down, and steer with their pectoral fins, which are actually modified hands. Like many modern cetaceans, orcas have a large "melon" organ in their foreheads, which is used to produce sonar and other sounds to echolocate obstacles and prey underwater. The cetacean hunter may use this ability on land as well as in the water.

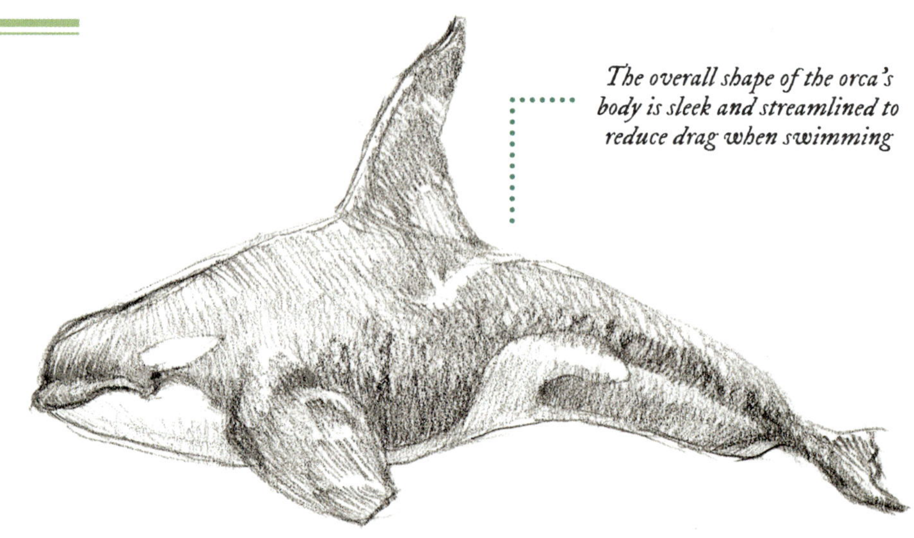

The overall shape of the orca's body is sleek and streamlined to reduce drag when swimming

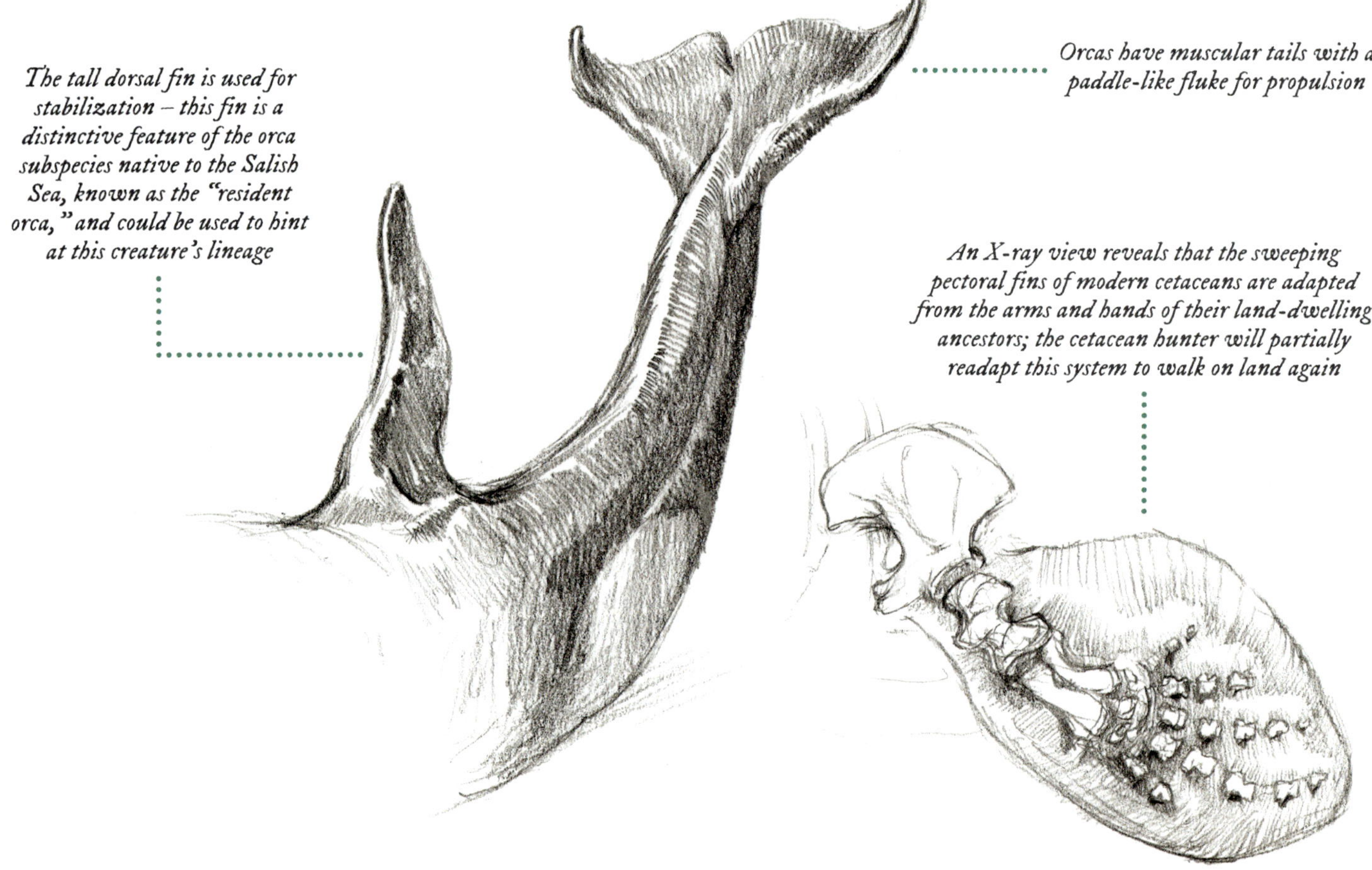

The tall dorsal fin is used for stabilization – this fin is a distinctive feature of the orca subspecies native to the Salish Sea, known as the "resident orca," and could be used to hint at this creature's lineage

Orcas have muscular tails with a paddle-like fluke for propulsion

An X-ray view reveals that the sweeping pectoral fins of modern cetaceans are adapted from the arms and hands of their land-dwelling ancestors; the cetacean hunter will partially readapt this system to walk on land again

Mudskipper

Before the ancestors of modern whales roamed the land, their own aquatic ancestors first had to leave the water. There is abundant fossil evidence that shows animals in this transitional phase between aquatic fish and terrestrial amphibians, but there are also modern animals that behave in very similar ways. Mudskippers are incredible fish capable of leaving the water for moderate periods of time. They drag themselves about on land with highly modified pectoral fins to escape predators and locate mates.

Strong muscles surrounding the pectoral fins allow the animal to pull its body through mud

This type of limb anatomy will make the cetacean hunter seem more plausibly amphibious

A large mudskipper rears up on land to impress potential mates

Turtles

The cetacean hunter will be moving on land like a mudskipper, so will need to have protection on its underbelly when navigating rough, rocky terrain. Modern cetaceans have layers of thick blubber and tough skin surrounding their bodies that insulate them in cold water. Including blubber would be appropriate, but exploring other ways to protect the creature's underbelly will elevate the design.

Turtles have developed a wonderful shell composed of bone, and this protects both the top of their bodies and their undersides. The plates seen on the underside of the snapping turtle interlock snugly, protecting the animal from any damage when navigating rough logs and rocks. Although turtle shells are composed of bone, many mammals form hard structures from modified hairs, called keratin, as seen in fingernails and the horns of rhinoceros. This material will be the basis of the protective plates on the creature's underside.

Snapping turtles have many wrinkles and layers of bumpy skin, which could add visual interest to the design

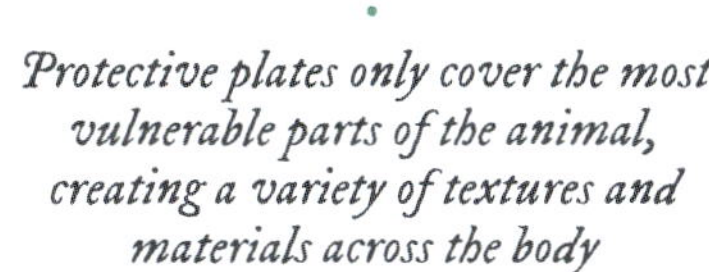

Protective plates only cover the most vulnerable parts of the animal, creating a variety of textures and materials across the body

Functionality research

Vision

As an amphibious ambush predator, this creature will be influenced by modern animals with similar lifestyles. Modern crocodilians are amphibious predators, and a large portion of their success is due to the position of their eyes. Their eyes are located on top of their heads, and this allows them to submerge most of their bodies in water while their eyes remain exposed to scan the landscape for unsuspecting prey. A prey animal might wander within striking distance of the predator before it realizes anything is amiss. This tactic would be especially useful for pack-hunting cetaceans; one creature on dry land could drive prey animals toward the water, where more members of the hunting pod lie in wait. Many other amphibious animals have similar eye positions, including mudskippers, frogs, and hippopotamuses.

Predatory

Modern toothed whales are formidable predators in the open seas. Most feed on fish, cephalopods, and other marine mammals. In order to hold onto such slippery prey, the teeth in cetaceans like the orca are curved and angled backward. This enables them to tear out large pieces of flesh with every bite. The jaws of these animals are also incredibly thick and powerful, able to apply immense pressure and crack through bone. The largest toothed whale ever to live, *Livyatan melvillei*, was a prehistoric giant with jaws over nine feet long and thick teeth more than a foot in length. It may have had the most powerful bite of any animal in existence. The cetacean hunter will make good use of these crushing jaws derived from a formidable evolutionary lineage, and will apply this anatomical advantage to land-dwelling prey.

Sound & communication

Cetaceans use sound not only to communicate with one another, but also to get a sense of their surroundings. Dolphins, orcas, and many other toothed whales possess an organ in their foreheads known as a "melon." The melon can amplify and direct sounds, especially long series of clicks created by the animal to produce a form of sonar, which bounces off nearby objects and is received through the animal's jaw in a process known as **echolocation**. This is useful when locating prey or obstacles in dark or kelp-dense waters. Our creatures will use a very large melon to amplify sounds they produce on land. Their specialized melon will not only help them to locate prey, but will also amplify sounds to be loud and focused enough to disorient and even disable the animals they hunt.

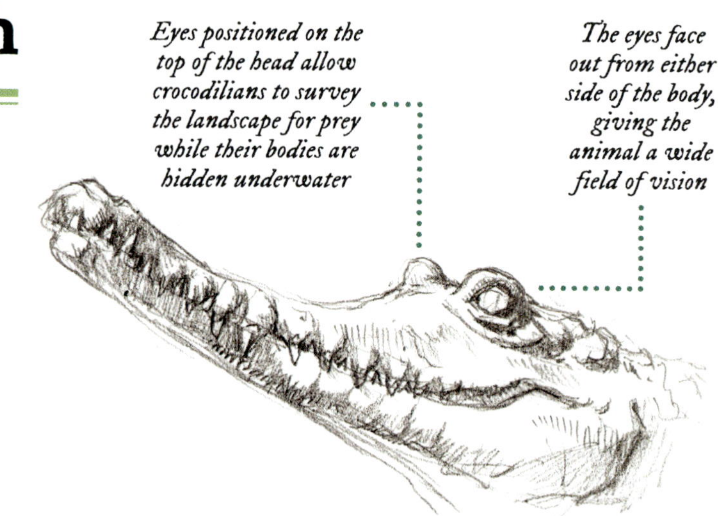

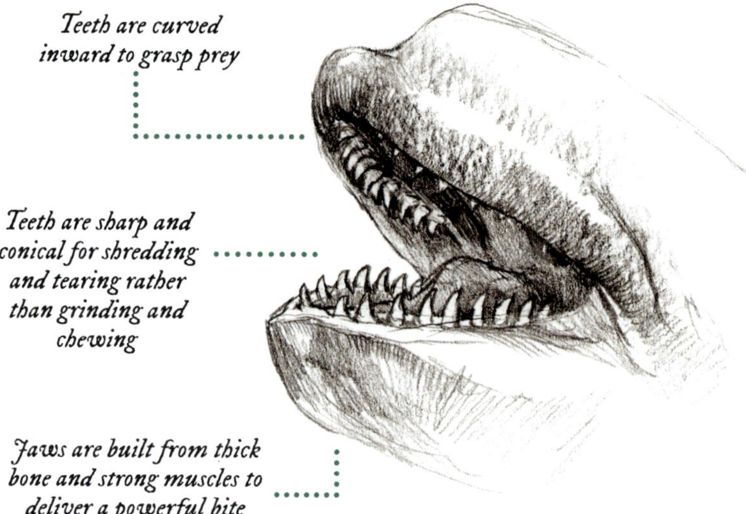

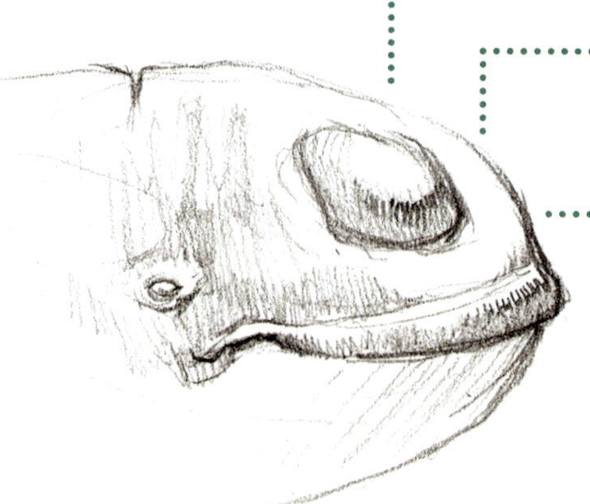

Evolution

Rodhocetus (see right) was an early whale ancestor from the Eocene era of what is now Pakistan. It is a prime example of the transition from predatory land-dwelling mammal to fully aquatic whale. Its limbs were adapted for swimming and its digits were likely webbed. Of the five fingers on its hands, three were capable of supporting weight on land, while two were reserved as attachments for flesh and webbing to aid with swimming. Its hip bones were suspended away from the spine, allowing for greater flexibility in the water.

It likely spent most of its life in the sea, and was only capable of pulling itself onto land for short periods of time. This lifestyle reflects the habits of the cetacean hunter, and the configuration of its forelimbs and fingers will aid in the final creature design.

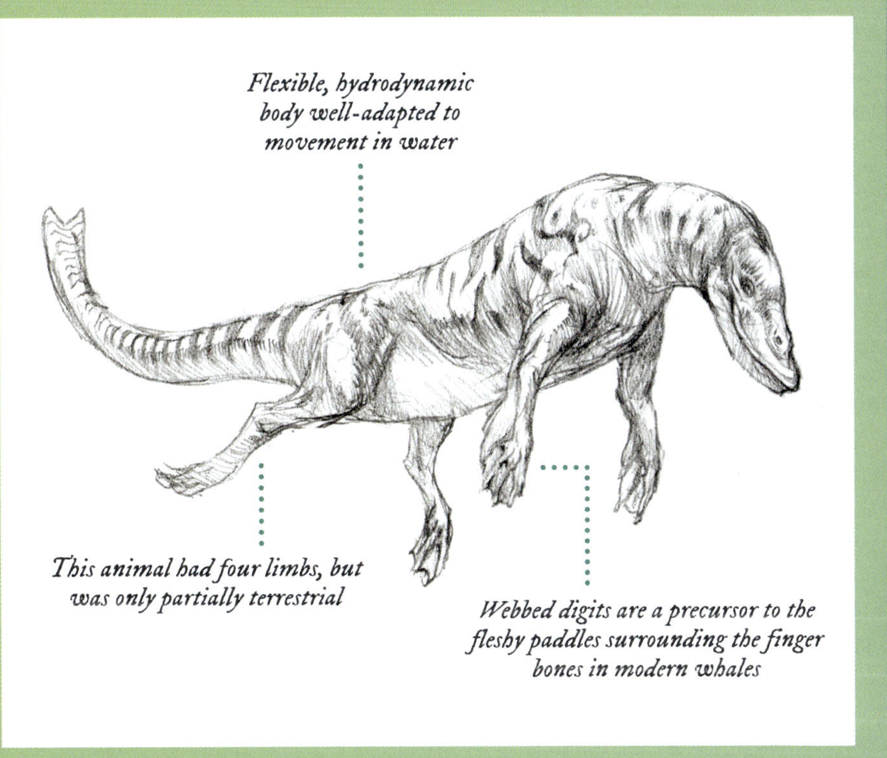

Coloration

As it is an ambush predator, camouflage will be a key component of the creature's design. Many animals that live in dense forests, both terrestrial and aquatic, make use of a series of disruptive patterns across their bodies to hide within their surroundings. This type of patterning, known as cryptic coloration, can take the form of high contrast rings, spots, or stripes that mimic the effect of light passing through dense foliage.

Bengal tigers (see right) are a great example of this effect. Their vertical stripes mimic the effect of trees in a forest or tall grasses in a savanna, and they can easily conceal themselves from their prey in these types of environments. The cetacean hunter will make use of cryptic coloration not only for hunting, but also to help hide young calves from rival pods in kelp forests.

Thumbnails

After gathering research about real-world animals to influence the design, it is time to work out the anatomy of the cetacean hunter. As this creature will be a direct descendant of modern resident orcas living off the northwest coast of North America, a large portion of its body shape will be derived from them. This includes a large tail fluke and dorsal fin, both essential for aquatic locomotion and highly distinctive as a species identifier.

One of the most prominent evolutionary adaptations will be the development of limbs capable of propelling the creature on land. The creature's front limbs will recall elements of *Rodhocetus* (see **page 169**), especially the use of some fingers to bear weight, while others function as part of a swimming paddle.

Modern orcas have lost all vestigial bone structures for the hind limbs, which their land-dwelling ancestors had, so the hind limbs of this creature will be composed of redistributed muscle and cartilage. These "legs" will be very rudimentary in comparison to the forelimbs, and bear more similarity to the appendages of mudskippers. Like the forelimbs, they should be equipped with fins or paddles to aid in aquatic locomotion.

This creature will often be dragging itself across the rocky, driftwood-studded shores of the Pacific Northwest, so it needs thick skin and protective armor on its underside, reminiscent of the snapping turtle's bony armor. As a semi-aquatic ambush predator, the cetacean hunter should have its eyes positioned toward the top of its head, in a manner suggestive of crocodilians. Large predatory jaws should be an important feature, and a specialized melon structure on the creature's head will help to provide a distinctive silhouette.

Since these will be territorial creatures that frequently find themselves in conflict with one another, it would be interesting to feature offensive structures, which can be used in battles for dominance or protecting young. It will be important to experiment with overall body shape and limb configuration. We want to place elements within the anatomy to create an exciting, unique creature, while also harking back to its evolutionary lineage.

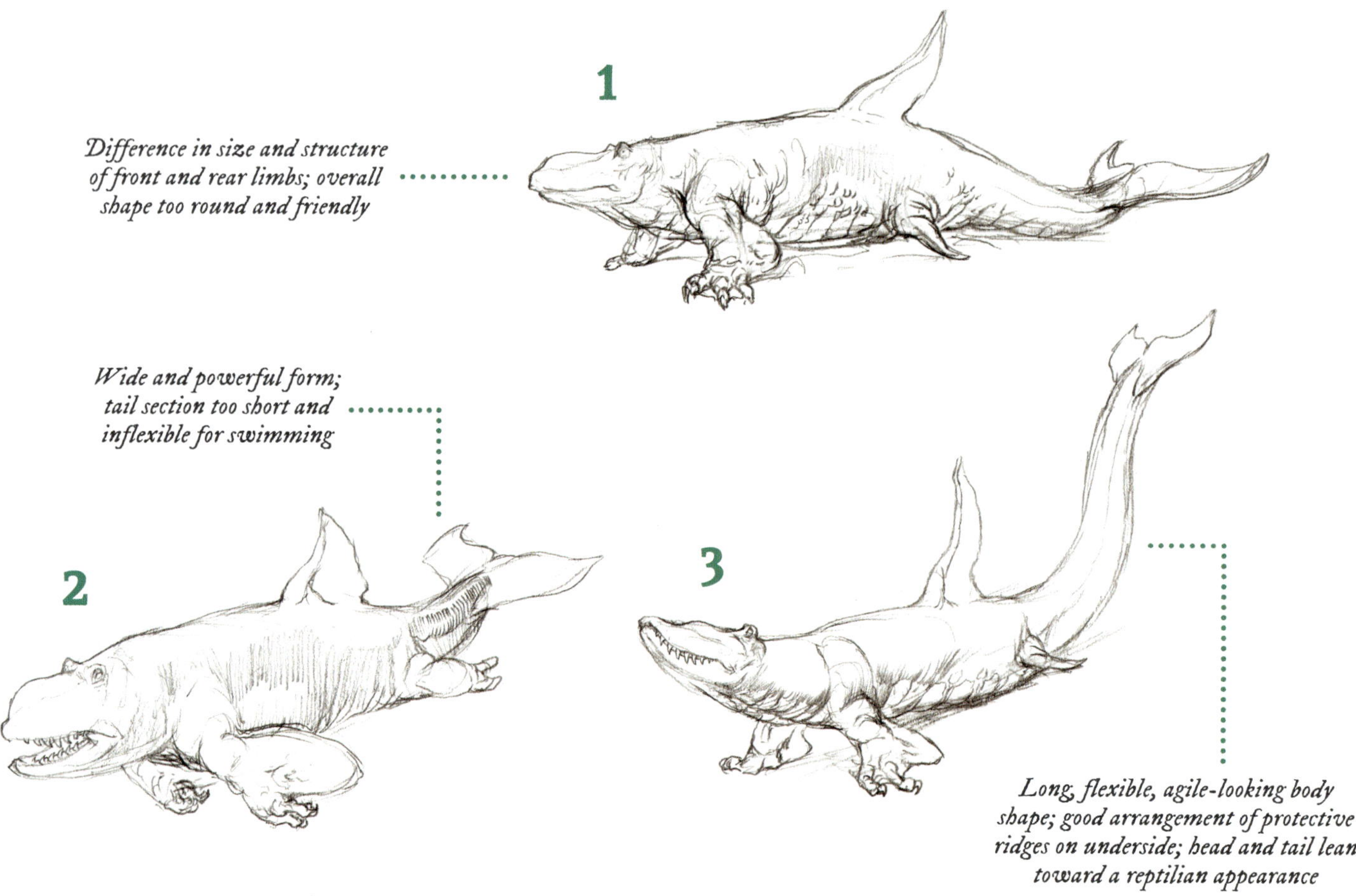

Difference in size and structure of front and rear limbs; overall shape too round and friendly

1

Wide and powerful form; tail section too short and inflexible for swimming

2

3

Long, flexible, agile-looking body shape; good arrangement of protective ridges on underside; head and tail lean toward a reptilian appearance

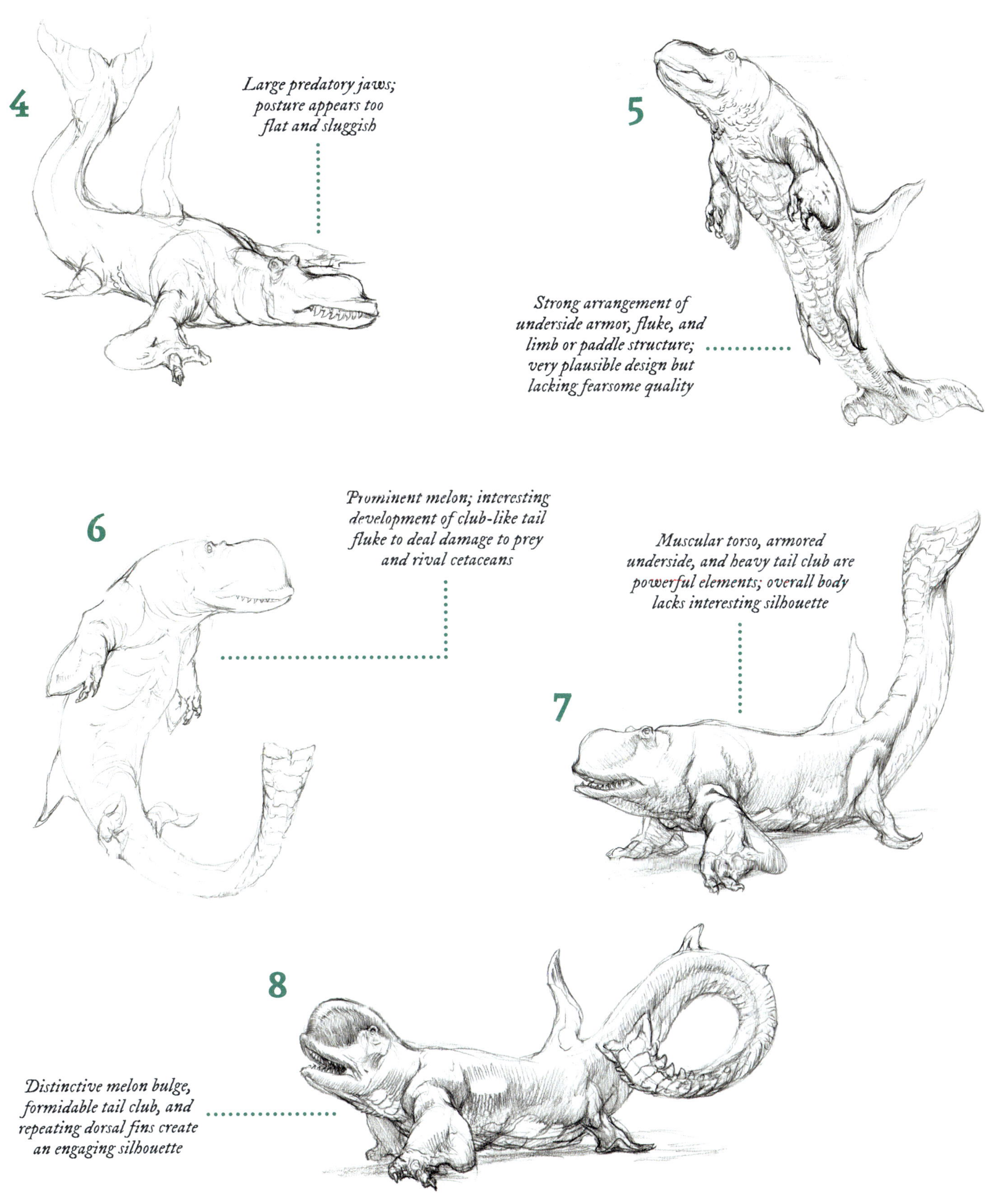

4

*Large predatory jaws;
posture appears too
flat and sluggish*

5

*Strong arrangement of
underside armor, fluke, and
limb or paddle structure;
very plausible design but
lacking fearsome quality*

6

*Prominent melon; interesting
development of club-like tail
fluke to deal damage to prey
and rival cetaceans*

*Muscular torso, armored
underside, and heavy tail club are
powerful elements; overall body
lacks interesting silhouette*

7

8

*Distinctive melon bulge,
formidable tail club, and
repeating dorsal fins create
an engaging silhouette*

DEVELOPMENT

Thumbnail 8 displays the most interesting anatomical shape language to fit the design brief. It appears to be the most capable of transitioning from swimming to walking on land effectively. Of all the designs, its limb configuration is most plausible, and its distinctive melon and tail club add interesting focal points to the design. I tend to incorporate the best ideas from earlier thumbnails into new ones as I draw, and since this was the last thumbnail I created it has the most promising design features.

Modern cetaceans still hold the vestiges of forelimbs in their flippers, and the cetacean hunter has readapted the concealed arm and finger bones of its ancestors into a functioning limb. Like *Rodhocetus*, the walking whale from ages past, it has adapted some of its fingers to bear weight while others are still incorporated into a paddle-like structure. Its rear limbs are derived from muscle and cartilage, and take on a structure analogous to the pectoral fins of a mudskipper.

The cetacean hunter is strongly tied to its pod, and must cooperate with its family members to successfully hunt. They can use their enlarged melon to produce a complex range of sounds that form a simple language, and can also modulate these to produce sonic pulses that disorient and incapacitate their prey. Individuals will often work together, with a few creatures on land emitting pulses that drive their prey toward the water, where the rest of the pod lies submerged in wait. When resources become scarce and competition between pods grows intense, these hunters will use their formidable tail clubs to protect their young and battle for dominance.

The forelimbs of the cetacean hunter are powerful enough to pull its body across the ground under a variety of conditions. Its fingers are capable of gripping rocky surfaces when needed, and the keratin plating on the creature's underside protects its body from being scraped against any rough terrain. Its rudimentary hind limbs are typically used as accessories to help push its body along or wiggle out of tight spaces, but are strong enough to be used as weight-bearing limbs for short sprints when pursuing prey.

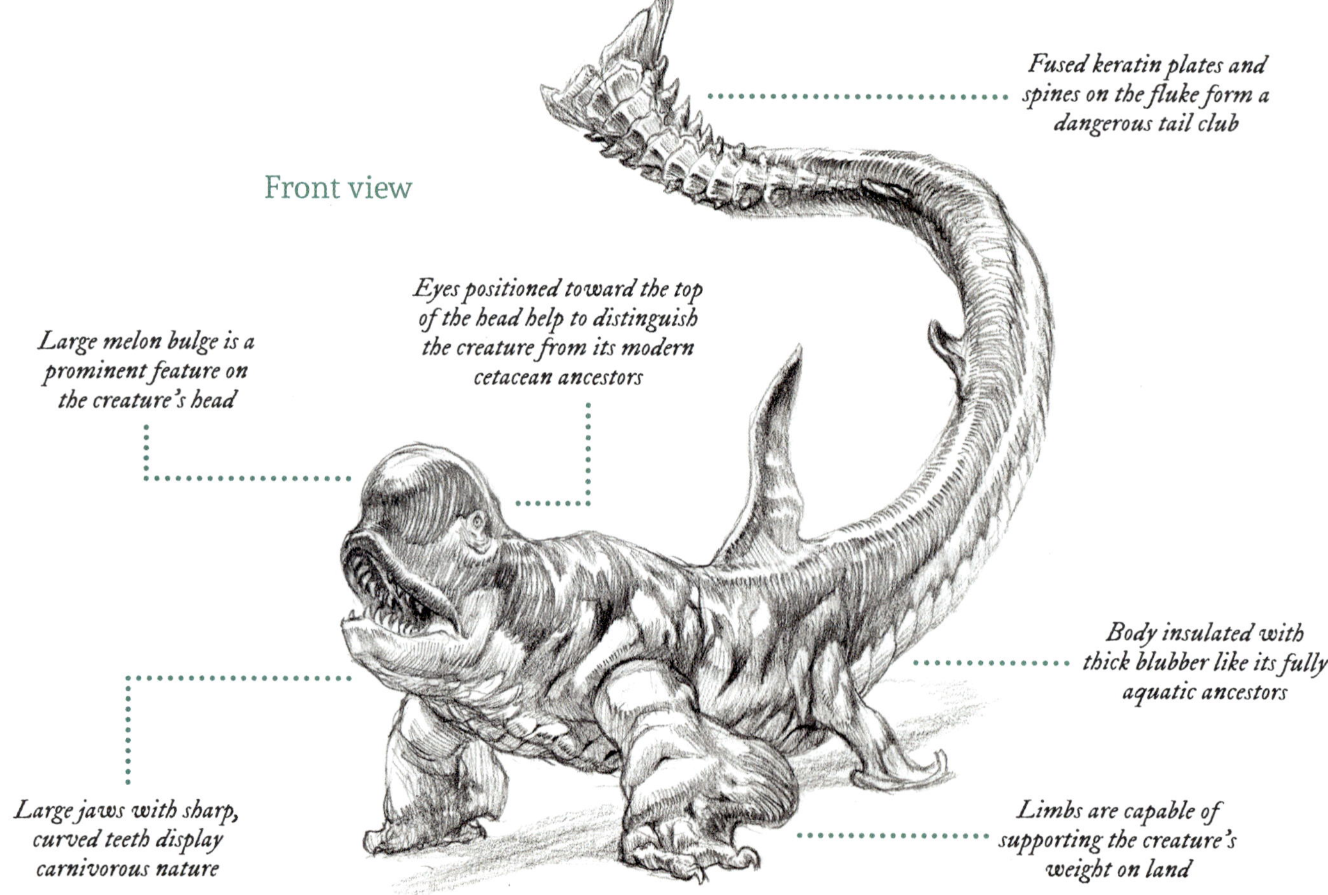

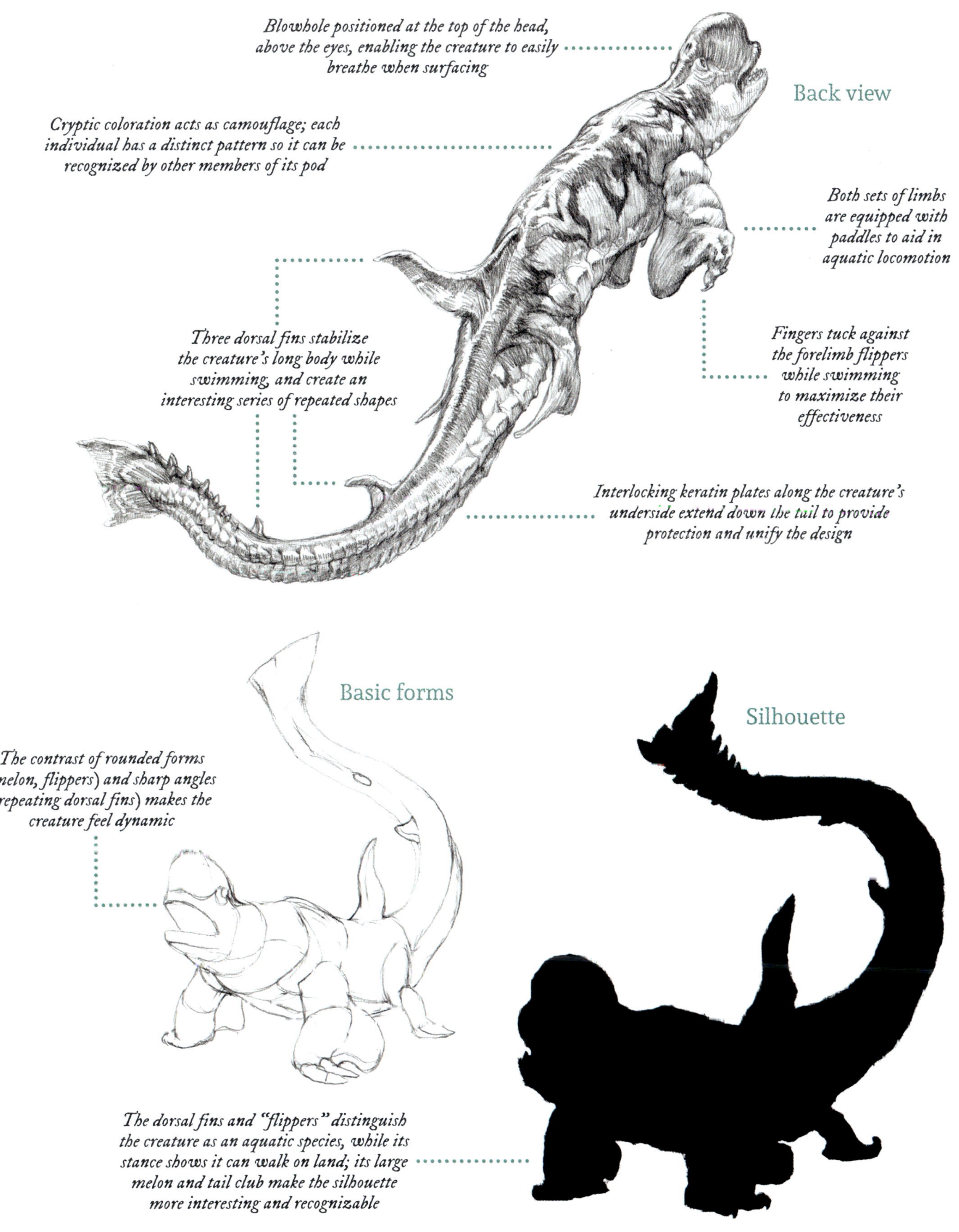

Blowhole positioned at the top of the head, above the eyes, enabling the creature to easily breathe when surfacing
Back view
Cryptic coloration acts as camouflage; each individual has a distinct pattern so it can be recognized by other members of its pod
Both sets of limbs are equipped with paddles to aid in aquatic locomotion
Three dorsal fins stabilize the creature's long body while swimming, and create an interesting series of repeated shapes
Fingers tuck against the forelimb flippers while swimming to maximize their effectiveness
Interlocking keratin plates along the creature's underside extend down the tail to provide protection and unify the design
Basic forms
Silhouette
The contrast of rounded forms (melon, flippers) and sharp angles (repeating dorsal fins) makes the creature feel dynamic
The dorsal fins and "flippers" distinguish the creature as an aquatic species, while its stance shows it can walk on land; its large melon and tail club make the silhouette more interesting and recognizable

173

Poses

To ensure the cetacean hunter is capable of moving comfortably in different environments, it is helpful to create a series of drawings showing different poses. The creature needs to be flexible enough to swim gracefully underwater, and should be able to use its fins in a variety of ways. There are a few elements (such as the dorsal fins and tail club) that might get in the way of movement if positioned in awkward locations, so it is important to explore the creature's range of motion and test these potential limitations.

Since the cetacean hunter will spend a lot of time navigating rocky shorelines, it will need to be able to grip surfaces securely. Pose A displays the creature tightly gripping onto a rock formation, using the strong fingers of its forelimbs and its long, semi-prehensile tail. This adaptation keeps it from being swept dangerously into crashing waves during stormy weather.

Pose B shows the force that the creature can exert when brandishing its tail club. By pushing off with its hind limbs, arching its back, and swinging its muscular tail, the creature can propel its formidable weapon at high velocities. The heavy weight at the end of the tail can act like a pendulum and often pulls the rest of the body off-balance after a heavy swing. This is another situation where the protective armor on the creature's underbelly can be useful. This tactic is sometimes used to overpower land-dwelling prey, but is more often used to defend young calves learning to take their first steps on land.

Although the cetacean hunter is relatively cumbersome on land, it is able to reach high speeds in short bursts. As shown in pose C, the shoulders allow the front limbs to rotate, and the muscle structures of the rear limbs can bend, allowing the creature to stand upright with its belly above the ground and "high walk" for short periods of time. This is a behavior observable in modern crocodilians, and will allow the creature to chase down prey disabled by its sonic pulses more effectively.

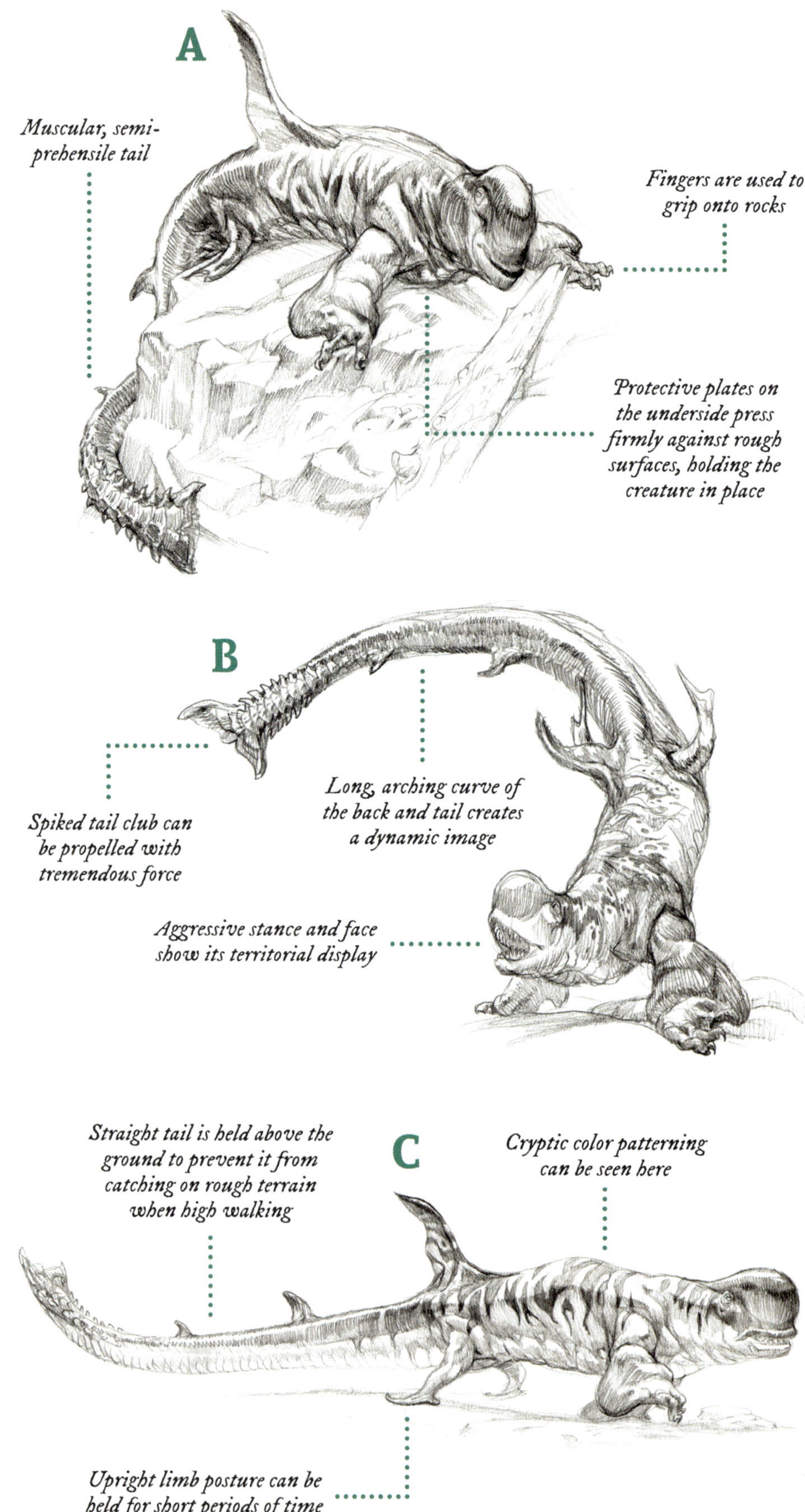

Color & pattern

As an ambush predator, the cetacean hunter will make use of cryptic coloration to conceal itself from its prey. This type of patterning will also help protect young creatures hiding in kelp forests from predators or rival pods. Another factor that provides the creature with camouflage, especially in the marine environment, is countershading. A light-toned underbelly will help the creature fade into the light coming from the water's surface when viewed from below, and darker shades on the creature's back will make it harder to spot from above. While the general patterns on the creature should be recognizable as a trait of the species, the markings should be complex, with enough variation between individuals that other members of their pod can easily recognize them. Contrast between dark and light will be important in these markings, and there is room to explore color variation and shape design as well.

The first color sketch is most reminiscent of modern orcas. Strong cryptic patterns adorn the creature's sides, and there is a good sense of countershading. More mottled greens and browns form the basis of the second color sketch, and these tones might help the creature conceal itself in forested environments. The third sketch focuses on a ring-based cryptic pattern, which creates a distinctive appearance.

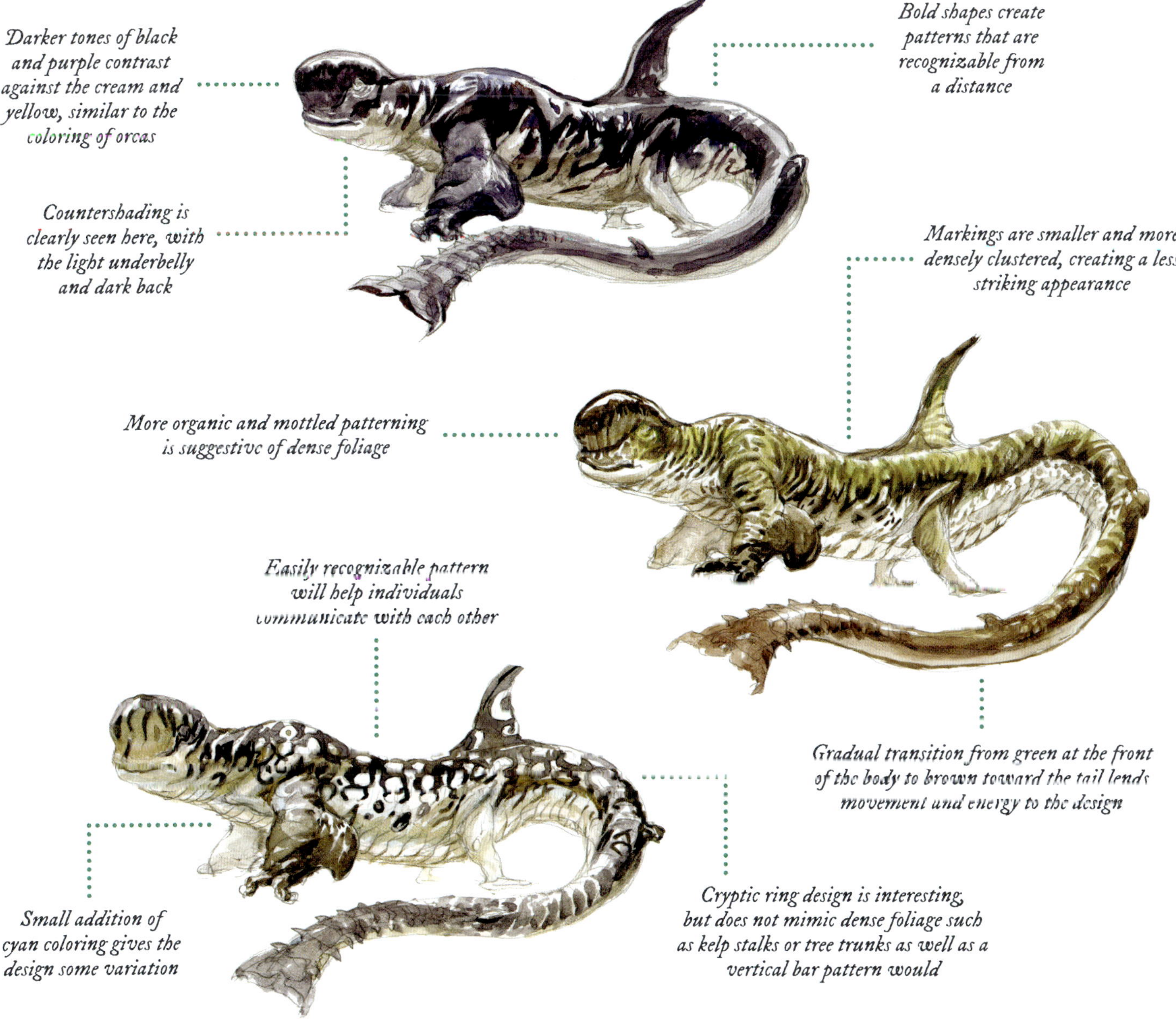

FINAL DESIGN

The final design incorporates all the best elements from earlier concepts, and emphasizes the amphibious, aggressive nature of the creature. The cetacean hunter is clearly aquatic in origin, with prominent dorsal fins and a tail fluke, but is depicted standing in a powerful posture on land with its modified limbs. The reference taken from modern and prehistoric whales, mudskippers, and crocodilians greatly informs the creature's body, so that it appears familiar and believable, yet it is still a unique species with its own anatomical solutions.

The creature is well adapted to its environment, with protective keratin plates on its underside to navigate rough terrain. These hard plates are covered with a thick layer of callused skin so they do not create drag when the creature is swimming. Cryptic patterns cover the body, aiding in camouflage and communication between individuals.

Modern cetaceans are known for being highly intelligent and social, and the cetacean hunter is no exception. The creature's distinctive enlarged melon is essential to its hunting strategy, and produces a wide range of sounds that form a simple language used to coordinate hunts. They can set up inescapable ambushes, using their melons to produce loud bursts to disorient prey and flush them out of the temperate forest toward other members of the pod. The creature's large predatory jaws make short work of prey, and bear a strong resemblance to those of its orca ancestors.

Young calves are reared in the safety of underwater kelp forests, but there comes a time when they must learn to walk and hunt on land. This is the most dangerous period of the cetacean hunter's life cycle, as calves are much smaller than their parents and require protection from predators such as wolves and rival cetacean pods.

The creature in the final design is a large male shown in an aggressive stance defending its young. It brandishes its barbed tail club menacingly and there are evident scars across its shoulders and neck, proclaiming past battles won.

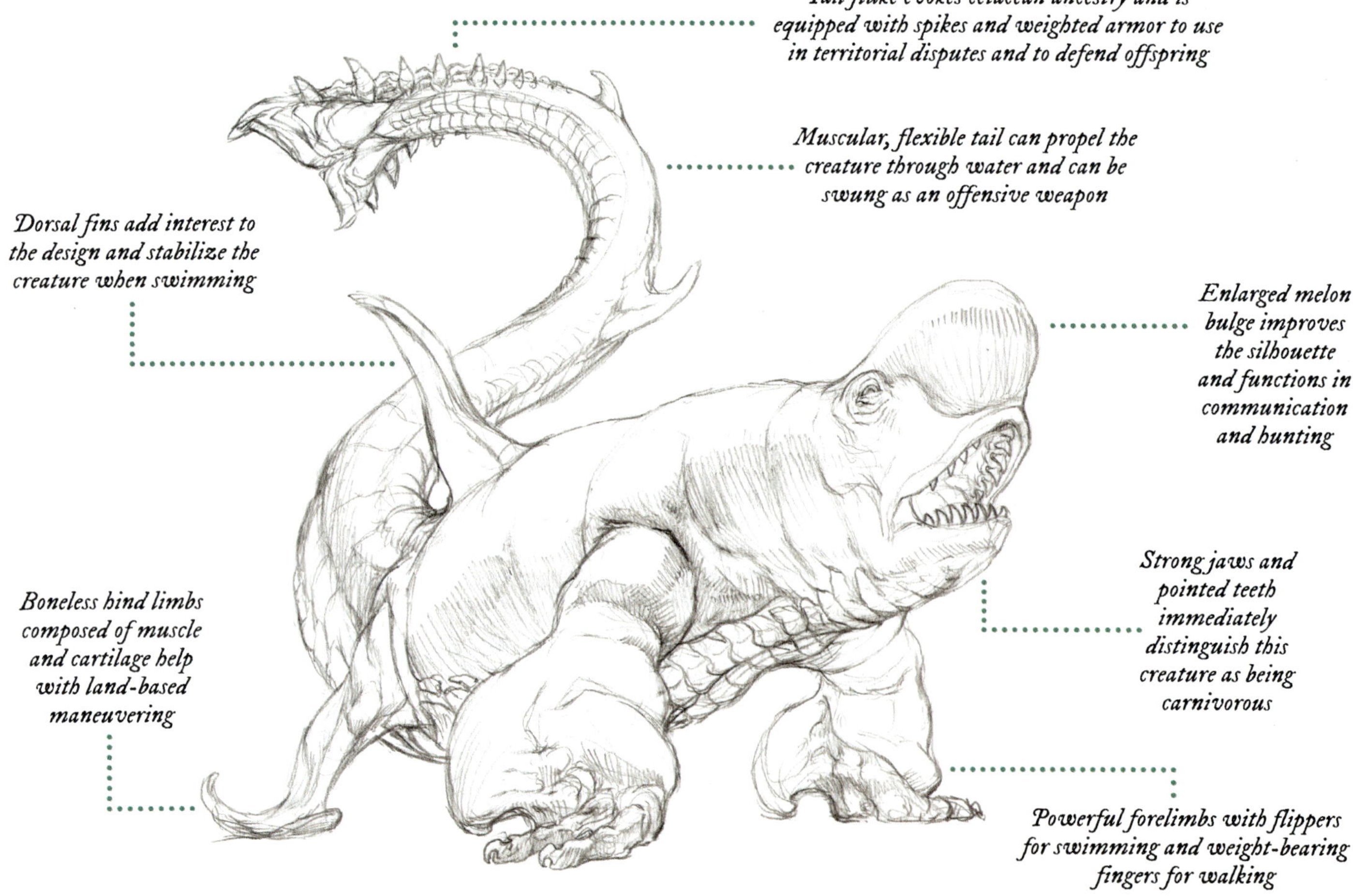

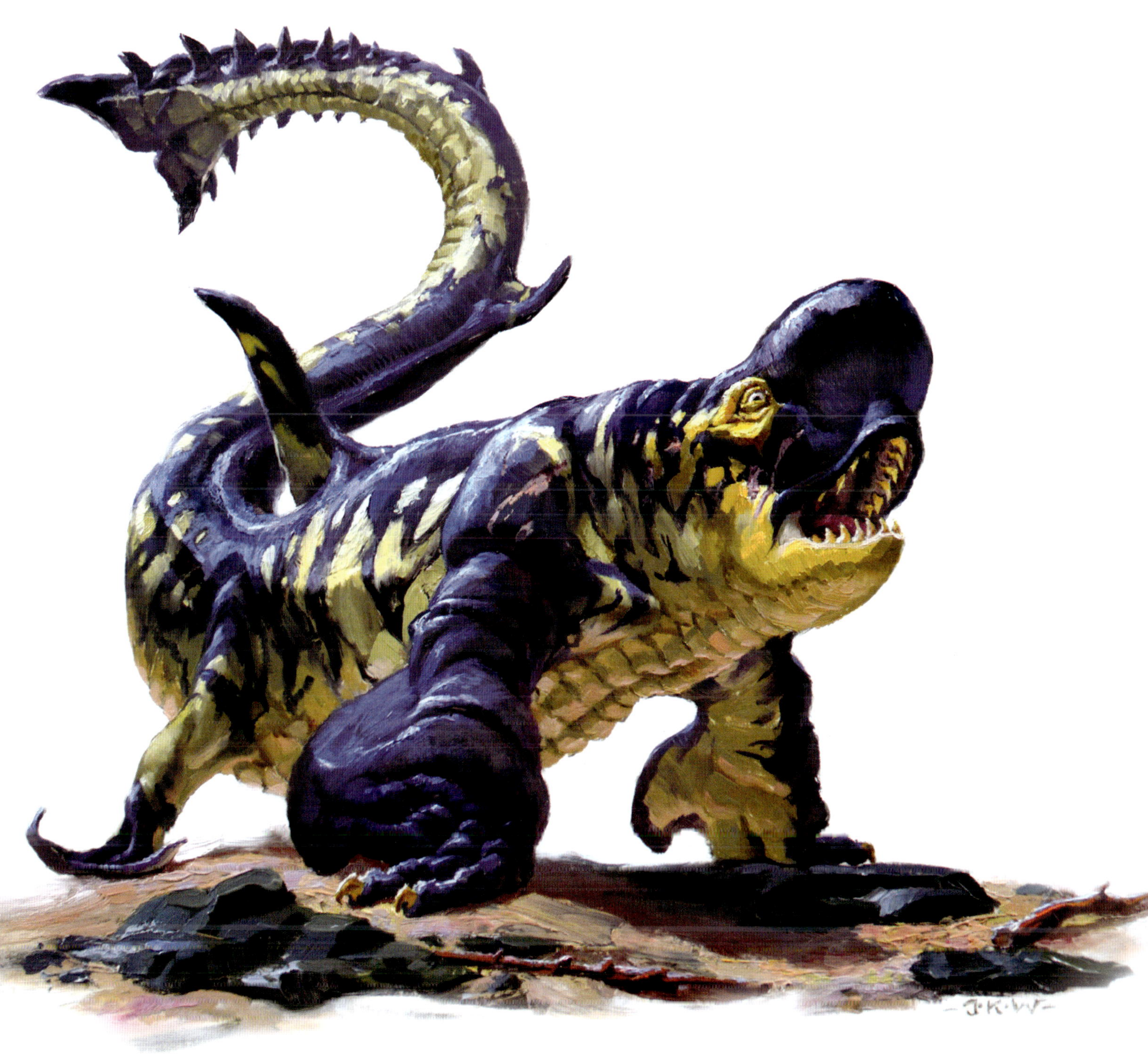

EVOLUTION

This section focuses on a speculative design based on the idea that as marine conditions change - possibly due to human-caused ocean acidification - the descendants of modern orcas might evolve to take advantage of resources on land.

In evolutionary terms, cetaceans are relative newcomers, with some of the earliest examples evolving around 50 million years ago. These early examples shared a common ancestor with the modern hippopotamus, and were comfortable moving across both land and water, spending their lives hunting in swampy environments. Over time these creatures adapted to take advantage of their watery surroundings. *Ambulocetus* is one of the first species known to have moved out of the brackish marshes and into a marine environment. Its jaws adapted to channel sound to its ears underwater.

With eyes positioned toward the top of its head, it would have been able to ambush prey from the water with ease.

Other aquatic cetacean species would develop, including *Rodhocetus*, and eventually some cetacean species would take fully to the sea. *Dorudon* was one of the first cetaceans to evolve the body shape evoking modern whales. Its forelimbs were modified into flippers but it still retained vestigial hind limbs. It likely led a solitary existence and preyed on fish in the open ocean. Changes in oceanic conditions allowed two distinct groups to develop. One group consisted of the filter-feeding baleen whales, and the other of toothed whales. After this period, melons began to appear in the anatomy of toothed whales, and their abilities to echolocate made them highly successful predators. Complex social behaviors eventually

became evident in modern toothed whales such as the orca, providing the basis for hunting strategies and strong family bonds.

Using knowledge of how animals adapt to their environments over time, it is possible to extend the cetacean lineage into the future. In this instance, the creature has developed a bipedal stance by developing its forelimbs to adapt to life on land. The creature's enlarged melon is capable of amplifying and directing sonic pulses that incapacitate prey. Without the need to maintain a hydrodynamic body it is now covered in dense rolls of insulating fat and blotchy patches of mottled fur. This nightmarish super-predator of the future Pacific Northwest barely resembles a whale at first glance, but by tracing its evolutionary history back in time, its resemblance becomes plain to see.

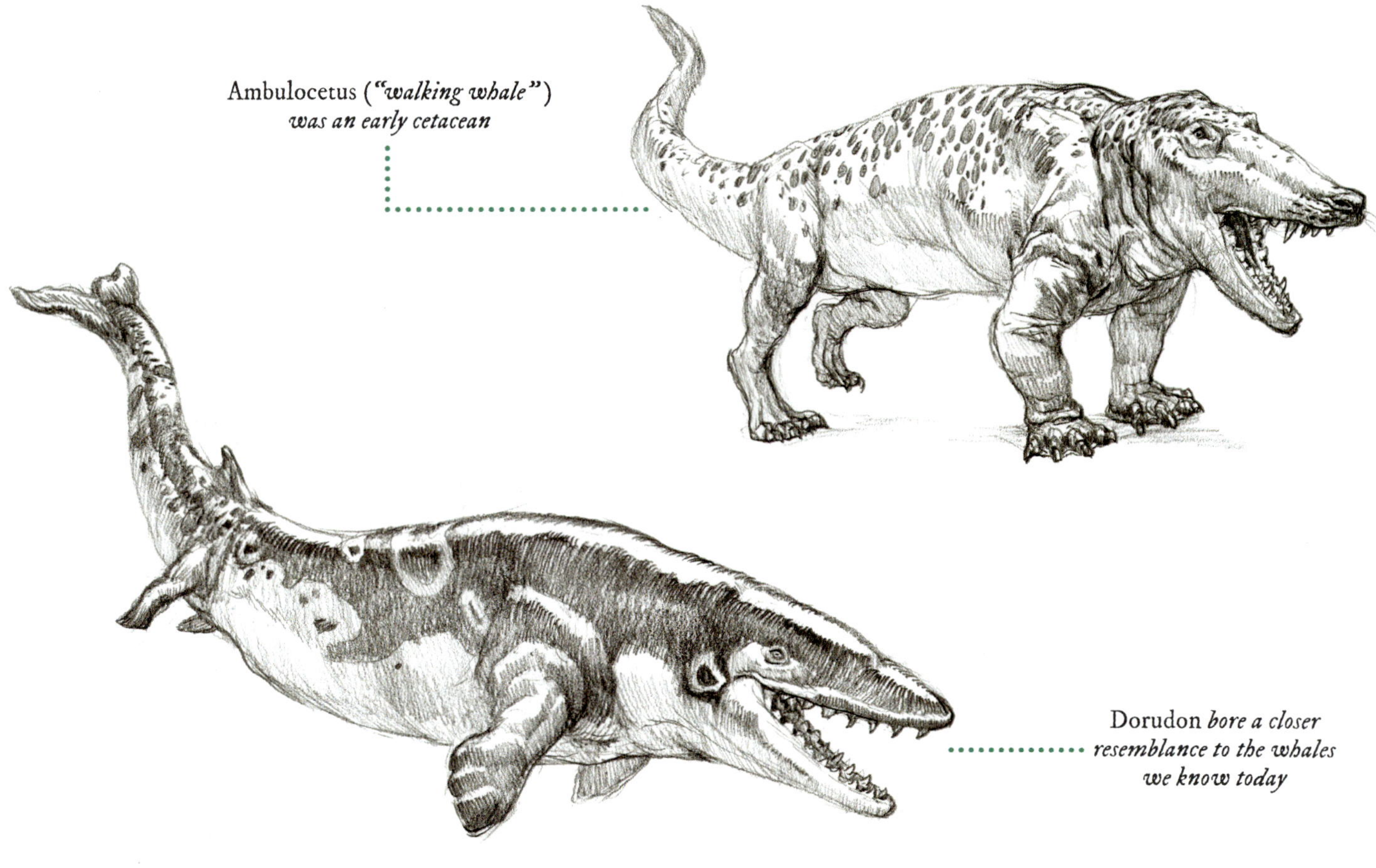

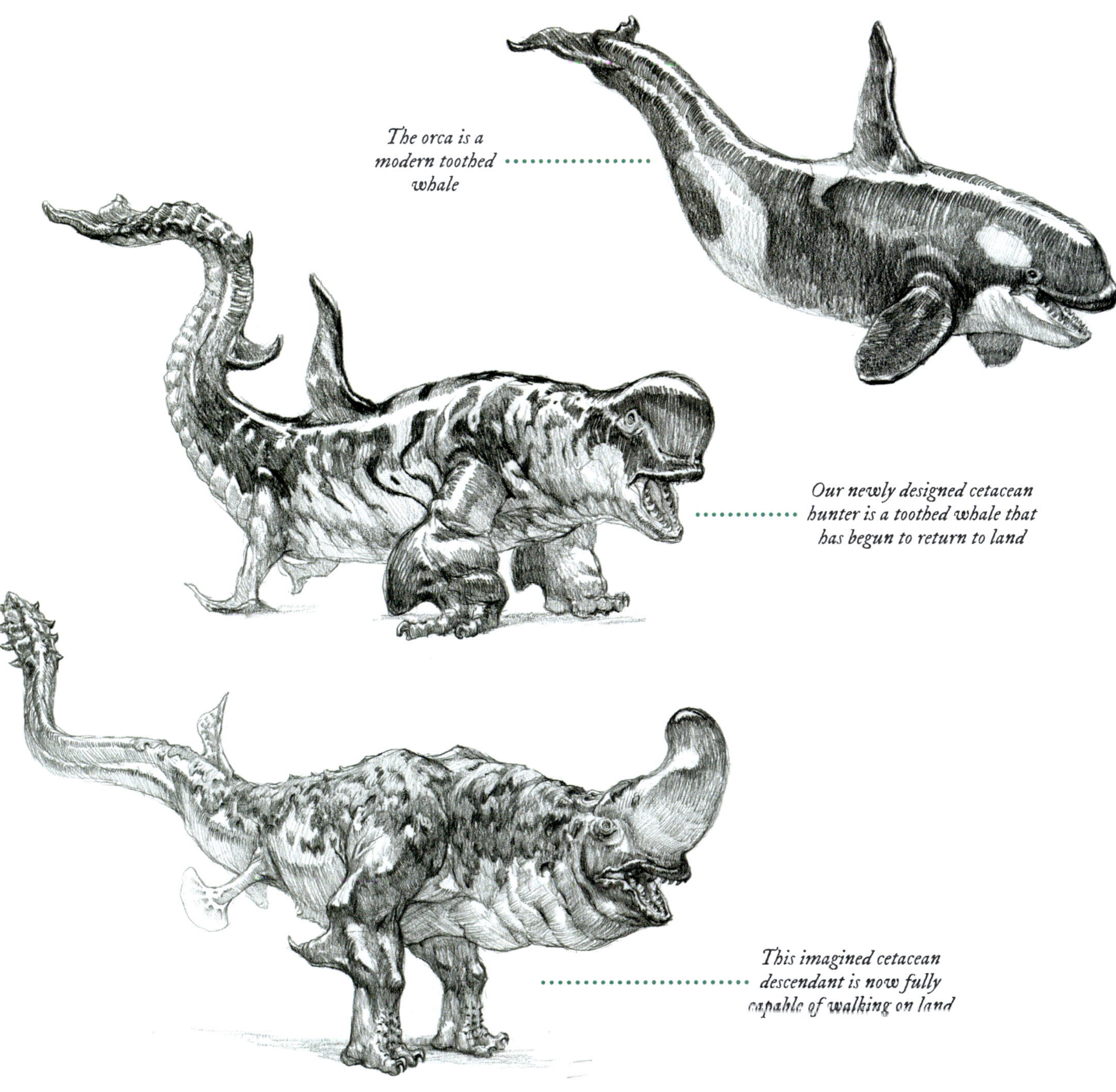

Industry tip

The fossil record is a wonderful place to explore when looking for creature design inspiration. Many of the most fascinating organisms to have lived on Earth are long dead, but that does not mean you cannot view and study them. Nothing beats examining fossil remains or artists' reconstructions up close. Next time you are looking for a good place to do some sketching, visit your local natural history museum and familiarize yourself with its collection. This will help you build up your visual library, and you can refer back to these studies when you need to come up with design elements for a specific creature.

Carrion scavenger

Kristina Lexova

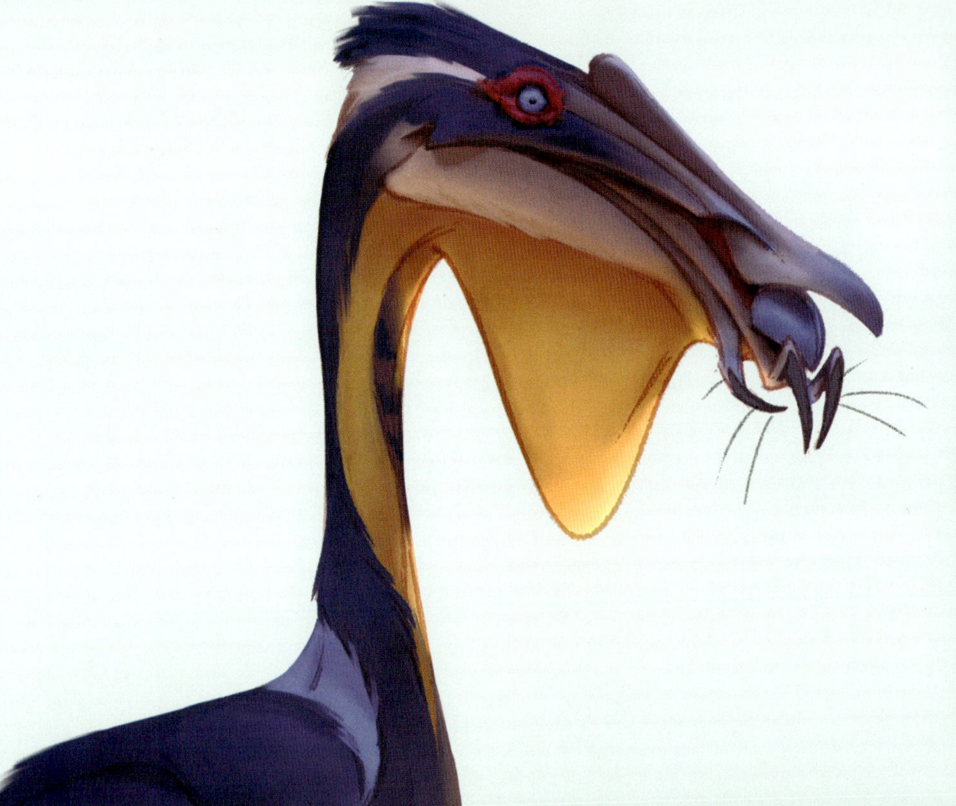

Key facts

- An avian creature capable of living in a variety of settings, including urban areas abandoned due to extreme heat as a result of climate change

- Scavenges carrion and sometimes catches small prey - its heavy beak and powerful claws help it crack open leftover bones

- Nests are protected by both parents, who return with scraps of food until their young are large enough to scavenge for themselves

- Capable of loud vocalization and physical intimidation to frighten away other creatures

IDEATION

First and foremost, aside from being avian in nature, this creature is a scavenger, meaning that its diet will largely consist of dead organisms. This kind of dietary specialization carries inherent risk to an animal - if it cannot find enough of its food source, it will perish. Because of this, so-called specialist animals tend to be highly adapted to make the most of a limited resource. In scavenger animals, these adaptations can be grouped broadly into these two categories:

- **Traits that increase the encounter rate of an organism**, meaning the number of carcasses an organism encounters to feed itself. These traits include well-developed senses, an efficient form of long-distance movement such as gliding flight, or attributes that allow for longer times between meals.

- **Traits that influence the handling time of an organism**, giving them time to access, defend, and process food while extracting the most nutrients possible. These traits include visual or audial displays to intimidate competition, an ability to quickly shred and gulp down food, or an ability to process bones and rotten meat.

The more of these attributes an organism possesses, the more effective it will be as a scavenger.

Lastly, we must consider the impact of this creature's environment on its appearance and behavior. For this particular design, we will focus on heat and urban environments.

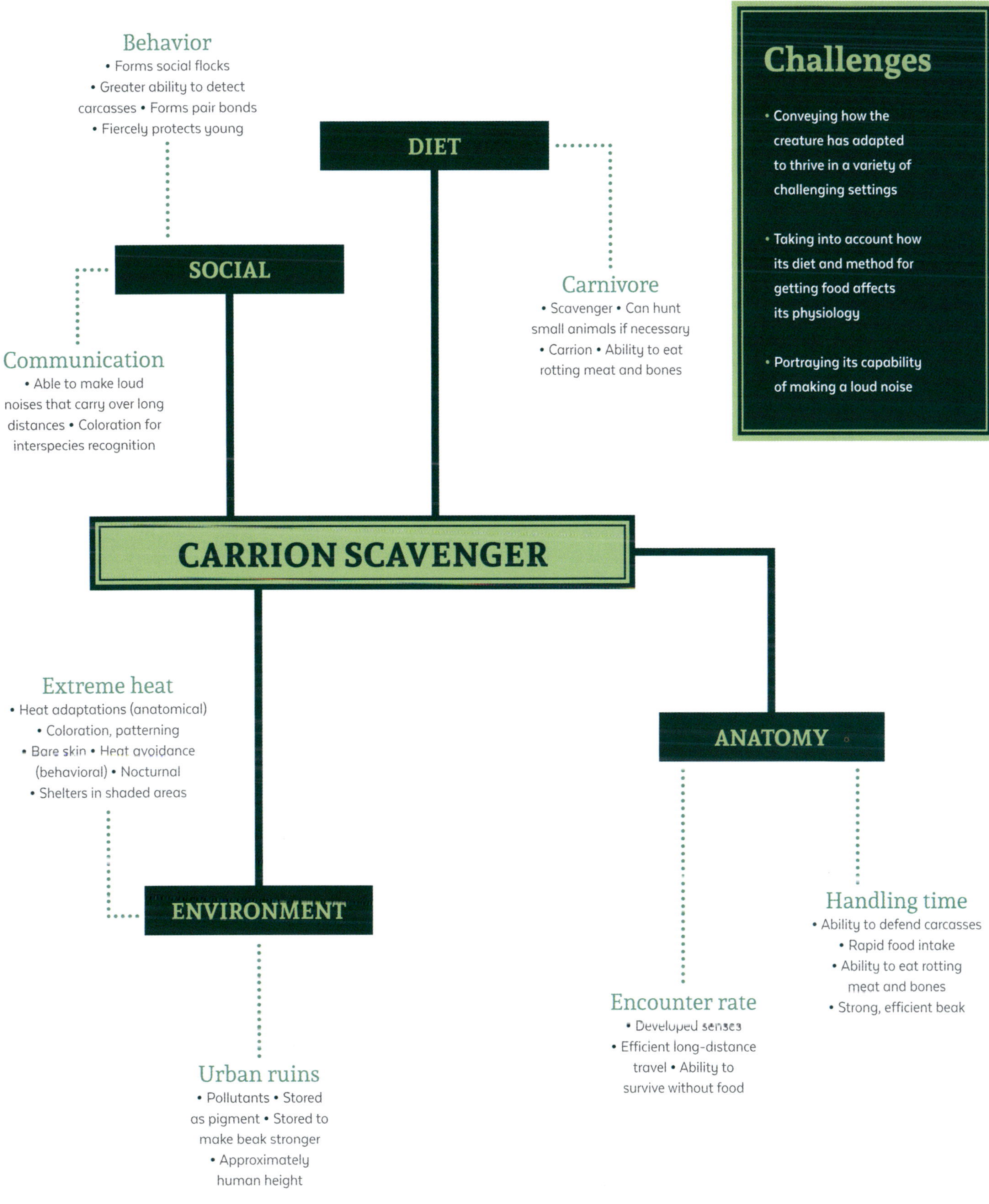
Behavior
• Forms social flocks
• Greater ability to detect carcasses • Forms pair bonds
• Fiercely protects young

DIET

SOCIAL

Challenges
• Conveying how the creature has adapted to thrive in a variety of challenging settings
• Taking into account how its diet and method for getting food affects its physiology
• Portraying its capability of making a loud noise

Carnivore
• Scavenger • Can hunt small animals if necessary • Carrion • Ability to eat rotting meat and bones

Communication
• Able to make loud noises that carry over long distances • Coloration for interspecies recognition

CARRION SCAVENGER

Extreme heat
• Heat adaptations (anatomical)
• Coloration, patterning
• Bare skin • Heat avoidance (behavioral) • Nocturnal
• Shelters in shaded areas

ANATOMY

Handling time
• Ability to defend carcasses
• Rapid food intake
• Ability to eat rotting meat and bones
• Strong, efficient beak

ENVIRONMENT

Encounter rate
• Developed senses
• Efficient long-distance travel • Ability to survive without food

Urban ruins
• Pollutants • Stored as pigment • Stored to make beak stronger
• Approximately human height

Anatomy research

Avian wing anatomy

Birds, bats, and other flying animals have bodies supremely well-adapted to flight. This is reflected in every layer of their anatomy, but the wings are undoubtedly an important feature to focus on. On a skeletal level, bones tend to be slender and light; some have even fused or have been lost entirely to shed excess weight. A large, keeled sternum (breastbone) serves as an attachment for flight muscles. Clavicles, too, are vital to flight.

Regarding the soft tissue of the wing, there are a few key features worth remembering. The first is the *pectoralis major*, one of two main muscles responsible for the action of flight; this massive muscle contributes to the rounded shape of the chest. Next, the *patagialis longus* is a band of fiber that runs from the shoulder area to the wrist. It is responsible for the shape of the wing's leading edge, and is therefore useful in a design sense.

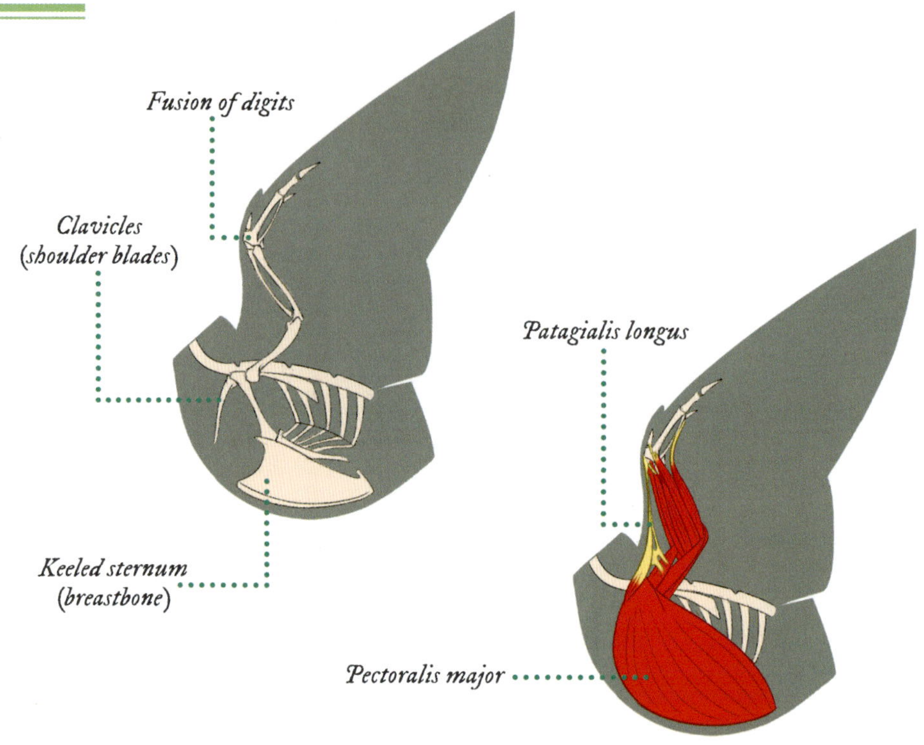

Evolution

"Tubenose" birds, such as albatrosses and petrels (pictured to the right), provide an excellent visual link between insectoid and avian features. The beaks of tubenose birds are composed of several horny plates, including a tubular nasal passage that gives them their common name. Even though the beaks are not technically related to the plates on the heads of insects, they are similar enough in appearance to allow for a merging of these two very different animal groups. Additionally, the aforementioned tubular nose provides these birds with an excellent sense of smell - something our creature is going to need to locate carcasses.

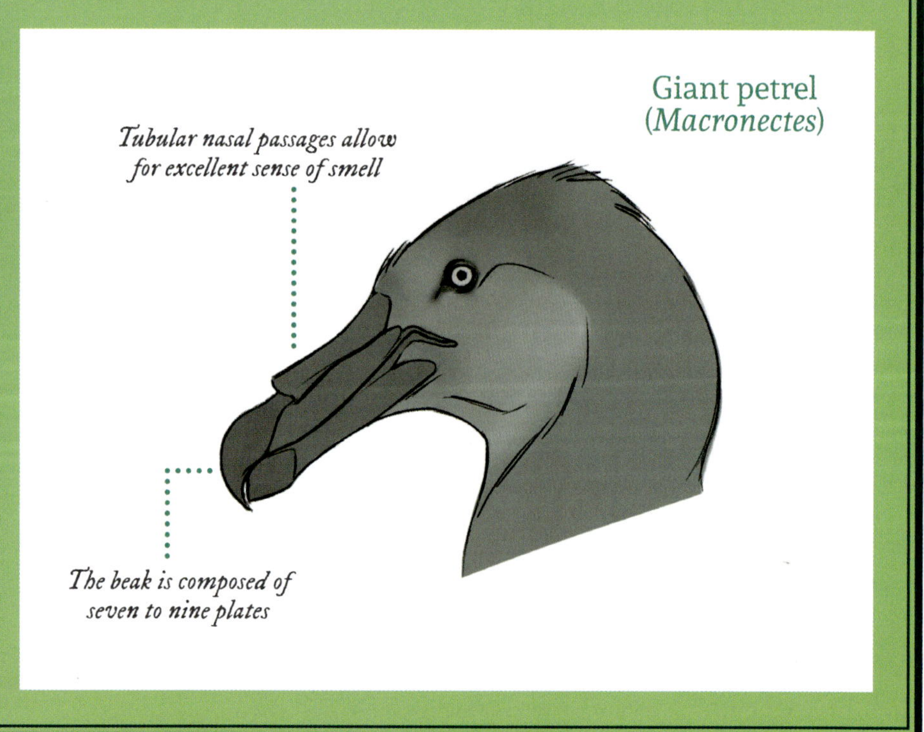

Insect mouthparts

When it comes to processing food, nothing comes close to the efficiency of insect mouthparts (pictured to the right). Adding insectoid features to the mouth of our creature will make it look like it can shred carcasses in minutes. As mentioned on **page 101**, the mouthparts of all insects consist of the same basic parts, stretched and skewed to suit their individual lifestyles.

- **Labrum** - a plate that acts as an upper "lip" to contain food

- **Mandibles** - a pair of jaws for crushing food

- **Maxillae** - paired appendages that work much like cutlery to manipulate food, with sensory organs attached

- **Hypopharynx** - acts as a "tongue" and mixes saliva into food

- **Labium** - acts as a bottom "lip" to contain food

Pictured right are chewing mouthparts, where the individual appendages are more or less neatly stacked, making them easier to remember.

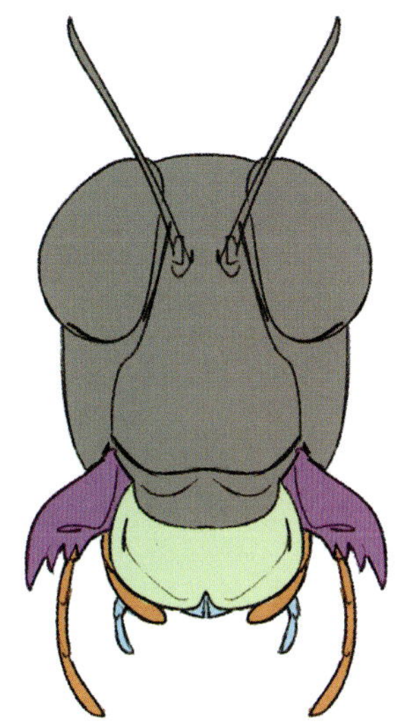

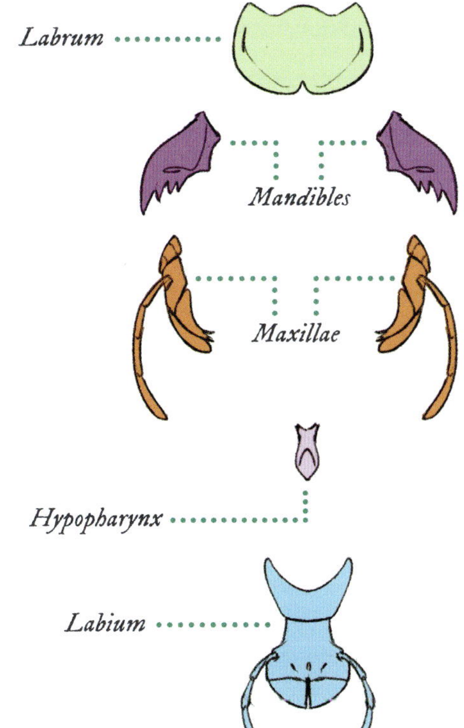

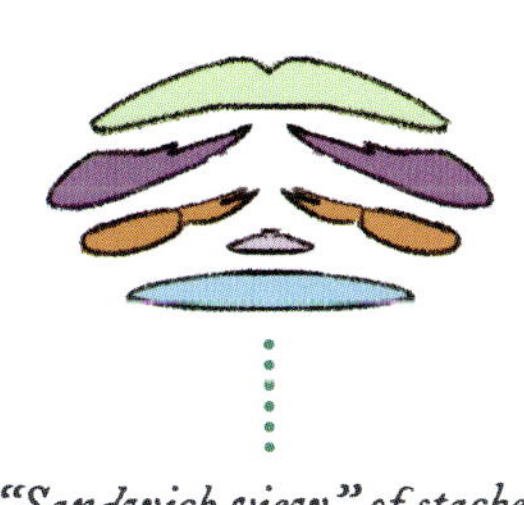

"Sandwich view" of stacked mouth appendages

Avian head structure

In order to blend insect features into this creature's avian anatomy, it will be helpful to understand the basic structure of a bird's head and beak (pictured to the left). The skull of a bird can be broadly divided into three parts:

- The **cranial area** containing the cranium (braincase), the back of which connects to the vertebrae of the neck. This is also where the eye sockets and ear openings are located.

- The **upper and lower jaws**, the former of which contains the nostril openings and is connected to the cranial area via a flexible border.

- The **hinge mechanism** consisting of three bones that push forward when the beak is opened, raising the upper jaw and enabling a wider gape than a fused jaw would allow. This is useful for swallowing food whole, which we will discuss later in this chapter.

The upper and lower jaws are covered in a keratinized sheath, the **rhampotheca**, which ends right before the nostril openings on the skull, and can be quite colorful in many species.

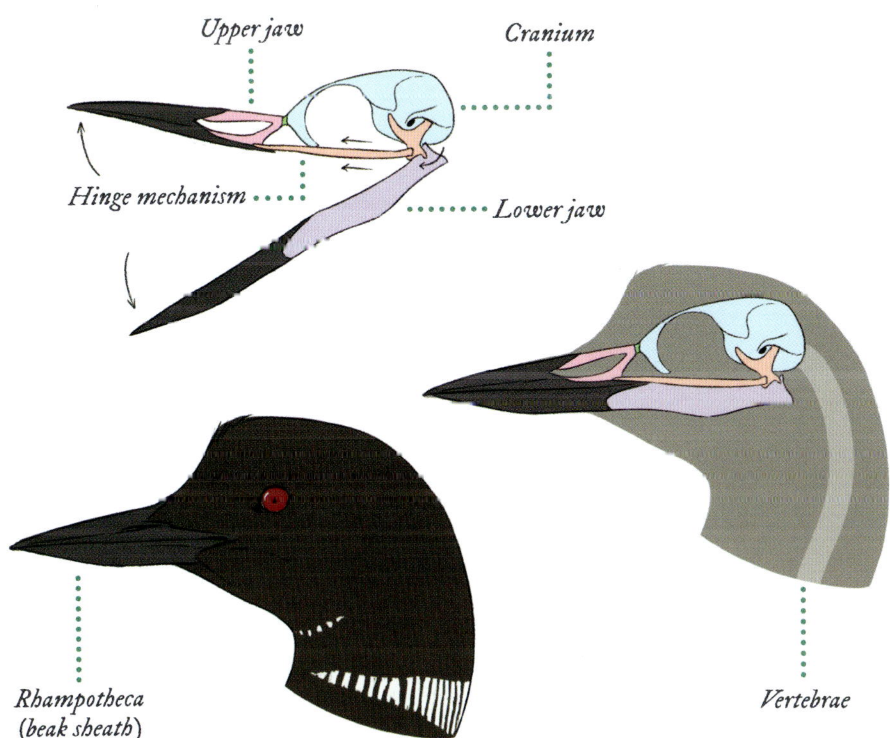

Functionality research

Types of avian wings

A bird's flying style is mirrored in the shapes of its wings. There are four main types of wing seen in flying birds:

- **Gliding wing** - long and slim for gliding on wind currents

- **Soaring wing** - broad and slotted for soaring on air thermals

- **High-speed wing** - short and pointed for speed

- **Elliptical wing** - short and wide for fast takeoffs and maneuverability

For this creature, gliding and soaring wings would make the most sense. They work for low-energy travel, as well as for rising high up into the air to spot prey. However, one of the best-adapted urban birds today, the peregrine falcon, has high-speed wings, making it adept at maneuvering in a packed urban environment. Even elliptical wings would have their benefits for our creature.

Heat adaptations

Our creature has adapted to living in a post-apocalyptic environment brought about by an extreme shift in climate. It might live in wastelands and urban ruins, alongside - or in competition with - a few remaining humans. To have any hope of surviving the scorching heat of an urban desert, it will need adaptations that prevent its body from overheating. It will need to thermoregulate. There are many ways animals achieve this, but for this creature, focusing on the role of skin in thermoregulation will create some interesting visuals.

Skin is integral to thermoregulation as it is the outermost layer of any animal, and therefore in direct contact with the environment. Animals can influence the flow of blood to the skin in order to control their body temperature - as blood flows through vessels near the surface, the skin loses heat to the environment, cooling the animal down. Bare skin areas are also used for display purposes, as found in vultures or the white ibis.

Because many animals need to survive both hot and cold temperatures, they will not be completely "naked," but rather have select areas of bare skin that are filled with many blood vessels and can act as a thermoregulatory device.

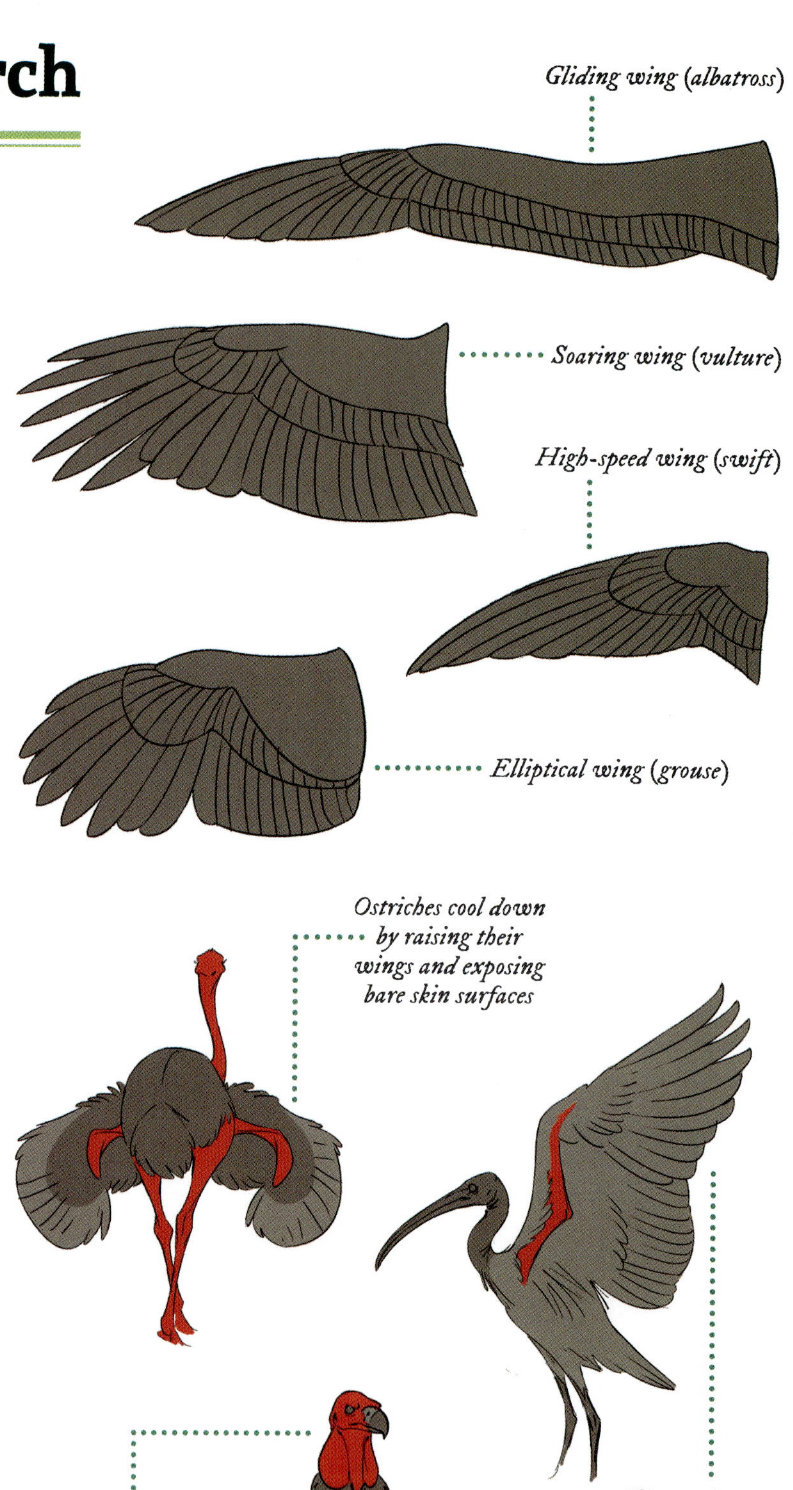

Digestive system

A scavenger's digestive system is one of the more important aspects of its anatomy, and it also has some effect on the outward appearance of the animal. Let us start at the beak. Birds have replaced their heavy teeth with a beak that is more lightweight, and consequently weaker. As a result of this, the food cannot be chewed, but is torn or crushed before being swallowed. If the animal would like to digest in a less exposed location, it can store food in a pouch or by channeling it into the crop (an area in the esophagus).

For digestion, the food moves into the proventriculus, a glandular tube that begins the process of breaking the food down by saturating it with acids. In vultures, this acid is extremely corrosive and can kill most pathogens, allowing it to digest rotting meat without getting sick. Finally, the food passes into the second part of the stomach, the gizzard. The gizzard has thick, muscular walls that "chew" the food. Not only is this an extremely effective replacement for teeth (the gizzard of a turkey is able to reduce surgical blades to grit!), it also shifts weight from the front of the bird, moving the center of gravity back - another benefit for flight.

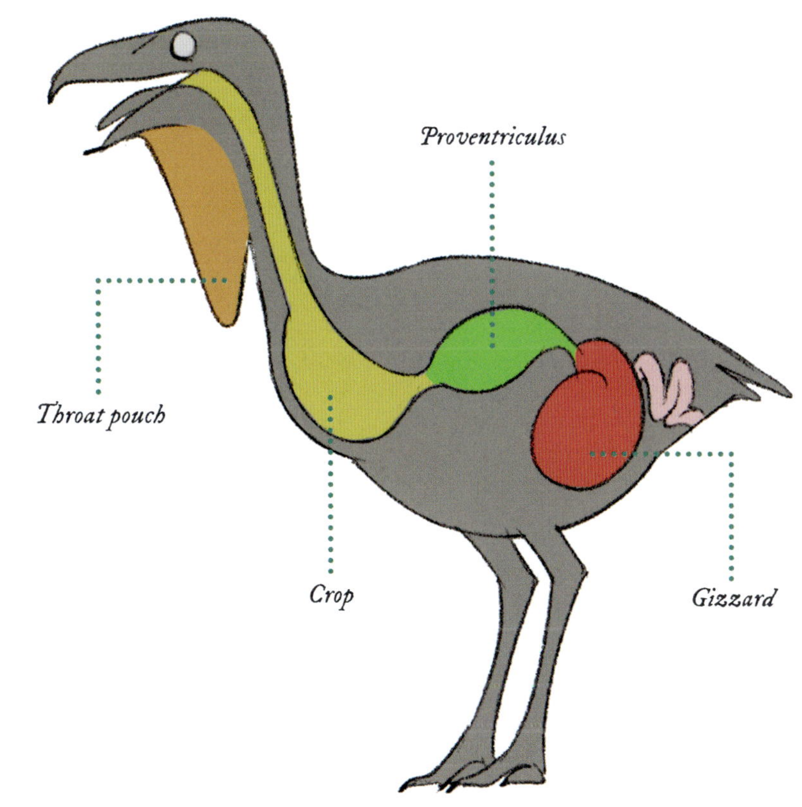

Coloration

Incorporating dark facial patterns on our creature will help it look like it lives in a desert - and these markings have several functional uses among real-world animals, too.

Facial stripes can serve to conceal the eyes, protecting them from injury by predators. In desert animals, dark areas around the eyes are thought to reduce glare, much like the "eye black" worn in some sports.

Lastly, these patterns can be a form of aposematism (use of bright colors or patterns to ward off predators), and could also help members of the same species to recognize each other (intra-species recognition).

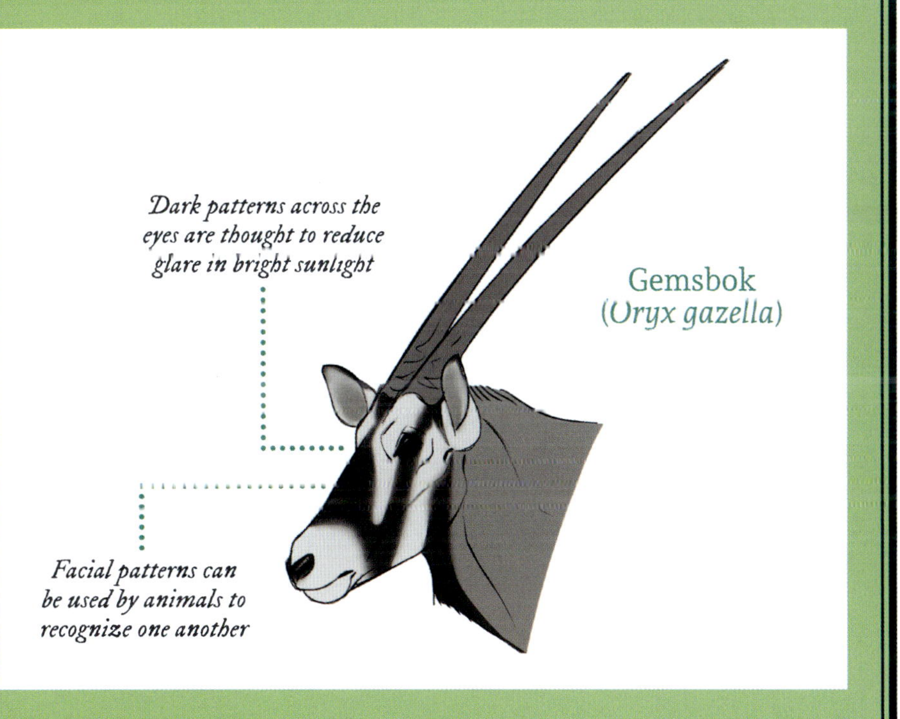

Thumbnails

Often, working against the norm can produce the best results. For this particular design, I made the thumbnails *before* I looked at references. If you find your drawings become stiff and uninteresting after doing too much planning, it could be because your brain is focused on too many things at once.

At this point in the design process the thumbnails can be loose and spontaneous - worry about any corrections or details later on. By drawing the thumbnails first, you effectively split up the process so that you can focus on one aspect at a time without getting overwhelmed. One size does not fit all - every artist will differ in their approach to designing creatures. Through trial and error, you will gradually learn what processes are most agreeable to you and how you work best, picking and choosing from a lot of different sources as you go.

In the case of thumbnails, the focus is on good gesture and interesting shapes and ideas, so just have fun during this stage. Once you are satisfied with the thumbnails you have made, you can revisit them and correct the anatomy, but over time you may find this a less necessary step. If your visual library has enough in it to work from, you will not make many major mistakes while sketching freely.

When creating thumbnails, it is important to depict the widest possible variety of "solutions" to a given brief. Cast a wide net in the beginning, both to make sure that you are choosing the best possible design and, in a commercial situation, to provide your client with the satisfaction that most avenues have been explored and a choice can be made on how to proceed. Of course, you will never be able to explore every single option out there on a single sheet! Some clients may not want to hear this, but the goal here is to provide a sufficient illusion of choice in order to move the design along.

For these thumbnails, variety is provided by showcasing the many directions in which a design can be pushed while still remaining under the umbrella of "scavenger." Insectoid mouthparts are particularly intriguing and so make an appearance in most of these designs. Sharp, triangular shapes are used to give these creatures an aura of danger.

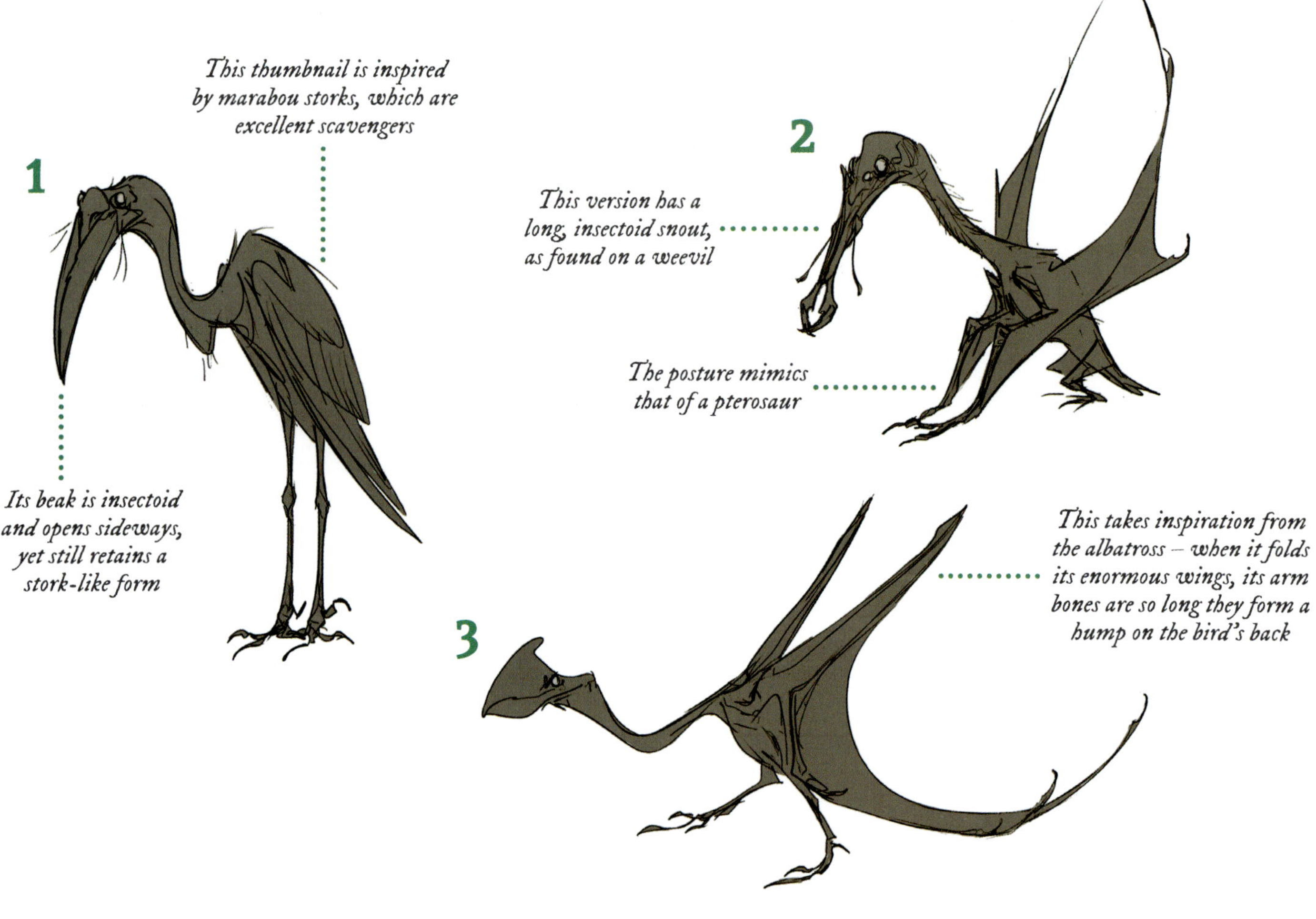

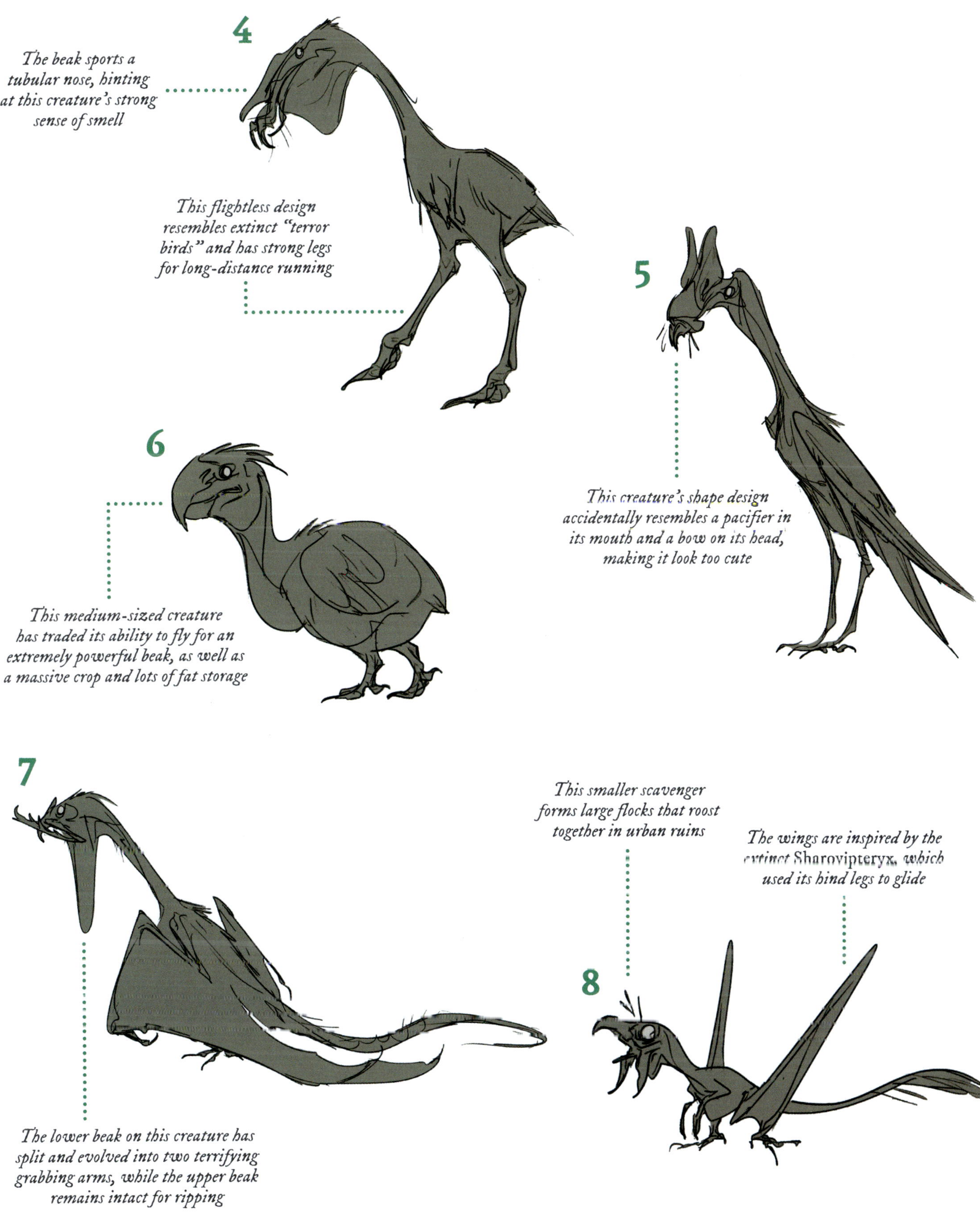

4
The beak sports a tubular nose, hinting at this creature's strong sense of smell
This flightless design resembles extinct "terror birds" and has strong legs for long-distance running
5
This creature's shape design accidentally resembles a pacifier in its mouth and a bow on its head, making it look too cute
6
This medium-sized creature has traded its ability to fly for an extremely powerful beak, as well as a massive crop and lots of fat storage
7
The lower beak on this creature has split and evolved into two terrifying grabbing arms, while the upper beak remains intact for ripping
This smaller scavenger forms large flocks that roost together in urban ruins
The wings are inspired by the extinct Sharovipteryx, which used its hind legs to glide
8

DEVELOPMENT

Thumbnail 4 is an original and interesting take on a scavenger - one that does not look explicitly vulturine. It also has the most appealing and novel beak out of all the thumbnails, merging the functions of smell, display, and call amplification, as well as an insectoid appearance, into a single focal point.

This design also succeeds in incorporating environmental adaptations, again without over-complicating the design and disturbing its flow. To cope with extreme temperatures, the creature possesses a wattle (a loose, fleshy flap) as well as plenty of bare skin areas to dissipate heat. To address the urban aspect of the setting, the creature's approximately human size would enable it to navigate easily through doorways and ruins.

Of all of the factors that influenced this design, the scavenger lifestyle is perhaps most strongly represented, as it informs the main focal point (the beak). Insectoid mouthparts allow this creature to break down carcasses at record speed, filling its crop/pouch and retreating to a cooler location to digest its meal.

The audial aspect of this creature is the most hidden element, as it would overcomplicate the design and compete with the already existing attributes if defined any further. Nevertheless, it is still there: the crest serves not only as a display feature but as an amplification device, and the throat pouch fulfills a similar double function, inflating to create sound.

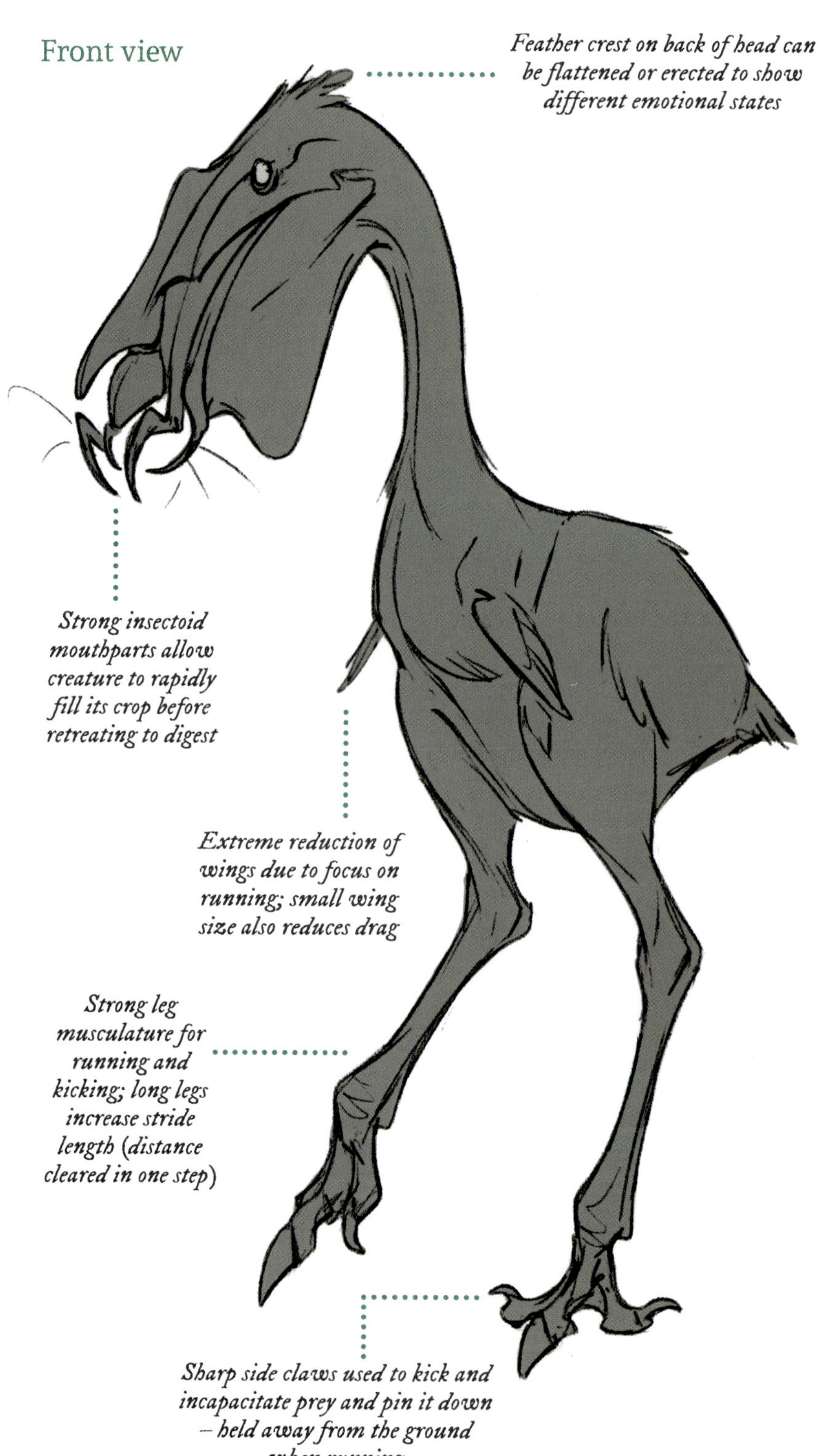

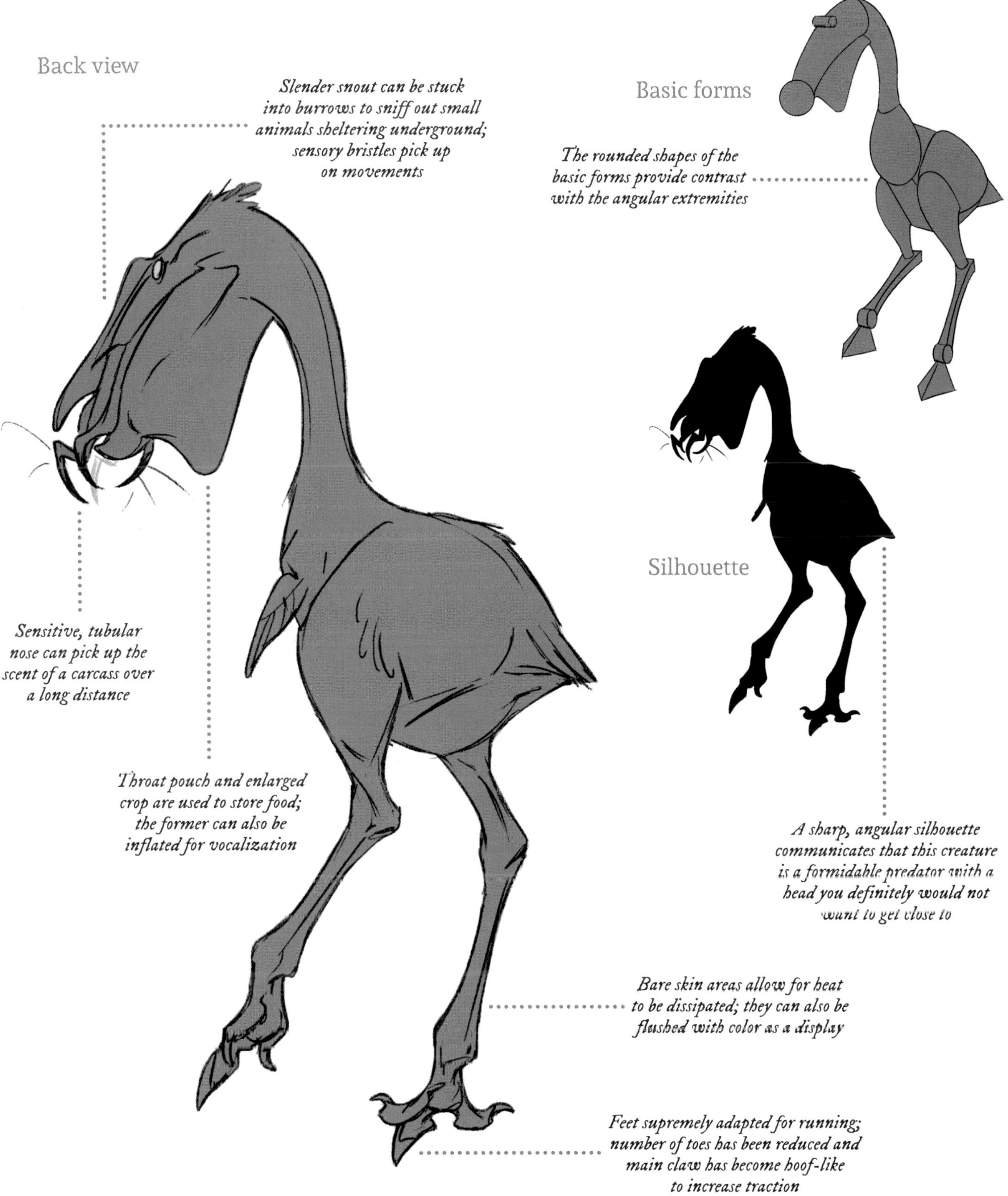

Back view
Basic forms
Silhouette
Slender snout can be stuck into burrows to sniff out small animals sheltering underground; sensory bristles pick up on movements
The rounded shapes of the basic forms provide contrast with the angular extremities
Sensitive, tubular nose can pick up the scent of a carcass over a long distance
Throat pouch and enlarged crop are used to store food; the former can also be inflated for vocalization
A sharp, angular silhouette communicates that this creature is a formidable predator with a head you definitely would not want to get close to
Bare skin areas allow for heat to be dissipated; they can also be flushed with color as a display
Feet supremely adapted for running; number of toes has been reduced and main claw has become hoof-like to increase traction

Poses

There are a few things to consider when choosing a pose to best represent your creature. You can go for something dynamic, action-packed, and full of movement, such as a fight between two creatures or a hunting scene. You could opt for something calmer - a glimpse into what the creature would probably spend the majority of its time doing, such as resting, grazing, or preening. It depends which side of your creature you would like to show.

Pose A falls into the former category. The creature is seen hunting down a small lizard at high speed, a supplement to its diet of carrion. The back leg is fully outstretched as if the creature has just launched itself forward with it, while the front leg is poised to kick and subdue the lizard. The jaws are open, ready to bite the prey as soon as it has been pinned down.

In contrast, pose B is calmer, showing the moment the creature has found (or perhaps stolen) a carcass to feed on. Its head is raised with the neck fully outstretched. The creature is sniffing the air to make sure no other creatures are around before it starts feeding.

Pose C is the calmest, depicting the creature as it rests in a shaded area. It has just finished eating, as evidenced by its bulging crop, and has now retreated to digest its meal away from the sun's scorching rays. The creature is relaxed yet alert - it is watching you closely, but knows that you could not possibly pose any kind of threat to it.

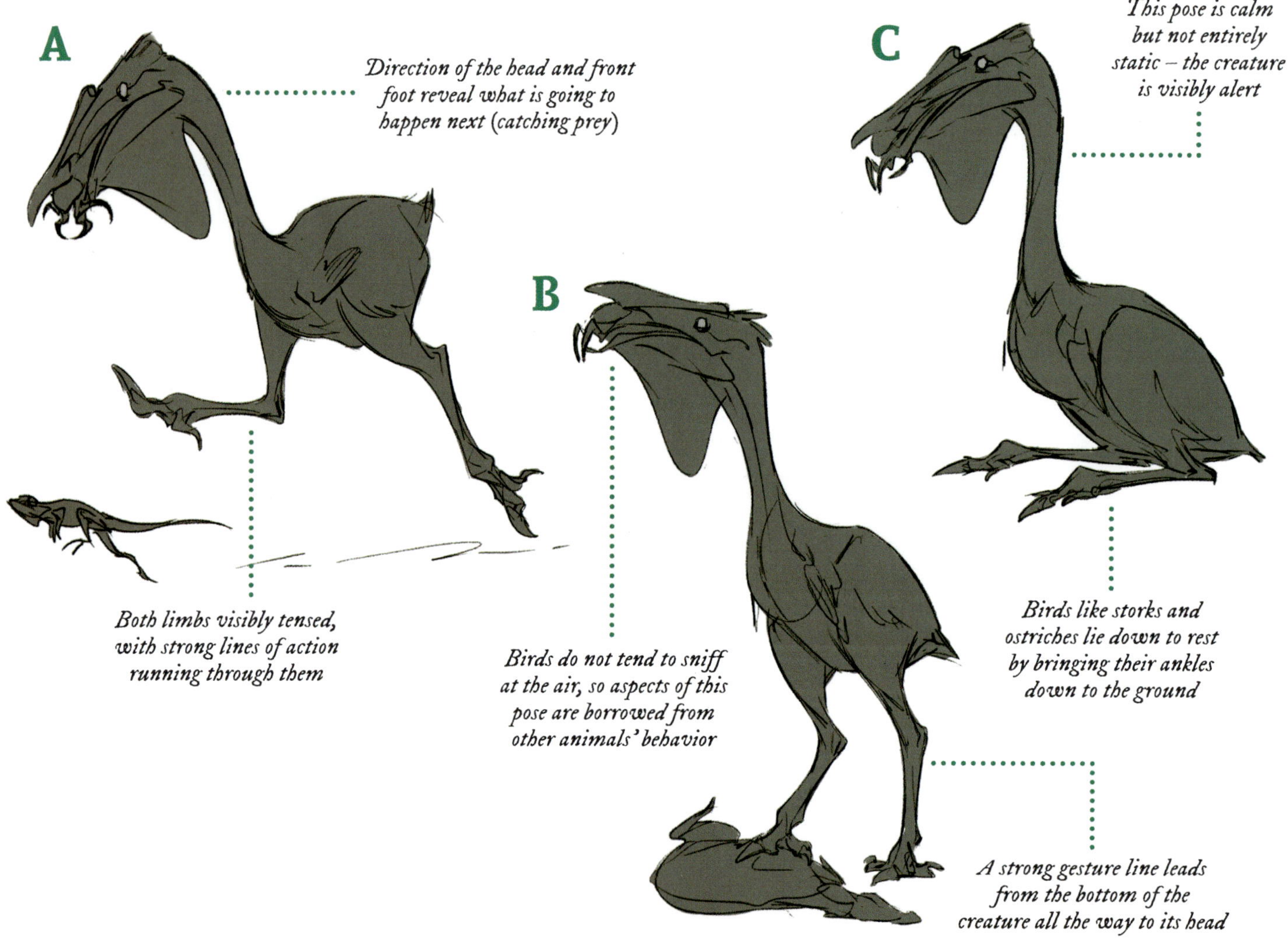

Direction of the head and front foot reveal what is going to happen next (catching prey)

Both limbs visibly tensed, with strong lines of action running through them

Birds do not tend to sniff at the air, so aspects of this pose are borrowed from other animals' behavior

This pose is calm but not entirely static – the creature is visibly alert

Birds like storks and ostriches lie down to rest by bringing their ankles down to the ground

A strong gesture line leads from the bottom of the creature all the way to its head

Color & pattern

Birds provide a vast amount of inspiration for creature designs, from the variety within their feathers and beaks to the vibrant patterns and colors they display. For every possible color combination or patterning you can think of, there is probably an existing bird that already has it, or at least comes close. And if there is not a bird, there is definitely a fish, lizard, or insect. Because of this, you can do nearly anything you please when it comes to creating coloration for your creatures.

One thing you do need to keep in mind is that the coloration must play well with the design you have already established. Ideally, the coloration should define and emphasize key areas (such as the eyes or beak), clarify portions of the design that were unclear in black and white (such as a white belly or dark back), and still manage to flow alongside the rest of the design.

The best way to learn when it comes to creature design is to look at real-world animals. After all, it is our brain's exposure to nature that helps it decide what we find visually appealing. Colors and patterning are no exception, so if you get stuck on this or any other part of the process, take a look at real animals for inspiration.

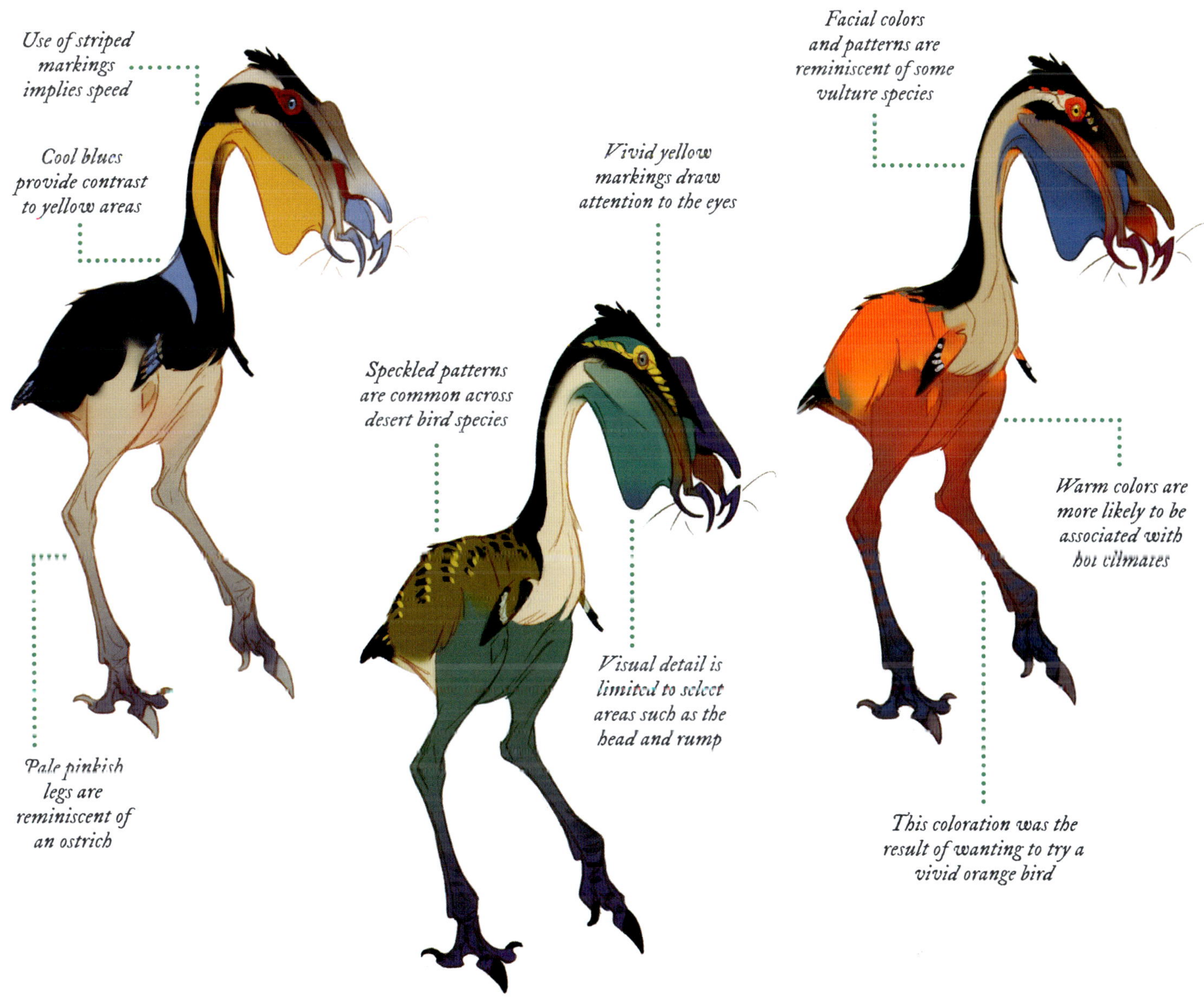

FINAL DESIGN

A variety of elements have contributed to making this final design a success. Looking first at the most basic building blocks, the design has an excellent gesture and flow to it, from the tip of the beak all the way down to the legs. A bulky body combined with a slender head, neck, and legs provides contrast in the base forms and contributes to an overall sense of strength and maneuverability. The silhouette is clearly readable, with flourishes of complexity in select areas such as the beak.

The design has also successfully combined biological information with aesthetics, creating the impression of believability without veering too far into overt realism. Key biological aspects of scavengers have been distilled down to their most basic components using diligent research, allowing them to be incorporated into the design in a subtle way without looking "Frankensteined" together. The physical attributes of this creature accurately reflect the functions they need to perform ("form follows function").

Avian and insectoid elements have been blended together seamlessly to create a creature that looks menacing and capable, yet still retains the elegance of its bird-like form. Bare skin, feathered areas, and hard surfaces such as the beak add interest in terms of textural variety. Coloration and patterning further emphasize the design elements established in the earlier stages of the process.

All of these factors combined make this creature pleasing to look at, and the character of the animal is well represented in the final version. If you can look at a design and are able to picture the creature alive - are enticed into imagining it running, squawking, feeding, tending to its young - that counts as a great success. The saddest reality of creature design is not being able to meet your creations in the flesh, but comfort can be found in getting as close as possible within the boundaries of art.

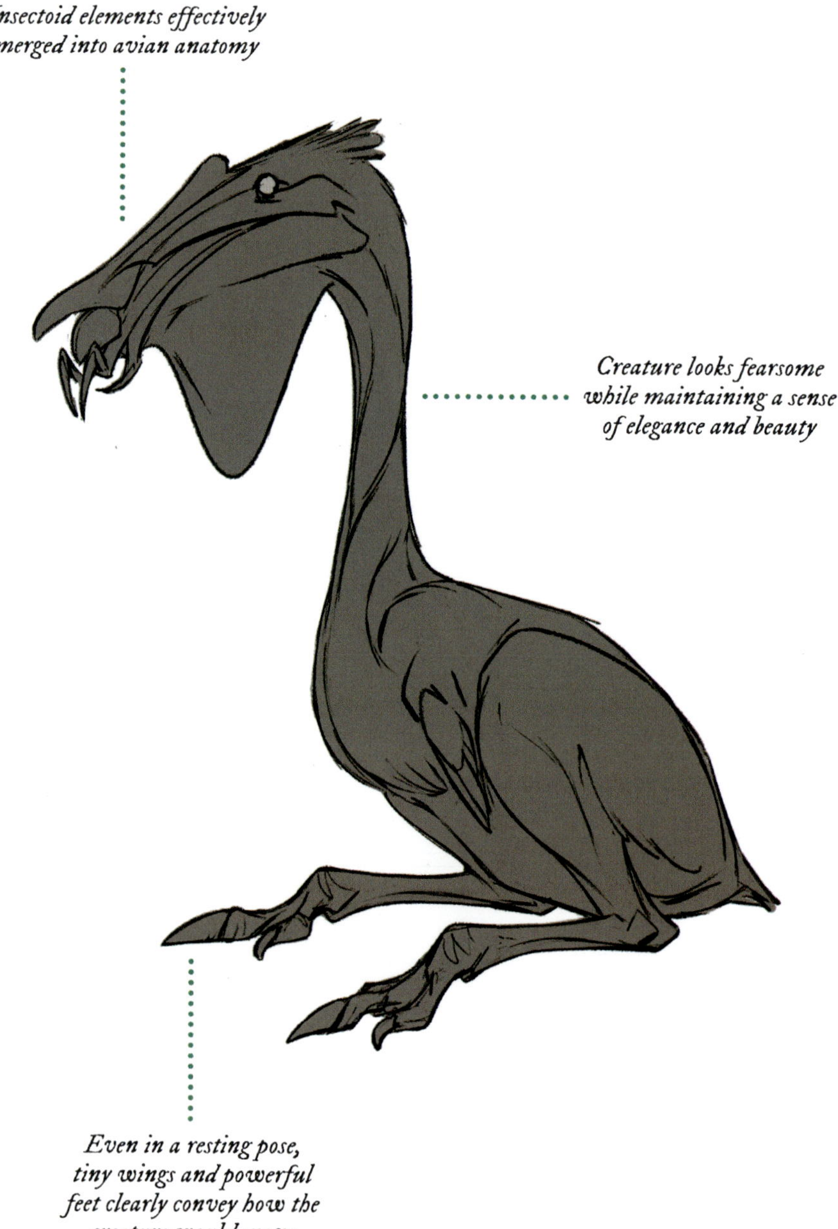

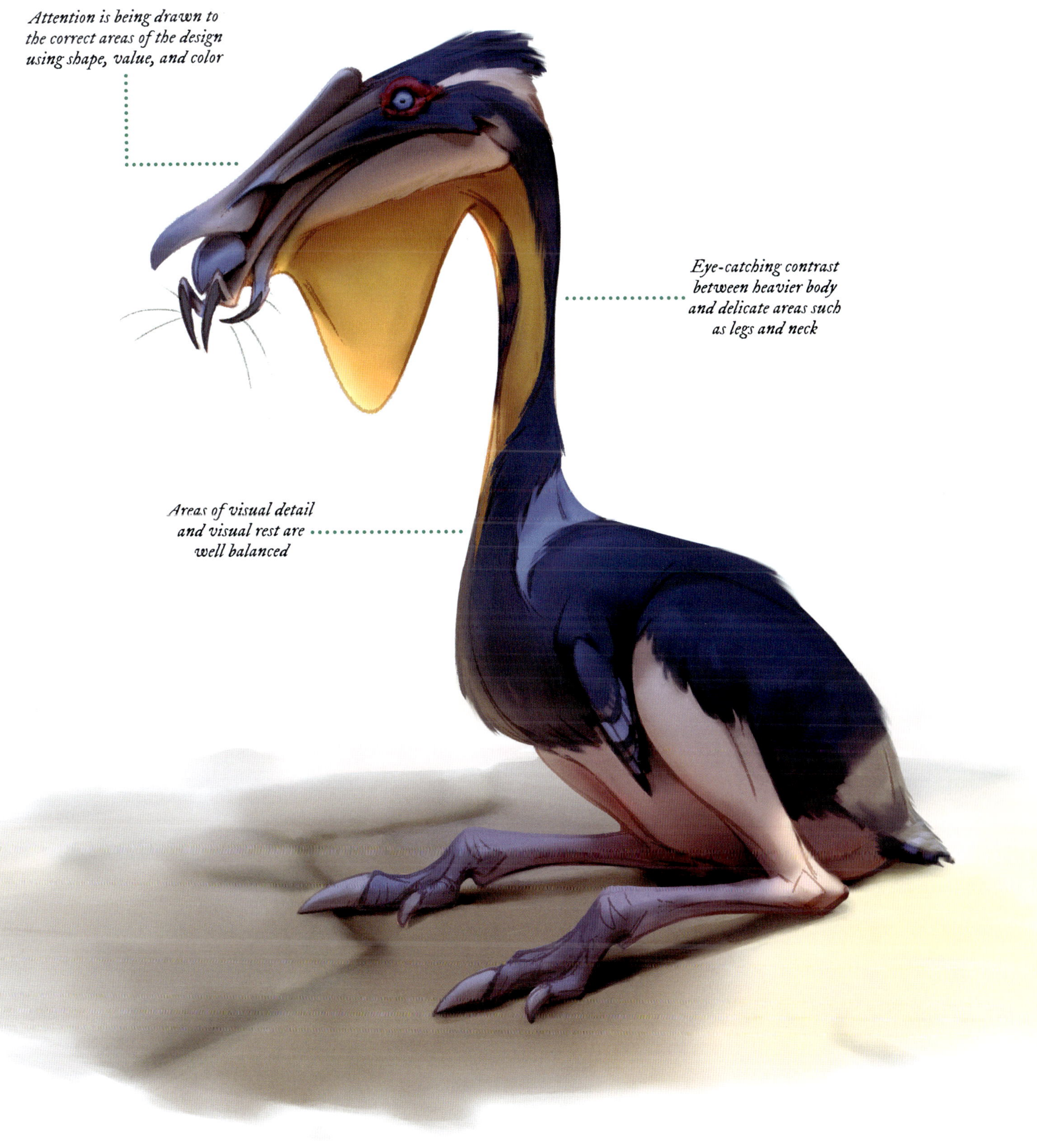

Final image © Kristina Lexova

VARIATIONS

Mountainous

This species of scavenger has adapted to survive the colder, harsher conditions of mountain ranges. It has a stouter stature, shorter neck and limbs, and smaller crest and wattle than its warmer-weather counterparts. This is due to Allen's rule in biology, which states that animals adapted to cold climates will have shorter limbs and appendages, minimizing the surface area exposed to the cold and helping them conserve heat.

The body of this species is covered in warm feathers; it even has feathers covering its nostrils to warm cold air as it inhales. The feet have adapted to act as snowshoes. Lastly, its beak is the strongest among all the avian scavengers, as it must be able to feed on carcasses that have been frozen solid.

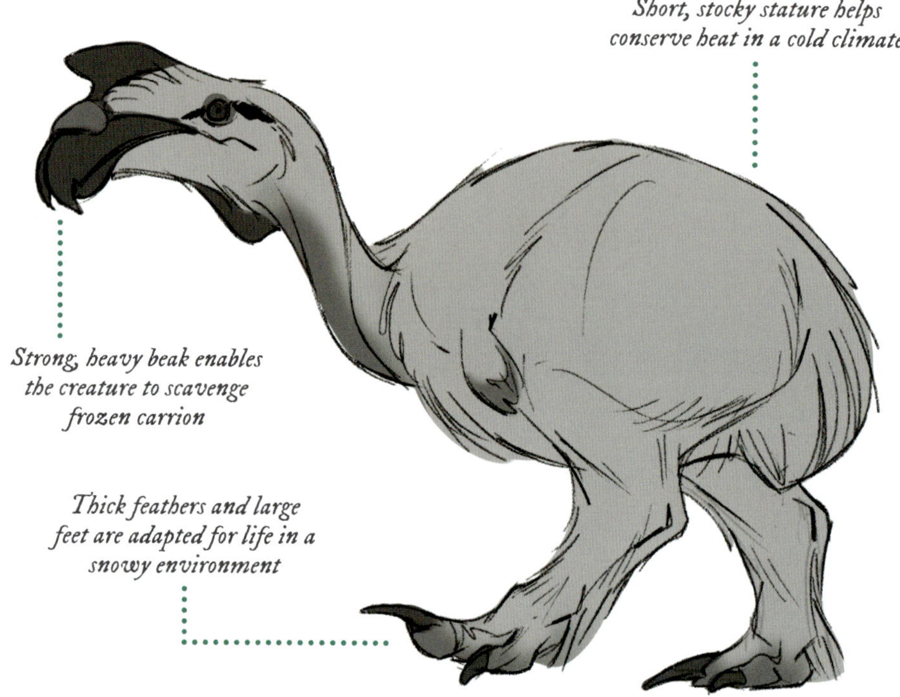

Insectoid

This adaptation was achieved by using the shapes of the base creature design to transform it into an insectoid, rather than focusing on realism like the other two versions. If you squint at it, the main shapes are all there, but their nature has been changed to reflect their new anatomy. The neck and chest have become hardened exoskeletal plates, and the wattle now resembles a pair of insect wings. The wings are now mantis-like arms, and the legs have also been changed, borrowing their shape language from the legs of a grasshopper. The abdomen, too, is now markedly insectoid in nature. The only features not changed much here are the mouthparts.

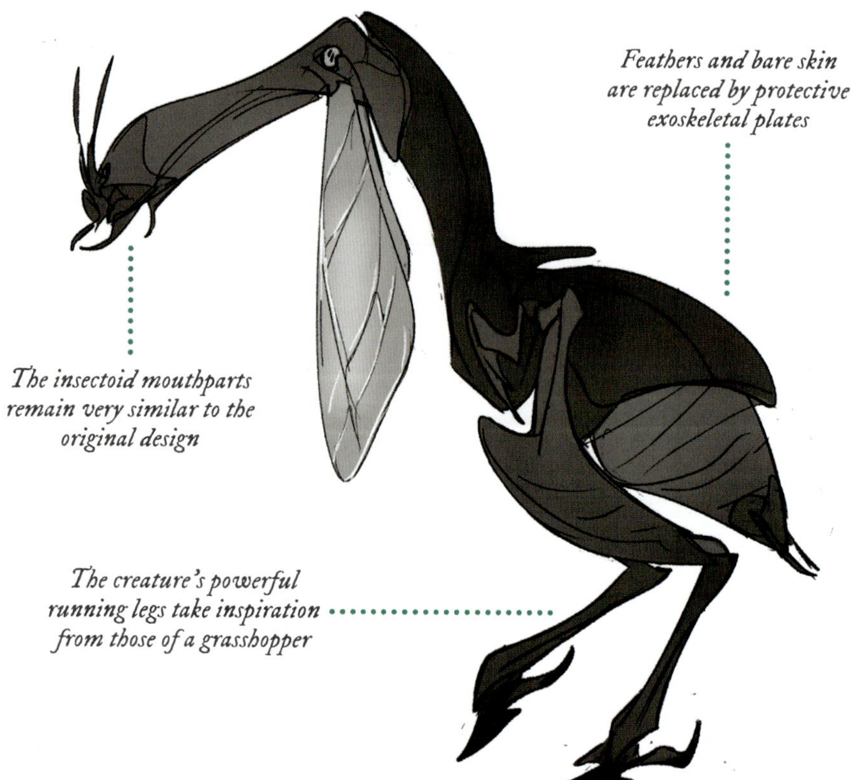

Tropical

This species is adapted to life in dense rainforests. Its most prominent feature is an enlarged crest. As this creature runs through the forest with its neck outstretched, its crest slices through the undergrowth and ensures easy passage (or protection, should a collision occur). It is also used to detect the rumbling calls of other members of its species, and to amplify its own calls.

The body is covered in rough, thick feathers for protection against thorns and branches. The eyes of this creature are larger than those of its cousins, to enable it to see in the lower light conditions of the forest. Finally, the wattle of this species can be folded flat against the neck so as not to snag on anything when not in use.

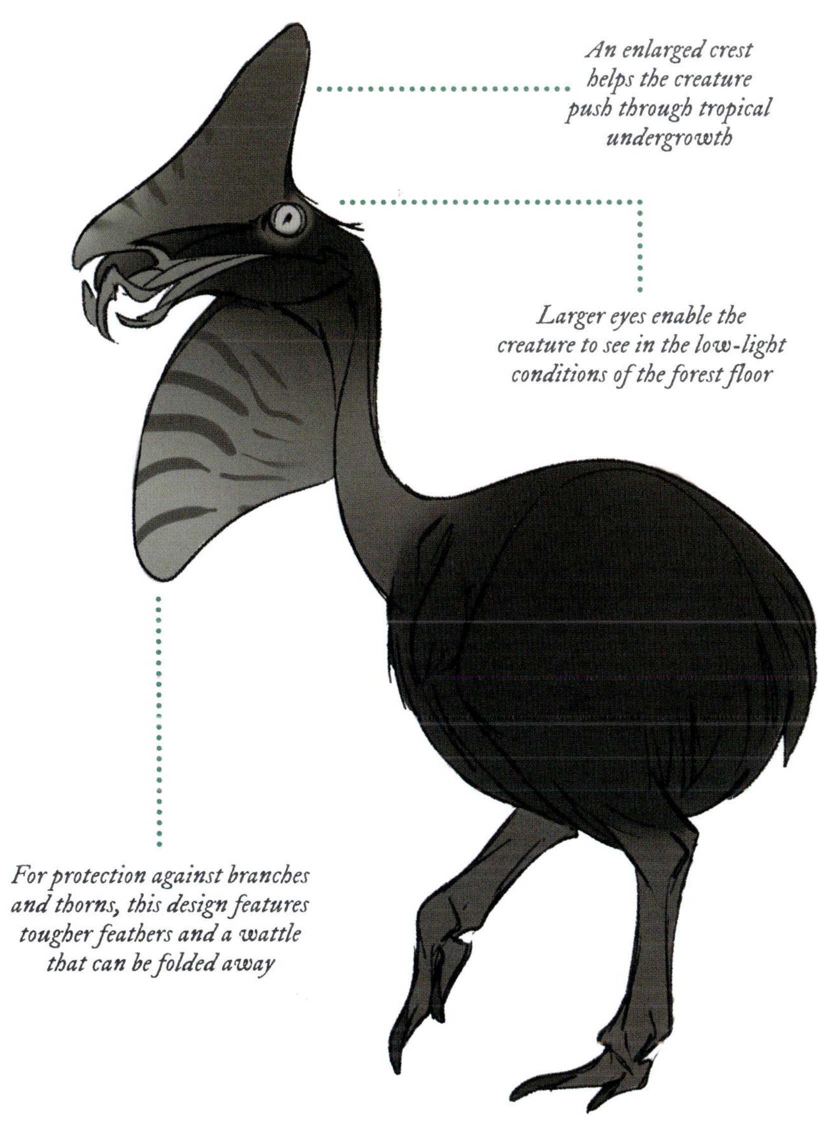

An enlarged crest helps the creature push through tropical undergrowth

Larger eyes enable the creature to see in the low-light conditions of the forest floor

For protection against branches and thorns, this design features tougher feathers and a wattle that can be folded away

Industry tip

Probably one of the most important (and frustrating) lessons I had to learn when I was getting into commercial creature art is this: *If the design doesn't look cool, people aren't going to like it, no matter how much research and effort has gone into making the design scientifically or anatomically accurate.* In the beginning, it can feel terrible that people are judging your art by its cover in this way, as if all your hard work means nothing. But this does not mean you have to abandon the science side of creature art – on the contrary. The beauty of a good design lies in creating something that looks wonderful and has layers to it. Good visuals will draw people in and get them interested in what you have to offer, and the thought you have put into the underlying aspects of a design is what will make it truly memorable. Creature design should be a marriage between these two aspects, working together to create that perfect balance.

Alien megafauna

Allison Theus

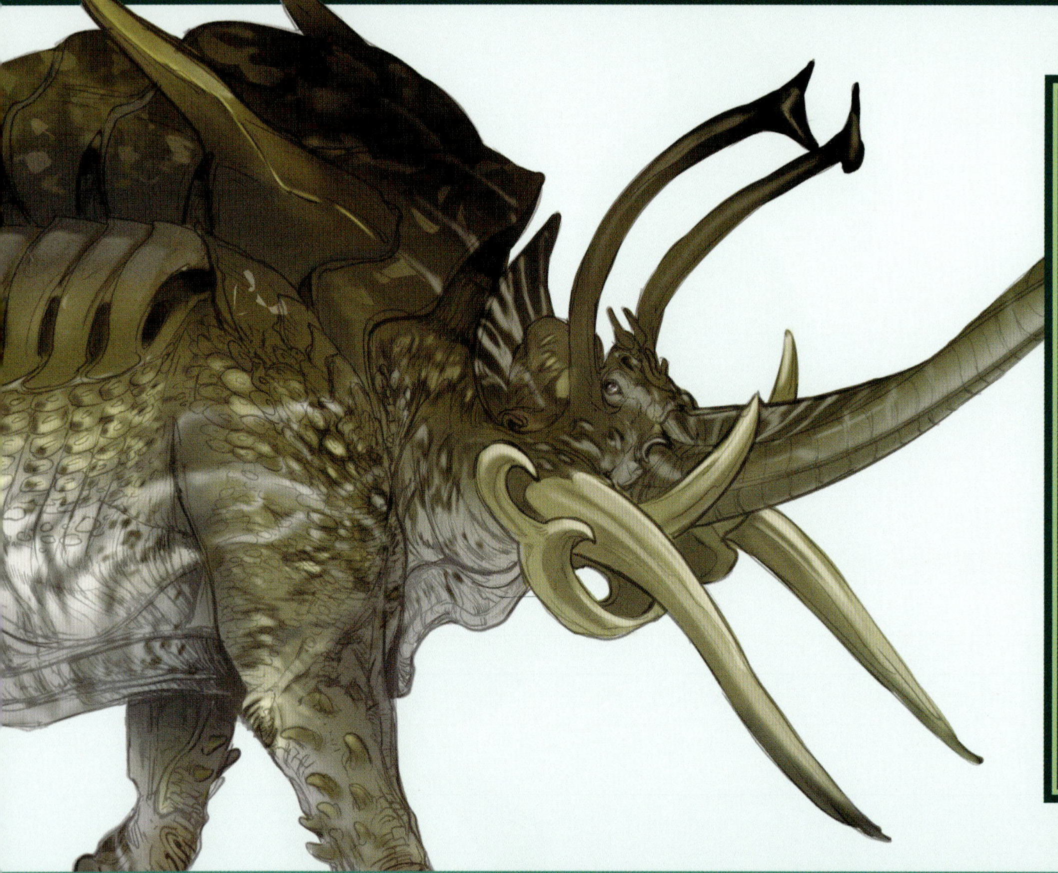

Key facts

- Long-legged and tall with insectoid mandibles and a protective shell

- Thrives in meadows and grasslands of an alien setting that may not have the same atmosphere and biology as Earth

- Herbivore, able to feed from lofty places using its mandibles

- Content to live and travel with small groups of its own kind; rarely completely solitary - its slow speed and gentle nature encourage smaller creatures to live on or near it

IDEATION

It can be helpful, if you have a first impression after reading a prompt, to scribble down that initial thought immediately - this frees up your mind to iterate on other solutions that may be more suitable for the task. The term "megafauna" refers to the large or giant animals of an area. The initial response to this design brief leads toward a large, long-legged, giraffe-like creature with a delicate shell, a reaching neck, and interesting jaws to add the "alien" element into the design. Taking a look at the phylogeny of modern day ungulates to derive further inspiration, there is a wealth of information on the evolution of grazing mammals that could prove useful. One well-known modern-day megafauna is the elephant, its tall and rounded body contrasting with the initial idea of a more slender creature. The specializations of insects (horned beetles in particular) are also a good reference for intriguing, varied silhouettes, as well as "alien" eating processes.

Designing a believable creature relies on the ability to fit it seamlessly into its environment. This requires considering how it responds to gravity, how it adapts to seasonal changes, its place in the food chain, its impact on the ecosystem, and the behaviors it displays in order to survive and procreate. This creature would likely need to be a wide-ranging herbivore, perhaps a highly specialized ruminant that lives in small family groups and migrates with the seasons to follow its primary food source. It may have an extensive proboscis to reach higher places, combined with the plant-stripping efficiency of a locust but on a larger scale. It may be adorned with beetle-inspired armor, chitin, or bone, to provide defense from aerial predators while maintaining optimum flexibility for movement - perhaps armor that starts out soft when the creature is young and hardens as the animal matures.

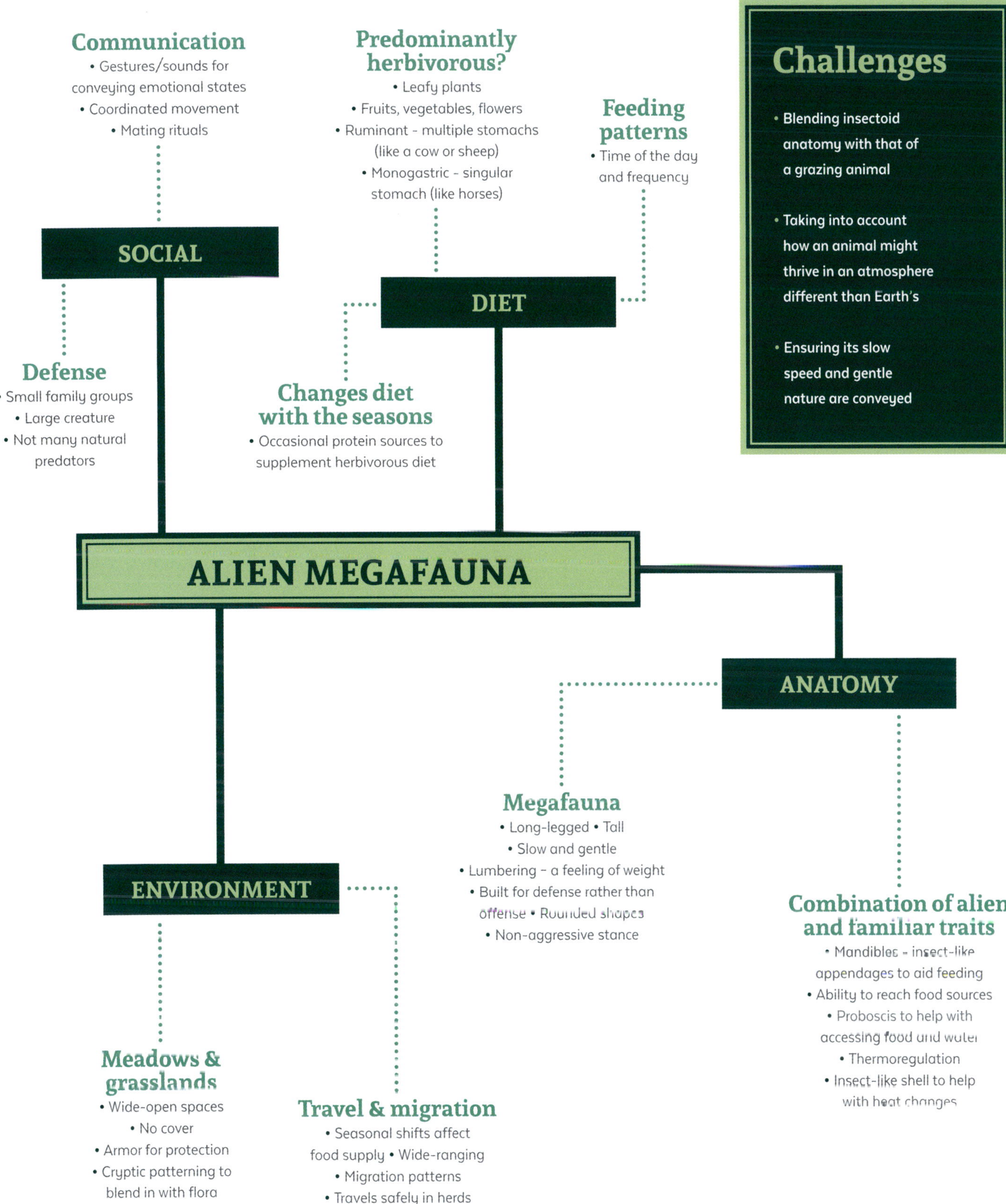
Communication
• Gestures/sounds for conveying emotional states
• Coordinated movement
• Mating rituals

SOCIAL

Defense
• Small family groups
• Large creature
• Not many natural predators

Predominantly herbivorous?
• Leafy plants
• Fruits, vegetables, flowers
• Ruminant - multiple stomachs (like a cow or sheep)
• Monogastric - singular stomach (like horses)

Feeding patterns
• Time of the day and frequency

DIET

Changes diet with the seasons
• Occasional protein sources to supplement herbivorous diet

Challenges
• Blending insectoid anatomy with that of a grazing animal

• Taking into account how an animal might thrive in an atmosphere different than Earth's

• Ensuring its slow speed and gentle nature are conveyed

ALIEN MEGAFAUNA

ANATOMY

Megafauna
• Long-legged • Tall
• Slow and gentle
• Lumbering – a feeling of weight
• Built for defense rather than offense • Rounded shapes
• Non-aggressive stance

Combination of alien and familiar traits
• Mandibles – insect-like appendages to aid feeding
• Ability to reach food sources
• Proboscis to help with accessing food and water
• Thermoregulation
• Insect-like shell to help with heat changes

ENVIRONMENT

Meadows & grasslands
• Wide-open spaces
• No cover
• Armor for protection
• Cryptic patterning to blend in with flora

Travel & migration
• Seasonal shifts affect food supply • Wide-ranging
• Migration patterns
• Travels safely in herds

Anatomy research

Weight distribution

Overcoming gravity is no easy task. Looking at examples from nature, you can see that the taller and larger the animal, the shorter and more rigid its spine tends to be. In a giraffe, this supports the long neck, whereas in an elephant it carries the massive muscles of the head, which support the teeth, tusks, and trunk. A bison's heavy appearance is driven by impressive neck muscles that support the animal's large head while grazing. The way a creature's skull is carried, the way it balances on its legs, and the way its belly hangs are all important to consider when designing for a feeling of weight. These aspects will assist you in evoking a "large and slow" feeling.

American bison
(*Bison bison*)

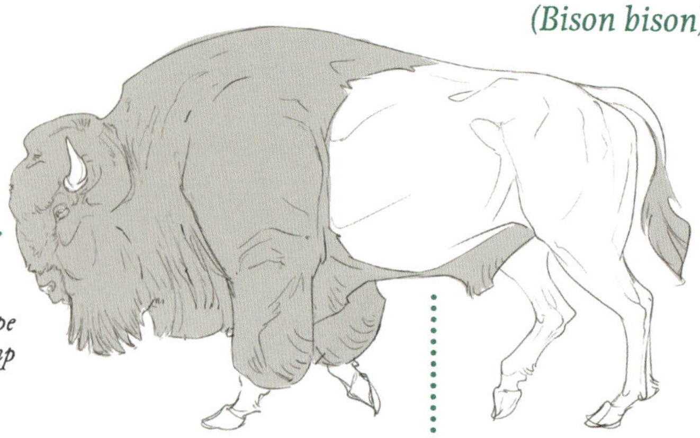

Compact, heavy shape with a rounded hump

Slight belly sway adds to the bison's sense of heaviness

African elephant
(*Loxodonta*)

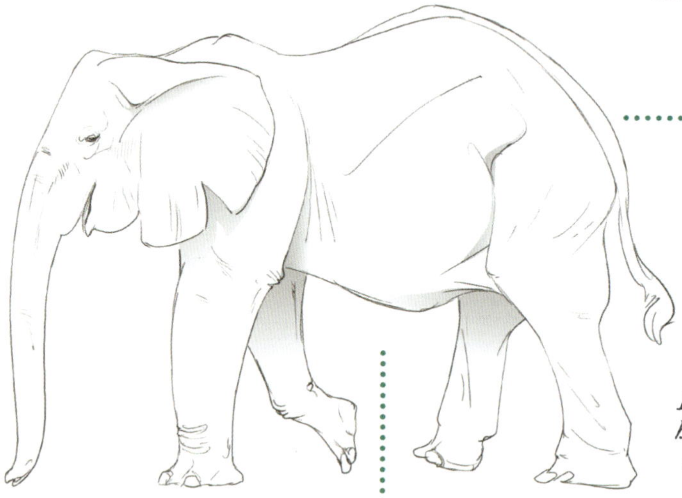

The elephant has a high, rounded, sloping back

The elephant's round head angles down into a long, flexible trunk

Like the bison, a low-hanging belly gives the impression of weight

Evolution

Samotherium is an extinct relative of the giraffe. It displays an elongated neck that was an intermediate stage between that of an okapi and a giraffe. It is likely that natural selection pressures, due to feeding and combat for mates, drove the length and shape of the giraffe's neck and allowed it to specialize. Our megafauna creature design may show similar adaptations in order to help with survival. An animal that must consume an enormous amount of food can make up some of that food debt by eating the most nutritious plant matter available - or by adapting to consume matter that other animals cannot reach.

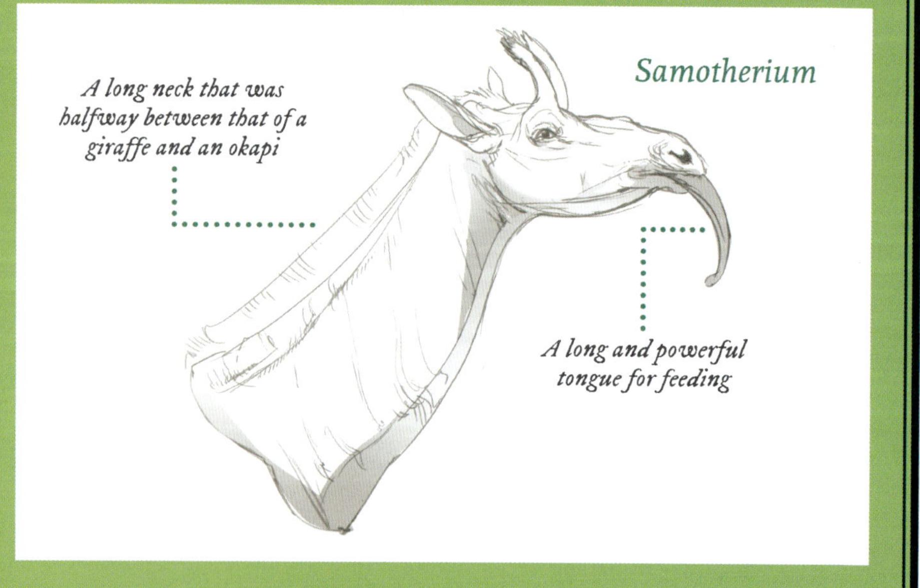

198

Insect mandibles

As mentioned on **page 101**, chewing insects, as opposed to insects that feed by piercing or sucking, have multiple mouthparts. Depending on the kind of food eaten, and what they are defending themselves against, their jaws are shaped to grasp, cut, or crush. Additionally, insects can use their maxillae as a means of offense or defense. It is important to consider the diet of the creature you are designing, as well as the threats it may encounter, as mouths often double as weapons.

Limbs

The shape of the creature's feet is dictated by the size and shape of the legs, how close they are to each other, and how much weight needs to be carried. All of Earth's megafauna carry their weight differently on their feet. Elephants put most of their weight on the outsides of their feet, while rhinoceros's weight is transferred to the insides of their feet. Both have significant padding behind their toes to assist in weight distribution, while giraffes can retain their long, thin limbs by having suspensory ligaments to support their legs.

Insects possess only striated muscle, adhering to the inside of the exoskeleton instead of attaching to an internal skeleton. Their legs can move even in the absence of muscles due to passive joint forces.

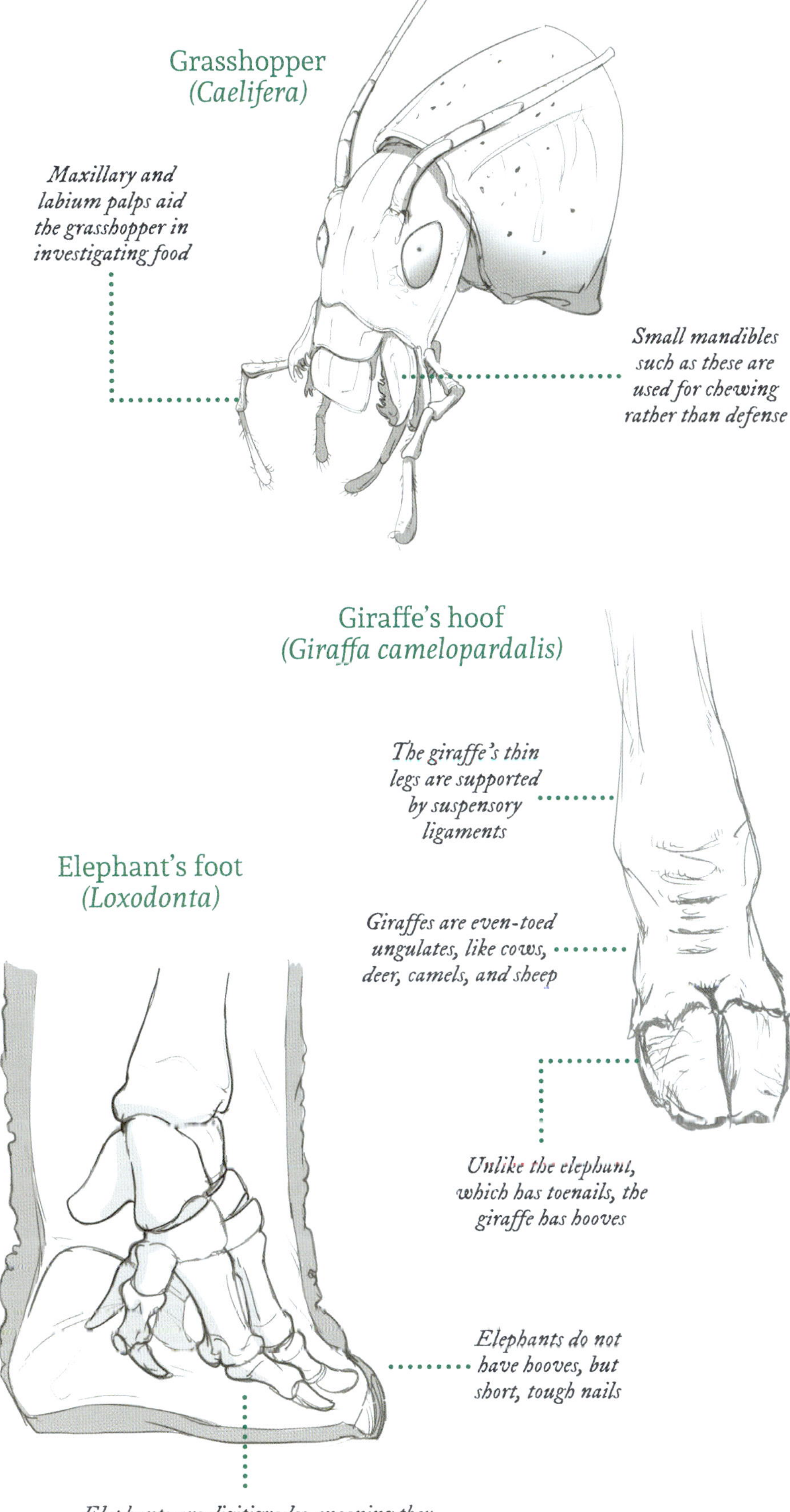

Grasshopper
(Caelifera)

Maxillary and labium palps aid the grasshopper in investigating food

Small mandibles such as these are used for chewing rather than defense

Giraffe's hoof
(Giraffa camelopardalis)

The giraffe's thin legs are supported by suspensory ligaments

Giraffes are even-toed ungulates, like cows, deer, camels, and sheep

Unlike the elephant, which has toenails, the giraffe has hooves

Elephant's foot
(Loxodonta)

The elephant has substantial padding behind its toes to help distribute weight

Elephants do not have hooves, but short, tough nails

Elephants are digitigrades, meaning they walk on their toes, similar to dogs and cats

Functionality research

Horns & tusks

Horns and tusks can serve multiple purposes when it comes to foraging, defense, and display. Tusks are elongated teeth, whereas horns typically originate on the head. From the rhinoceros to the rhinoceros beetle, the shape of a creature's horns may speak to the style of fighting employed. Elongated horns can wrestle and fence; curved horns appear to be adept at ramming; and smooth, straight horns are used to injure. The same could be said about tusks, although the kind of foraging the animal does is more likely to influence the shape of these specialized teeth. Some ornamental aspects of beetle horns combined with straighter tusks could give this creature a striking look, as well as driving some interesting social behaviors.

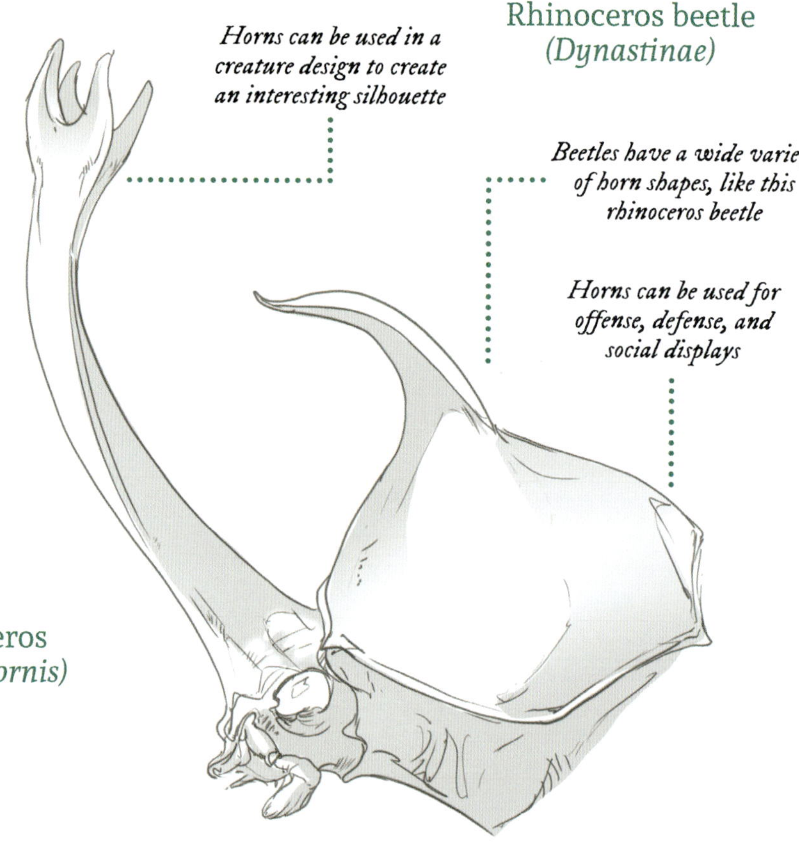

Horns can be used in a creature design to create an interesting silhouette

Rhinoceros beetle
(Dynastinae)

Beetles have a wide variety of horn shapes, like this rhinoceros beetle

Horns can be used for offense, defense, and social displays

Indian rhinoceros
(Rhinoceros unicornis)

Some rhinoceroses have thick folds of skin that resemble armor plates

Segmented appearance would blend well with insect inspirations

A tough hide protects against thorns and grass

Armor

Many mammals have evolved thick skin to protect them from thorns and sharp grasses. For most insects, their tough exoskeleton is protection enough, but soft-bodied insects can build their own armor. Scale insects, for instance, secrete a waxy substance that becomes a shield for protection against various predators.

In addition to defense, armor can often aid in thermoregulation. "Osteoderms" (such as those present in armadillos and spectacled caimans) and "dermal scutes" (such as in turtles and birds) are tough scales and plates that can be highly vascularized (full of blood vessels) and help to change body temperature. In many crocodilians, the osteoderms help combat acidosis when they are submerged for long periods and accumulating carbon dioxide. Thermoregulation plays a key role in the activity levels of all living things, so a mix of chitin carapace and osteoderms could produce an interesting appearance and variety of textures that add believability to the creature.

Communication

A number of larger animals use infrasound to communicate - for example, giraffes, elephants, and crocodiles. This low-frequency sound can also be produced by large natural events, such as volcanic eruptions, earthquakes, thunderstorms, and other geographic or atmospheric occurrences, giving the animals able to hear at those frequencies a distinct advantage over those that cannot.

Low-frequency communications can travel for miles uninterrupted, which allows isolated herds or groups to "message" back and forth and potentially coordinate movements around food, mating, or seasonal migrations. Infrasound can also be used to intimidate and potentially stun in close proximity, as in the case of a tiger's roar. It is easy to envision this large herbivore communicating with other family groups across long distances in such a manner, or using a powerful burst of infrasound to dissuade smaller attackers. Taking visual cues from the aforementioned animals in our research, such as elephants, will help convey that this creature can produce similar infrasound.

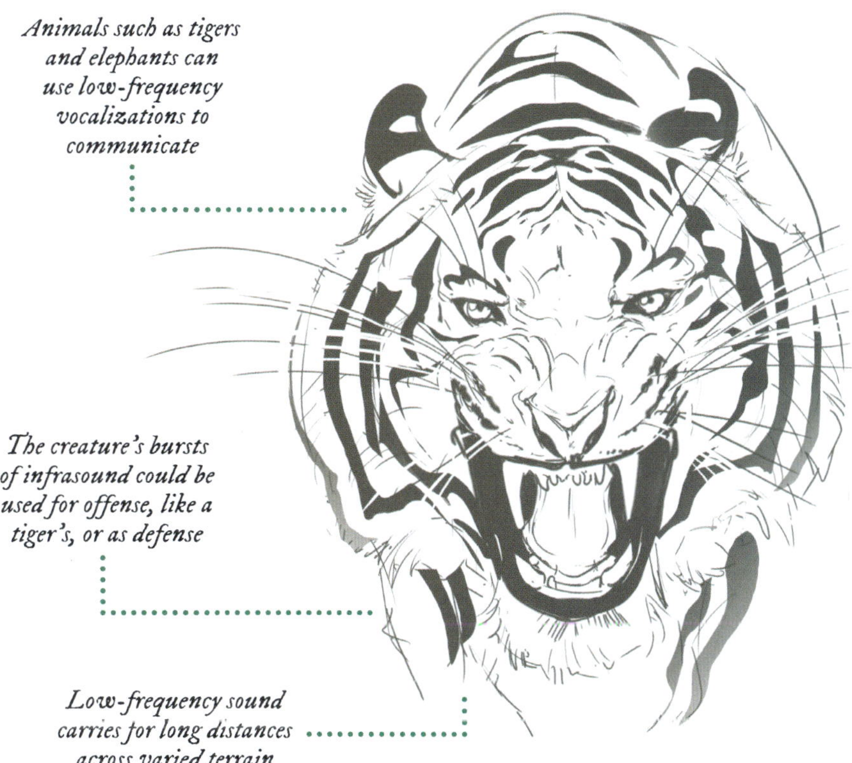

Coloration

Animals wield a variety of cryptic abilities to avoid detection. Disruptive camouflage is one of these, and can be utilized by predator and prey alike, as it breaks up an animal's silhouette using a highly contrasting pattern. It works especially well when combined with mimicry or countershading, where lighter colors are present on the ventral surface and darker colors along the back, which in turn disrupts shadows. These combinations are typically pitched to the visual acuity of prey and predator. For example, a deer's vision is based on motion, as well as acuity in low-light situations. Its ability to see mid- to low-color wavelengths is limited, and it is essentially colorblind, so the orange of a tiger or a hunter's vest is not so recognizable. Recognizing these functions in animals will help you to design creatures that are believable as predator or prey.

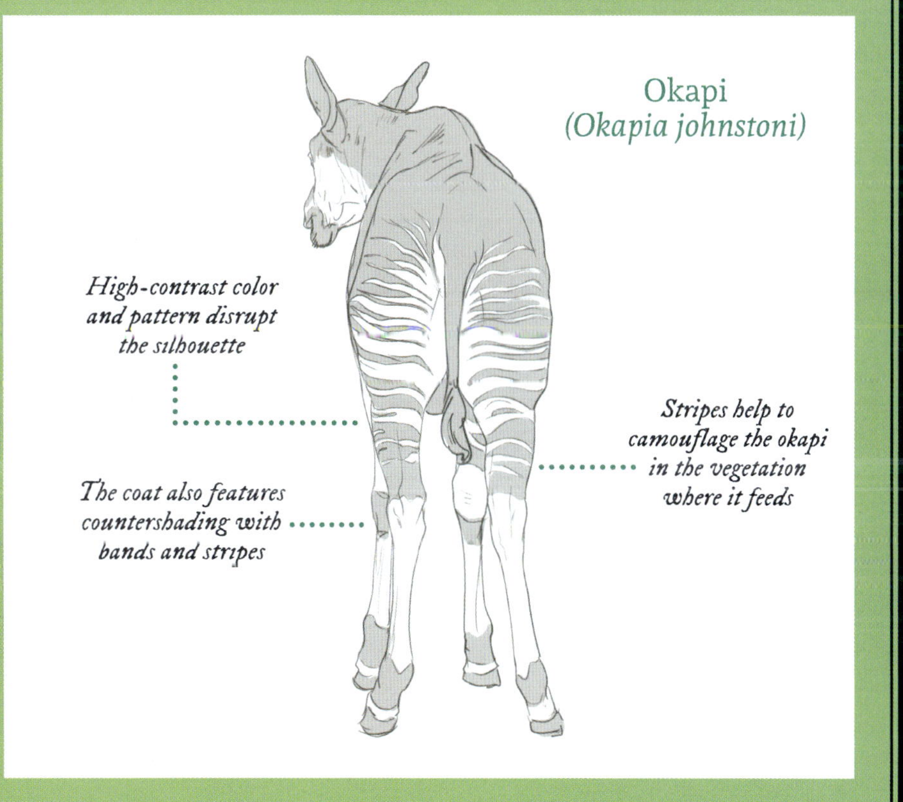

Thumbnails

Important features to consider when designing a larger, slow creature are the positioning of the skull, the shape of the pelvis, the proximity of the legs, and the way the body is carried. A low-slung skull adds to the impression of weight, but can also be interpreted to suggest unpredictability and aggression. This creature's appearance needs to announce its docile and gentle nature, so a higher head with a shorter neck may be the preferred route for this design.

Spine flexibility will influence how fast the creature is likely to move. From our research, we found that spine length can be affected by the height of the animal: the taller the animal, the shorter the spine.

A shorter back gives a feeling of compactness and decreased mobility, lessening any threat implied by the creature's size. If it is adorned with defensive horns or armor, they would be interpreted primarily as a means of defense. Incorporating rounded shapes into the design will further emphasize its gentle nature.

The creature's proportions may be difficult to convey due to its large size. Its weight needs to be supported with large legs, but the alien "longness" of the legs may not seem very apparent if the creature lives in gravity similar to Earth's. Body length will either assist or confound in this endeavor - a shorter body will emphasize the long legs, while a longer body has the potential to make the same legs look shorter. A smaller head will accentuate the feeling of bulk, and that sense of heaviness will play into the desired feeling of slowness.

Depending on how familiar versus how alien the design is, a long neck or proboscis would be the most straightforward ways of reaching high-level foliage. A telescoping proboscis design - one that mimics the shape of an elephant's trunk but is instead a very elongated esophagus tipped with mandibles - would enable the animal to feed from high places.

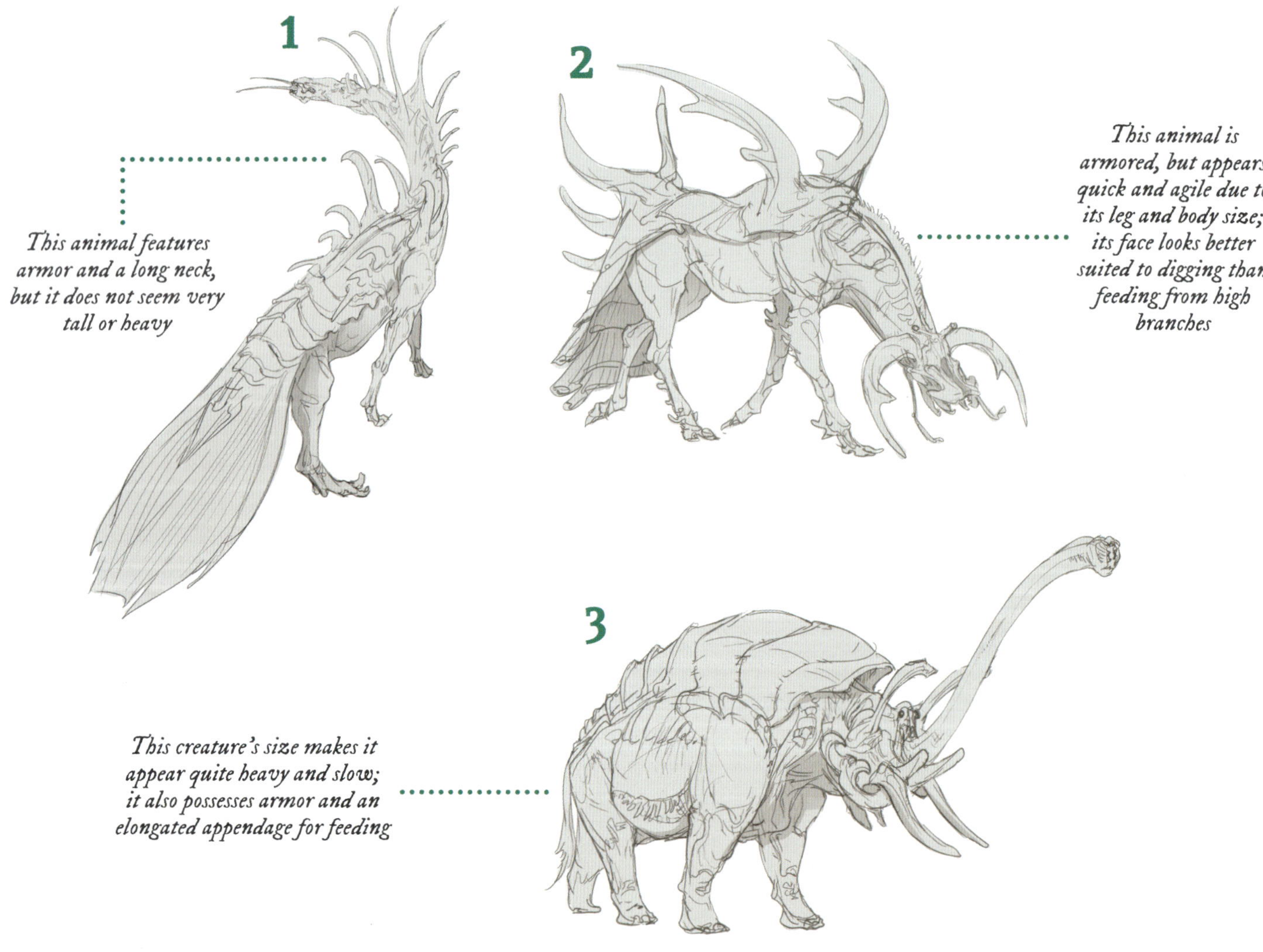

This animal features armor and a long neck, but it does not seem very tall or heavy

This animal is armored, but appears quick and agile due to its leg and body size; its face looks better suited to digging than feeding from high branches

This creature's size makes it appear quite heavy and slow; it also possesses armor and an elongated appendage for feeding

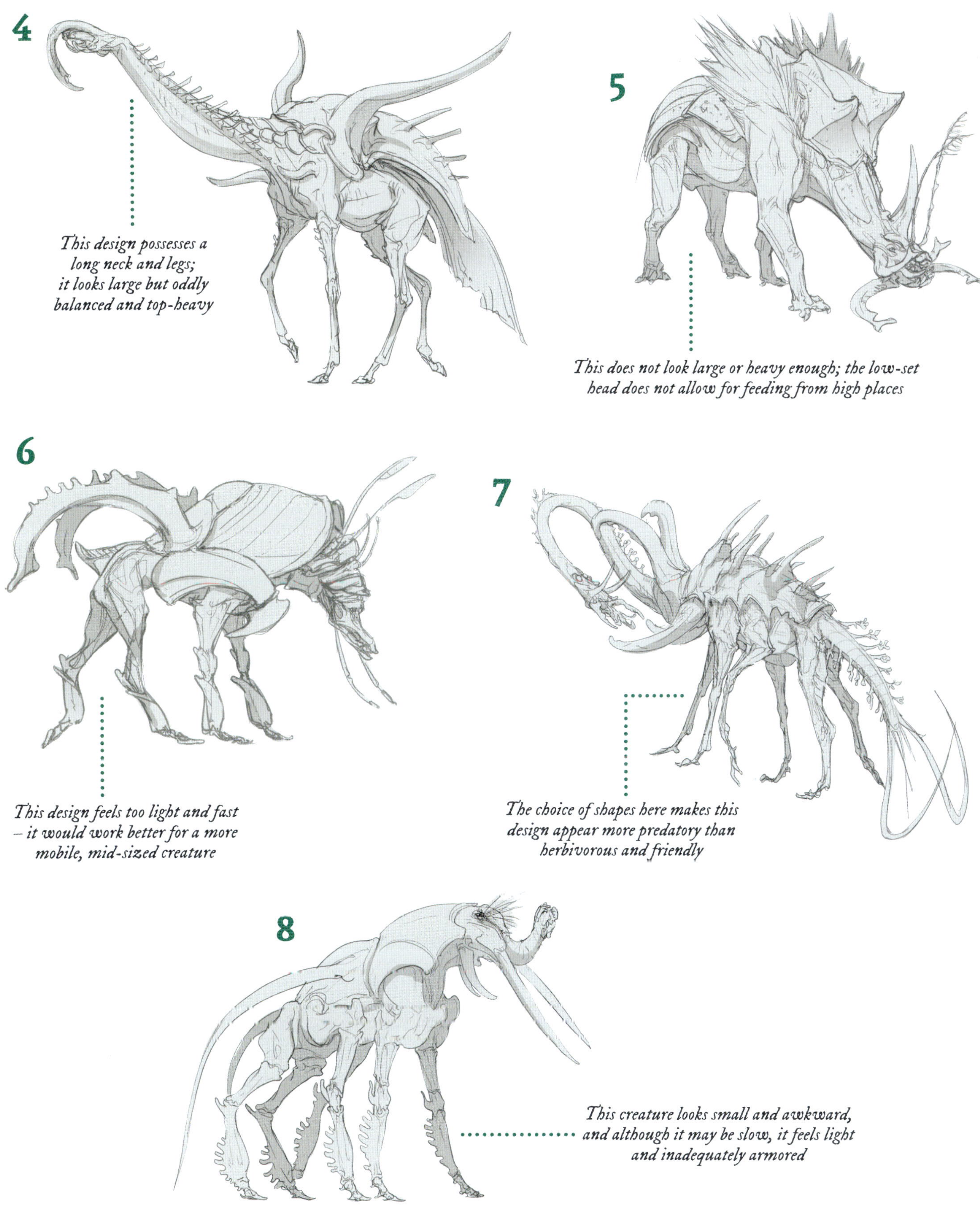

4

This design possesses a long neck and legs; it looks large but oddly balanced and top-heavy

5

This does not look large or heavy enough; the low-set head does not allow for feeding from high places

6

This design feels too light and fast – it would work better for a more mobile, mid-sized creature

7

The choice of shapes here makes this design appear more predatory than herbivorous and friendly

8

This creature looks small and awkward, and although it may be slow, it feels light and inadequately armored

DEVELOPMENT

The elephant-like silhouette of thumbnail 3 clearly conveys the creature's size; it appears large, slow and friendly, although it looks like it possesses the capability to defend itself if necessary. Small eyes and a lumbering gait help in conveying a relatively docile nature, as it does not appear intense or ready to strike, but instead seems mostly unconcerned.

Highly vascularized osteoderms and a shell covering help this animal heat and cool quickly, allowing it to feed uninterrupted during shifting weather conditions. As a result, its migration patterns are driven by social needs and food availability rather than changes in temperature. The shell on its back and sides provides convenient cover and shade

for smaller animals, which can in return keep the creature's back free of parasites. Overall, the design emanates a gentle, rather harmonious nature, while also feeling rugged and able to survive in the wild.

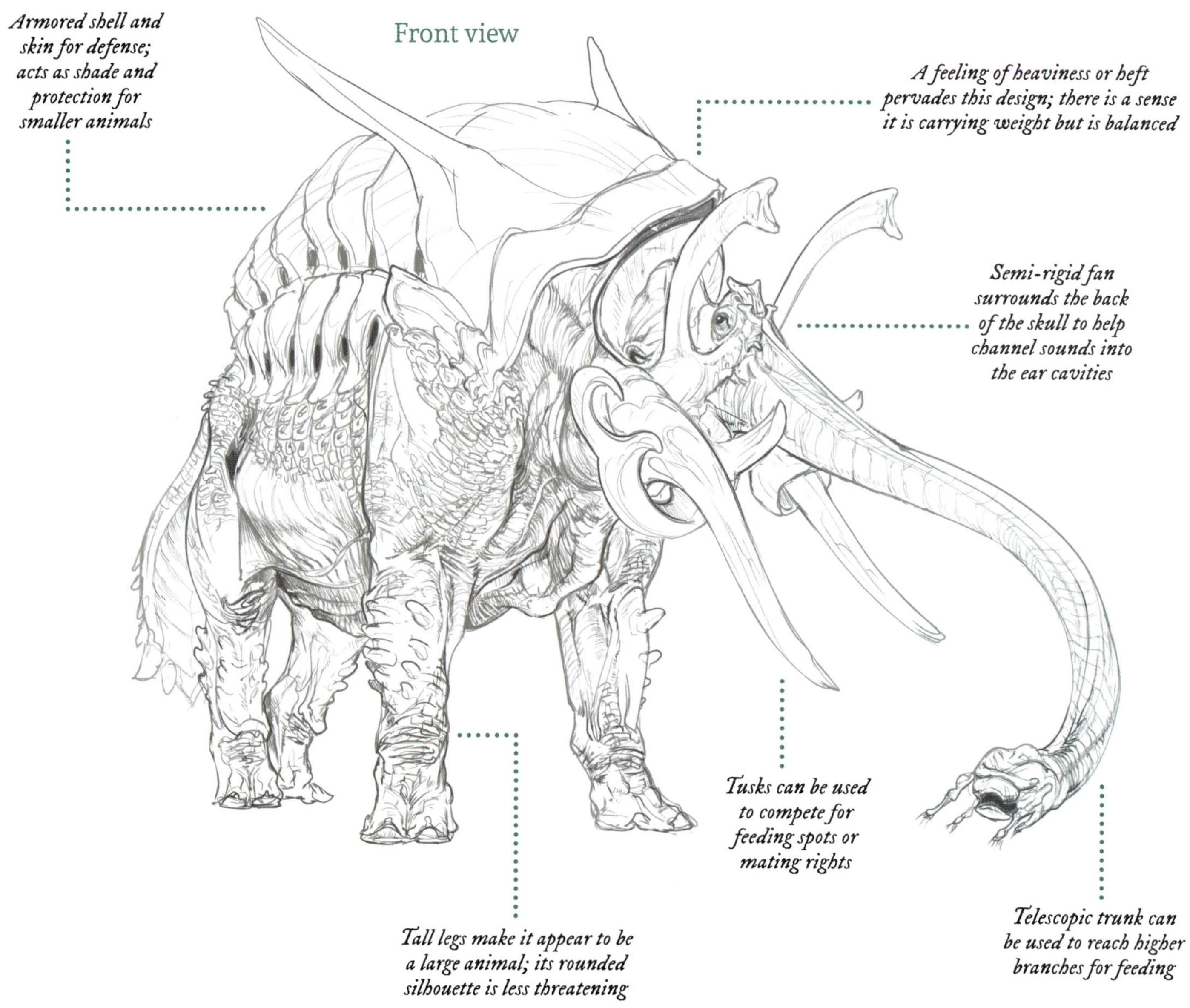

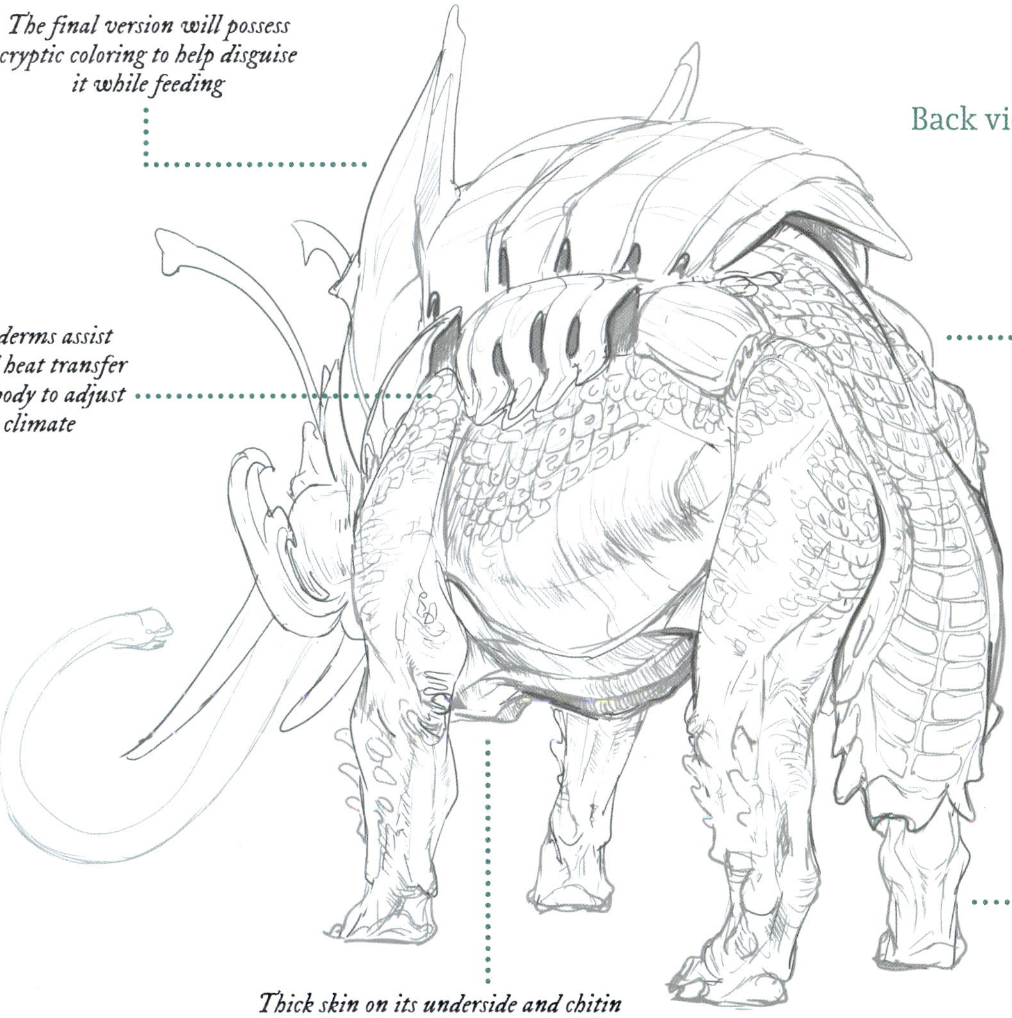

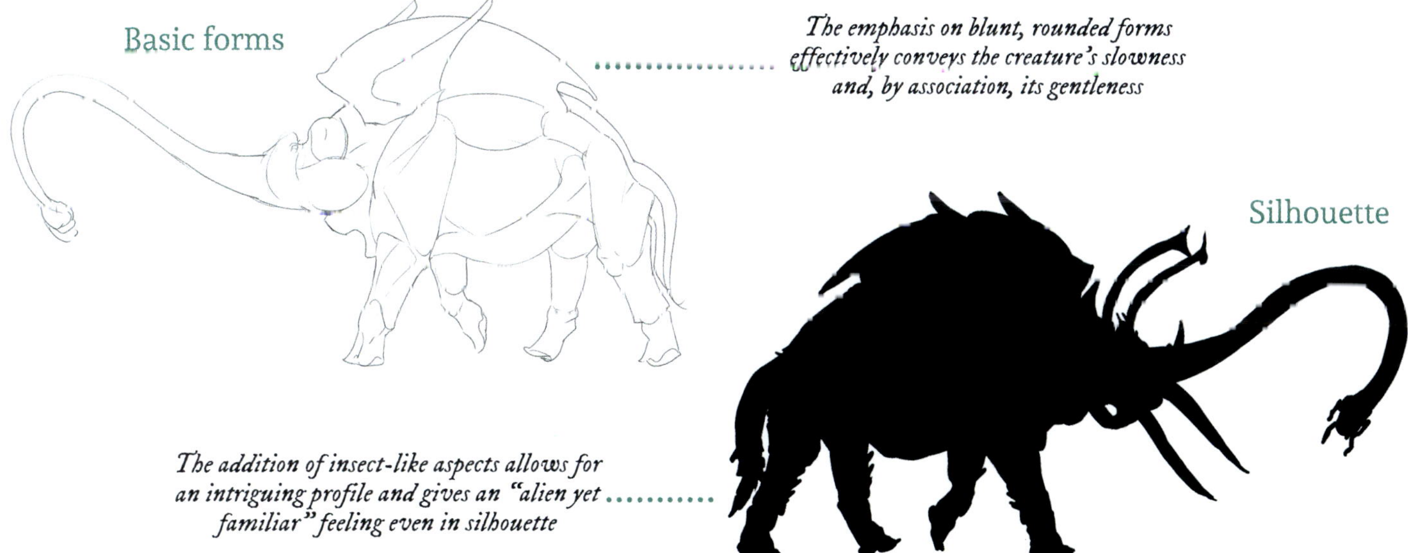

The final version will possess cryptic coloring to help disguise it while feeding

Back view

The osteoderms assist with rapid heat transfer across the body to adjust to the climate

A relatively short spine will limit its gait cycle, which will emphasize its slow nature

A wide, flat tail covered in osteoderms protects its vulnerable back

Thick, padded feet balance its weight

Thick skin on its underside and chitin growths on the legs protect softer locations from spiny brush

Basic forms

The emphasis on blunt, rounded forms effectively conveys the creature's slowness and, by association, its gentleness

Silhouette

The addition of insect-like aspects allows for an intriguing profile and gives an "alien yet familiar" feeling even in silhouette

205

Poses

Now you can begin to play around with different poses that show the creature's behavior in its environment. Outside of a lumbering walk, its range of motion is limited. As a rather tall and short-bodied creature, it likely spends the majority of its life on its feet and very rarely lies down.

To recline on the ground, it must bend its legs in a particular fashion, likely starting with the knees first, and then once "sitting" it is able to walk itself forward into a flat position. Exhaustion or injury may be the primary drivers of this particular behavior, but the occasional reclining position may allow non-flying smaller animals to take up residence in the hollow armor on its back.

Although this animal cannot run or gallop owing to the rigidity of its spine, it can perform a fast shuffle to charge. The charge would be used primarily as intimidation against competition or to dissuade attacking predators. Its telescopic mouth would be almost completely retracted behind the safety of the tusks to prevent injury, as its mandibles are not suitable for biting and fighting. The pair of secondary tusks and accompanying bone growths would be more appropriate for sparring at close quarters.

In order to support its massive bulk, the creature would have to spend the majority of its time feeding. The mandibles at the end of the "trunk," which functions more like an extended esophagus than a proboscis, would serve to harvest plant material and, with the help of the segmented muscles surrounding it, move it all down into the body. Once the esophagus is full of material, it could use the retraction function to push food through to the stomach much faster.

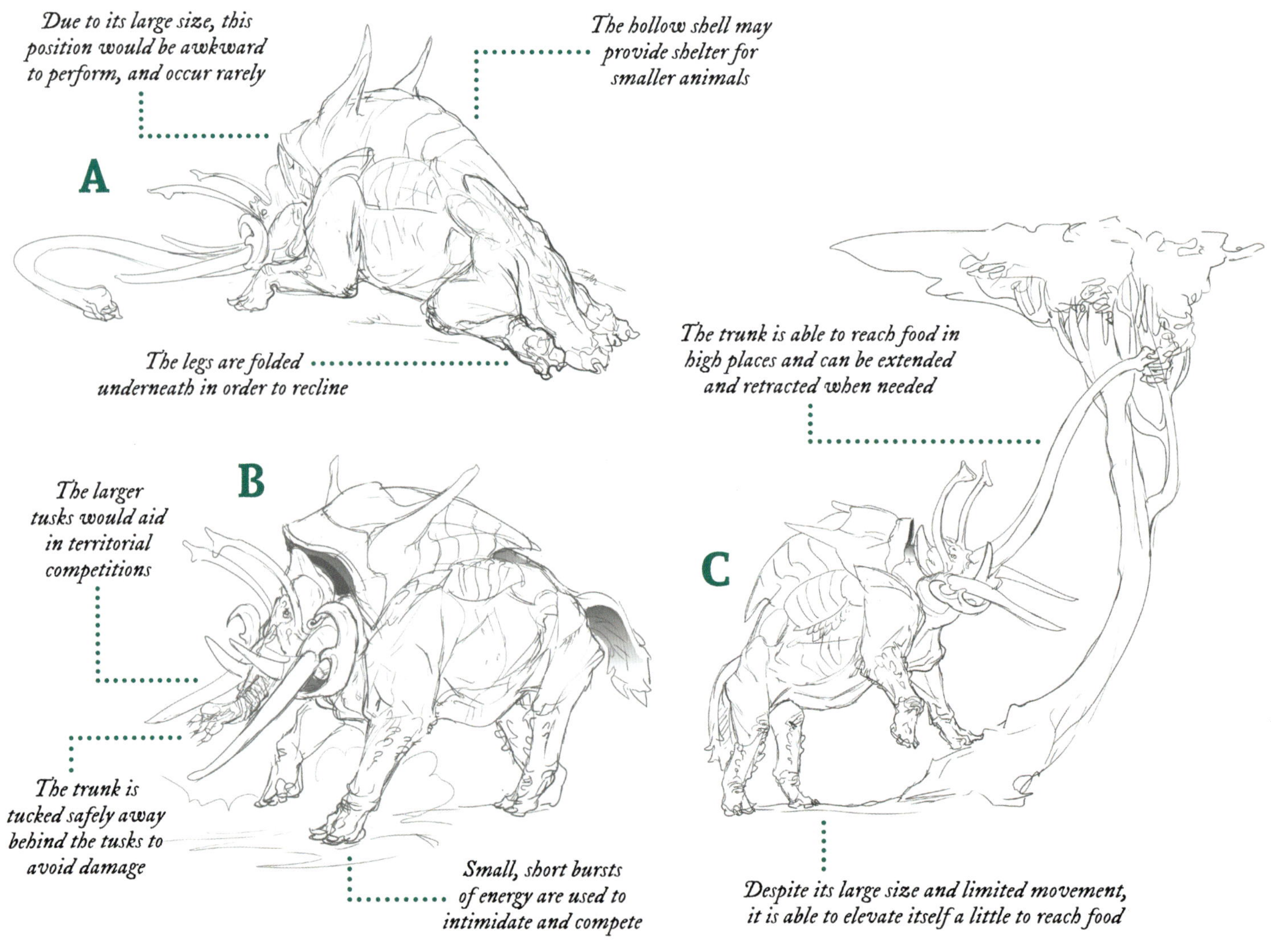

Color & pattern

Important factors to consider when finalizing a color palette are whether it is suited to your creature and its environment. Several color combinations are possible in this case. A creature this large is best suited to neutral base tones, perhaps with patterning that would help it blend in with the foliage while it feeds. Muted colors and patterns can lack interest, but overly bright colors would suggest a threat or dominance that does not fit the creature's profile. Countershading can be useful to break up shadows to aid with camouflage; our creature could benefit from this to obscure its many appendages. An earthy palette of oranges, yellows, or browns, with speckles that complement and occasionally accentuate the thick, textured skin, could be suitable here.

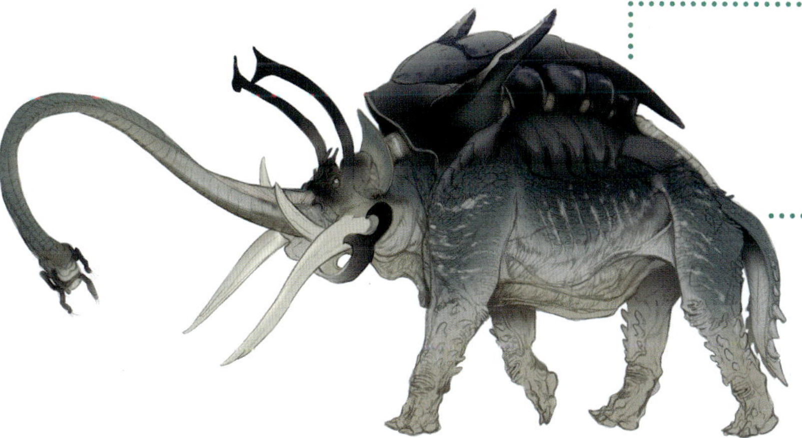

Solid blocks of color and brighter streaks make the creature stand out too much

The base tones are too rich and do not mesh well; a blended look would be more appropriate

Countershading on the underside helps break up shadows, but does little for the overall design

A darker back has the added benefit of attracting heat in colder temperatures

The muted blue is interesting, but may stand out too much in the environment

These small, cryptic pattern details do not feel like enough for camouflage

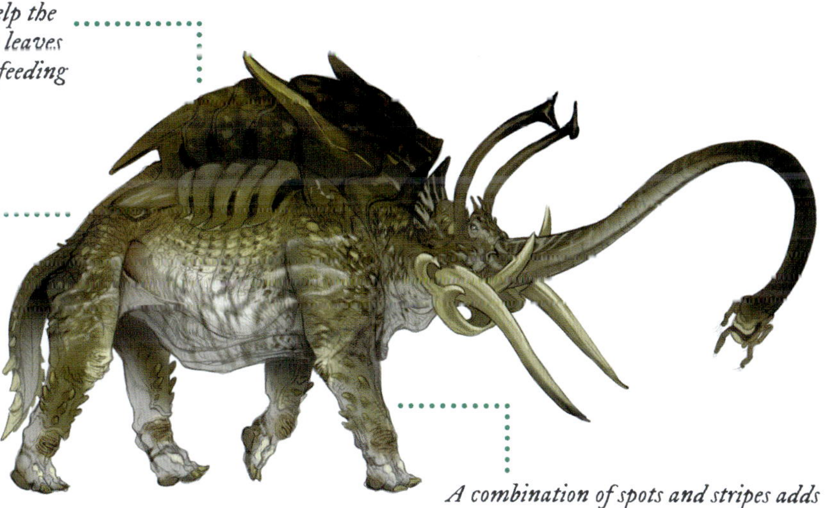

Subtle mottling on the dark back would help the creature blend with leaves and branches while feeding

Muted yellow and brown tones are more fitting for the grassland environment

A combination of spots and stripes adds interest to the cryptic pattern details

FINAL DESIGN

The final design reflects elements of elephants, rhinos, beetles, and various other armored creatures, combined to produce a slow, harmless grazing animal. One can easily envision it being domesticated over hundreds to thousands of years - perhaps for varying colors and patterns, rather than for a smaller size and compliant temperament, as the creature is already very docile.

The animal looks appropriately rugged and equipped for survival, protected by its tough hide and armor plating. Its skin is patterned to blend in with the kinds of plant growth it feeds from, and makes it more intriguing than something with a flat color. Looking at it should lead to further questions about the setting it exists in - what its predators are and what flora and fauna exist in its world.

Hollow back armor provides protection as well as shelter for small creatures

Pebble-like osteoderms regulate heat and provide flexible protection for the creature's flanks

Fleshy, padded feet help distribute the creature's weight

Thick, elephantine legs give the impression of a slow gait and heavy weight

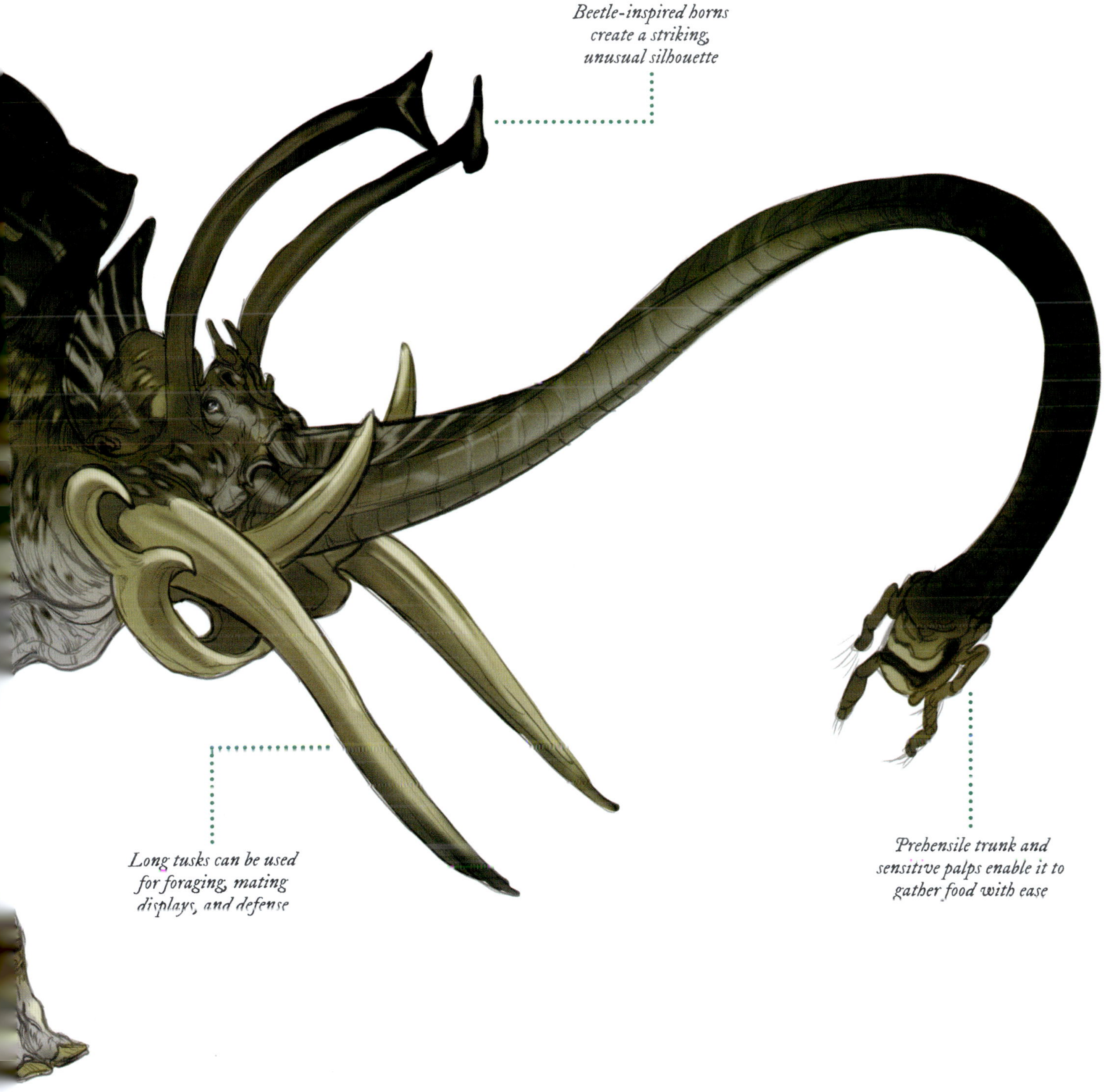

Final image © Allison Theus

ADAPTATIONS

Forest-dwelling

A forest-dwelling subspecies of this animal (shown right) would require a smaller stature and a leaner profile. There is less need for the heavy armor of its kin due to the thick cover of branches and foliage, and its hide may be smoother or less pronounced for easy passage through branches. With foliage providing an abundance of shade, there is no need for relief from the heat and therefore its shell may be tucked closer to its body. The shapes of tusks and horns may be streamlined to help with travel through the bush, and angled to help it fence and wrestle vigorously when competition for food and mates occurs.

Carnivorous

A carnivorous version (shown below) would require a shorter, leaner body with a more flexible back for spry movement. In order to make it lighter, it would have a sleeker look, accentuated with spiny hairs as opposed to armor. The feet may be a little wider and the skin less tough to make movement less restricted. Its tusks would be better suited to grappling, and the trunk not as long, as it diminishes in usefulness for the creature. The mandibles could be large and clawed or more pincer-like, to grab and hold prey, so that sharpened tusk-like maxillae could punch forward and deal fast, devastating blows. The legs are lightly armored with the same chitinous leg bumps for protection against dangerous brush.

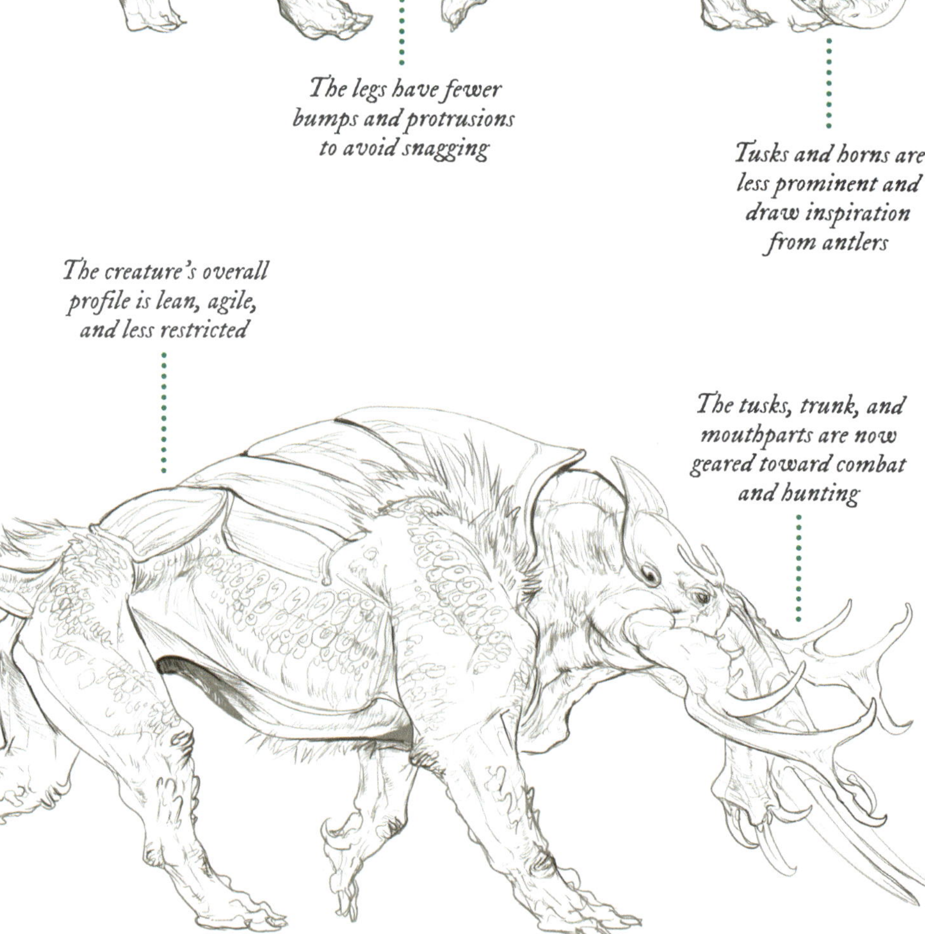

Domesticated

A domesticated version of this creature (shown below) would likely have rounder, softer shapes. One can envision it being bred to be meatier and more docile, with less defensive armor. Domestication may require certain attributes from the creature; one variation could be bred for large tusks and another for more aesthetic reasons. Easier access to food would lead to a softer, more vulnerable body; the extendable trunk would be considerably shorter as it no longer needs to reach into the trees for sustenance. The mouth may change and simplify, losing sensitive palps in favor of dense whiskers.

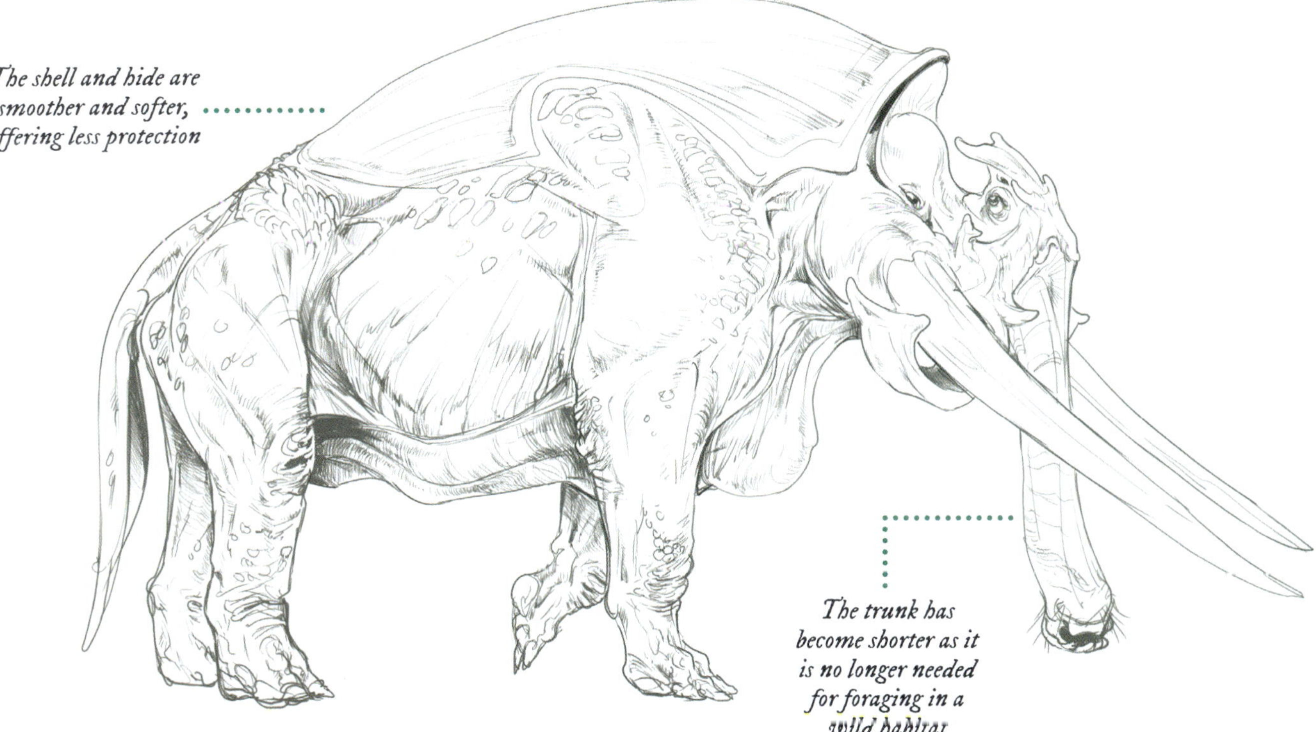

Industry tip

Reference is your best friend. The natural world can be extremely strange, and with enough research you will uncover a wealth of information you can use to your advantage in design. When providing work for games, do not get emotionally attached to your first couple of attempts, or the designs you really like, and be ready and willing to experiment to find something that fits the brief. Each iteration is an opportunity to explore your options. If you like animals and are constantly learning about them, your visual knowledge will be expansive and you will never be at a loss for ideas to mash together. Ensure that you have a good grounding in animal anatomy, especially if you are using specific animals to convey a feeling to the viewer. You must be able to replicate the shape language of an animal successfully while determining how much you can distort or stretch it to create something different.

Post-apocalyptic swamp fish

Damien Mammoliti

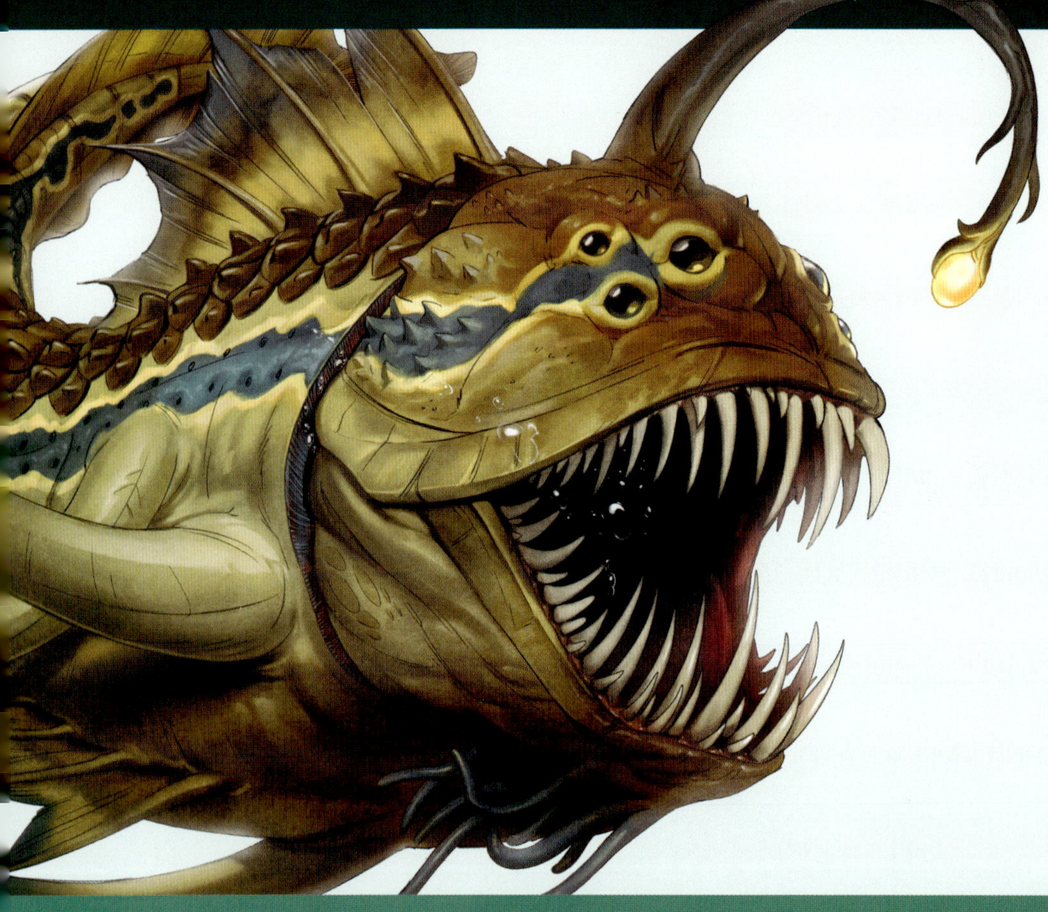

Key facts

- A fish designed to thrive in a post-apocalyptic swamp

- Has features similar to an anglerfish, helping it to see in dark, murky water

- Has a crocodile-like appearance and is developing the ability to walk on land

- A terrifying predator - can use jolts of electricity to stun its prey, like an electric eel

- Highly intelligent

IDEATION

This animal will be unique in that it derives from both crocodilian and fish-like anatomy. As fish and crocodiles are different classes of creature, their anatomical differences are profound. Fish breathe solely underwater, while reptiles are air-breathing terrestrial creatures that must regulate their temperatures to digest and survive. Despite their differences, fish and crocodiles both live and feed primarily in the same environment - water. They share some anatomical quirks such as scales and webbing. The predatory instinct of the crocodile is also a trait of some deep-sea fish, such as anglerfish, which hunt in complete darkness. The anglerfish could inspire the combination of fish and crocodile features - its grotesque appearance offers interesting ways to convey mutation and shifts in texture and anatomy.

As well as borrowing physical and behavioral aspects from the anglerfish and crocodile, the design will feature adaptations from mutations due to possible toxicity and radiation. This animal will have reproduced and thrived in murky, unclean water, eating and hunting anything that it can, potentially even its own mate. Mixing two types of scales, to provide the effect of combining crocodile and fish anatomy, will be important to fully sell the idea of a mutation of the two. Harder dorsal scales could potentially act like armor, combined with a softer, fish-like underbelly.

Subjects to explore will include the scale pattern, the overall silhouette for readability on combined reptile-fish anatomy, and how to convey ferocity and hunger due to a potential shortage of food. We could also include a sense of unique anatomy that is not inherent for its species, as mutation and radiation will potentially have changed this creature's DNA greatly from its original form.

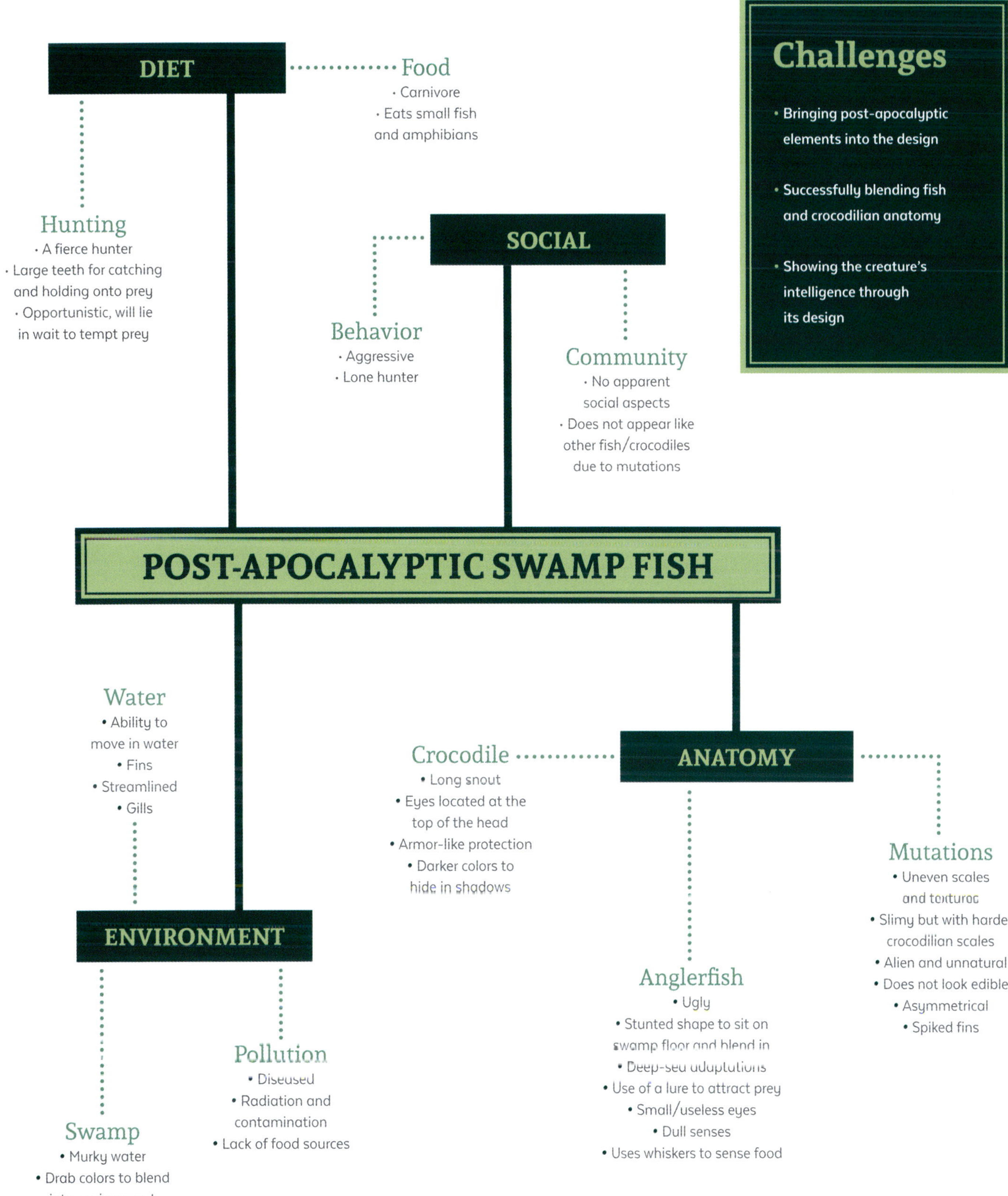
DIET

Food
· Carnivore
· Eats small fish
and amphibians

Hunting
· A fierce hunter
· Large teeth for catching
and holding onto prey
· Opportunistic, will lie
in wait to tempt prey

SOCIAL

Behavior
· Aggressive
· Lone hunter

Community
· No apparent
social aspects
· Does not appear like
other fish/crocodiles
due to mutations

Challenges
· Bringing post-apocalyptic
elements into the design

· Successfully blending fish
and crocodilian anatomy

· Showing the creature's
intelligence through
its design

POST-APOCALYPTIC SWAMP FISH

Water
• Ability to
move in water
• Fins
• Streamlined
• Gills

Crocodile
• Long snout
• Eyes located at the
top of the head
• Armor-like protection
• Darker colors to
hide in shadows

ANATOMY

Mutations
· Uneven scales
and textures
• Slimy but with harder
crocodilian scales
• Alien and unnatural
• Does not look edible
• Asymmetrical
• Spiked fins

Anglerfish
• Ugly
• Stunted shape to sit on
swamp floor and blend in
• Deep-sea adaptations
• Use of a lure to attract prey
• Small/useless eyes
• Dull senses
• Uses whiskers to sense food

ENVIRONMENT

Pollution
• Diseased
• Radiation and
contamination
• Lack of food sources

Swamp
• Murky water
• Drab colors to blend
into environment

Anatomy research

Anglerfish

Fish are often found in swamp ecosystems, though for the sake of creating the most grotesque and otherworldly form of a fish, we are going to take a deeper look at the oceans. Anglerfish are a species that spend their lives in the deepest, darkest places in the ocean. They never see the sun and barely have scales; instead, their bodies are smooth and fleshy in appearance.

The grotesque appearance of the anglerfish will help us to understand odd mutations that happen during evolution, when stressors such as a lack of sun and a smaller pool of resources are presented to a group of fish. Their eyes are fairly useless, as they spend most of their time hunting with small sensory "whiskers" around their face and body. They lure their prey to them with a strange appendage, an aspect which can be transferred to the new creature design.

Anglerfish
(Ceratioidei)

The mouth of this predator is long and widens considerably, allowing extra reach toward its prey

The impossibly wide mouth takes up the majority of this frontal view

The profile of the anglerfish is lumpy and misshapen compared to other, sleeker fish

Crocodile

Crocodiles and alligators are ambush predators that spend a considerable amount of time in swamps and shallow rivers to hunt prey. Despite their great size, they are able to camouflage themselves in the murky water, thanks to their drab coloration, and still retain the ability to see just above the water.

Crocodile and alligator skin is tough and rigid, providing excellent protection against thrashing prey much larger than they are. It also keeps them protected during territorial disputes with others of their species – fights will often break out.

Crocodiles have highly sensory skin and sensitive pits on their jaws. They can feel potential prey passing near their hungry mouths in the murky water.

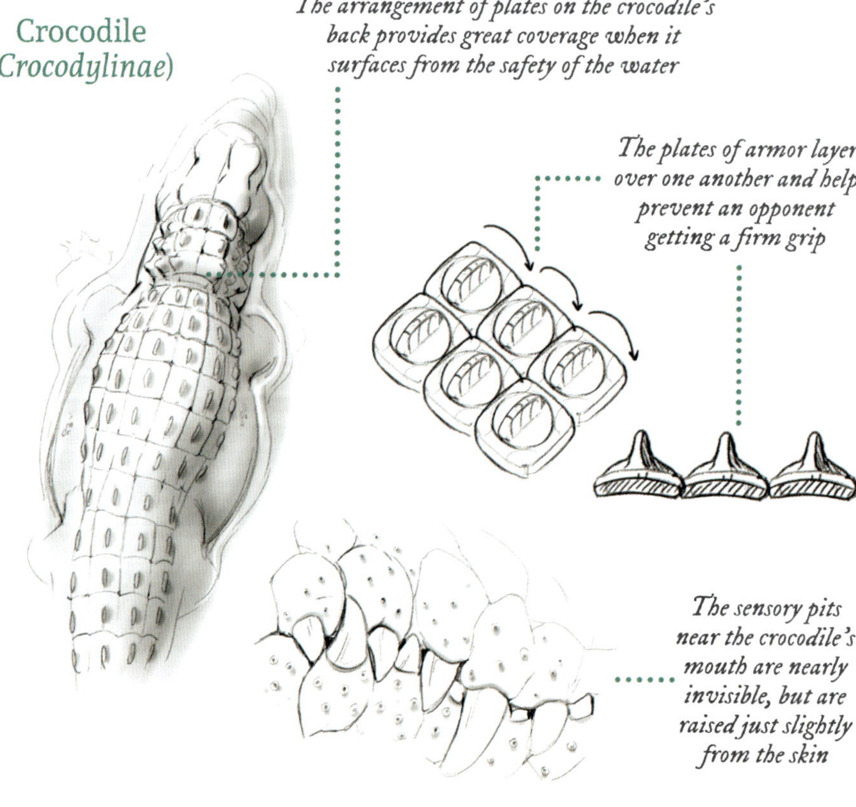

Crocodile
(Crocodylinae)

The arrangement of plates on the crocodile's back provides great coverage when it surfaces from the safety of the water

The plates of armor layer over one another and help prevent an opponent getting a firm grip

The sensory pits near the crocodile's mouth are nearly invisible, but are raised just slightly from the skin

Electric eel

Eels can be found in all kinds of watery environments, swamps included. For this design we will be focusing on a specific eel known colloquially as the "electric eel," due to its ability to create electric shocks through its skin. The electric eel is a species of fish that uses its skin in a defensive and predatory manner, which works well for this design. However, the eels also use it as a means to sense the environment around them, in a similar way to a crocodile or anglerfish.

Despite many fantastical visual interpretations of electricity being used in creature design, the reality is that these pulses are invisible to the eye. The imperceptible Sach's organ produces the deadly volts. Introducing an element like this to our creature would reinforce its ferocity.

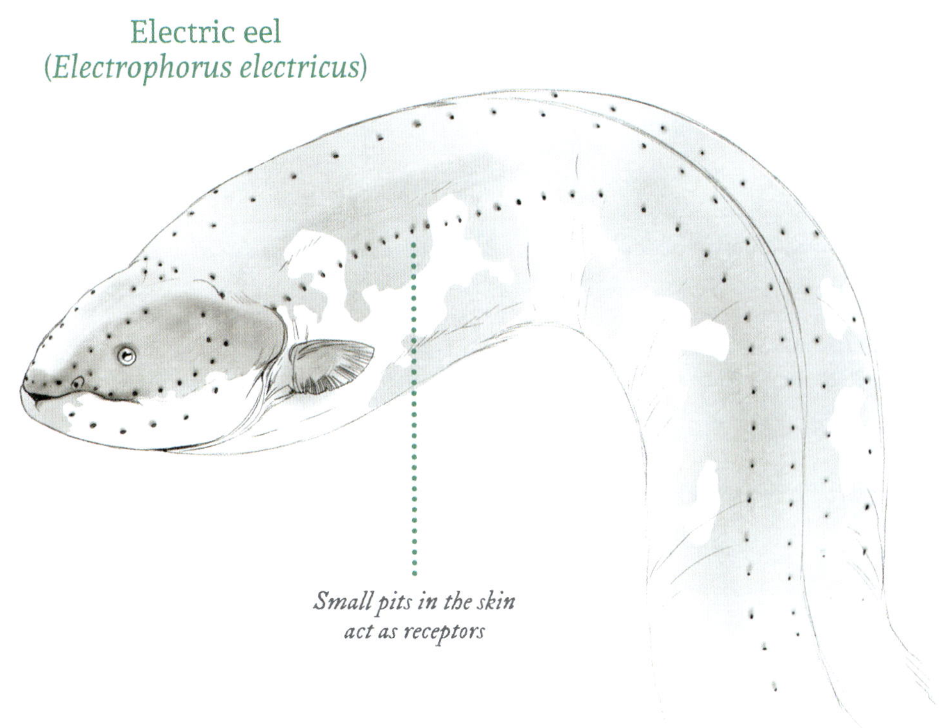

Electric eel
(*Electrophorus electricus*)

*Small pits in the skin
act as receptors*

Evolution

To understand how our creature might have mutated and evolved in its new post-apocalyptic environment, it is helpful to study the lineage of fish adapting gradually to walk on land like their tetrapod (four-limbed animal) descendants.

One real-world example of evolution from fish to four-legged amphibian is the *Tiktaalik*, an extinct lobe-finned fish from 375 million years ago. *Tiktaalik* is special because it is the first fish fossil to have been found with legs strong enough, both skeletally and anatomically, to support itself on land. It also features many adaptations we have been discussing in our other real-world examples, such as eyes set high up on its head, and a large mouth that takes up most of its face. How *Tiktaalik*'s anatomy proves its capacity for walking in shallow waters is great inspiration for our creature design.

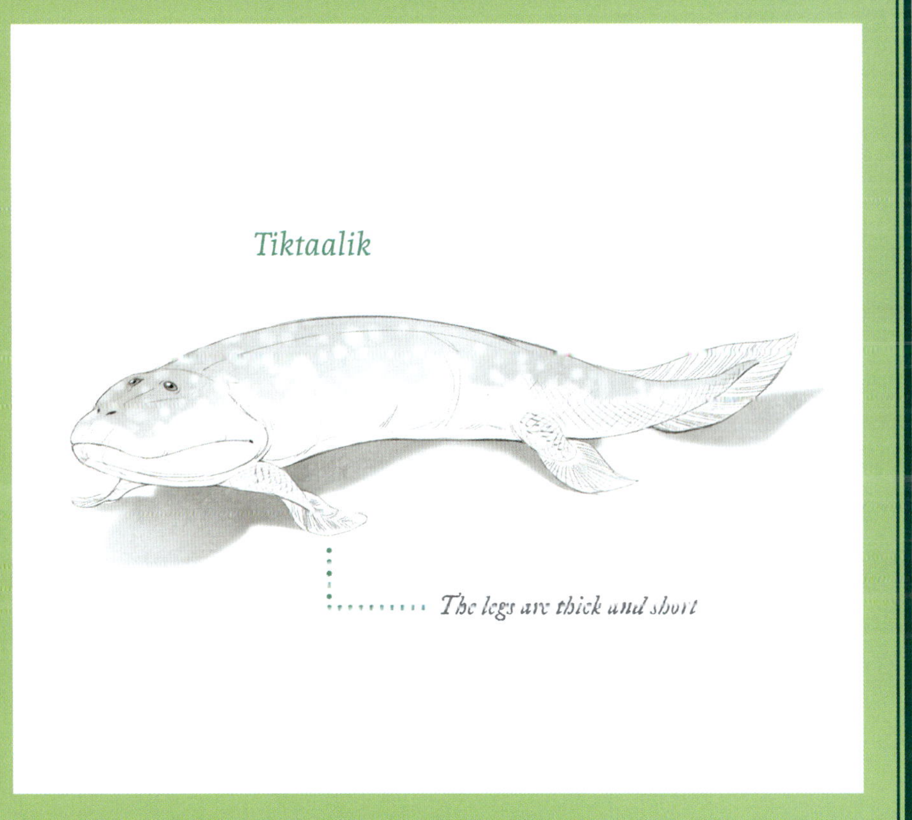

Tiktaalik

The legs are thick and short

Functionality research

Legs

There are many types of fish that are known to have adapted to "walk" on land. One of these is the lungfish, a living fossil from the Triassic period. The fins of the lungfish have a well-developed skeletal structure that allows them to be used as primitive legs. Our design may require a similar ability, especially as we consider the need to walk from one small pool of water to another. A post-apocalyptic setting may have made bodies of water scarcer, forcing our creature to move briefly across land in order to reach food. The lungfish's fin anatomy also provides a convenient "tentacle-like" appearance, which lends us a great visual to convey mutation in our creature's design.

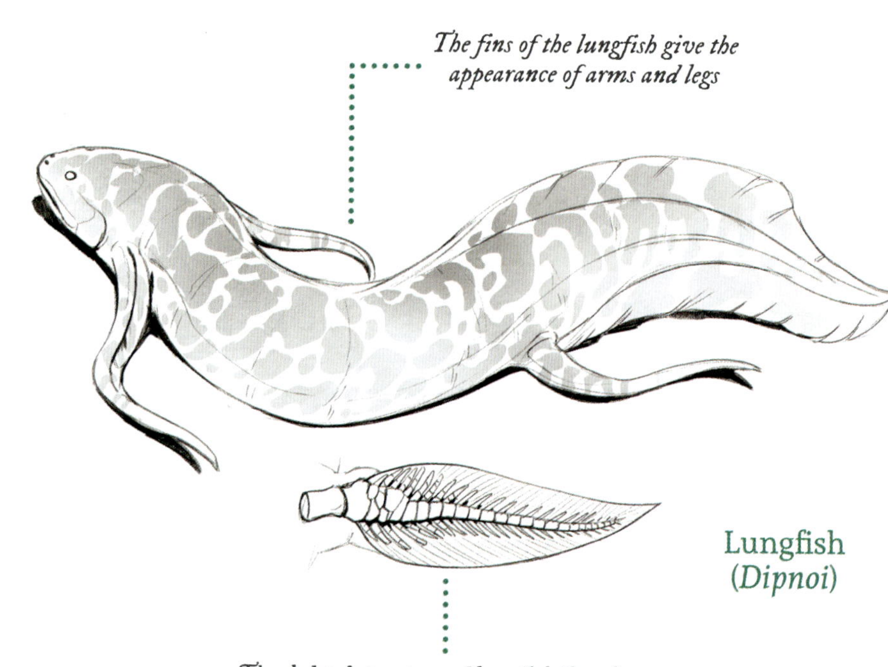

The fins of the lungfish give the appearance of arms and legs

Lungfish
(Dipnoi)

The skeletal structure of lungfish fins shows how sturdy and versatile they are

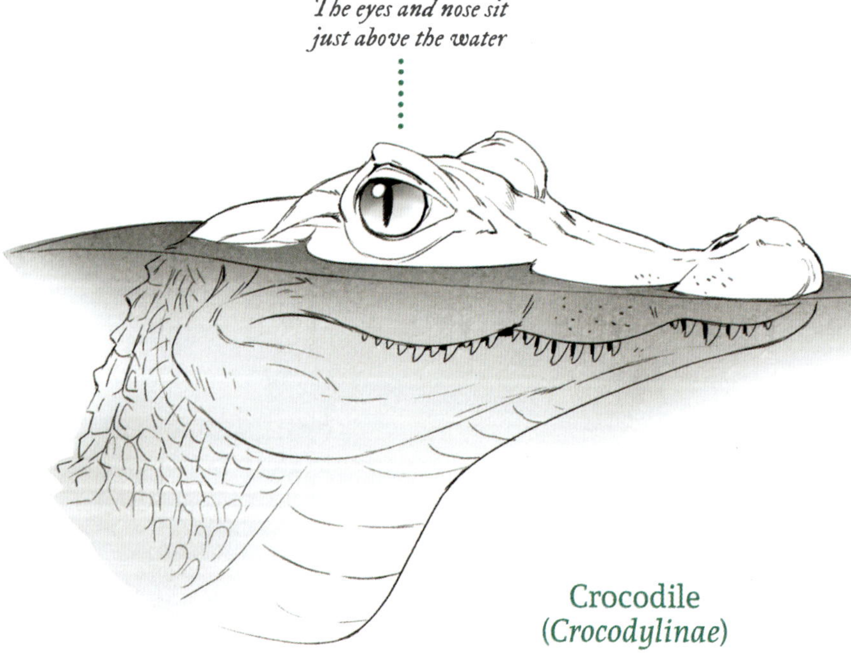

The eyes and nose sit just above the water

Crocodile
(Crocodylinae)

Eyes

The crocodile is an expert hunter with many tricks to spot prey on land without being detected. Its adaptations include the eyes and nose, which sit high on the head so they can imperceptibly emerge from the water while the crocodile's massive bulk and silhouette is hidden beneath the surface. This anatomical detail would help convey the potential hunting capability of our creature. Setting the eyes forward and high up on the head will give the impression that our predator can see and stalk animals just beyond reach on land.

Lure

The alligator snapping turtle is another swamp predator that can provide some design inspiration for our creature. The snapping turtle will often sit motionless at the bottom of the swamp for extended periods of time, waiting with its mouth wide open. The turtle has a small adaptation in the form of a lure on its tongue, which entices prey to move closer - the same technique as the anglerfish. The turtle's tongue appears like worms, wriggling in the dark. Our creature will most likely use this same luring method to capture its prey.

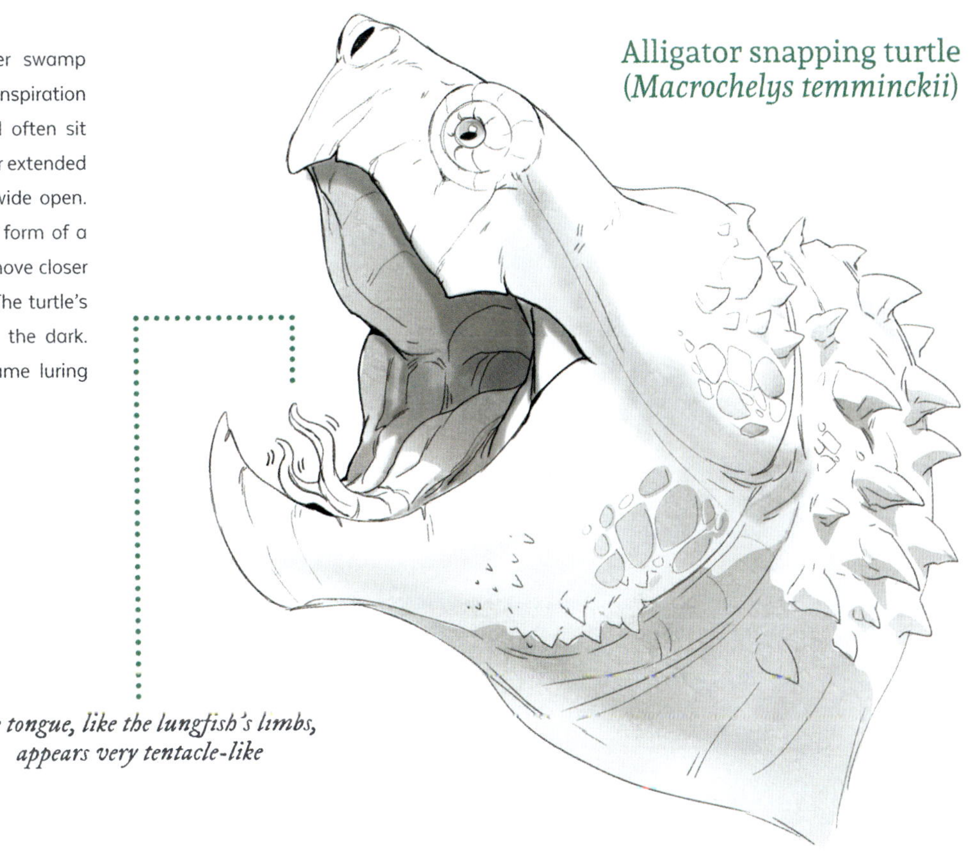

Alligator snapping turtle
(*Macrochelys temminckii*)

The tongue, like the lungfish's limbs, appears very tentacle-like

Coloration

Swamp creatures are rarely colorful. In fact, most adaptations for predators in murky water share similarities in their color-coding. Predators attempting to camouflage in a swamp will often have slight stripes, which help diffuse their form in the waves and light passing through the water. A lighter belly compared to their backs (known as "countershading") also helps confuse prey from all directions. If their prey is below, the silhouette of the animal is diminished by its lighter belly, with the darker back providing the same effect from above.

The crocodile provides a great example of how a predator's color has adapted to its environment.

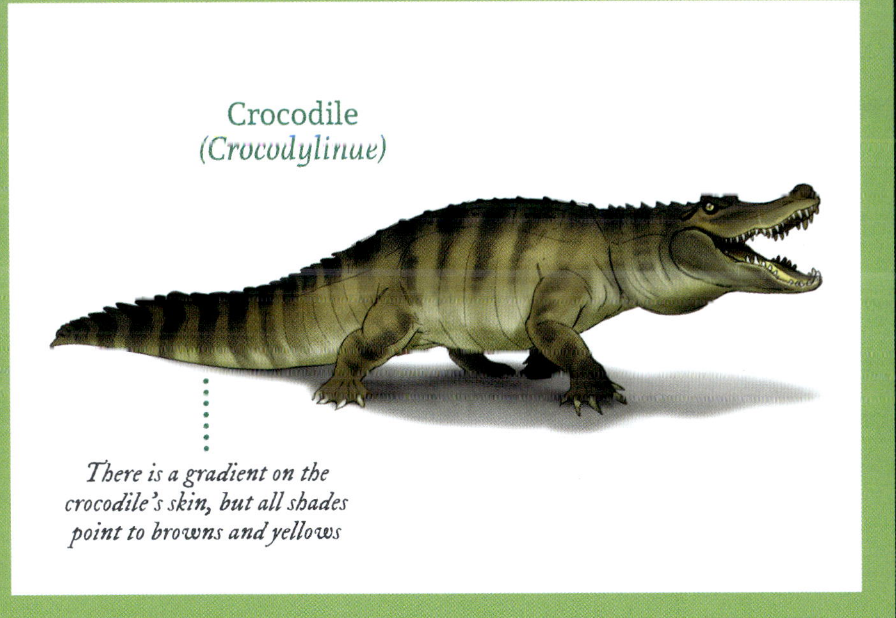

Crocodile
(*Crocodylinae*)

There is a gradient on the crocodile's skin, but all shades point to browns and yellows

Thumbnails

Combining our knowledge of the creatures we have studied, and taking into account the mutations that may have occurred from radioactive water in our post-apocalyptic setting, we can start to form visual ideas of this predatory swamp fish. The main aspects to take into account are: the predatory adaptations, such as a lure; a large mouth with long teeth; front-facing and high-set eyes; fins strong enough to carry it from one pool to another; and some armor along its back to protect it during territorial disputes with other mutated creatures.

In order to give the creature a grotesque nature, our design will align with the large mouth and smooth, squat body of the anglerfish, while attempting to mutate in a believable way with aspects of other predators. One thing we do not want is to create impractical and unbelievable mutations that would make the creature appear incapable of survival. Bearing in mind the environmental factors that could affect the appearance and functionality of the design, we should avoid an animal that appears mutated beyond the ability to function.

Large, mutated monsters are great for creature design, but if we were to see repeated examples of them in our fictional world, the realistic quality would begin to diminish. It should be realistic to see multiple variations of these animals in the same swamp, and have them exist and function in that ecosystem together.

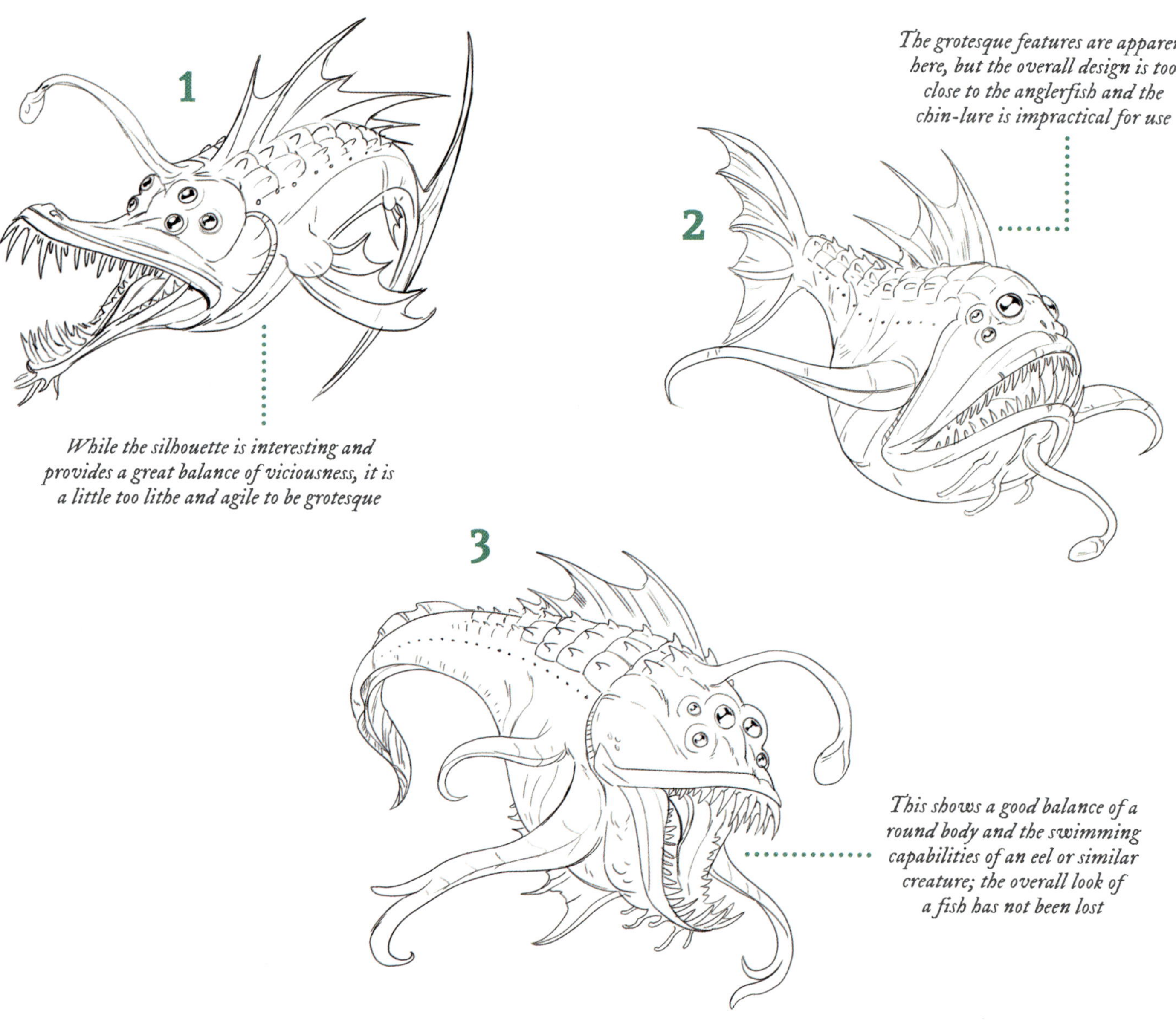

While the silhouette is interesting and provides a great balance of viciousness, it is a little too lithe and agile to be grotesque

The grotesque features are apparent here, but the overall design is too close to the anglerfish and the chin-lure is impractical for use

This shows a good balance of a round body and the swimming capabilities of an eel or similar creature; the overall look of a fish has not been lost

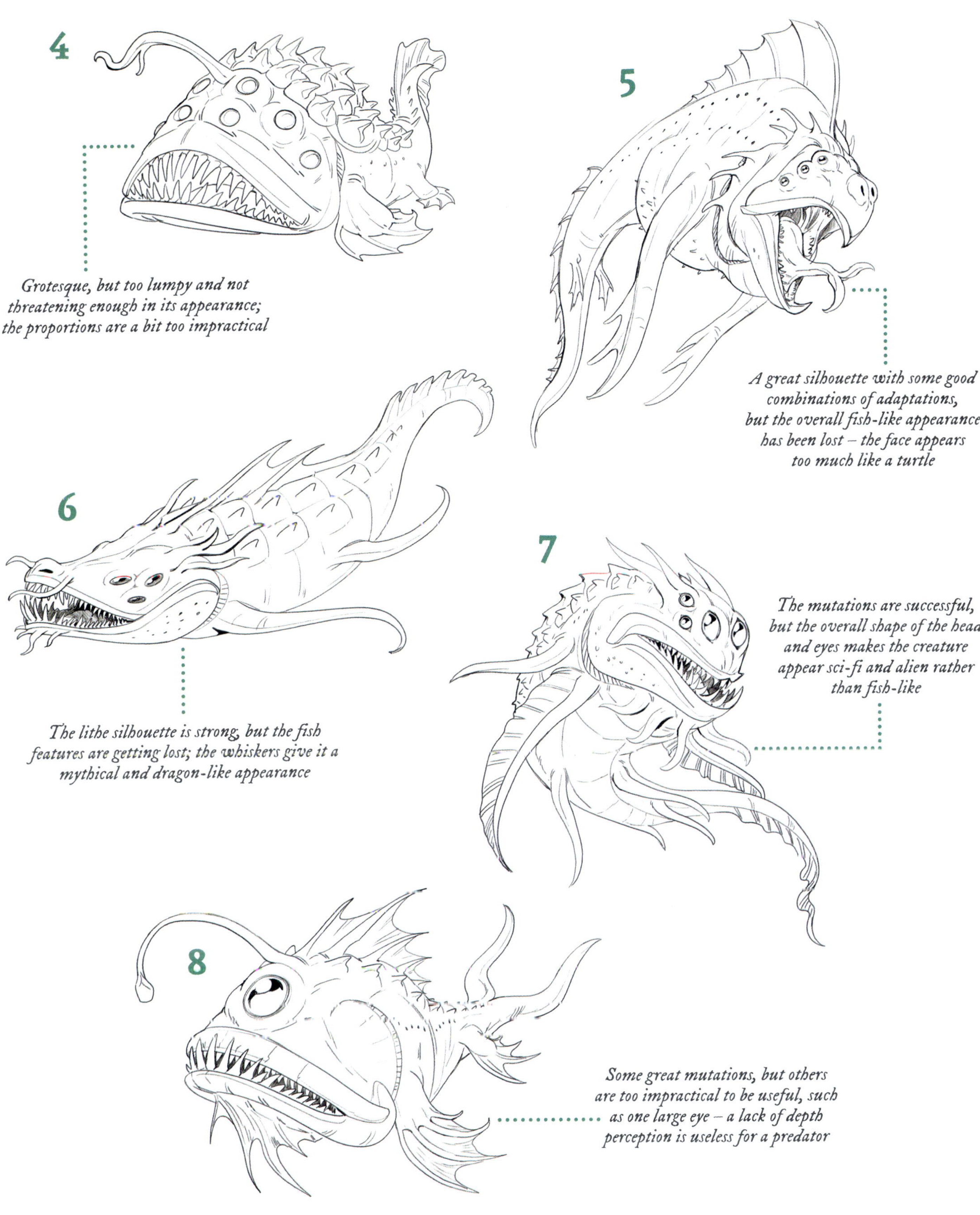

4

Grotesque, but too lumpy and not threatening enough in its appearance; the proportions are a bit too impractical

5

A great silhouette with some good combinations of adaptations, but the overall fish-like appearance has been lost – the face appears too much like a turtle

6

The lithe silhouette is strong, but the fish features are getting lost; the whiskers give it a mythical and dragon-like appearance

7

The mutations are successful, but the overall shape of the head and eyes makes the creature appear sci-fi and alien rather than fish-like

8

Some great mutations, but others are too impractical to be useful, such as one large eye – a lack of depth perception is useless for a predator

DEVELOPMENT

Thumbnail 3 is selected for further development, as it matches most of the criteria set out earlier in the design process. Mutations are seen across the form of the creature, blending varying features of swamp-dwelling animals together without losing the core appearance of a fish. It features long, tentacle-like limbs and multiple eyes that provide a great sense of unnatural mutation without leaving the creature handicapped. Multiple tentacle-like appendages make the creature appear deformed,

but not unbelievably so. It can still hunt and thrive in its post-apocalyptic environment.

The creature features predatory signifiers from both fish and crocodile anatomy. Combining scale types provides it with a plated and armored look like a crocodile, with high-set eyes that allow it to stalk its prey from below the surface. The fish elements are maintained in the silhouette; the overall shape still appears like a fish, not veering too heavily toward

an eel or crocodile, with fins and gills ensuring the creature does not appear too reptilian.

Forward-facing eyes, a lithe and powerful tail, and an attached lure give the animal a great sense of predatory intelligence. It is a creature that can hide on the floor of a swamp, between piles of debris or long weeds, waiting for prey to stumble upon it.

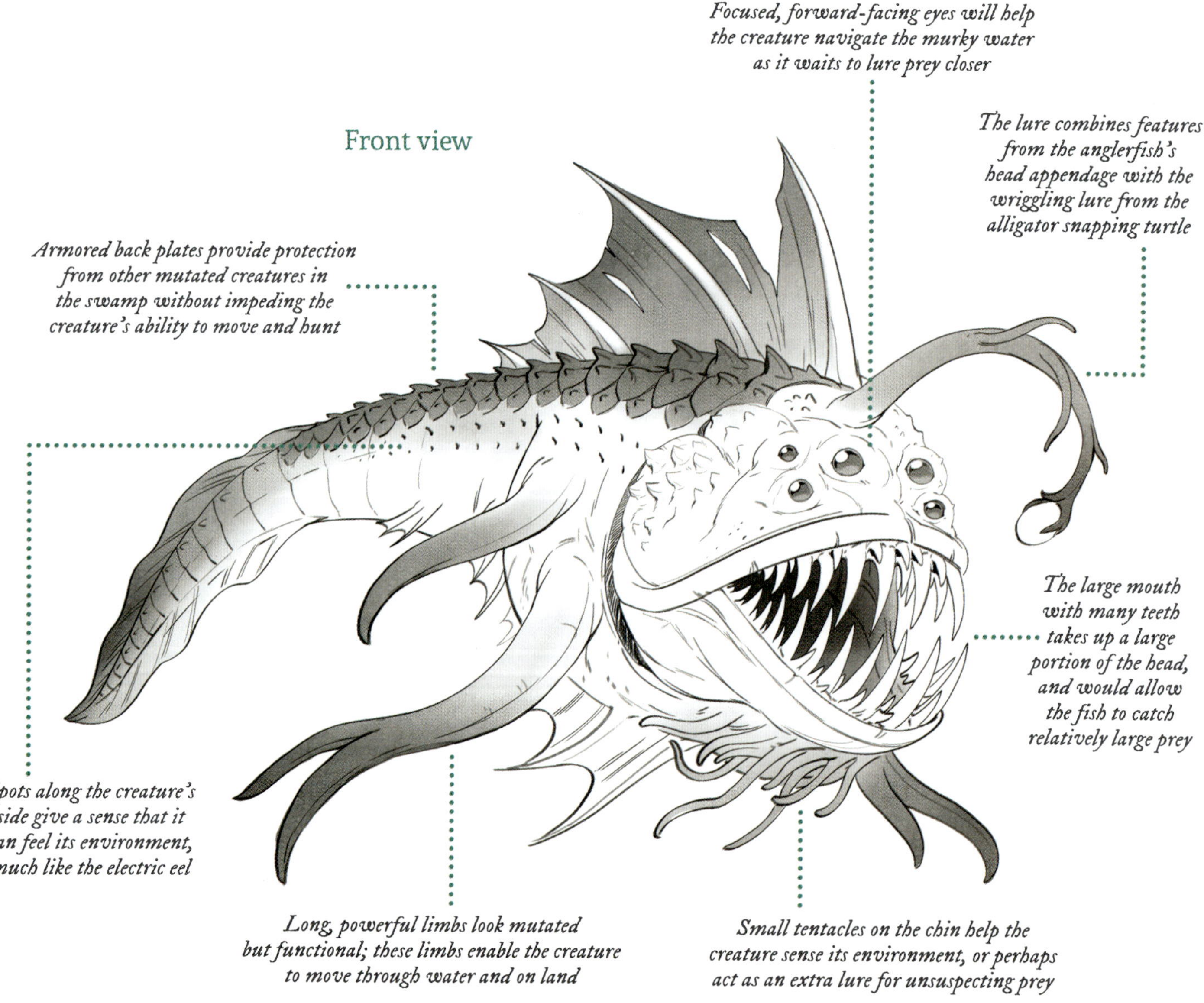

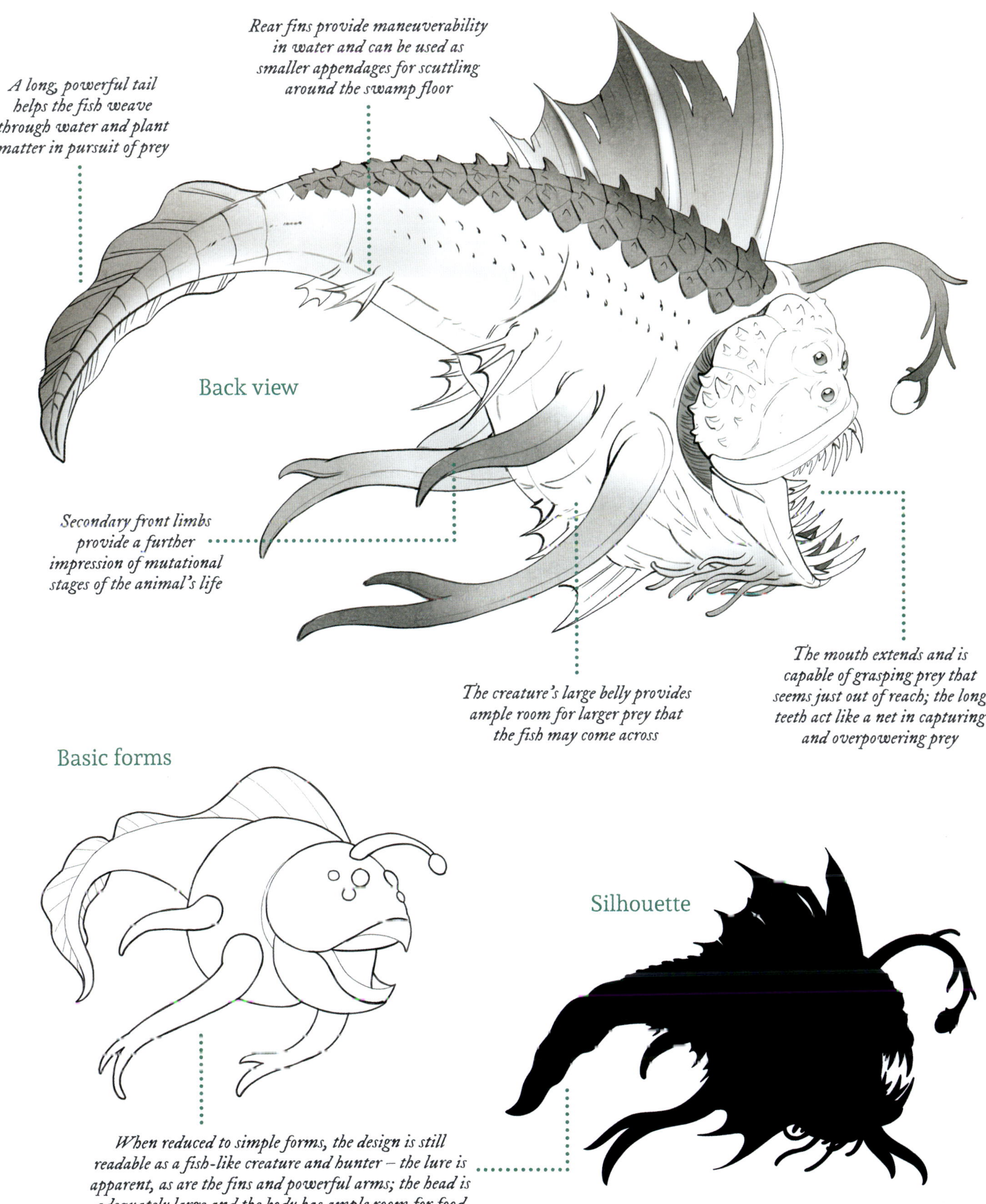

Rear fins provide maneuverability in water and can be used as smaller appendages for scuttling around the swamp floor

A long, powerful tail helps the fish weave through water and plant matter in pursuit of prey

Back view

Secondary front limbs provide a further impression of mutational stages of the animal's life

The creature's large belly provides ample room for larger prey that the fish may come across

The mouth extends and is capable of grasping prey that seems just out of reach; the long teeth act like a net in capturing and overpowering prey

Basic forms

Silhouette

When reduced to simple forms, the design is still readable as a fish-like creature and hunter – the lure is apparent, as are the fins and powerful arms; the head is adequately large and the body has ample room for food

Poses

Testing out the design in different circumstances helps iron out any potential issues with the creature in motion. The first pose tests the fish's swimming capabilities, the second tests its ambushing capabilities, and the third any defensive measures. The animal seems to pass multiple conditions of living in these poses, which is a positive sign.

Pose A is a swimming pose that shows how the fish arranges its limbs to become more hydrodynamic and produce bursts of speed through the water. The powerful tail and fins act as rudders to pivot and weave as needed, and all of the creature's appendages can fold neatly against its body to reduce friction in the water.

The ambushing pose (pose B) explores how the creature lies in wait for prey. The powerful front limbs can act as leverage for the creature to reach up and grab prey, with the tail acting as a counterbalance.

The defensive pose (pose C) shows how the creature might attempt to defend itself. While the electrical quality of its skin might not be the main feature of the design, the other advantages of the creature can be made more obvious to reinforce its predatory nature. Not only does the massive mouth provide an intimidating presence, but the fish can fold its body neatly and expose its armored back to any potential threats to its life.

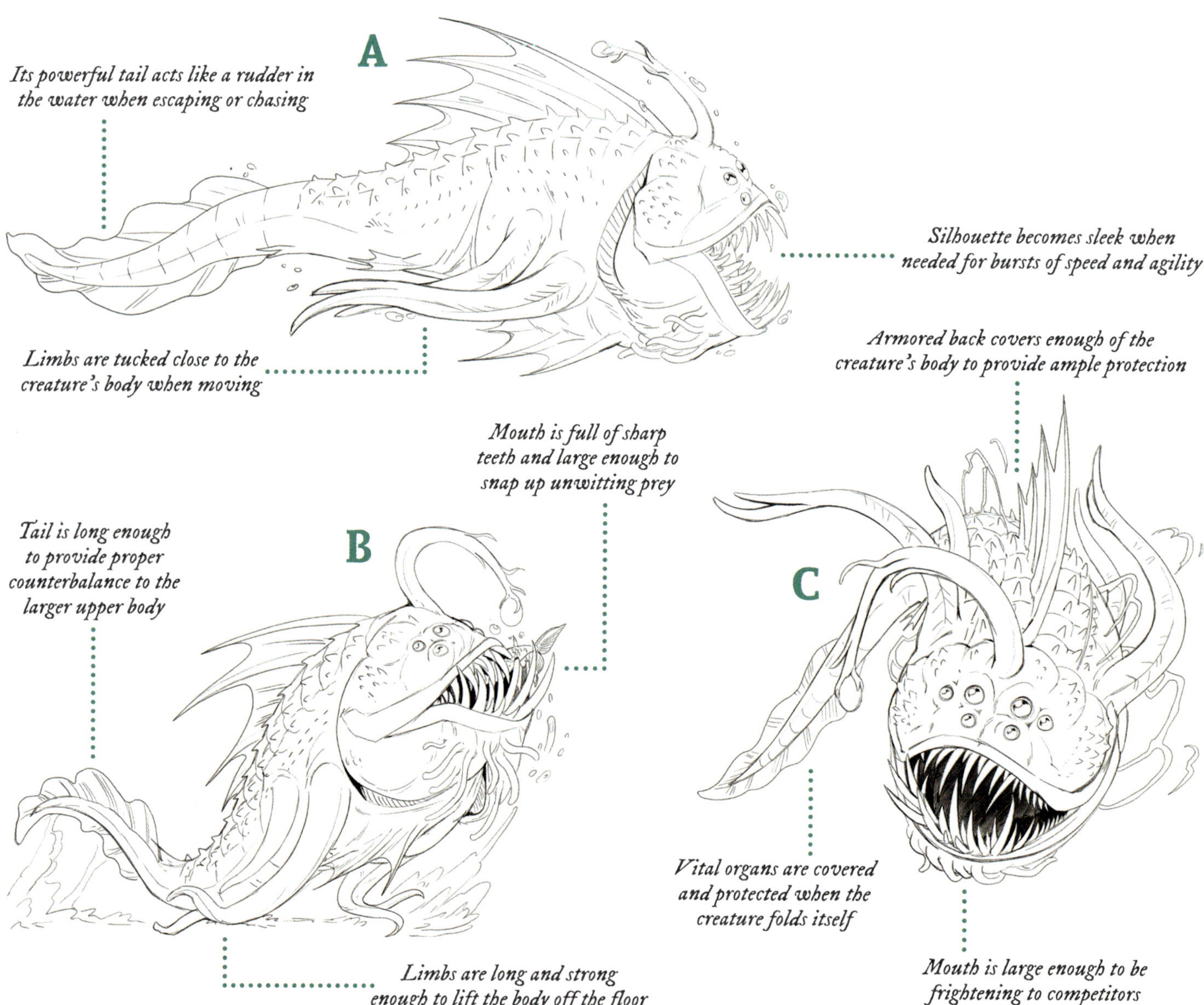

Color & pattern

Swamp creatures tend to have subtle color combinations to blend in with their environment. The primary color palette for swamp-dwelling animals seems to stay within the brown, yellow, and sometimes green-yellow spectrum.

When deciding the creature's coloration, we must consider how it functions as a predator but also as an interesting design. While it is true to nature that swamp predators will have yellows and browns for camouflage, it is also a particularly dull design feature, so we must be careful when considering what colors to work with. This design has the added benefit of the post-apocalyptic environment, which could influence some more interesting coloration.

If we maintain known color qualities of similar predators and apply them to this design, the colors reflect crocodilian palettes: subtle stripes with a gradient of greens, browns, and yellows. The creature also has a darker back and lighter belly, reflecting our crocodile example earlier. Another route to explore is that of the anglerfish and other deep-sea creatures. Hints of blue allude to the electric qualities of the creature and aspects of countershading reinforce its predatory stalking nature. Spots act as camouflage in the dark water, breaking up the fish's silhouette as it stalks its prey.

Exploring more fantastical colors and combining them with colors from nature can create a more unique palette. A blue stripe warns foes of the creature's dangerous nature – a type of patterning seen naturally in fish species. The stripe also breaks up the countershading of the dark back and the light belly.

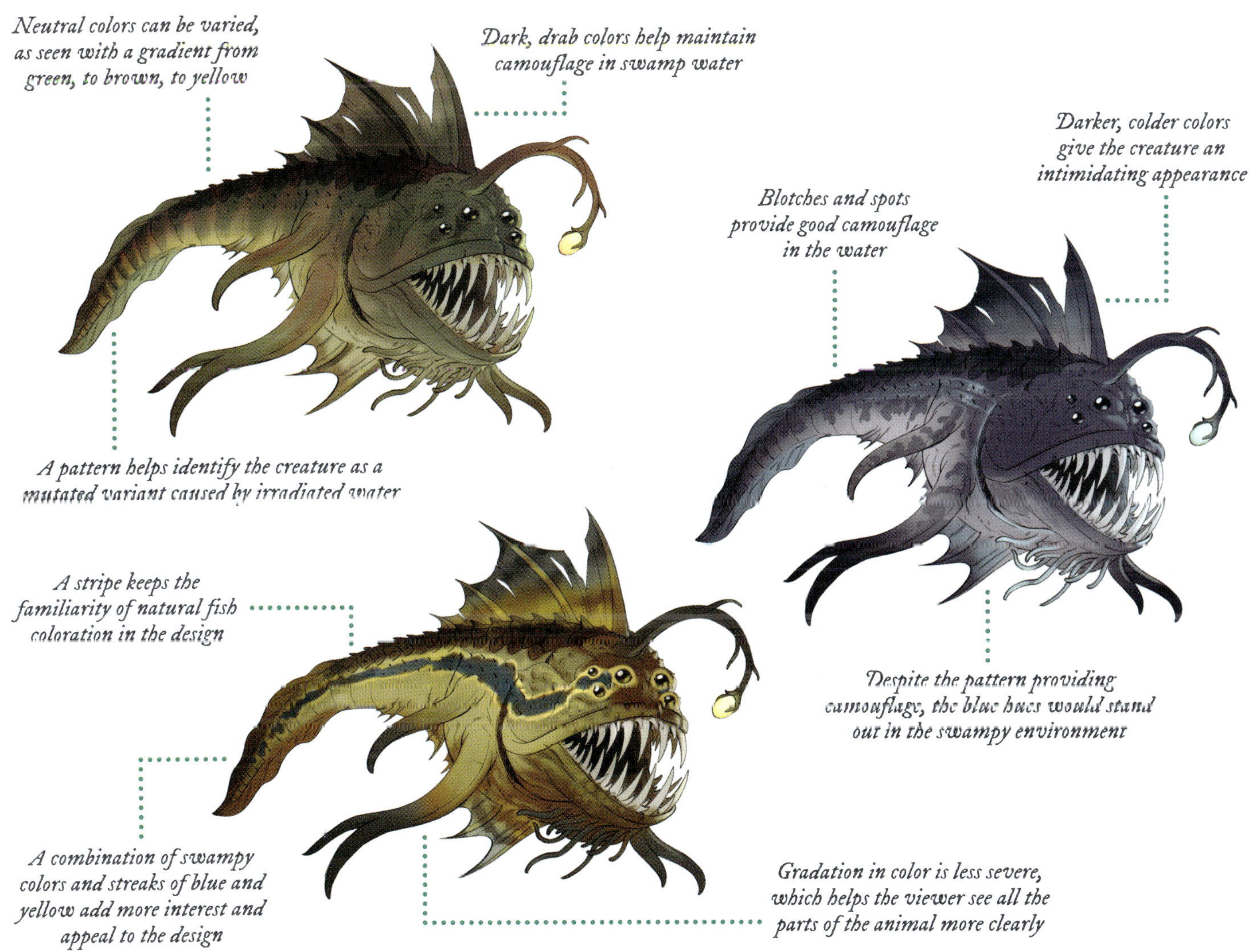

FINAL DESIGN

In the final design, the different elements that have come from experimentation through the research stages are all applied. The armor, legs, fins, and overall flow of the design read as intentional to the creature itself. By tracing out a clear path of research and execution, the design fits together naturally instead of haphazardly.

Researching different animals has given the design room to accommodate unique touches and variables, like offering the lungfish's long, tubular fins for arms, and giving the creature a thicker armor, which is not seen in many fish species naturally. Small details like this ground the predatory and unnerving features of the design in its post-apocalyptic environment and reinforce its believability.

The ferocity and dazzling color combinations should help viewers easily recognize the creature and its attributes. Unique designs hinge on the sum of their anatomical parts and design aspects such as pattern and color combination. With this creature, we have a great variety of textures and patterns along the body, which shows the viewer a unique design they cannot mistake for any creature they may have seen before. Readability in pattern and form are essential to a great and memorable creature design.

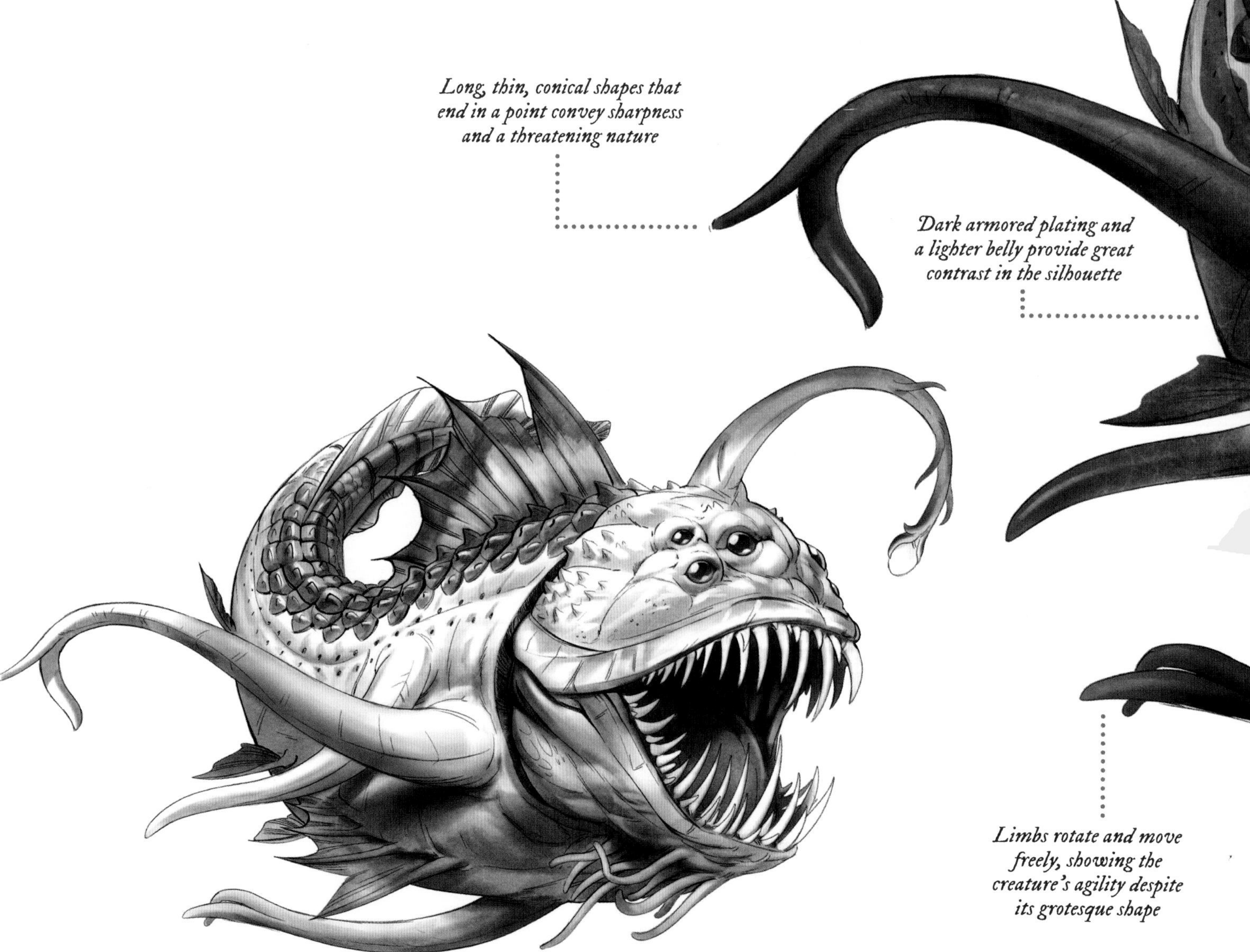

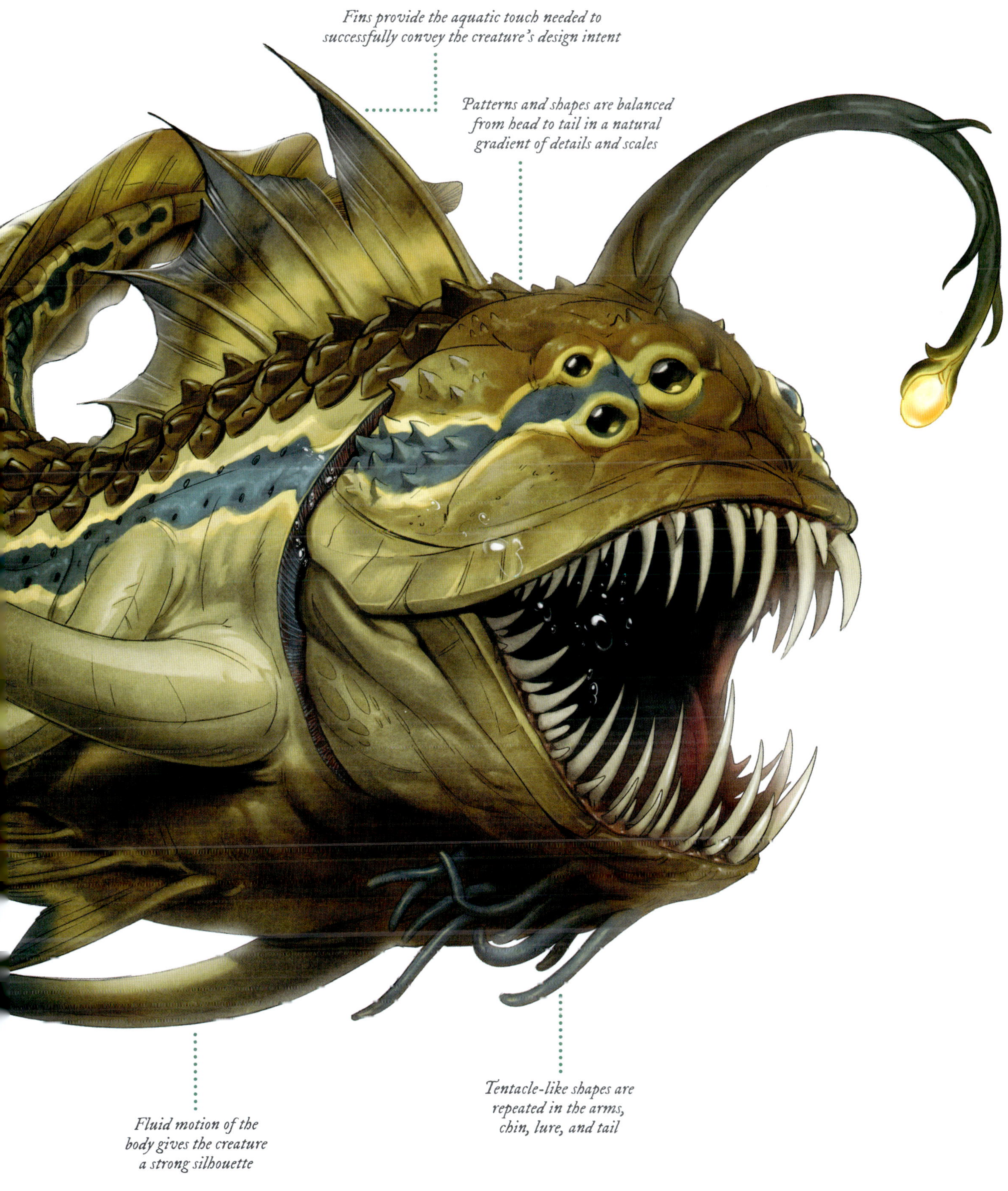

Final image © Damien Mammoliti

ADAPTATIONS

Terrestrial

A slightly more terrestrial version of the species would appear more crocodilian than fish-like in shape. Crocodilian features can be seen in the longer snout and shorter legs, which make the fins appear more like clawed, webbed hands. The back legs have a slight bend in them, as seen in crocodiles, and there are hints at reptilian hips. The armored plating flows all the way down to the end of the tail to provide full-body coverage.

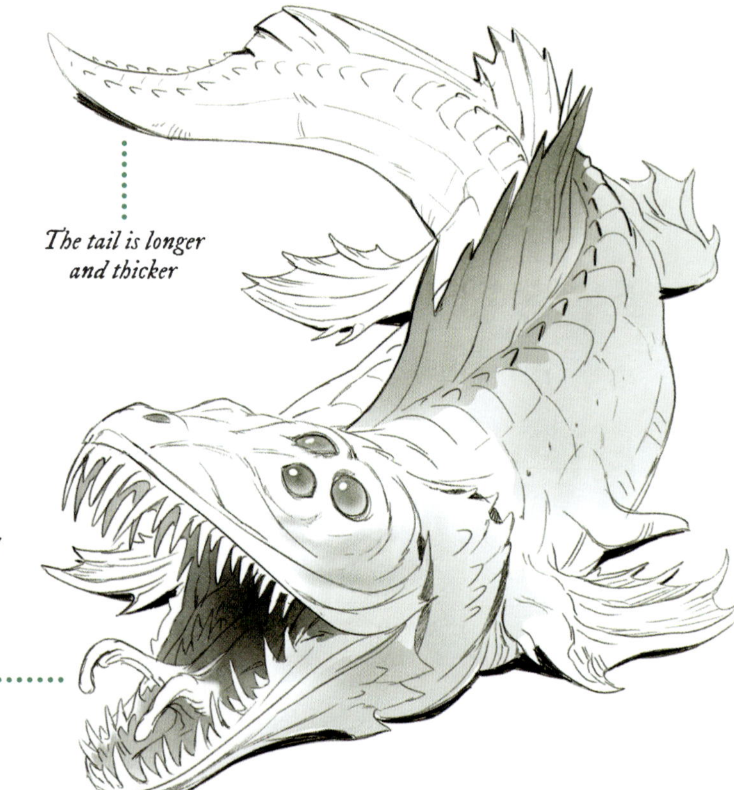

The tail is longer and thicker

A mouth lure is more effective for hunting on land than a head lure

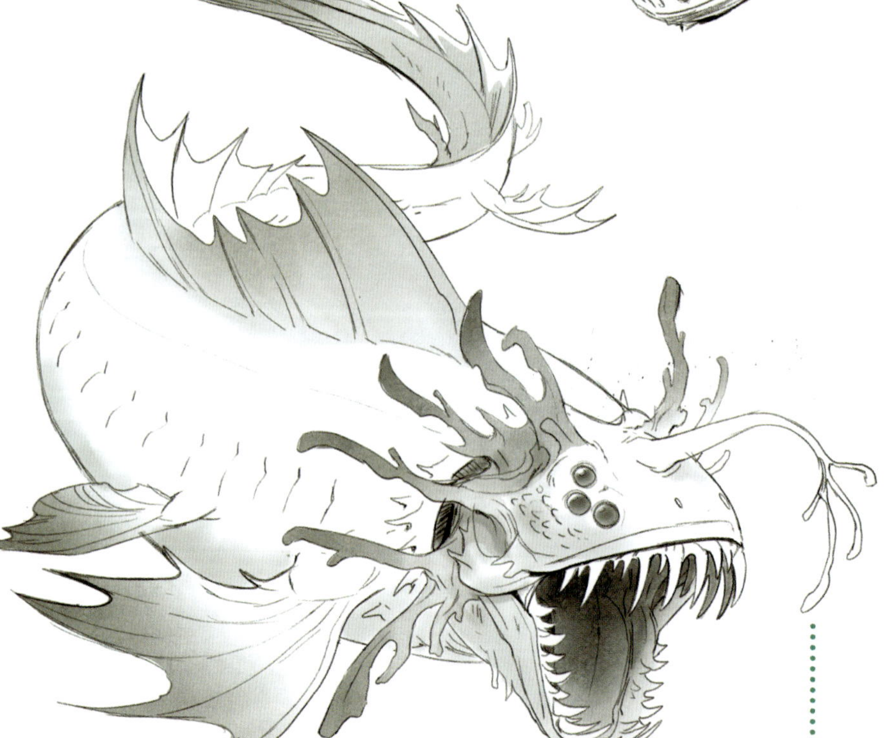

Coral reef

Reefs are thick and make it hard to maneuver, due to the strange and cryptic pattern of the coral. Small prey can take advantage of the many small holes in the textured reef when escaping predators, so our post-apocalyptic creature would have to be longer and more slender to reach them. The sensory appendages appear more coral-like in appearance, camouflaging the creature as it lurks in crevices. The long limbs are not as necessary now that the body itself is long and flexible, so the fins are shorter and can lie against the body in tight spaces.

The lure has a more cryptic form so it is less obvious in the reef

Arctic

The larger and more impressive predators of the Arctic provide great inspiration for tweaking the design. Orcas have powerful bodies and sleek profiles, so borrowing some of these traits helps give the creature a larger and more impressive form. Arctic animals also need thicker skin and blubber to prevent them freezing in the water. As our creature does not have a thick layer of fur like a walrus or seal, it will rely on having a slightly thicker and heavier body compared to the other variations.

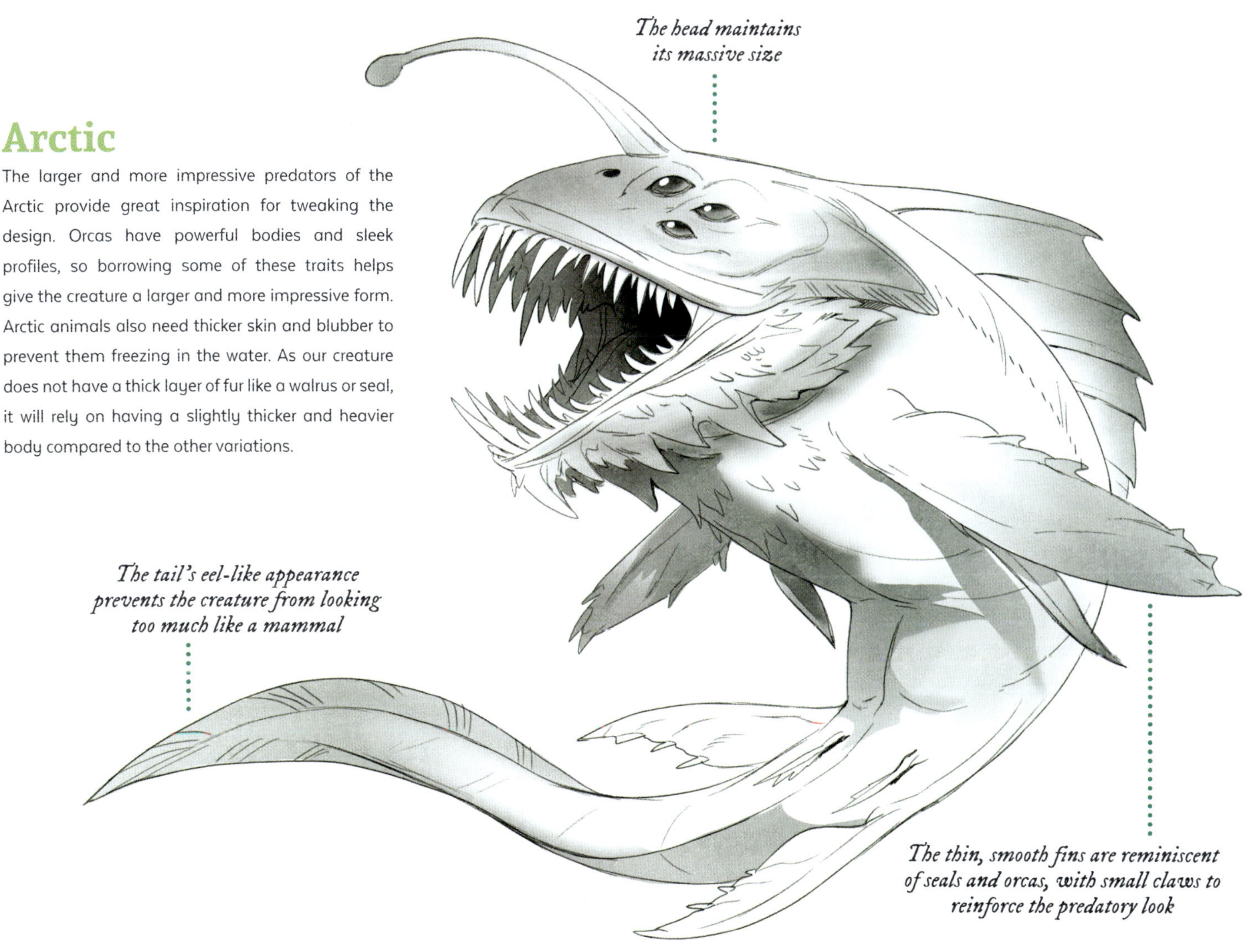

Industry tip

In the career of concept art and illustration, achieving readability is key, and this relies heavily on knowing how to work with and adapt to your medium. When designing creatures for games or books, for example, there are different considerations to make during the design process.

Games need quick readability and strength in the creature's silhouette and pattern. This is because when players approach other creatures, they need to be able to recognize them immediately as an enemy or a friend, and act accordingly.

When creating illustrations for books and other less interactive media, your focus should be on memorable design and impact on the viewer. Creating something beautiful or ferocious will make your design memorable – which is particularly important for potential intellectual property recognition.

What separates your design from those in another game, book, or movie? What unique features are included that will be instantly recognizable to anyone familiar with that intellectual property? These are questions you should ask yourself at every stage of your creation process.

Alien crustacean

Oriana Menendez

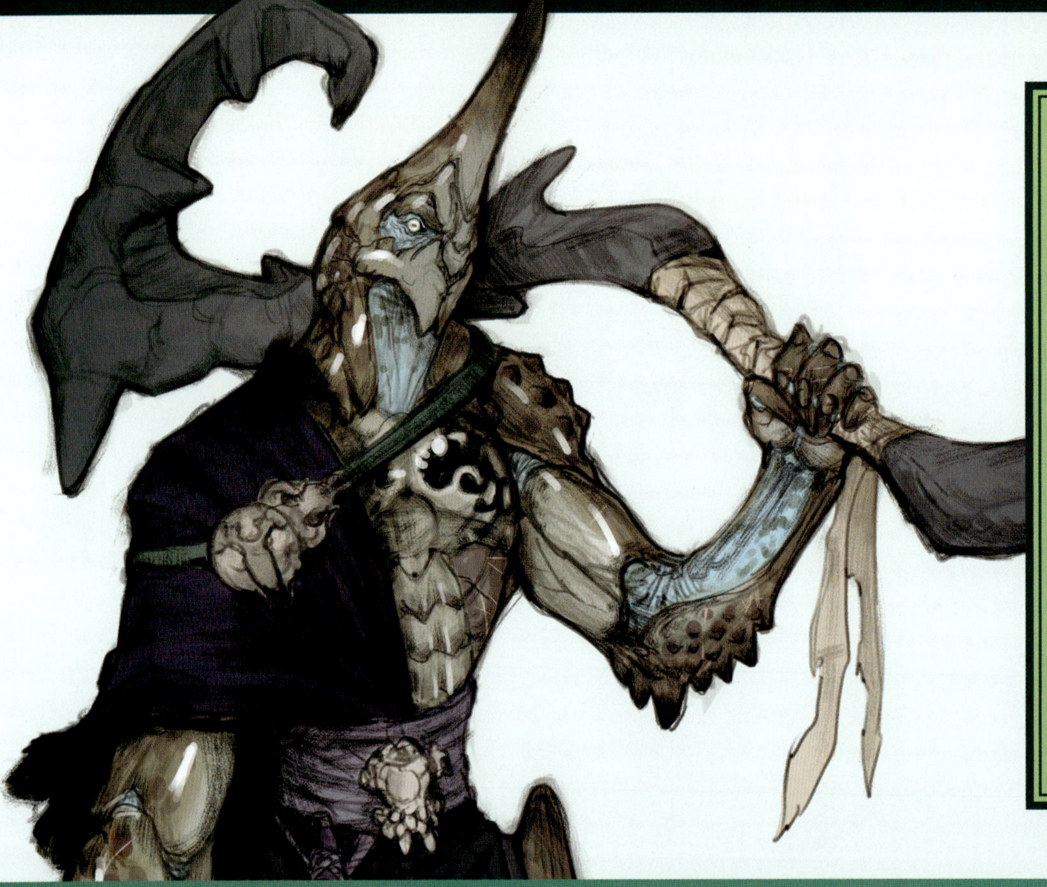

Key facts

- Capable of thriving in a dry, dusty/sandy environment

- Anthropomorphic qualities: basic tribal adornment/ weaponry, bipedal, expressive, communicative, and indications of social behavior/hierarchy

- Omnivorous diet

- Primate influence adds humanoid qualities

- Crustacean element acts as armor

IDEATION

For this alien warrior, a good balance between crustacean and primate will be important in achieving a design that feels alien but can still emote to us. The creature will need some humanoid facial features to be able to quickly communicate its intelligence to an audience. A crustacean's exoskeleton and social behavior, on the other hand, can help emphasize its otherness and avoid making it too close to human. Bipedalism and adaptation to a dry climate are both featured in primates, so it will be ideal to look to primate anatomy for the overall body plan. Humans and many other simians originally evolved on dry savannas, while most crustaceans are aquatic. Even terrestrial crabs return to the sea to reproduce.

As this species is planned to have comparable levels of intelligence to humans, it will be able to use collaboration and invention to thrive in its dry steppe (grassland) habitat - rather than using purely biological adaptations. Cultural elements like weapons, tools, and art emerge from that environmental pressure. Many non-human primates, such as baboons, also adapt to dry climates by finding hidden sources of water and collaborating with their group.

A crustacean-like exoskeleton could lend the creature a fierce appearance befitting a warrior. Some species of crustacean also have interesting social behaviors, such as the eusocial snapping shrimp, *Synalpheus*. Our creature could be part of their colony's soldier caste, defending their home from invaders. Eusociality and castes will be explained further on page 233. *Synalpheus* also live symbiotically with sponges, using them as shelter and a food source. To survive the cold, dry, alien steppe, the colony could rely on a gigantic, immobile, plant or sponge-like organism for shelter. From there, we have plenty with which to get started.

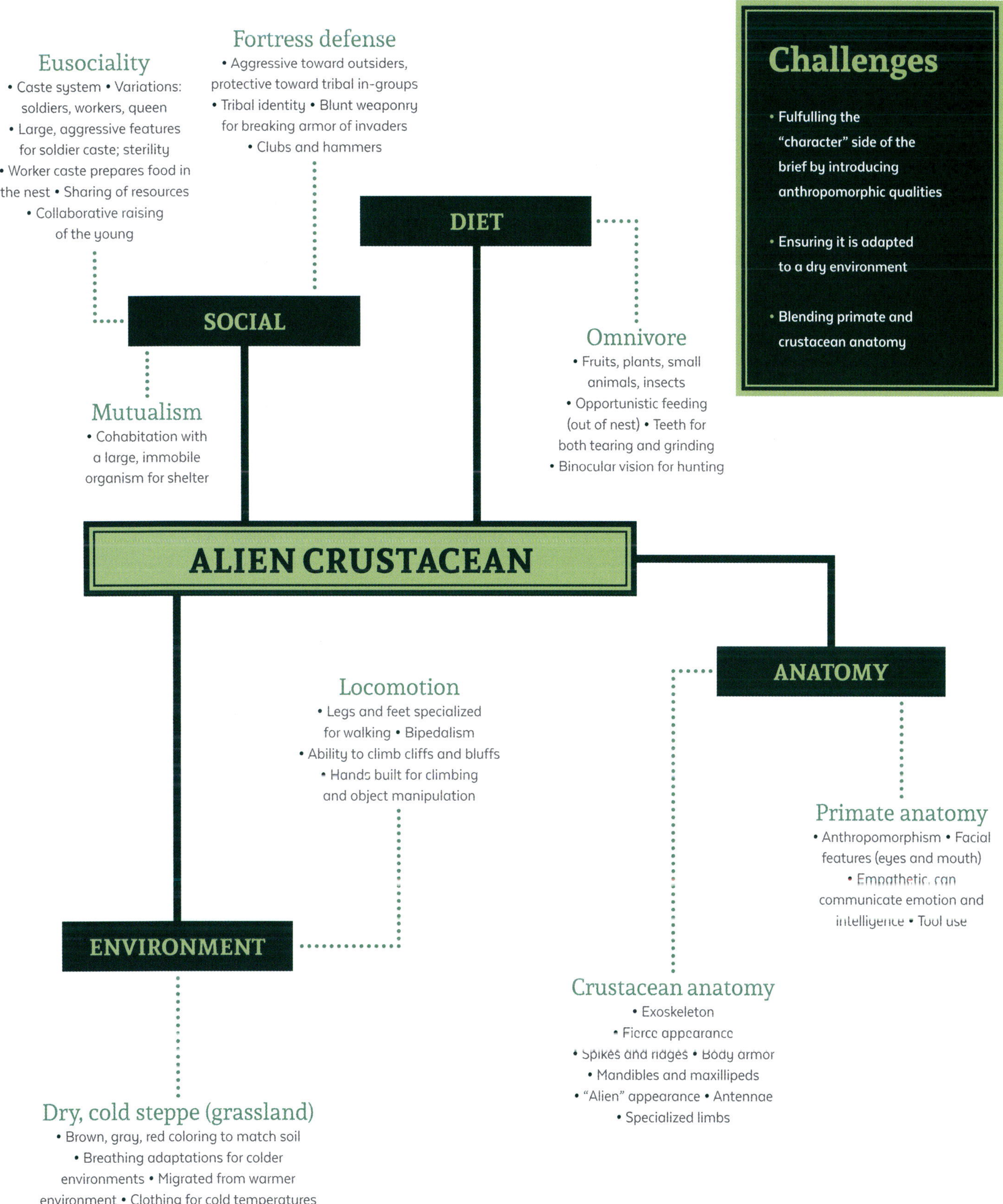
Eusociality
• Caste system • Variations: soldiers, workers, queen • Large, aggressive features for soldier caste; sterility • Worker caste prepares food in the nest • Sharing of resources • Collaborative raising of the young

Fortress defense
• Aggressive toward outsiders, protective toward tribal in-groups • Tribal identity • Blunt weaponry for breaking armor of invaders • Clubs and hammers

DIET

Challenges
• Fulfulling the "character" side of the brief by introducing anthropomorphic qualities
• Ensuring it is adapted to a dry environment
• Blending primate and crustacean anatomy

SOCIAL

Omnivore
• Fruits, plants, small animals, insects • Opportunistic feeding (out of nest) • Teeth for both tearing and grinding • Binocular vision for hunting

Mutualism
• Cohabitation with a large, immobile organism for shelter

ALIEN CRUSTACEAN

Locomotion
• Legs and feet specialized for walking • Bipedalism • Ability to climb cliffs and bluffs • Hands built for climbing and object manipulation

ANATOMY

Primate anatomy
• Anthropomorphism • Facial features (eyes and mouth) • Empathetic, can communicate emotion and intelligence • Tool use

ENVIRONMENT

Crustacean anatomy
• Exoskeleton • Fierce appearance • Spikes and ridges • Body armor • Mandibles and maxillipeds • "Alien" appearance • Antennae • Specialized limbs

Dry, cold steppe (grassland)
• Brown, gray, red coloring to match soil • Breathing adaptations for colder environments • Migrated from warmer environment • Clothing for cold temperatures

Anatomy research

Human bipedalism

Revisiting human anatomy is helpful for studying adaptations that have specifically occurred to aid bipedalism. This includes an S-curve to the spine, a broad pelvis, and longer hind limbs to support body weight. Humans are built for endurance, using much less energy for locomotion than other apes and quadrupedal animals. This requires the skeleton to be well-balanced to conserve energy. In humans, the bicondylar (inward) angle of the femur is critical for maintaining balance, and is a unique visual feature in the human skeleton. Human feet are also adapted for walking (as opposed to grasping), with a large heel and an arch for shock absorption.

Since human forelimbs no longer need to support weight, they are smaller and much more dexterous and flexible. This allows them to be specialized for manipulating and throwing objects.

Primate anatomy

Primates are a very varied group of animals, with the "great apes" (such as bonobos, chimpanzees, gorillas, and orangutans) being quite close to humans in terms of anatomical structure. In comparison, monkeys (such as baboons, macaques, tamarins, and langurs) have more cat-like anatomy, with scapulae on the sides of the ribcage in a manner more typical of quadrupedal animals.

Non-human primates are a good source of inspiration for human-like features adapted to different environments. One example of this is the hands - some baboons have hands and feet adapted to terrestrial foraging as well as climbing up the rocks and cliffs of the steppe they inhabit. Gorillas' feet and hands allow them to climb up trees, even though they live mostly on the ground.

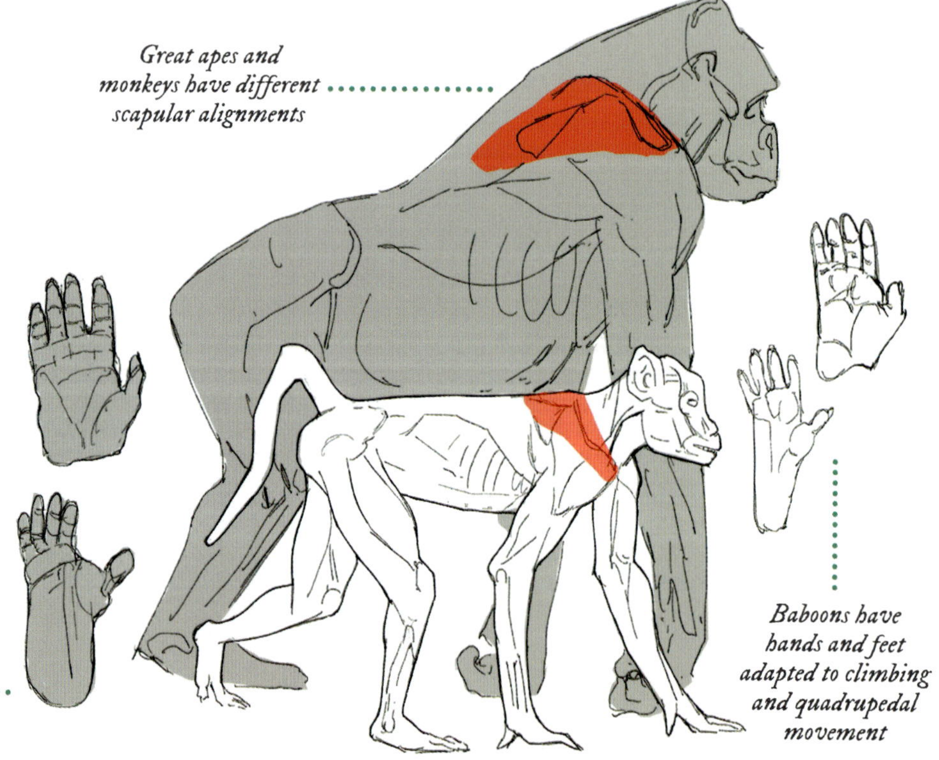

Crustacean anatomy

A crustacean's exoskeleton protects it from predators and provides stability for its soft internal body. In order to design natural body armor for a bipedal creature, it is important to study the shapes and points of articulation.

The lobster shown here has repeated body segments that form the abdomen, and fused plates to form the cephalothorax. Several pairs of jointed limbs are specialized into claws, walking legs, and sometimes a pair of paddle-like swimming legs in crabs. The swimmerets (feathery hair-like stuctures beneath the abdomen) are used for locomotion and for holding eggs in females. These features could add a strange or alien element to this species.

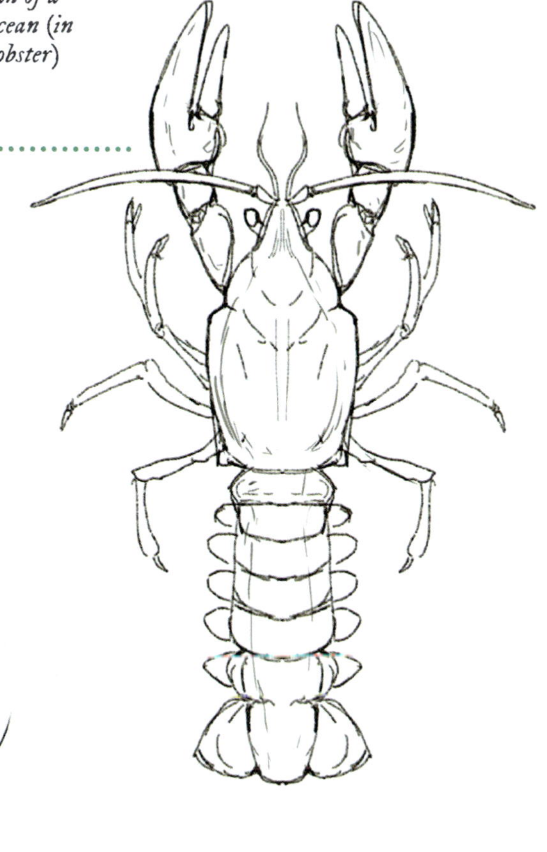

The body plan of a typical crustacean (in this case, a lobster)

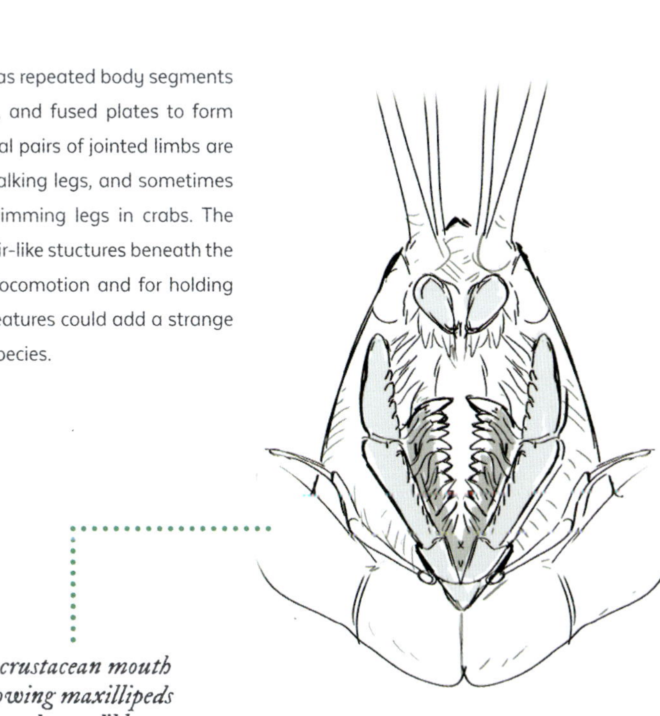

A crustacean mouth showing maxillipeds and mandibles

Evolution

Primates (including humans) communicate with facial expressions, body language, and vocalizations. Eyes and mouths, for example, can be very expressive while being nonverbal, and serve as a good basis for anthropomorphization.

For some species, like the gelada pictured right, threat displays from the leader of the group are often used to keep the peace between individuals. These evolutionary adaptations can speak to a human audience on a fundamental level, helping to make an emotional connection with a non-human subject.

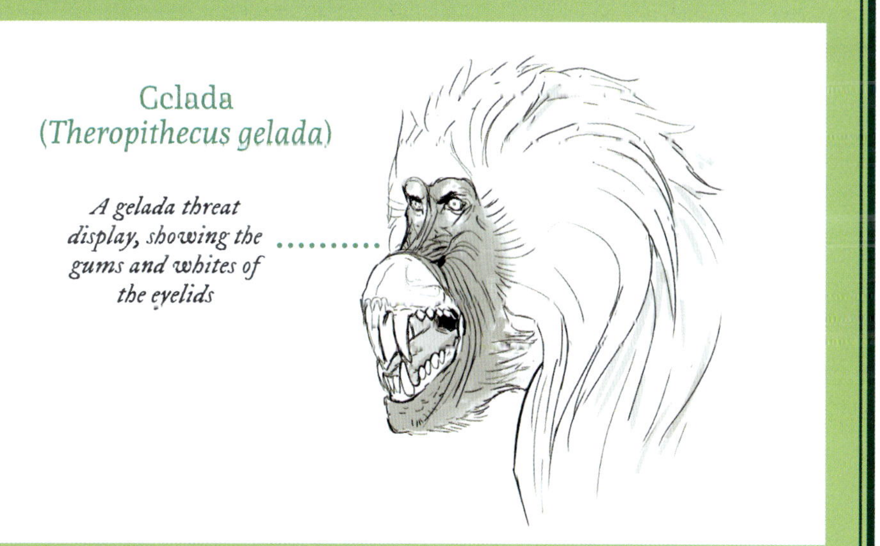

Gelada (*Theropithecus gelada*)

A gelada threat display, showing the gums and whites of the eyelids

Functionality research

Crustacean carapace

Crustacea comprises an incredibly diverse range of species, including lobsters, shrimp, and crabs. Crustaceans originally developed in "the Cambrian explosion," a time with great variation of species using a similar body plan. As a result, a bounty of inspiration can be found for shape language and design in crustaceans. For example, many species of crabs have long spines or other features on their exoskeletons to protect them from predators. Although the species pictured here are small animals, their defensive shells are an exciting look into how body armor evolves in nature. The thorny shell of a crab could add fierce character to an alien warrior.

Lollipop crab
(*Ixa cylindrus*)

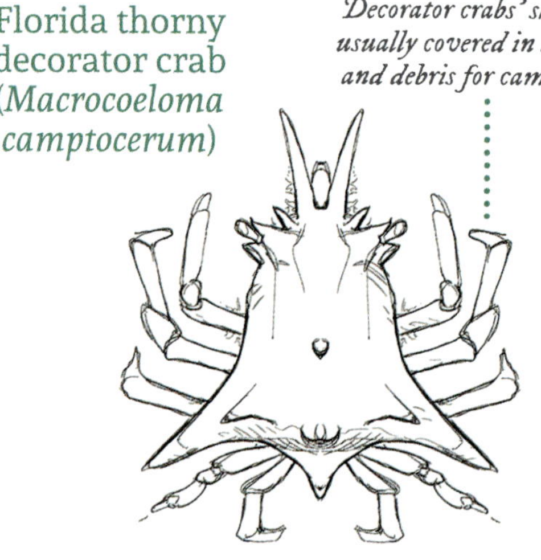

Cylindrical knobs give this crab's shell a uniquely memorable shape

Sand or mole crab
(*Albunea*)

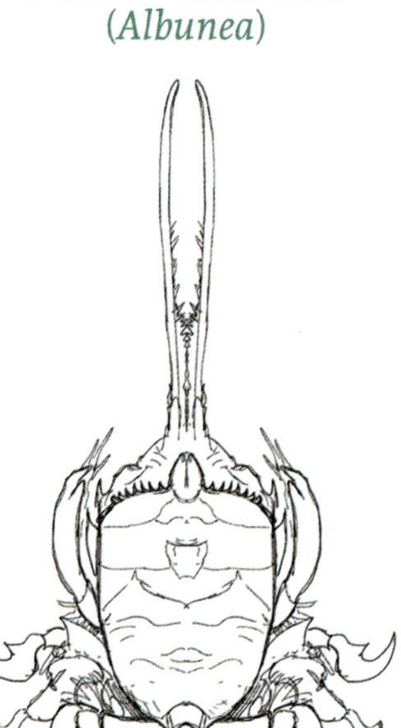

Shovel-like claws help when burrowing in sand

Florida thorny decorator crab (*Macrocoeloma camptocerum*)

Decorator crabs' shells are usually covered in seaweed and debris for camouflage

Technological invention

Since this alien is a warrior with human-like intelligence, and is part of a tribe, it is helpful to look into different human cultures and how they adapted to hostile environments. Textiles, agriculture, architecture, and metallurgy, for example, were all important human inventions influenced by the society in which they were created.

Studying these areas can inspire clothing or other elements that imply the alien's own unique culture. This particular species could have been biologically adapted to a desert environment and later moved to a cold, steppe-like climate. Rather than developing fur or thicker shells, they could have made clothes or adapted their living space to survive. Researching peoples that developed in similar environments will help inform what this species may have invented in order to thrive.

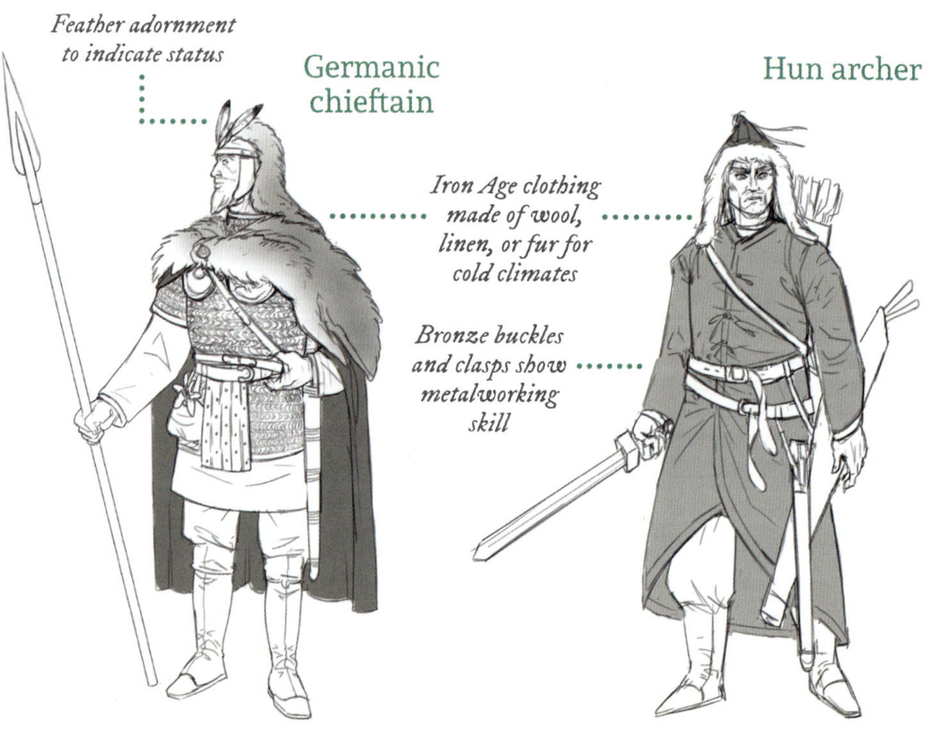

Feather adornment to indicate status

Germanic chieftain

Hun archer

Iron Age clothing made of wool, linen, or fur for cold climates

Bronze buckles and clasps show metalworking skill

Eusociality

Eusocial animals such as bees and termites act as a group, with adults living and collaborating together to maintain their nest. Division of labor defines eusocial animals, where one individual (the queen) is in charge of reproduction while others are tasked with defending the nest from invaders and tending to the young. This collaboration enables the group to thrive in places where an individual would fail.

For this design, considering the social behavior of the alien creature will help differentiate individuals and avoid having an entire species defined by one characteristic. Since the brief mentions that the alien is a warrior, for example, they would be part of a warrior or defender caste (social class) with characteristics appropriate for that role.

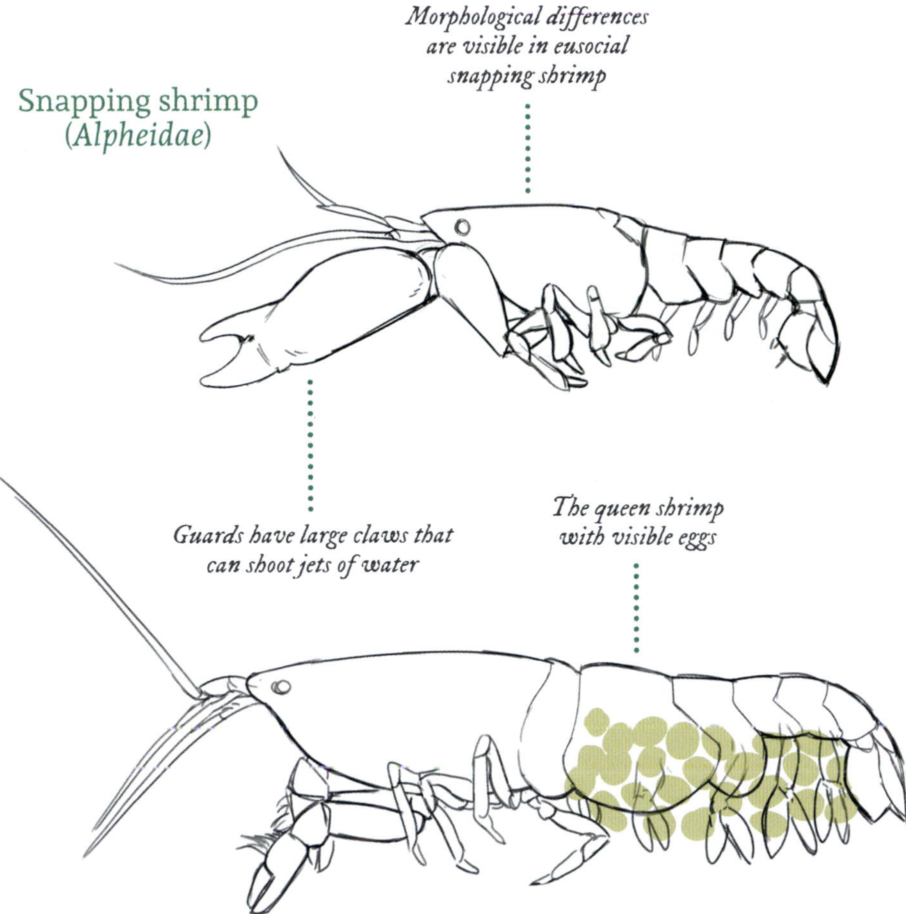

Coloration

Fiddler crabs can change their color for courtship displays, camouflage, thermoregulation, and distinguishing neighbors from strangers. This is similar to cuttlefish and chameleons, and can solve a lot of design problems that a static color scheme could not. For the visual elements of the design, the most relevant use would be in identification. Since this character is eusocial, each caste could have a unique color demarcating its role, and each tribe could also have a specific marking on its carapace. Along with having varied patterns between members of the same species, this color-changing ability could also help solve this alien creature's problem of adapting to the colors and temperatures of a cold environment.

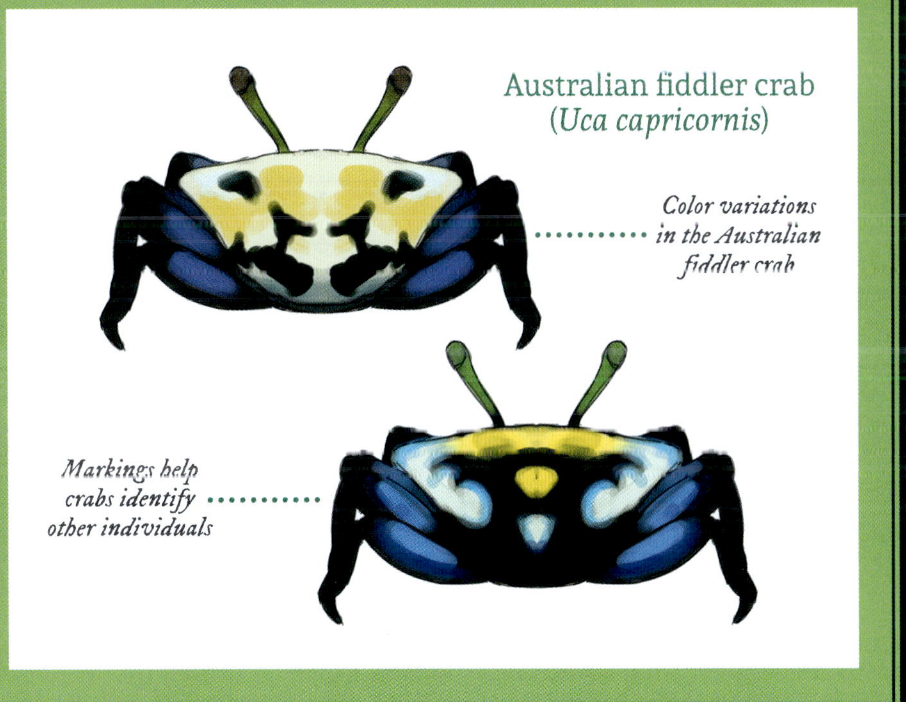

Thumbnails

This design requires a good visual balance between the alien warrior, its clothing, and its weapon. Too much or too little emphasis on any of these elements could diminish the effectiveness of the design, both as a memorable alien creature and as an individual character with a clear role. These thumbnails explore some very different proportions and appearances that could fulfill the brief, all drawing inspiration from the tough shells of crustaceans and the postures of humans and primates. Being a warrior or soldier, the design requires a tough, naturally armored body, and a weapon effective against enemies of the same and other species.

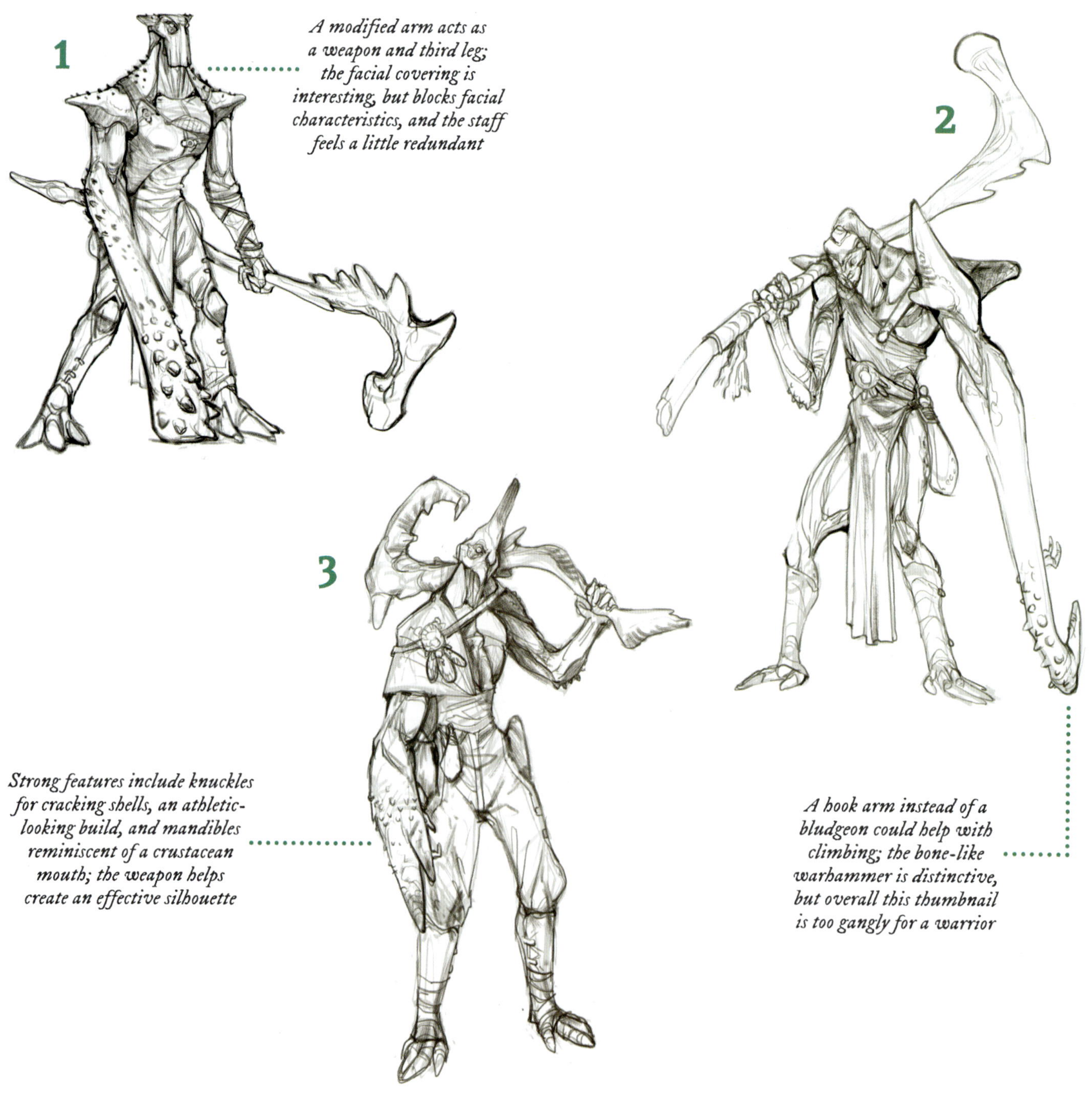

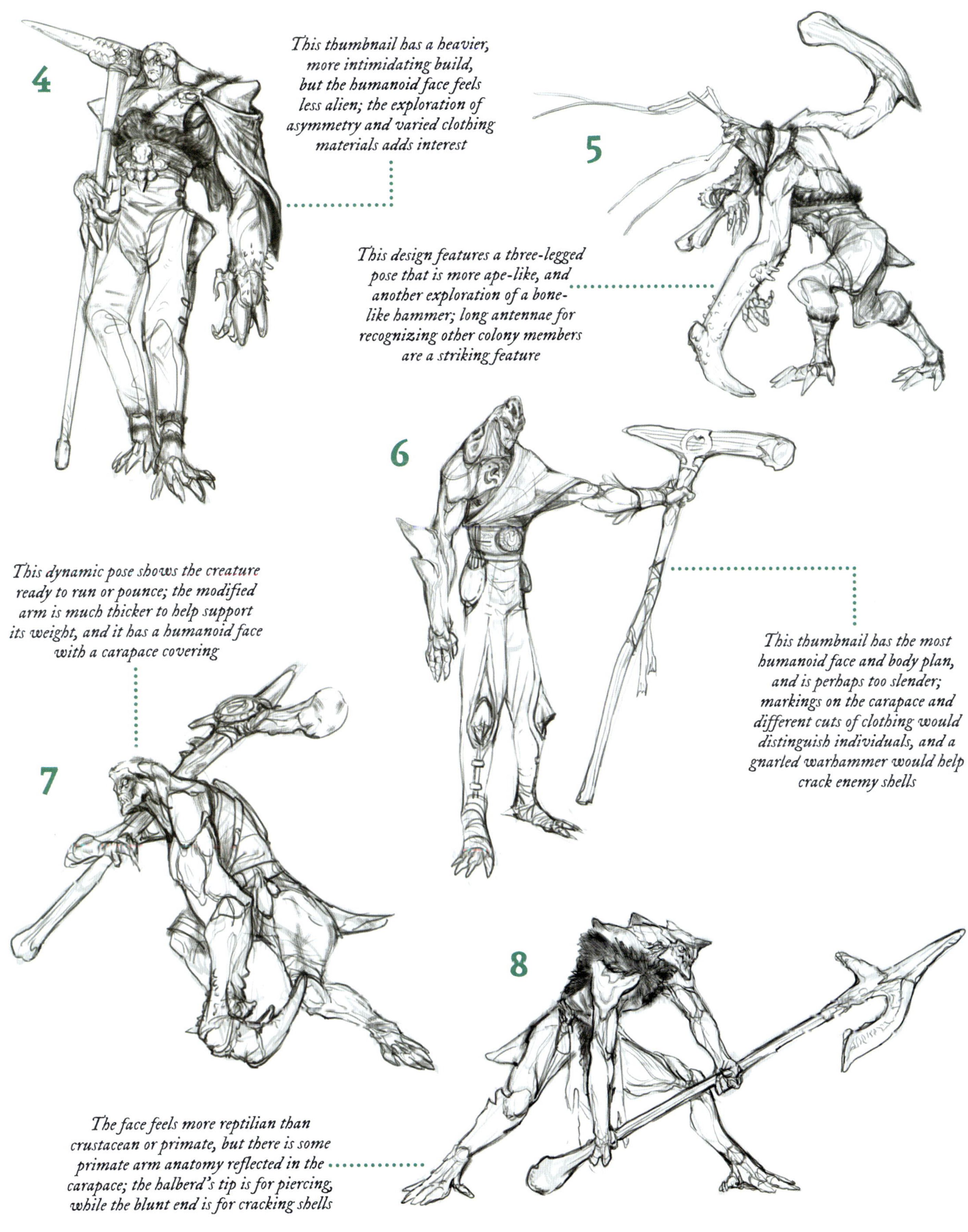

4

This thumbnail has a heavier, more intimidating build, but the humanoid face feels less alien; the exploration of asymmetry and varied clothing materials adds interest

5

This design features a three-legged pose that is more ape-like, and another exploration of a bone-like hammer; long antennae for recognizing other colony members are a striking feature

6

This dynamic pose shows the creature ready to run or pounce; the modified arm is much thicker to help support its weight, and it has a humanoid face with a carapace covering

7

This thumbnail has the most humanoid face and body plan, and is perhaps too slender; markings on the carapace and different cuts of clothing would distinguish individuals, and a gnarled warhammer would help crack enemy shells

The face feels more reptilian than crustacean or primate, but there is some primate arm anatomy reflected in the carapace; the halberd's tip is for piercing, while the blunt end is for cracking shells

8

DEVELOPMENT

Thumbnail 3 achieves a good balance of human and crustacean, while giving an impression of a tribal warrior. The silhouette of this thumbnail is the strongest as well, being clear at first glance, while also being interesting due to the hook-shaped motif created by the weapon and armor pieces.

Anthropomorphic qualities are important to show attitude. On a more practical level, they allow the creature to emote in its own way, while also remaining alien. Having visible eyes creates opportunities to show emotion in a recognizable way. A bipedal body plan also allows for body language that can be similar to humans - another way of communicating the alien's character.

Although crustaceans specifically are aquatic, carapaces (outer shells) help certain species of arthropods survive in the desert by trapping moisture in their bodies. Showing evidence of social structure and intelligence, such as a gourd or pouch for extra water, also addresses the creature's desert survival abilities. It can be assumed that life in a dry climate is possible with the help of the larger group.

Primate and crustacean characteristics are tricky to mix together, but the combination of a bipedal body plan with a crustacean carapace is a strong start. The textures and patterns are inspired by crustaceans to create interesting markings, while the posture and proportions are clearly derived from humans and other primates.

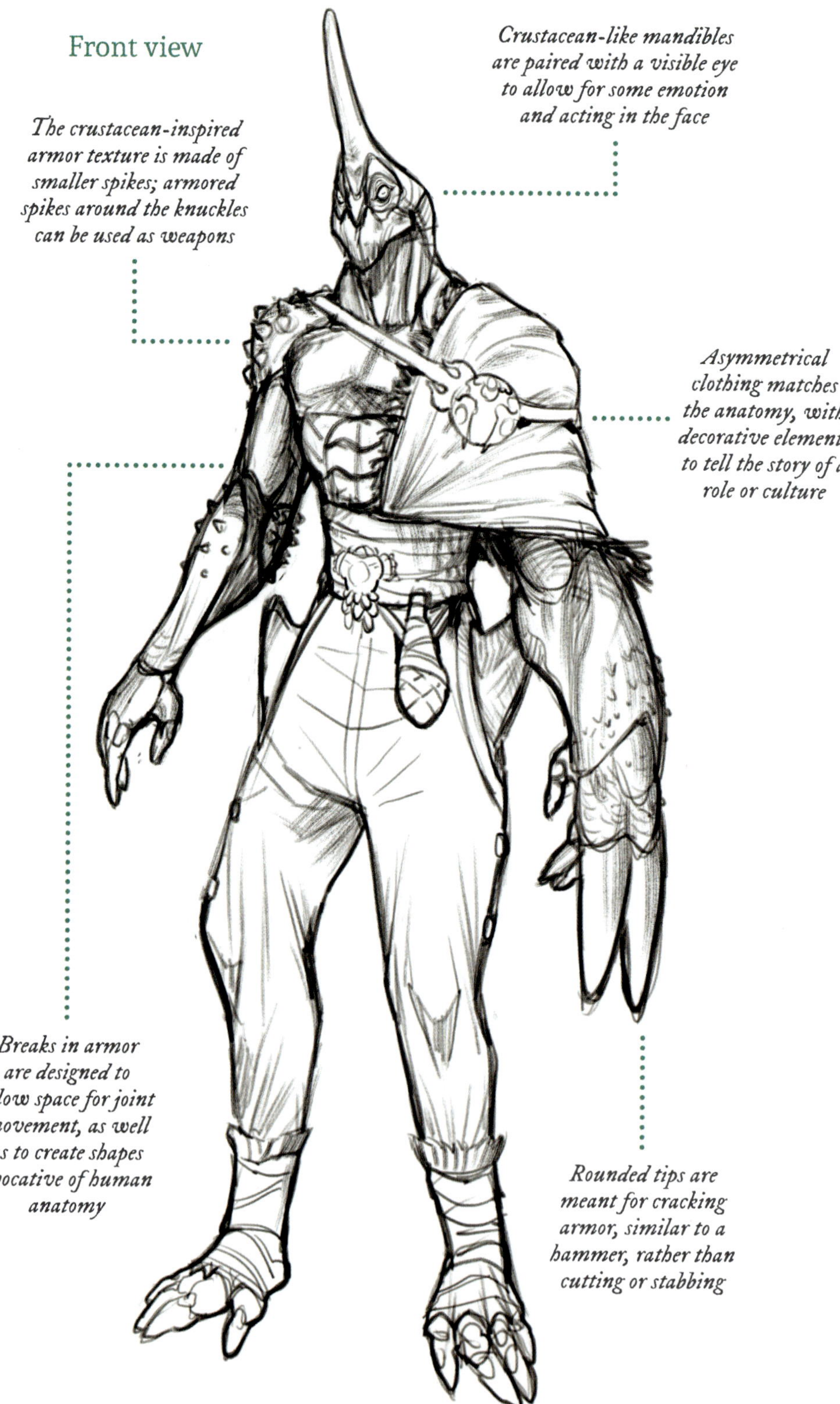

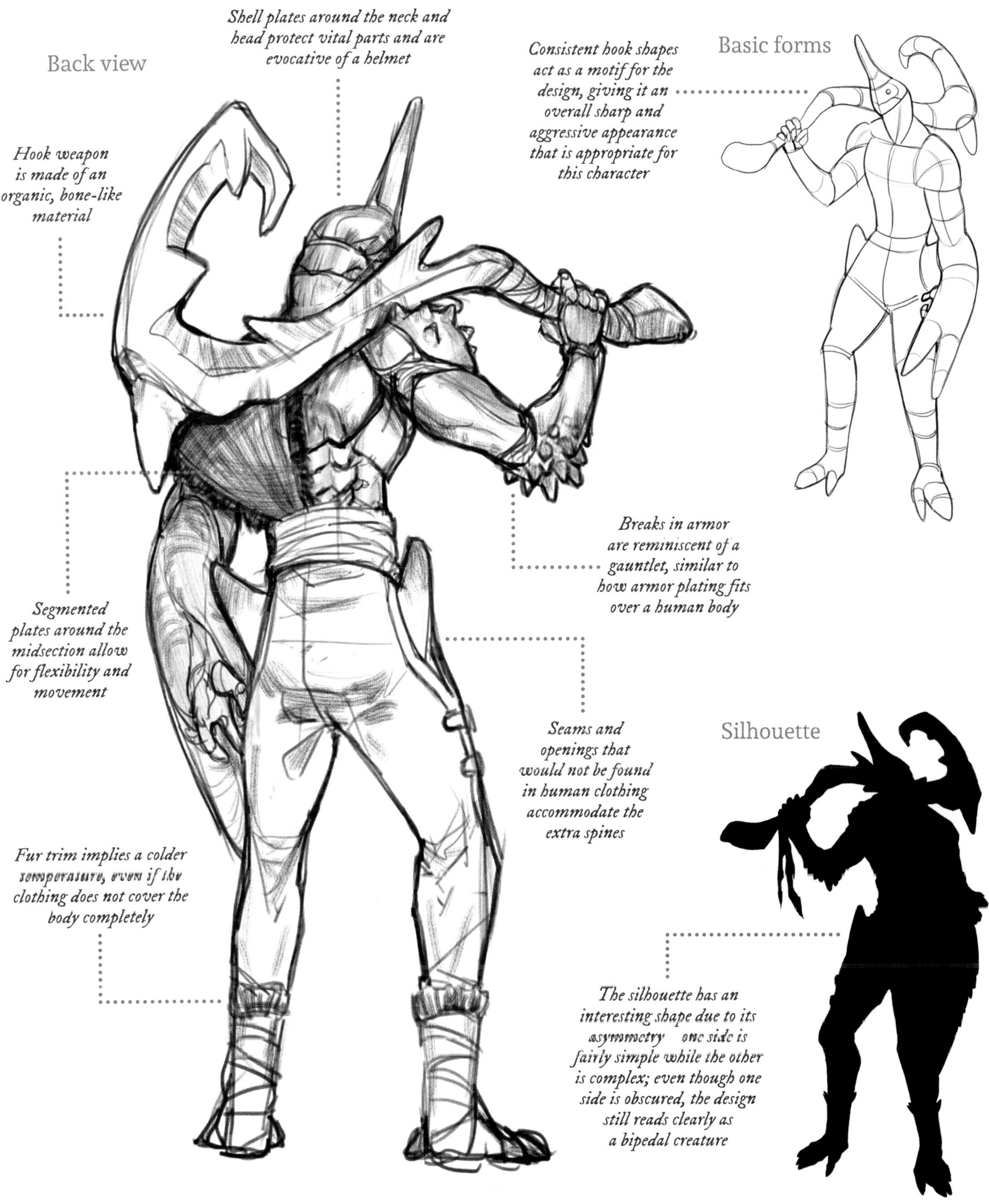

Back view

Shell plates around the neck and head protect vital parts and are evocative of a helmet

Consistent hook shapes act as a motif for the design, giving it an overall sharp and aggressive appearance that is appropriate for this character

Basic forms

Hook weapon is made of an organic, bone-like material

Breaks in armor are reminiscent of a gauntlet, similar to how armor plating fits over a human body

Segmented plates around the midsection allow for flexibility and movement

Seams and openings that would not be found in human clothing accommodate the extra spines

Silhouette

Fur trim implies a colder temperature, even if the clothing does not cover the body completely

The silhouette has an interesting shape due to its asymmetry — one side is fairly simple while the other is complex; even though one side is obscured, the design still reads clearly as a bipedal creature

Poses

Posing a character in multiple ways helps test the viability of a design. For the crustacean warrior, it is important that it is able to emote through the face, but also through body language. On a more practical note, it should also be flexible and agile enough to fight if need be. These poses will explore attitude while also testing the creature's range of motion.

Important elements that need to be brought out are the creature's aggression, which in this case would be for the purpose of defending its colony. Imagining specific scenarios can help avoid a generic approach to a pose.

Pose A is a threat display - aggression for the purpose of frightening off a foe. It tests how the carapace might move around the shoulder and elbow joints, and also explores how the mouth might look under the mandibles. Though not visible in a neutral pose, the mouth is a mix of primate-like canines with the crustacean mandibles over them, which this pose shows. The pose also tests how the creature looks with its limbs extended and stretched out.

Pose B is a compact, crouched position. This explores an earlier idea of using the larger, armed limb as support or for climbing. It tests how natural the faux three-legged pose looks on a creature that ordinarily moves on its two feet. It is also helpful to see how the hip spines can fit onto the body in different positions. While large spikes are useful for a dramatic silhouette and add a crustacean quality, they can be an obstructive feature if not properly explored.

Pose C is an upright, alert position, with the shoulders back. This pose allows for the exploration of the design from the rear. When including a large limb, as in this design, it is important to make sure it does not obstruct the clarity of the silhouette as a whole in its different poses.

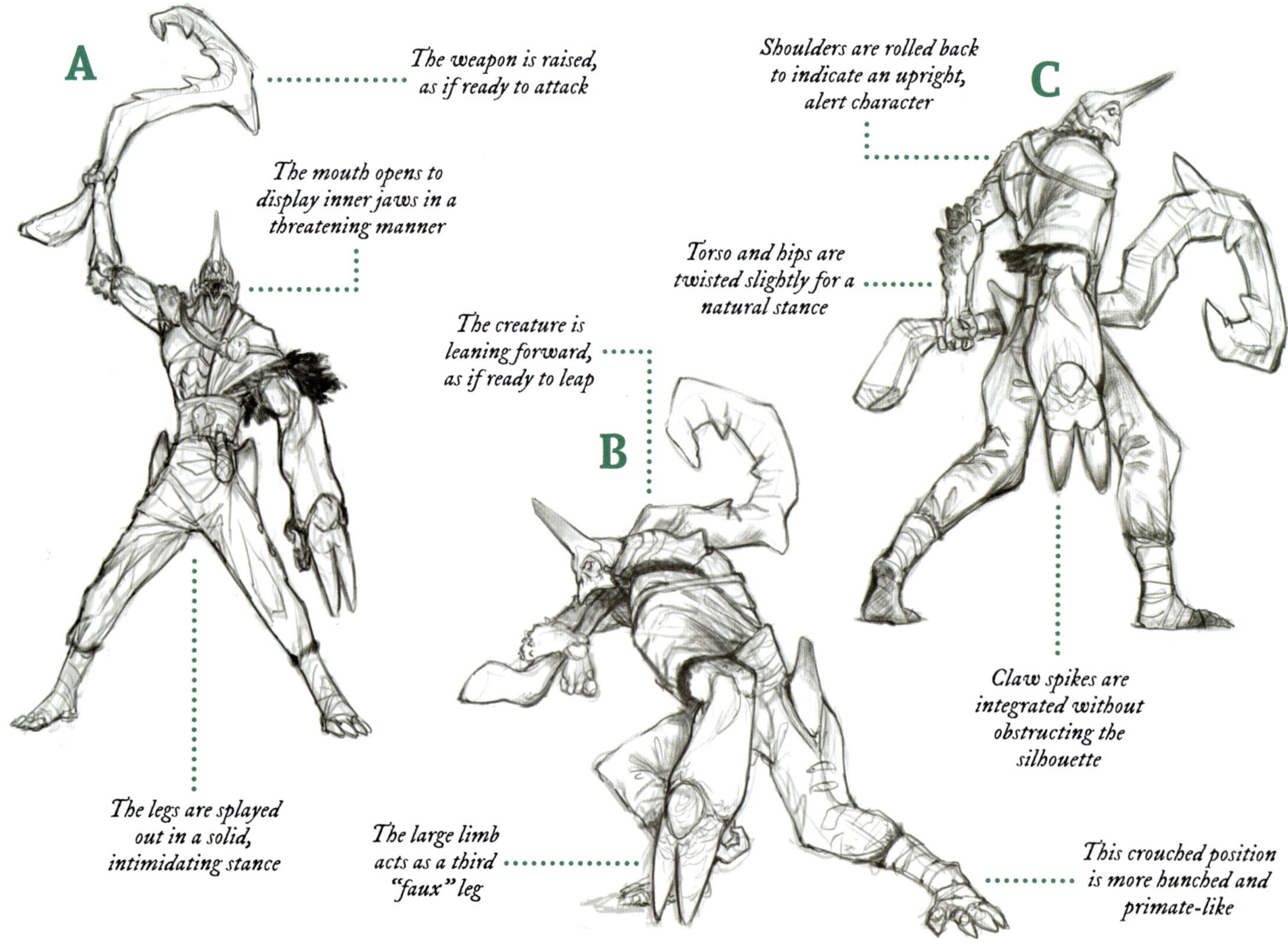

Color & pattern

Crustaceans offer a variety of bright colors to be inspired by, and it can be tempting to go for a more flashy design. However, for this creature, the dry environment narrows down the believable choices for its color palette. Since the colony would be living on a cold steppe, cool or warm grays evocative of a rocky, dusty habitat would be the best camouflage.

However, this does not necessarily mean all the colors need to be muted. Because the crustacean warrior is a guard, not necessarily a hunter, it would make sense to have some brighter warning colors to threaten potential attackers. This is a feature found in some species of primate, where individuals with brighter colors are usually more dominant.

The first two options explore a mix of bright flesh with muted base shell colors for camouflage. The third goes for a more full-on "stay away from me" color set. It includes an iridescent white that would be easier to see against gray stone and dust - perhaps this variation could be a rarer and more extreme coloration in the species.

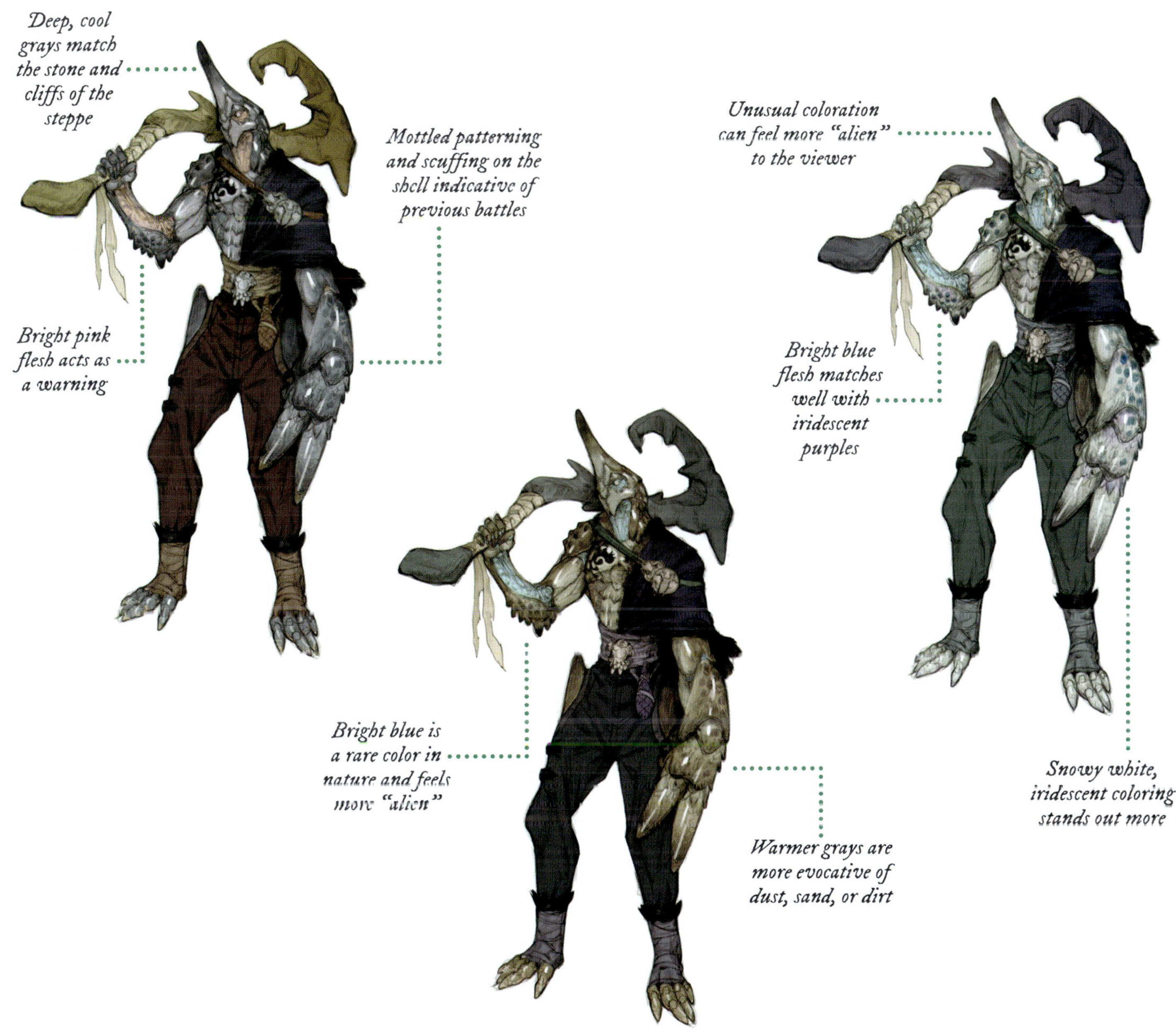

FINAL DESIGN

The final design shows an alien-looking tribal warrior, mixing the features of various animals while also indicating it is part of a larger society with the use of clothing, decoration, and tools. While the body plan is very much human, there are various details that give it a more otherworldly appearance. The mandibles and crustacean carapace are the biggest contributors to this. A balance between human and alien is struck by allowing the eyes to feature prominently on the face, giving the creature a way to emote and show what it may be thinking. Its coloration is a mix of familiar earthy tones with a more alien bright blue, giving it believability without sacrificing bolder color elements.

The pose of its body also adds to its character, even if its position is relatively relaxed here. The sharp hook motif is reflected in both its tool of choice and in the spines and armored spikes of its carapace, giving it an aggressive appearance. Its asymmetrical stance helps give weight to the larger, heavier limb used to attack, while also adding to its strong silhouette.

Elements of the warrior's eusocial society show up as biological marks as well as cultural ones - the most obvious being the larger limb and specialized markings indicating its caste. Its clothing is adapted to its anatomy, accommodating the large spines protruding from its leg and hip area. The use of fur detailing helps evoke the image of a cold-weather ancient warrior, appropriate for life on a chilly steppe. Metallic decorations indicate the creation of art, suggesting intelligence and craftsmanship. The liquid pouch is also a helpful element, showing how the creature has adapted to travel in a dry habitat where water would be sparse.

All these elements of environment, society, and character come together to help make a memorable and unique design. The more specific you can get with your research and ideas, the easier it is to avoid getting caught in tropes.

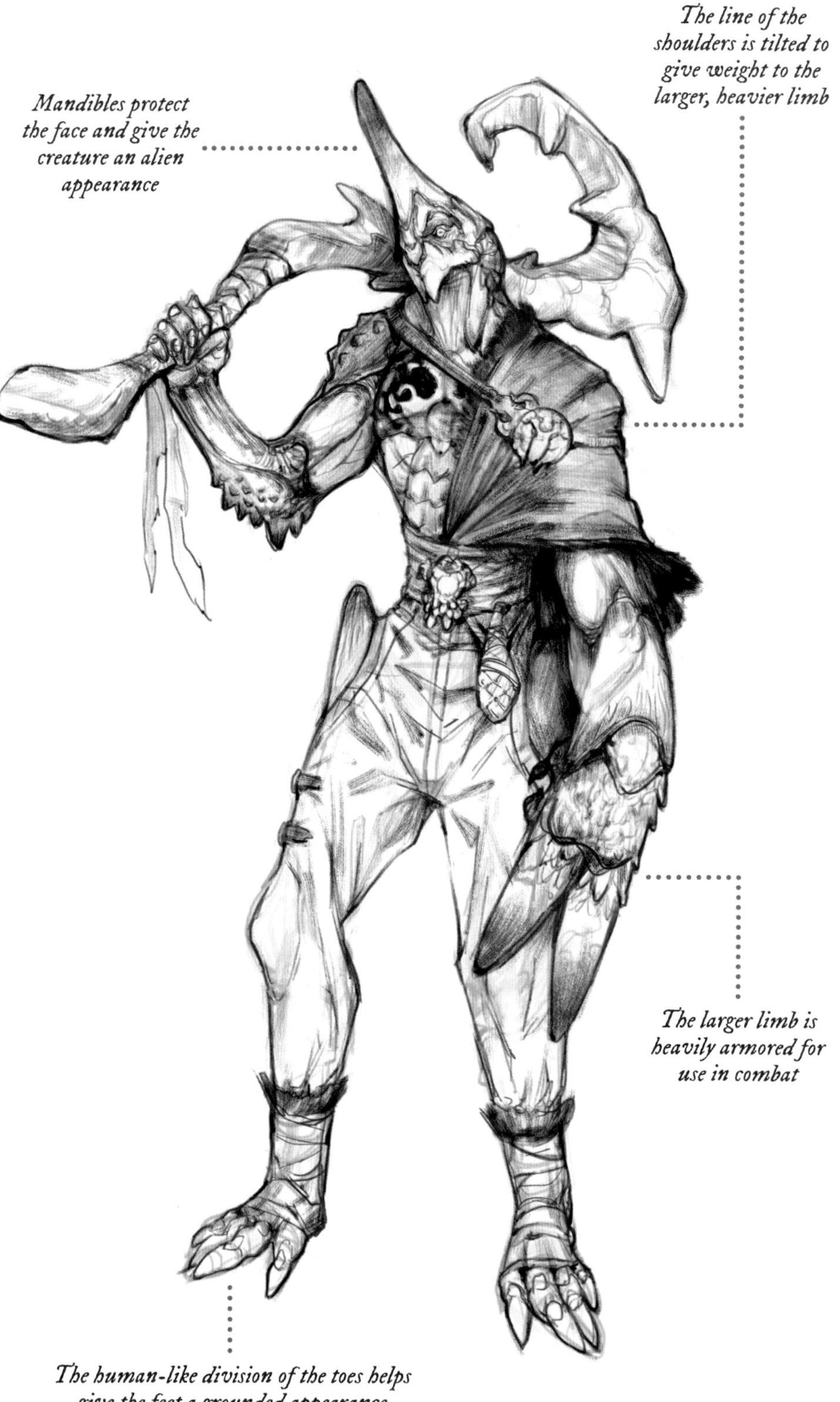

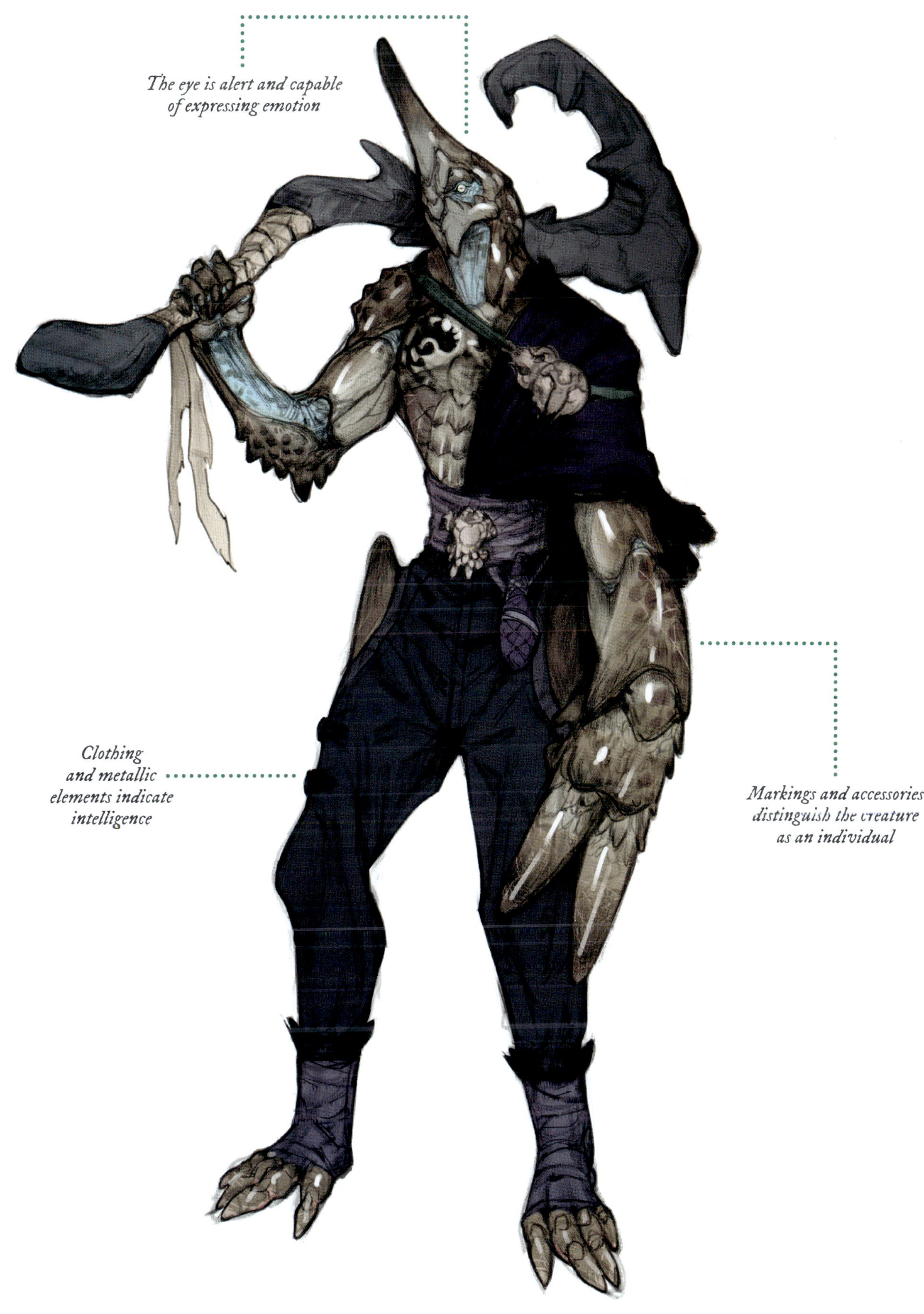

Final image © Oriana Menendez

VARIATIONS

Retainer

Borrowing from the initial thumbnails of the tribal warrior, the retainer variant (shown below) has a lankier build and facial covering, linking it to the queen (see opposite page) and denoting a different social role in the colony. The queens in eusocial insect colonies have individuals to help take care of them, which is where the idea of this retainer comes from. Rather than being a generic worker-type individual, this creature has the specific role of caring for the colony's queen. It is fitting that it has a more mysterious, docile appearance than the warrior.

Juvenile

Juvenile crustaceans often look just like smaller adults, and molt to get bigger, so it is more helpful to look at the proportions of humans for this design. This helps to create a version that reads as a "child," rather than as another species or caste. The design's proportions are the most generalized and basic of the different versions; these young aliens have a bipedal body plan that later specializes into different roles as it grows. The carapace armor has larger gaps between the plates, inspired by the fontanels, or soft spots of the skull, which fuse together as a human baby matures.

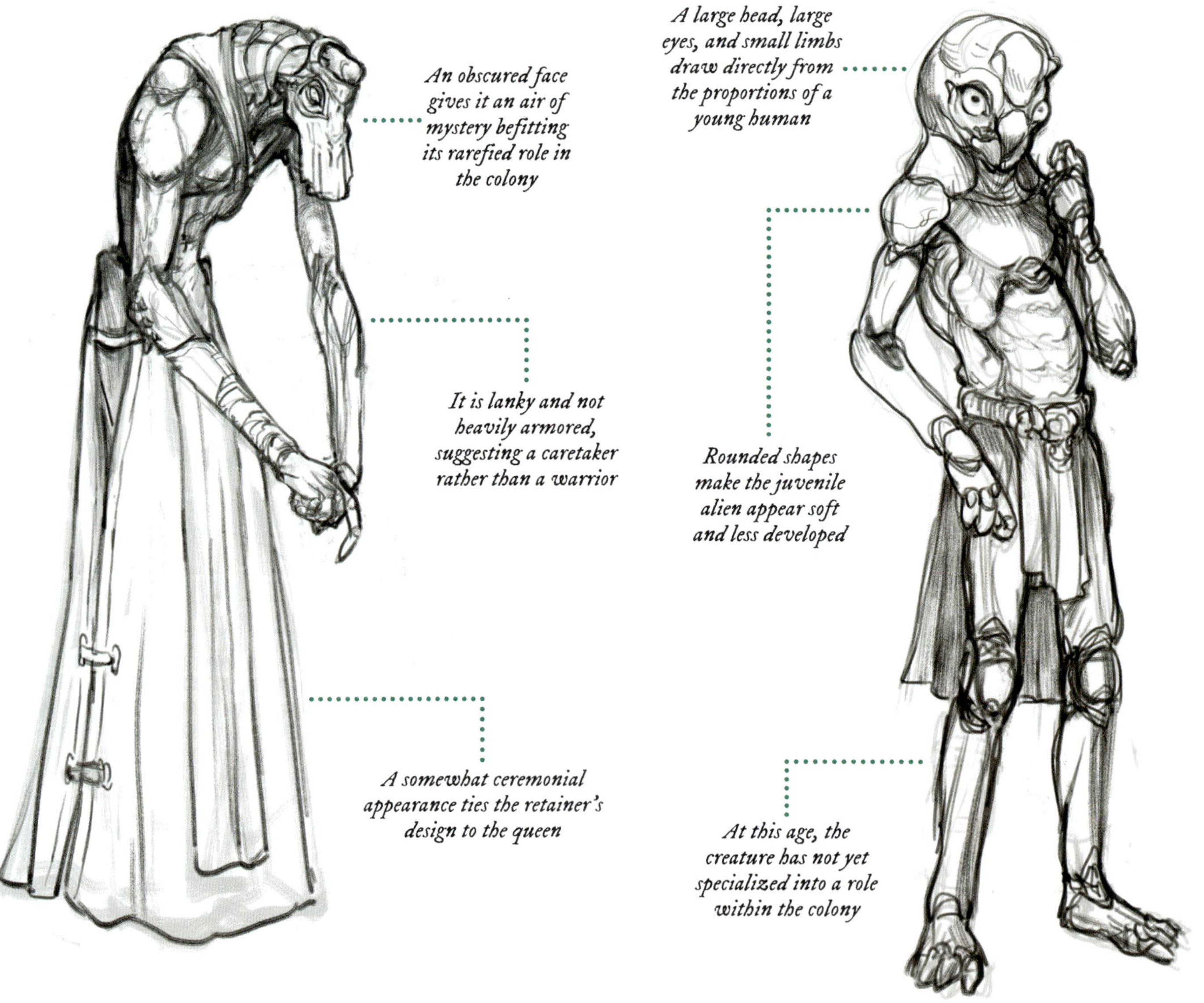

Queen

When designing the different variants, it is only natural to include a queen solely focused on reproduction, as this is a defining characteristic of eusocial animals. Her front pouch and armor are inspired by the segmented abdomens of crabs and snapping shrimp, which are used to hold eggs. Queens are often larger than other members of the colony, so she has a smaller face and hands to help imply that extra size. Her higher social status is also suggested by her ceremonial clothing and authoritative pose.

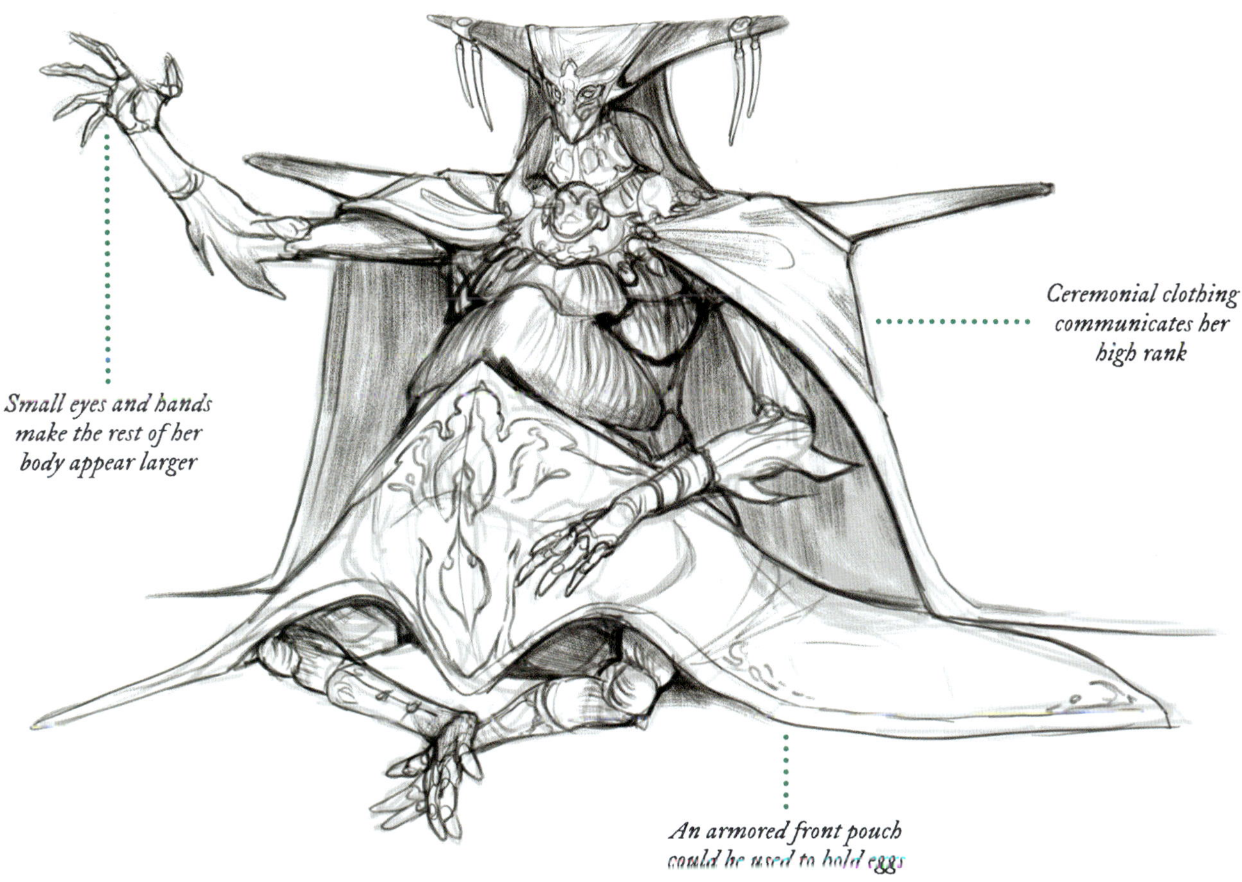

Industry tip

A good way to approach creature design is to extract the core character or personality of the brief and focus on that for the design. A "guarded alien warrior" is what was used for this brief, and it was expanded from there with the details available. It is easier to explore core visual elements once you have these goalposts in mind, as you will always have a rough direction to keep heading toward, even if some attempts are less successful than others.

Interesting elements for design can be found in any part of nature, even if something does not seem immediately relatable. It just takes a little creativity and exploration to push into the weird or unexpected aspects of the natural world - and they make for the most interesting creatures.

Tundra werebear

Edin Durmisevic

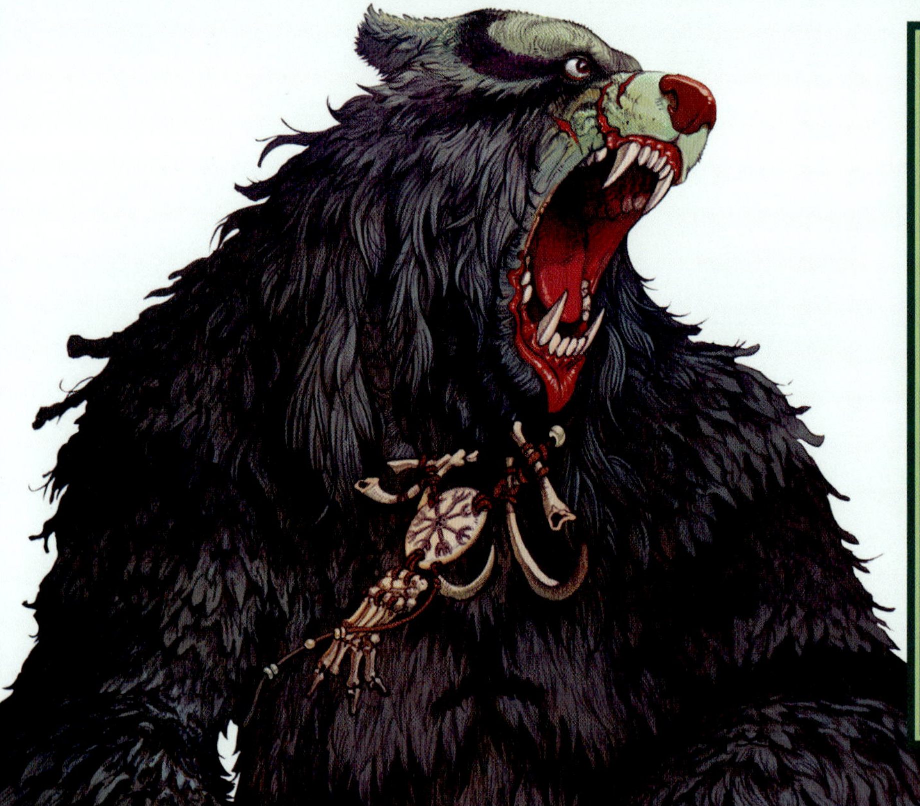

IDEATION

Let us now try incorporating some elements of myth and magic into a design. This werebear will be a mythological type of creature, similar to the traditional concept of a werewolf or "lycanthrope." Were-creatures are humans that have the ability to transform into a kind of animal - in this case, a bear. This creature will have three forms: an ursine form, a human form, and a hybrid form that is bear-like but bipedal with grasping paws.

This design's ursine form will be the main focus of this chapter and will resemble a wild bear, but it must also be a character to some degree, reflecting a human intelligence and spirit. The key to making this design interesting and unique will be successfully blending a human's nature with that of a wild beast. Standing upright on two legs and having a distinct human expression, as well as human accessories and artifacts such as tattoos, body paint, or tribal ornaments, will be a strong approach for this design.

Another way to incorporate more human elements is to think about this creature's human form, then transfer as many design elements as possible from human to bear. For example, if werebears choose to live in isolation, away from other humans, it would be logical for this human to be self-sufficient and close to nature - a kind of hermit, shaman, and hunter. Having these somewhat opposing professions would add more layers to the character: a hermit or shaman suggests wisdom and a spiritual connection with nature, while a hunter demands more physical strength and skill in combat.

This specific werebear lives in a tundra habitat - an open, windy, and rocky environment with low temperatures and no tree cover. All forms of the design should reflect the endurance, resilience, and strength needed to survive in this harsh setting.

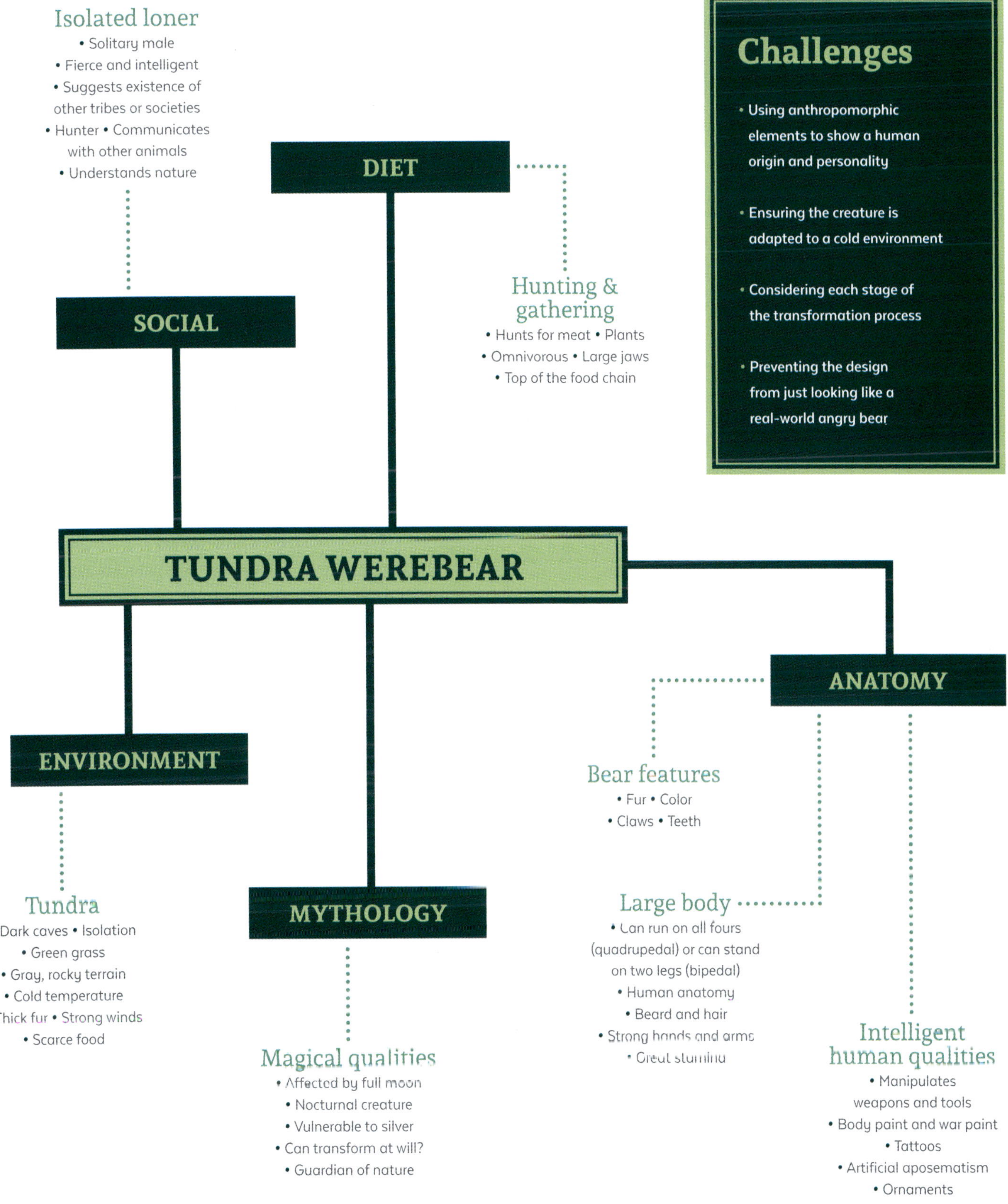

Isolated loner
• Solitary male
• Fierce and intelligent
• Suggests existence of other tribes or societies
• Hunter • Communicates with other animals
• Understands nature

DIET

SOCIAL

Hunting & gathering
• Hunts for meat • Plants
• Omnivorous • Large jaws
• Top of the food chain

Challenges
• Using anthropomorphic elements to show a human origin and personality
• Ensuring the creature is adapted to a cold environment
• Considering each stage of the transformation process
• Preventing the design from just looking like a real-world angry bear

TUNDRA WEREBEAR

ANATOMY

Bear features
• Fur • Color
• Claws • Teeth

ENVIRONMENT

Tundra
• Dark caves • Isolation
• Green grass
• Gray, rocky terrain
• Cold temperature
• Thick fur • Strong winds
• Scarce food

MYTHOLOGY

Large body
• Can run on all fours (quadrupedal) or can stand on two legs (bipedal)
• Human anatomy
• Beard and hair
• Strong hands and arms
• Great stamina

Magical qualities
• Affected by full moon
• Nocturnal creature
• Vulnerable to silver
• Can transform at will?
• Guardian of nature

Intelligent human qualities
• Manipulates weapons and tools
• Body paint and war paint
• Tattoos
• Artificial aposematism
• Ornaments

Anatomy research

Bear

Bears are mammals of the family *Ursidae*. In general, they are carnivores, but they can eat plants too, making them omnivorous. Bears have strong, muscular necks and large heads with powerful jaws. They are quadrupedal but can stand on two legs in specific circumstances, such as for defense and out of curiosity or aggression. This will be an important element of the werebear's design, as this creature needs to be very mobile when on two legs. When standing on two legs, its forelegs and powerful claws will be free for fighting or defense.

Some bears, such as the polar bear and brown or grizzly bear, are huge and powerful animals covered with thick fur, helping them to thrive at low temperatures. Grizzly bear fur is typically brown with darker legs, and commonly white- or blond-tipped on the flank and back.

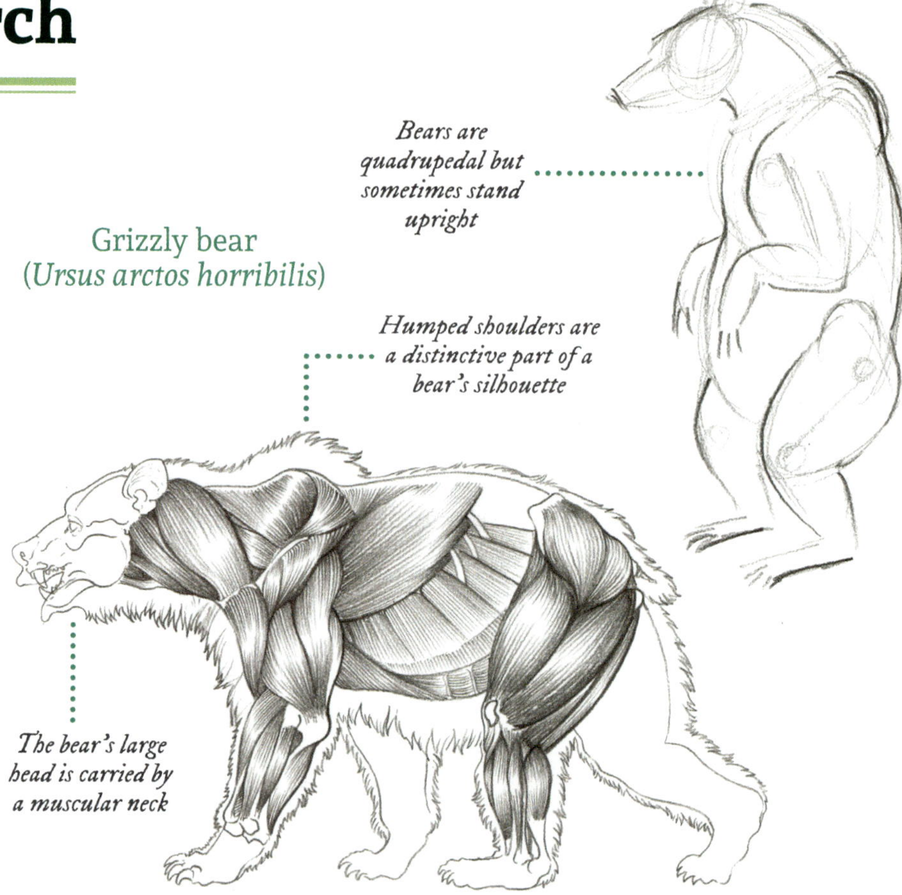

Evolution

Tundra is a very harsh habitat with few or no trees, and few animals. The soil is permanently frozen in temperatures that can reach minus 30 to minus 50 degrees Fahrenheit. Animals that live in tundra usually have small ears and tails, helping them to lose less heat in the cold. Tundra animals such as musk oxen have a double layer of fur to protect them from icy winds. This fur is a combination of a thick undercoat and long hairs, and is dark-colored so the animal can blend with the dark brown, rocky ground. This long fur can sometimes resemble human hair and could be used for our werebear, implying the human origin underneath its ferocious exterior. The longer fur could even be braided, giving an additional human aspect to the character's ursine and hybrid forms.

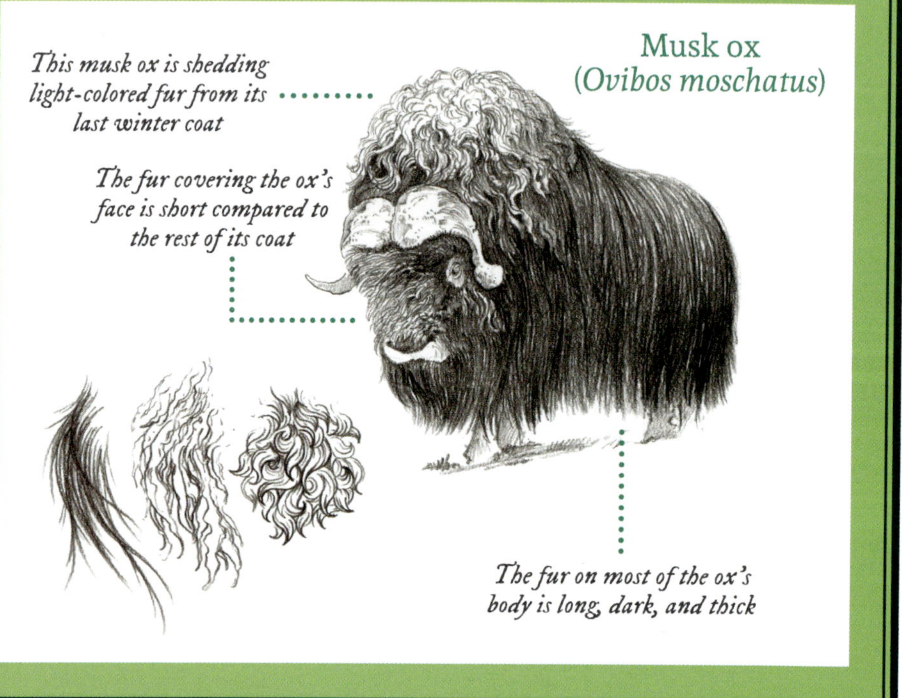

Head & jaws

Bears' heads are massive, usually long with a wide forehead, prominent eyebrow ridges, strong jaw muscles, and broad nostrils. The brown or grizzly bear does not usually bite to kill, so its teeth are more designed for grinding and crunching, aided by large masseter and temporalis muscles. Polar bears are true carnivores that bite to kill their prey, with sharper teeth than a grizzly but a less robust build. The anatomy of the grizzly bear would fit the werebear well, with a high forehead, brows, and concave face that would suit the creature's humanoid intelligence.

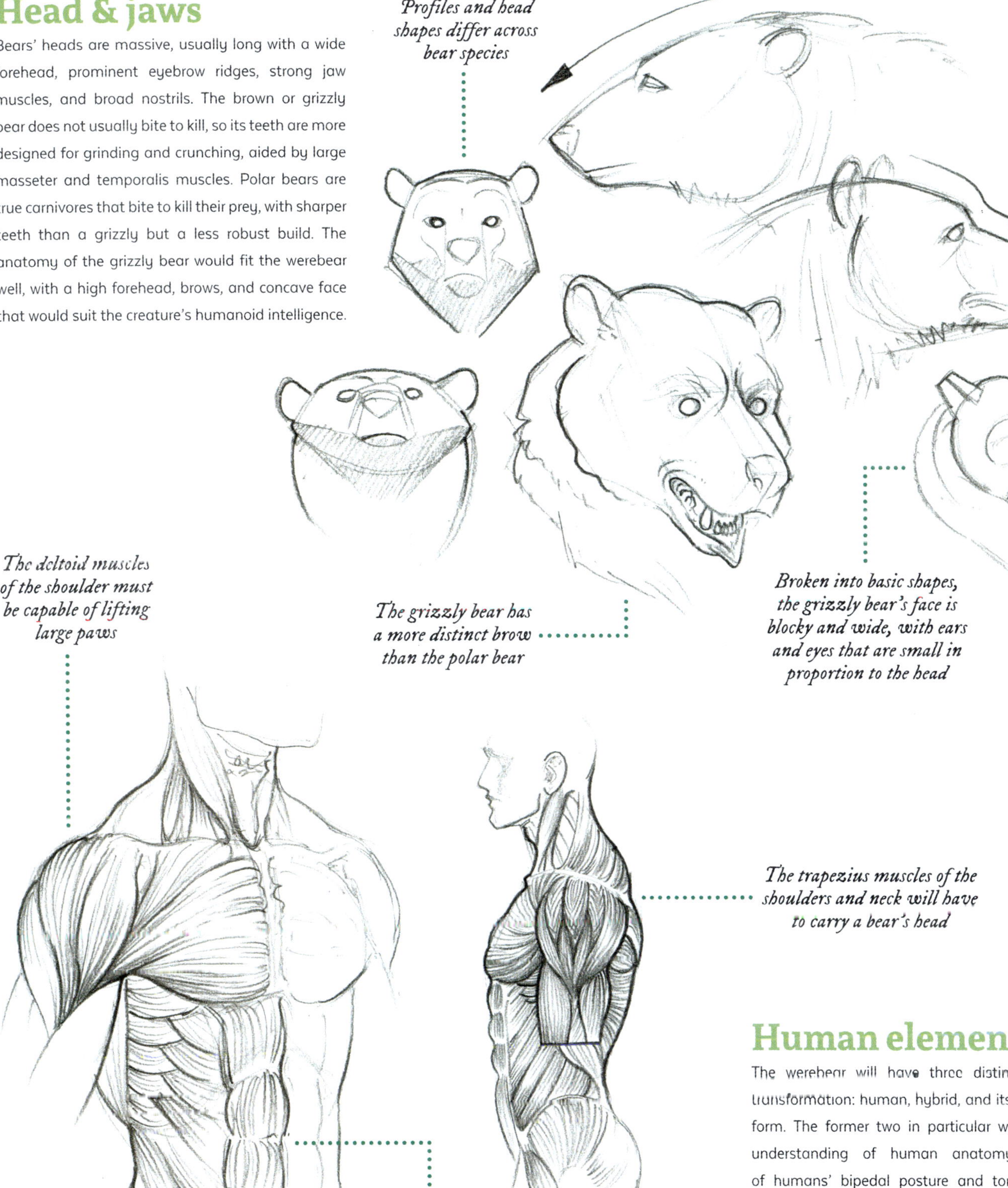

Profiles and head shapes differ across bear species

The deltoid muscles of the shoulder must be capable of lifting large paws

The grizzly bear has a more distinct brow than the polar bear

Broken into basic shapes, the grizzly bear's face is blocky and wide, with ears and eyes that are small in proportion to the head

The trapezius muscles of the shoulders and neck will have to carry a bear's head

Defined rectus abdominis muscles will add a recognizably human aspect to the hybrid werebear's torso

Human elements

The werebear will have three distinct states of transformation: human, hybrid, and its final animal form. The former two in particular will require an understanding of human anatomy, especially of humans' bipedal posture and torso structure. The humanoid elements of the design will be very muscular, with strong deltoids for lifting heavy claws, and large trapezius muscles to connect the human body to the large bear's head in the creature's half-transformed hybrid state.

Functionality research

Communication

Bears usually communicate through body language, vocalization, and different odors. Posture says a lot about a bear's intentions: if standing on its hind legs, it may be curious or warning away a potential combatant. Bears use sounds such as bellowing, grunting, puffing, and teeth-clacking to communicate. As a werebear is a human as well, we can also explore nonverbal human communication through visual means such as tattoos and body art. Traditional tattoos from all around the world have different social meanings, such as indicating a person's social standing, as a means of individual recognition, or even for invoking divine protection in battle. The main inspirations here are tattoos of the Inuit peoples and the Scottish Pict warriors; these tattoos will suggest that this is an individual who once belonged to a social group of similar people.

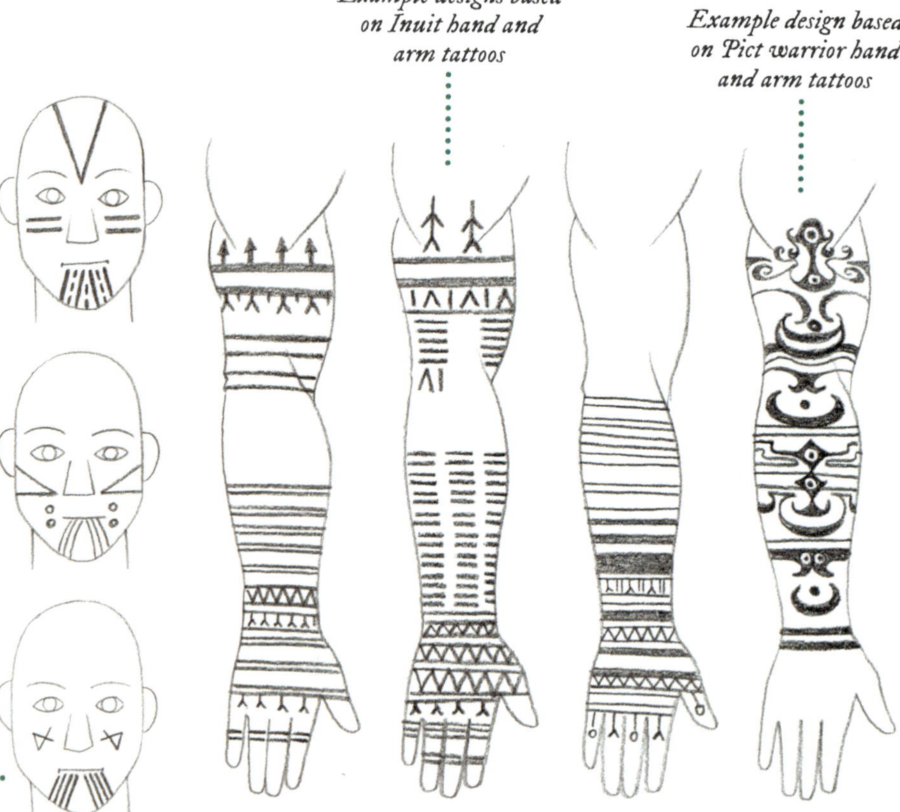

Example designs based on Inuit hand and arm tattoos

Example design based on Pict warrior hand and arm tattoos

Example designs based on Inuit facial tattoos

Movement

The werebear is essentially a quadruped, but needs to be able to move and operate as a bipedal creature. Orangutans, chimpanzees, and especially gorillas are a useful reference point for this. Gorillas are powerful animals that usually walk on all fours, but in some instances use their hind legs to successfully walk short distances. Their legs are short but very strong and muscular. This could be used as a design element of the werebear's hybrid form, giving its hind legs an anatomical structure similar to that of a human. The gluteus maximus (buttock) and muscles of the upper legs could be enlarged in volume to make the creature appear strong and agile.

Bears, like humans and other large primates, have plantigrade feet that stand flat on the ground, and sometimes stand in the iconic upright pose that will be familiar to most viewers. This ability will help reinforce the idea that the werebear can walk upright like a human.

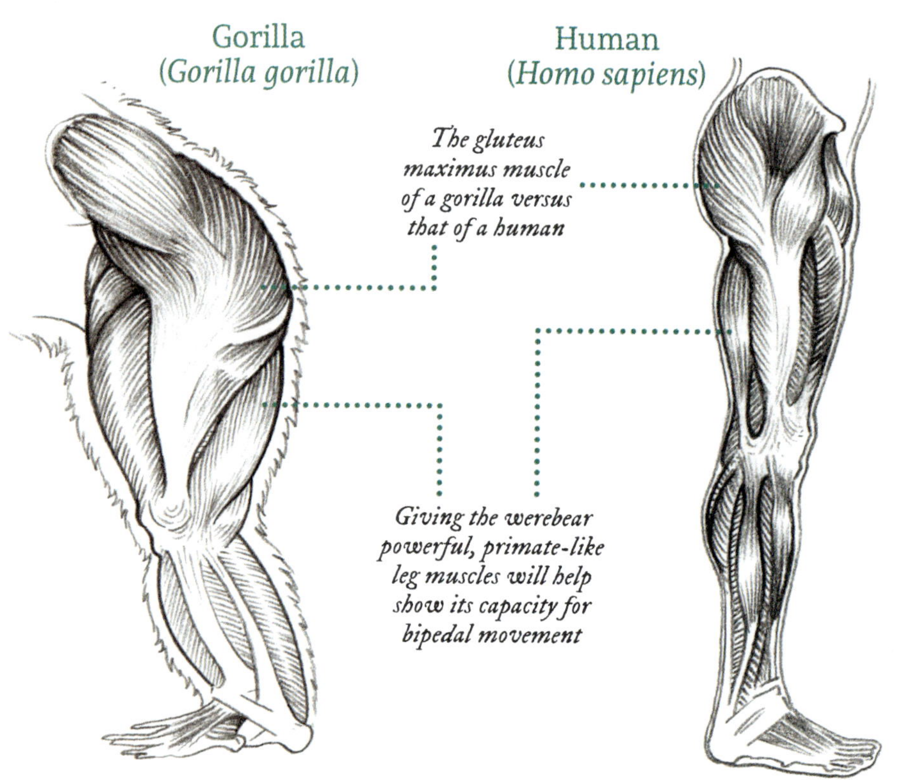

Gorilla
(*Gorilla gorilla*)

Human
(*Homo sapiens*)

The gluteus maximus muscle of a gorilla versus that of a human

Giving the werebear powerful, primate-like leg muscles will help show its capacity for bipedal movement

Combined features

Were-creatures are usually presented in mythology and folklore as aggressive and bloodthirsty, but this creature must incorporate other qualities that show an element of human wit and awareness. The creature's human form is a spiritually enlightened person with a great connection to nature; he understands plants, protects other animals, and loves the wilderness, only tapping into his ursine strength during the full moon or times of need. This would create an engaging contrast with the fearsome appearance of the hybrid and bear forms, adding depth and narrative to the character's nature. Combining the expressive face and domed skull of a human with the heavy head of more wild or primal mammal could achieve this.

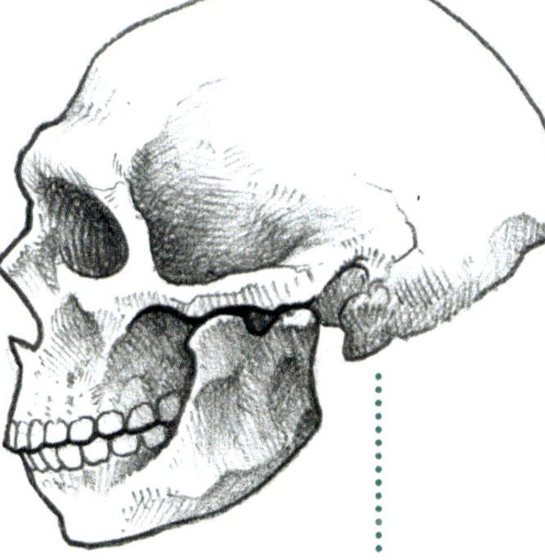

The human skull is rounded to house a large, intelligent brain, but will be too small and fragile for most of the werebear's forms

A Neanderthal skull could provide good reference for a more primal, heavyset human

A bear skull has a long muzzle with powerful jaws and teeth

Patterns

This werebear would be a creature at the top of the food chain - an intelligent hunter and a capable warrior in any form, not necessarily reliant on camouflage. If a werebear's fur color is derived from the hair colors (and even textures) of its human form, werebears could come in many colors ranging from white to dark. This individual could have long, dark brown hair, or a color such as black that would be uncommon among non-magical bears.

As explored earlier, this werebear will have tattoos - an important detail that establishes a direct human connection between its three forms. Icelandic magical staves could be a reference here, as they are purported to have great symbolic meaning and magical power.

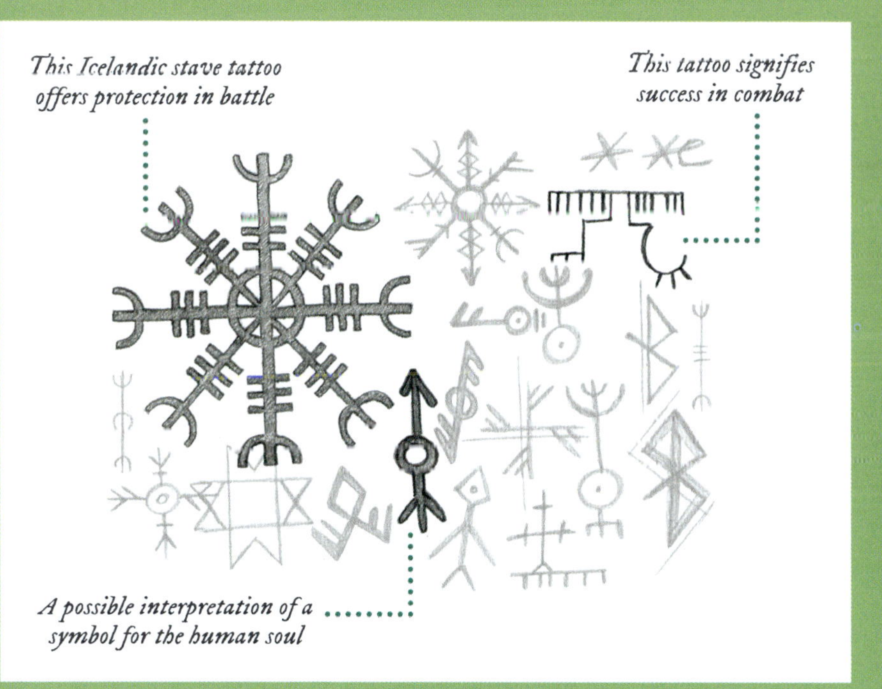

This Icelandic stave tattoo offers protection in battle

This tattoo signifies success in combat

A possible interpretation of a symbol for the human soul

Thumbnails

Werebears would fall under the same category as lycanthropes and other were-creatures - humans that transform into animals during the full moon. This adds some challenges to the design process, as we need to portray a familiar, realistic animal that is in some way special or magical, with a clear connection to its original human form.

One way of approaching this design is by thinking about the human and animal forms at the same time. We know from the brief that the bear form will exhibit human traits like standing on two legs, with visible tattoos or some other color patterns. The werebear's arms should be muscular, with strong shoulders, and hands or paws with long, powerful claws for offense and defense. These arms could be tattooed or painted with tribal patterns and colors. The werebear's head, based on a grizzly's, would be wide and heavy with a distinct brow. Longer fur on the back of the head and neck would transfer a humanoid element to the bear form, possibly with a human hairstyle such as braids.

In these thumbnails, I try to represent a large, strong warrior creature that might still possess a gentle, more human side. Blocky shapes make the werebear look heavy and powerful, capable of both aggression and a solid defense that fits its protective nature.

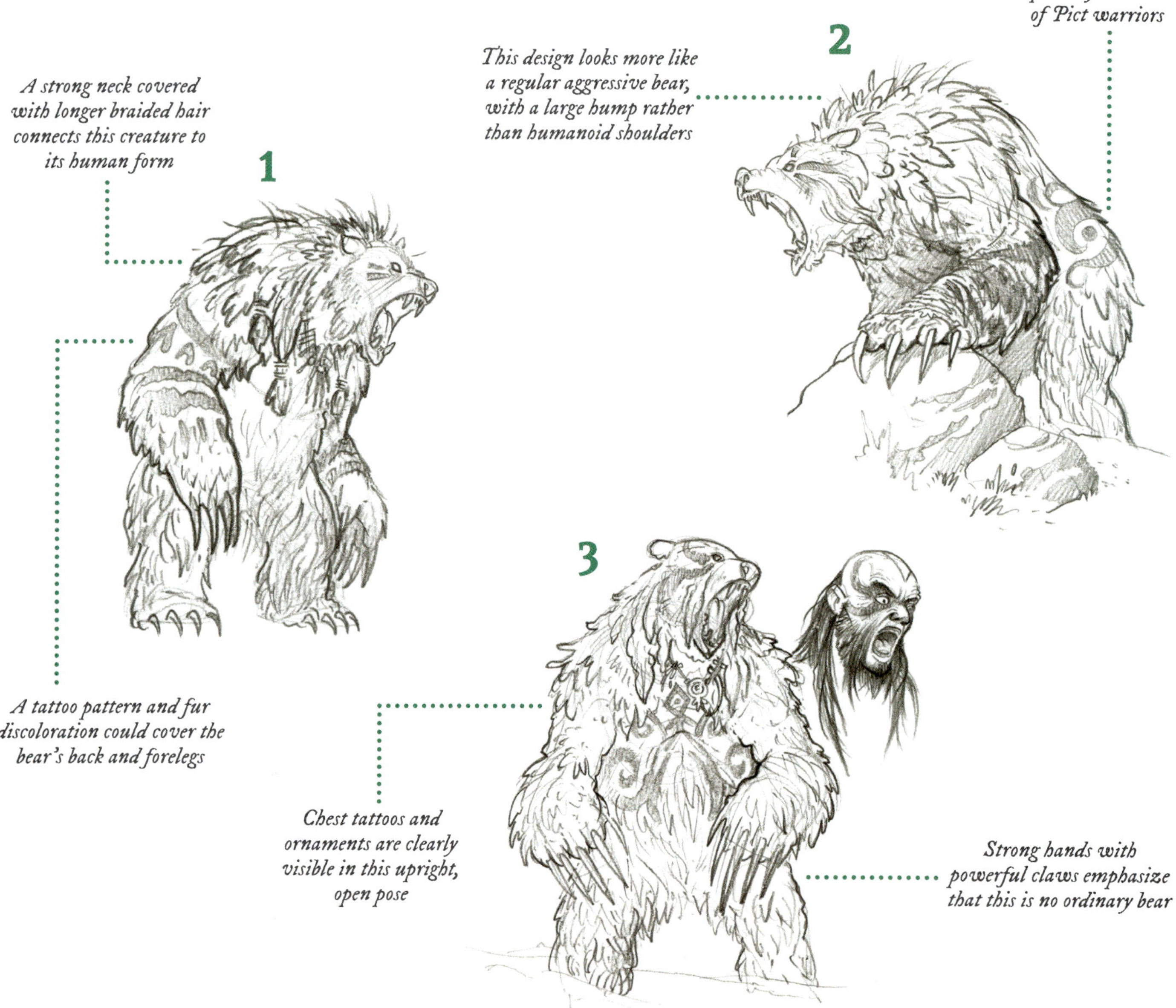

A strong neck covered with longer braided hair connects this creature to its human form

This design looks more like a regular aggressive bear, with a large hump rather than humanoid shoulders

An ornamental tattoo covers the bear's back, inspired by the tattoos of Pict warriors

A tattoo pattern and fur discoloration could cover the bear's back and forelegs

Chest tattoos and ornaments are clearly visible in this upright, open pose

Strong hands with powerful claws emphasize that this is no ordinary bear

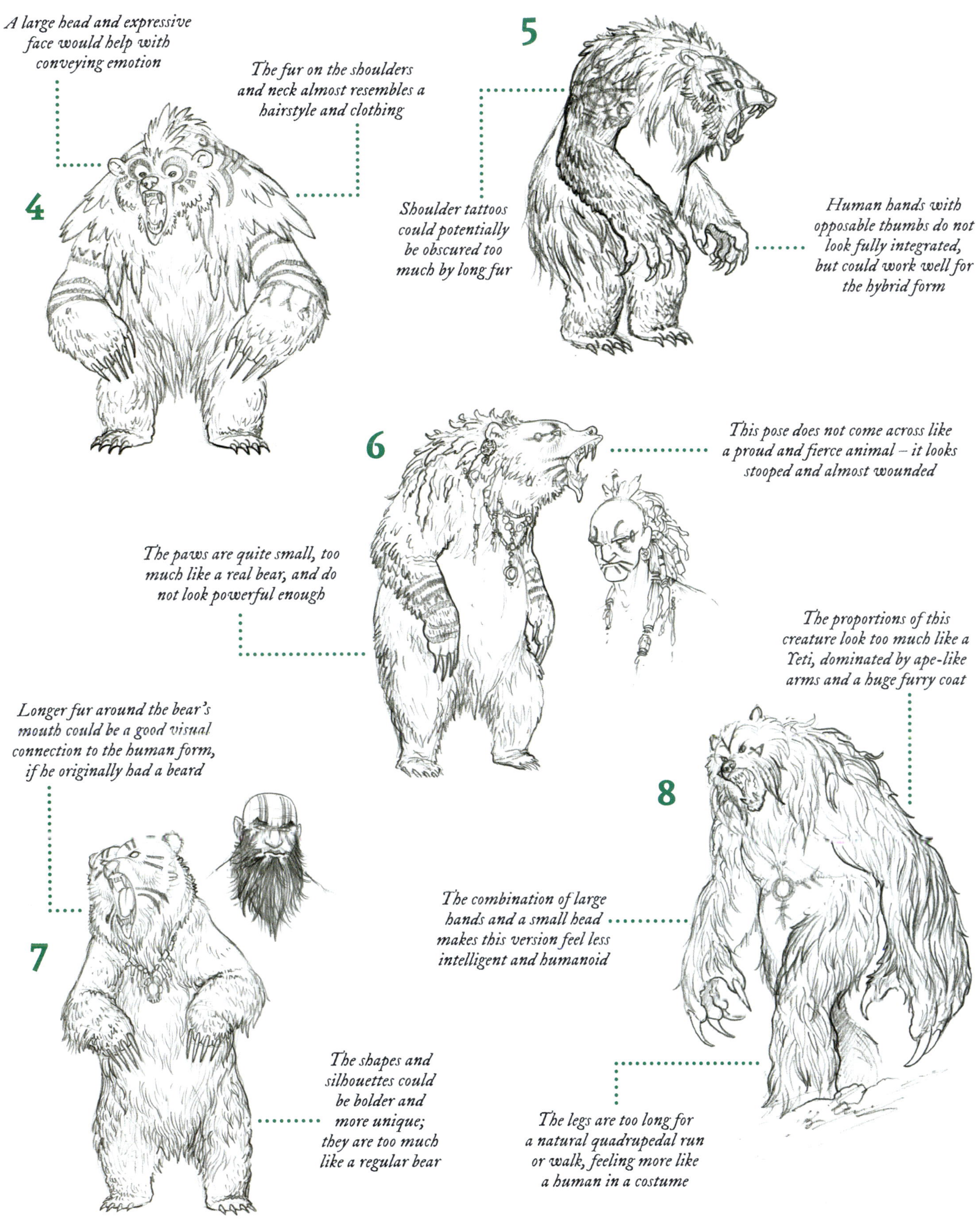
A large head and expressive face would help with conveying emotion
The fur on the shoulders and neck almost resembles a hairstyle and clothing
4
5
Shoulder tattoos could potentially be obscured too much by long fur
Human hands with opposable thumbs do not look fully integrated, but could work well for the hybrid form
6
This pose does not come across like a proud and fierce animal – it looks stooped and almost wounded
The paws are quite small, too much like a real bear, and do not look powerful enough
The proportions of this creature look too much like a Yeti, dominated by ape-like arms and a huge furry coat
Longer fur around the bear's mouth could be a good visual connection to the human form, if he originally had a beard
8
The combination of large hands and a small head makes this version feel less intelligent and humanoid
7
The shapes and silhouettes could be bolder and more unique; they are too much like a regular bear
The legs are too long for a natural quadrupedal run or walk, feeling more like a human in a costume

DEVELOPMENT

The thumbnail explorations for this creature were mainly guided by its original human form, so the design would not lose sight of that human intelligence, awareness, and movement. In the chosen concept, mixing elements of thumbnails 1 and 3, we can see a powerful beast capable of inflicting serious damage. At the same time, its posture is defensive and reserved, with lowered claws, as if it is only warning off a potential enemy rather than charging to attack.

The werebear's size and upright stance communicate that this creature is powerful and alert. Its large claws and muscular body are great natural weapons, and the addition of war paint would be a good sign for enemies to stay away. The war paint mimics the warning markings often found on real-world dangerous animals, and also hints at the creature's human narrative.

The biggest challenge of this design is in creating something that looks like a beast but is not just a real-world angry bear. Personal ornaments, such as a necklace and tattoos, tell the story of a proud warrior and a protector of nature. They also imply a connection with some kind of society, even if this individual lives in isolation. These details will intrigue the viewer, encouraging them to question who this creature is and how it lives. The human and hybrid forms would wear clothes and be capable of carrying more weapons and accessories.

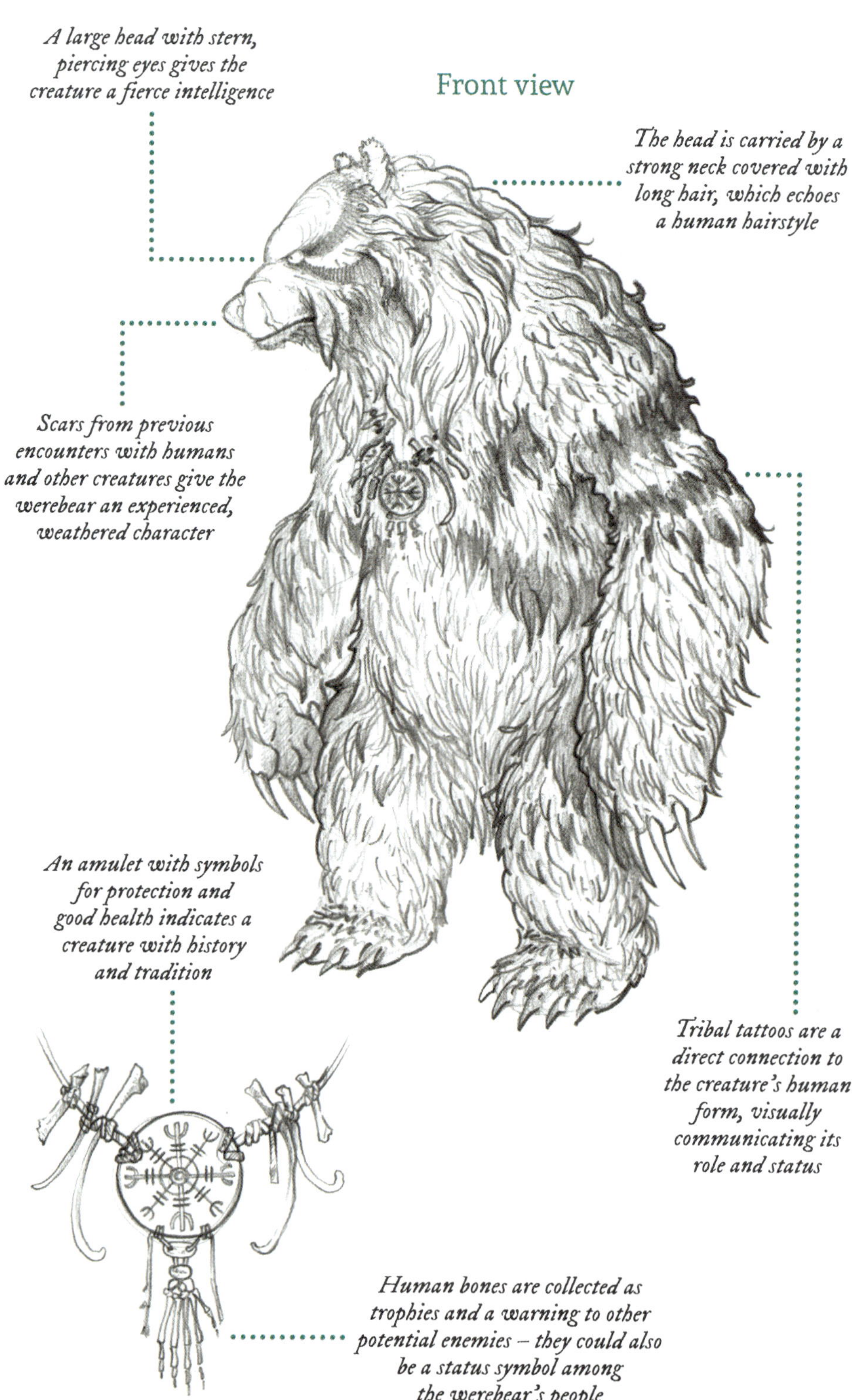

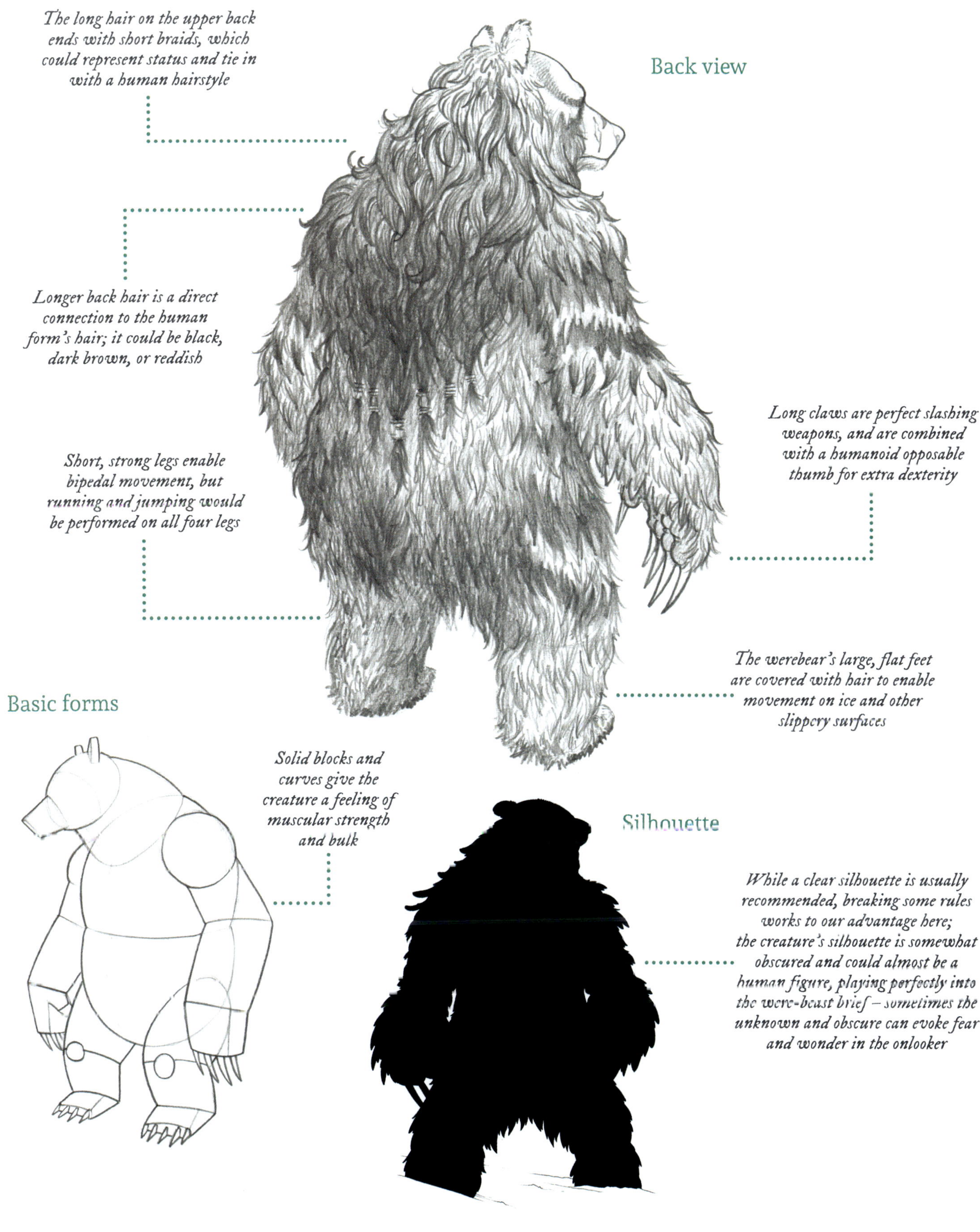

Back view

The long hair on the upper back ends with short braids, which could represent status and tie in with a human hairstyle

Longer back hair is a direct connection to the human form's hair; it could be black, dark brown, or reddish

Short, strong legs enable bipedal movement, but running and jumping would be performed on all four legs

Long claws are perfect slashing weapons, and are combined with a humanoid opposable thumb for extra dexterity

The werebear's large, flat feet are covered with hair to enable movement on ice and other slippery surfaces

Basic forms

Solid blocks and curves give the creature a feeling of muscular strength and bulk

Silhouette

While a clear silhouette is usually recommended, breaking some rules works to our advantage here; the creature's silhouette is somewhat obscured and could almost be a human figure, playing perfectly into the were-beast brief — sometimes the unknown and obscure can evoke fear and wonder in the onlooker

Poses

Think about the actions and poses that are natural, organic, and iconic to your creature design. The anatomy and nature of your creature will affect the range of actions it can perform and look believable doing. This werebear is a massive and powerful creature that is not able to perform rapid and flexible movements. It is tough, muscular, and somewhat rigid, so would move in a deliberate, calculated manner. This does not mean it is lazy or low-energy, but its actions would instead need to emphasize its explosive energy and strength.

Pose A illustrates the werebear in mid-run. Though the creature is designed to have some bipedal capability, running on all fours looks more animalistic and menacing. A gorilla or grizzly bear attack was in mind when developing this pose; studying these animals in motion, for example in videos, will help you capture that power and strength.

Pose B shows an upright, bipedal attack stance with aggressive claws. To accentuate the force and power of an action pose, you need to focus on a gesture and push it a little over the top to fully convey its energy and movement, as you can see in the dramatic, foreshortened paws.

Pose C explores the more complex human aspects of the creature, with a softer expression and a gently curious posture. An additional portrait sketch shows the potential for expressiveness in the werebear's eyes, though these do not fully convey how powerful and intimidating the creature can be.

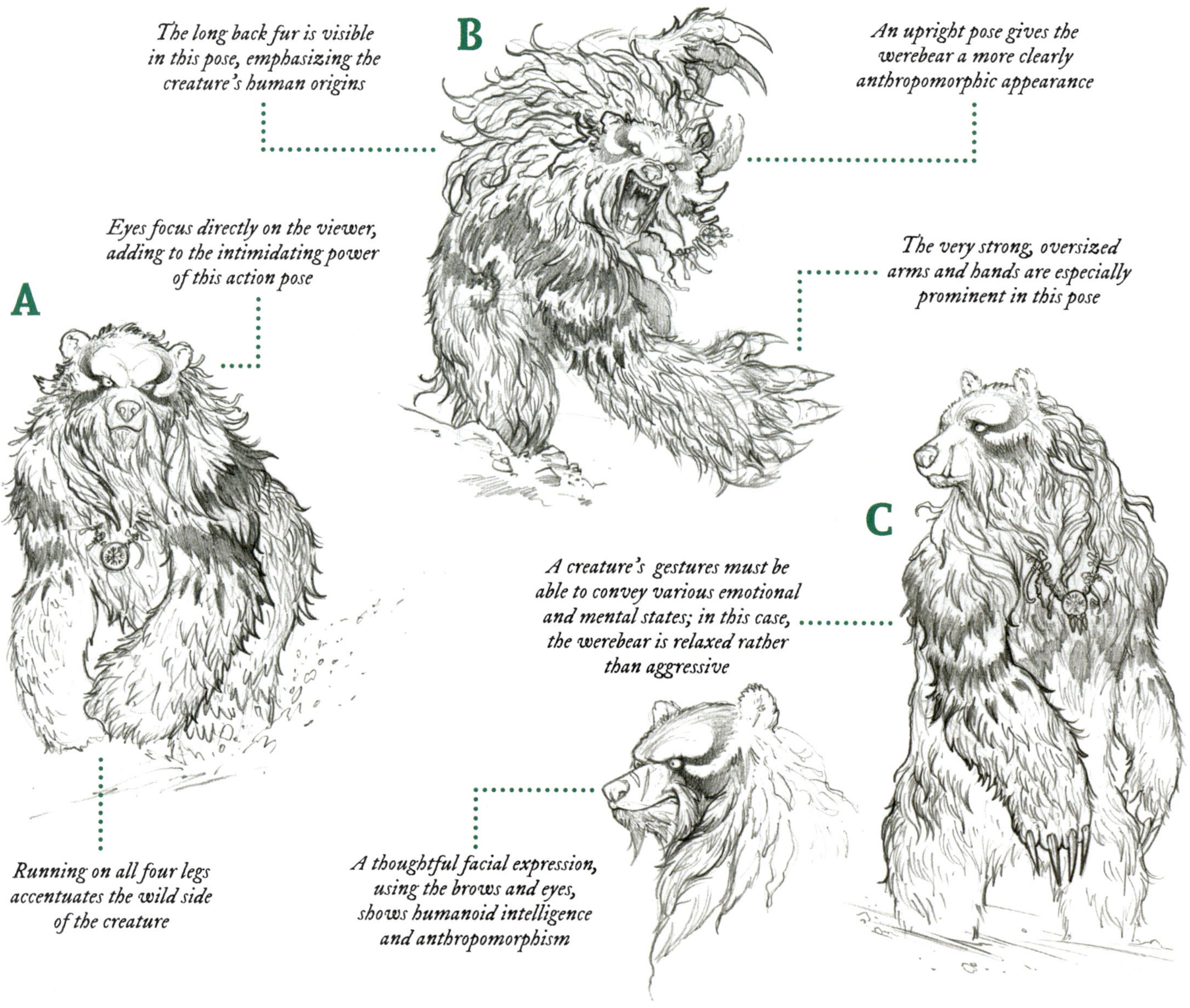

The long back fur is visible in this pose, emphasizing the creature's human origins

B

An upright pose gives the werebear a more clearly anthropomorphic appearance

Eyes focus directly on the viewer, adding to the intimidating power of this action pose

A

The very strong, oversized arms and hands are especially prominent in this pose

C

A creature's gestures must be able to convey various emotional and mental states; in this case, the werebear is relaxed rather than aggressive

Running on all four legs accentuates the wild side of the creature

A thoughtful facial expression, using the brows and eyes, shows humanoid intelligence and anthropomorphism

Color & pattern

The natural color of real bears ranges from white polar bears to dark brown bears, to the combined black and white of panda bears. This werebear lives on the open tundra plains, which will affect our choice of color palette. A combination of greens and grays would help the creature belong to an environment of grass and low vegetation. Camouflage for defense and protection would not play a big factor here, and, as the creature is able to hunt in any form, we can use colors less conducive to stealth. Its fur color would need to have some resemblance to the hair or beard of the werebear's human form.

Werebears in any of their forms can communicate with other werebears and humans through ornamental symbols, tattoos, and paint, so the colors of those elements must be considered in relation to the overall fur color.

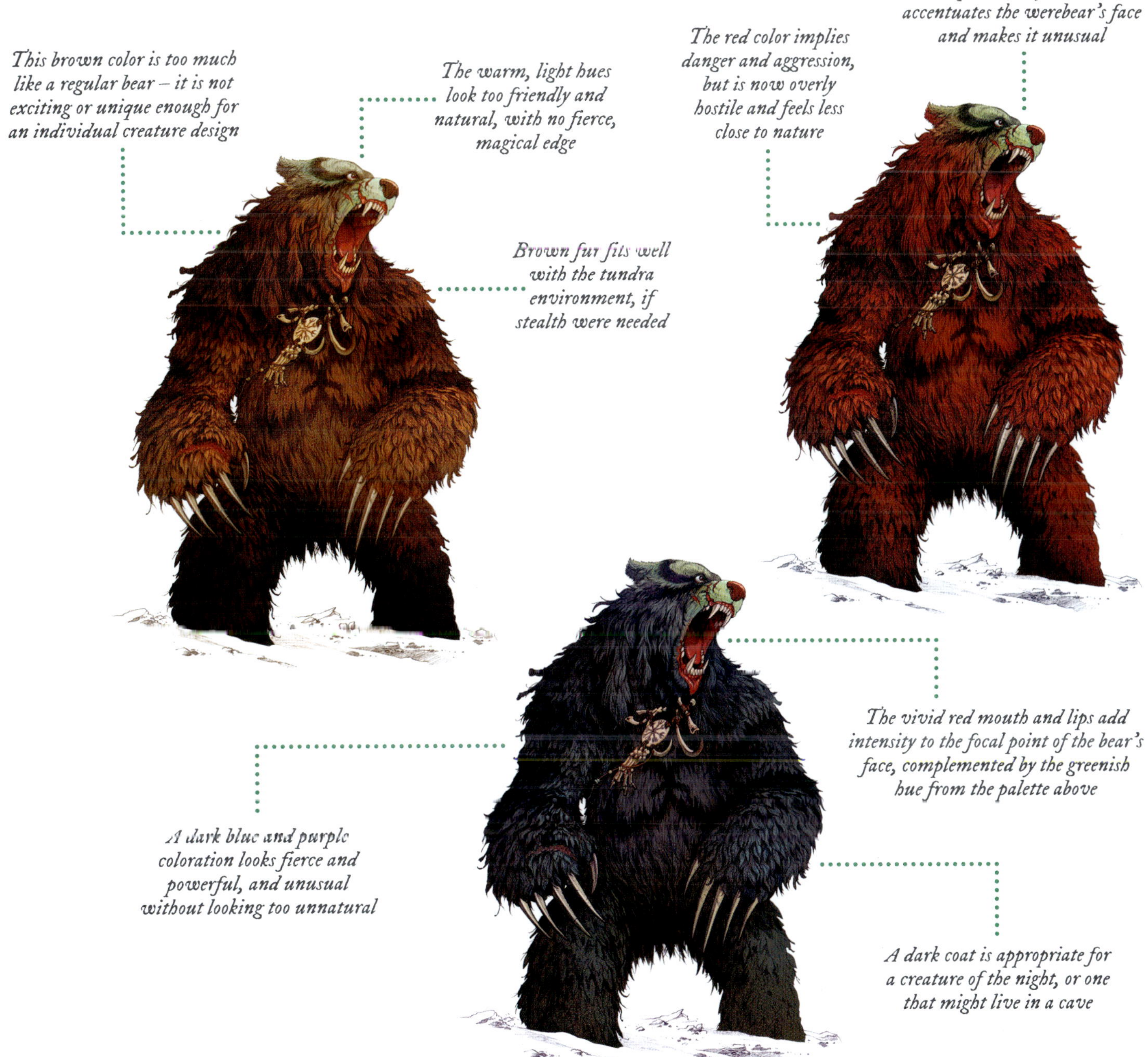

This brown color is too much like a regular bear – it is not exciting or unique enough for an individual creature design

The warm, light hues look too friendly and natural, with no fierce, magical edge

Brown fur fits well with the tundra environment, if stealth were needed

The red color implies danger and aggression, but is now overly hostile and feels less close to nature

A complementary green color accentuates the werebear's face and makes it unusual

The vivid red mouth and lips add intensity to the focal point of the bear's face, complemented by the greenish hue from the palette above

A dark blue and purple coloration looks fierce and powerful, and unusual without looking too unnatural

A dark coat is appropriate for a creature of the night, or one that might live in a cave

FINAL DESIGN

The final design represents a being of human intelligence transformed into a powerful and potentially destructive force of nature. It takes a familiar animal from nature and pushes it to the extreme, accentuating its strength and power. Elements of anthropomorphization, such as the tattoos, paint, and focused humanoid eye, establish that this beast is more than a typical bear. Details such as the human bone necklace give a clue as to the huge size of the creature, as well as to its intelligence by showing it has aesthetic taste and interest in status symbols. The dark blue-gray color palette, with contrasting colors and war paint for the head, makes a visual impact and distances the creature from a regular bear.

This design is tied in closely with the creature's other two forms, which can be seen on the next pages. The details and relationships between the human and bear elements of each design can be appreciated more fully when the three are considered together.

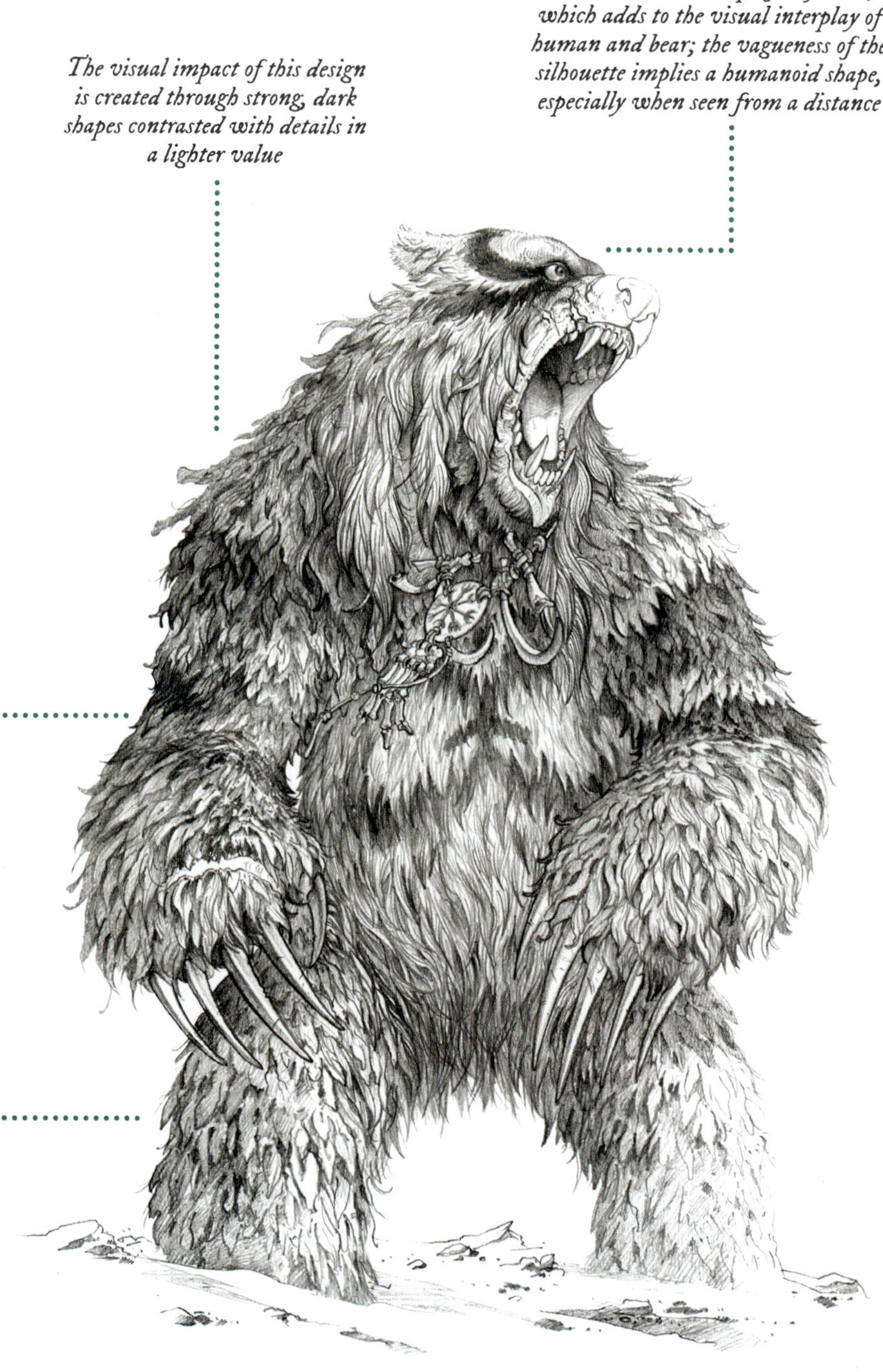

The visual impact of this design is created through strong, dark shapes contrasted with details in a lighter value

The silhouette is not perfectly clear, which adds to the visual interplay of human and bear; the vagueness of the silhouette implies a humanoid shape, especially when seen from a distance

Though there is some movement in this design, the relative restraint of the pose adds to the werebear's sense of immense strength and contained power

The scale of the werebear is defined by the human bones on its necklace, which seem small and thin compared to the creature

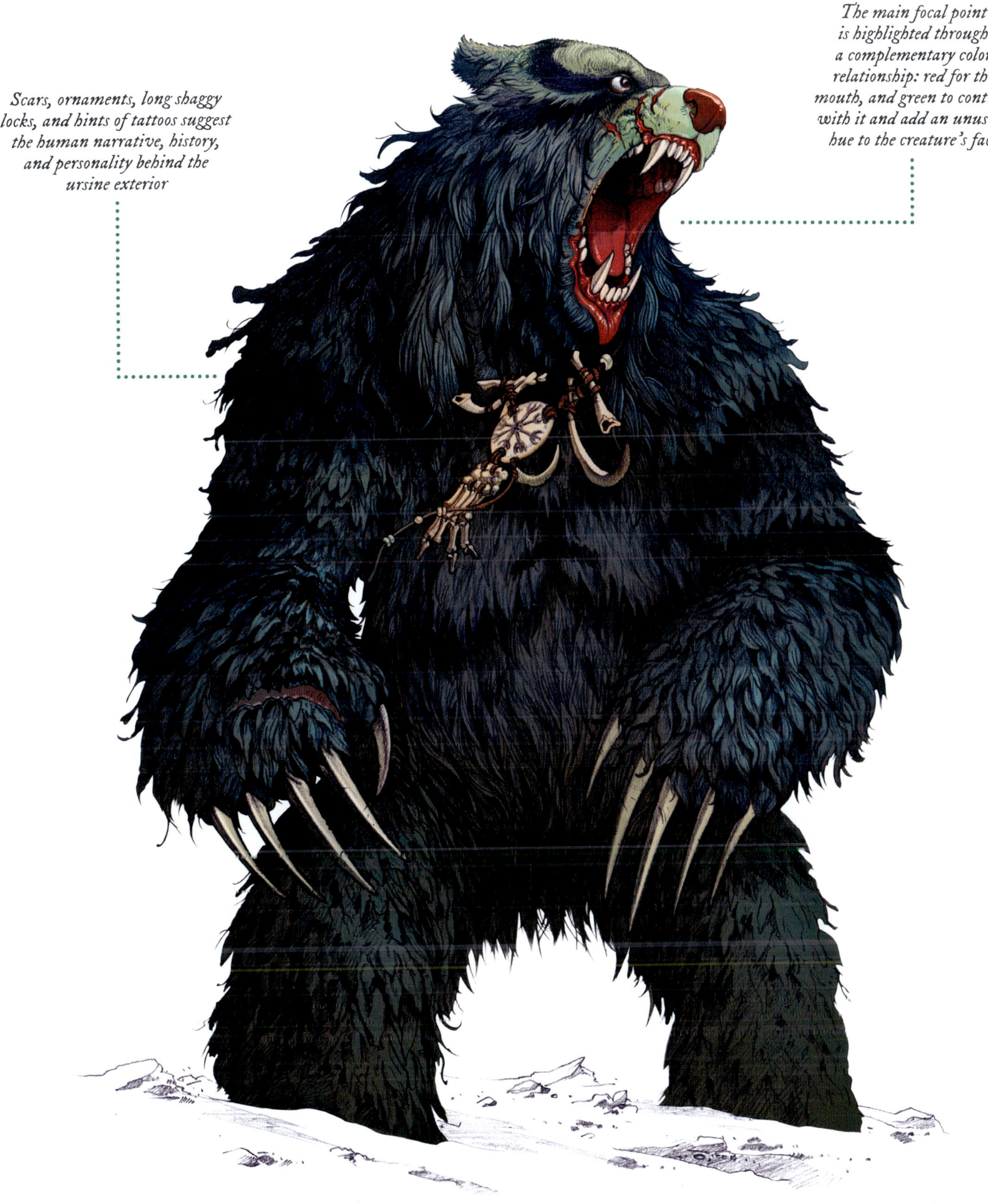

Final image © Edin Durmisevic

TRANSFORMATIONS

Human state

The werebear's human form has been an essential subject to consider when developing the creature's final animal form, as all of its humanoid qualities derive from this. In its human form, the bear is a character used to living in very harsh conditions. Due to the permafrost (permanently frozen ground) of the tundra, agriculture would not be a part of this man's lifestyle. Instead, he would be a fierce hunter, living off the scarce animal life, and perhaps foraging for plants with his keen understanding of local flora and their properties.

He is clad in warm animal furs and a long tunic, including bear-paw boots that hint at his later transformation. These handmade clothes, sewn from natural materials, show his closeness to nature and protect him from freezing temperatures. Clothing such as capes and tunics would also be easy to remove when shapeshifting. His tribal tattoos and markings are easily visible here, indicating his status in a wider community, though his equipment suggests a lone wanderer who enjoys a solitary life.

A long, warm fur cape protects the werebear's human form from low temperatures and constant freezing wind

Tribal tattoos represent his status and cultural heritage, in a form of visual communication both to the viewer and to other beings in the character's world

The bag would be used for collecting different herbs and rare plants found on the tundra, showing a less combative side to the character

Mid-transformation

This hybrid form of the werebear is a partially transformed state between human and animal, which could be a form the character adopts at will. The creature has a large bear's head and powerful, heavily furred hands with opposable humanoid thumbs, allowing it to carry weapons and objects. The legs are short but strong with large claws, and allow the werebear to walk bipedally. It is capable of moving and living like a human, but its enormous strength allows it to use heavy weapons with ease. Like the fully human form, it wears clothing and trophies made from animal pelts and bones, and its areas of bare skin show a humanoid torso posture and predilection for tattoos.

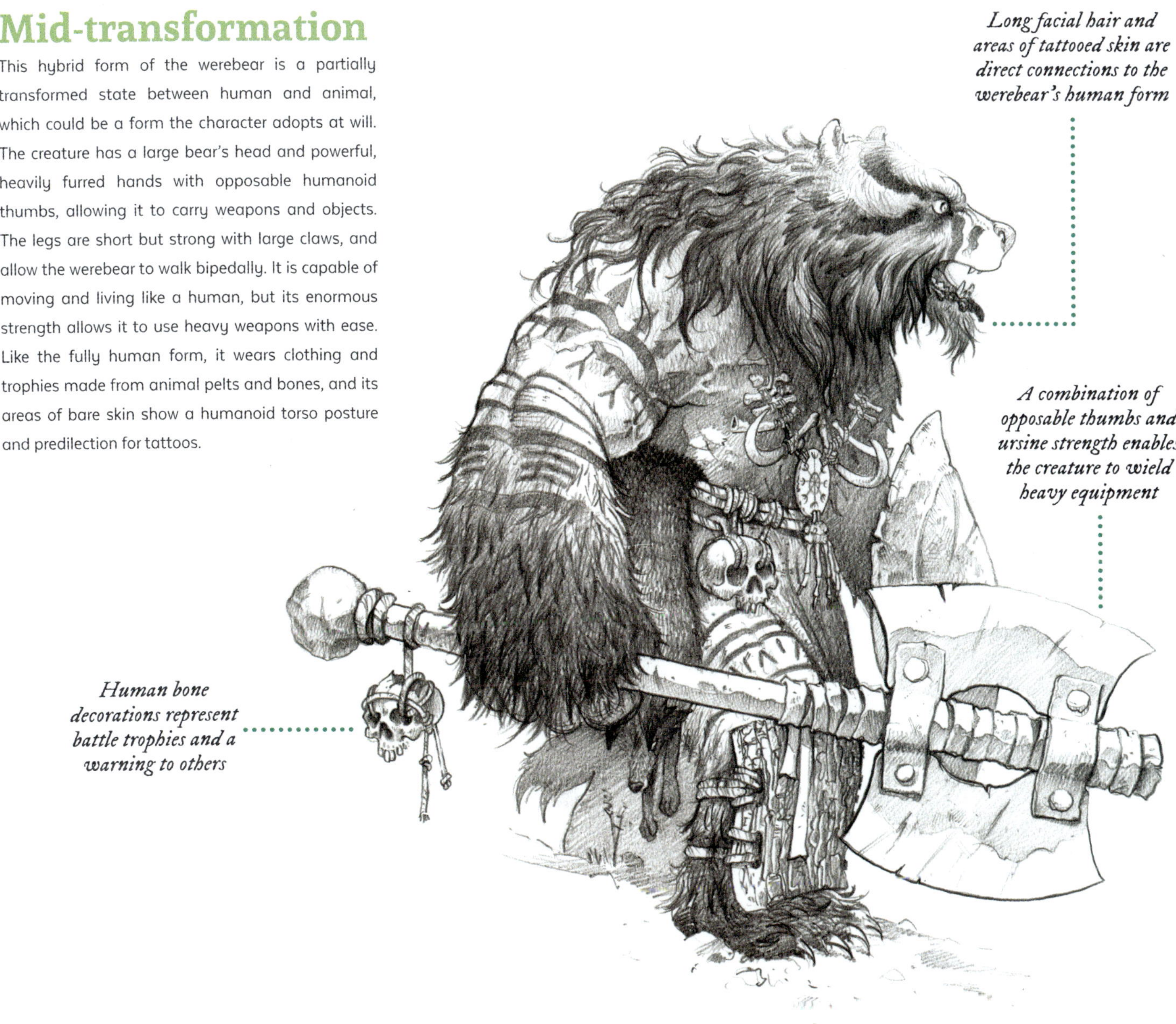

Industry tip

To create an interesting and believable creature design, or any design, you need to develop your "creative muscle." Be brave and think of strange, even outrageous combinations of different elements. Knowledge of the animal world, plant world, psychology, anatomy, and nature in general will always be helpful to you as a creature designer. In my experience, the most important thing is to be brave. Take your sketchbook with you everywhere you go, and be like a child exploring the world for the first time.

People are usually impressed by technique, and it is important in some ways, but the most important thing is the idea and the creative process. Do not overthink "style," as this is something that will come naturally with time. Instead, learn the essence of good design. Do not hold back from making "bad" creative choices - everything you do is an experience that will guide you on the journey of creativity.

Gallery

Swamp critter

Ken Barthelmey

Research

Exploration

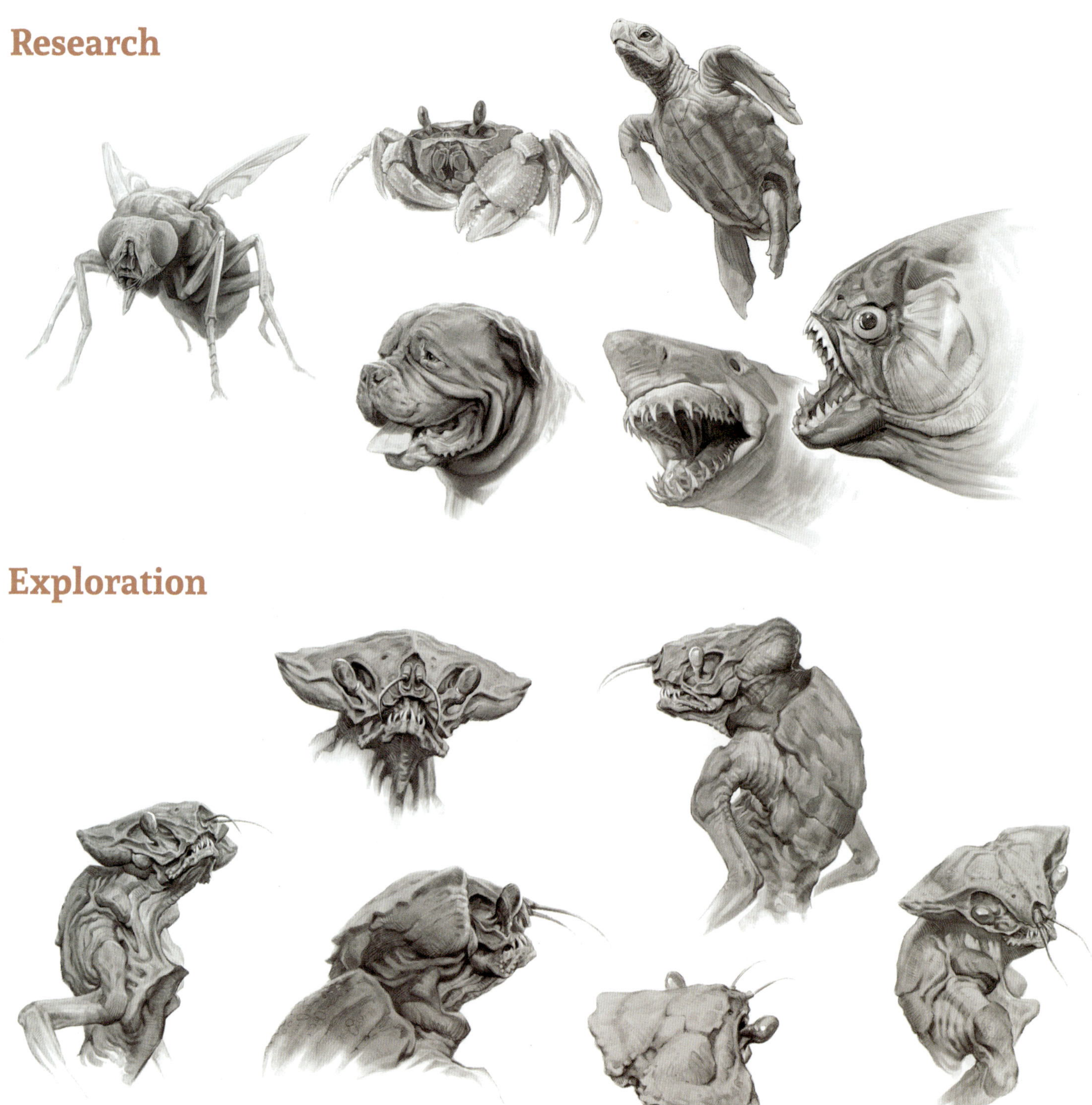

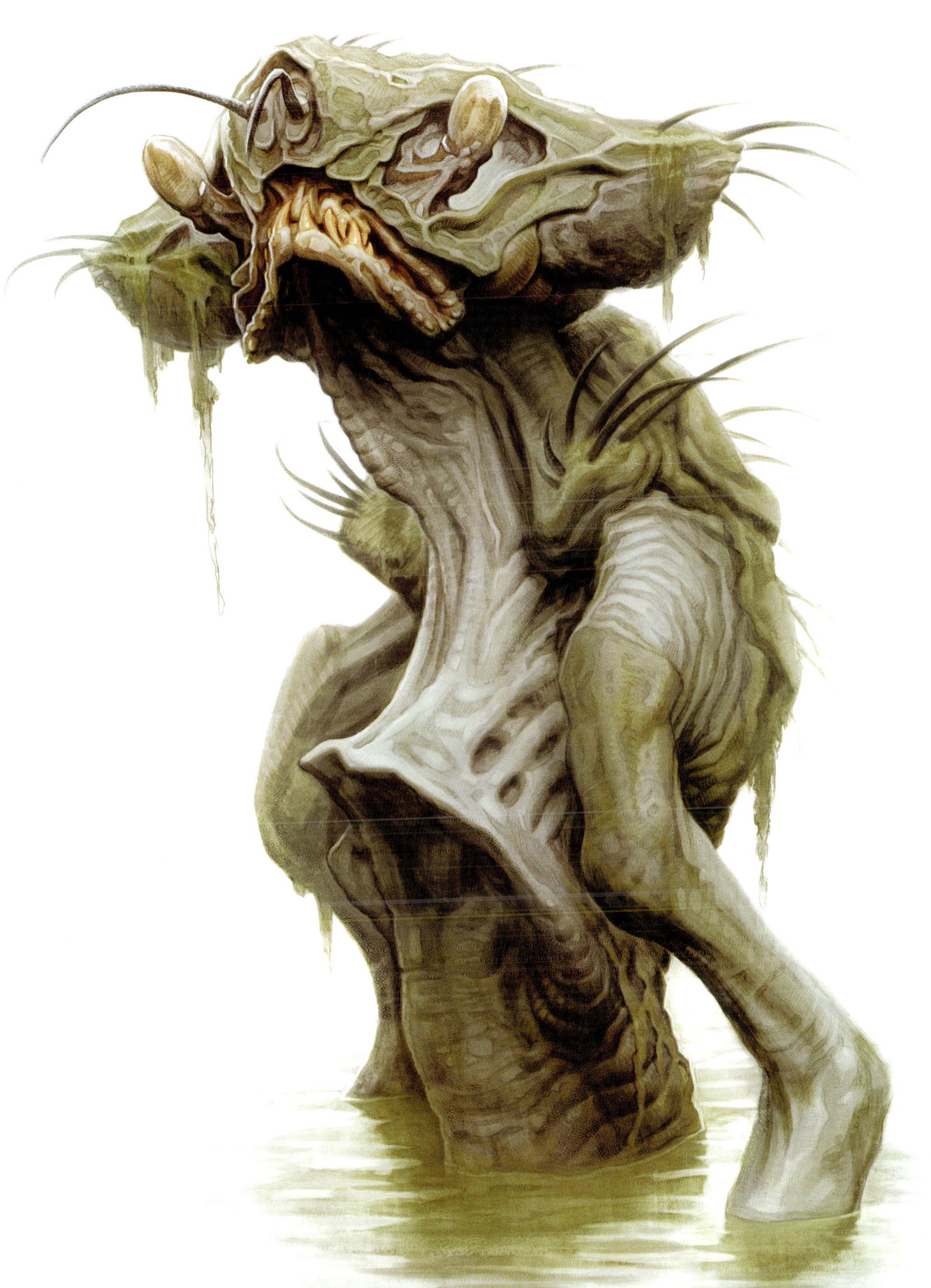

White striped savanna wyvern

Brian Valeza

Research

Exploration

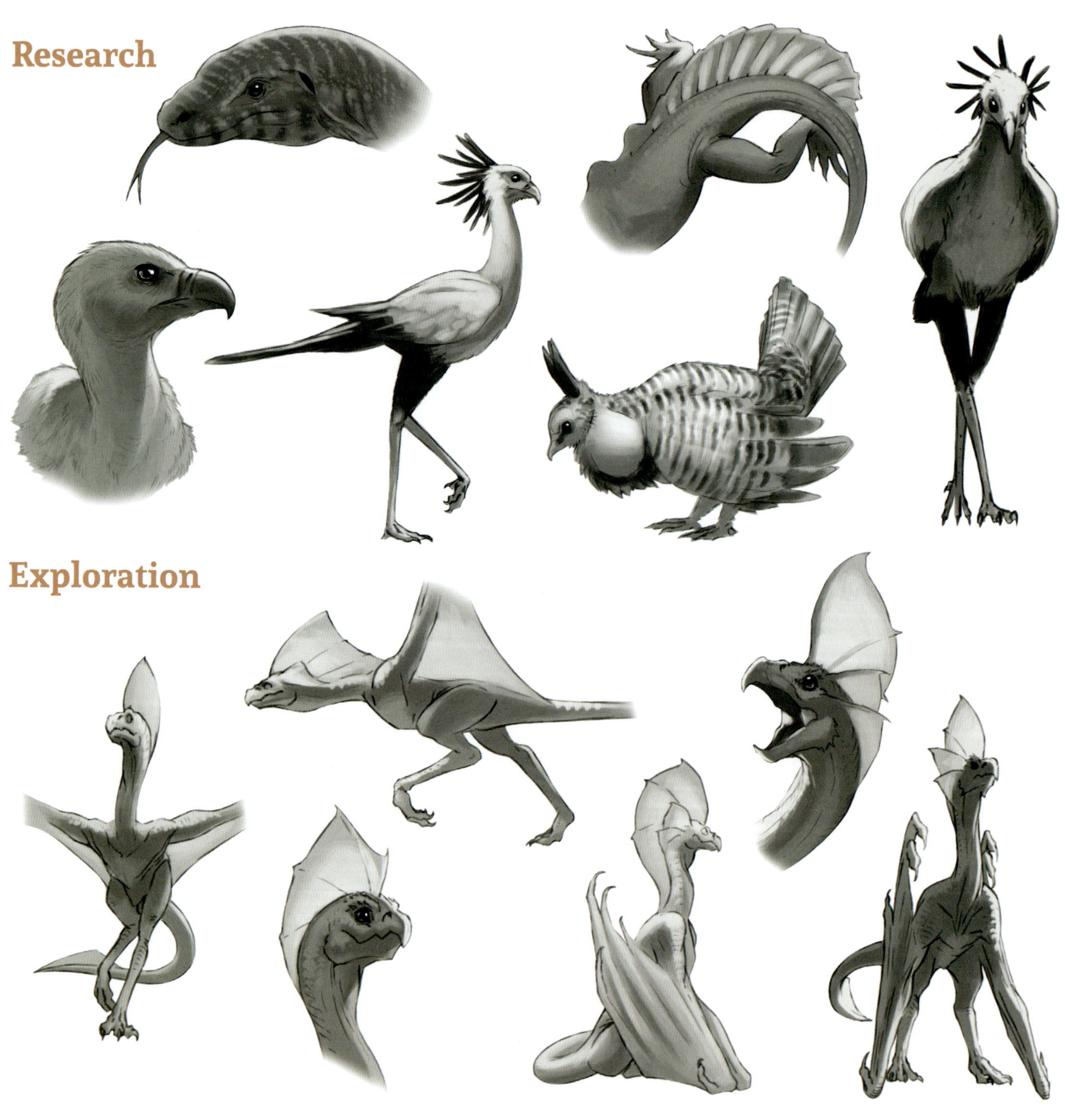

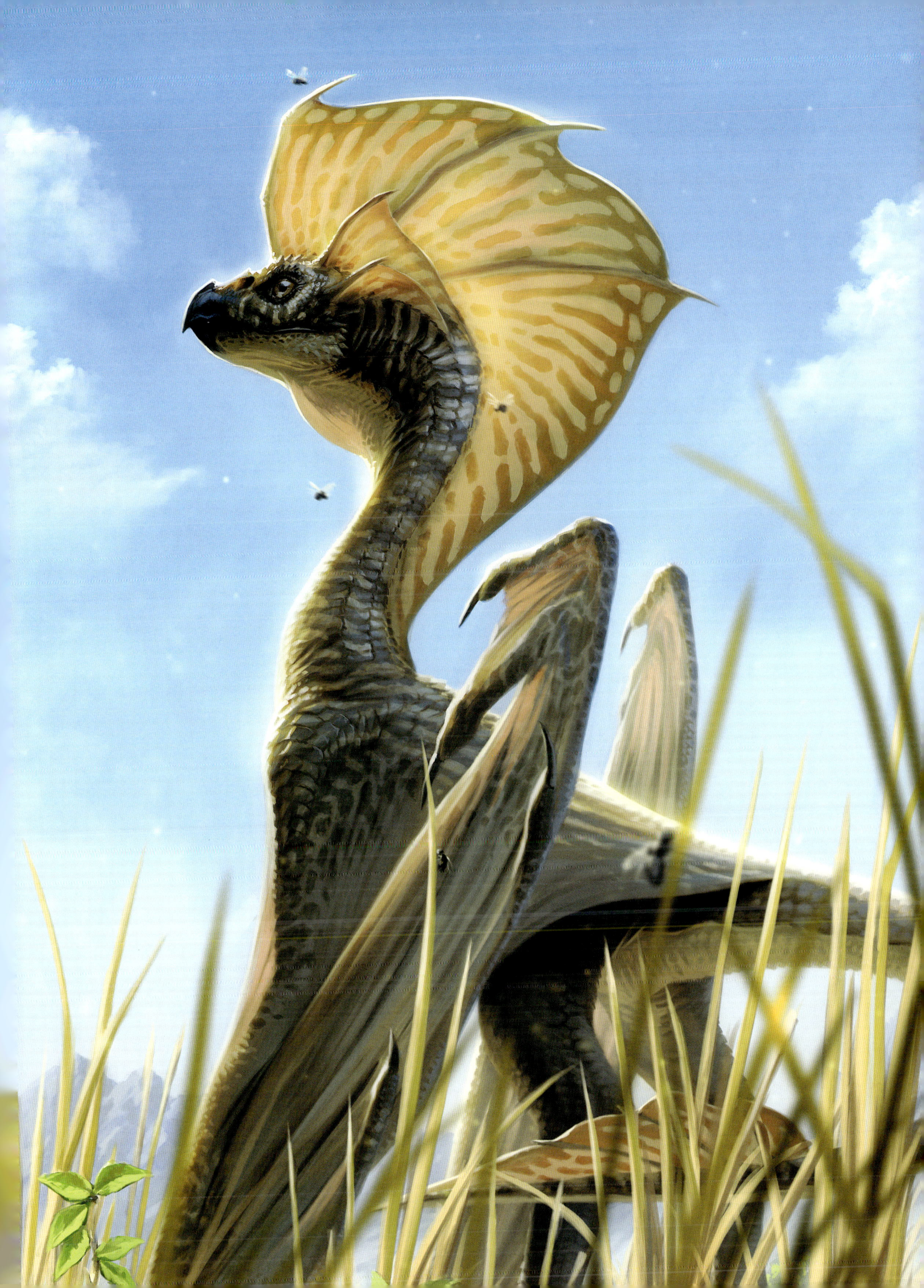

Rock eater

Gabe McAlpine

Research

Exploration

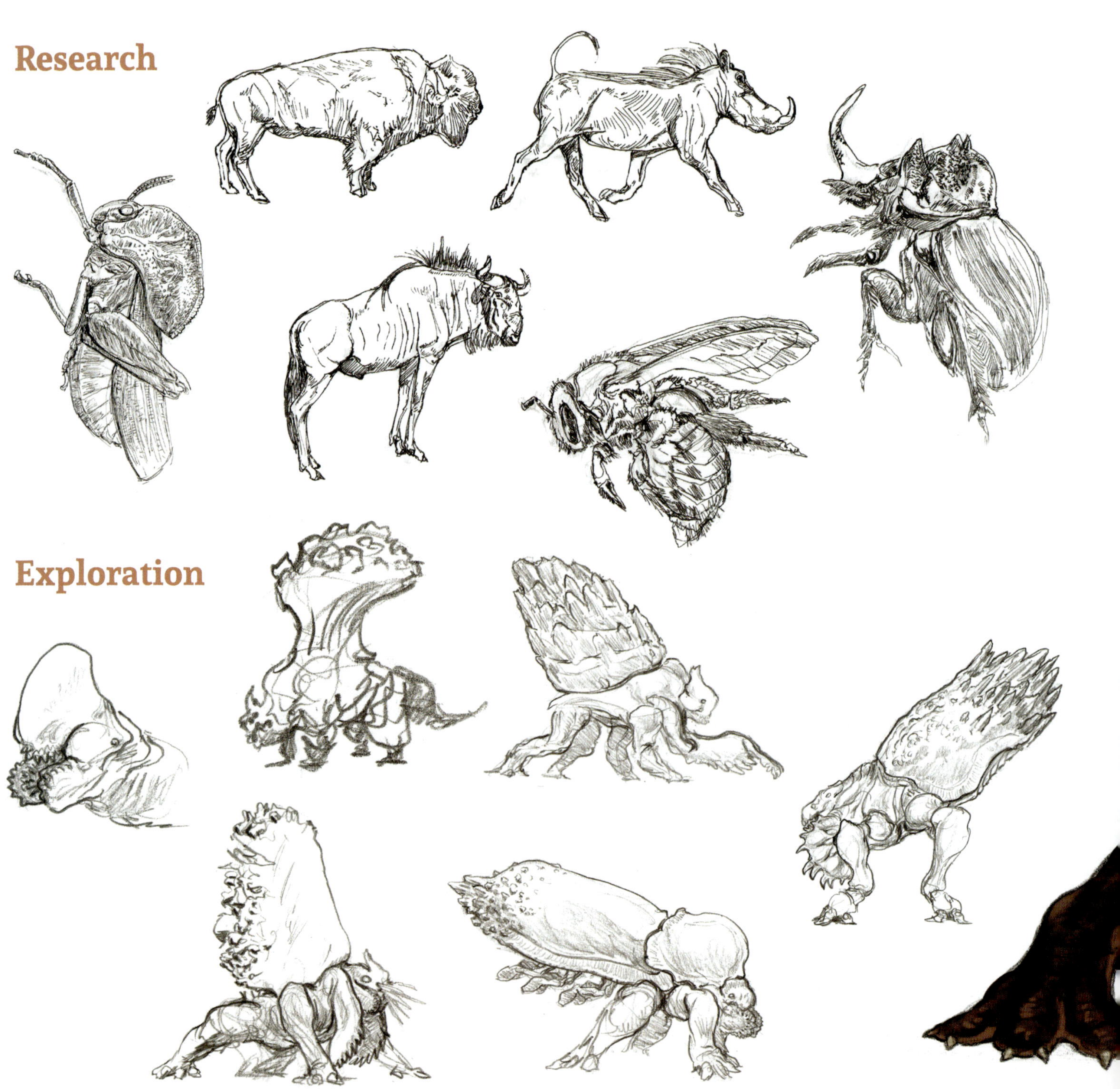

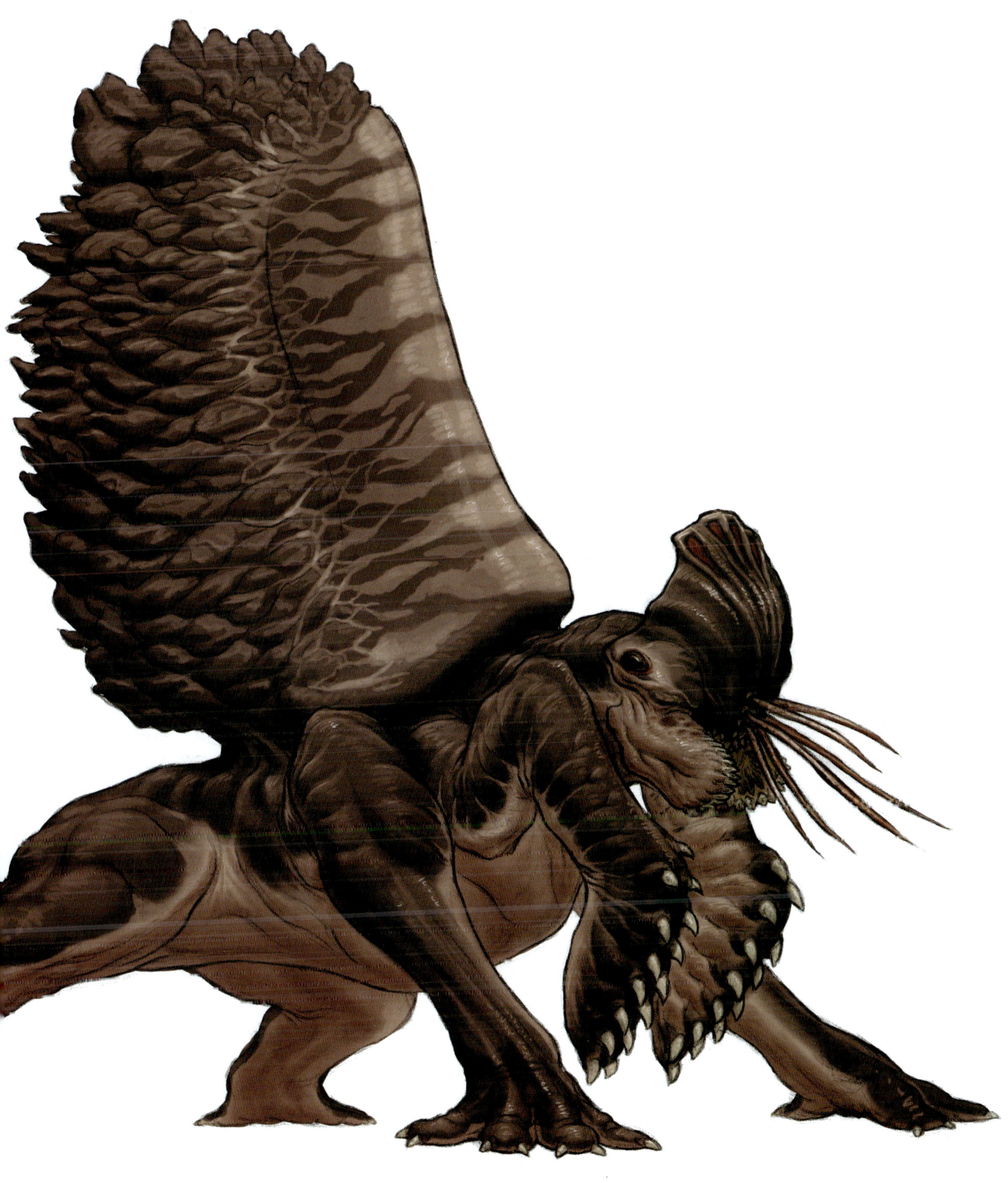

Stalker

Max Duran

Research

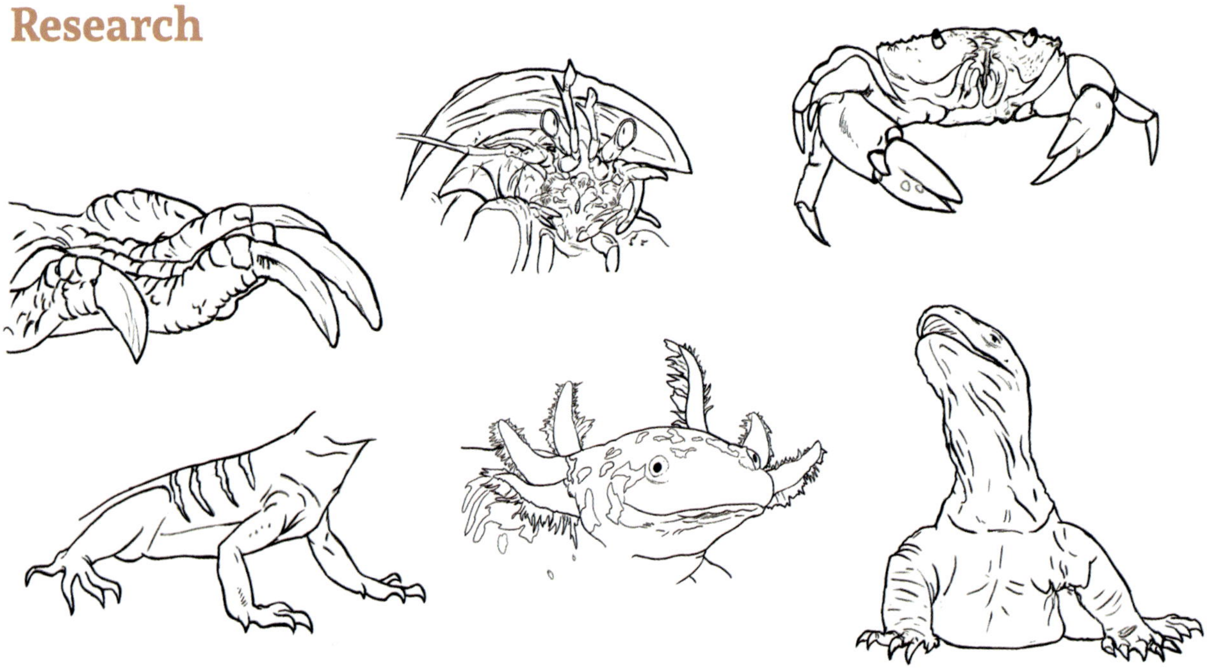

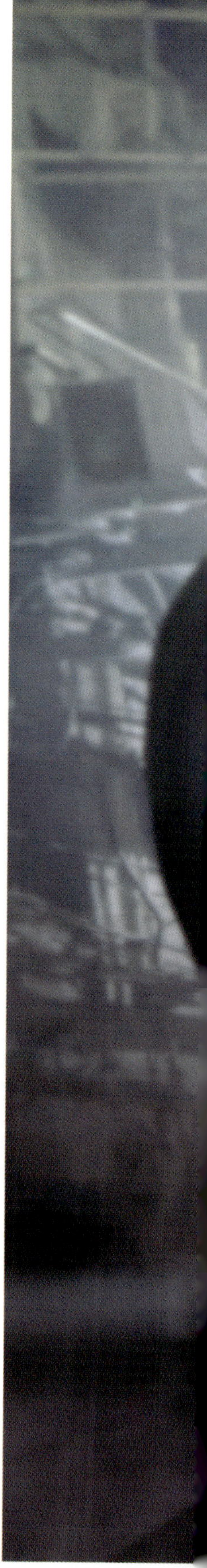

Exploration

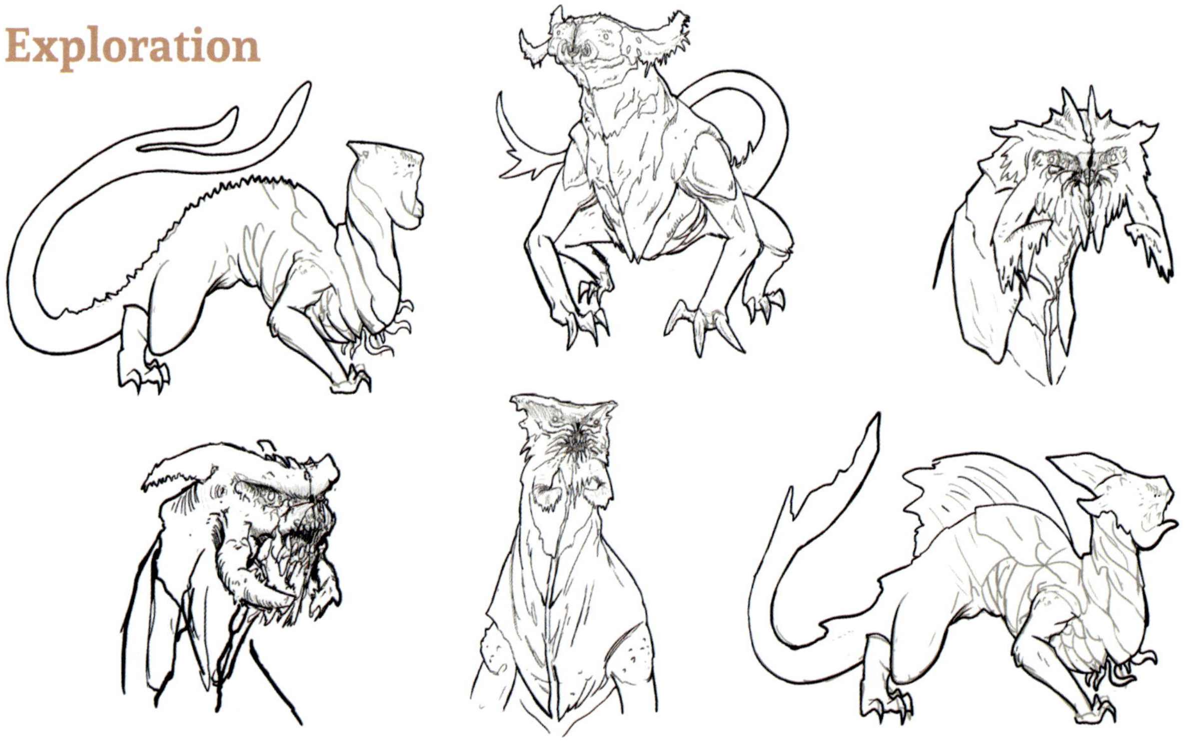

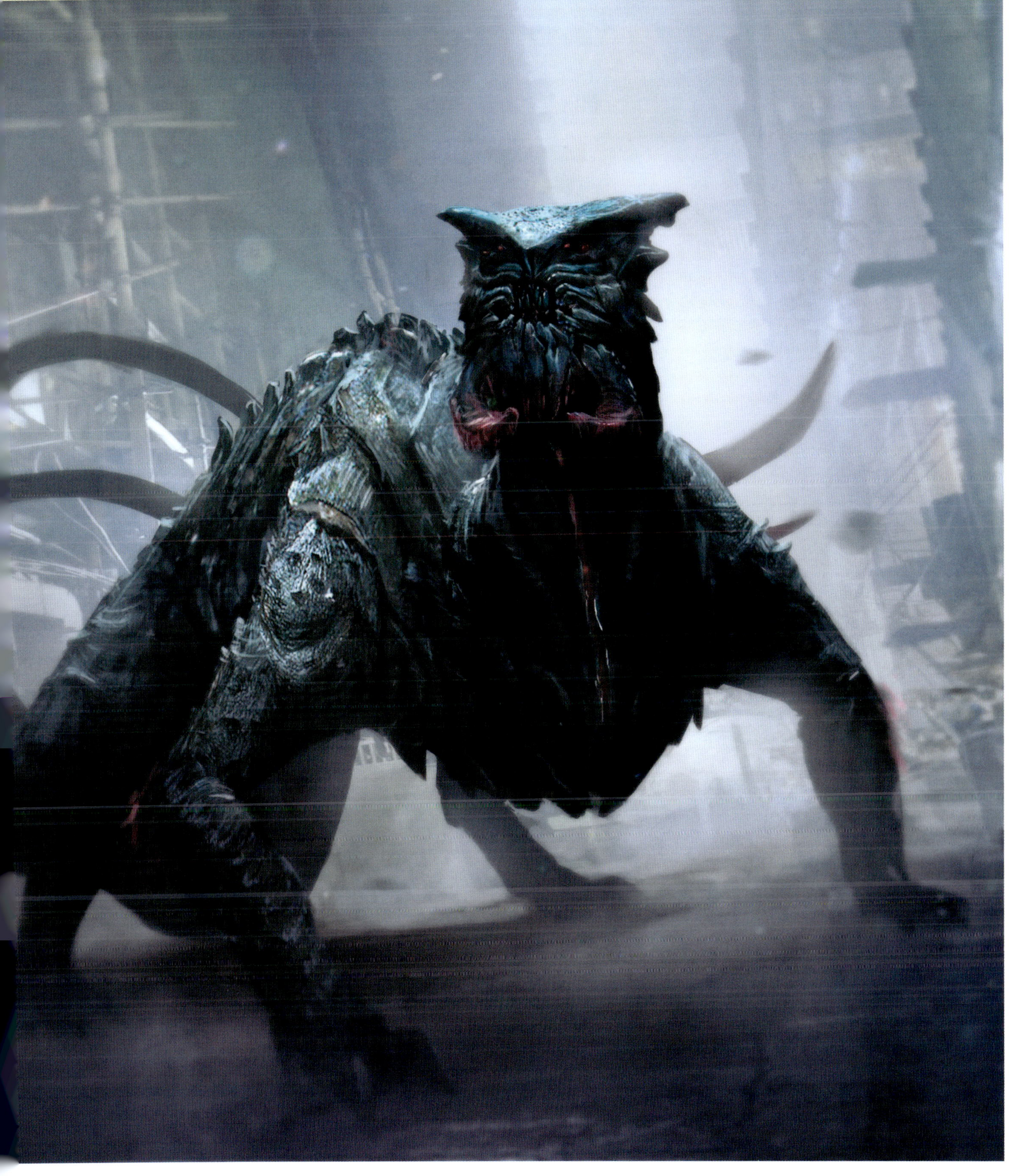

Dragonfly dragon
Le Yamamura

Research

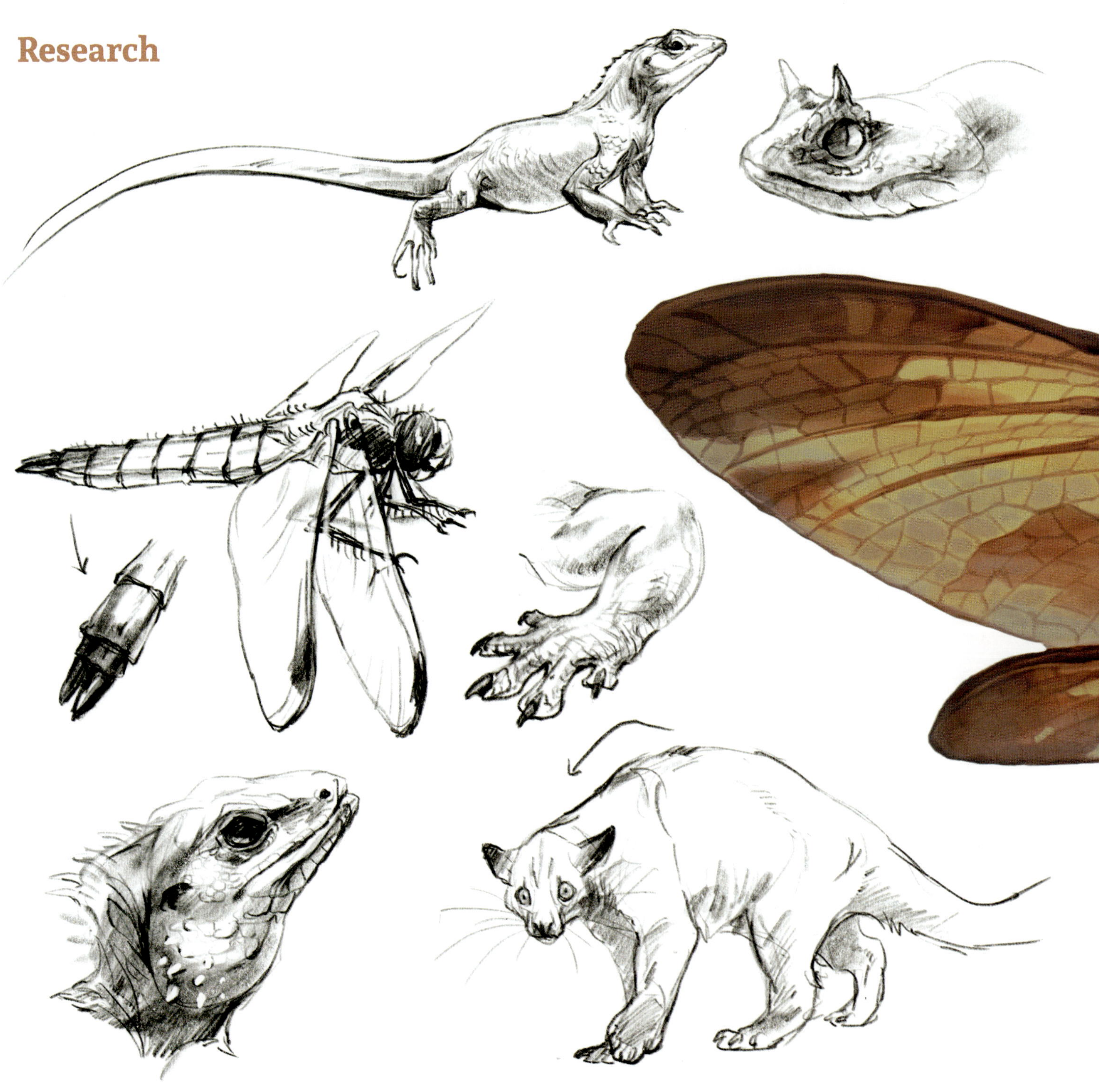

Exploration

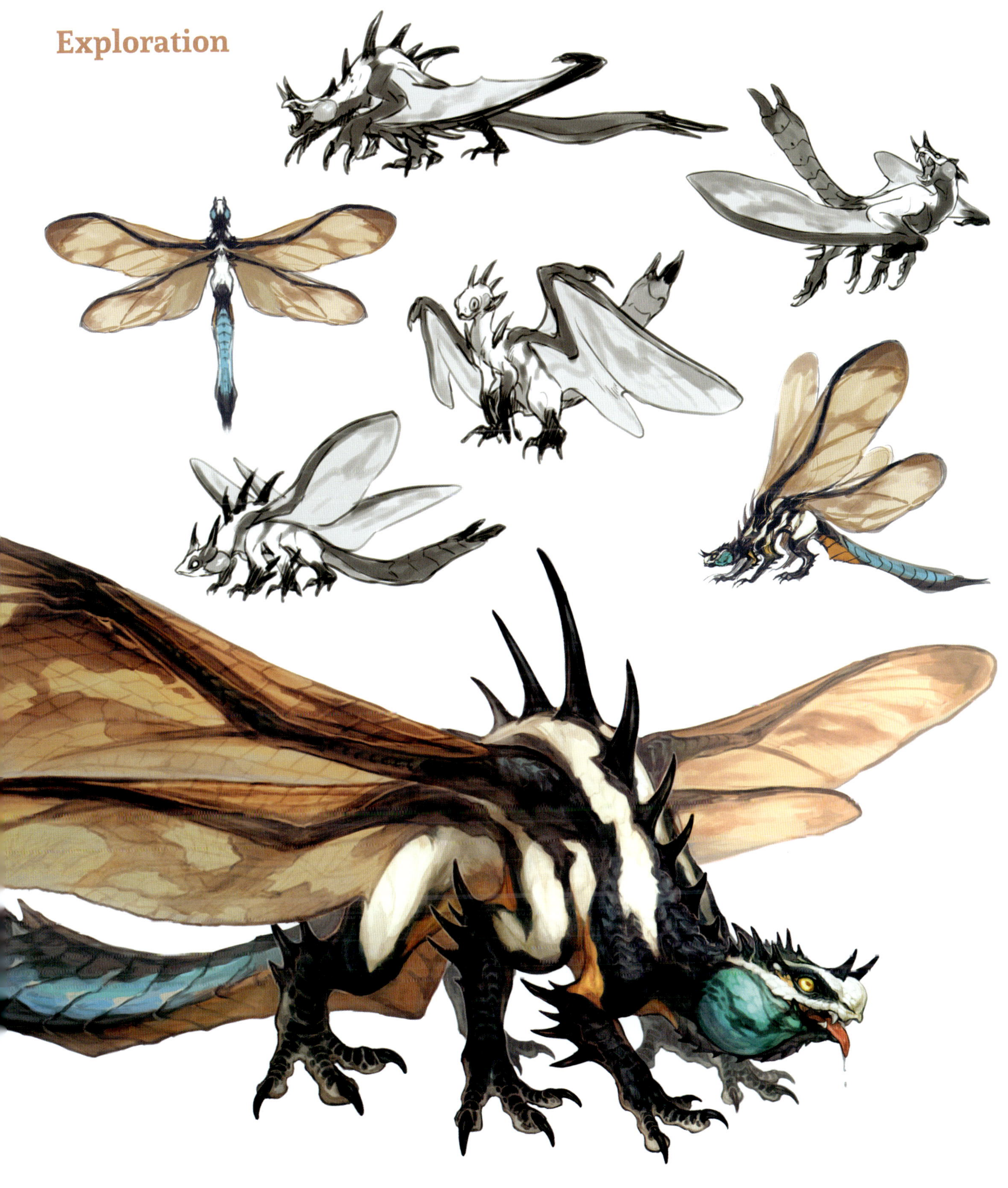

Blue griffin

John Tedrick

Research

Exploration

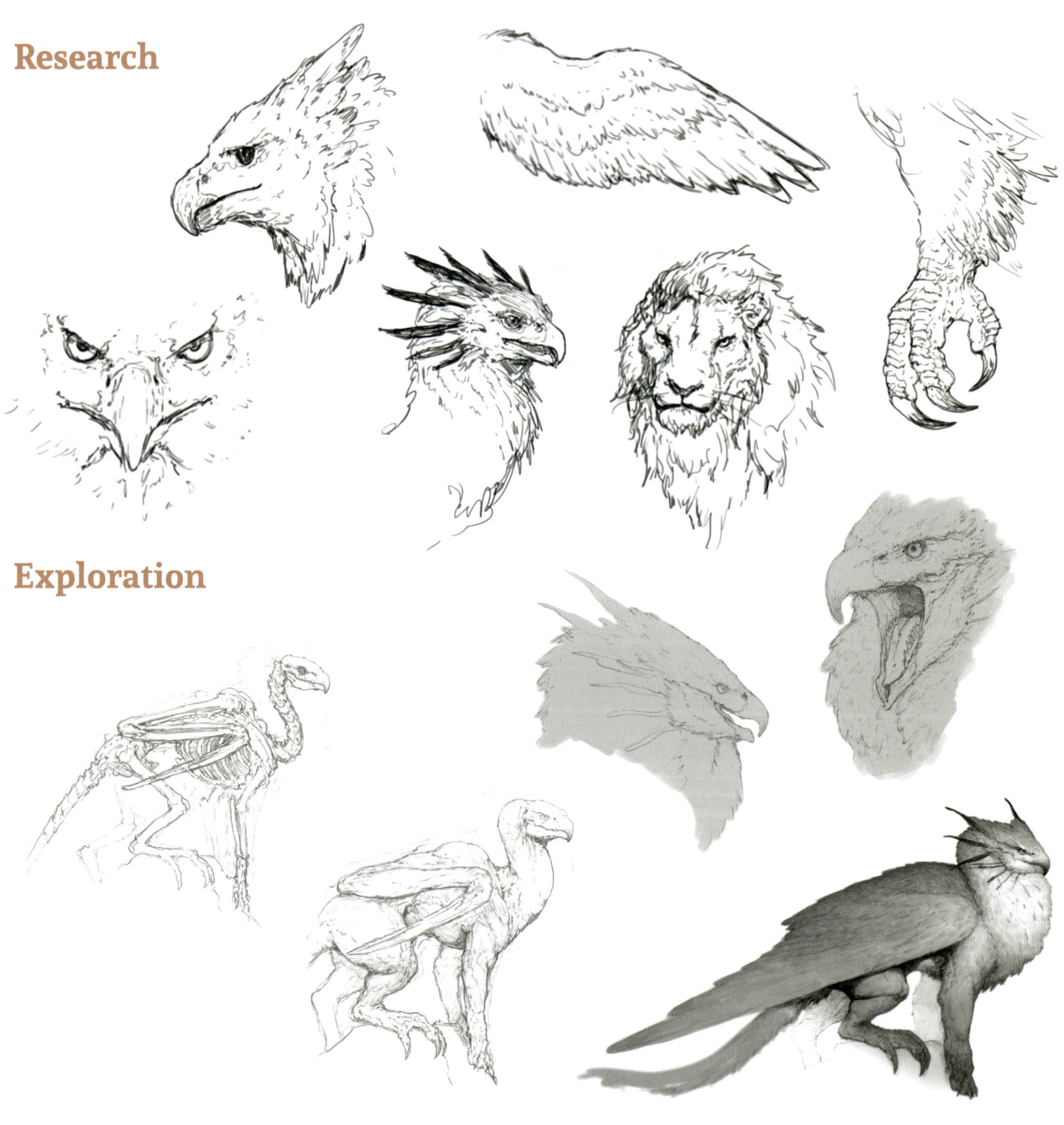

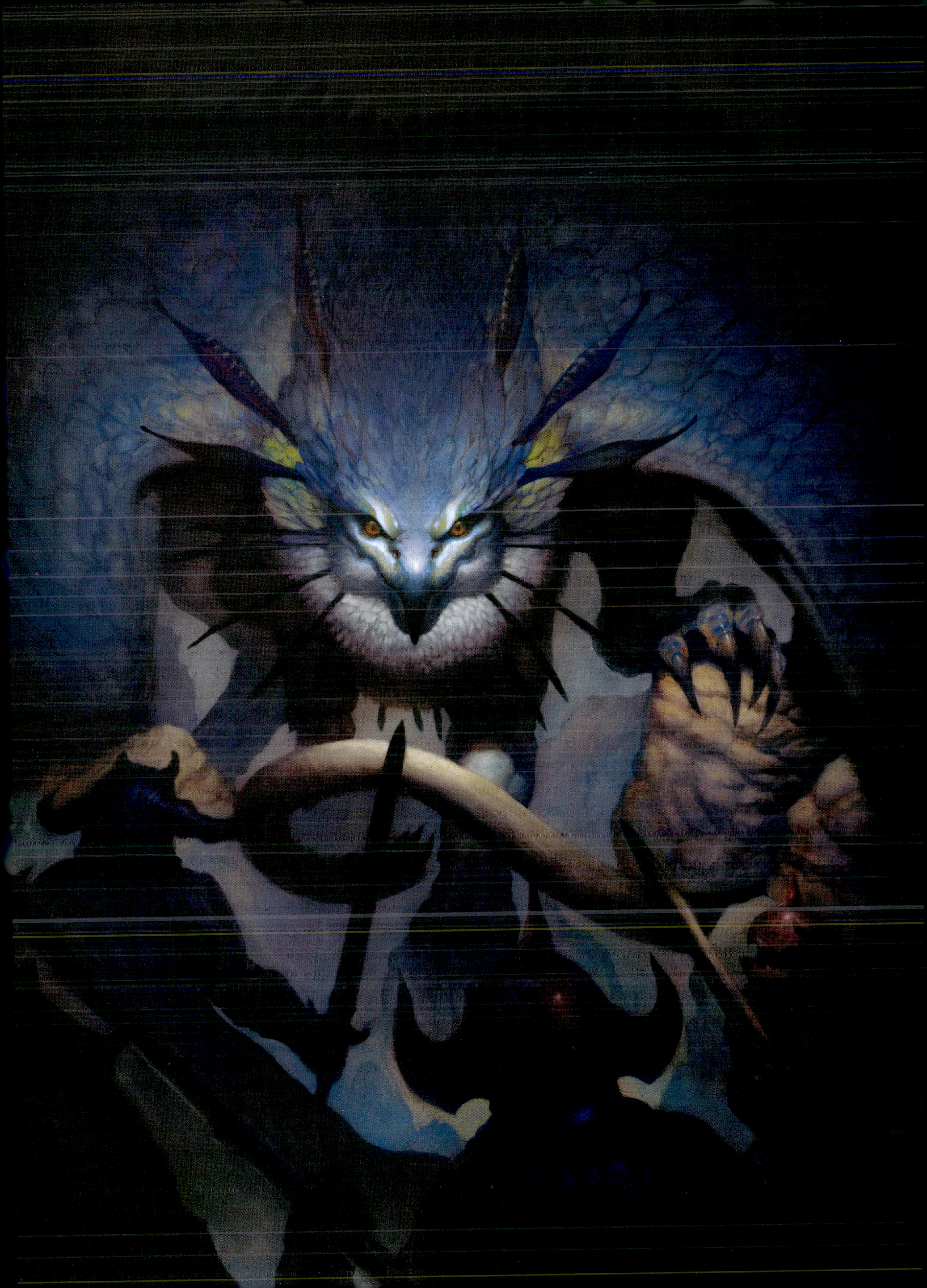

Flying wyvern

Joseph Lin

Research

Exploration

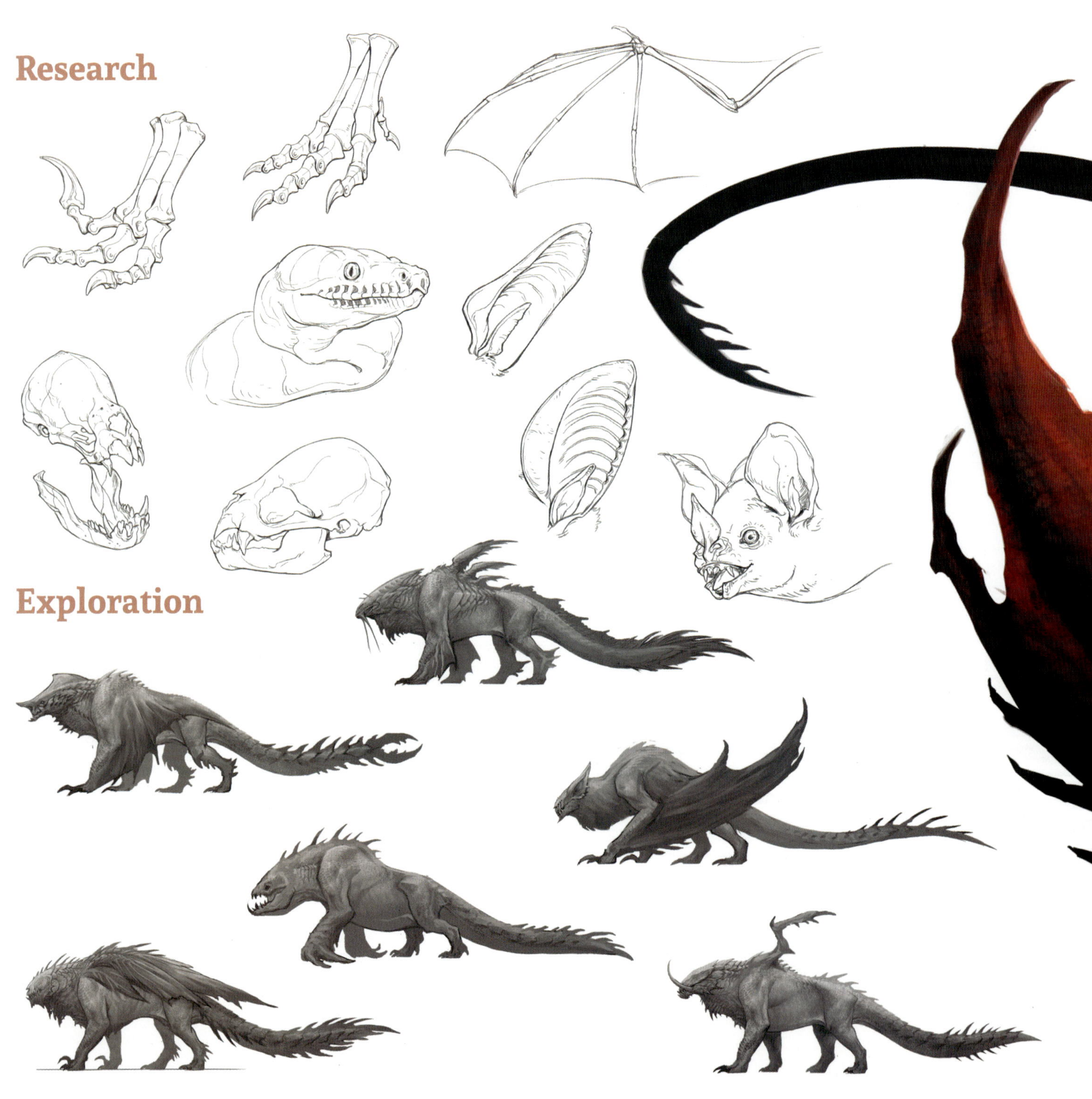

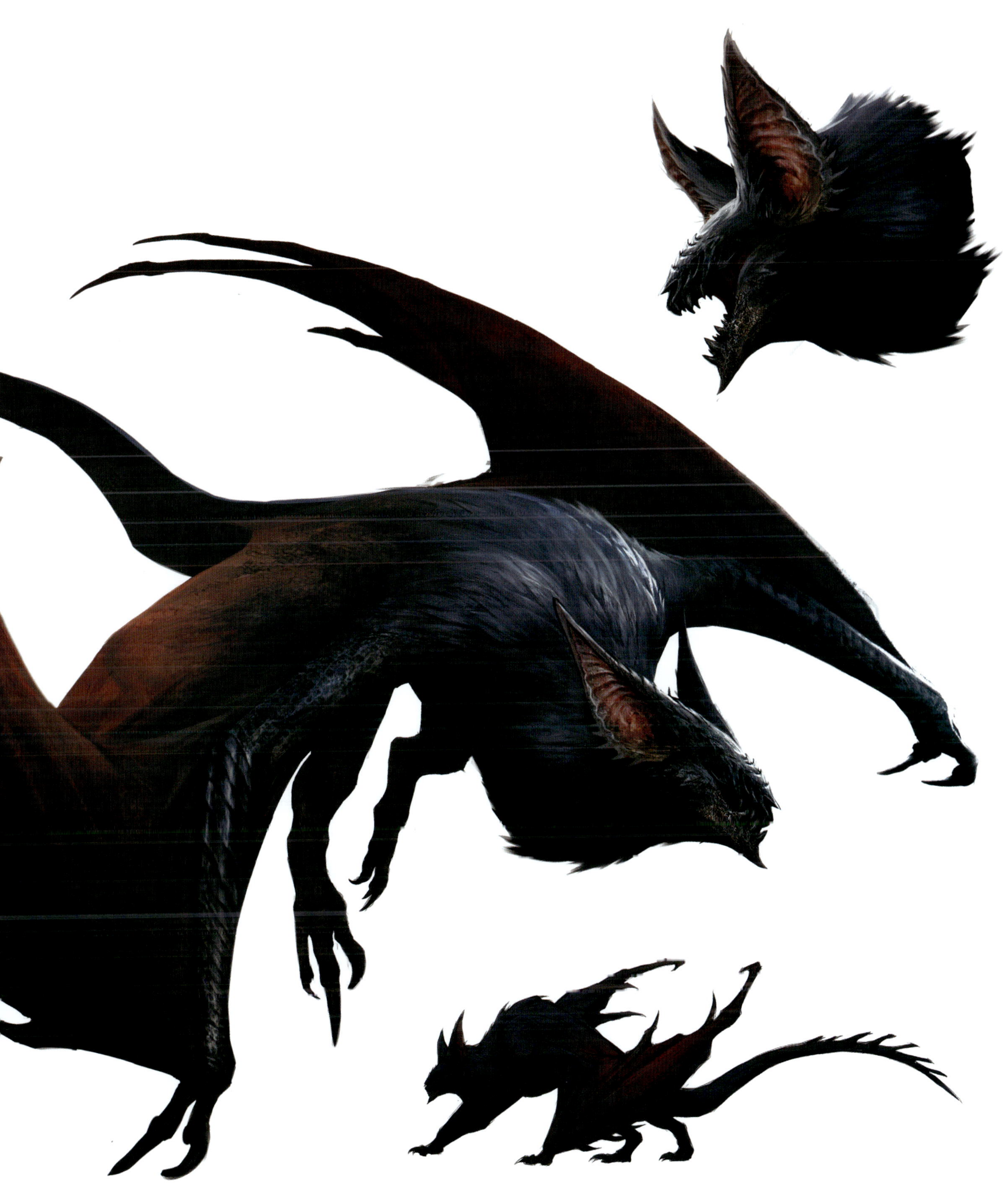

EXERCISES

Use the prompts on these pages to jump-start
your next creature-design project or encourage
a new avenue of research.

- A rainforest-dwelling creature with six limbs

- A slow-moving creature with poor vision and tough armor

- A creature that lives and hunts in coastal rockpools

- An insectoid hunter that disguises itself as a flower

- An aquatic creature with a sharp, rough shell

- An insectivore that can fly or glide using webbed limbs

- An avian predator that spears fish with its unusual beak

- A flightless bird with poisonous barbs or spurs

- An ungulate creature with blotchy camouflage

- An intelligent alien creature with multiple antennae

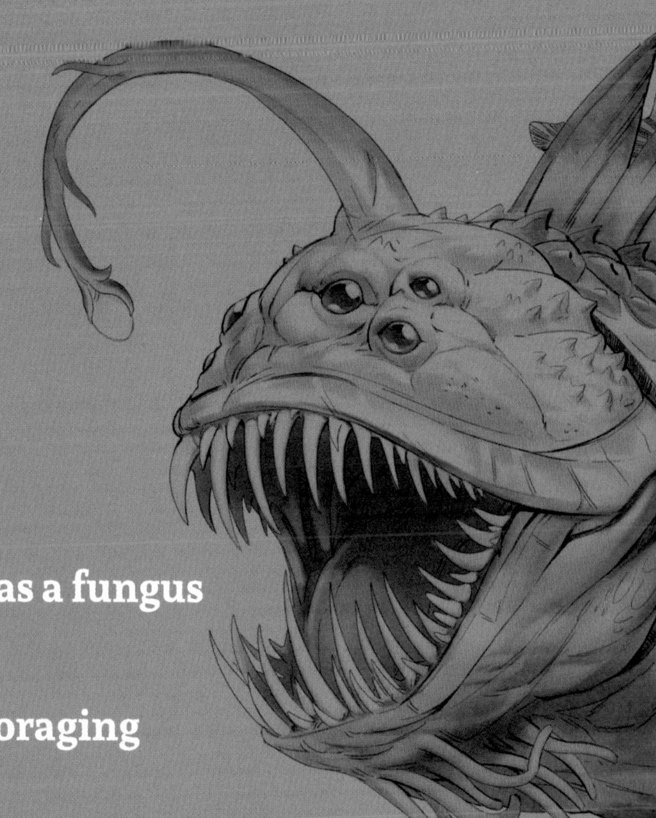

- A frog-like creature that can disguise itself as a fungus

- A spiny woodland creature with tusks for foraging

- A large, armored creature that has been domesticated for riding

- A nocturnal desert-dweller that eats scorpions and toxic bugs

- A semi-aquatic creature that can crack open tough shellfish

- A reptile that can camouflage itself in a rainforest habitat

- A colorful invertebrate that produces a foul toxin in self-defense

- A fruit-eating mammal with a powerful prehensile tail

- A docile aquatic alien that lives off algae and plant life

- A pack-hunting creature that disorients its prey with loud noises

GLOSSARY

Amphibious

Adapted to, or living in, both land and water.

Antennae

A pair of sensory appendages, such as insects have, sometimes called "feelers."

Anthropomorphism

Assigning human characteristics to a non-human subject such as an animal.

Aposematism

A feature that deters predators from attacking, such as bright warning colors on a toxic animal.

Arachnid

An arthropod that typically has eight legs, such as a spider or scorpion.

Arboreal

Related to or living in the trees.

Arthropod

An invertebrate animal with segmented body parts and an exoskeleton rather than an internal skeleton.

Avian

Of or relating to birds.

Bipedal

Walking on two legs, as humans do.

Camouflage

Coloration or other visual features that allow something to blend in with its environment.

Carnassial

A carnivore's large back teeth, used for shearing through meat.

Carnivore

An animal that lives on a diet of meat.

Chelicerate

A subdivision of arthropod that includes spiders, scorpions, and horseshoe crabs.

Chitin

A tough, fibrous material that forms the exoskeletons of arthropods (for example, a crab's shell).

Countershading

A type of camouflage where one side of a creature is light and the other is dark.

Crustacean

A type of arthropod that is mostly aquatic and includes crabs, lobsters, and shrimp.

Digitigrade

Walking on tip-toe without the heels touching the ground, as a dog or cat does.

Domestication

Taming an animal, for example for companionship or agriculture.

Echolocation

The process of using sound waves to detect objects in the environment.

Ecosystem

A community of organisms and their environment when considered together.

Eusociality

When animals live in an organized colony comprised of multiple generations and groups (or castes) with specialized roles and cooperative behaviors. Bees and ants are examples of eusocial creatures.

Exoskeleton

An external skeleton, such as a beetle's or crab's shell, that supports the body from the outside. The opposite is an internal skeleton (an "endoskeleton"), such as humans have.

Herbivore

An animal that lives on a diet of plants.

Hexapod

Having six legs.

Insect

A group of invertebrate hexapods with features including an exoskeleton, jointed legs, and antennae.

Insectivore

A type of carnivore that eats a diet of insects.

Integument

The protective outer covering of an organism, such as a creature's skin or shell.

Invertebrate

An animal that does not have a backbone, such as a worm or a creature with an exoskeleton.

Keratin

A fibrous substance that forms hair, skin, hooves, horns, feathers, claws, and fingernails.

Larvae

The juvenile form of an insect; for example, a grub or caterpillar.

Locomotion

The ability to move or the act of moving.

Mandible

An animal's lower jaw. In insects, mandibles are paired mouthparts often used for gripping or cutting.

Megafauna

Large animals from any period, though especially Ice Age animals such as mammoths.

Myriapod

A group of many-legged arthropods including centipedes and millipedes.

Nectarivore

An animal that lives on a diet of sugary plant nectar.

Olfactory

Of or related to the sense of smell.

Omnivore

An animal that eats a diet of both plants and meat.

Osteoderm

A tough deposit of bone that forms a protective scale or plate on the skin.

Paleontology

The scientific study of plant and animal fossils.

Pheromone

A chemical released by a creature that alters the behavior of other creatures of the same species.

Plantigrade

Walking on the flat soles of the feet, as humans do.

Prehensile

Capable of grasping something (especially when referring to a tail or similar appendage).

Proboscis

A mammal's nose, especially when long, or the long, tubular mouthpart of a sucking insect such as a butterfly.

Quadrupedal

Moving on four legs, as a dog or horse does.

Sexual dimorphism

When the male and female of a species have different physical characteristics (beyond their reproductive organs), such as birds with notable differences in size and color.

Terrestrial

Relating to or living on the land, rather than in the air, trees, or water.

Thermoregulation

The process of controlling and maintaining a specific body temperature.

Thumbnail

In concept art, a small sketch used to quickly explore an idea.

Ungulate

A mammal with hooves.

Unguligrade

Walking on hooves, as a horse or cow does.

Vestigial

In biology, this refers to a leftover feature that no longer serves a function.

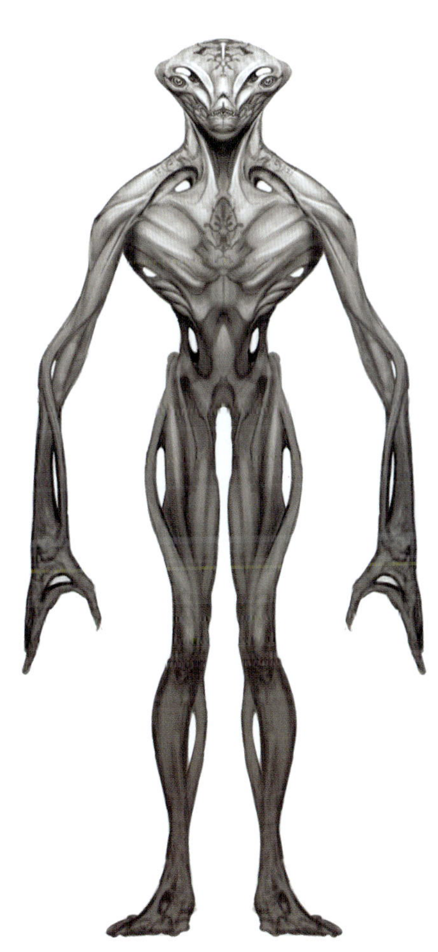

CONTRIBUTORS

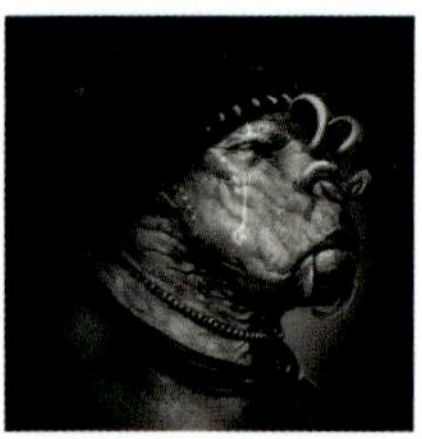 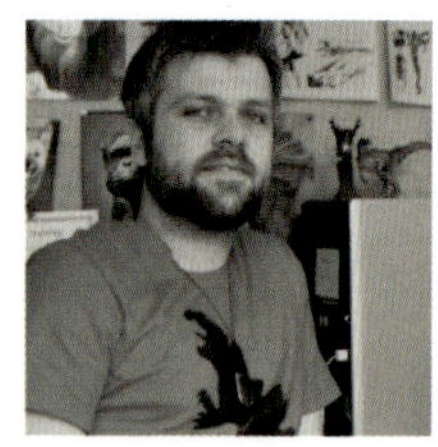

Andrew Baker

Senior concept artist | andrewbakerdesigns.com

Andrew Baker is currently a senior concept artist at A44 games in Wellington, New Zealand. He spent ten years as a senior designer at Weta Workshop, working on *Ghost in the Shell, Godzilla,* and the *Hobbit* trilogy. Andrew enjoys infusing his passion for worldbuilding into all aspects of his work.

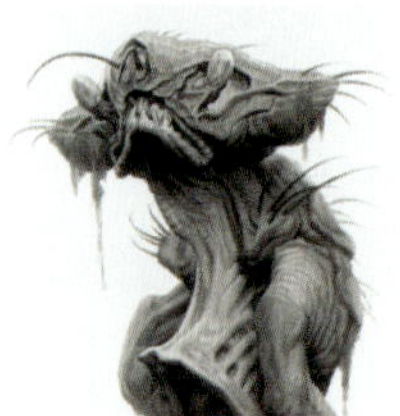 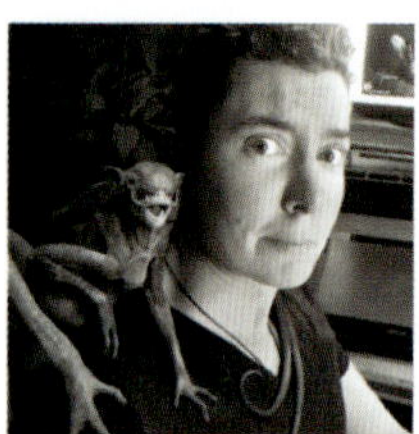

Ken Barthelmey

Creature & character designer | theartofken.com

Ken Barthelmey is a passionate creature and character designer who has worked in the film industry since 2012, and is experienced in 2D and 3D art.

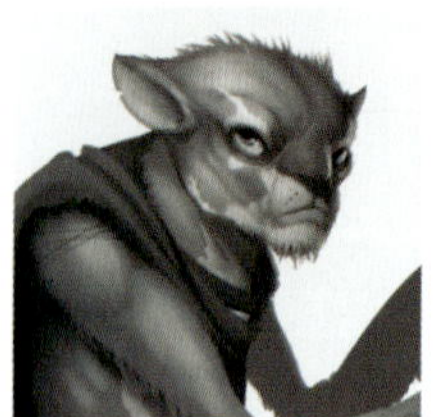 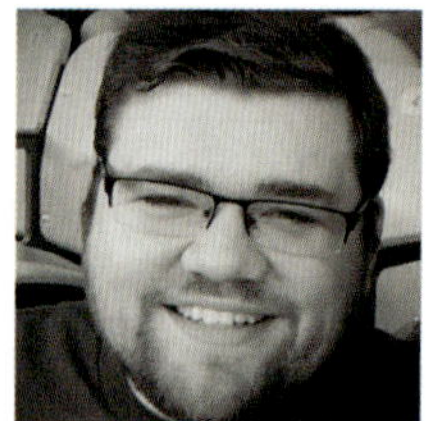

Kyle Brown

Concept artist & instructor | kylebrowndesign.com

Originally from Dublin, Ohio, Kyle Brown now works as a concept artist for film and television in Los Angeles, California, hoping to follow in the footsteps of those who inspired him to do what he does today.

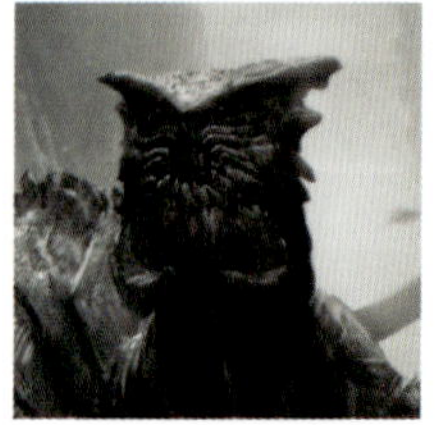 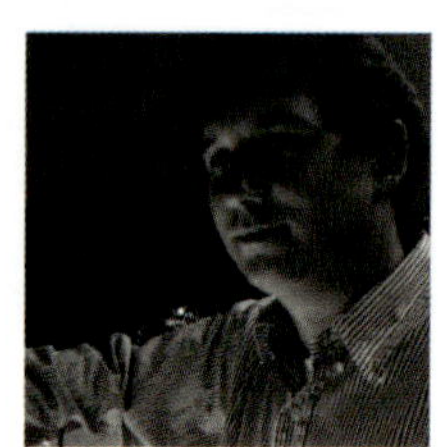

Max Duran

Concept artist | artstation.com/maxduran

Max Duran is from Colombia but has lived in Chengdu, China, since 2018, working as a lead concept artist and illustrator at Virtuos Games.

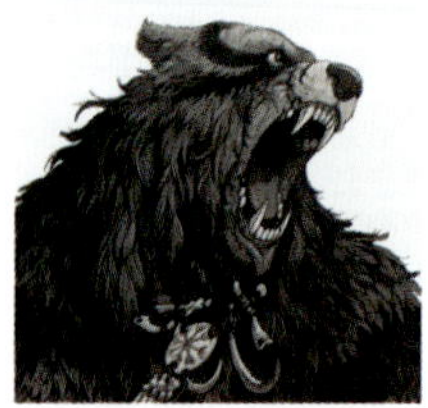 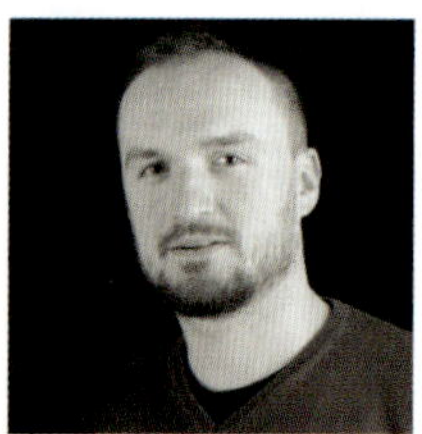

Edin Durmisevic

Freelance concept artist & illustrator | edind.artstation.com

Edin Durmisevic lives in Sarajevo, Bosnia and Herzegovina, and graduated from the Academy of Fine Arts there. He is passionate about creating interesting concepts and illustrations for games and movies - especially designing characters and creatures.

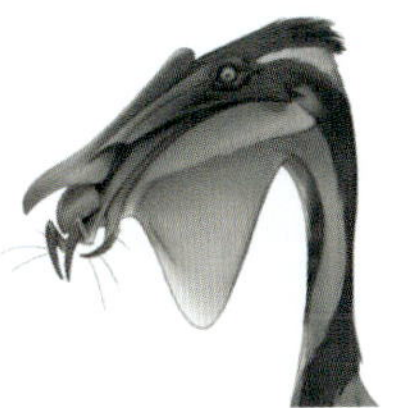 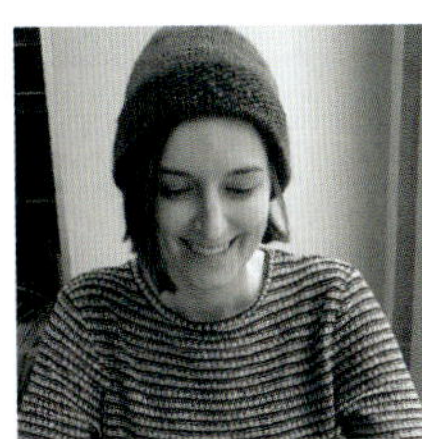

Kristina Lexova

Concept & creature artist | klexova.com

Kristina Lexova is a concept artist specializing in creature design. Having recently wrapped up work on Rare Ltd's *Everwild*, she is currently enjoying recording wildlife and foraging near her home in the Czech Republic.

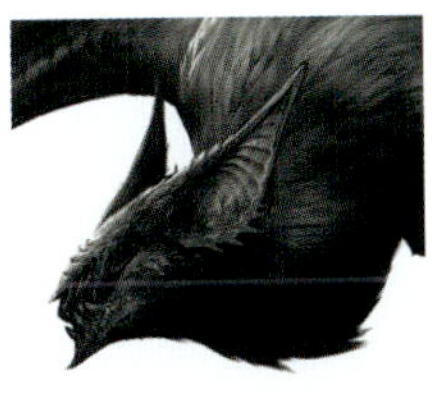 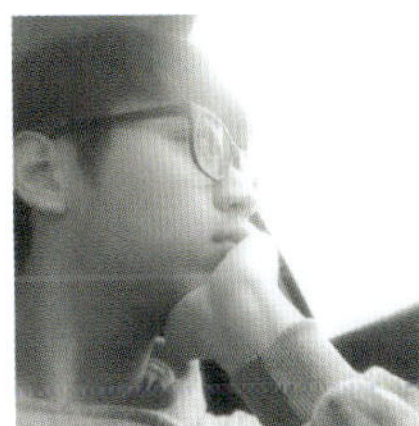

Joseph Lin

Freelance concept artist | artstation.com/simca1017

Joseph Lin is a freelance creature and character concept artist, born and raised in Taiwan. He has loved watching, reading about, and drawing creatures since childhood. Nowadays, dragons are his favorite subject.

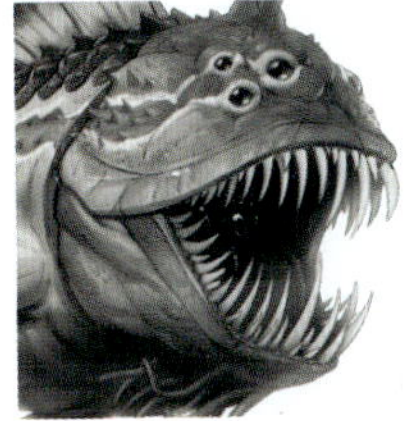 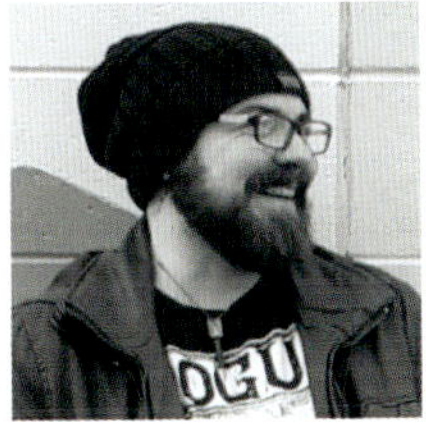

Damien Mammoliti

Freelance concept artist | boneandbrush.com

Damien Mammoliti is a freelance concept artist working with game and tabletop roleplaying companies across the world, such as CD Projekt Red, Paizo Publishing, and Modiphius Entertainment.

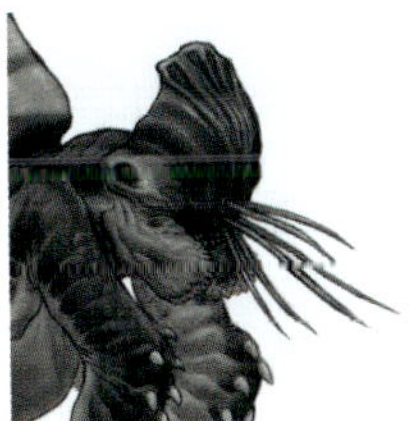 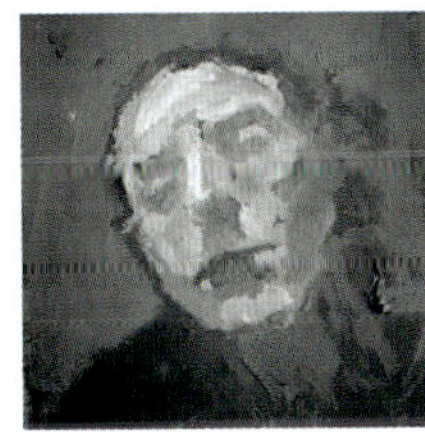

Gabe McAlpine

Concept artist | artstation.com/gabemcalpine

Gabe McAlpine is a freelance concept artist and illustrator from the south coast of England, specializing in creature design.

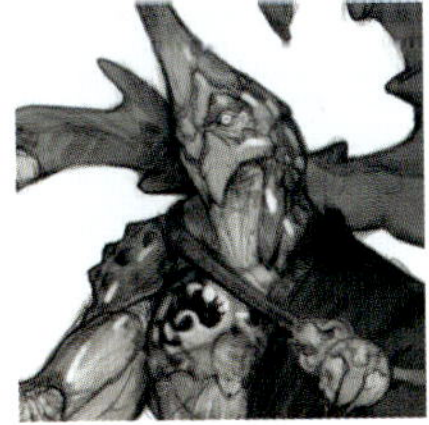 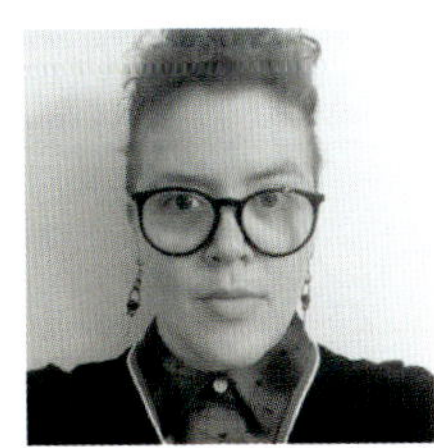

Oriana Menendez

Concept artist | orianamdz.artstation.com

Oriana Menendez is a Los Angeles-based freelance concept artist. She has made creature and character concept art for video games and tabletop games.

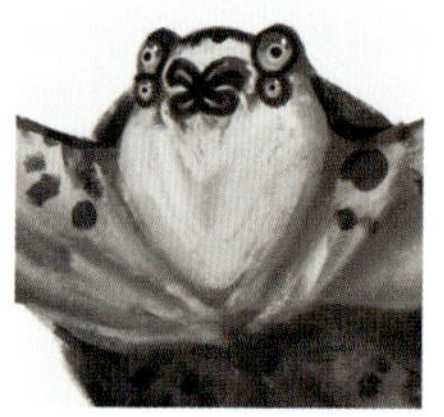 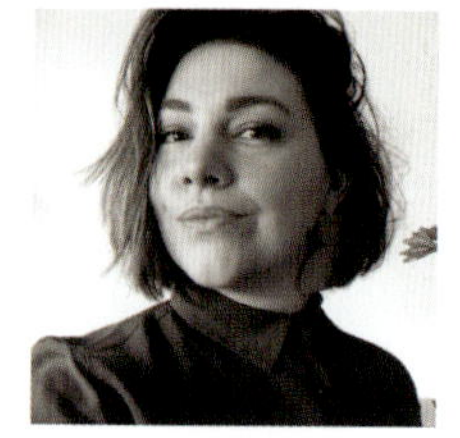

Brynn Metheney

Concept artist & illustrator | brynnart.com

Brynn Metheney is a Los Angeles-based concept artist specializing in creature design for entertainment. She has worked on projects including *Ghostbusters*, *Men in Black: International*, *Sorry to Bother You*, *Scoob!*, and *Dungeons & Dragons*.

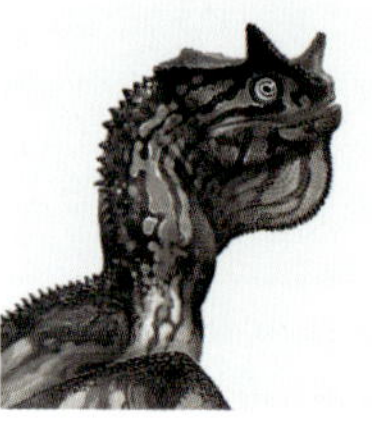 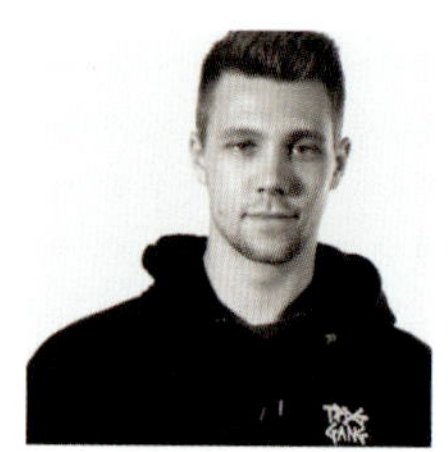

Alexander Ostrowski

Creature designer & concept artist | alexander-ostrowski.artstation.com

Alexander Ostrowski is a creature designer and concept artist based in Germany. He works with various clients, including SIXMOREVODKA Studio, West Studio, and Ready At Dawn.

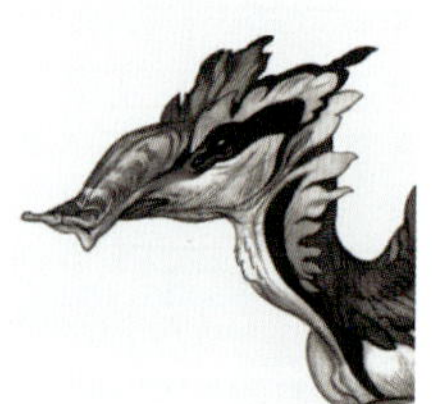 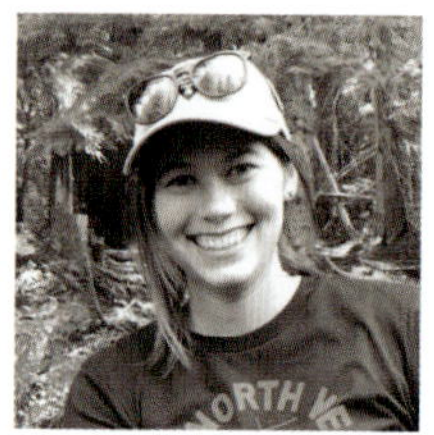

Kate Pfeilschiefter

Creature artist | katepfeilschiefterart.com

Kate Pfeilschiefter is a concept artist and illustrator in the Pacific Northwest. She specializes in 2D and 3D creature design, and her inspirations span the gap between science and myth - from cryptids and mythological monsters to zoology, ecology, and speculative biology.

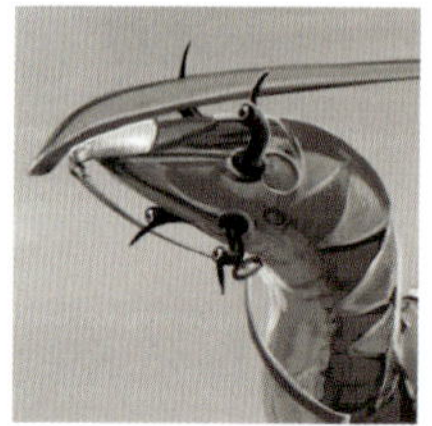 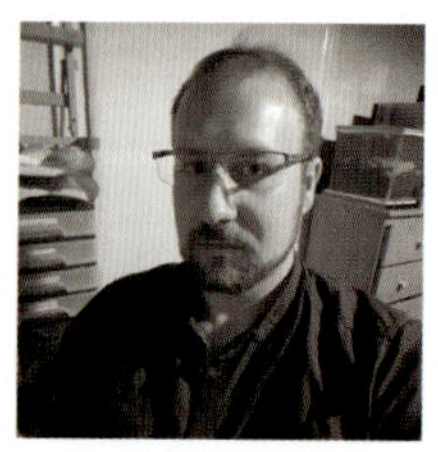

Alex Ries

Concept artist & illustrator | alexries.com

Raised in rural Australia, Alex Ries produces art for films, games, and publishing. He creates natural history art, as well as creature designs for games such as *Subnautica: Below Zero*.

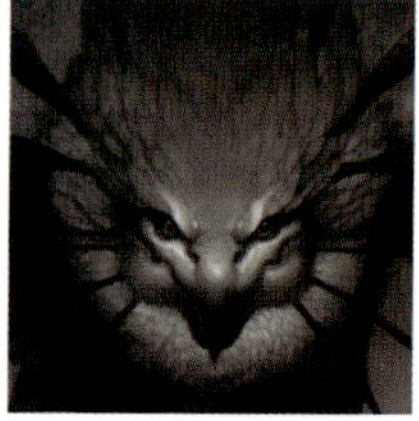 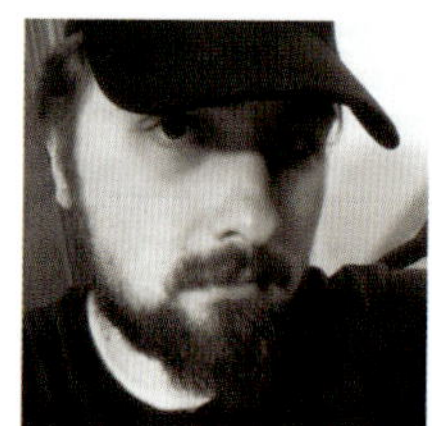

John Tedrick

Concept artist & illustrator | artstation.com/tedrick94

John Tedrick is an illustrator and concept artist. Currently living in Ohio, he enjoys creating, especially when it involves a good creature.

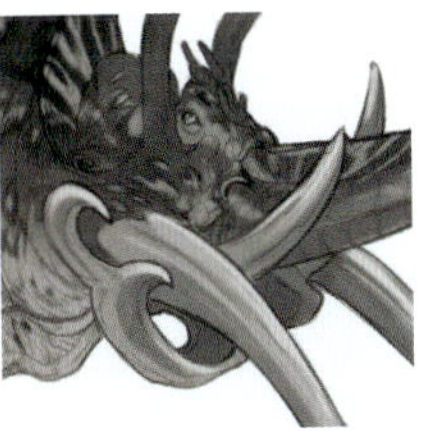 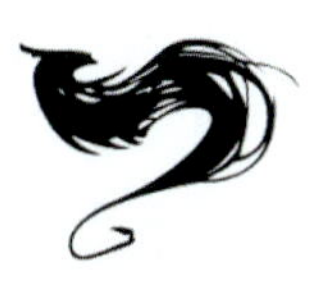

Allison Theus

Concept artist | allisontheus.com

Allison Theus is a creature concept artist and illustrator working in the games industry.

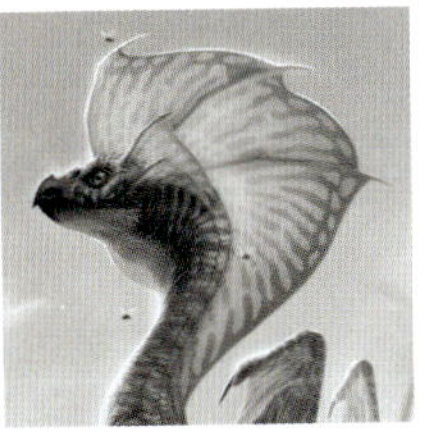 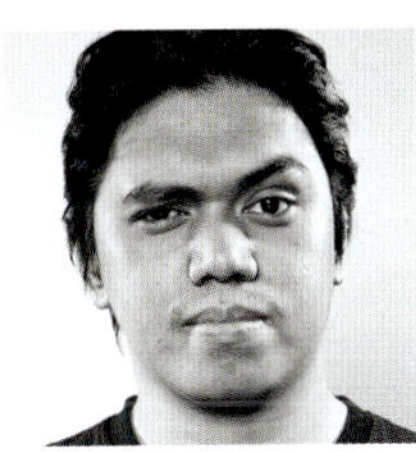

Brian Valeza

Freelance illustrator | artstation.com/tots

Brian Joseph P. Valeza is the co-owner of an online art studio called Gunship Revolution, as well as a freelance illustrator who has worked for Wizards of the Coast, Paizo Publishing, Volta, and many more studios.

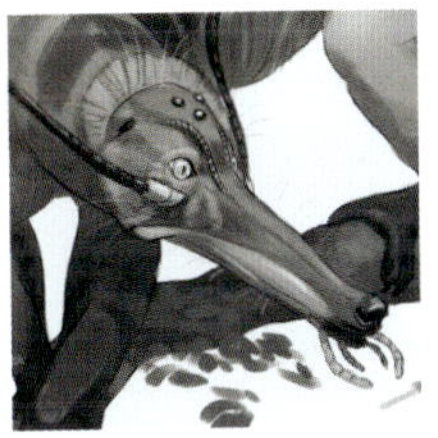 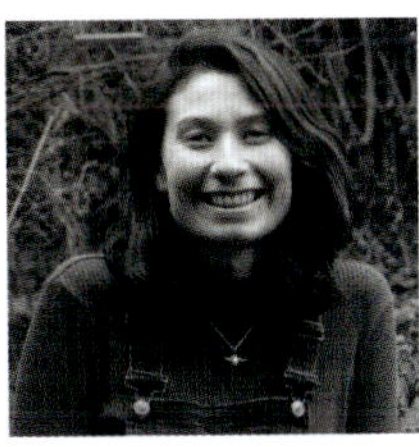

Dominique Vassie

Freelance artist & biologist | dominiquevassie.com

Dominique Vassie is an artist with an equal passion for science. She studied biology at the University of Oxford while maintaining art in her free time, and loves to mix the two.

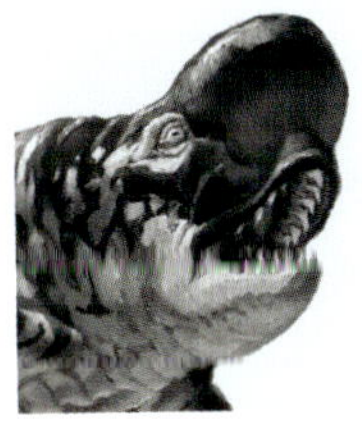 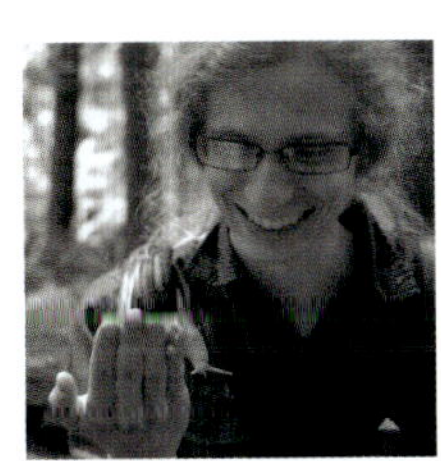

Jordan K. Walker

Fantasy & natural history illustrator | jordankwalkerart.com

Jordan K. Walker is an illustrator and fine artist based in western North America. His work has been featured in galleries across the United States, and appears in numerous print and digital publications.

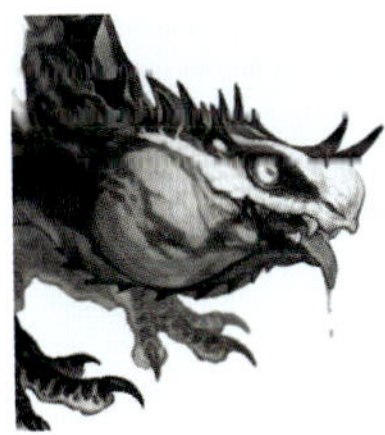 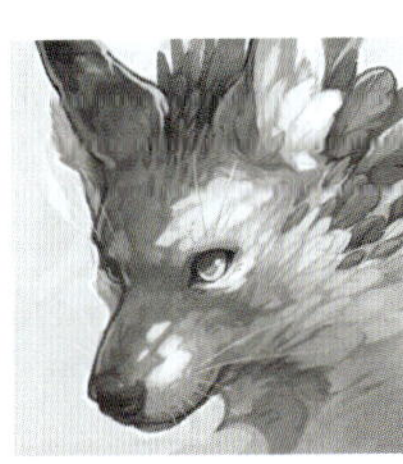

Lē Yamamura

Freelance creature designer | gomalemo.tumblr.com

Le Yamamura is a Japan-based creature artist who, after working for a Japanese game company, went freelance to design imaginary creatures for games, books, and movies.

INDEX

coloration, 60, 63-64, 133, 137, 143, 149, 153, 156, 158-159, 169, 173, 175, 181, 185, 191-192, 201, 214, 217, 223, 233, 239-240, 255

communication, 40, 43, 111, 118-119, 133, 149, 160, 165, 168, 176, 181, 197, 201, 248, 258

contrast, 25, 36, 40, 44, 106, 109-110, 112-113, 135, 143, 150, 153-154, 159, 161-162, 169, 173, 175, 189-193, 201, 224, 249, 257

countershading, 39, 153, 159, 175, 201, 207, 217, 223

crab, 94, 97, 228, 231-233, 243

crocodile, 36, 39, 86, 201, 212-217, 220, 223, 226

crustacean, 12, 94, 97, 131, 228-229, 231-241, 234, 236, 239, 242-243

cuttlefish, 72, 233

O

ocean, 12, 28, 30-31, 52, 88, 164-165, 178, 214
octopus, 132-133
okapi, 198, 201
olfactory, 28, 43, 78, 154, 160
oligopod, 102
omnivore, 32, 55, 149-150, 229, 245-246
orangutan, 32, 66, 74, 230, 248
orca, 54, 82, 164-166, 168, 170, 175-176, 178-179, 227
osteoderm, 200, 204-205, 208
owl, 39, 88

P

paleontology, 12, 151, 162
pangolin, 151, 160
physiology, 25, 32, 36, 48, 52, 181
pig, 61, 155
pincer, 94, 96, 210
plantigrade, 74-75, 248
polypod, 102
porpoise, 82, 164, 168
prehensile, 34, 62, 74, 132-133, 136, 138-142, 144, 146, 174, 209
prehistoric, 168, 176
primate, 74-75, 133, 228-230, 235-236, 238-239, 248
proboscis, 101, 196-197, 202, 206
Psittacosaurus, 151
pterosaur, 13-14, 133-135, 186

Q

quadruped, 66-68, 151, 230, 245-246, 248, 251

R

rainforest, 14, 28, 32, 165, 195
reindeer, 24, 28
reproduction, 44-45, 94, 233, 243
reptile, 12, 28, 66, 84, 90, 131-135, 137-139, 141, 143-145, 147, 153, 160, 212
rhinoceros, 64, 89, 156, 167, 199-200
Rodhocetus, 53, 169-170, 172, 178

S

salamander, 153
salmon, 90-91

scale, 107, 113-115, 118, 141, 144, 150-151, 157, 196, 200, 212, 220, 256
scales, 31, 46, 55, 60, 84-85, 110, 133, 137-138, 140-142, 144, 147, 154, 200, 212-214, 225
scavenger, 116, 131, 180-181, 183, 185-189, 191, 193-195
scorpion, 94, 96
sea, 30, 32, 52-53, 70, 73, 153, 164-166, 169, 178, 212-213, 223, 228 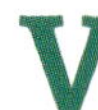
sexual dimorphism, 44
shark, 39, 90-91, 165
shell, 47, 167, 196-197, 204, 206, 210-211, 232, 234-237, 239
shrimp, 15, 97, 228, 232-233, 243
skeleton, 67, 75, 77, 79, 81-83, 85-87, 91, 199, 230
skull, 53, 76, 78-79, 90, 108, 113-115, 150, 152, 156, 158, 183, 198, 202, 204, 242, 249
snapping shrimp, 228, 233, 243
snapping turtle, 167, 170, 217, 220 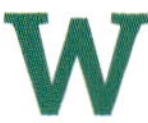
snow, 22, 25, 28, 32-33, 39
spider, 13, 74, 94-95, 137, 139
swamp, 131, 212-215, 217-221, 223, 225, 227
swimming, 12, 31, 52-54, 58, 82-83, 90, 92, 97, 100, 166, 169-170, 172-173, 176, 218, 222, 231

T

tadpole, 46
tapir, 16, 80, 148-149
tattoo, 244-245, 248-252, 255-259
teeth, 36-39, 46, 52-53, 64, 71, 78, 81-84, 86, 103, 117, 140, 165, 168, 172, 176, 185, 198, 200, 213, 218, 220-222, 229, 245, 247-249
temperature, 25, 34, 133, 136, 184, 200, 204, 237, 245
terrain, 22, 25, 28, 32, 35, 52, 55, 152, 167, 172, 174, 176, 201, 245
terrestrial, 66, 69, 82, 98, 165, 167, 169, 212, 226, 228, 230
territorial, 43, 132-134, 136, 139-140, 143, 147, 170, 174, 176, 206, 214, 218, 244
thermoregulation, 16, 184, 197, 200, 233
Tiktaalik, 215
tongue, 23, 36, 38, 84, 137-139, 183, 198, 217
toothed whale, 82-83, 168, 178-179
transformation, 245, 247, 258-259
tree, 25, 32-33, 52, 66, 74, 85, 132-133, 137, 139-140, 142-144, 146, 175, 244
tribal, 124, 228-229, 236, 240, 242, 244, 250, 252, 258
tropical, 32, 39, 74, 133, 143, 153, 195

trunk, 144, 198, 202, 204, 206, 209-211
tuna, 30, 90, 92
tundra, 24, 28, 131, 244-247, 249, 251, 253, 255, 257-259
turtle, 30, 167, 170, 217, 219-220
tusk, 24, 27, 35, 51, 116, 198, 200, 204, 206, 209-211

U

underwater, 30-31, 46, 165-166, 168, 174, 176, 178, 212
ungulate, 131, 148-151, 153, 155, 157, 159-161, 163
urban, 163, 180-181, 184, 187-188
ursine, 244, 249, 257, 259

V

value, 48-50, 106, 108-109, 111-112, 153, 159, 193, 256
vegetation, 22, 36, 39, 149, 151, 153, 156, 158-160, 162-163, 201, 255
venom, 39, 96, 99
vertebrate, 12, 66, 73, 86, 94, 164
vocalization, 40, 43, 152, 163, 165, 180, 189, 201, 231, 248
vulture, 37, 184-185, 191

W

walrus, 24, 227
warrior, 228, 232-234, 236, 238-240, 242-243, 248-250, 252
werebear, 131, 244-259
whale, 52-55, 59, 82-83, 164, 168-169, 172, 176, 178-179
wing, 13, 16, 28-29, 43, 52, 58, 69, 82, 86-89, 94, 100, 103, 133-135, 138-144, 182, 184, 186-188, 192, 194
wolf, 39-40, 48, 78, 95, 165, 176
worm, 12, 15, 217
wyvern, 132, 134-144, 146-147

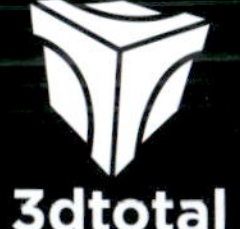

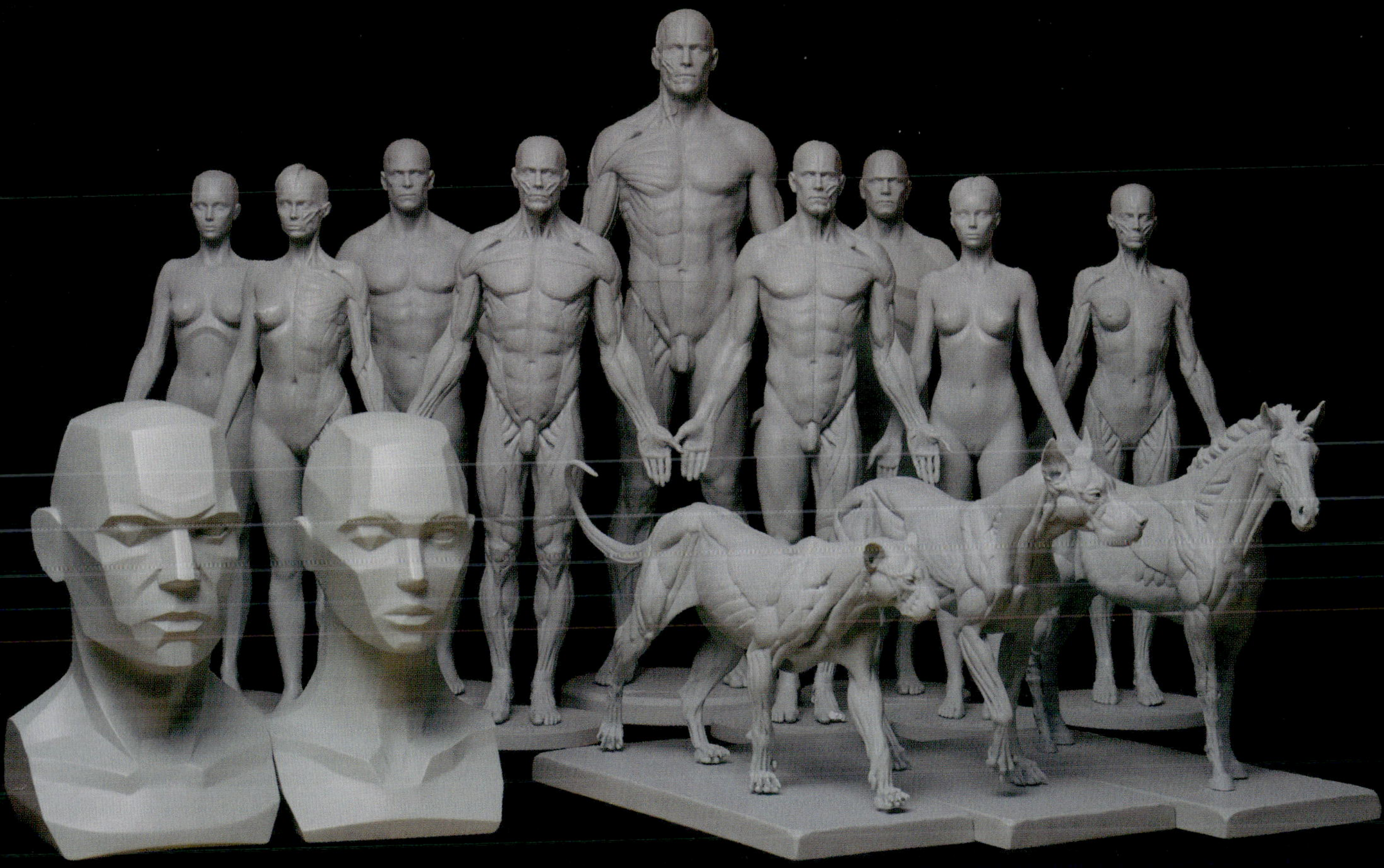

3dtotalAnatomy

Whether you use pencil and paper, paintbrushes, clay, Blender, ZBrush, Procreate, or Photoshop, our anatomical reference figures are invaluable if you want to understand the form and structure of human and animal bodies.

Available now at
store.3dtotal.com

3dtotalPublishing

3dtotal Publishing is a trailblazing, creative publisher specializing in inspirational and educational resources for artists.

Our titles feature top industry professionals from around the globe who share their experience in skillfully written step-by-step tutorials and fascinating, detailed guides. Illustrated throughout with stunning artwork, these best-selling publications offer creative insight, expert advice, and essential motivation. Fans of digital art will enjoy our comprehensive volumes covering Adobe Photoshop, Procreate, and Blender, as well as our superb titles based around character design, including *Fundamentals of Character Design* and *Creating Characters for the Entertainment Industry*. The dedicated, high-quality blend of instruction and inspiration also extends to traditional art. Titles covering a range of techniques, genres, and abilities allow your creativity to flourish while building essential skills.

Well-established within the industry, we now offer over 100 titles and counting, many of which have been translated into multiple languages around the world. With something for every artist, we are proud to say that our books offer the 3dtotal package:

LEARN · CREATE · SHARE

Visit us at store.3dtotal.com

3dtotal Publishing is part of 3dtotal.com, a leading website for CG artists founded by Tom Greenway in 1999.